THE YALE EDITION

OF

HORACE WALPOLE'S

CORRESPONDENCE

EDITED BY W. S. LEWIS

VOLUME FORTY

HORACE WALPOLE'S MISCELLANEOUS CORRESPONDENCE

I

EDITED BY W. S. LEWIS

AND

JOHN RIELY

WITH THE ASSISTANCE OF

EDWINE M. MARTZ

AND

RUTH K. McCLURE

NEW HAVEN

YALE UNIVERSITY PRESS

OXFORD · OXFORD UNIVERSITY PRESS

1980

Library of Congress catalog card number: 65-11182

International standard book numbers:
0-300-02608-0 (*Miscellaneous Correspondence*, vols. 40–42)
0-300-01769-3 (vol. 40)

10 9 8 7 6 5 4 3 2 1

ADVISORY COMMITTEE

ADVISORY COMMITTEE

John Brooke, Editor, The Yale Edition of Horace Walpole's Memoirs

[illegible] Brinton [illegible], Ph.D., Professor of History, Trinity College, Hartford, Connecticut

The Honourable [illegible], London

Herman Warner Liebert, Librarian Emeritus, The Beinecke Rare Book and Manuscript Library, Yale University

[illegible], Ph.D., Litt.D., [illegible] Professor of English, [illegible] University

Stephen Robert Parks, Ph.D., Curator, The James Marshall and Marie-Louise Osborn Collection, Yale University Library

[illegible], Ph.D., Director, the Yale [illegible], Yale University

Frederick [illegible] Pottle, Ph.D., Litt.D., LL.D., Sterling Professor of English, Emeritus, Yale University

[illegible] David [illegible], M.A., [illegible], Librarian of the [illegible] Society

Charles [illegible] Ryskamp, Ph.D., Litt.D., L.H.D., Director, The Pierpont Morgan Library

[illegible] Robert [illegible], [illegible] Mary College

The [illegible] Waldegrave, K.G., T.D., [illegible]

Secretary: [illegible]

TABLE OF CONTENTS

VOLUME I

LIST OF ILLUSTRATIONS

VOLUMES I, II, AND III

Unless otherwise noted, the originals of these illustrations are in the Lewis Walpole Library, Farmington, Connecticut. Grateful acknowledgment is made to the Earl of Normanton, the Trustees of the British Museum, Sir John Soane's Museum, Messrs Christie, Manson & Woods, the Yale Center for British Art, and the Yale University Library for permission to reproduce the paintings, drawings, or prints in their possession.

LADY NORTHUMBERLAND'S INVITATION CARD TO HORACE WALPOLE, ?JANUARY 1759 i. 153

The card, designed by Richard Bentley, is pasted in an extra-illustrated copy of the *Description of Strawberry Hill,* 1784, that probably belonged to Walpole's printer and secretary, Thomas Kirgate.

BENTLEY'S DESIGN FOR ROGER TOWNSHEND'S MONUMENT i. 167

Bentley drew the design from a 'rude' sketch by Walpole, whose proposed epitaph appears below. Neither the design nor the epitaph was used.

CHARLES LYTTELTON, BISHOP OF CARLISLE, AFTER FRANCIS COTES i. 271

From the mezzotint by James Watson, after the painting by Cotes (present whereabouts unknown), first published in 1770; plate XXVIII in *Vetusta monumenta,* vol. II, 1789 (published by the Society of Antiquaries of London; copy in the Yale University Library).

THE HON. MRS KEPPEL AND LADY HUNTINGTOWER, BY ALLAN RAMSAY, 1765 i. 370

From the painting (present whereabouts unknown) commissioned by Walpole that hung in the Gallery at Strawberry Hill.

ROBERT ADAM'S DESIGNS FOR THE ROUND DRAWING-ROOM AT STRAWBERRY HILL ii. 39

The original drawings for the ceiling and the chimney-piece, inscribed by Adam and dated 1766 and 1767, are in Sir John Soane's Museum, London.

VERTUE'S DRAWING OF RICHARD III AND QUEEN ANNE ii. 132

The original from which Vertue made this copy has not been identified. The drawing was engraved by Charles Grignion for Walpole's *Historic Doubts on . . . Richard the Third,* 1768.

VOLTAIRE, BY JEAN HUBER ii. 146

This *découpure* by the Swiss artist Jean Huber (1721–86) is probably that sent to Walpole by Madame du Deffand in her letter of 15 Nov. 1772 (DU DEFFAND iii. 285–6, 438–9).

painting, which hung in the Beauclerk Closet at Strawberry Hill, was copied from the original portrait by Reynolds painted when Lady Di was Viscountess Bolingbroke.

SCENE FROM 'THE CASTLE OF OTRANTO,' BY BERTIE GREATHEED, THE YOUNGER iii. 430

The younger Greatheed made four drawings illustrating scenes from Walpole's novel. This is one of the copies (in pen and sepia wash) executed at Walpole's request, depicting the episode in which the spectre of the holy hermit is discovered by Frederic in Hippolita's oratory (Chapter V). The copies of Greatheed's originals are bound in Walpole's copy of the Bodoni *Castle of Otranto,* Parma, 1791.

MAP OF HORACE WALPOLE'S TWICKENHAM 1747–1797 iii. 477

WILMARTH SHELDON LEWIS
1895–1979

WILMARTH SHELDON LEWIS, the founder and editor-in-chief of this edition, died on October 7, 1979, shortly before his 84th birthday, which he would have celebrated on November 14. Birthdays were significant events to him, and so were celebrations. He had at first hoped to complete the edition by his fifty-fifth birthday, but World War II, together with newly discovered letters and increasing complexities of annotation, kept postponing the final day of triumph.

Yet he saw his edition complete though not all in print. He read most of the annotation (and two-thirds of the galley proof) of the present three volumes; he wrote the introduction to them; he was even able to glance at the typescript of the final index though failing eyesight kept him from reading it. The concluding celebration alone escaped him—and what a jubilee it would have been!

He started to collect Walpole's letters in 1924, and he began this edition of the correspondence in 1933. In his *Collector's Progress* and *One Man's Education* he tells how he, at that time a collector rather than a scholar, persuaded Yale University to entrust this monumental editorial enterprise to him. The edition has ever since been guided by his good taste, and publicized by his extraordinary genius for promotion.

The edition profited by his ingenuity too. Previous editors had always numbered their letters for purposes of cross-reference, and then had encountered difficulties when letters had to be switched, or when new ones were inserted. He decided to cross-refer to letters merely by their dates, printing the dates in the running-heads of the pages, so that the reader could find them more readily. He insisted on a preliminary index before the editing was begun. He devised various space-saving devices to shorten the annotation, introducing new abbreviations and cue-titles.

Style was always important to him. Yale's English department, when he was a student, had been a galaxy of brilliant lecturers; they were thorough scholars but they were never dull; they had flair and panache; mere plodding pedantry was beneath them. From them he imbibed his aim for accuracy and also a feeling for artistry—he said that there was need for art even in footnotes; they must be factual but they need not be pedantic. His volumes were handsomely designed by Carl Rollins; the illustrations, brilliantly executed by the Meriden Gravure Company, were selected from the rarest items in his collection. He wrote graceful introductions to each of the correspondences or groups of volumes.

Mrs Lewis, until her untimely death in 1959, aided him financially and stylistically. When he showed her his first draft of the introduction to the opening volume, she told him to tear it up and start all over again. His easy informal introductions were actually the result of hard work and many re-writings—and, at first, of her wise counsel.

He sought and received advice from his scholarly colleagues also. Should the letters be arranged chronologically or by separate correspondences? Should the spelling and punctuation be 'normalized'? His Advisory Committee helped him in such choices, and the Advisory Committee itself exemplified his feeling for style and also his flair for publicity. It included Lord Waldegrave as the representative of Walpole's family, together with distinguished English and American scholars, librarians, and curators, and even a novelist (his old schoolmate, Thornton Wilder). Their names were on the edition's letter-head, and in the front pages of each of the correspondences. Professor Pottle used to predict that Queen Mary, who was a Walpolian, would join the illustrious list, but she withdrew her subscription on hearing that her son, through the Royal Library at Windsor, was already a subscriber so that she didn't need a set herself.

The List of Subscribers, likewise printed at the beginning of each of the correspondences, was instituted by Mr Lewis as a 'snob-sheet.' It was headed by his Majesty King George VI, and was originally expected to consist chiefly of connoisseurs, collectors, English noblemen, and American millionaires, together with various institutions. He was surprised to discover that the English regarded the volumes as too expensive, and that most of the subscriptions came from American colleges and universities —whereupon he shifted the emphasis of snobbery from social to academic spheres, and prodded the Yale Press into employing a special salesman to round up subscriptions from American schools and universities. He kept a map dotted with the locations of sets of the Yale Walpole, so that less enlightened institutions would realize that they inhabited waste lands which could only be redeemed by promptly signing up.

His approach to editing was similarly modified over the years, chiefly through the influence of his staff. In bibliography, he was aided by the expertise of the late Allen T. Hazen of Columbia University, who compiled bibliographies of Walpole's writings and of the imprints of the Strawberry Hill Press, as well as the monumental catalogue of Walpole's library.

The earliest collaborator on the Yale Edition of Horace Walpole's Correspondence was the late A. Dayle Wallace, who had been a graduate student at Yale (and so had most of his successors, including the late Charles H. Bennett), but it was a Cornell Ph.D., the late George L. Lam, who had the greatest impact on our annotation. Lam believed in basing the footnotes, whenever possible, on primary sources, carrying the edition's foundations down to bed-rock; he felt that there should be no room for 'happy discoveries' in scholarship, since nothing should be left to accident—the field was to be systematically combed by the process which he called 'the bulldozer method.' Therefore he prodded Mr Lewis into procuring a veritable library of microfilms: the Newcastle Papers from the British Museum, the diplomatic dispatches (for France and Tuscany) from the Public Record Office, a complete run of the *Daily Advertiser*. Furthermore, he did not trust Mr Lewis to remember and insert all the pertinent passages from the unpublished MSS at Farmington, and so he insisted on having those MSS on microfilm in New Haven.

With these resources at his command, his footnotes grew so

much longer and so much more technical that Mr Lewis and I had some difficulty in reducing them to manageable size, and still more trouble in dissuading Dr Lam from too much time-consuming research into peripheral problems. Even so, the footnotes tended to be less concentrated on Walpole's personal life, and much more on world events. We were not just making a charming letter-writer more accessible and intelligible, we were converting Walpole's references to current events into a sort of documentary history.

Mr Lewis accepted this shift because it elevated Walpole from a mere dispenser of gossip into a serious historian; our indexes were to be indexes of history, social and political. He still balked, however, at footnotes that were too repellent: if they were full of symbols and abbreviations he called them 'algebra'; uncouth foreign names were to be avoided; when the note on a naval event listed the names of the Russian ships involved, he shuddered, and struck out the barbarous names with exclamation marks of horror.

In such ways, our editor-in-chief adjusted to new situations without ever swerving from his original drive for completeness, accuracy, and distinction; above all, distinction. In reminiscing about the Elizabethan Club at Yale, he said that its founders did a wise thing—they made it 'smart.' It had elegance and style and so did his edition of Walpole.

Towards Walpole himself, Wilmarth Lewis had an almost mystical feeling of identification; in fact he wrote that at one period he had to be rescued from a real obsession with this idea. He felt special guidance whenever he entered a room and turned towards the very cabinet where 'a bit of the True Cross' was concealed. When he was writing an introduction to Walpole's correspondence with Mme du Deffand, he attributed Walpole's tenderness for the old lady to a 'mother complex.' I differed with him about this, since Walpole's mother had died comparatively young, and Mme du Deffand may have seemed a much older and different person at the time when Walpole met her, but Mr Lewis confessed that he felt an instinctive insight into Walpole's feelings. He, Wilmarth Lewis, had suffered from a mother complex, as he later stated in *One Man's Education.*

This feeling of identification with his subject sometimes made him impervious to certain suggestions; he simply *knew* how Horace Walpole would have talked and acted, even if the evidence for it was not entirely convincing.

His other activities, and they were many, are described in his various reminiscences—his trusteeship at Yale where he emphasized the building-up of the Yale collections, his championship of such libraries as the Watkinson in Hartford and the Redwood at Newport, his interest in art (exemplified in his *See for Yourself,* and in his own collections of paintings and prints), his pride in the Indian artifacts discovered by his gardener, William Day, on his own grounds at Farmington, his services in the two World Wars, his work as 'ambassador of good will' in Peru and Canada.

Before his death, he arranged for the editing and eventual publication of Walpole's historical memoirs, under the guidance of John Brooke, thus continuing to bolster Walpole's reputation as the interpreter and historian of his own time.

Above all, Wilmarth Lewis's personal charm and ingratiating manner won him a host of friends, and indeed made possible the success of our edition. Most of the choicest items in his collection, and many letters in this edition, were procured from English owners who would never have opened their doors to any other American collector. His tactful approach, his sensitivity to English oddities and prejudices, his network of warm friends all over the British Isles (the President of Ireland visited him in Farmington) broke down the defences of even the crustiest curmudgeons.

It was fitting that he should receive from Prince Philip the Benjamin Franklin medal for Anglo-American cooperation, since his edition and other writings made bridges across great oceans of international misunderstanding; he was so careful of English sensibilities that our edition uses English rather than American spellings; he was meticulous in seeing that the titles and honours of his British advisers and subscribers were printed in correct British form. He became Yale's unofficial ambassador to the British 'establishment.'

We are sorry that he had to leave us before the fanfare of our final volume's publication, but we feel that he was assured of that fanfare and was already hearing distant echoes of it.

* * * * * *

Since the publication of our last preceding volumes in 1974, we have lost seven members of our Advisory Committee, whose deaths, with one exception, preceded that of our founder.

Allen T. Hazen, Emeritus Professor at Columbia University, was the bibliographer of our project. He prepared bibliographies of the Strawberry Hill Press (1942) and of Horace Walpole's writings (1948), ending with the monumental three-volume *Catalogue of Horace Walpole's Library* (1969).

Frederick W. Hilles, Emeritus Professor at Yale, was C. B. Tinker's successor in teaching the course in the Age of Johnson at Yale, and he joined our Advisory Committee when 'Tink' was no longer able to be active in it.

Sir Owen Morshead, G. C. V. O. and K. C. B., sometime librarian to King George VI and to Queen Elizabeth II at Windsor Castle, was helpful in getting us access to many private collections in England.

A. N. L. Munby, who was Fellow and Librarian at Horace Walpole's former college (King's, at Cambridge), was instrumental in procuring for us several of the letters which are printed in these volumes.

James M. Osborn's name is perpetuated in the great Osborn Collection in the Beinecke Library at Yale, from which we are able to print letters in these volumes; he has enriched all of Yale's eighteenth-century projects.

Thornton Wilder, novelist and playwright, was a schoolmate of our founder during their early days in California. His interest in Walpolian studies is displayed in his annotated set of our edition, which has appropriately been given to the Lewis Walpole Library at Farmington.

A. Hyatt Mayor, Curator of Prints, Emeritus, at the Metropolitan Museum of Art in New York, was helpful to us in procuring information concerning prints which had been collected by Walpole.

In addition to these seven deaths, we must notice those of two former members of our staff, who died very soon after the death of their erstwhile employer.

Miss Julia T. McCarthy had served for twenty-six years as secretary at the Lewis Walpole Library in Farmington when she retired in 1965. She prepared thousands of index cards for the MSS there, and she typed the texts of many of the letters which are included in our edition, some of which appear in these present volumes.

Miss Emma H. E. Stephenson, who died at the end of 1979, had been librarian at the American Library in Paris in the 1920s. After a year at the library of the University of California at Berkeley, she came in 1932 to the Reference Department in the Yale University Library; she was briefly Acting Head of the Department before coming to us in 1956–7. She did proof-reading and indexing at various intervals, and she prepared some preliminary annotation for most of the letters in the first two volumes of the present series. She retired in 1966 after nearly ten years with our project. Her knowledge of the Yale Library's resources helped to enlarge the scope of our researches, and her gracious presence made the 'Walpole Factory' a pleasanter place for us all.

W. H. S.

INTRODUCTION

THIS is the final instalment of the Yale Walpole except for the five or six volumes of index, which we hope to have out in two years. My initial guess in 1933 that the edition would take seventeen years and fill thirty volumes has been thirty years and twenty volumes off.

These final letters are not the sweepings of the ballroom floor. They include Garrick, Burke, Boswell, Fanny Burney, Chesterfield, Gibbon, Hume, and Voltaire; the elder Pitt, C. J. Fox, and Lord North; George IV, Princess Amelia, and Stanislas II of Poland; Robert Adam, Sir William Chambers, and J. S. Copley. We have printed the few letters to and from the correspondents chronologically, a course that has provided a conspectus of Walpole's life. It has also highlighted his five chief interests—politics, the great world, literature, the fine arts, and antiquarianism. These last three volumes are a happy conclusion to the whole undertaking.

We celebrated its fortieth year with a 'Jubilee' in October 1973. There were publications, exhibitions, speeches, dinners, and a concert by the wife of one of our colleagues, Beth Riely. I repeat my tributes to the five Yale Librarians, Andrew Keogh, Bernhard Knollenberg, James Babb, James Tanis, and Rutherford Rogers, who headed the staff that for forty years has done all in its great power to help us. My gratitude to the Yale Library goes back fifty years to May Humphreys and descends through Donald Wing, John Ottemiller, Emily Hall, and Radley Daly. Invaluable aid was given at Farmington by my wife, and by Catherine Jestin and Joan Sussler who put our library and print room there in order.

Besides sponsoring us, the members of our Advisory Committee have read our proofs and reviewed us favourably in major periodicals. Of the initial Committee, only Lord Waldegrave and F. A. Pottle remain. Each of its members has made his own special contribution to our welfare. Their original colleagues were R. W. Chapman, Leonard Whibley, Lewis Namier, Robin Flower, H. M. Hake, and Wyndham Ketton-Cremer in England, and C. B. Tinker, Andrew Keogh, Wallace Notestein, E. S. Furniss, Albert Feuillerat, and Karl Young at Yale. Later members of the Committee have also served with zeal and fidelity, reading proof, reporting discoveries of Walpoliana, and, in the case of A. N. L. Munby, H. W. Liebert, and J. M. Osborn, giving me originals of Walpole's letters and drawings, prints, and books from his library. It is impossible to exaggerate the help given by the Advisory Committee through the years. Among its members a special word of gratitude is owing Allen Hazen, whose bibliographies of Walpole's works and the Strawberry Hill Press, and catalogue of the Strawberry Hill Library, the labour of thirty years, are indispensable.

Tinker once said, 'The Walpolians lead dedicated lives.' This has been true from the first. Our title-pages bear many of their names: Dayle Wallace, Warren Smith, Ralph Brown, George Lam, Charles Bennett, Edwine Martz, Grover Cronin, Robert A. Smith, Ralph Williams, Joseph Reed, Lars Troide, John Riely, and Ruth McClure.

We bless George Lam daily. For thirty-three years he compiled vast indexes to Walpole's manuscripts and marginalia at Farmington and the letters of the eighteenth-century men and women there. He once estimated that there are a million cards referring to the books, manuscripts, prints, and drawings at Farmington and to various indexes in the Walpole Room in Sterling. Of these he contributed and supervised a high percentage with infectious cheerfulness. Thanks to him we can find what we want when we want it and enrich our annotation with unpublished material. His bulldozing excavations in our five miles of microfilm were historic. They took days, weeks, *months*, but he would emerge at last glistening in triumph with another contribution to Walpolian studies that only he could have made, having used perhaps half a dozen languages, ancient and modern, on the way.

Such an exploration produced the phrase that became our motto. George wrote the Librarian of the Vatican Library for help with the election of Pope Benedict XIV, which he confessed he had pursued *diligenter sed frustra,* and *diligenter sed frustra* became our motto forthwith.

Warren Smith was a gift to the Yale Walpole from Chauncey Tinker in 1934. For the past many years he has presided over Room 331B in the Sterling Library, editing the six volumes of the correspondence with Mme du Deffand and, partnered by George Lam, the eleven Mann volumes. He has saved us from ourselves so successfully that we have few corrigenda, editing with judgment and common sense, making indexes that have won the gratitude of our readers, guiding and counseling our newcomers, earning the respect and affection of all his colleagues. When at last some curious traveller from Lima studies the making of the Yale Walpole he will see how great a part was played in it by Warren Smith.

The Yale Edition of Horace Walpole's Correspondence comes to its last page, but the completion of the Yale Edition of Horace Walpole's Memoirs is many years off. It is moving steadily ahead in London under the shaping hand of John Brooke, Lewis Namier's collaborator and successor as the historian of eighteenth-century Parliaments. Owing to the generous cooperation of the Memoirs' owner, Lord Waldegrave, and Lady Waldegrave's knowledge of the material and her skill in research, the Yale Edition of Horace Walpole's Memoirs is proceeding with every advantage. How thankful Walpole must be that he entrusted his future to the descendants of his niece, Maria Waldegrave, for they are being, as he hoped they would be, his emissaries to Posterity.

W. S. L.

MANUSCRIPTS AND EDITORIAL METHOD

THESE three volumes contain 886 letters, comprising Walpole's correspondence with 330 different persons. The correspondence is 'miscellaneous' in the sense that none of these persons exchanged more than a few letters with Walpole, or, if they exchanged a substantial number (as must have been the case, for example, with the Duke of Richmond), only a few of their letters are known to have survived.

Of the 592 letters written by Walpole, 507 are printed from the manuscripts (or from photostats or copies of them); 181 are 'new' and 44 others are printed in full for the first time. There are 294 letters written to Walpole, of which 225 are printed from the manuscripts; 92 of these letters are previously unpublished and ten have been printed hitherto only in part.

The correspondents are so numerous and the manuscripts so widely dispersed that it would be pointless to attempt any summary of provenance. The history of each letter, as far as it is known to us, is given in the headnote to the letter. Nevertheless, we must record here changes in ownership of seven letters from the Lyttelton Papers at Hagley Hall that were sold at Sotheby's on 12 December 1978 (lots 84–88, 136–37), while these volumes were in the press. Walpole's letters to Charles Lyttelton of 27 July 1736 OS and 18 September 1737 OS were acquired by the Hon. William Waldegrave, of London; his letters to Lyttelton of 28 August 1734 OS and 22 May 1736 OS were purchased at the sale by 'Milton,' about whom we have no further information; his letter to Lyttelton of 23 March 1758 was bought by Messrs Quaritch (anonymous commission); his letter to Lyttelton of 10 July 1763 was acquired by Messrs Maggs Bros.; and his letter to George, 1st Baron Lyttelton, of 25 August 1757 was sold to Messrs Quaritch and is now owned by Dr Gerald E.

Slater, of Deephaven, Minnesota. The three other letters from Walpole to Charles Lyttelton that are described in the headnotes as being in the possession of Viscount Cobham were not offered for sale and are still at Hagley.

In the third volume, the last dated letter (February 1797) is followed by a group of undated letters arranged alphabetically by correspondent. New information made it possible to date some of these letters, but the information came too late for them to be placed in their proper chronological sequence.

The editorial method for the miscellaneous correspondence has been that described in earlier volumes of this edition. Spelling and capitalization have been modernized, except for proper names and certain characteristic words such as 'cotemporaries.' Walpole's punctuation has been followed exactly, but that of his correspondents has been normalized to some extent. Square brackets are used for editorial emendation and angular brackets for restoration of a mutilated text. In biographical notes we assume the use of the *Dictionary of National Biography*, the *Complete Peerage*, and the *Complete Baronetage*; for members of Parliament we further assume the use of Romney Sedgwick's and Namier and Brooke's histories (full citations given in the list of cue-titles). All English books are assumed to be published in London and all French books in Paris, unless otherwise stated. Manuscripts and printed books cited as being in the British Museum are now in the British Library, and items described as being 'now WSL' are in the Lewis Walpole Library, Farmington, Connecticut.

J. R.

ACKNOWLEDGMENTS

OUR first acknowledgment is due to the private owners and institutional custodians who have generously allowed us to publish letters in their possession; their names are gratefully recorded in the headnotes to the letters. We deeply appreciate their kindness in furnishing us with photostats or transcripts of the manuscripts.

It gives us pleasure to acknowledge our debt to past and present members of the Advisory Committee. Mr John Brooke and Professor George B. Cooper read the proof and made valuable additions to the footnotes. Dr Stephen Parks, Professor Frederick A. Pottle, and Dr Charles Ryskamp were ready sources of information and advice, as was Lady Waldegrave in questions concerning the genealogy of the Walpole family. The late Allen T. Hazen was unfailingly helpful with bibliographical problems. Other late members of the Committee who particularly assisted us in these volumes were A. N. L. Munby, Sir Lewis Namier, James M. Osborn, and Romney Sedgwick.

We wish to thank the many scholars, librarians, archivists, and others who answered our inquiries or volunteered information. Whenever possible, their contributions have been acknowledged in the headnotes. We have also to thank Mlle Annie Angremy, Mr Jack Baldwin, Professor Maurice W. Barley, Mr Alan Bell, the late Theodore Besterman, Professor Edward A. Bloom, Professor Frank Brady, Mr Andrew Brown, Dr L. Brummel, Mrs Nancy N. Coffin, Miss Winifred Collins, Miss Margaret Cooke, Dr Timothy J. Crist, the Very Rev. K. P. Cronin, C.M., Mr G. F. J. Cumberlege, Professor Bertram H. Davis, Mrs Althea Douglas, Dr David Fairer, Dr B. D. Greenslade, Professor Robert Halsband, Mr John Harris, Professor Joyce Hemlow, Mr Felix Hull, Professor Martin Kallich, Dr Mary E. Knapp, Professor

Roy Lamson, Jr, Mr James Lawton, the late Sir Shane Leslie, Bt, Dr Michael Liversidge, Dr Michael McCarthy, Mrs Mary A. McKenzie, Mrs Sarah Markham, Mr George Milne, Professor Ronald Paulson, Dr John V. Price, Professor Jules David Prown, Professor Joseph W. Reed, Jr, Mr Alvaro Ribeiro, Mrs Elizabeth Riely, Miss Marjorie Robertson, Mrs Isobel J. Sayer, Dr Barbara Schnetzler, Professor Arthur Sherbo, Professor Alastair Smart, Mr R. O. C. Spring, Dr J. E. A. L. Struick, Sir John Summerson, Professor James E. Tierney, Mr and Mrs P. A. Tritton, Mr D. E. Williams, Miss M. G. Williams, Mr G. M. V. Winn, and Mr Paul Woudhuysen.

Elizabeth A. Porter reviewed our texts of the letters in French, and Professor Thomas G. Bergin gave similar help with the Italian letters.

We are indebted to many members of the staffs of the following libraries: Bodleian, British Library, Harvard, Huntington, Pierpont Morgan, and Yale. We should also like to thank those in the antiquarian book trade who patiently dealt with our requests for information about the provenance of manuscripts, in particular Mr Theodore Hofmann, Mr H. Clifford Maggs, the late Michael Papantonio, Mr P. N. Poole-Wilson, Mr Jeffrey Thomas, Mr John Wilson, and the staffs of Sotheby's and Christie's.

The Walpole staff in New Haven has worked together over many years in the editing of this correspondence. The late Emma H. E. Stephenson prepared preliminary annotation for most of the letters in the first two volumes, and her work was being continued by Dr George L. Lam at the time of his death in 1970. Professor Grover Cronin, Jr, did some preliminary work on the French letters, and Dr Lam annotated the correspondence with the Duke of Newcastle. Dr Edwine M. Martz and Dr Ruth K. McClure annotated the letters of the 1790s and the undated letters. Dr Martz oversaw the proofreading of the volumes; Dr McClure verified the footnotes and references, making important contributions to the notes and to the appendices. In addition to writing the memoir of W. S. Lewis that precedes the Introduction in this volume, Dr Warren Hunting Smith read the typescript and proof at every stage and made many valuable suggestions; he also prepared the working index to the correspondence (to be published with the comprehensive index to the Walpole edition). Other present or former members of the staff to whom we are indebted for assistance of various kinds are the late Charles H. Bennett, Mr William LaMoy, Miss Barbara Stoops, and Dr Lars E. Troide. We are grateful to have had the services of Mr Andrew L. McClellan, who performed research tasks for us in London.

Finally, we offer our thanks to the members of the staff at Farmington, past and present, who devotedly supported every aspect of our work: in the library, Mrs H. William Day, Mrs H. A. Jestin, the late Julia T. McCarthy, Miss Mabel Martin, and Mrs James M. Peltier; and in the print room, Mrs Richard D. Butterfield, Mrs Warren M. Creamer, Mrs Richard Schatten, and Mrs Frank Sussler.

W. S. L.
J. R.

CUE-TITLES AND ABBREVIATIONS

Anecdotes of Painting, Works iii . . .	Horace Walpole, *Anecdotes of Painting in England,* in *The Works of Horatio Walpole, Earl of Orford,* 1798, vol. iii.
Army Lists . . .	[Great Britain, War Office], *A List of the General and Field Officers as they Rank in the Army,* 1740–1841.
Berry	*The Yale Edition of Horace Walpole's Correspondence: The Correspondence with Mary and Agnes Berry,* New Haven, 1944, 2 vols.
Bibl. Nat. Cat. . .	*Catalogue générale des livres imprimés de la Bibliothèque nationale,* 1897– .
BM Add. MSS . .	Additional Manuscripts, British Museum.
BM Cat. . . .	Catalogue of Printed Books in the British Museum.
BM Cat. of Engraved British Portraits .	British Museum, Department of Prints and Drawings. *Catalogue of Engraved British Portraits Preserved in the Department of Prints and Drawings in the British Museum,* by Freeman O'Donoghue and Henry M. Hake, 1908–25, 6 vols.
'Book of Materials' .	Three manuscript volumes, the first two entitled by Walpole 'Book of Materials,' the third entitled 'Miscellany,' begun in 1759, 1771 and 1786 respectively; now in the collection of W. S. Lewis.
'Book of Visitors' . .	Horace Walpole's manuscript list of visitors to Strawberry Hill, printed in *The Yale Edition of Horace Walpole's Correspondence: The Correspondence with Mary and Agnes Berry,* New Haven, 1944, ii. 221–74.

Burke, *Peerage* . .	Sir John Bernard Burke and Ashworth P. Burke, *A Genealogical and Heraldic History of the Peerage and Baronetage.*
CHATTERTON . . .	*The Yale Edition of Horace Walpole's Correspondence: The Correspondence with Thomas Chatterton . . .*, New Haven, 1951.
CHUTE	*The Yale Edition of Horace Walpole's Correspondence: The Correspondence with John Chute . . .*, New Haven, 1973.
Cobbett, *Parl. Hist.* .	*The Parliamentary History of England,* ed. William Cobbett, John Wright, and T. C. Hansard, 1806–20, 36 vols.
Coke, MS Journals .	Photostats of unpublished journals (1775–91) of Lady Mary Coke in the possession of Lord Home.
COLE	*The Yale Edition of Horace Walpole's Correspondence: The Correspondence with the Rev. William Cole,* New Haven, 1937, 2 vols.
Collins, *Peerage,* 1812 .	Arthur Collins, *The Peerage of England,* ed. Sir Samuel Egerton Brydges, 1812, 9 vols.
CONWAY . . .	*The Yale Edition of Horace Walpole's Correspondence: The Correspondence with Henry Seymour Conway . . .*, New Haven, 1974, 3 vols.
Country Seats .	'Horace Walpole's Journals of Visits to Country Seats, etc.,' ed. Paget Toynbee, in *The Walpole Society 1927–1928,* vol. xvi, Oxford, 1928.
Cunningham . .	*The Letters of Horace Walpole, Earl of Orford,* ed. Peter Cunningham, 1857–59, 9 vols.
Daily Adv. . . .	*The Daily Advertiser,* 1731–95. Film in the Yale University Library from the file in the Library of Congress.
DALRYMPLE . . .	*The Yale Edition of Horace Walpole's Correspondence: The Correspondence with Sir David Dalrymple . . .*, New Haven, 1951.

Damer-Waller . .	The MS passed on HW's death to Mrs Damer, who bequeathed it to Sir Wathen Waller, 1st Bt.
'Des. of SH,' *Works* ii .	Horace Walpole, 'A Description of the Villa of Mr Horace Walpole at Strawberry Hill near Twickenham,' in *The Works of Horatio Walpole, Earl of Orford,* 1798, vol. ii.
Dict. de biographie française . . .	*Dictionnaire de biographie française,* sous la direction de J. Balteau . . . M. Barroux . . . M. Prévost . . . avec le concours de nombreux collaborateurs . . . , 1933– , 10 vols.
DNB	*Dictionary of National Biography,* ed. Leslie Stephen and Sidney Lee, reissue, 1908–9, 22 vols.
DU DEFFAND . . .	*The Yale Edition of Horace Walpole's Correspondence: The Correspondence with Mme du Deffand,* New Haven, 1939, 6 vols.
Eton Coll. Reg. . .	R. A. Austen-Leigh, *Eton College Register 1698–1752,* Eton, 1927; *1753–1790,* Eton, 1921.
FAMILY	*The Yale Edition of Horace Walpole's Correspondence: The Correspondence with the Walpole Family,* New Haven, 1973.
Foster, *Alumni Oxon.* .	Joseph Foster, *Alumni Oxonienses: The Members of the University of Oxford, 1500–1714,* Oxford and London, 1891–2, 4 vols; *1715–1886,* London, 1887–8, 4 vols.
GEC	George Edward Cokayne, *The Complete Peerage,* revised by Vicary Gibbs *et al.*, 1910–59, 13 vols.
GEC, *Baronetage* . .	George Edward Cokayne, *The Complete Baronetage,* Exeter, 1900–9, 6 vols.
GM	*The Gentleman's Magazine.*
GRAY	*The Yale Edition of Horace Walpole's Correspondence: The Correspondence with Thomas Gray, Richard West, and Thomas Ashton,* New Haven, 1948, 2 vols.

Hazen, *Bibl. of HW* .	Allen T. Hazen, *A Bibliography of Horace Walpole,* New Haven, 1948.
Hazen, *Cat. of HW's Lib.*	Allen T. Hazen, *A Catalogue of Horace Walpole's Library,* New Haven, 1969, 3 vols.
Hazen, *SH Bibl.* . .	Allen T. Hazen, *A Bibliography of the Strawberry Hill Press,* New Haven, 1942; new edn, 1973.
Hist. MSS Comm. .	Historical Manuscripts Commission.
HW	Horace Walpole.
Isenburg, *Stammtafeln* .	Wilhelm Karl, Prinz von Isenburg, *Stammtafeln zur Geschichte der europaeischen Staaten,* Berlin, 1936, 2 vols.
Journal of the Printing-Office . .	Horace Walpole, *Journal of the Printing-Office at Strawberry Hill,* ed. Paget Toynbee, 1923.
Journals of the House of Commons . .	[Great Britain, Parliament, House of Commons], *Journals of the House of Commons . . . Reprinted by Order of the House of Commons,* 1803, 51 vols.
Journals of the House of Lords . . .	[Great Britain, Parliament, House of Lords], *Journals of the House of Lords* [ca 1777–] 1891, 123 vols.
Last Journals . .	Horace Walpole, *The Last Journals of Horace Walpole during the Reign of George III from 1771–1783,* ed. A. Francis Steuart, 1910, 2 vols.
London Stage . .	*The London Stage 1660–1800 . . .*, Pt I: 1660–1700, ed. W. Van Lennep, Carbondale, Illinois, 1965; Pt II: 1700–1729, ed. E. L. Avery, 1960; Pt III: 1729–1747, ed. A. H. Scouten, 1961; Pt IV: 1747–1776, ed. G. W. Stone, Jr, 1962; Pt V: 1776–1800, ed. C. B. Hogan, 1968.
MANN	*The Yale Edition of Horace Walpole's Correspondence: The Correspondence with Sir Horace Mann,* New Haven, 1954–71, 11 vols.
MASON	*The Yale Edition of Horace Walpole's Correspondence: The Correspondence with William Mason,* New Haven, 1955, 2 vols.

Mem. Geo. II . .	Horace Walpole, *Memoirs of the Reign of King George the Second,* 2d edn, ed. Henry R. V. Fox, Lord Holland, 1847, 3 vols.
Mem. Geo. III . .	Horace Walpole, *Memoirs of the Reign of King George the Third,* ed. G. F. Russell Barker, 1894, 4 vols.
MONTAGU	*The Yale Edition of Horace Walpole's Correspondence: The Correspondence with George Montagu,* New Haven, 1941, 2 vols.
MORE	*The Yale Edition of Horace Walpole's Correspondence: The Correspondence with Hannah More . . . ,* New Haven, 1961.
N & Q	*Notes and Queries.*
Namier and Brooke .	Sir Lewis B. Namier and John Brooke, *The History of Parliament: The House of Commons 1754–1790,* 1964, 3 vols.
NBG	*Nouvelle biographie générale,* ed. Jean-Chrétien-Ferdinand Hoefer, 1852–66, 46 vols.
Nichols, *Lit. Anec.* .	John Nichols, *Literary Anecdotes of the Eighteenth Century,* 1812–15, 9 vols.
Nichols, *Lit. Illus.* .	John Nichols, *Illustrations of the Literary History of the Eighteenth Century,* 1817–58, 8 vols.
OED	*A New English Dictionary on Historical Principles,* ed. Sir James A. H. Murray *et al.,* Oxford, 1888–1928, 10 vols.
OSSORY	*The Yale Edition of Horace Walpole's Correspondence: The Correspondence with the Countess of Upper Ossory,* New Haven, 1965, 3 vols.
'Paris Journals' . .	Horace Walpole, 'Paris Journals,' in *The Yale Edition of Horace Walpole's Correspondence: The Correspondence with Mme du Deffand,* New Haven, 1939, v. 255–417 (Appendix 1).
Scots Peerage . .	*The Scots Peerage,* ed. Sir James Balfour Paul, Edinburgh, 1904–14, 9 vols.

Sedgwick . . .	Romney Sedgwick, *The History of Parliament: The House of Commons 1715–1754*, 1970, 2 vols.
SELWYN . . .	*The Yale Edition of Horace Walpole's Correspondence: The Correspondence with George Selwyn . . .*, New Haven, 1961.
SH	Strawberry Hill.
'Short Notes' . .	Horace Walpole, 'Short Notes of the Life of Horatio Walpole,' in *The Yale Edition of Horace Walpole's Correspondence: The Correspondence with Thomas Gray, Richard West, and Thomas Ashton*, New Haven, 1948, i. 3–51.
sold London . .	*A Catalogue of the Collection of Scarce Prints* [also MSS and books] *Removed from Strawberry Hill*, 13–23 June 1842. The number following each entry is the lot number in the sale.
sold SH . . .	*A Catalogue of the Classic Contents of Strawberry Hill Collected by Horace Walpole*, 25 April–21 May 1842. The roman and arabic numerals which follow each entry indicate the day and lot number in the sale.
Thieme and Becker .	Ulrich Thieme and Felix Becker, *Allgemeines Lexikon der bildenden Künstler von der Antike bis zur Gegenwart*, Leipzig, 1907–50, 37 vols.
Toynbee . . .	*The Letters of Horace Walpole*, ed. Mrs Paget Toynbee, Oxford, 1903–5, 16 vols.
Toynbee, *Supp.* . .	*Supplement to the Letters of Horace Walpole*, ed. Paget Toynbee, Oxford, 1918–25, 3 vols.
Venn, *Alumni Cantab.*	*Alumni Cantabrigienses*, Part I to 1751, compiled by John Venn and J. A. Venn, Cambridge, 1922–27, 4 vols; Part II 1752–1900, ed. J. A. Venn, Cambridge, 1940–54, 6 vols.
Vict. Co. Hist. . .	*The Victoria History of the Counties of England* [with name of county].

Walpole Society . .	The annual volumes of *The Walpole Society*, Oxford, 1911/12– .
Works	Horace Walpole, *The Works of Horatio Walpole, Earl of Orford*, 1798, 5 vols.
Wright	*The Letters of Horace Walpole, Earl of Orford*, ed. John Wright, 1840, 6 vols.
WSL (now WSL) . .	In the collection of W. S. Lewis, The Lewis Walpole Library, Farmington, Connecticut.

LIST OF LETTERS

The dates of the letters to Walpole are printed in italics. Page references to earlier editions are given in the headnotes to the letters.

To Charles Lyttelton,[1] Wednesday 28 August 1734 OS

Printed from a photostat of the MS in the possession of Viscount Cobham, Hagley Hall, Stourbridge, Worcs. First printed in N&Q 1869, 4th ser., iii. 2–3. Reprinted, Toynbee i. 2–3. The MS descended in the Lyttelton family to the present owner.

Eton, August 28, 1734.

My dearest Charles,

I FIND we not only sympathize in the tenderest friendship for one another, but also in the result of that, which is the jealousy you mention.[2] If you have given me a kind trial in your own mind and condemned me, I assure you I have over and over, though unwillingly, returned you the compliment: but to set the matter to rights, in which I have had the pleasure first to acquit you, you must know I came here but yesterday from home,[3] where I have been, almost ever since I saw my dear Charles, detained with a violent cold and fever, and through the ill-natured stupidity of our people here, who can't judge of what friends suffer by not hearing from one another, I did not receive so much as the alleviation of my illness by my dear Charles's letters,[4] which they had hoarded up here for me like old gold, equally dear to me indeed with that, but hoarded up without my having the pleasure of knowing my riches. But I am afraid my eagerness to clear myself from the imputation of neglecting to answer my dear Charles's letters, has made me tire your patience with a tedious roll of excuses, when I know one word would have satisfied my dear Charles's good na⟨ture⟩ of my innocence. I wish Randal[5] were but as sensible of the pleasure I take in writing to you, as I am, and then

1. (1714–68), 3d son of Sir Thomas Lyttelton, 4th Bt, of Hagley Hall, Stourbridge, Worcs; educated at Eton and University College, Oxford; D.C.L., 1745; Bp of Carlisle 1762–8; P.S.A. 1765–8; antiquary and divine (COLE i. 144 n. 3). Along with HW and George Montagu, Lyttelton was a member of HW's Eton 'triumvirate' (MONTAGU i. 4).

2. Lyttelton's letter is missing.

3. Sir Robert Walpole's house, Orford House, adjoining the Royal Hospital at Chelsea (DALRYMPLE 4 n. 1).

4. All missing.

5. Perhaps Thomas Randal, Eton College postman (*Eton Coll. Reg.*).

he would indulge me a few more minutes, without forcing me so hastily to repeat how much

I am
My dearest Charles
Your most sincere friend

Hor. Walpole

Tell me immediately that you have sealed my pardon.

To Charles Lyttelton, Thursday 7 August 1735 OS

Printed from a photostat of the MS in the possession of Viscount Cobham, Hagley Hall, Stourbridge, Worcs. First printed in N&Q 1869, 4th ser., iii. 2 (misdated 'August 7, 1732'). Reprinted, Toynbee i. 1–2 (likewise misdated). The MS descended in the Lyttelton family to the present owner.

Chelsea, August 7, 1735.

My dearest Charles,

The pleasure that the interview, though so very short, that I had with you the night before you left town,[1] gave me, has I think made your absence seem still more insupportable. That little snatch of conversation was so agreeable, that I am continually thinking how happy we should be in a much longer. I can reflect with great joy on the moments we passed together at Eton, and long to talk 'em over, as I think we could recollect a thousand passages, which were something above the common rate of schoolboy's diversions. I can remember with no small satisfaction that we did not pass our time in gloriously beating great clowns, who would patiently bear children's thumps for the collections, which I think some of our cotemporaries were so wise as to make for them afterwards. We had other amusements which I long to call to mind with you: when shall I be so happy? Let me know, my dear Charles, how far you are from Ragley[2]; I have some thoughts of going down thither this summer, and if it is not too far, I will spend a day with you in Worcestershire.[3] You may assure yourself I am mightily put to it for news, when for want of

1. The date and place of this 'interview' are not known.

2. Ragley Hall, the seat of HW's cousin Lord Conway (after 1750, Earl of Hertford), near Alcester, Warwickshire.

3. That is, at Hagley Hall, the seat of the Lytteltons (see heading). It is about twenty miles from Ragley.

4. Missing.

JOHN DODD, BY JOHN VANDERBANK, 1739

that, I send you some trifling verses[4] of my own, which have nothing to recommend 'em but the subject. I know you will excuse 'em, when you consider they come from

My dearest Charles
Your sincere friend and servant
HOR. WALPOLE

From JOHN WHALEY,[1] Sunday 10 August 1735 OS

Printed from Toynbee *Supp.* iii. 83–6, where the letter was first printed from the MS formerly in the Waller Collection. The eight letters from Whaley were bequeathed by Mrs Damer to Sir Wathen Waller, Bt, in 1828; sold Sotheby's 5 Dec. 1921 (first Waller Sale), lot 196, to Sutton; not further traced.

Rye,[2] Aug. 10th 1735.

Dear Sir,

WHEN we came into Canterbury[3] with our attendance and unloaded our sumpter horse, the people of the inn took us for mountebanks, and treated us accordingly till Mr Dodd[4] put a letter[5] into the post-house, directed to you which a little opened the good

1. (1710–45), educated at Eton 1724–8 and King's College, Cambridge (B.A. 1731/2, M.A. 1735); fellow of King's 1731–45; ordained deacon, 1745; editor of *A Collection of Poems,* 1732 and 1745; tutor to John Dodd and HW at King's College (*Eton Coll. Reg.*). William Cole wrote of him: 'He was the son of a tradesman of Norwich, whose father dying when he was young, left him to the care of his mother, a very sensible, active and stirring woman, who . . . sent him to Eton school, where he was observed to be a boy of a sprightly and toward genius. . . . Soon after his removal to King's College in Cambridge, he began to indulge his propensity to the Muses, such as it was; but much more his turn for a dissolute and debauched kind of life . . . yet as he was reckoned a man of genius and a poet, a good jolly companion, a singer of a good song, and rather a genteel person, his company was sought after, and he spent his time in a continual scene of jovial amusements and mirthful society: nor was this train of life at all altered, when he became the private tutor in college of John Dodd Esquire . . . a young gentleman of excellent parts, lively genius, and uncommon understanding . . . and had it not happened that this young gentleman was the master of as good a judgment, as his parts were lively, it could not have been but that his tutor would have ruined him forever' (*A Journal of my Journey to Paris in the Year 1765,* ed. F. G. Stokes, 1931, pp. 73–5).

2. Whaley was at this time travelling on a 'long vacation' tour of parts of England. The party consisted of Whaley, John Dodd, Francis Shepheard (a student at Clare College, Cambridge), and Shepheard's governor and companion, George Reste. They left London 28 July and returned to Cambridge 19 October. Whaley's MS journal (missing) of the 'Tour through England in the Year 1735' was transcribed by William Cole in 1775 and this transcript is now among Cole's papers in the BM (Add. MS 5842, ff. 122–35). The section of the journal dealing with Kent (28 July–9 Aug.), which is the subject of the present letter, has been printed by V. J. B. Torr in 'A Tour through Kent in 1735,' *Archæologia Cantiana,* 1931, xliii. 267–80.

3. 'Aug. 3. We came to the King's Head in Canterbury' (Whaley's Journal).

4. John Dodd (1717–82), of Swallowfield, Berks; HW's contemporary at Eton and King's; M.P. (*Eton Coll. Reg.;* Constance, Lady Russell, *Swallowfield and Its*

folks eyes and changed our titles from doctors and pickled herrings, to your Lordship and your honour. We stayed three days at Canterbury the first of which, being Sunday, we spent in the cathedral, which is the most magnificent I have seen, for a description of its curiosities I refer you to some acquaintance of yours in leather jackets[6] who can inform you of them much better than I. On Monday we took a coach and four and went into the Island of Thanet, where from a hill we had a most charming view of the sea almost all round us, and also of Deal, Sandwich, Ramsgate and Margate. Tuesday we went to the horse race[7] and at night to the assembly, where we saw a great deal of good company, and some pretty ladies with three of which Mr D. fell in love successively, *velut unda impellitur unda.*[8] The top company were Lord Romney,[9] Sir James Grey,[10] Sir Thomas D'Aeth,[11] Sir W[yndha]m Knatchbull,[12] Lord Winchelsea,[13] Sir Edw[ard] Dering[14] and Colonel Paget[15] whose regiment[16] is quartered in the city.

On Wednesday we went in the morning to Sir George Oxenden's[17] at Deane House in the parish of Wingham, which is a good old home, but made worth seeing by some very fine pictures, particularly one in water colours of Christ disputing with the doctors, and another in oil of the Roman slave plucking the thorn out of his foot. But who were they done by, you'll say? In truth I had not skill enough to distinguish the hand, and according to the taste of England the person that showed it knew no more of the matter than I did, but I must not pass over one extraordinary thing we met in this gentle-

Owners, 1901, pp. 228–9). For Cole's affectionate references to him and to Sneyd Davies's verses 'On Two Friends Born on the Same Day' see COLE ii. 299, 303. On his death HW wrote to Cole: 'He and I were born on the very same day, but took to different elements' (COLE ii. 299).

5. Missing.

6. Presumably a guide-book.

7. 'Aug. 5. We went to the races on Barham Downs, about 4 miles from Canterbury' (Whaley's Journal).

8. *Ut unda impellitur unda:* 'wave is pushed on by wave' (Ovid, *Metamorphoses,* xv. 181).

9. Robert Marsham (1712–93), 2d Bn Romney, 1724.

10. Presumably Sir James Gray (ca 1708–73), 2d Bt, 1722; diplomatist.

11. (1670–1745), cr. (1716) Bt; M.P.

12. Sir Wyndham Knatchbull (after 1746, Knatchbull-Wyndham) (d. 1749), 5th Bt, 1730.

13. Daniel Finch (1689–1769), 8th E. of Winchilsea, 1730.

14. (1705–62), 5th Bt, 1711; M.P.

15. Thomas Pagett (d. 1741), Brig. Gen., 1738; deputy governor of Minorca (Society for Army Historical Research, *Army List of 1740,* Sheffield, 1931, p. 34; GM 1741, xi. 332).

16. 'Pagett's Regiment of Foot' (after 1751, 22d Foot).

17. (1694–1775), 5th Bt, 1720; M.P. HW visited his seat, Deane, in 1780 (*Country Seats* 77).

man's house, which was a glass of wine and some bread and cheese. From hence we went to Waldeshare[18] the seat of the late Sir Henry Furnese,[19] and had we seen only this house, you, Sir, I am sure would think our journey not in vain, when I tell you we there saw a capital picture of Guido,[20] representing liberality and modesty, but one that has seen it must indeed have no judgment in painting should he attempt to describe it. There are a great many other fine pictures in this house, but what particularly pleased me was one which represents the Duke of Tuscany's gallery,[21] the pictures of which are copied in this. It was drawn by David Teniers[22] in 1651. The gardens are very fine and in the park is the case of a most beautiful belvedere, which is 80 foot high and commands both land and sea.

Dover is a Cinque Port and situated on the sea shore between two prodigious hills, it is built in the form of a crescent, on the south side is the famous cliff, to look from whose top is indeed as dreadful as even Shakespear's description of it.[23] On the north side is the ruins of a magnificent old castle from which we very plainly beheld the cliffs of Calais, you may easily guess how much we wished ourselves on t'other side, but it was a Pisgah[24] that we were mounted on. From Dover we came through Hithe and Romney to this place, from which we shall make the best of our way by the sea side to Chichester, till we come to which place I doubt we shall have nothing curious to inform you of. We rode to Winchelsea this afternoon where we had a melancholy conviction of the influence commerce has on places; it was once a large flourishing town of trade, was built in squares like Babylon, had nine churches, and in Edward III's[25] time it supplied the government with 49 ships of war, for its quota. But now *seges ubi Troja fuit,*[26] there is not a good house in the town, of all its churches but one poor chancel remaining, and under

18. Waldershare Park, now the seat of the Earl of Guilford.

19. (ca 1716–35), 3d Bt, 1733. He died at Montpelier, France 28 March 1735.

20. Guido Reni (1575–1642).

21. Archduke Leopold Wilhelm of Austria was the patron of David Teniers, who painted the Archduke's gallery at Brussels in 1651 and did various views of the gallery at other times (A. Rosenberg, *Teniers der Jüngere,* Bielefeld and Leipzig, 1895, pp. 48–55). Whaley had perhaps mistaken a copy of one of these for a painting of the Uffizi at Florence.

22. David Teniers, the younger (1610–90), Flemish painter.

23. In *King Lear* IV. i. 72–5 and IV. vi. 11–22.

24. The mountain east of Jordan from which Moses viewed the Promised Land; hence used allusively, as in 'a Pisgah view' (OED).

25. (1312–77), K. of England 1327–77.

26. *Iam seges est, ubi Troia fuit:* 'Now are fields of corn where Troy once was' (Ovid, *Heroides* i. 53).

the cornfields are magnificent and extensive empty wine vaults *non ita pridem.*[27] This town of Rye is in little better plight, having with its trade lost its inhabitants also.

From Rye we went most pleasantly by sea to Hastings, from hence to Eastbourne where Lord Wilmington[28] has laid out a great sum of money about an old house,[29] to inform posterity how much he wants taste; there is a profuseness of gilding and carved work in rooms you can scarce stand right *up in.*

Lewes in Sussex, Aug. 13th 1735.

We came hither last night and have spent this whole day at a cricket match between the gentlemen of Kent and Sussex, which was won by the latter at which they seem as much pleased as if they had got an election. We have been at supper with them all, and have left them at this one o'clock in the morning laying bets about the next match; Lord Middlesex[30] and Sir W[illia]m Gage[31] are the rivals of the bat. We are to dine at Mr Pelham's[32] at Stanmer tomorrow, and shall be at Portsmouth on Sunday, if you will honour me with a line[33] by Saturday's post directed to be left for me at the post-house in Portsmouth you will oblige

Your most obedient humble servant,

JOHN WHALEY

From Portsmouth I or Mr Dodd will inform you of what we find curious at Chichester or there.

27. 'Not long ago.'

28. Sir Spencer Compton (ca 1674–1743), cr. (1728) Bn Wilmington and (1730) E. of Wilmington; K.G., 1733.

29. For an illustrated description of it see Christopher Hussey, 'Compton Place, Eastbourne, Sussex,' *Country Life,* 1953, cxiii. 734–7, 818–21.

30. Charles Sackville (1711–69), styled E. of Middlesex; 2d D. of Dorset, 1765; M.P. 'The greatest of all the "feudal lords" of cricket were the Sackvilles of Knole. In the very earliest county matches we find the two sons of the first Duke of Dorset, the Earl of Middlesex and Lord John Sackville, championing their county's players' (H. S. Altham, *A History of Cricket,* 1926, p. 37).

31. (1695–1744), 7th Bt, 1713; M.P. 'Sussex, under their patrons Sir William Gage and the second Duke of Richmond, had a fine side in the thirties and forties' (ibid. 33).

32. Thomas Pelham (ca 1705–37), of Stanmer, Lewes, Sussex; M.P. A cousin of the Duke of Newcastle, he succeeded his brother Henry to the family estates in 1725 (Sedgwick ii. 333).

33. No letter from HW to Whaley has been found.

TO CHARLES LYTTELTON, Monday 18 August 1735 OS

Printed from a photostat of the MS in the possession of Viscount Cobham, Hagley Hall, Stourbridge, Worcs. First printed in N&Q 1869, 4th ser., iii. 3. Reprinted, Toynbee i. 3–4. The MS descended in the Lyttelton family to the present owner.

August 18th 1735.

Dear Charles,

IF I WAS impatient to see you to talk with you, I am much more so now to thank you for being so extremely obliging in your invitation to Hagley. My Lord[1] is come to town, but I believe he will go down to Warwickshire[2] in September, when if you are at Hagley I will certainly make myself so happy as to pass a day with you.[3] My Lord Conway thinks himself no less obliged to my dear Charles than I do, and has given me a very hard task, which is to return you the thanks your civility deserves. While I say this, I fear you will think as we are friends I might have spared these speeches; but, my dear Charles, tho' friends ought not to stand on compliments, they ought the more to say what they think, and I hope friends are capable of thinking as fine things of each other, as the most polite courtier could say without meaning. Such a one would tell you out of mere civility, that he was, what I am with the greatest sincerity,

My dear Charles

Your most affect[ionate] friend and humble servant

HOR. WALPOLE

1. Francis Seymour Conway (1718–94), 2d Bn Conway, 1732; cr. (1750) E. and (1793) M. of Hertford; HW's cousin and correspondent.

2. That is, to Ragley, his country seat in Warwickshire.

3. We do not know whether a meeting took place.

From John Whaley, Wednesday 27 August 1735 OS

Printed from Toynbee *Supp.* iii. 86–8, where the letter was first printed from the MS formerly in the Waller Collection. For the history of the MS see *ante* 10 Aug. 1735.

Dorchester, Aug. 27, 1735.

Dear Sir,

I WAS favoured with yours[1] at Portsmouth, from which place Mr Dodd wrote to you on the 20th instant,[2] and desired the favour of an answer at Salisbury, which he was really disappointed in not meeting, and begs you would not fail writing to him on Saturday night directed to the post-house at Bath. Portsmouth and the fleet gave us such a pleasure as they must give to every lover of liberty in Britain; Mr Dodd and I ventured our carcasses in a sloop to the Isle of Wight to and from which we had a most delightful passage, and in our return went on board the *Blenheim* a second rate of 90 guns completely manned and the admiral[3] on board, a sight which no man that don't see it can conceive. There were about 23 more of these noble guardians of our liberty at Spithead. From Portsmouth we went to Winchester, the college of which is far inferior to ours at Eton in building and situation; as to their numbers and performances I leave you to judge from what I have enclosed, a catalogue[4] of the present school, and some of their top exercises. From Winchester we went through Stockbridge to Salisbury, a very ill built town, and famous for nothing but its fine spire, and for making scissors and flannel for under-petticoats. On Monday we were at Lord Pembroke's[5] at Wilton, where we were most elegantly entertained with the best remains of Greek and Roman statuary, of which I will give you a full account when I have the pleasure of seeing you. Yesterday we went to Stonehenge, the most surprising relics of some ancient building, but of what *adhuc sub judice lis est.*[6] We likewise

1. Missing.
2. Also missing.
3. Probably Hon. Charles Stewart (1681–1741), Vice-Adm., 1734; M.P. In 1734 he was made second-in-command to Sir John Norris in the Channel. 'Sir John Norris with the British fleet is arrived at Lisbon to the no small joy of that city. . . . Another squadron is fitting out under Admiral Stewart in order to join Sir John Norris' (GM *sub* 30 June 1735, v. 331).
4. Missing; the catalogue does not appear in the SH records.
5. Henry Herbert (ca 1689–1750), 9th E. of Pembroke, 1733.
6. 'The case is still before the court' (Horace, *Ars poetica* 78).

saw yesterday some other stones as unaccountably put together by Sir John Vanbrugh[7] at Eastbury,[8] the seat of Mr Dodington,[9] whom we saw seated in state at dinner between Lady Dudley[10] and Mrs Beagham,[11] *cætera quis nescit?*[12] The inside of the house is all designed by its master and is fitted up in the same taste as the lady[13] in Virgil is dressed

Aureus arcus erat, crines nodantur in aurum
Aurea purpuream subnectit fibula vestem.[14]

I believe I quote the lines wrong but you will both correct and excuse me. We laid last night in Blandford, a very pretty new town, occasioned by the dreadful fire there about four years ago;[15] from thence we came this morning through a prodigious pleasant country to this place, where I beg leave to assure you,

I am
Sir
Your most obliged friend and humble servant,
J. WHALEY

Mr Dodd's best compliments wait you. We did not forget a bowl of arrack punch in honour of yesterday.[16]

7. (1664–1726), Kt, 1714; architect and dramatist.

8. Near Blandford, Dorset; built by Vanbrugh 1716–18.

9. George Bubb Dodington (?1691–1762), cr. (1761) Bn Melcombe; M.P.

10. Elizabeth Kennedy (d. ca 1750), m. (1719) Sir William Dudley, 3d Bt, 1721.

11. Katherine Beaghan (d. 1756), m. (1725, acknowledged 1742) George Bubb Dodington (MANN ii. 105, 424).

12. 'Who does not know the rest?' (Ovid, *Amores* I. v. 25).

13. Dido, Queen of the Carthaginians.

14. *Cui pharetra ex auro, crines . . . vestem:* 'her quiver is of gold, her tresses are knotted into gold, golden is the buckle to clasp her purple cloak' (Virgil, *Æneid* iv. 138–9).

15. In 1731 all but forty houses in Blandford-Forum were destroyed by fire. By an act of Parliament the following year, the town was rebuilt (S. Lewis, *Topographical Dict. of England,* 1842, i. 274–5).

16. Sir R[obert] W[alpole]'s birthday (HW). He was born 26 Aug. 1676.

From JOHN WHALEY, Friday 19 September 1735 OS

Printed from Toynbee *Supp.* iii. 88–91, where the letter was first printed from the MS formerly in the Waller Collection. For the history of the MS see *ante* 10 Aug. 1735.

Buckingham, September 19th 1735.

Dear Sir,

MR DODD was favoured with yours[1] at Oxford, for which he begs you to accept his thanks by me; which if you do you will indeed be as generous as Diomede χρύσεα χαλκείων, μεταβαλλόμενος.[2] You found him I think last at Bath, where we stayed about a week; and in compliance to the taste of the place, drank the waters and lounged from morning till night; it is indeed a very proper place to do nothing in; very widely differing from its neighbouring city of Bristol, in which we may truly say an idle man has no business: where the Bath music was (in our ears at least) far exceeded by the creaking of ropes, and rumbling of sledges; and Harrison's room[3] and its gaudy company deservedly contemptible when compared with the sweating greasy crowds of the custom house; as widely does this flourishing city differ from its neighbouring city of Wells, which is indeed only the skeleton of a city at present, and has nothing in it worth observation; within two miles of it is a famous subterraneous cavern called Wookey Hole,[4] which runs 312 yards underground amidst craggy rocks, and murmuring waters. To the farther end of this we went, armed with a dram of brandy, a quid of tobacco, and each man a candle in his hand. Can you forgive me for carrying your friend into so dismal a place, where only a Bajazet[5] could have desired to have been?

Far from the hated sight of man and day.[6]

Tamerlane[7] did not deserve such usage, but his courage and brandy brought him safe out again. From Wells we came back to Bath, from

1. Missing.

2. 'Giving golden for brazen.' Whaley has freely adapted the phrase from Homer, *Iliad* vi. 236.

3. The fashionable ballroom built in 1708 by Thomas Harrison, at the instigation of 'Beau' Nash, and enlarged in 1720. Known later in the century as the Old Assembly Rooms, it was located on the east side of the Orange Grove, near the bowling-green (Lewis Melville, *Bath under Beau Nash*, 1907, pp. 47, 116–17).

4. A cavern in the Mendip Hills, about a mile and a half from Wookey.

5. A character (emperor of the Turks) in Marlowe's and Rowe's *Tamerlane*.

thence made to Glocester, in our way to which we saw, about six miles from Bath, the gardens of Mr Blaithwaite[8] which are exceeding well disposed on the side of a hill, beautified by several fine waterworks, and a very noble terrace, the motto on which is

Dispicere unde queas alios passimque videre
Errare, atque viam palantes quærere vitæ.[9]

Six miles beyond these is Badminton, a magnificent seat of the Duke of Beaufort.[10] Had I time I could say a great deal more of it, so, perhaps you'll say, I might about its master, but you know 'em both too well, to leave any room for my encomiums or criticisms.

From Badminton we went about 15 miles to Cirencester, near which is a good pretty house of Lord Bathurst's,[11] with a very pretty park;[12] the middle view of the house is terminated by the statue of a slave in chains;[13] the noble peer might perhaps have been blessed with many originals, had the work of December 11, 1713[14] taken its desired effects. From hence we went to Gloucester, a neat little city enough; 12 miles from thence we came to Sandywell[15] where we were in hopes to have met Lord Conway,[16] but he was gone. Mr Dodd begs to know where he is now, please to tell me in your next; I cannot say Sandywell answered our expectation, it is a tolerable pretty little box, but most dirtily situated. From Sandywell we came

6. Rowe, *Tamerlane* II. ii. 196–7:
Come, lead me to my dungeon; plunge me down,
Deep from the hated sight of man and day.

7. Mr Dodd had acted the part of Tamerlane at Eton (HW).

8. William Blathwayt (1688–1742), of Dyrham Park, near Marshfield, Glos (Burke, *Landed Gentry*, 4th edn, 1868, p. 114). The house, designed by Hauduroy, a French architect, and William Talman, was built 1692–1704 by his father William Blathwayt (d. 1717), secretary of state to William III. The gardens were probably laid out by George London (Mark Girouard, 'Dyrham Park, Gloucestershire,' *Country Life* 1962, cxxxi. 335–9, 396–9).

9. *Despicere unde queas alios passimque videre*
Errare atque viam palantis quærere vitæ.
'Whence you may look down from the height upon others and behold them all astray, wandering abroad and seeking the path of life' (Lucretius, *De rerum natura* ii. 9–10).

10. Henry Somerset (1707–45), 3d D. of Beaufort, 1714. No evidence has been found that HW visited either house.

11. Allen Bathurst (1684–1775), cr. (1712) Bn and (1772) E. Bathurst.

12. For detailed accounts of Cirencester House and its park see James Lees-Milne, *Earls of Creation*, 1962, pp. 33–56, and Christopher Hussey, *English Gardens and Landscapes 1700–1750*, 1967, chap. xi.

13. Probably a statue of Prometheus (information given by the 6th Earl Bathurst to Paget Toynbee).

14. Possibly a reference to the grant of the Asiento, a monopoly of the slave trade with Spanish America, in the Treaty of Utrecht, signed 11 April 1713.

15. Sandywell Park, five miles from Cheltenham, built ca 1680 by Henry Bret (M. E. Macartney, *English Houses and Gardens in the 17th and 18th Centuries*, 1908, p. 18).

16. See *ante* 18 Aug. 1735 OS, n. 1.

to Woodstock; please to ask Mr Pope[17] what I should say of Blenheim,[18] and Anthony Wood[19] what is [to] be said of the antiquities of Oxford,[20] they are both too copious for me [to] tell of, till you indulge me with a pipe at King's College.

Chalbury in Oxfords[hire]
September 20th 1735.

We have this day seen Ditchley about two miles from hence, the seat of the Earl of Litchfield,[21] which is indeed most delightfully situated, looking down (with no great satisfaction I fancy) on Bleinheim,[22] but for which, all Tories might at present have been as well situated.

We are now within half a mile of Cornbury,[23] where we have this afternoon been most elegantly entertained by Sir Anthony Vandyke,[24] and were almost apt to cry out that Charles I did nothing wrong, from the noble appearance around us of the brave Royalists that favoured his cause. I'll say no more of the paintings than that your friend Mr Dodd chose rather to gaze on the portrait of the Duchess of Orléans,[25] stuck up over the chimney-piece, than on the real flesh and blood of Lady Charlotte Hyde[26] walking in the gardens.

I beg, dear Sir, you would favour me with a line by next Thursday's post, directed to me at the post-house in Shrewsbury, in which I shall be glad to be informed when you design being at Cambridge again. Mr Dodd's most sincere respects wait on you, and I am,

Dear Sir,

Your most faithful friend and most humble servant,

J. WHALEY

If my Lord Conway is with you, Mr Dodd begs you would present his service to him.

17. Alexander Pope (1688–1744), poet.

18. Presumably an allusion to the verses 'Upon the Duke of Marlborough's House at Woodstock,' first published in 1714 and attributed to Pope.

19. Anthony à Wood (1632–95), antiquary and historian.

20. An allusion to Wood's *Historia et antiquitates Universitatis Oxoniensis*, Oxford, 1674.

21. George Henry Lee (1690–1743), 2d E. of Lichfield, 1716. HW visited Ditchley in 1760; see *Country Seats* 26.

22. Five miles from Ditchley.

23. The seat of Henry Hyde (1672–1753), 4th E. of Clarendon, 1723.

24. There were many portraits by Van Dyck at Cornbury; see V. J. Watney, 'Inventory of the Pictures at Cornbury . . .

From JOHN WHALEY and JOHN DODD, Friday 3 October 1735 OS

Printed from Toynbee *Supp.* iii. 92–4, where the letter was first printed from the MS formerly in the Waller Collection. For the history of the MS see *ante* 10 Aug. 1735.

Shrewsbury, October 3d 1735.

Dear Sir,

TO endeavour to express my thanks to you for your goodness would be much to undervalue them for the overflowings of a grateful heart are like the sublime conceptions of a grateful poet's imagination, too strong to be expressed, *quod nequeo monstrare et sentio tantum.*[1] Could anything add to my esteem for you, it would be that affection you express for one[2] whom I love equal to myself, and who will always be an honour to himself and his tutor while he is a friend to Mr Walpole: he I think in his last[3] informed you of what we met worth observation between Charlbury and Worcester where we stayed till Monday last. It is as pretty a city as we have seen in our journey, very well built and very populous; it had formerly a great trade in clothing, but its present manufacture is gloves, in which above ten thousand people are constantly employed. The Severn which runs by this town adds much to its beauty, its cathedral is but mean and old.

Near Worcester we saw some very good houses; Holt Castle a very pleasant old house of Mr Bromley's[4] of Cambridgeshire, but too far from Newmarket to be agreeable to him. Both Mr Dodd and myself are not a little concerned at the pains he takes in the education of Lord Conway.[5] Two miles from Holt is Ambersley[6] a new

in 1751,' *Cornbury and the Forest of Wychwood*, 1910, pp. 235–44.

25. Henrietta Anne (1644–70) of England, m. (1661) Philippe de Bourbon, Duc d'Orléans.

26. Lady Charlotte Hyde (d. 1740), dau. of the 4th E. of Clarendon (GM 1740, x. 148).

1. *Qualem nequeo monstrare et sentio tantum:* 'such an one as I cannot point to, and only feel' (Juvenal, *Satires* vii. 56).

2. John Dodd.

3. Missing.

4. Henry Bromley (1705–55), of Horseheath Hall, Cambs; cr. (1741) Bn Montfort; M.P.

5. Presumably on the turf. See MANN iv. 74.

6. Ombersley Court, about five miles from Worcester. The house, designed by Francis Smith of Warwick, was built 1723–30 (Arthur Oswald, 'Ombersley Court, Worcestershire,' *Country Life* 1953, cxiii. 34–7, 94–7, 152–5).

and very good seat of Samuel Sandys Esqr.[7] Three miles from that is Westwood,[8] the seat of Sir Herbert Packington,[9] a knight of high renown in the camps of Cupid. It is a very old house, built more in the Chinese taste than the English, but situated in the midst of a most delightful wood. In the park is a most noble lake of above 100 acres of water; but how dreadful is it to think that these may perhaps ere long by the turn of a die

Permutare dominos et cedere in altera jura.[10]

In our way from Worcester to Bridgnorth we came through Hartlebury, the palace of the bishop of Worcester,[11] to whom we were introduced, being very desirous of the pleasure of seeing so great and good a prelate to whose virtue and resolution we in some measure owe our present happy establishment.[12] From thence we went to Bridgenorth, a large corporation town situated on the banks of the Severn; it is built on a rock, the sides of which being excavated in many places afford little snug houses . . .[13]
[Tro]glodytes of this . . .
to Parliament . . .
almost the whole town belongs to Watkyn Williams Wynn.[14] Seven miles more brought us on Tuesday night to this town, which in its situation exceeds all towns I ever saw or read of. It stands on a gently rising hill, and the Severn almost quite surrounds it, on whose banks are most agreeable walks, on which I doubt not but you have often walked in imagination with Melinda and Silvia.[15] And now dear Sir (as I have been writing a long hour by Shrewsbury clock)[16] I suppose you are sufficiently tired with this long winded and insipid narration, from which (were I inclined to be more im-

7. (1695–1770), cr. (1743) Bn Sandys; M.P.

8. Westwood Park, near Droitwich, Worcs. Originally built as a hunting lodge in the late sixteenth century, it became the seat of the Pakington family in the mid-seventeenth century, when various additions to the house were made ('Westwood Park, Worcestershire,' *Country Life* 1902, xii. 688–97).

9. Sir Herbert Perrott Pakington (ca 1701–48), 5th Bt, 1727; M.P.

10. *Permutet dominos et cedat in altera jura:* 'changes owners and passes under the power of another' (Horace, *Epistles* II. ii. 174).

11. John Hough (1651–1743), Bp of Oxford, 1690; Bp of Lichfield and Coventry, 1699; Bp of Worcester, 1717.

12. Hough had successfully withstood James II's illegal attempts to oust him from the presidency of Magdalen College, Oxford.

13. 'Piece cut out [of the MS], carrying with it a part of the text on the opposite side' (Toynbee).

14. Sir Watkin Williams (after 1719, Williams Wynn) (?1693–1749), 3d Bt, 1740; M.P.

15. Characters (cousins) in Farquhar's *The Recruiting Officer,* 1706.

16. Falstaff 'fought a long hour by Shrewsbury clock' (1 *Henry IV* V. iv. 151).

pertinent) I am obliged to release you, we having just received a summons from Sir Richard Corbet,[17] mayor of this town, to attend him and his brethren to dinner, a command which out of our loyalty to this burgh and roast beef we cannot disobey . . .[18]

shall always be the study of him who is,

Dear Sir
Most faithfully yours,

J. WHALEY

Mr Dodd desires me to beg you would write to him by next Tuesday's post to the post-house at Derby, where I also shall hope to find a letter from you. He is in reality at present writing letters of business which prevents his answering yours.[19] We hope to meet you at college in a fortnight or three weeks at farthest.

Dear Walpole, excuse my silence here, I will make you amends from Derby.

Yours most faithfully,

JOHN DODD[20]

From JOHN WHALEY, Saturday 11 October 1735 OS

Printed from Toynbee *Supp.* iii. 94–7, where the letter was first printed from the MS formerly in the Waller Collection. For the history of the MS see *ante* 10 Aug. 1735.

From the Devil's Arse,[1]
Oct. 11th 1735.

Dear Sir,

MR Dodd tells me he concluded his letter[2] to you with an account of Chester; I don't doubt but he was large in his encomiums, though I doubt not but his being born there[3] would

17. Sir Richard Corbet (1696–1774), 4th Bt, 1701; M.P.
18. See n. 13 above.
19. Missing.
20. 'These two last lines are in Dodd's handwriting' (Toynbee).

1. In the Derbyshire Peak, about six miles NW of Tideswell (*A New Display of the Beauties of England,* 1776, ii. 101).
2. Missing.

easily prejudice you in its favour, as it would have done me had it wanted partiality to be commended. We met nothing worth observation between this and Manchester, which is a most noble and flourishing town of trade, making vast quantities of thread, and all sorts of linen and cotton goods. Here is a very fine collegiate church and pretty college for a warden and four fellows, with an hospital for 60 boys, founded by Humphry Cheetham,[4] who likewise built a library and endowed it with £116 a year to buy books, of which there is a very good collection, enslaved like those at King's College, for the common use of all people that come there. We met little worth note between Manchester and Buxton Wells in Derbyshire, where we lay last night, which is really a very pretty place, being an epitome of Bath and Tunbridge, but free from their coquetry and extravagance. Here are warm, cold, and chalybeate springs, and within half a mile of it another Wookey hole; and forgive me when I tell you your friend Dodd has out-Theseused Theseus,[5] for he has been both in that, and the Devil's Arse today, which you know make three descents; but, as I need not tell you, he is of too volatile a nature to stay long at the bottom of anything. The last place mentioned is really dreadful, into which we were conducted by old women whom we could not help fancying so many sibyls, though instead of golden branches they clapped candles into our hands, and were very quiet at our first appearance to them, and all the way of our subterraneous journey; but at our return, on not giving them just what they demanded, they scolded and sputtered as furiously as a thousand sibyls, and were truly *non mortale sonantes*.[6] But we got off safe at last and rode ten miles over a most bleak and dismal country, when in the midst of an amphitheatre of barren and craggy hills our eyes were struck with the glittering of the windows of Chatsworth,[7] and truly refreshed with the beauty of so elegant a

3. Dodd was born at Chester 5 Oct. 1717 (Constance, Lady Russell, *Swallowfield and its Owners*, 1901, p. 227).

4. Humphrey Chetham (1580–1653), founder of the Chetham Hospital and Library at Manchester. Established under Chetham's will, the Hospital and Library occupied the building to the north of the collegiate church (since 1847 Manchester cathedral) that had formerly been used as the residential college for priests serving the church (W. R. Whatton, *A History of the Chetham Hospital and Library*, Manchester, 1833, pp. 173–80; Thomas Perkins, *The Cathedral Church of Manchester*, 1901, pp. 63–7).

5. Who entered a cave to seek the Minotaur.

6. *Nec mortale sonans:* 'not sounding human' (Virgil, *Æneid* vi. 50).

7. The seat of William Cavendish (?1698–1755), 3d D. of Devonshire, 1729. HW visited Chatsworth in 1760; see *Country Seats* 28–9.

pile of building, which exactly answers the idea one has of Milton's Pandaemonium a palace in hell, and seems to

Rise like an exhalation from the ground.[8]

All that it differs from his diabolical majesties palace in is in being well supplied with fine waters, which are formed into most beautiful fountains and cascades. But I beg pardon for detaining you in the Peak of Derbyshire, while your thoughts might be so much better employed on the other side of the Ganges; perhaps this may stop you while you are eagerly pursuing some nymph with eyes of the size of a period, or break off your devotion while you are sticking a pig with a mandarin on the top of a mountain in the province of Quenton;[9] but why do I jest with sacred things; some angry deity of rice has just leaped over the table and kicked down my ink pot.[10]

Derby, October 13th 1735.

Dear Sir,

I WAS favoured with your letter[11] here and rejoice that you are got again to college, where we hope to be on Sunday or Monday next at farthest,[12] and have the pleasure (which we both most eagerly long for) of meeting you well, so that we can trouble you no more to write to us. We are this morning setting out for Nottingham, from whence we[13] shall hasten, by Belvoir Castle,[14] Burleigh House,[15] Stamford and Stilton to Cambridge, till which time I can only by dead letters tell you that

I am
With the utmost sincerity
Your most affectionate friend and humble servant,

J. WHALEY

8. 'Anon out of the earth a fabric huge
Rose like an exhalation, with the sound
Of dulcet symphonies and voices sweet'
(Milton, *Paradise Lost* i. 710–12).

9. Perhaps a phonetic rendering of Kwang-tung. HW had apparently written Whaley an enthusiastic account of a book on China similar to the one he sent to Lord Hervey (see following letter). The book was doubtless Jean Baptiste du Halde's *Description géographique, historique, chronologique, politique, et physique de l'Empire de la Chine*, 4 vols, 1735. HW's copy, now WSL, is Hazen, *Cat. of HW's Lib.* 874.

10. 'There is a great ink blot at this place in the original' (Toynbee).

11. Missing.

12. They arrived at Cambridge on Sunday, 19 October (*ante* 10 Aug. 1735, n. 2).

13. 'MS "she"' (Toynbee).

14. The seat, near Grantham, of John

From LORD HERVEY,[1] Tuesday 21 October 1735 OS

Printed from the MS now WSL. First printed, Toynbee *Supp.* iii. 97–8. Damer-Waller; the MS was sold Sotheby's 5 Dec. 1921 (first Waller Sale), lot 144, to Maggs; offered by them, Cat. Nos 433 (Christmas 1922), lot 3342; 471 (1925), lot 2831; and 501 (Spring 1928), lot 322; resold Sotheby's 4 May 1942, lot 255, to Maggs for WSL.

Kensington,[2] Oct. 21st 1735.

Dear Sir,

I RETURN you many thanks for the favour of the letter[3] I received from you yesterday and am extremely glad to hear the History of China[4] has so strong an effect upon you, as it is the surest sign of your being pleased with what you read, and that your being pleased is the most agreeable effect I could propose from procuring you the book.

You describe in a very entertaining manner the change it has made in you, but whatever that alteration may be it can never be more extraordinary than that any alteration should make you agreeable to me: and notwithstanding my partiality to China, I advise you if you can to continue an Englishman. Upon the whole it will be better for you; that your father[5] is one, is the better for us.

The Prince of Modena[6] is at last arrived, and has been several times at Court,[7] but I cannot say I am so much charmed with an Italian prince realized, as you are with a mandarin in description. They are most of them haughty and dull, and ignorant of everything but forms and genealogies; they seem to measure all merit by the length of a pedigree, as if the esteem of mankind was to be purchased like the knighthood of Malta or preferment in the Teutonic Order;

Manners (1696–1779), 3d D. of Rutland, 1721.

15. Burghley House, near Stamford, Northants, the seat of Brownlow Cecil (1701–54), 8th E. of Exeter, 1722. HW visited the house 24 July 1763 (*Country Seats* 58–9; MONTAGU ii. 91).

1. John (1696–1743), styled Lord Hervey 1723–33; summoned to Parliament as Bn Hervey of Ickworth, 1733; M.P.; memoirist; Pope's 'Sporus.'

2. Hervey was vice-chamberlain of the Household 1730–40.

3. Missing.

4. See previous letter, n. 9.

5. At this time Hervey was a supporter of Sir Robert Walpole's ministry, and through his influence with the Queen rendered Walpole valuable service.

6. Francis III (Francesco Maria d'Este) (1698–1780), D. of Modena 1737–80 (GRAY i. 242 n. 5).

7. 'Saturday, 18 [October 1735]. The hereditary Pr[ince] of Modena arrived here, to solicit (as reported) his Majesty's good offices with the allied powers, for the restitution of his father's revenues, which they had sequestered for his attachment to the Emperor' (GM 1735, v. 617).

and that the world would pay the same regard to the virtues of our ancestors, that the second commandment tells us God almighty does to their sins, whilst the one should revere as the other punishes to the third and fourth generation, though the traces of both are lost in the offsprings that were notorious in their progenitors.

When you see Dr Middleton[8] I shall be obliged to you if you will make my compliments to him: it is an acquaintance I dare say you cultivate, and one I should wish you to cultivate for both your sakes. It will certainly be agreeable and may be useful to both. If there is anything in which I can be serviceable to you in this part of the world you will oblige me by employing me. I am with the greatest truth

Dear Sir,

Your most obedient and faithful servant,

HERVEY[9]

The King will not be here till Sunday at soonest.[10]

TO CHARLES LYTTELTON, Saturday 22 May 1736 OS

Printed from a photostat of the MS in the possession of Viscount Cobham, Hagley Hall, Stourbridge, Worcs. First printed, Toynbee i. 15–16. Reprinted (with brief omissions) in *Horace Walpole's Fugitive Verses,* ed. W. S. Lewis, 1931, pp. 100–1. The MS descended in the Lyttelton family to the present owner.

King's Coll[ege],[1] May 22d 1736.

Dear Charles,

I HAVE been at Oxford; how could you possibly leave it? after seeing that charming place, I can hardly ask you to come to Cambridge. But when will you? I long to talk it all over with you. I

8. Conyers Middleton (1683–1750), D.D., fellow of Trinity College, Cambridge; author and controversialist, whose deistic views had a strong effect on HW; HW's correspondent (DALRYMPLE 1 n. 1). Hervey was Middleton's chief patron.

9. John Lord Hervey, eldest son to the Earl of Bristol, vice-chamberlain to the King, and afterwards lord privy seal (HW).

10. George II landed at Harwich from Hanover on Sunday, 26 October (GM 1735, v. 618).

1. HW was admitted as a fellow-commoner at King's College, Cambridge, 11 March 1735.

just saw Sir Edward Noel[2] there, but had hardly time to exchange a syllable with him; he looks just what he always was; I wanted mightily to shake him into a fat good-natured laugh. Maudlin[3] Walks please me most; I felt a pensive joy in 'em occasioned by thinking two Lytteltons[4] had been drowned in the adjoining stream; and another[5] had so often walked there.

The frolic boy, unfortunately gay,
Too near the current urg'd his little play;
The yielding bank beneath his feet retir'd,
And his soft soul absorb'd by waves expir'd.
The pious youth (ah' tyrant of the flood,
Why vainly pious, why untimely good?)
Plung'd after him precipitate; and try'd
To save his brother; but in trying, dyed.
Go, gentle pair, nor at your fate repine;
Earth or Elysium would to neither shine,
Unless to share the joys of both, both join.
 Mov'd at our tears; and mov'd to see no more
The hapless striplings sporting on his shore,
The River God sunk his flag-waving head,
And melancholy winding thro' the mead,
In bubbling murmurs told his grief; till here
He saw another Lyttelton appear;
No more a double loss he could bemoan,
Finding the worth of two compris'd in one.[6]

Excuse this flight, Charles; Oxford inspired me; Maudlin Walks gave me the hint, and friendship dictated to

Yours sincerely

H. Walpole

I received yours,[7] since I wrote this. Dodd is at your service. I wish you joy! Adieu!

2. Sir Edward Noel (1715–74), 6th Bt, 1733; 9th Bn Wentworth, 1745; cr. (1762) Vct Wentworth. He had been at Eton with Lyttelton and HW; he matriculated at New College, Oxford 23 July 1733.

3. That is, Magdalen College, Oxford.

4. The two eldest sons of Sir Thomas Lyttelton, 1st Bt, John and Thomas, were drowned in the Cherwell 9 May 1635. HW had doubtless seen their tomb in Magdalen College chapel. See *Anecdotes of Painting, Works* iii. 168.

5. Charles Lyttelton had been a student at University College, Oxford.

6. HW had perhaps read Abraham Cowley's 'Elegy on the death of John

TO CHARLES LYTTELTON, Tuesday 27 July 1736 OS

Printed from a photostat of the MS in the possession of Viscount Cobham, Hagley Hall, Stourbridge, Worcs. First printed in N&Q 1869, 4th ser., iii. 3. Reprinted, Toynbee i. 19–20. The MS descended in the Lyttelton family to the present owner.

K[ing's] Coll[ege], July 27, 1736.

Dear Charles,

I AM returned again to Cambridge,[1] and can tell you what I never expected, that I like Norfolk. Not any of the ingredients, as hunting or country gentlemen, for I had nothing to do with them,[2] but the county; which a little from Houghton is woody, and full of delightful prospects. I went to see Norwich and Yarmouth, both which I like exceedingly. I spent my time at Houghton for the first week almost alone; we have a charming garden all wilderness; much adapted to my romantic inclinations. The last week I had company[3] with me. I don't hear whether George Mountagu[4] is gone[5] yet or not; I conclude he is by not hearing from him.

Adieu! dear Charles
Yours in haste
H. WALPOLE

From JOHN WHALEY, Sunday 19 September 1736 OS

Printed from Toynbee *Supp.* iii. 98–100, where the letter was first printed from the MS formerly in the Waller Collection. For the history of the MS see *ante* 10 Aug. 1735.

Address: To Horatio Walpole Esq. at the Right Honourable Sir Robert Walpole's at Chelsea, Middlesex. *Postmark:* LEOMINSTER. 22 SE.

Memorandum (by HW, on the verso of the MS): On my reading Lord Hervey the epigram in this letter he composed this answer ex tempore.

Littleton, Esq.; son and heir to Sir Thomas Littleton, who was drowned leaping into the water to save his younger brother,' printed in Cowley's *Works,* 10th edn, 1707–8, iii. 49–51. HW's copy of the *Works* is Hazen, *Cat. of HW's Lib.* 1823.

7. Missing.

1. HW had been with his father at Houghton for a fortnight (*Daily Adv.* 5 July 1736; HW to Sir Robert Walpole 27 July 1736 OS, FAMILY 5).

2. Thomas Gray wrote sympathetically to HW 15 July 1736 about imagining him

I read your compliment, but there I see
Not what I am, but what I ought to be;
Thus Trajan's character when Pliny rais'd,
'Twere better so to praise, than to be prais'd[1] (Toynbee).

Kingsland,[2] September 19th 1736.

Dear Sir,

I WAS this morning favoured with your short epistle,[3] but it was indeed short and sweet; the epigram is very pretty. And in return take two from me. Perusing Camden's *Britannia* I met four lines on Sir Francis Drake which I thought worth translating:

Drake, pererrati novit quem terminus orbis,
Quemque semel mundi vidit uterque polus;
Si taceant homines, faizent[4] *te sidera notum.*
Sol nescit comitis immemor esse sui.[5]

To the world's bound, that saw him, Drake is known
With pride his presence either pole will own,
Silent were men, the stars would tell his name,
And the sun speak his fellow traveller's fame.

I have so often with pleasure heard you speak in praise of the author[6] of the epigram you sent me and particularly in relation to his learning, and correspondence about the Roman senate,[7] that I have long entertained the same opinion of him which you do, as you will see from the under lines, which perhaps you will not esteem poems, because they are so plain and true.

at Houghton 'in a confusion of wine and bawdy and hunting and tobacco' (GRAY i. 104).

3. Not identified.

4. George Montagu (ca 1713–80), HW's correspondent and member of the 'triumvirate' with HW and Lyttelton at Eton.

5. On his Grand Tour, which he made with HW's cousin, Lord Conway. Conway left England 17 June (GRAY i. 166 n. 34; MONTAGU i. 9).

1. HW quoted the last two lines in his letter of 30 Dec. 1736 to Conyers Middleton (DALRYMPLE 3)

2. Whaley was staying with his friend Sneyd Davies, who had a living at Kingsland, near Leominster, Herts (Nichols, *Lit. Illus.* i. 509).

3. Missing.

4. *Facient.*

5. William Camden, *Britannia: or a Chorographical Description of Great Britain and Ireland,* ed. Edmund Gibson, 2d edn, 1722, i. 34. HW's copy of this edition is Hazen, *Cat. of HW's Lib.*, No. 563.

6. Lord Hervey (see below).

7. Later published as *Letters between Lord Hervey and Dr Middleton concerning The Roman Senate,* ed. Thomas Knowles, 1778. HW's copy is Hazen, op. cit. 3168.

To Lord Hervey, on his discourse on
the Rom[an] sen[ate].

How Roman senates once were fill'd
From thy judicious pen we know;
That virtue calls up Britain's peers
Yourself to future times will show.

Mr Dodd and all here join in best respects to you, and it is with pleasure I find myself every day more

Your obliged friend and servant,

J. WHALEY

TO CHARLES LYTTELTON, Sunday 18 September 1737 OS

Printed from a photostat of the MS in the possession of Viscount Cobham, Hagley Hall, Stourbridge, Worcs. First printed in N&Q 1869, 4th ser., iii. 2 (misdated 'Sept. 18, 1732'). Reprinted, Toynbee i. 24–5. The MS descended in the Lyttelton family to the present owner.

Sept. 18, 1737.

Dear Charles,

YOU will not wonder that I have so long deferred answering your friendly letter, as you know the fatal cause.[1] You have been often witness to my happiness, and by that may partly figure what I feel for losing so fond a mother. If my loss consisted solely in being deprived of one that loved me so much, it would feel lighter to me than it now does, as I doated on her. Your goodness to me encourages me to write at large my dismal thoughts; but for your sake I will not make use of the liberty I might take, but will stifle what my thoughts run so much on. There is one circumstance of my misfortune which I am sure you will not be unwilling to hear, as no one can that loved

1. HW's mother, Lady Walpole, died 20 Aug. 1737 at Chelsea. He was so affected by her death that his friends became concerned about his health, as their letters to him show. The present letter is the only one extant written by HW during the twenty months following his mother's death.

her, and among the many that did, I have reason to flatter myself that you was one. I mean, the surprising calmness and courage which my dear mother showed before her death. I believe few women would behave so well, and I am certain no man could behave better. For three or four days before she died, she spoke of it with less indifference, than one speaks of a cold; and while she was sensible, which she was within her two last hours, she discovered no manner of apprehension. This my dear Charles was some alleviation to my grief. I am now got to Cambridge out of a house which I could not bear; wherever I am, believe me

Yours ever

H. Walpole

Mr Dodd desires his compliments.

From James Anstey,[1] Wednesday 2 November 1737 OS

Printed from Toynbee *Supp.* iii. 102–4, where the letter was first printed from the MS formerly in the Waller Collection. Damer-Waller; the MS was sold Sotheby's 5 Dec. 1921 (first Waller Sale), lot 87, to Field; not further traced.

Eton, November 2, 1737.

Sir,

Having an opportunity of writing by Mr Naylor[2] I could not let slip the occasion, though I have nothing to say but what, I believe, you are already very well assured of, that I highly respect and value you. I remember you once expressed a desire of seeing some of our school performances; had I any of them by me, the other leaf perhaps might furnish out a more agreeable entertainment. The half dozen of epigrams with which I have blotted it had the good luck not to be disliked here, but I suspend my judgment of them till I know yours. The Dean[3] told me he liked them so well, particularly

1. (1714–42), Eton 1727–31; fellow of King's College, Cambridge 1735–42; private tutor to HW at King's and tutor to the eldest son of the 3d Earl of Cholmondeley (Gray i. 5 n. 19).

2. Probably John Naylor (1709–61), Eton 1718–27; fellow of King's College, Cambridge 1730–47; assistant clerk in the House of Commons 1740–4 (*Eton Coll. Reg.*).

3. Henry Bland (d. 1746), D.D., second chaplain to Chelsea Hospital, 1715, and chaplain, 1724; chaplain to the King, 1716; canon of Windsor, 1723; Dean of

the first, that he would show them to Sir Robert: but the author's ambition will amply be satisfied, if they are approved of by Sir Robert's son. But enough of these trifles—what is more material, my Lord[4] and his brother[5] are extremely well and proceed in their business with pleasure. Bob is just gone to school prepared with his prosodia, and at his return I expect to hear he is advanced to the next remove. Their dutiful respects attend upon you. I am in the true, genuine, original meaning of the words,

Your most obedient and affectionate servant,

JAMES ANSTEY

[Enclosure]

Ad Hispanos.

Quæ nova devotos leti sitis urget, Iberi,
Quis deus in Britonas vos malè amicus agit?
Virginis arma olim, et flammas sensistis Elizæ;
Nuper et Herculeum contudit Anna jugum.
Fatalis furor est incendere Cæsaris iras,
Fœmineæ toties quos domuere manus!

In ægrotantem Lumlium.

Duceret extremam cum nuper Lumlius horam,
Intremuit Cæsar nescius ante metûs.
Arbiter Europæ stetit omnis fixus in uno,
Et populi lacrymis miscuit Ipse suas.
Plaude malis, Dux magne, tuis morboque fruare,
Qui tibi dat vivo posteritate frui.

In eundem.

Invida Lumleium cum nuper fata vocabant
Lapsura et Britonum magna columna fuit;

Durham 1728–46; headmaster (1720–8) and provost (1733–46) of Eton; friend of Sir Robert Walpole (*Eton Coll. Reg.*; C. G. T. Dean, *The Royal Hospital Chelsea*, 1950, pp. 193, 309–10).

4. George Cholmondeley (1724–64), styled Vct Malpas; eldest son of George, 3d E. of Cholmondeley, and Mary, dau. of Sir Robert Walpole; M.P.; HW's nephew.

5. Hon. Robert Cholmondeley (1727–1804), second son of George, 3d E. of Cholmondeley; Eton, 1742; served in the army in early life; afterwards rector of St Andrew's, Hertford; m. (1746) Mary Woffington, sister of 'Peg' Woffington, the actress (*Eton Coll. Reg.*).

Immisit se mæsta pavor per pectora cunctis,
Et Georgi lachrymis non caruere genæ.
Ægrotent alii; sentit domus una dolorem:
At pro Lumleio Rex, populusque gemit.

In eundem.

Quis novus hic horror Georgi subrepit in artus?
Quid fletu insolito Cæsaris ora madent?
Jacturam chari capitis timet ille; tributum
Hoc poscunt Lumlî fata propinqua pium.
O quantum, Princeps, moveant te publica fata,
Cum tibi privati non aliena putas!

In præcocem Augustæ prolem.

Longa decem portant aliæ fastidia menses
Augusta et citiùs dulce profundit onus.
Parcite natales, medici, numerare deorum
Caesaribus nasci contigit ante diem.

In eandem.

Indignata moras, et lenti tempora partûs
Augusta in lucem prosilit ante diem.
Sit præcox virtute, ut erat natalibus, infans
Matris et ante annos mentem animumque gerat.

I have subjoined a translation of the first, which was wrote by another hand.[6]

Sure! some judicial wrath fond Spain misleads,
And ruin points at their devoted heads.
Th' Armada shatter'd, and Gibraltar won,
Eliza's arms, and Anna's thunder own.
'Tis woman's easy task proud Spain to scourge;
Think they of this, and learn to dread a George!

From Mrs Porter,[1] ?1738

Printed from the MS now WSL, inserted in HW's *MS Poems,* p. 250. First printed in Toynbee *Supp.* iii. 105. The volume of *MS Poems* was acquired from Lord Waldegrave by WSL in 1942.

6. Not identified.

Dated conjecturally by the reference to the 'ingenious paper' which may have been, as Toynbee suggests, the 'essay' on Mrs Porter as Clytemnestra in James Thomson's *Agamemnon,* referred to in Thomas Gray to HW 23 Feb. 1738 (GRAY i. 151 and n. 2). Mrs Porter played Clytemnestra at the first performance of *Agamemnon* 6 April 1738 at Drury Lane (*London Stage* Pt III, ii. 710). HW had apparently written to Gray on the subject while the play was in rehearsal.

Address: To the Honourable Horace Walpole.

MRS Porter is not at present able to write, being much indisposed today. Is extremely sorry she cannot herself make proper acknowledgments to her kind and generous friend and benefactor Mr Walpole for all his goodness. She cannot see a fault in his ingenious paper,[2] nor she does not think there is one. Hopes he will soon recover [from] his cold and that she shall have the honour of seeing him and telling him how infinitely she thinks herself obliged.

From JOHN SELWYN the Younger,[1] ca May 1739

Printed from a photostat of the MS in the Bodleian Library (MS Toynbee c. 1). First printed, Toynbee *Supp.* iii. 105–7. The MS was *penes* the 9th Earl Waldegrave in 1925; presumably given by him to Paget Toynbee, who presented it to the Bodleian.

Dated approximately by the reference to Lord Conway's return to England (see n. 4 below).

Endorsed in an unidentified hand: From Mr John Selwyn.

Dear Sir,

YOU are excessively good to a very dull correspondent; how have I deserved it? How shall I thank you? If I had the same opportunity, my letters should interest you as much as yours do me,[2] and yet I have pleasure in thinking how *far* that is out of my power, because I remember you used to think that a safe place.

My Lord Conway[3] is come.[4] I met him in the park[5] the first night, both of us in chairs; if he had taken no notice of me, he would have

1. Mary Porter (d. 1765), actress (GRAY i. 96 n. 10).
2. See heading.

1. (ca 1709–51), son of Col. John Selwyn (1688–1751) and Mary (Farrington) Selwyn (ca 1690–1777), brother of HW's friend and correspondent George Selwyn; M.P.
2. None of HW's letters to John Selwyn has been found.
3. HW's cousin, Francis Seymour Conway.
4. He had returned to England from making the Grand Tour at the end of April 1739 (*Daily Adv.* 1 May 1739; *ante* 27 July 1736, n. 5).
5. St James's Park.

passed by unknown, but seeing somebody make me a bow put me upon thinking who it could be, and in a minute I recollected him. He was then gone too far, but I had the good fortune to meet him again the same evening at Sir R.W.,[6] who had whisk there, and I think him very little altered, but rather more like his brother and improved extremely by his heighth; he has said so many obliging things from Mr C[onway][7] that I feel myself in vast spirits.

I have delivered all your compliments to Lady Hervey,[8] and I told my Lord[9] that you inquired after him. He bid me say that he is 'quite recovered, but I mill[10] myself three or four times a day.' 'How, my Lord, do you mill yourself?' 'Why, I am like a cup of chocolate: I grow cold and dead, then I mill myself again and in a little while I grow cold again and am fit for nothing but to catch dead flies.' For want of public news I tell you private conversation and cannot omit a story of an English servant of the Duchess of Richmond's[11] which I heard yesterday and may be of use to you in your journey. When she went from Paris to Aubigny[12] he was sick and she left him to follow her, which he did in a few days; he had learned the cant of postilions, and when he arrived she asked him how he made his journey. 'Oh, Madam, I foutred and bougred my way along very well.' Another of Mrs Pulteney;[13] she was playing at whisk with my Lord Tullimore[14] for her partner; he played abominably, she scolded and he laughed till she grew out of patience, got up, took hold of his ears across the table and shook him for two minutes. Upon which he said very coolly, Madam you confound me; I am at a loss how to behave; if you were a man I must kill you, and by God I will see whether you are a man or not. Which point they say he made clear both to himself and the whole company. I have nothing else worth telling; you see that I am in spirits at present, but I fancy I shall

6. Sir Robert Walpole's house in Downing Street (GRAY i. 98 n. 1).

7. Hon. Henry Seymour Conway (1719–95), Lord Conway's younger brother; HW's intimate friend and correspondent. He was then at Paris, and was joined by HW and Thomas Gray the first week in April (GRAY i. 8 and n. 45).

8. Mary Lepell (1700–68), m. (1720) Hon. John Hervey, styled Bn Hervey of Ickworth, 1733; HW's correspondent.

9. Hervey.

10. 'To beat or whip (chocolate, etc.) to a froth' (OED).

11. Sarah Cadogan (1706–51), m. (1719) Charles Lennox, 2d D. of Richmond, 1723.

12. In 1734 the Duke of Richmond succeeded to the Seignory of Aubigny, which had been given to his grandmother, the Duchess of Portsmouth, by Louis XIV. The Duke and Duchess went to France for three months in 1735 (GEC).

13. Anna Maria Gumley (1694–1758), m. (1714) William Pulteney, cr. (1742) E. of Bath.

14. Charles Moore (1712–64), 2d Bn Moore of Tullamore, 1725; cr. (1758) E. of Charleville.

want milling often and soon, at least I did very lately. Pray make my compliments to Mr. C. and tell him, that I have sent him a book[15] which a gentleman was to leave at Calais to be forwarded to Alexander;[16] 'it has more nastiness than wit in it, but it is new.' I cannot conclude without repeating my thanks to you, and assuring you how much I am your obliged humble servant.

TO UNKNOWN, ca 1740

Printed from *Letters of Anna Seward,* Edinburgh, 1811, v. 431. Reprinted, Toynbee *Supp.* ii. 198–9. The history of the MS and its present whereabouts are not known.

The present text is an extract (or paraphrase) included by Anna Seward in her letter of 27 Dec. 1801 to Mrs Childers and introduced as follows: 'I lately met with a passage in one of Lord Orford's juvenile letters to this effect. . . .' It is dated conjecturally by the reference to Richardson's *Pamela; or, Virtue Rewarded,* published 6 Nov. 1740 (W. M. Sale, Jr, *Samuel Richardson: A Bibliographical Record,* New Haven, 1936, p. 14). HW's letter was doubtless written not long after, while he was on the Grand Tour. As Toynbee suggests, his correspondent may have been Richard West, Thomas Ashton, or H. S. Conway.

I can send you no news; the late singular novel is the universal, and only theme—Pamela is like snow, she covers everything with her whiteness.

From CARDINAL ALBANI,[1] Sunday 3 July 1740 NS

Printed from the MS now WSL. First printed, Toynbee *Supp.* iii. 107–8. Damer-Waller; the MS was sold Sotheby's 5 Dec. 1921 (first Waller Sale), lot 86,

15. Probably *Gustavus Vasa, the Deliverer of his Country,* a tragedy by Henry Brooke, published 5 May 1739. In a letter to West 18 June 1739 NS, HW mentions receiving a copy of the play from England (GRAY i. 171 and n. 7).

16. Alexandre Alexander (fl. 1727–41), banker in the Rue St-Apolline, Paris (GRAY i. 184 n. 1).

1. Alessandro Albani (1692–1779), Clement XI's nephew; cardinal, 1721; librarian of the Vatican 1761–79; collector of coins and medals (GRAY i. 208 n. 11). HW wrote H. S. Conway 23 April 1740 NS that Albani was 'one of the most agreeable' cardinals of the papal conclave at Rome, from whom he had 'received great civilities' (CONWAY i. 57). He wrote Horace Mann the same day: 'Alex. Albani has sent me sundry civil messages, and commissioned his friend Count Petronio to usher me about [Rome]; and three days ago Lord D[eskford] and I went to visit him at the door of the Conclave' (MANN i. 9).

bought in; resold Christie's 15 Dec. 1947 (second Waller Sale), lot 55 (with other letters to HW), to Maggs for WSL.

Endorsed by HW: From Cardinal Alex. Albani.

Du conclave,[2] 3me juillet 1740.

Monsieur,

Je suis sensible aux marques d'amitié, que votre Excellence a la bonté de me donner dans son billet[3] d'aujourd'hui au sujet de son départ,[4] dont je suis d'autant plus fâché, que mon séjour du conclave m'a ôté la consolation de la voir, et de lui témoigner mon particulier attachement à votre Excellence, et à toute sa famille.[5] Je souhaite, que le voyage soit heureux, et [que] le retour[6] que vous me faites espérer soit prochain pour avoir occasion de m'employer en son service, et avoir le plaisir de la convaincre par des preuves effectives de ma parfaite reconnaissance aux bontés, qu'elle a pour moi, et que personne n'est avec plus d'estime et de sincérité, Monsieur,

Votre véritable serviteur de tout mon cœur,

Alexandre Cardinal Albanj[7]

From the Prince de Beauvau,[1] Wednesday 19 October 1740 NS

Printed from the MS now WSL. First printed, Toynbee *Supp.* iii. 108–9. Damer-Waller; the MS was sold Sotheby's 5 Dec. 1921 (first Waller Sale), lot 91, to

2. The papal conclave at Rome lasted from 19 Feb. to 17 Aug. 1740, when Benedict XIV (d. 1758) was elected successor to Clement XII (d. 6 Feb. 1740) (*Enciclopedia Cattolica,* Vatican City, 1950, iv. 178).

3. Missing.

4. HW wrote Conway 5 July from Radicofani: 'You will wonder . . . to find me on the road from Rome' (Conway i. 66). Accompanied by Thomas Gray, HW left Rome 12 June, spent about nine days at Naples, and arrived ca 8 July at Florence, where they stayed with Horace Mann until May 1741. HW explained in his 'Short Notes' that 'the Conclave continuing, and the heats coming on' prompted their departure for Florence (Gray i. 9 and nn. 56–7).

5. Mann was a distant cousin of HW. Albani, who was in Austrian service, was a friend of Mann and keenly interested in supporting George II against the Pretender at Rome.

6. HW never returned to Rome.

7. Only the last line and the signature are in Albani's hand.

1. Charles-Just de Beauvau (1720–93), Prince de Beauvau; son of Marc de Beauvau (1679–1754), Prince de Craon; Maréchal de France, 1783 (Mann i. 11 n. 43).

Wells; given by him to Thomas Conolly of Chicago, from whom WSL acquired it in 1937.

Endorsed in an unknown hand: The Prince de Beauvau to Mr Walpole.

Lunéville,[2] le 19 octobre 1740.

J'AI toujours fait trop de cas, Monsieur, de notre amitié,[3] pour n'être pas extrêmement sensible au souvenir dont vous voulez bien m'honorer, ma mère[4] m'a fait un plaisir infini, en m'apprenant que vous n'oubliez pas la personne du monde qui se sait le meilleur gré de vous être attaché par l'estime et l'amitié la plus sincère, je voudrais fort être à portée de cultiver la vôtre, et rien ne me flatte plus dans le projet que j'ai formé, comme vous savez, d'aller en Angleterre,[5] que l'espérance d'y vivre quelque temps avec vous. La satisfaction que j'ai goûté dans votre commerce, me fera toujours souhaiter d'être partout où je vous saurai; c'est pourquoi je vous demande en grâce de m'informer[6] de vos allures pour cet hiver, si vous resterez en Italie ou si vous passerez quelque temps en France en retournant en Angleterre: si je pouvais être assez heureux pour vous voir à Paris en attendant que ce soit à Londres, je ne négligerais rien pour m'y trouver en même temps que vous; mandez-moi sans aucune façon si je pourrais vous être bon à quelque chose quelque part où ce fut, mon zèle et mon empressement à vous marquer ma consideration, et tous mes sentiments pour vous, ne pourront jamais être surpassés, que par le désir que j'aurai toute ma vie de mériter la continuation de votre bienveillance, et quand même toutes les flottes d'Angleterre auraient coulées à fond toutes celles de France, vous pouvez toujours me regarder comme votre très humble et très obéissant serviteur,

LE PRINCE DE BEAUVAU[7]

2. In the duchy of Lorraine, ca 15 miles SE of Nancy. Beauvau had received command of a peacetime guard regiment assigned to Stanislas, Duc de Lorraine, and stationed at Lunéville (MANN i. 11 n. 45, i. 28 n. 5).

3. HW had made Beauvau's acquaintance at Rome during the spring of 1740 (MANN i. 11).

4. Anne-Marguerite de Ligniville (1686–1772), m. (1704) Marc de Beauvau, P. de Craon (MANN i. 3 n. 8). HW met the Prince and Princesse de Craon during his stay in Florence, where they became great friends. He wrote Mann 18 Sept. 1748 OS: 'I profess great attachment to that family for their civilities to me' (MANN iii. 503).

5. Beauvau never went to England, although he had hoped to visit HW there during the winter of 1749–50 (MANN iv. 87). After seeing Beauvau again during his trip to Paris in 1769, HW described him as 'by no means the amiable man we thought he would prove, but at once full of all the pride and meanness of Versailles' (MANN vii. 142; DU DEFFAND v. 328).

6. No letters from HW to Beauvau have been found.

Oserais-je vous prier de faire un peu ma cour à Milady Pomphret[8] et à sa famille, vous n'oublierez pas j'espère que Milady Sophie[9] en fait partie, mettez-moi aux pieds de cette adorable fille.

Je vous prie encore *di portar i miei saluti* à Monsieur Men,[10] *per il quale ho sempre avuto tutta la stima dovuta al suo merito*, et de vouloir bien aussi faire mille compliments à tous les anglais de ma connaissance qui pourraient être à Florence.

From GIOVANNI BATTISTA MARIA UGUCCIONI,[1] Saturday 3 December 1740 NS

Printed for the first time from the MS now WSL. The MS descended in the Waldegrave family to the 12th Earl Waldegrave, from whom WSL acquired it in 1948.

Di casa 3 Xbre [dicembre] 1740.

A Monsieur Walpole fa umilissima reverenza Gio. Batt[ist]a Uguccioni, e La fa noto come il Sig[nor] Francesco Pepi[2] non ha più intenzione di tagliare stante l'essere continuam[en]te in gran disdetta, che però supponendo lo scrivente, che sì sua Sig[no]ria come il Sig[nor] Man[3] avranno piacere il potere avere un piccolo taglio di faraone nel futuro lunedi, quindi è che si prende la libertà di proporre alle Signorie[4] Loro, come crede che il Sig[nor] Abb[at]e Dini[5] acceterà di venire a trattenere la Loro bella conversazione col fare d[et]to taglio,[6] che però potranno, o darne incumbenza a d[et]to Gio.

7. Prince de Beauvau, son to the Prince de Craon (HW).

8. Hon. Henrietta Louisa Jeffreys (ca 1700–61), m. (1720) Thomas Fermor, 2d Bn Leominster, cr. (1721) E. of Pomfret. She stayed at Florence with her husband and two eldest daughters, Lady Sophia and Lady Charlotte, from 20 Dec. 1739 NS until 13 March 1741 NS (MANN i. 4 n. 18).

9. Lady Sophia Farmor [Fermor (1721–45)], eldest daughter to Lord Pomfret, afterwards Countess of Granville (HW). She m. (1744) John Carteret, 2d E. Granville, 1744 (MANN i. 4 n. 23).

10. Horace Mann (1706–86), cr. (1755) Bt; diplomatist; HW's correspondent.

1. (1710–82), Florentine senator, 1761; at this time employed in the office of records at Florence (MANN i. 129 n. 15).

2. Francesco Gaspero Pepi (1708–64), impresario of the Theatre of the Via del Cocomero at Florence (MANN ii. 41 n. 28).

3. Horace Mann.

4. The MS reads 'SS:rie'.

5. Not identified; perhaps a relation of Cavaliere Agostino Dini (1694–1741), whom HW knew at Florence (MANN i. 95 n. 6).

6. It is not known whether this card-party took place. HW wrote Richard West 4 Dec. 1740 NS: 'For this last month we have passed our time but dully . . . I have seen nothing but cards and dull pairs of cicisbeos. I have literally seen so much love and pharaoh since being here, that I believe I shall never love either again as long as I live' (GRAY i. 237–8).

Batt[ist]a, acciò ne parli a detto Dini, oppure vorranno da per Loro fargl[i]ene sapere, il tutto come piacerà alla di Loro gentilezza, alle quale lo scrivente si fa pregio di dirsi il Suo vero e sincero servitore obbligato.

From VITTORIA TESI,[1] Tuesday 13 December 1740 NS

Printed for the first time from the MS now WSL. The MS descended in the Waldegrave family to the 12th Earl Waldegrave, from whom WSL acquired it in 1948.

[Di] casa, 13 dicembre 1740.

Monsieur,

SICCOME Lei ebbe la bontà di dirmi che sarà venuto a prendermi una sera per andare all' accademia di Monsieur Dasciut,[2] e sapendo che la fanno domani a sera; io li invio il presente foglio acció mi favorisca di mandarmi a dire s'è domani che mi viene prendere. Mi perdoni tanto incomodo, e con tutto l'ossequio li faccio profonda riverenza e del simile la supplico all' gentilissimo Monsieur Mains[3] e di novo mi rassegno la vostra, Monsieur,

v[ostra] de[votissima] e obb[edientissima] serva,

VITTORIA TESI

1. Vittoria Tesi (1700–75), m. (before 1735) Giacomo Tramontini; Italian singer (Benedetto Croce, *Un prelato e una cantante del secolo XVIII*, Bari, 1946, pp. 27–43; *Grove's Dict. of Music and Musicians*, 5th edn, ed. Eric Blom, 1954, viii. 401–2).

2. Probably Samuel Dashwood (?1717–93), grandson of Sir Samuel Dashwood, lord mayor of London (SELWYN 7 n. 32; MANN ii. 451 n. 28). He was staying at Rome and Florence in 1740–1 (ibid. i. 125 and n. 12). Lady Pomfret wrote Lady Hertford 20 Nov. 1740 NS: 'Every Monday Mr Mann, at whose house Mr Walpole is on a visit, has a select set, and a sixpenny pharo-table. We have the same on Thursday; and Mr Dashwood has a concert every Wednesday' (*Correspondence between Frances, Countess of Hartford . . . and Henrietta Louisa, Countess of Pomfret between the years 1738 and 1741*, 1805, ii. 176–7). Dashwood's Wednesday 'accademia' is presumably the subject of the present letter.

3. Horace Mann.

To the REV. JOSEPH SPENCE,[1] Tuesday 21 February 1741 NS

Printed from a photostat of the MS in the Henry E. Huntington Library. First printed in *Anecdotes, Observations, and Characters, of Books and Men. Collected . . . by the Rev. Joseph Spence,* ed. S. W. Singer, 1820, pp. 405–6. Reprinted in Spence's *Anecdotes,* ed. Singer, 2d edn, 1858, pp. 313–14; Wright i. 65–6; Cunningham i. 64–5; Toynbee i. 93–5; *Joseph Spence: Letters from the Grand Tour,* ed. Slava Klima, Montreal, 1975, pp. 354–5. The MS is pasted in an extra-illustrated copy of Spence's *Anecdotes,* ed. Singer, 1820, vol. IV, opp. p. 406; this copy probably composed by Singer from Spence's papers) was sold Sotheby's 19 Feb. 1867 (Sir Charles Rugge Price Sale), lot 2203, to Quaritch; resold American Art Galleries 20 March 1900 (Augustin Daly Sale, Part II), lot 3137; subsequently acquired by Huntington.

Endorsed by Spence: Walpole, Feb. 24. Verses by Mr Pope. Epitaph and Grotto-verses by Mr Pope.

Florence, Feb. 21st 1741 NS.

Sir,

NOT having time last post, I begged Mr Mann to thank you for the obliging paragraph for me in your letter[2] to him. But as I desire a nearer correspondence with you than by third hands, I assure you in my own proper person, that I shall have great pleasure on our meeting in England to renew an acquaintance[3] which I began with so much pleasure in Italy. I will not reckon you among my modern friends, but in the first article of virtu: you have given me so many new lights into a science that I love so much, that I shall always be proud to own you as my master in the antique, and will never let anything break in upon my reverence[4] for you,[5] but a warmth and

1. (1699–1768), professor of poetry at Oxford 1728–38 and regius professor of modern history, 1742; prebendary of Durham, 1754; friend of Pope; anecdotist. Spence travelled abroad with various young men of rank as companion and tutor. On his third and last tour (1739–41), while travelling with Lord Lincoln, he made the acquaintance of HW.

2. Missing.

3. Spence first met HW at Turin in Nov. 1739 and again during HW's residence at Florence. In May 1741 Spence and Lord Lincoln went to Reggio, where Spence, finding HW seriously ill, attended him until Dr Cocchi arrived from Florence. Upon his recovery HW joined Spence and Lincoln in Venice and travelled with them to Paris ('Short Notes,' GRAY i. 10–11 and n. 62; SELWYN 17).

4. 'Reverence' is written over 'esteem' in the MS, apparently by HW.

5. In later years HW expressed something less than reverence for Spence. He wrote William Cole 19 May 1780 that Spence was a 'good-natured harmless little soul, but more like a silver penny than a genius. It was a neat fiddle-faddle bit of sterling, that had read good books and kept good company, but was too trifling for use, and only fit to please a child' (COLE ii. 216–17).

freedom that will flow from my friendship, and which will not be contained within the circle of sacred[6] awe.

As I shall always be attentive to give you any satisfaction that lies in my power, I take the first opportunity of sending you two little poems,[7] both by a hand that I know you esteem the most: if you have not seen them, you will thank me for lines of Mr Pope; if you have, why, I did not know it.

On the Grotto at Twickenham.

Thou, who shalt stop where Thames' translucent wave
Shines a broad mirror thro' the shadowy cave,
Where ling'ring drops from mineral roofs distill,
And pointed chrystals break the sparkling rill,
Unpolish'd gems no ray on pride bestow,
And latent metals innocently glow;
Approach! Great Nature studiously behold,
And eye the mine without a wish for gold:
Thou see'st that country's wealth, where only free
Earth to her entrails feels not slavery;
Enter! but awful this inspiring grot,
Here wisely pensive St John sat and thought;
Here British sighs from dying Windham stole,
And the bright flame was shot thro' Marchmont's soul;
Let such, such only tread this sacred floor,
Who dare to love their country, and be poor.

Epitaph for Himself.

Under this marble or under this hill,
Under this turf or e'en what you will,
Whatever my heir or some friend in his stead,
Or any good Christian lays over my head,
Lies one who ne'er car'd and still cares not a pin
What they said or may say of the mortal within;
But who living and dying resign'd still and free,
Trusts in God that as well as he was, he shall be.

6. All previous editions read 'a severe' for 'sacred.'

7. Pope's 'Verses on a Grotto by the River Thames at Twickenham' and the 'Epitaph on Himself.' HW may have obtained them from Lady Pomfret, who had been sent a copy of the 'Verses on a Grotto' in a letter of 29 Nov. 1740 from Lady Hertford (Pope's *Minor Poems*, ed. Norman Ault and John Butt, 1954, p. 384n). The 'Verses on a Grotto' had appeared in GM 1741, xi. 45, and the 'Epitaph' in *The Publick Register: or, the Weekly Magazine* of 10 Jan. 1741. West's parody of 'Verses on a Grotto' is quoted by HW (GRAY ii. 235).

I don't know whether Lord Lincoln[8] has received any orders to return home:[9] I had a letter[10] from one of my brothers last post, to tell me from Sir Robert[11] that he would have me leave Italy as soon as possible,[12] lest I should be shut up unawares by the arrival of the Spanish troops;[13] and that I might pass some time in France[14] if I had a mind. I own I don't conceive how it is possible these troops should arrive without its being known some time before. And as to the Great Duke's[15] dominions,[16] one can always be out of them in ten hours or less. If Lord Lincoln has not received the same orders, I shall believe what I now think, that I am wanted for some other reason. I beg my kind love to my Lord,[17] and that Mr Spence will believe me

His sincere humble servant

HOR. WALPOLE

TO HENRY PELHAM,[1] Monday 17 May 1742 OS

Printed from a photostat of the MS in the British Museum (Add. MS 32,699, f. 234). First printed, Toynbee i. 224.

Endorsed in an unidentified hand: May 17, 1742. Mr H. Walpole (for a living in Lancashire).

Downing Street, May 17th.

Sir,

I HAVE no pretence in the world to give you this trouble, but by knowing from your own example how right it is to undertake anything for a friend. Yet, Sir, if the favour I am going to ask is the

8. Henry Fiennes Clinton (after 1768, Pelham Clinton) (1720–94), 9th E. of Lincoln; 2d D. of Newcastle-under-Lyne, 1768; HW's correspondent.

9. The Duke of Newcastle wrote Lincoln 16 March 1741 OS to come home to settle his estate and to avoid the impending Spanish invasion of Italy (BM Add. MS 33,065, f. 398).

10. Missing; see FAMILY 6.

11. Sir Robert Walpole.

12. HW did not start home until May 1741 (GRAY i. 9).

13. Six or seven thousand Spanish troops were said to have disembarked at Spezia, near the border of Tuscany, on 29 Jan. 1742 (MANN i. 305 n. 17).

14. He landed at Antibes from Genoa and was at Aix by 7 Aug. He left Spence and Lincoln at Paris and landed at Dover 12 Sept. 1741 ('Short Notes,' GRAY i. 11).

15. Francis II (1708–65), Grand Duke of Tuscany 1737–65; Holy Roman Emperor (as Francis I) 1745–65.

16. His dominions in Tuscany extended from the Mediterranean to the Marches and Umbria on the east, and from Liguria and Emilia-Romagna southward to the Province of Rome.

17. All previous editions read 'Lord Lincoln.'

1. Hon. Henry Pelham (1695–1754), M.P.; first lord of the Treasury 1743–54.

least impertinent, I beg you will punish it, by taking no notice of it.

There is fallen a small living in Lancashire in the gift of the Crown,[2] by the death of Mr Tully[3] the incumbent; 'tis called Adlington or Adlingham,[4] and is worth about an hundred a year.[5] If I could obtain it for Mr Ashton[6] of Lancaster, a clergyman who lives with me,[7] and who is reckoned to have some merit, I should think myself extremely happy, and much more so, if I could add it to the very great obligations, which we already have to Mr Pelham.

I am Sir
Your most obedient humble servant

Hor. Walpole

From the Prince and Princesse de Craon,[1] Monday 9 July 1742 NS

Printed from the MS now wsl. First printed, Toynbee *Supp.* ii. 80–1. Damer-Waller; the MS was sold Sotheby's 5 Dec. 1921 (first Waller Sale), lot 113, to Wells; given by him to Thomas Conolly of Chicago, from whom wsl acquired it in 1944.

The first two paragraphs of the letter are in the Princesse de Craon's hand; the concluding paragraph was written by the Prince. The original spelling, capitalization, and punctuation of the letter have been preserved.

2. Pelham, at this time paymaster-general of the forces, did not have the disposal of Crown livings, but his brother, the Duke of Newcastle, did, when secretary of state. Since HW was not on good terms with Newcastle at this time, he approached him through Pelham. The late Romney Sedgwick called our attention to *Mem. Geo. III* i. 163, where HW wrote: 'The seals of secretary of state, with the *feuille de bénéfices,* were once more offered to the Duke of Newcastle.' See Norman Sykes, 'The Duke of Newcastle as Ecclesiastical Minister,' *English Historical Review,* 1942, lvii. 59–84.

3. Thomas Tullie (d. 1742), presented as rector of Aldingham by George I and instituted 20 April 1727 (Edward Baines, *History of . . . Lancaster,* 1893, v. 576; *Vict. Co. Hist. Lancs* viii. 327; John Le Neve and T. D. Hardy, *Fasti Ecclesiæ Anglicanæ,* 1854, iii. 255).

4. Aldingham, in north Lancs, five miles NE of Barrow.

5. It was worth £200 per annum ca 1714 (Francis Gastrell, *Notitia Cestriensis* ii. 494, in Chetham Society, *Remains,* 1850, xxii).

6. Thomas Ashton (1715–75), divine; HW's friend at Eton and correspondent. He was presented by George II in succession to Thomas Tullie and instituted as rector of Aldingham 12 July 1742. After resigning the living in 1749, he was followed by his brother, John Ashton (*Eton Coll. Reg.*).

7. Ashton was living in Downing Street as chaplain to Sir Robert Walpole (*Daily Adv.* 19 June 1742).

1. Marc de Beauvau (1679–1754), Prince de Craon, m. (1704) Anne-Marguerite de Ligniville (1686–1772) (*ante* 19 Oct. 1740 NS, n. 4).

HW wrote Horace Mann ca 21 July 1742 OS: 'I have just now received . . . a married letter from both Prince and Princess: but sure nothing ever equalled the setting out of it! She says "The generosity of your friendship for me, Sir, leaves me nothing to desire of all that is precious in England, China and the Indies"' (MANN i. 505). HW quoted from memory these words of the Princesse in his letter of 14 Aug. 1743 OS to Mann (ibid. ii. 291).

Endorsed by HW: From the Princess and Prince de Craon.

de la Paetraia[2] le 9 juillet 1742.

LA GENEROSITÉ de vostre amitie pour moy monsieur ne me laisse rien a desirer de tous se qui se trouve de precieus en engletere den la chine et aus indes, le motif qui vous a enguagé a me prevenire sur tous cela et pour moy monsieur dun prix infinis rien ny et oublié et les offres que vous me faite pour mon fils[3] ne luy seronst pas ignoré pour long temp Sy mes lettres pour luy onst plus de succest desormais quels nans ont eu jusqua presen ne luy en estan parvenus que tres peus non plus que des sienes a nous, je luy feré bien conoitre en trentes ocasions que de tous se que nous avons conus de cavalier de vostre nation monsieur aucuns nexsiges plus que vous de reconoissence et datachement de sa part sil va jamais en angletere[4] il profitera sil mans croit des offres obligens que vous luy faite et vous prouvera tan quil poura monsieur lestime que je conserveré pour vous toute ma vie

je natandre pas de vous monsieur un compliman sur la perte que nous avons fait de mon fils le primat de lorraine[5] pour me persuader de linterest que vous y prenez cest un amis que vous avez de moin den le monde

Made de Craon a eté obligé monsieur de laisser cette lettre imparfaite et me charge dy adjouter tout ce qui manque a la decoration des sentiments quelle a pour vous, je vous dois aussi un nouveau remerciment de la lettre[6] dont vous mavez honoré, je me rejouis

2. Petraia a villa of the Gr[and] Duke's near Florence (HW). HW greatly admired Petraia, situated about three and a half miles NW of Florence and occupied at this time by the Prince de Craon (MANN i. 95 n. 11).

3. Charles-Just de Beauvau (1720–93), Prince de Beauvau (*ante* 19 Oct. 1740 NS, n. 1).

4. See ibid. n. 5.

5. François-Vincent-Marc de Beauvau (1713–42), second son of the Prince de Craon; Primate of Lorraine of the collegiate church of St Georges of Nancy, 1722 (MANN i. 12 n. 49).

6. Missing.

davoir a mander a mon fils les nouvelles marques damitié dont vous lhonorez, jen suis penetré de reconnoissance ainsy que du plus parfait attachement avec le quel on puisse etre

Monsieur
Votre tres humble et tres obeissant servateur

LE PRINCE DE CRAON

From HENRY PELHAM, Friday 16 July 1742 OS

Printed for the first time from the MS now WSL. Damer-Waller; the MS was sold Sotheby's 5 Dec. 1921 (first Waller Sale), lot 61, bought in; resold Christie's 15 Dec. 1947 (second Waller Sale), lot 49, to Maggs for WSL.

On the second leaf of the letter HW copied the revised text of his *Lesson for the Day*, 1742 (Hazen, *Bibl. of HW* 19; Toynbee *Supp.* ii. 78).

July the 16, 1742.

Dear Sir,

I HOPE you will forgive the trouble I am obliged to give you at the request of several friends. I am told Mr Ashton, the gentleman you recommended to the Duke of Newcastle for a living in Lancashire,[1] is at present a Fellow of King's in Cambridge.[2] He can't keep it long, and if he makes his resignation now, it will be of great service to some young gentlemen at Eton,[3] that the Speaker[4] and the Chancellor of the Exchequer[5] are concerned for. The only objection, as I understand, is on account of a young Paxton[6] and Mr Naylor[7]

1. Pelham had doubtless forwarded HW's request (*ante* 17 May 1742 OS) to his brother, the Duke of Newcastle.

2. Ashton was a fellow of King's 1737–42. Having been instituted as rector of Aldingham, Lancs, on 12 July, he probably resigned his fellowship at King's soon after this date on Pelham's urging (see below).

3. Scholars were preferred from Eton to King's College as scholarships became vacant there (Henry Malden, *An Account of King's College Chapel,* Cambridge, 1769, p. 5).

4. Arthur Onslow (1691–1768), M.P.; Speaker of the House of Commons 1728–61.

5. Samuel Sandys (1695–1770), cr. (1743) Bn Sandys; M.P.; chancellor of the Exchequer Feb. 1742 – Dec. 1743.

6. Probably William Paxton (1723–95), Eton 1735–42; admitted as a scholar at King's College, Cambridge, 3 Nov. 1742 (B.A. 1746/7; M.A. 1750); fellow of King's 1745–51; vicar of Padstow, Cornwall, and of Buckland, Devon, 1752, through presentation of the Earl of Orford; rector of Taplow, Bucks, 1788 (*Eton Coll. Reg.*) His father, Nicholas Paxton (d. 1744), solicitor to the Treasury 1730–42, had been taken into custody for refusing to answer the Committee of Secrecy's questions about Sir Robert Walpole's conduct, on the grounds that 'it may tend to accuse

the assistant clerk of the House of Commons tells me, there is an expedient that will equally excuse young Paxton. If so, I shall be much obliged to you, if you can procure Mr Ashton's resignation forthwith. I understand no time is to be lost, probably you know the circumstances of this affair better than I do, I shall therefore leave it to your management. I know you must have the trouble of writing to Mr Ashton by the first post, and if he sends his resignation to Mr Naylor at Eton, that will do. I can't finish without congratulating you upon the happy conclusion of this session.[8] I sincerely wish it may put an end to all future trouble to your father, which no one can have a great[er] pleasure in, than

Dear Sir, your most obedient humble servant,

H. PELHAM

TO CHARLES [?LYTTELTON], May – September 1743

Printed from an extract quoted in the Sotheby's auction catalogue of the John Taylor Sale, 22–3 March 1855. The MS was sold 23 March 1855, lot 450, to 'M'; not further traced. According to the catalogue, the MS was accompanied by a 'Parody on the 4th Chapter of Genesis' in HW's hand.

Dated approximately by HW's visits to Houghton in 1743. He arrived there in late May, returned to London in mid-July, then went to Houghton again from 15 Aug. until the end of September (MANN ii. 232, 267, 292, 311). The surviving text of the letter suggests that it was written to a close friend of similar interests. The only such 'Charles' of HW's acquaintance at this time was Charles Lyttelton, his schoolmate at Eton (HW addressed his friend Sir Charles Hanbury Williams as 'Williams').

Houghton, 1743.

Dear Charles,

. . . Men of wit and pleasure about town understand not the language, nor taste the charms of the inanimate world.

myself.' He was sent to Newgate 15 April and not released until the end of the session (*Report from the Committee of Secrecy appointed to enquire into the Conduct of Robert Earl of Orford*, 1742, pp. 1–8). HW wrote Horace Mann ca 21 July 1742 OS that 'the long session is over, and the Secret Committee already forgotten—Nobody remembers it but poor Paxton, who has lost his place by it' (MANN i. 502).

7. John Naylor (1709–61), assistant clerk in the House of Commons 1740–4 (*ante* 2 Nov. 1737 OS, n. 2).

8. The session of Parliament ended 15 July 1742, when it was clear that the

GROSVENOR BEDFORD, BY AN UNKNOWN ARTIST

To Grosvenor Bedford,[1] Monday 29 August 1743 OS

Printed for the first time from the MS now WSL. The MS descended in the Bedford family to Grosvenor Bedford's great-niece, Mrs Erskine, of Milton Lodge, Gillingham, Dorset; sold Sotheby's 15 Nov. 1932 (property of Mrs Erskine), lot 492, to Maggs for WSL.

Houghton, Aug. 29, 1743.

Dear Sir

YOUR letter[2] gave me great pleasure to hear how obliging Mr Fowle[3] has been in your affair.[4] I showed my Lord[5] your letter. He does not think there is the least probability of any danger from the Treasury: however you will easily hear if there is any thoughts of such a thing, and if you will let me know, my Lord will immediately write to Mr Pelham[6] to prevent it. Be so good at the same time to name me the place,[7] for having sent your letter to Mr Fowle, I have really forgot it.

You will believe, dear Sir, how happy I shall be to have done you any service, not only on your aunt's[8] account, but very particularly on your own and on Mrs Blechenden's:[9] and if ever it shall be in my power again, I hope you will not think I would stop at what I have done, for I am

Very sincerely yours

H. Walpole

Committee of Secrecy's investigation into Sir Robert Walpole's affairs would come to nothing.

1. (d. 1771), son of Thomas Bedford (1673–1710) and Elizabeth (Grosvenor) Bedford. His mother may have been governess of HW's sister, Catherine Walpole, who died in 1722 (J. H. Plumb, *Sir Robert Walpole: The Making of a Statesman,* 1956, p. 320). He succeeded William Swinburn (d. 1755) as HW's deputy usher of the Exchequer.

2. Missing.

3. Presumably John Fowle (d. 1772), of Broome, Norfolk; bencher of Gray's Inn, 1732; auditor of excise 1750–72; m. Elizabeth Turner (d. 1763), HW's cousin (GRAY ii. 198 n. 24).

4. With the change of ministry Bedford was no doubt afraid of losing his post as collector of customs for Philadelphia, to which, through the influence of Sir Robert Walpole, he had been appointed 29 June 1732 at £160 per annum (*Calendar of Treasury Books and Papers 1731–1734,* pp. 357, 474).

5. HW's father, cr. (6 Feb. 1742) E. of Orford.

6. Henry Pelham had been appointed first lord of the Treasury 25 August.

7. Philadelphia.

8. Anne Grosvenor (1679–1750), housekeeper of Somerset House 1739–50; friend of HW's mother (GRAY i. 220 n. 17).

9. Perhaps Mrs Lidia Blechinden (ca 1712–43), widow of Thomas Blechinden (ca 1709–40) of Swanscombe, Kent (Edward Hasted, *The History of . . . Kent,* 2d edn, Canterbury, 1797–1801, ii. 412, 419).

From JOHN WHALEY, Monday 12 September 1743 OS

Printed from Toynbee *Supp.* iii. 111–13, where the letter was first printed from the MS formerly in the Waller Collection. For the history of the MS see *ante* 10 Aug. 1735.

Burton upon Trent, Staffordshire, September 12, 1743.

Dear Sir,

YOUR very kind letter[1] reached me on the road on a ramble with Mr Davies,[2] and I thank you for it, and for doing me the honour of showing anything of my poor performance to Lord Orford, and your saying he was pleased with it gave me a satisfaction beyond expression. I have a copy of the verses at King'sland where I shall be again in a week, and I will endeavour to make them as much better as I can, and dress them up as clean as possible that they may appear with decent modesty, in company so far above them as you will condescend to introduce them to. I should be greatly obliged to you for a catalogue of the pictures now at Houghton[3] as soon as you can conveniently, or rather to see it in London where I propose being about the same time you mention. I purpose leaving out the trifling circumstances of the journey and leave nothing in the poem[4] but what relates to Houghton if you think proper, which I should be glad to know.

In my way hither I passed through Bewdley in Worcestershire, a town situated delightfully on the banks of the Severn, and the great mart of business for the midland parts of England; within five miles of it in Shropshire, is a seat of Sir Edward Blount,[5] a Roman Catholic baronet, most charmingly situated, and fitted up to the perfection of elegance, the whole designed and directed by himself. Wolverhampton, next to Birmingham is the most large and populous town I ever saw, the second forge of Vulcan, and every corner of it as full of life

1. Missing.

2. Sneyd Davies (1709–69), Eton 1724–9 and King's College, Cambridge (B.A. 1732, M.A. 1737, D.D. 1759); fellow of King's 1732–4; rector of Kingsland, Hereford, 1732; prebendary of Lichfield; archdeacon of Derby 1755–69 (*Eton Coll. Reg.*).

3. The MS of HW's *Ædes Walpolianæ*, the dedication of which is dated 'Houghton, Aug. 24, 1743.'

4. 'A Journey to Houghton,' subsequently printed, with several unsigned poems by Davies, in Whaley's *A Collection of Original Poems and Translations,* 1745, pp. 29–51, and included by HW in *Ædes Walpolianæ*, 1747, and later editions.

5. (d. 1758), 4th Bt, 1717. His seat, Mawley Hall, near Cleobury Mortimer, is described and illustrated in *Country Life,* 1910, xxviii. 18–27.

as a pismires nest and its inhabitants as black. Twelve miles from it is Litchfield, as indolent as the former was busy. The bog in which the cathedral (a very fine one) stands, stagnates I believe midst beds of poppy, and makes all its inhabitants as sleepy as its bishop[6] and canons.

Qui s'eveillent à dîner, et laissent en leur lieu
À des chantres gagez le soin de louer Dieu.[7]

If I write false French you must excuse me. This town also is pretty much of the drowsy, its chief manufacture being ale, with too frequent draughts of which, it is said the great Czarina[8] killed herself. The bridge over the Trent into Derbyshire is a very fine one, and has 37 large arches. It will be a great pleasure to know Lord Orford enjoys his health and you yours, and that he received no great harm from his fall.[9] Mr Dodd[10] writes me word his brother St Leger[11] died of his wounds at Dettingen.

I beg leave to wish you all joy and health, and to subscribe myself,

Dear Sir,

Your ever obliged friend and humble servant,

J. WHALEY

If you are so good as to write to me in a post or two after you have this it will find me at Kingsland.

I have lately been employed in putting a story into verse in imitation of Dryden's tales,[12] and style, which with some other small things I hope to have the pleasure of communicating to you in London;

6. Richard Smalbroke (1672–1749), Bp of St David's, 1724; Bp of Coventry and Lichfield, 1731.

7. Veillaient à bien dîner, et laissaient en leur lieu
À des chantres gagés le soin de louer Dieu
(Boileau, *Le Lutrin* I. 23–4).

8. Anna Ivanova (1693–1740), Empress of Russia 1730–40.

9. HW wrote Horace Mann 19 July 1743 OS: 'my father had a most dreadful accident; it had near been fatal; but he escaped miraculously. . . . his foot slipped, and he . . . fell at once down the stairs. . . . He cut his forehead . . . but most luckily did himself no other hurt, and was quite well again before I came away' (MANN ii. 277 and n. 8).

10. John Dodd (*ante* 10 Aug. 1735, n. 4).

11. That is, Dodd's brother-in-law, Henry St Leger (ca 1722–43), aide-de-camp to the Marquess of Granby at the Battle of Dettingen (Constance, Lady Russell, *Swallowfield and its Owners,* 1901, p. 231). Dodd married Jane St Leger in 1739 (ibid. 229).

12. Probably, as Toynbee suggests, 'Cornaro and the Turk,' the first poem in Whaley's *Collection of Original Poems and Translations.*

but lest they find not admittance alone, Mr Davies shall contribute to their reception. He begs his best respects to you.

Epigram. On a statue of Q[ueen] Anne at Gloc. standing with its back to one of K[ing] Cha[rle]s II.

Ye Glocester men, 'tis sure no handsome thing,
To turn the Queen's tail to her Uncle King;
Deserving less such usage there is no man
Who in his life time ne'er turn'd tail to woman.

On a Gentleman's singing at request of his Mistress.

Wretched the foreign songster who must part,
With dearest manhood to complete his art;
Whilst Beauty strains our English artist's strings,
And 'tis because he is a man he sings.

From the Hon. Mary Townshend,[1] Friday 30 September 1743 OS

Printed from the MS now WSL. First printed, Toynbee *Supp.* iii. 114–16. Damer-Waller; the MS was sold Sotheby's 5 Dec. 1921 (first Waller Sale), lot 186 (with three letters from Viscountess Townshend to HW), to Quaritch; resold Sotheby's 25 May 1948 (Harmsworth Sale), lot 4977, to Maggs for WSL.

Dated by the reference to Augustus Townshend's visit to China (see n. 7 below).

Midgham[2] Sept. 30th [1743].

Sir,

THERE was so much good humour in your last,[3] I fancy you would be disappointed if I did not send you a proof of its having given me great pleasure, for you could not write such a letter without having a desire to please; neither am I vain in this supposition. I believe you have this inclination in general to all the people you

1. (ca 1720–76), youngest dau. of Charles, 2d Vct Townshend, by his second wife Dorothy Walpole, sister of Sir Robert Walpole; m. (1753) Lt-Gen. Edward Cornwallis (1713–76); HW's cousin (CONWAY i. 115 n. 23).

2. The seat of Stephen Poyntz (1685–1750), near Newbury, Berks. Poyntz had been tutor to Lord Townshend's sons and was often visited by Mary Townshend, her sister Dorothy, and Dorothy's husband, Spencer Cowper, dean of Durham. Mary Townshend lived nearby at Ewhurst, near Basingstoke (*Letters of Spencer Cowper, Dean of Durham, 1746–74,* ed. Edward Hughes [Pub. of the Surtees Soc., vol. clxv], 1956, pp. 79, 82–3).

3. Missing; from what follows it is apparent that the letter was written in the character of HW's dog Patapan.

converse with, and it does not require your taking much pains to make yourself agreeable; but you are to remember I did not intend to draw myself into a serious correspondence with you, and like most women of spirit, my wit ceases when I am no longer at liberty to use you like a dog. Your flattery is dangerous, many a woman has lost the use of a good understanding intoxicated with the praise of her genius; and if Patapan[4] according to the usual wisdom of his sex, intends his wife should be his companion, but not his counsellor, he should not have employed a writer so likely to destroy the humility of his wife.

I can easily believe the historian is faithful, and Prince Floridan refused the kingdom at the price of his dog;[5] the dog was given to him by a fairy who was in love with him. Men are sometimes so grateful upon this subject, they are as romantic as the ladies. Indeed you appear to want sentiment; Lady C. F.[6] would have thought your doubt unpardonable, I dare say she would give twenty kingdoms for twenty dogs.

Augustus[7] being in a great hurry has desired me to make his excuses to you for not writing himself, and to acquaint you, he has just received a letter from China, with an account of an unfortunate accident, that all the china and other things that were made for him to be brought home this year, were burnt at Inquais Hong[8] by the great fire[9] which burnt almost all the merchants' houses, three weeks before the ships came away. The value of these things is a trifle, but the disappointment to his friends gives him great concern.

I don't exactly know how long we shall stay here, but I fancy I

4. A white Roman spaniel which HW brought back from Italy in 1741. Patapan had been taken to Houghton for the summer holidays. The dog was a favourite of Sir Robert Walpole and a curiosity to the visitors who came to see the house (GRAY i. 14, n. 90; MANN ii. 299).

5. Doubtless a reference to HW's 'Patapan or the Little White Dog,' written at Houghton during the summer of 1743 in imitation of La Fontaine's 'Le Petit Chien.' It is printed as Appendix 1 in SELWYN 287–306.

6. Probably Lady Caroline Fitzroy (1722–84), dau. of the 2d D. of Grafton; m. (1746) William Stanhope (1719–79), styled Vct Petersham 1742–56, 2d E. of Harrington, 1756.

7. Hon. Augustus Townshend (1716–46), Mary Townshend's older brother. He was captain of the East Indiaman *Augusta* and had been sent to Canton in 1742 to engage in trade with the Hong merchants (H. B. Morse, *Chronicles of the East India Company Trading to China 1635–1834*, Oxford, 1926–29, i. 283).

8. A warehouse or factory belonging to the Hong merchants of Canton, who had the privilege of trading with foreigners. Inquais was possibly a patois term for the English traders (ibid. 163–5; E. H. Pritchard, *Anglo-Chinese Relations during the Seventeenth and Eighteenth Centuries*, Urbana, Illinois, 1929, p. 109).

9. 'A fire broke out at Canton, which destroyed one hundred shops and eleven streets of warehouses' (Peter Auber, *China*, 1834, p. 165).

shall be in town as soon as you,[10] and shall be impatient for an opportunity of showing Patapan and his master they will have free admittance into the house in Brutton Street, and wish I may reconcile them to the Small Closet as I pass many evenings there.

There is nothing so advantageous to a female writer as a hurry. I was in luck this morning, and desire you would impute the deformities of this letter to my being too late for the post. You may also conclude I had bad pens and ink; but I am not quite sure it is sentimental to write better, carelessness is very becoming, and really to do anything of this sort with exactness looks as if one never thought of anything else.

I am Sir your very
humble servant

M. TOWNSHEND

TO LADY TOWNSHEND,[1] Saturday 25 August 1744 OS

Printed for the first time from the MS now WSL, who acquired it (with four other letters from HW to Lady Townshend) from Maggs in Aug. 1946; its previous history is not known.

Endorsed in an unidentified hand: Aug. 25, 1744. Hor. Walpole to Visc[ounte]ss Townshend.

Houghton, Aug. 25, 1744.

I BEG your Ladyship's pardon for encroaching on Mrs Gardiner's[2] province of sending you an account of your children,[3] but as none of them are at the point of death, perhaps you may not hear from her

10. HW was back in London within a week (MANN ii. 315).

1. Etheldreda, or Audrey, Harrison (ca 1708–88), m. (1723) Charles Townshend (1700–64), 3d Vct Townshend, 1738. HW wrote of her wit and malice 'the latter of which, without any derogation to the former, had vastly the ascendant' (*Mem. Geo. II* i. 39).

2. Possibly Hannah Turner (d. 1759), dau. of John Turner of Saffron Walden; m. (1722) the Rev. John Gardiner (ca 1702–70), domestic chaplain at Houghton and (1731) rector of Great Massingham, Norfolk. The Gardiner family had become associated with members of the Walpole and Townshend families in various ways (R. W. Ketton-Cremer, *Norfolk Portraits,* 1944, pp. 110–12; *Eton Coll. Reg.;* [M. J. Armstrong,] *History and Antiquities of the County of Norfolk,* Norwich, 1781, v. 235).

3. Hon. George Townshend (1724–1807), 4th Vct Townshend, 1764; cr. (1787) M. Townshend; Hon. Charles Townshend (1725–1767); Hon. Roger Townshend (ca 1731–59); and Hon. Audrey Townshend (d. 1781).

this post. If my Lord[4] was, I don't know whether I should not be as indiscreet as she was, and tell you the worst at once. Mr Charles Townshend is extremely well at Scarborough[5] and Miss Townshend[6] as well as anybody, who was born with sentiments can be at Raynham.[7] After these, it is very vain to tell you I am as well as anybody can be, that has Augustus[8] skipping and hollowing all day before him. The anecdotes of the family say he is in love with Lady Mary,[9] but I see no symptoms of it; unless his courtship is like Prince Cormorant's in the *Écumoire*,[10] who was continually turning over head and heels to charm the fairy Moustache.

I have not seen Mrs Ethelreda[11] yet; and when I do your Ladyship knows I dare not be very particular with her: but as I am sure my Lord Townshend can't discover sentiments when wrapped up in anything that looks like politics, I design instilling into her a passion for Prince Esterhasi,[12] whom I imagine your Ladyship can spare to your daughter, since you have seen Mr Nightingale;[13] unless you have made over that Prince to Miss Dives.[14] Except the death of Mr Hoste,[15] *my Muster Hoste,* I can tell you no news. The last piece of news they have heard in this world was Sacheverel's[16] trial. Indeed a

4. Lady Townshend had left her husband ca 1741 (MANN i. 173).

5. Lady Townshend wrote Lady Denbigh in July 1744 of 'having been extremely uneasy for some time about my second son Charles, who is in a very melancholy state of health now at Scarborghe' (Hist. MSS Comm., *Report on Denbigh MSS,* pt v, 1911, p. 253).

6. Probably Hon. Mary Townshend (*ante* 30 Sept. 1743, n. 1).

7. Raynham Hall, Norfolk, the seat of the Townshends.

8. Hon. Augustus Townshend (*ante* 30 Sept. 1743, n. 7), HW's cousin.

9. Lady Maria Walpole (ca 1725–1801), m. (1746) Charles Churchill; HW's half-sister.

10. *L'Écumoire, ou Tanzaï et Néadarné, histoire japonaise,* 1734, by Claude-Prosper Jolyot de Crébillon (1707–77). HW's copy of the 1740 edition is Hazen, *Cat. of HW's Lib.,* No. 979.

11. Hon. Audrey Townshend (d. 1781), m. (after 1756) Robert Orme (d. 1790), of Devonshire and of Bergham, Brabant, the Netherlands, aide-de-camp to Gen. Braddock during his American campaign (GM 1781, li. 94; ibid. 1790, lx pt i. 577; Collins, *Peerage,* 1812, ii. 473; MONTAGU i. 188 n. 8).

12. Paul Anton (1711–62), Prince Eszterházy von Galántha; army officer and diplomatist (MANN iv. 349 n. 2).

13. Probably Edward Nightingale (1726–82), 8th Bt (but never assumed the title), of Kneesworth, Cambs (COLE i. 238–40 and n. 2).

14. Charlotte Dyve (ca 1712–73), m. (1762) Samuel Masham, 2d Bn Masham, 1758. She was at this time a maid of honour to the Princess of Wales.

15. James Hoste (1705–44), son of James Hoste of Sandringham; m. Susan Hamond (ca 1710–59), HW's cousin. The Hostes and the Hamonds were Norfolk families 'nearly allied' to the Walpoles. James Hoste died 20 Aug. 1744 (MANN ii. 238 n. 10; Edmund Farrer, *The Church Heraldry of Norfolk,* Norwich, 1885–93, ii. 267; C. R. Jones, *Sandringham, Past and Present,* 1883, p. 107).

16. Henry Sacheverell (ca 1674–1724), D.D., whose trial and impeachment for printing seditious libels took place in 1710. Sir Robert Walpole supported the Godolphin ministry on the impeachment.

few more knowing have been let into the secret of my Lord Orford's being out of place, but they know no more who has succeeded him than the Duke of Newcastle[17] does. Some conclude my Lord Walpole[18] has, as he is his eldest son and is not in Norfolk.

I flatter myself the air of Brumpton[19] has done your Ladyship a great deal of good, though I fear you don't use enough exercise with it. The vast piece of work, the travelling library, and the great number of crow quills you carried with you, make me fear you will sit too much. Apropos, I have taken the liberty to send you by the Lynn coach half a hundred quills, which I have plucked myself from the most charming breed of crows I ever saw. The jet of their feathers is remarkably black, their eyes a fine expressive blue, and instead of a hoarse quack like others of the species, they have the softest nervous notes I ever heard. I forgot to tell you that their feathers grow excessively low over their beaks.

I beg your Ladyship's pardon for the liberty I have taken, and am

Your most obedient, humble servant

Hor. Walpole

From John Whaley, Tuesday 4 December 1744 OS

Printed from Toynbee *Supp.* iii. 120–2, where the letter was first printed from the MS formerly in the Waller Collection. For the history of the MS see *ante* 10 Aug. 1735 OS.

King's Coll[ege], December 4, 1744.

Dear Sir,

I HAVE endeavoured to the best of my power to give in verse[1] some idea of the glorious collection of paintings at Houghton, though I am thoroughly conscious of the inequality of my Muse to such a task. If my attempt is fortunate enough to give any sort of

17. Thomas Pelham Holles (1693–1768), cr. (1715) D. of Newcastle.

18. Robert Walpole (1701–51), 2d E. of Orford, 1745.

19. Brompton. J. de Pesters, a cousin of Lady Denbigh, wrote to her 27 Aug. 1744: 'Lady T[ownshend] a une demie campagne. Elle couche à Brumpton et trôle les rues de Londres le reste du jour' (Hist. MSS Comm., op. cit. 182).

1. Whaley's 'A Journey to Houghton' (*ante* 12 Sept. 1743, n. 4).

pleasure to my Lord Orford and yourself it will answer the utmost of my ambition. I beg you would make any sort of alteration you shall think proper; and if you should choose to have any additions made to it and will point out to me in what manner you should choose 'em, I will take what pains I can to make them. I shall be pleased to have your opinion of my performance as soon as you have leisure to give it me, and to know you have still a regard to the welfare of

Your truly faithful, though
unfortunate friend

J. WHALEY

As you have the first part of this copy of verses (which you were pleased to say you would have continue as it was) I thought there was no occasion to send you that again, till I have your opinion of this latter part,[2] and I shall correct 'em both together, and present the whole to you; so that when you have marked this, and given me your opinion (which I beg you would do fully) about it, please to send it me again.

[Enclosure]

Albi Nostrorum, etc.[3]

O, Walpole, to whose keen yet candid sense
My scenes I trust, and judge their value thence,
While rattling coaches just beneath me roll,
Ruffle my thoughts, and discompose my soul,
How shall I guess my friend his time employs,
In London fixed, yet rescued from its noise?
Flows from thy pen the sweet spontaneous line
While Seymour's[4] look supplies the absent nine?
Or do you through ideal China rove,
And mix with Brachmans in the hallow'd grove?[5]
Or are you posting o'er some Roman road,
By captive kings and conqu'ring consuls trod,
By which the world's remotest ends were join'd
And Rome's commands were issu'd to mankind?
Or dost thou sit in pensive musing mood

2. These 'latter' verses of 'A Journey to Houghton' must have been enclosed in the present letter, along with the verses printed below.

Weighing within thy mind what's right and good,
Teaching thyself, without the aid of school's,
True Wisdom's,[6] Honesty's, and Friendship's rules?
For thou, my friend, art not mere breathing clay
But all thy thoughts the strongest sense display.
To thee the gods sufficient wealth have given
And taught thee too its use, the greatest gift of heav'n.
What for his child would more a parent have,
What for his pupil[7] more could tutor crave,
Than that with health heav'n would him bless,
Make him think right, and what he thinks, express?
Midst hope and cares, and jealous fears and rage,
Expect each coming day to close thy age;
Then if propitious fate shall add one more,
Happier you'll pass the sweet unthought for hour,
When[8] you would laugh, come to the Hoop and dine
There shall you see me eat and drink and shine
Of Epicurus' herd the fattest swine.

J. WHALEY

From THOMAS COPLESTON,[1] Sunday 27 January 1745 OS

Printed for the first time from the MS fragment now WSL, who acquired it from Lord Waldegrave in 1948.

Memoranda (by HW, on the verso):[2] Fox, Yonge, Fox, Yonge, Sir F. Dashwood, Pelham, Fazakerley, Fox, Knight, Winnington, Pelham, Hume Campbell, Sir F. Dashwood, Sir W. Yonge, Sir J. Cotton, Winnington, Lord Cornbury, Boone, H. Walpole, Fox, H. Walpole, Sir W. Yonge.

89/170/ on renewing the new reg[iment]s for four months.[3] Jan. 31, 1746.

3. An imitation of Horace's *Epistle* I. iv, subsequently much revised by Whaley and printed in his *A Collection of Original Poems and Translations,* 1745, pp. 83–5.

4. Hon. Jane Conway (1714–49), only dau. of Francis Seymour Conway, cr. (1703) Bn Conway, by his second marriage (MANN i. 274 n. 32; GRAY i. 235 n. 4). In the printed poem 'Seymour' has been changed to 'Cælia.'

5. 'And Brachmans [brahmins] deep in desart woods rever'd' (Pope, 'The Temple of Fame,' l. 100).

6. 'Wisdom' changed to 'Virtue' in the printed version.

7. Mr Whaley had been Mr Walpole's tutor at Cambridge (HW).

8. The last three lines of the poem were omitted in the printed version.

1. (1688–1748), of Bowden, Devon; M. P. Callington 1719–48. HW and Copleston were the successful candidates for the

St James's, [Jan]uary 27th 1745.

a son of Lord Orford's
rs, in his Lordship's
that office, but no
been only employed
[w]ithout a salary in
vacancy in your
that of the Earl
commands about it
can be had from
earnest request, that
[s]ubmit it to you
n, I heartily wish
[s] as well as ready
[f]riends. I know Lord
[opp]ortunity offers, but
open in his Lordship's

[Your obedi]ent and [humble servant,]

[THO]s COPLESTON

TO LADY TOWNSHEND, ca March 1745

Printed for the first time from the MS now WSL, who acquired it from Maggs in Aug. 1946; its previous history is not known.

Dated approximately by the references to Sir Robert Walpole's last illness and the return of George Townshend from his travels.

Endorsed in an unidentified hand: No date. Horace Walpole to Visc[ounte]ss Townshend.

AFTER all your Ladyship's extreme goodness to me, I have no excuse for having been anywhere before I waited on you, but that I really went to air myself—not to take off the smell of physicians and

borough of Callington in 1741 and again in 1747. Copleston, who received an equal number of votes in 1741 but fewer than HW in 1747, was first returned for Callington 4 Dec. 1719 (GRAY i. 11 n. 71; Sedgwick i. 207).

2. Presumably a list of the speakers in a debate in the House of Commons.

3. 'A motion was made . . . that the proper officers do lay before this House, the certificates from the commanding officers of the fifeen regiments commanded by certain noblemen, setting forth when they were half complete; as also copies of all the rolls of muster of the said regiments, with the dates thereof; and also by what general officer or officers the said regiments have been respectively re-

medicines,[1] two things which I know your Ladyship's delicacy has unfortunately reduced you to endure,[2] but the more offensive scent of volunteer-nurses, and cousin-distempers. Durst I enter the pure Pekin,[3] reeking out of a sick waiting room? or having been so long used to whispers that are louder than any laugh that is ever let loose in your Ladyship's dressing-room, durst I risk shaking ornaments of Bateman-architecture[4] when every Chinese shelf has weak nerves?

However since your Ladyship's goodness will give me leave, I will incense myself abundantly tomorrow evening, and find half an hour to wait on you and thank you. In the meantime I wish you joy of Mr Townshend's arrival,[5] and if you give me leave and tell me I shall not be troublesome, will wait on him.

I am, Madam,

Your Ladyship's most obedient humble servant

Hor. Walpole

viewed.' The motion was defeated 170 to 89 on 31 Jan. 1745 OS (*Journals of the House of Commons* xxv. 49). On 1 Feb. 1745 OS the House of Commons voted a sum 'for continuing two regiments of horse, and thirteen regiments of foot, now in his Majesty's service, under the command of several noblemen, for the further time of one hundred twenty-two days' (ibid. xxv. 50).

---

1. During the 'melancholy two months' of his father's last illness HW reported to Horace Mann that he had 'been out but twice' (Mann iii. 16, 24). Sir Robert Walpole died 18 March 1745.

2. Lady Townshend wrote Lady Denbigh 4 Oct. 1744: 'I am . . . nursing my mother, who has had a horrible accident, she having fallen from the top of her stairs nearly to the bottom with her head doubled under her' (Hist. MSS Comm., *Report on Denbigh MSS*, pt v, 1911, p. 257).

3. Lady Townshend had purchased in the previous year a lease on the house at No. 4 Whitehall Yard owned by Lord Holdernesse (J. de Pesters to Lady Denbigh 23 June 1744, ibid. 180). She apparently introduced *chinoiserie* into the remodelled house.

4. Richard ('Dicky') Bateman (ca 1705–73), antiquary and collector. HW claimed to have converted Bateman's house at Old Windsor from the Chinese to the Gothic style. He wrote Lord Strafford 13 June 1781: 'Though he [Bateman] was the founder of the Sharawadgi taste in England, I preached so effectually that his every pagoda took the veil' (Chute 359). See also Montagu ii. 43.

5. Doubtless George Townshend, who arrived in London 2 March 'from his travels in foreign parts' (*Daily Adv.* 5 March). See Mann ii. 566.

From the PRINCE DE CRAON, Saturday 1 May 1745 NS

Printed for the first time from the MS now WSL, acquired presumably in 1934 from Richard Bentley along with Mann's letters to HW (MANN i. pp. xlviii–xlix).

The letter was enclosed in Horace Mann's letter of 4 May 1745 NS to HW. Mann wrote: 'Prince Craon has just sent me the enclosed for you' (MANN iii. 38).

Florence ce 1 de mai 1745.

Monsieur,

JE SUIS trop sensible à tous les événements qui vous intéressent pour vous laisser ignorer la part que je prends à la perte que vous venez de faire de Monsieur votre père.[1] Nous connaissons, Mme de Craon et moi, la bonté de votre cœur et nous ressentons vivement ce qui lui en a coûté dans cette occasion; nous ne pouvons, Monsieur, vous rien offrir de plus propre à servir à votre consolation que ces sentiments dont nous sommes pénétrés, qui sont si conformes aux vôtres.

J'ai l'honneur d'être avec l'attachement le plus inviolable et le plus fidèle,

Monsieur,

Votre très humble et très obéissant serviteur,

LE PRINCE DE CRAON

Le Prince de Beauvau est marié depuis un mois avec Mlle d'Auvergne.[2] J'ai l'honneur, Monsieur, de vous en donner part, persuadé que vous lui continuez l'amitié dont vous l'avez honoré ici.

From LORD EDGCUMBE,[1] Thursday 26 September 1745 OS

Printed from the MS now WSL. First printed, Toynbee *Supp.* iii. 123–4. Damer-Waller; the MS was sold Sotheby's 5 Dec. 1921 (first Waller Sale), lot 119 (with

1. Sir Robert Walpole died 18 March 1745.
2. Marie-Sophie-Charlotte de la Tour d'Auvergne (1729–63), m. (3 April 1745) Charles-Just de Beauvau, Prince de Beauvau (MANN iii. 1 n. 4).

1. Richard Edgcumbe (1680–1758), cr. (1742) Bn Edgcumbe; M.P.

Hon. Richard Edgcumbe to HW 10 Aug. and 10 Sept. 1744), to Maggs; offered by them, Cat. No. 433 (Christmas 1922), lot 3206; sold by them to WSL, 1932.

Mount Edgcumbe,[2] 26th September 1745.

Dear Sir,

THOUGH you seemed to think in your last kind letter,[3] that our affairs do not grow worse, yet I cannot find they grow better, unless it be by the arrival of the Dutch troops[4] in aid of his Excellency Sir John Cope.[5]

The great city of Edinborough having received the rebels without the least resistance, as our papers mention,[6] I must own surprises very much; what is become of that boasted number of inhabitants able to bear arms, or where hath been their loyalty, or courage? But I will wait for the next post before I say any more about them, hoping to hear a good account from our army, which we are told are at full march within 18 miles of the town.[7] And so much for politics at present.

I have made your compliments to Dick,[8] and told him the piece of news[9] you sent him. He takes you for a wag, but is much your humble servant.

As to Mr Chasselup's[10] affair, or any other that you would mention to me, you need not make any excuses for it, nor will I use any ceremony with you, but plainly tell you, that I have had an eye to that employment[11] for a very particular person,[12] whom I will name to you when we first meet, which will be very soon, I hope, for I design to be with you at the opening of the Parliament.[13] Though I can send you no news from hence, yet I sit down with great pleasure to thank you for your kind remembrance, and to assure you that I am most truly and affectionately

Your very humble servant, etc.

EDGCUMBE

I am just stepping into my coach, bound for Mr Moyle's.[14]

2. Lord Edgcumbe's seat in Cornwall, near Plymouth.

3. Missing.

4. About 2,500 Dutch troops arrived at Gravesend 17 Sept. to oppose the Young Pretender's forces in Scotland; also one regiment at Bridlington Bay, Yorks, 17 Sept. and two more regiments at Gravesend 20 Sept. (SELWYN 97, nn. 16, 17).

5. (1690–1760), K.B., 1743; Lt-Gen., 1743; commander-in-chief in Scotland against the insurgents; M.P.

6. They took possession of the city 17 Sept. (*London Gazette*, No. 8468, 17–21 Sept.). 'Edinburgh surrendered to the rebels, without firing a gun' (*Daily Adv.* 24 Sept.).

7. Cope's army landed at Dunbar, 18 miles east of Edinburgh, and was defeated by the rebels at Prestonpans, only six

From the HON. EDWARD CORNWALLIS,[1] Wednesday 18 December 1745 OS

Printed from Toynbee *Supp.* ii. 85, where the letter was first printed from the MS formerly in the Waller Collection. Damer-Waller; the MS was sold Sotheby's 5 Dec. 1921 (first Waller Sale), lot 112, to Field; not further traced.

Preston,[2] December the 18th.

I HAVE just time, dear Hor., to tell you where I am in pursuit of the rascally rebels[3] but despair much of getting up with them. Our only hopes was part of Wade's[4] army stopping them, but such is the inactivity of that army[5] that I have no hopes; the Duke[6] is forty miles before us with a body of horse.[7] This is the sixth day's march without halt with a thousand volunteers from the army and Bligh's[8] reg[imen]t, our men much fatigued but in great spirits. How far we

miles from the city, 21 Sept. (*London Gazette*, op. cit.; SELWYN 97 nn. 14–15).

8. Hon. Richard Edgcumbe (1716–61), eldest son of Lord Edgcumbe; 2d Bn Edgcumbe, 1758; M.P.; HW's friend and correspondent.

9. Not explained.

10. Possibly a member of the Chasseloup-Laubat family, which included several distinguished military officers, but not further identified (NBG x. 47).

11. As Lord Lieutenant of Cornwall, chancellor of the Duchy of Lancaster, and chief government manager in the Cornwall boroughs, Edgcumbe had numerous 'employments' in his gift.

12. Not identified.

13. It was originally scheduled to meet on 19 Sept., but was further prorogued to 17 Oct. (SELWYN 97 n. 10).

14. Possibly a son of Joseph Moyle (d. 1742), M.P. Saltash during Q. Anne's reign (GM 1742, xii. 218).

---

1. (1713–76), Lt-Gen., 1760; M.P. Eye 1743–9, Westminster 1753–62; governor of Nova Scotia 1749–52 and of Gibraltar 1762–76; groom of the Bedchamber, 1747; m. (1753) Hon. Mary Townshend, HW's first cousin (MANN iii. 177 n. 37). At this time he was Lt-Col. of the 20th Foot, commanded by Thomas Bligh (ibid.).

2. Henry Seymour Conway wrote HW 13 Dec. 1745 from Wigan, near Preston, that 'Ned Cornwallis has just joined us with his regiment and is of our expedition' (CONWAY i. 215).

3. The Scottish rebels arrived at Preston 12 December and left the following morning on their retreat toward the border (W. B. Blaikie, *Itinerary of Prince Charles Edward Stuart*, Edinburgh, 1897, p. 31; James Ray, *A Compleat History of the Rebellion*, Bristol, 1750, pp. 191–2).

4. George Wade (1673–1748), Lt-Gen., 1727; field marshal, 1743; commander-in-chief in the north of England during the Jacobite rebellion, 1745; M.P.

5. 'Wade . . . made no attempt to intercept the northward march of Charles' (J. W. Fortescue, *History of the British Army*, 2d edn, 1910, ii. 137).

6. William Augustus (1721–65), D. of Cumberland; son of George II.

7. On 13 Dec. a body of horse and dragoons reinforced by volunteers had arrived under Oglethorpe, having marched 100 miles in three days through snow and ice. Cumberland arrived in the afternoon of the same day and immediately gave his orders for continuing the pursuit of the rebels (ibid.; *Daily Adv.* 11 Dec. 1745; Ray, op. cit. 200).

8. Thomas Bligh (1685–1775) Lt-Gen., 1754; M.P. (Ireland) (MANN v. 238 n. 7). He was at this time in command of the 20th Foot.

shall pursue I know not, but see them out of England.[9] I dare say we have picked up a few.[10] The Pretender's son[11] flies before the army—I mean, of rascals.

I am
Ever yours,
Ed. Cornwallis

From John Hobart,[1] Tuesday 21 June 1746 NS

Printed for the first time from the MS now WSL, who acquired it from Maggs ca 1930; its previous history is not known.

The year is established by Hobart's known period of residence at Florence.

Florence, Jun[e] the 21st NS.

YOU cannot conceive how much I am ashamed at having so long deferred acknowledging the infinite obligation I have to Mr Walpole for his letter to Mr Mann.[2] Had I wrote when it was my duty my thanks might then perhaps have borne a little more proportion to it, but his goodness has increased so much upon me every day, that all I now can say will express very faintly how excessively I feel myself obliged to you. We are very glad to send our friends in England, with our thanks for the good news from Scotland,[3] that of the victory at Piacenza;[4] the Spaniards are said to have lost in all above twelve

9. The rebels crossed the Esk into Scotland unmolested 20 December (Fortescue, loc. cit.; Chevalier James de Johnstone, *Memoirs of the Rebellion in 1745 and 1746*, 1820, pp. 74–6).

10. 'The King's troops continued under arms all night [18 Dec.] . . . and in the morning we had about sixty of the rebels prisoners, many of them being picked up by the country people' (Ray, op. cit. 205). See also MANN iii. 172–7.

11. Charles Edward Louis Philip Casimir (Stuart) (1720–88), the Young Pretender.

1. (1723–93), styled the Hon. John Hobart 1728–46, and Lord Hobart 1746–56; 2d E. of Buckinghamshire, 1756; M.P. Norwich 1747–56 (MANN iii. 60 n. 1). HW wrote Horace Mann 6 June 1746 OS: 'I used to call him the *clear cake;* fat, fair, sweet, and seen through in a moment' (ibid. iii. 263).

2. June 1745 OS, 'recommending you a new acquaintance, for which I am sure you will thank me' (MANN iii. 60). Mann reported to HW 24 May 1746 NS: 'Your *reccomandé* Mr Hobart is come at last, and is so unlike all the English that I adore him. . . . he is extremely well bred, introduces himself vastly well to all your acquaintance, and is by them as well received' (ibid. iii. 252).

3. Prince Charles Edward's highlanders had been routed by the Duke of Cumberland's forces at Culloden 16 April 1746. HW reported the news to Mann 25 April 1746 OS (ibid. iii. 247–9).

thousand men.[5] I shall not trouble you with the detail as you will see so many better than I can possibly send you. Mr Whitehead[6] and Mr Chute[7] left us three weeks ago;[8] you are acquainted with them; guess, therefore, how cruel it was for me only to know them, that I might so soon feel their loss. I like Florence extremely, and am happy in many agreeable acquaintance that Mr Mann has procured me. The people in general seem very amiable; at least their appearing so very sensible of the merit of Mr Walpole has prepossessed me infinitely in their favour. Believe me, with the greatest regard,

Your most obedient humble servant,

JOHN HOBART

From LORD HOBART, Saturday 8 July 1747 NS

Printed from Toynbee *Supp.* iii. 125–6, where the letter was first printed from the MS formerly in the Waller Collection. Damer-Waller; the MS was sold Sotheby's 5 Dec. 1921 (first Waller Sale), lot 99, to Oppenheim; not further traced.

The year of the letter is determined by the reference to the creation of Cardinal York.

Address: To the Honourable Horace Walpole Esq., Member of Parliament, in Arlington Street, À Londres. *Postmark:* IY 18.

Rome, July the 8th, NS.

Dear Sir,

THOUGH I have an infinite pleasure in putting you in mind of me, I should not have troubled you with this, if I did not flatter myself that you would receive some pleasure from the enclosed.[1] I have had great trouble in getting it and have but just time enough to read it once over before I send it. It is certainly a most

4. The Battle of Piacenza, 15–16 June 1746 NS. Predictions of surrender were common, but the siege was not lifted until 16 July NS (ibid. iii. 291 n. 6).

5. The enemy's losses were reported to be 'above 10,000 men killed, wounded, and taken prisoners' (ibid. iii. 291 n. 9).

6. Francis Whithed (formerly Thistlethwayte) (1719–51), of Southwick Park, Hants; lived in Italy with his cousin John Chute 1740–6; M.P. Hampshire 1747–51.

7. John Chute (1701–76), of the Vyne, Hants; HW's correspondent.

8. They left Florence 26 May 1746 NS (MANN iii. 252).

1. Missing; it was a printed copy of Benedict XIV's speech on creating the younger son of the Old Pretender Cardinal York 3 July 1747 (MANN iii. 422 n. 4).

original piece, and I fancy a translation of it would not make a bad figure in the *Evening Post*.[2] The young gentleman[3] was half cardinalised a week ago, and this morning I saw him receive the hat by which the finishing stroke was put to that great work; the Pretender was present at the ceremony and seemed most extremely pleased. I have not time to say anything of myself, nor if I had would I venture to tire your patience with it. The paper that is enclosed[4] with the Pope's speech is the summons that was sent to the cardinals this morning. I shall leave this place in a few days to go to Florence in my way to England,[5] where I hope soon to have the pleasure of assuring you that I am,

With great regard,

Your most obedient humble servant,

JOHN HOBART[6]

From STEPHEN POYNTZ,[1] Wednesday 1 July 1747 OS

Printed from the MS now WSL. First printed, Toynbee *Supp.* ii. 88. Damer-Waller; the MS was sold 5 Dec. 1921 (first Waller Sale), lot 170, to Wells; given by him to Thomas Conolly, of Chicago, from whom WSL acquired it in 1937.

Dated by the Battle of Laeffeld 2 July 1747 NS; HW reported details of the battle to Horace Mann 3 July 1747 OS (MANN iii. 423–4).

Wed. morning.

Sir,

I HAVE the pleasure to acquaint you that Colonel Conway[2] and Lord Robert Sutton[3] are safely arrived at the Headquarters on their parole.[4] My letter is from Sir Everard Fawkener[5] of the 6th

2. 'Rome, July 8. Prince Henry Benedict Stuart, second son of the Chevalier de St George, having resolved to take up with an ecclesiastic life, the Pope performed on the 30th of last month the ceremony of shaving the crown of his head. The 3d instant the Holy Father held a public consistory, at which the whole Sacred College assisted; and the Pontiff made an eloquent harangue. . . . All the Sacred College having given their approbation, Prince Henry was introduced into the Consistory, and made a Cardinal with the usual ceremonies; and is to be styled from henceforth, *Cardinal Duke of York*' (*London Evening Post*, No. 3075, 18–21 July 1747).

3. Henry Benedict Maria Clement (Stuart) (1725–1807).

4. Also missing.

5. He arrived at Florence 11 July 1747 NS and left 22 July NS. Although returned to Parliament for Norwich 29 June OS, he was not back in England until well after the elections (MANN iii. 421 and nn. 2–3).

6. Lord Hobart, eldest son to the Earl of Bucks (HW).

1. (1685–1750), of Midgham, near Newbury, Berks; chargé d'affaires at Paris 1730; envoy extraordinary and plenipotentiary to Sweden 1724–7; governor and

NS by Mr George Townshend.[6] I have sent it to Mr Pelham,[7] and as soon as it comes back shall forward it to you. Colonel Conway brings an account that the French own the loss of *1,000* officers and *9,000* private men, but we compute it at upwards of *12,000*.[8] I am,

Sir,

Your most humble and obedient servant,

STE. POYNTZ

From LORD CHEDWORTH,[1] Friday 23 September 1748 OS

Printed from Toynbee *Supp.* iii. 130–1, where the letter was first printed from the MS formerly in the Waller Collection. Damer-Waller; the MS was sold Sotheby's 5 Dec. 1921 (first Waller Sale), lot 103, to Stuart; not further traced.

September the 23d 1748.

Sir,

I RECEIVED your letter[2] this morning which I was extremely glad to do, as it gives me an opportunity of communicating to you what little I know concerning Lord Walpole's[3] affairs. I was not at home till after my Lord had been some time at Cheltenham; as soon as I knew his Lordship was there with Lord Orford's[4] consent, I took the liberty to use all the arguments I could to persuade my

steward of the Duke of Cumberland's household (D. B. Horn, *British Diplomatic Representatives 1689–1789*, 1932, pp. 19, 142; *ante* 30 Sept. 1743 OS, n. 2).

2. Henry Seymour Conway, HW's cousin and correspondent, at this time Col. of the 48th Foot (Namier and Brooke).

3. Lord Robert Manners Sutton (1722–62), second son of John, 3d D. of Rutland; Lt-Col. of the D. of Cumberland's Dragoons 1746–8, serving in Flanders 1747–8; M.P. Notts 1747–62.

4. They had been captured at the Battle of Laeffeld 2 July NS and held prisoners by the French for three days. Their release on parole enabled them to return to Cumberland's headquarters at Maestricht (MONTAGU i. 50). For Conway's account of the affair see his letter of 9 July 1747 NS to HW (CONWAY i. 273–4).

5. (1684–1758), Kt, 1735; secretary to the D. of Cumberland (MANN iii. 26 n. 15).

6. (1724–1807), 4th Vct Townshend, 1764; cr. (1787) M. Townshend. Poyntz had been his tutor.

7. First lord of the Treasury.

8. HW reported this last total to Mann 3 July 1747 OS, but the official figure was 9,409 (MANN iii. 424 and n. 10).

1. John Thynne Howe (1714–62), 2d Bn Chedworth, 1742.

2. Missing.

3. George Walpole (1730–91), styled Vct Walpole 1745–51; 3d E. of Orford, 1751; HW's nephew.

4. Robert Walpole (1701–51), cr. (1723) Bn Walpole; 2d E. of Orford, 1745; HW's brother.

Lord to return home. When I found I could not prevail on him to do so immediately, I then invited his Lordship to my house,[5] thinking that his Lordship would be more out of the way of any bad company he might by chance fall into, and that I might have a better opportunity of talking with him. I have had a great deal of conversation with my Lord, and by what I can learn of him, he thinks that his father is so angry with him, that till there is some person so good as to make some mediation between them, he is unwilling to return. He tells me he imagines things have been represented to Lord Orford in as bad a light as possible and he is afraid to return till he has some hopes of his father's forgiving him.[6] I have not nor shall mention that I have had a letter from you. But Lord Walpole told me before I had your letter that he had wrote to you concerning this affair,[7] and said he had not heard from you lately and that he did intend to send his servant to you if he did not hear from you soon. You may depend that the great regard I have for Lord Orford, and the obligation I think myself under to his family,[8] will make me use my utmost endeavours to persuade his Lordship to return, and to take all the care that I possibly can of Lord Walpole while he is with me, and I will do all I can to keep him with me till he returns home. Any commands you have for me I will punctually observe, and shall be very glad to receive them. My Lord Orford knows that my Lord Walpole is with me, and I hope he is well assured that I wish nothing more than the welfare of his Lordship and of my Lord Walpole, and that I will do all that is in [my] power to persuade my Lord Walpole to return as soon as possible. As soon as I can learn anything more of my Lord Walpole's thoughts I will be sure to communicate them to you, and am,

Sir,

Your most obedient humble servant,

CHEDWORTH

5. Stowell Park, near Chedworth, about nine miles SE of Cheltenham (Samuel Rudder, *A New History of Gloucestershire,* Cirencester, 1779–?83, pp. 707–8).

6. The reason for Lord Orford's anger at his son is not known, but Lord Chedworth's reference to 'bad company' is suggestive. Writing to Horace Mann ca Aug. 1748, HW called George 'a wild boy of nineteen.' He informed Mann 24 Oct. OS that 'Lord Walpole is setting out on his travels' to the Continent (MANN iii. 496, 510–11).

7. The letter is missing.

8. His father, John Howe, 1st Bn Chedworth, after supporting Sir Robert Walpole in Parliament, had received a peerage on Sir Robert's recommendation (GEC iii. 156*n*).

From MRS CLIVE,[1] ?Saturday 3 December ?1748 OS

Printed, with spelling and punctuation preserved, from a facsimile of the MS in the catalogue of the first Waller Sale, facing p. 25. First printed, Toynbee *Supp.* iii. 139. Reprinted, *SH Accounts,* p. 85. Damer-Waller; the MS was sold Sotheby's 5 Dec. 1921 (first Waller Sale), lot 108, to Maggs; not further traced.

Dated conjecturally 1755 by Paget Toynbee, who assumed that Little Strawberry Hill (where Mrs Clive came to live ca 1754) is the 'little cottage' mentioned in the letter. It more likely refers to the cottage near Marble Hill, where she lived previously (see n. 3 below). HW was personally acquainted with Mrs Clive in 1748 (MONTAGU i. 70, 72). She presumably sought his advice in improving the Marble Hill cottage (acting 'a good sort of a countrey gentlewoman at twickenham') soon after becoming a Twickenham neighbour ca 1748.

Great Queenstreet Lincone inn feilds, Decem. ye 3d.

Sir

I HOPE you will pardon my takeing this liberty. I am inform'd that you have lately made some very advantadgeous allterations in your garden[2] at twickenham and as your tast is unquestionable, I shou'd be glad to have a shadow of it at my little cottage;[3] therefore beg the favour to know who is your gardener,[4] for th'o I am now representing women of qualitty and Coblers wives[5] &c &c to Crowded houeses, and flattering applause; the Charecture I am most desierous to act well is; a good sort of a Countrey gentlewoman at twickenham; and therefore must endeavour to have everything thats convenient there, th'o perhaps not all I shoud like; for there is such a thing as exspence, which I am oblidged to avoid.

I am exstreamly sorry I happend to be abroad when you did me the

1. Catherine Raftor ('Kitty Clive') (1711–85), m. (1732) George Clive; actress (GRAY i. 44 n. 298).

2. During 1748–9 HW was engaged in extensive landscaping of the grounds at SH; see *SH Accounts,* pp. 36–8. He wrote Henry Seymour Conway 29 Aug. 1748 OS: 'My present and sole occupation is planting, in which I have made great progress' (CONWAY i. 292).

3. Near Marble Hill, Twickenham, which she occupied ca 1748–54 (R. S. Cobbett, *Memorials of Twickenham,* 1872, p. 245).

4. Not identified. At this time HW employed a jobbing gardener, who was paid off in Sept. 1749. He subsequently hired a Scotsman, John Cowie, as his permanent gardener (*SH Accounts,* pp. 38–9).

5. During the 1748–9 season at Drury Lane Mrs Clive appeared frequently in the rôles of Mrs Riot, the 'fine lady' in Garrick's *Lethe,* and Nell, the cobbler's wife in Charles Coffey's *The Devil to Pay* (*London Stage* Pt IV, i. 64–5, 86, *et passim*). She was particularly noted for her portrayal of Nell (Percy Fitzgerald, *The Life of Mrs Catherine Clive,* 1888, pp. 42, 44, 58, 60).

honour to Call on me;[6] but hope I shall have the favour to see you some other time.

I am Sir your Most
humble Ser't

CATH: CLIVE

To the REV. JOSEPH SPENCE, Tuesday ?1749

Printed for the first time from a photostat of the MS deposited in the University of Nottingham Library (Newcastle MS Ne C 4108), by kind permission of the Trustees of the 7th Duke of Newcastle deceased. The letter was presumably passed by Spence to Lord Lincoln at the time Spence received it, and it has descended among the Newcastle papers (deposited at the University of Nottingham in 1955).

Dated conjecturally by the reference to 'selling a house' at Twickenham (see n. 2 below).

Endorsed in an unidentified hand: H. Walpole. No. 11.

Address: To the Reverend Mr Spence at Lord Lincoln's.[1]

Tuesday morning.

Dear Sir,

I MUST beg you to tell my Lord Lincoln how very sorry I am that he is out of order and that I cannot have the honour of waiting on him this morning. I am obliged to go to Twickenham on unavoidable business. I am selling a house there,[2] and am to meet the purchaser,[3] who is a difficult person, and one whom I must take when I can. I will undoubtedly pay my duty to my Lord on Thursday or Friday morning, but as he knows he may command me at any time or all times, I will take my chance, and if he is busy, call again, when it is more convenient, for I would by no means have him confine himself a moment for me, who am totally at his disposal.

Yours ever

HOR. WALPOLE

6. The date of this visit is not known.

1. 2d D. of Newcastle-under-Lyne, 1768; HW's correspondent. Spence lived in London from Nov. 1741 until the spring of 1749, when he moved to a house at Byfleet, Surrey, given to him by his former pupil, Lord Lincoln. Spence doubtless spent many days at Lincoln's during his residence in London (Austin Wright, *Joseph Spence*, Chicago, 1950, pp. 69, 114–15).

JAMES MACLEANE EXECUTED OCT. 3. 1750. AGED 26 YEARS
Now, for those foolish days of wanton pride,
My Soul is justly humbled in the dust.
——— all judging Heav'n,
Who knows my Crimes has seen my Sorrow for 'em.
Engrav'd from the Original Drawn from the Life
while under Sentence, by L.P. Boitard.

JAMES MACLAINE, BY L. P. BOITARD, 1750

From JAMES MACLAINE,[1] Friday 10 November 1749 OS

Printed from the MS now WSL, with the original spelling and punctuation preserved. First printed in the *Times Literary Supplement,* 5 Feb. 1920, p. 86. Reprinted, Toynbee *Supp.* iii. 132–5. Damer-Waller; the MS was sold Sotheby's 5 Dec. 1921 (first Waller Sale), lot 145, bought in; resold Christie's 15 Dec. 1947 (second Waller Sale), lot 17, to Maggs for WSL.

Dated by the newspaper notices of the robbery. The letter is written on gilt-edged paper.

Address: To the Honourable Horatio Walpole Esquire. (The letter was apparently delivered by hand to HW's house in Arlington Street.)

friday Evening.

Sir,

SEEING an advertisement in the papers of to Day giveing an Account of your being Rob'd by two Highway men on Wedensday night last in Hyde Parke[2] And during the time a Pistol being fired whether Intended or Accidentally was Doubtfull Oblidges Us to take this Method of Assureing you that it was the latter And by no

2. By Private Act of Parliament (22 Geo. II, c. 44) HW purchased 'divers lands and tenements in Twickenham' in 1749. The property included the original five acres of SH and other parcels of land nearby. The 'house' sold by HW was presumably part of the other property that HW disposed of, although no record of this particular transaction has been found ('Short Notes', GRAY i. 17; *Strawberry Hill Accounts . . . Kept by Mr Horace Walpole from 1747 to 1795,* ed. Paget Toynbee, Oxford, 1927, pp. 47–8, 183–9).

3. Not identified.

1. James Maclaine (1724–50), son of the Rev. Thomas Maclaine (d. 1740), a Presbyterian minister in Ireland, and brother of the Rev. Archibald Maclaine (1722–1804), author and divine. HW described him as 'a fashionable highwayman, who . . . robbed me among others' (MANN iv. 168 and nn. 24, 31–2). The robbery, recounted in HW's 'Short Notes,' took place in Hyde Park 8 Nov. 1749 as HW was returning from Holland House at night. Maclaine's accomplice was William Plunket (GRAY i. 23; *A Complete History of James Maclean,* [1750], p. 51). HW's essay in the *World,* No. 103, 19 Dec. 1754, remarks upon the episode.

2. 'The night before last, as Mr Horace Walpole was returning from Holland House, between nine and ten, he was stopped in Hyde Park by two men on horseback, masked, one of which held a blunderbuss to the coachman, while the other came up to the chariot, and, thrusting a pistol into it, demanded Mr Walpole's money and watch; he gave the fellow his purse, and as he was giving him the watch, the pistol, which was held close to his cheek, went off (by accident or design is uncertain); but, though it was so near that the force struck Mr Walpole backwards, the ball luckily missed him, and went through the corner of the chariot just above his head, only scorching his face, and leaving several marks of powder. The coachman started, and said, What is that? The man with the blunderbuss swore he would shoot him too, if he spoke, bid him give him his watch, and then riding up to the chariot, they took Mr. Walpole's sword, and some silver from the footman, and rode off to Kensington gate' (*Daily Adv.* 10 Nov. 1749).

means Design'd Either to hurt or frighten you for tho' we Are Reduced by the misfortunes of the world and obliged to have Recourse to this method of getting money[3] Yet we have Humanity Enough not to take any bodys life where there is Not a Nessecety for it. We have likewise seen the advertisem^t offering A Reward of twenty Guineas for your watch and sealls[4] which are very safe and which you shall have with your sword and the coach mans watch for fourty Guineas and not a shilling less As I very well know the value of them and how to dispose of them to the best Advantage therefore Expects as I have given You the preference that you'll be Expeditious in your Answering this which must be in the daily Advertiser of Monday;[5] And now S^r to Convince you that we are not Destitute of Honour Our selves if you will Comply with the above terms and pawn your Honour in the publick papers that you will punctually pay the fourty Guineas after you have Reced the things and not by any means Endeavour to apprehend or hurt Us I say if you will agree to All these particulars we Desire that you'll send one of your Serv^ts on Monday Night next between Seven and Eight O Clock to Tyburn and let him be leaning ag^st One of the pillers[6] with a white handkerchif in his hand by way of Signall where and at which time we will meet him and Deliver him the things All safe and in an hour after we will Expect him at the same place to pay us the money Now S^r if by any means we find that you Endeavour to betray us (which we shall goe prepaird against) and in the attempt should Even succed we should leave such friends behind us who has a personall knowledge of you As would for Ever seek your Destruction if you occasion ours but if you agree to the above be assurd you nor none belownging to you shall Receive Any or the least Injury further as we depend upon your

3. HW related to Horace Mann 2 Aug. 1750 OS that Maclaine had formerly been 'a grocer, but losing a wife that he loved extremely about two years ago, and by whom he has one little girl, he quitted his business with £200 in his pocket, which he soon spent, and then took to the road with only one companion, Plunket, a journeyman apothecary. . . . their faces are as known about St James's as any gentleman's who lives in that quarter' (MANN iv. 168).

4. HW inserted the following advertisement in the *Daily Adv.* 10 and 11 Nov.: 'Taken on Wednesday night last, by two highwaymen in Hyde Park, a gold repeating watch in a shagreen case, with gilt edges, maker's name Benjamin Gray, London, mark *Vin*. It had a black ribband with two seals, one a white cornelian with a coat of arms; the other a small onyx with a head. Whoever will bring the above watch and seals to Mr Gray, watchmaker, near St James's House, shall have twenty guineas reward, and no questions asked.'

5. The same advertisement appeared in the *Daily Adv.* on Monday, 13 Nov., with the addition: 'No greater reward will be offered.'

6. The three wooden stilts of the Tyburn gallows, a triangular structure.

Honour for the punctuall paym^t of the Cash if you should in that Deceieve us the Concaquence may be fattall to you—if you agree to the above terms[7] I shall Expect your Answer in the following words in Mondays Daily Advertiser—

Whereas I Reced a letter Dated friday Evening last sign'd A:B and C:D: the Contents of which I promise in the most sollemn manner upon my Honour strictly to Comply with to which you are to sign your name—if you have any thing to Object ag^st any of the Above proposalls[8] we Desire that you'll let us know them in the Most Obscure way you Can in mondays paper but if we find no notice taken of it then they will be sold A tuesday morning for Exportation

A:B & C:D:

P:S: the same foot man that was behind the Chariot when Rob'd will be Most Agreeable to us as we Intend Repaying him a triffle we took from him[9]

To the Duke of Bedford,[1] Sunday 11 February 1750 OS

Printed for the first time from a photostat of the MS in the possession of the Duke of Bedford, Woburn Abbey, kindly furnished by the late Sir Lewis Namier.

Endorsed by Bedford: Feb. 11 1749/50. Mr H. Walpole jun[io]r. R[eceived] 11 at night.

Arlington Street, Sunday night.

My Lord,

IT HAPPENED fortunately that your Grace's servant[2] did not find me in the country, for having engaged my interest[3] for Mr Parry[4] to Mr Churchill,[5] I could not have taken any step in favour

7. 'Mr Walpole did not think [these terms] proper to comply with' (*Daily Adv.* 15 Nov.).

8. 'Friday, Nov. 17, 1749. Whereas I have received a second letter [missing], signed A.B. and C.D. offering to restore my watch and seals on payment of twenty guineas: if any person will bring them to Mr Cates, pawnbroker, at the Five Balls in Chandos Street, Covent Garden, I promise upon my honour that they shall receive the money without any inquiry or molestation. Hor. Walpole' (*Daily Adv.* 18 Nov.).

9. Maclaine was apprehended 27 July 1750 OS after robbing the Salisbury coach and, under examination, confessed to the Hyde Park robbery. He was tried at the Old Bailey, condemned 19 Sept. 1750 OS, and executed at Tyburn 3 Oct. OS. HW recovered his property for the twenty guineas originally offered (Gray i. 23 n. 148; Mann iv. 199 and nn. 21–2).

1. John Russell (1710–1771), 4th D. of Bedford, 1732.

2. Not identified.

of any other person without his leave; but your Grace's man came back to me here, and I went immediately to Mr Churchill, and obtained his consent to write to Mr Ashton[6] for Mr Hetherington,[7] in case Mr Parry declines or cannot succeed. I dispatched the messenger to Eton without letting him return to your Grace, for fear of his not being time enough, and with a letter[8] to Mr Ashton, which I flatter myself will have the success your Grace desires.[9] I am extremely glad to be at liberty to obey your Grace's commands, and beg leave to thank you for honouring me with them.

I am, my Lord

Your Grace's most obedient and most faithful humble servant

Hor. Walpole

To George Lee,[1] Saturday 23 March 1751 OS

Printed for the first time from the MS now WSL. The MS was sold Sotheby's 8 March 1939 (property of Mrs Benedict Eyre), lot 738, to Maggs for WSL; its earlier history is not known.

The year of the letter is established by the reference to the Prince of Wales's death.

Arlington Street, March 23d.

Sir,

GIVE me leave to condole with you very sincerely on the loss you have had in the Prince of Wales,[2] who had so just a sense of your merit and abilities. Nobody has a stronger conviction than

3. Apparently on the request of Lord Sandwich. HW wrote Horace Mann 25 Feb. 1750 OS: 'He [Sandwich] had made interest for these two years for one Parry, a poor clergyman, schoolfellow and friend of his, to be fellow of Eton, and had secured a majority for him' (MANN iv. 121).

4. Perhaps Gregory Parry (ca 1717–85), rector of Vaynor, Brecon, 1749; prebend of Worcester, 1772 (MANN iv. 121 n. 13).

5. Presumably Charles Churchill (?1720–1812), M.P.; HW's brother-in-law.

6. Thomas Ashton (1715–75), divine; fellow of Eton 1745–75; HW's correspondent.

7. William Hetherington (1698–1778), rector of Dry Drayton, Cambs, 1728–53, of Farnham Royal 1753–78. His brother, John Hetherington, was tutor to the Duke of Bedford (*Eton Coll. Reg.* 174).

8. Missing.

9. William Hetherington was made fellow of Eton on 16 Feb. 1750 OS (ibid.).

1. George Lee (ca 1700–58), Kt, 1752; M.P.; lawyer and politician. He was one of the chief advisers to Frederick, Prince of Wales, and was appointed treasurer of the household to the Princess of Wales after Frederick's death in 1751, a post he resigned in 1757.

myself of the misfortune His Royal Highness's death is to this country; nobody can be more convinced than I am how extensively you, Sir, must foresee the fatal consequences it may be attended with. As I flatter myself you have always seen that my regard for you, Sir, was really founded on the most sincere esteem, I can't help taking the earliest opportunity of renewing my professions of attachment to you, and of assuring you that no alteration of circumstances, as none ever have, can affect the personal regard[3] (and if you will give me leave to say the friendship) with which I am

Sir,

Your most obedient and most sincere humble servant

Hor. Walpole

To the Duke of Bedford, Wednesday 3 April 1751 OS

Printed for the first time from a photostat of the MS in the possession of the Duke of Bedford, Woburn Abbey, kindly furnished by the late Sir Lewis Namier.

Endorsed by Bedford: Arlington Street. April 3d 1751. Mr H. Walpole.

Arlington Street, April 3d 1751.

My Lord,

I AM EXTREMELY sensible of your Grace's kind intentions to Lord Orford[1] and me, and am persuaded he will think himself as much obliged to your Grace as I do, and that he would be very

2. Frederick (1707–51), P. of Wales, who died suddenly at Leicester House 20 March 1751 OS.

3. After Pelham's death, when Lee was talked of for lord treasurer, HW remarked to Horace Mann: 'he is an unexceptional man, sensible, of good character, the ostensible favourite of the Princess, and obnoxious to no set of men; for though he changed ridiculously quick on the Prince's death, yet as everybody changed with him, it offended nobody' (Mann iv. 412–13). HW's good opinion of him is also expressed in *Mem. Geo. II* i. 90–1.

1. George, 3d E. of Orford, who had succeeded to the title on his father's death 31 March 1751 OS.

2. Robert Walpole, 2d E. of Orford, was Lord Lieutenant of Devon 1733–51. Bedford had apparently consulted HW as to whether Lord Orford wished to succeed his father in the lieutenancy.

3. His mother's estates in Devon and Cornwall were legally hers during her lifetime, although she could not deprive the 3d Earl, an only son, of the reversion of the properties (Mann iv. 424 nn. 18–19). The obituary notice of his father's death in GM 1751, xxi. 187, noted that Lady Walpole 'has a large jointure, so that a very small estate is left to [her son] his Lordship.'

sorry to interfere in any shape with your views for the lieutenancy of Devonshire,[2] where at present he will not even have any property.[3] However, my Lord, I must not take upon myself to answer absolutely for Lord Orford, though I must think I do him a much greater service if I have interest enough to recommend him to your Grace's protection, than I could by obtaining him the honour in question.[4] Give me leave at least, my Lord, to say for myself, that I am extremely obliged to your Grace for this mark of your friendship, and that I shall always be,

My Lord

Your Grace's most faithful
and obedient humble servant

Hor. Walpole

To the Rev. Joseph Spence, Monday 3 June 1751 OS

Printed from a photostat of the MS in the Henry E. Huntington Library. First printed in Spence's *Anecdotes, Observations, and Characters, of Books and Men,* ed. S. W. Singer, 1820, pp. 439–41. Reprinted, Toynbee iii. 55; *Horace Walpole's Fugitive Verses,* ed. W. S. Lewis, 1931, pp. 117–18 (closing, signature, and postscript omitted in both).

Arlington Street, June 3d 1751.

Dear Sir,

I HAVE translated the lines[1] and send them to you, but the expressive conciseness and beauty of the original and my disuse of turning verses, made it so difficult, that I beg they may be of no other use than of showing you how readily I complied with your request.

Illam, quicquid agit, quoquo vestigia vertit,
Componit furtim subsequiturque decor.

If she but moves or looks, her step, her face
By stealth adopt unmeditated grace.

4. 'Whitehall, April 13. The King has been pleased to appoint the D. of Bedford, one of his Majesty's principal secretaries of state, to be Lord Lieut. and Custos Rot. of Devonshire, and of the city of Exeter, and county of the same, in the room of the Earl of Orford, dec.' (ibid. xxi. 187–8).

1. 'Illam quidquid agit, quoquo vestigia movit,
Componit furtim subsequiturque,
Decor'
(Tibullus III, 'De Sulpicia,' viii. 7–8).

There are twenty little literal variations that may be made, and are of no consequence, as mov*e* or loo*k; air* instead of *step,* and adop*ts* for adop*t:* I don't know even whether I would not read, *steal and adopt,* instead of *by stealth adopt.* But none of these changes will make the copy half so pretty as the original: but what signifies that, I am not obliged to be a poet because Tibullus[2] was one, nor is it just now that I have discovered I am not.[3] Adieu!

Yours ever

H. WALPOLE

PS. Was not Milton's paraphrase, Grace was in all her steps, etc.[4] even an improvement on the original? It takes the thought, gives it a noble simplicity, and don't screw it up into so much prettiness.[5]

To the REV. HENRY ETOUGH,[1] Saturday 12 October 1751 OS

Printed for the first time from a photostat of the MS in the Hornby Library, Liverpool City Libraries. The MS was sold Sotheby's 24 [25] May 1893 (other properties with Harries Sale), lot 244, to Pearson.

Arlington Street, Oct. 12, 1751.

Reverend Sir,

IT IS impossible to drop so lively a correspondent,[2] without thanking you very particularly for these new obligations. I own I was hurt at being told that the lies[3] you had dispersed of me, came from

2. Albius Tibullus (ca 50–19 B.C.), Roman poet.

3. HW enclosed a transcript of his verse 'Inscription for the Neglected Column in the Place of St Mark at Florence,' written in 1740, in this letter (*Horace Walpole's Fugitive Verses,* pp. 21–2). The transcript, now in the Henry E. Huntington Library, is pasted in an extra-illustrated copy of Spence's *Anecdotes,* ed. S. W. Singer, 1820, Vol. IV, opp. p. 440 (Hazen, *Bibl. of HW* 42; *ante* 21 Feb. 1741 NS, heading). Also included in this volume is a sheet on which Spence copied translations by various persons (including HW) of the Latin verses.

4. 'Grace was in all her steps, heav'n in her eye.
In every gesture dignity and love'
(*Paradise Lost* viii. 488–9).

5. As Singer notes, several of Spence's friends submitted translations of these lines, and Spence himself wrote a version of them (op. cit. 439).

---

1. (ca 1687–1757), M.A. (Cantab.), 1717; vicar of Cringleford, Norfolk, and of Eaton, Norwich; rector of Therfield, Herts, 1734–57 (Nichols, *Lit. Anec.* viii. 261–4; GRAY ii. 42 n. 58). He married Sir Robert Walpole to Maria Skerrett in 1737 or 1738.

my uncle.[4] As he is thought a man of veracity, and of some character, I did not know but some credit might be given to those improbable tales, though he knows they are utterly false. Had I suspected their having no better foundation than your authority,[5] (who by your own account report comments as facts and inferences as causes, and don't seem to know the difference) believe me they would never have given me a moment's uneasiness: and whether they were coined in that productive mint your own brain, or only dispersed by that equally active engine your tongue; whether picked up in *places of polite resort*[6] (do forgive my laughing) or came accidentally in your way, which with equal propriety you call *such evidence of publication;* I assure you, you have my free leave for the future to repeat them, and any other lies of my love, ambition, writings in prose or verse, inclinations or aversions to marriage, that you shall either invent, or be fool enough to believe; and who ever knows Parson Etough so little as to believe the scandal he either makes or propagates, will give me leave to have the same contempt for their understanding, that I should have for his, if I were to judge by the sample[7] he has sent me of it, or by his own picture of himself, and not by my obligations to him.

Adieu! Sir; if *I have more wit than you can answer, which I firmly believe,* yet as your folly is full as unanswerable, for, my dear Doctor, how is it possible to argue with a man who is capable of telling one that he thought it his duty to repeat tittle tattle which he picked up at *places of polite resort,* you will excuse me (though I shall be very glad to laugh at more of your letters) if I don't take the trouble of replying to them, but content myself once for all with assuring you

2. The letters are missing.

3. Circulated at the time of the Nicoll affair (Gray ii. 193–233). Writing to HW 26 Nov. 1751, Thomas Gray mentions Etough's 'constant practice twice in a year to import [to Cambridge] a cargo of lies and scandalous truths mixed' (ibid. ii. 56).

4. Horatio Walpole (1678–1757), cr. (1756) Bn Walpole of Wolterton.

5. Etough is described by HW's friend William Cole as a 'pimping, tale-bearing dissenting teacher, who by his adulation and flattery, and an everlasting fund of news and scandal made himself agreeable to many of prime fortune, particularly Sir Rob[ert] Walpole' (BM Add. MS 5829, f. 184b). Cole also refers to him as 'the memorable vendor of scandal, Mr Etough' (Montagu App. 4, ii. 343).

6. The words and phrases in italics are extracted from Etough's missing letter.

7. Missing.

8. Etough was caricatured in a drawing, ca 1749, by William Mason, which inspired the following satirical verses by Gray:

'Such *Tophet* was; so looked the grinning Fiend
Whom many a frighted Prelate calld his friend;
I saw them bow & while they wishd him dead

upon my honour that I am in perfect charity with you, should even like sometimes to see you as a buffoon,[8] and am

Your very humble servant

Hor. Walpole

PS. I don't think I have much pretensions or much reason to expect favours from you, yet I can't help begging that if you will not distribute my letters,[9] you will at least yours to me, which not only contains the fullest justification of me, but will give the world a clear idea of the excellent foundation of all that has been said of me in this business.

To the Duke of Bedford, Wednesday 22 January 1752 OS

Printed from a photostat of the MS in the possession of the Duke of Bedford, Woburn Abbey, kindly furnished by the late Sir Lewis Namier. First printed in *Correspondence of John, Fourth Duke of Bedford,* ed. Lord John Russell, 1842–6, ii. 107.

Endorsed by Bedford: Arlington Street. Jan. 22, 1752. Mr Walpole. R[eceived] 23 [Jan.].

Arlington Street, Jan. 22d.

My Lord,

I HAVE taken the liberty to send your Grace the enclosed short notes[1] of the debates today.[2] If they are of any use towards next Tuesday,[3] by informing you on what foot the question has been put

With servile simper nod the mitred head.
Our Mother-Church with half-averted sight
Blushd as she blesst her griesly proselyte:
Hosannahs rung thro Hells tremendous borders
And Satans self had thoughts of taking orders.'

(*The Complete Poems of Thomas Gray,* ed. H. W. Starr and J. R. Hendrickson, Oxford, 1966, p. 75; *Correspondence of Thomas Gray,* ed. Paget Toynbee and Leonard Whibley, Oxford, 1935, i. 302 n. 50).

9. Gray reported to HW that this letter (in which 'you took him to task') was circulated by Etough in Cambridge (Gray ii. 56, 58).

1. See Appendix 3.

2. On the treaty between Great Britain and the States General of the Low Countries on the one part, and Saxony on the other part, concluded at Dresden, Sept. 13th 1751 (*Journals of the House of Commons* xxvi. 398, 400; Cobbett, *Parl. Hist.* xiv. 1132–75). 'The prospect of allies in opposition was immediately hung out to the Duke of Bedford, by some

by the ministry, I shall be happy—at least I flatter myself you will forgive a well-meant intention in your Grace's

Much obliged and most obedient servant

Hor. Walpole

From Lord Chesterfield,[1] Thursday 2 April 1752 OS

Printed from the MS now WSL. First printed, Toynbee *Supp.* iii. 135–6; Chesterfield's *Letters,* ed. Bonamy Dobrée, 1932, v. 1855–6. Damer-Waller; the MS was sold Sotheby's 5 Dec. 1921 (first Waller Sale), lot 104, to Maggs; offered by them, Cat. No. 433 (Christmas 1922), lot 3087; *penes* Capt. Frank L. Pleadwell, M.D., USN, of Honolulu; resold Parke-Bernet Galleries 7 Oct. 1958 (Pleadwell Sale), lot 90, to Seven Gables for WSL.

The letter was apparently delivered by hand to HW's house in Arlington Street.

Thursday morning, Apr. 2d 1752.[2]

Sir,

IT IS very true that I told Mr Mann[3] some time ago, that I believed I had in my possession a counterpart of the late Lord Orford's[4] marriage settlement. He desired me to look for it, and if I could find it, to lend it him, as what might be of use to the family. Accordingly I had it carefully looked for among my writings, both in town[5] and in Derbyshire.[6] But in this search, I only found the cause of my mistake, which was this: my grandfather[7] had purchased two small estates in Derbyshire of the Lady Philips[8] and her sister the Lady Rokesby,[9] which purchase deeds were signed as trustee by the

who wished to fix him against the Court, and who wanted to engage him to speak against the treaty' (*Mem. Geo. II* i. 242).

3. On Tuesday, 28 Jan., when the Treaty of Dresden was debated in the House of Lords, Bedford opened the opposition to it (ibid. i. 244–7; Cobbett, *Parl. Hist.* xiv. 1175–84).

1. Philip Dormer Stanhope (1694–1773), 4th E. of Chesterfield, 1726; diplomatist and author.

2. The date was added by HW.

3. Galfridus Mann (1706–56), twin brother of Sir Horace Mann; army clothier.

4. Sir Robert Walpole, not HW's recently deceased brother (see below).

5. Chesterfield House, South Audley Street.

6. Bretby, near Derby, the seat of Lord Chesterfield.

7. Philip Stanhope (ca 1634–1714), 2d E. of Chesterfield, 1656.

8. Catharine Darcy (ca 1641–1713), m. (1660) Sir Erasmus Philipps, 3d Bt; granddaughter of Philip Stanhope, 1st E. of Chesterfield; HW's great-grandmother.

9. Dorothy Darcy (d. 1729), m. 1 (ca 1676) Sir William Rokeby, 2d Bt; m. 2 Col. the Hon. Thomas Paston.

late Lord Orford, then Mr Walpole.[10] They consisted of almost as many acres of parchment as the estates did of land. You will easily believe that I read no part of them but the signatures, among which remembering Mr Walpole's, and the bulk of the parchment, I took it into my head that they were a counterpart of his marriage settlements. If I had them or anything else that could be of use to you, I hope you do me the justice to believe that you might command, Sir,

Your most faithful humble servant,

CHESTERFIELD

To the HON. HENRY PELHAM, Saturday 25 November 1752

Printed from HW's MS draft, now WSL. First printed, Cunningham ii. 312–13. Reprinted, Toynbee iii. 132–33. The MS was sold by the Waldegrave family to Richard Bentley, the publisher, ca 1843; acquired from his grandson's wife, Mrs Richard Bentley, by WSL, 1951. The original letter is missing.

Endorsed by HW: To Mr Pelham.

Strawberry Hill, Nov. 25, 1752.

Sir,

WHEN I did myself the honour to apply to you last, to beg your interest with the King, that I might obtain the enjoyment of the patent for my own life, which now depends upon that of my brother;[1] you told me, that if I could prevail upon my brother to

10. Upon Sir Robert's marriage to Catherine Shorter in 1700 (marriage settlement, 25 May 1700), he was to receive as part of her dowry £2,500, secured on lands in Warwickshire and Derbyshire, belonging to Catherine Shorter's grandmother, Lady Philipps. It was probably the deeds to part of this land that Chesterfield had seen among his family papers (J. H. Plumb, *Sir Robert Walpole: The Making of a Statesman,* Boston, 1956, pp. 89–90). He had been 'Mr Walpole' until 1725, when he persuaded George I to revive the Order of the Bath and accepted a knighthood in it.

1. Sir Edward Walpole (1706–84). George I had bestowed upon Sir Robert Walpole the patent place of Collector of Customs for his lifetime and the lifetimes of his two elder sons Robert and Edward. He was also given the right to decide who should receive the income from the patent after his death and exercised this right to give HW the greater part of such income, which would cease upon the death of the survivor of his two brothers. In early 1751, before the death of his brother Robert on 31 March OS, HW asked Pelham, the prime minister, to intercede with the king for an amendment of the patent so that it would not terminate until the death of the survivor of the three brothers, thereby assuring HW of the income as long as he lived. 'I was at last over-persuaded to make application

consent that his life might be changed for mine, you would willingly undertake to serve me: and you added very kindly (for which, Sir, whatever success I may have, I must always thank you) that no interest of your own should interfere with my suit. Indeed Sir, the consideration of that would have prevented me, who am neither apt to ask, nor disposed to think that I have much title to favours, from troubling you at first, if I had not reflected that what I begged was not so unreasonable, either from my brother's life being as good as my own, or at least if the event should happen of his death before mine, that the other large reversions attending it, would make the emolument which I must be obliged to hope to receive from it, appear of the less value to you. I do not mean, Sir, to detract from the very handsome manner in which you treated it, though I am desirous of not being thought to prefer an extravagant suit.

My reason for troubling you again, Sir, is to represent to you, how impossible it will be for me to make any advantage of the method you proposed, as I cannot undertake the necessary steps. As the patent now stands, it is for my brother's life, but far the greater profits are given to me. If he dies,[2] the whole drops: if I die first, the whole falls to him. What, therefore, I must have asked of him, would be, not only to risk upon my life what he now enjoys for his own, but to resign his chance of the great benefit which he would reap from my death: in short, I must ask him to run all the risk instead of me. This, Sir, would be difficult to ask of any brother or any friend; unreasonable, I am afraid, to ask of one who has a large family;[3] and impracticable, I am very sure, to obtain from one, who, though I believe he loves me very well, I have no reason to think prefers me to himself.

You will excuse my stating the case thus plainly, Sir, which, after long consideration[4] I think myself obliged to do, lest you should suppose that I have neglected to make advantage of your kindness to me. I hope you see that it is out of my power to obtain the previous

to Mr Pelham—how unwillingly will appear by my behaviour on that occasion, which did not last two minutes' ('Account of my Conduct relative to the Places I Hold under Government, and towards Ministers,' *Works* ii. 364–5, 366–7).

2. Sir Edward died first (12 Jan. 1784) and HW lost £1400 a year by his death (MANN x. 53).

3. Three daughters and a son, his natural children by Dorothy Clement.

4. Before sending the present letter to Pelham, HW submitted it to Henry Fox for his opinion of it. Fox approved this 'very proper and genteel application to Mr Pelham' and the letter was accordingly sent as written (Fox to HW 23 Nov. 1752, SELWYN 119).

conditions. If without them, you will be so good as to serve me by adding my life, a request which I again make to you,[5] there is nobody will be more pleased to be

Sir

Your much obliged and most obedient servant

HOR. WALPOLE

From MARY ASTON,[1] Friday 23 February 1753

Printed for the first time from a photostat of the MS given by Sir Wathen A. Waller, 5th Bt, to WSL in 1935. Damer-Waller; the MS was not offered in the first Waller Sale; sold Christie's 15 Dec. 1947 (second Waller Sale), lot 3, to unknown; not further traced.

Feb. 23d 1753.

Sir,

ENCLOSED I send you three guineas for the use of his Corsican Majesty,[2] the first as a free gift, the second to show I am not a Jacobite,[3] and the third, to gratify the humane author of our new *World*,[4] to whom my thanks are due for this opportunity of trebly gratifying his constant reader,

MARY ASTON

5. 'Dec. 3d 1752 NS. I went to Mr Pelham; he told me he had received my letter, and should have been very glad if I could have prevailed upon my brother to have consented to the alteration of the patent. . . . That as to asking a reversion, that was what he had never done, and what the King did not love to grant. That if he did ask it, the King would probably mention what I have already for my life: however if I desired it he would mention it to the King, though he did not believe it would succeed. I replied, he knew best, and took my leave' (HW's MS note, written at the end of the letter). The application to the King was apparently not made at this time. Later HW was twice offered the reversion but refused it (MASON ii. 327 n. 4).

1. (1706–ca 1765), dau. of Sir Thomas Aston (1666–1725), 3d Bt; m. (31 May 1753) David Brodie (ca 1709–87), Capt. R. N. (GM 1753, xxiii. 296; A. L. Reade, *Johnsonian Gleanings*, 1909–52, v. 245, 249). '"Molly (says Dr Johnson) was a beauty and a scholar, and a wit and a Whig . . . she was the loveliest creature I ever saw!"' (H. L. Piozzi, *Anecdotes of the late Samuel Johnson*, 1786, p. 157).

2. Theodore (1694–1756), Baron de Neuhoff; elected 'King of Corsica,' 1736 (MANN ii. 145 n. 1). At this time he was imprisoned for debt in the King's Bench prison. HW's espousal of his cause and its outcome are described in GRAY i. 28 n. 186. In Sept. 1757 HW erected a monument to Theodore in the churchyard of St. Anne's, Soho, and composed an epitaph for it.

3. HW's contribution to the *World*, No. 8, 22 Feb. 1753, solicited aid for 'his Corsican Majesty.' It acquainted the readers of the *World* 'that a subscription

To Henry Fox,[1] Monday 20 August 1753

Printed for the first time from a photostat of the MS in the British Museum (Add. MS 51,404, f. 180). The MS descended in the Fox-Strangways family and is among the Holland House papers acquired by the British Museum in 1963.

Arlington Street, Aug. 20, 1753.

Dear Sir,

I TAKE the liberty you gave me of troubling you with the enclosed for my Lady Hervey,[2] and at the same time of putting you in mind that when you have nothing to do, you said you would call for me at Liotard's;[3] I know he is very tedious, and shall take care not to be too pressing.

Since I saw you, I have found among my Gothic studies an account of a very odd custom, which from some circumstances about the idol and the person under whose patronage this rite was last performed I think worth transcribing and sending you. In Dr Plot's *Natural History of Staffordshire*[4] is an image as like as I can draw it to the following extraordinary Lar—[5]

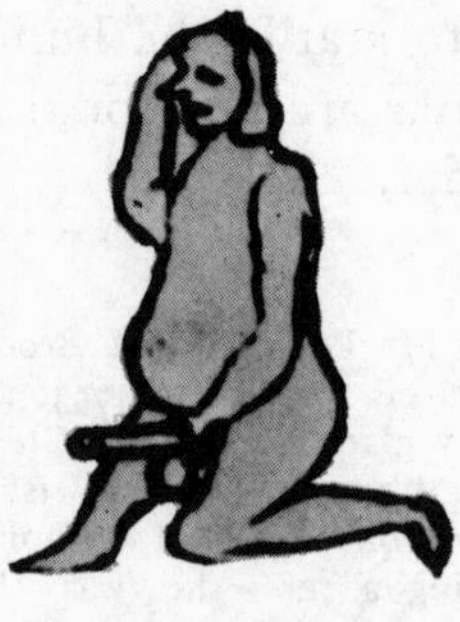

and the account the Dr gives of it is this:[6]

The service due from the Lord of Essington to the Lord of Hilton:[7] The Lord of Essington shall bring a goose every New Year's

for a subsidy for the use of his Corsican Majesty is opened at Tully's head in Pall Mall, where all the generous and the fair are desired to pay in their contributions to Robert Dodsley. . . . declaring by my censorial authority all persons Jacobites, who neglect to bring in their free gift for the use of his majesty of Corsica.'

4. The *World* was published weekly from 4 Jan. 1753 to 30 Dec. 1756. HW contributed eight issues (Hazen, *Bibl. of HW* 157). The Earl of Corke and Orrery's complete annotated set of the *World* is in the Osborn Collection, Yale University Library. On this essay (No. 8) he noted: 'There seems a farther meaning in this paper than is easily perceptible. The author always writes with vivacity, generally with wit, never without politeness.'

1. (1705–74), cr. (1763) Bn Holland; M.P.; HW's friend and correspondent.

day, and drive it round the fire in the Hall at Hilton at least three times, whilst Jack of Hilton is blowing the fire. Now *Jack of Hilton* is a little hollow image of brass of about 12 inches high, kneeling upon his left knee, and holding his right hand upon his head, and his left upon Pego or his *veretrum* erected; having a little hole in the place of the mouth, and another in the back, at which last hole it is filled with water, which when set to a strong fire, evaporates, and vents itself at the smaller hole at the mouth in a constant blast, blowing the fire so strongly that it is very audible. After the Lord of Essington or his bailiff has driven the goose round the fire, at least three times, whilst this image blows it, he carries it into the kitchen of Hilton Hall, and delivers it to the cook, who having dressed it, the Lord of Essington or his bailiff, brings it to the table of the Lord Paramount of Hilton and Essington, and receives a dish of meat from the said Lord of Hilton's table, for his own mess. Which service was last performed[8] by James Wilkinson then bailiff of Sir Gilbert Wakering,[9] the *Lady Townshend*[10] being Lady of the Manor.

Adieu! my dear Sir,

I am

Your most obedient servant

HOR. WALPOLE

2. HW's letter to Lady Hervey is missing.

3. Jean-Étienne Liotard (1702–89), pastel and enamel painter. HW wrote Mann 4 March 1753: 'Liotard the painter is arrived [from Paris], and has brought me Marivaux's picture' (MANN iv. 362). HW had doubtless commissioned the pastel portrait of Fox by Liotard that later hung in the Gallery; sold SH xxi. 74* ('Des. of SH,' *Works* ii. 464).

4. Robert Plot (1640–96), *The Natural History of Stafford-shire,* Oxford, 1686, folio. HW's copy is Hazen, *Cat. of HW's Lib.,* No. 579.

5. This Lar, or household deity, was an æolipile, 'a pneumatic instrument or toy, illustrating the force with which vapour generated by heat in a closed vessel rushes out by a narrow aperture' (OED). The engraving of it is fig. 12 in plate XXXIII of Plot's *Natural History,* facing p. 404. A similar æolipile is described in *Archæologia,* 1800, xiii. 410; illustrated plate XXVII.

6. Plot, op. cit. 433–4; HW does not quote verbatim.

7. The manors of Essington and Hilton, near Wolverhampton, Staffs, were about half a mile apart. In the mid-sixteenth century the two manors, which had been united for many years in the Swynnerton family, came by marriage to Henry Vernon, of Sudbury, Derbyshire, and remained in the Vernon family (Rev. Canon Bridgeman, 'An Account of the Family of Swynnerton, of Swynnerton and Elsewhere in the County of Stafford,' *Collections for a History of Staffordshire,* 1st ser., 1886, vii pt ii. 59, 97, 105).

8. 'about fifty years since' omitted by HW, who also omits Plot's statement that he examined the æolipile in operation on 26 May 1680 (Plot, op. cit. 433). The 'service' is thus said to have been last performed ca 1630.

9. Sir Gilbert Wakering, 'of Sussex,' Kt, 1604 (W. A. Shaw, *The Knights of England,* 1906, ii. 129).

10. Presumably the Hon. Mary Vere (ca 1611–69), m. 1 (ca 1628) Sir Roger Townshend, 1st Bt; m. 2 (1638) Mildmay Fane, 2d E. of Westmorland, 1629.

To Robert Dodsley,[1] Sunday 4 November 1753

Printed from Cunningham ix. 485 (no source given). Reprinted, Toynbee iii. 195. The history of the MS and its present whereabouts are not known.

Strawberry Hill, Nov. 4, 1753.

I AM SORRY you think it any trouble to me to peruse your poem[2] again; I always read it with pleasure. One or two little passages I have taken the liberty to mark and to offer you alterations; page 79 I would read *thrust to thrust;* I believe *push* is scarce a substantive of any authority. Line 449, and line 452, should I think be corrected, as ending with prepositions, disjoined from the cases they govern. I don't know whether you will think my emendations for the better.[3] I beg in no wise that you will adopt any of them out of complaisance; I only suggest them to you at your desire, and am far from insisting on them. I most heartily wish you the success you so well deserve, and am

Your very humble servant,

Hor. Walpole

PS. I shall beg you to send me a piece I see advertised, called, 'A True Account of Andrew Frey,' etc.[4]

From Charles Pratt,[1] Saturday 2 February 1754

Printed for the first time from the MS now wsl. Damer-Waller; the MS was sold Sotheby's 5 Dec. 1921 (first Waller Sale), lot 9, bought in; resold Christie's 15 Dec. 1947 (second Waller Sale), lot 39 (with two other letters), to Maggs for wsl.

1. (1703–64), bookseller, dramatist, and poet. He was HW's bookseller and publisher, and presumably helped him start the SH Press.

2. According to Cunningham, Isaac Reed thought the poem was *Public Virtue: A Poem in Three Books*, 1753, of which only the first book, 'Agriculture,' was printed. Selections from it appeared in GM 1753, xxiii. 533. The *Daily Adv.* 5 Dec. 1753 announced: 'This day is published . . . the first book of *Public Virtue: A Poem.*'

3. It is not known whether Dodsley adopted HW's 'emendations.'

4. Andreas Frey, *A True and Authentic Account of Andrew Frey; Containing the Occasion of his Coming among the Herrnhuters, or Moravians, his Observations . . . and the Reasons for which he left them . . . Translated from the German*, 1753. It was advertised in the *Daily Adv.* 5 Nov. HW's copy, now wsl, is Hazen, *Cat. of HW's Lib.*, No. 1608:75.

The MS is dated 'February 2, 1753' but the letter refers to events following the death of Erasmus Shorter on 23 Nov. 1753 and thus clearly belongs to the next year.

Endorsed by HW: From Mr Ch. Pratt, afterwards attorney general.

Serjeants' Inn,[2] February 2, 175[4].

Sir,

I HAVE the favour of yours[3] to which I cannot give a precise answer as to the nature of the security that ought to be given, because that depends in great measure upon your own discretion, the fortune or the character of those persons that are to give it. A bond from some persons is better than a mortgage from others. Some security is certainly proper for you to take upon this occasion,[4] because if a will should be found, you will be liable to restore the whole to the devisee, if there should be any such. However, as the persons concerned are people of fortune as well as rank and very nearly related to you, a less security from such might satisfy you better than a greater from strangers. The safest way would be to pay these shares under a decree of the Court of Chancery upon a bill brought against yourself for a distribution; but that will be attended with delay and some expense. Therefore I do not advise it. You know better than I do the fortune and honour of the parties concerned and are therefore better able to point out what kind of security would be sufficient. Perhaps the easiest way would be to lodge the several share[s] in the stock in trustees' hands for a year or two in which time you may be morally certain no will can ever be produced.[5]

I am Sir your most obedient servant,

C. PRATT

1. Charles Pratt (1714–94), cr. (1765) Bn and (1786) E. Camden; lord chancellor, 1766; M.P.; HW's contemporary at Eton and King's College, Cambridge.

2. One of the houses of law in Chancery Lane and Fleet Street, originally set aside for the Honourable Society of Judges and Serjeants-at-Law.

3. Missing.

4. 'In December [23 Nov. 1753] died Erasmus Shorter Esq. the last and youngest of my mother's brothers. He dying without a will, his fortune of £30,000 came in equal shares between my brother Sir Edward, me, and my cousins, Francis Earl of Hertford, Colonel Henry Seymour Conway and Miss Anne Seymour Conway' (HW's 'Short Notes,' (GRAY i. 25). For the letters which passed between HW, Conway, and Hertford on the proper handling of the estate, see CONWAY i. 372–3. HW apparently then consulted Pratt on the legal questions discussed in this letter.

5. No will was ever found and accordingly the estate was divided among the five heirs. HW wrote George Montagu 6 Dec.: 'it is not uncomfortable to have a little sum of money drop out of the clouds, to which one has as much right as anybody, for which one has no obligation, and paid no flattery' (MONTAGU i. 156–7).

From JOHN MICHAEL RYSBRACK,[1] Wednesday 26 June 1754

Printed from Toynbee *Supp.* iii. 137, where the letter was first printed. Damer-Waller; the MS was sold Sotheby's 5 Dec. 1921 (first Waller Sale), lot 179, bought in; not further traced.

Wednesday, June 26th 1754.

Sir,

I WAITED upon Mr Davies,[2] according to your order; and he was glad to hear the monument[3] was ordered to be put up, it being so long since everything was settled[4] that he had forgot it. And I expected to have had the pleasure of seeing you the beginning of last week, for the addition your Honour mentioned; because I thought to have sent it away directly, it being very much in my way.[5] If your Honour please to inform the bearer what addition[6] you will please to have, you will very much oblige,

Sir,

Your Honour's most respectful and obedient servant,

MICH. RYSBRACK

1. (1694–1770), sculptor.

2. Owen Davies (ca 1699–1759), receiver-general of Westminster Abbey (E. W. Brayley, *The History and Antiquities of the Abbey Church of St Peter, Westminster,* 1818–23, ii. 293).

3. In 1741 HW commissioned Filippo Valle (1693–1770) to copy an antique 'Pudicitia,' perhaps representing the Empress Livia, in the Villa Mattei in Rome as a monument to his mother, Lady Walpole. The statue arrived in 1743; Rysbrack carved the pedestal for it (ibid. i. 70–1; GRAY i. 26 nn. 170–1; M. I. Webb, *Michael Rysbrack, Sculptor,* 1954, p. 48). Rysbrack's original design for the pedestal is now WSL; see illustration.

4. Leave was given on 30 May 1747 for the erection of the monument in the south aisle of Henry VII's Chapel in the Abbey ('Short Notes,' GRAY i. 25 n. 169).

5. The cenotaph for Lady Walpole is described in [William Combe or Rudolph Ackermann], *The History of the Abbey Church of St Peter's Westminster,* 1812, ii. 157–8, and illustrated facing p. 157; it is also illustrated in GRAY i, facing p. 26.

6. The 'addition,' if made, could not have been elaborate, for HW wrote Richard Bentley 9 July 1754: 'The monument for my mother is at last erected' (CHUTE 178). HW's inscription on the pedestal was first published in the *Whitehall Evening Post* 2–4 July 1754; it was reprinted in his *Fugitive Pieces,* SH, 1758, pp. 44–5, and in *Works* i. 131.

RYSBRACK'S ORIGINAL DESIGN FOR
LADY WALPOLE'S MONUMENT

From SIR GEORGE LYTTELTON,[1] Monday 30 September 1754

Printed from the MS now WSL. First printed, Toynbee *Supp.* iii. 137–8. Damer-Waller; the MS was sold Sotheby's 5 Dec. 1921 (first Waller Sale), lot 155, to Maggs; offered by them, Cat. Nos 471 (1925), lot 2928, and 504 (summer 1928), lot 1149; sold by Schindler's Antique Shop, Charleston, South Carolina, to WSL, 1959.

Hagley, Sept. the 30th 1754.

Dear Sir,

AS MUCH the humble servant as I am of King Henry[2] I had rather have had you at Hagley[3] this summer[4] than him in your library a year or two hence. However I have given some of that time which I should have employed more agreeably in your conversation and that of some other friends who have disappointed me of their company in revising and correcting some part of my history and flatter myself that I may be able to begin printing it early next summer, in which case it may be published within a twelvemonth more.[5] Your partiality to it animates me extremely, but at the same time makes me more cautious not to let it come out uncorrect, or without all the perfection that I can give to it, for fear your judgment should be disgraced. We shall not build our grotto this year, and therefore the shells[6] you are so kind to offer to it may as well be brought to Lady Lyttelton[7] in Hill Street[8] as sent hither now. We

1. (1709–73), 5th Bt, 1751; cr. (1756) Bn Lyttelton.

2. Lyttelton was writing a life of Henry II.

3. Hagley Park, Worcs, Lord Lyttelton's seat. HW described it in a letter of September 1753 to Richard Bentley, after a visit there during which Lyttelton apparently showed HW the MS of his life of Henry II (CHUTE 147–9).

4. HW wrote Henry Seymour Conway 6 Aug. 1754: 'I believe I shall be able to come to you [at Park Place, Berks] any part of the first fortnight in September, for though I ought to go to Hagley, it is incredible how I want resolution to tap such a journey' (CONWAY i. 383). There is no evidence that HW visited Hagley or Park Place in 1754.

5. Lyttelton's *History of the Life of King Henry the Second,* 4 vols, was not published until 1767–71. HW queried George Montagu 31 July 1767, 'Have you waded through or into Lord Lyttelton? How dull one may be, if one will' but take pains for six or seven and twenty years together!' (MONTAGU ii. 244–5). He wrote Lady Ossory 14 Dec. 1771: 'Lord Lyttelton has published the rest of his *Henry the Second,* but I doubt has executed it a little carelessly, for he has not been above ten years about it' (OSSORY i. 69). HW's copy is Hazen, *Cat. of HW's Lib.*, No. 3173.

6. Ormer shells, from the Channel Islands, which HW had asked Richard Bentley to obtain for Lady Lyttelton's grotto (CHUTE 175).

don't intend to place it in the shrubbery according to our first purpose, but in a very romantic part of the park, which situation we think you will approve of when you see it, and count upon your giving us your judgment upon it as soon as it is finished.[9] Your own enchanted palace will then be completed and you may have leisure to visit ours. I only wish that the weather may be as fine as it has been this autumn and the park as pleasant.

All here desire their best compliments to you and amongst them the Dean of Exeter[10] who is returned to us from Spa.

I am most affectionately,

Dear Sir,

Your most faithful and devoted friend and servant,

G. LYTTELTON

I am your most devoted friend and servant too, but in a violent hurry: however I actually love you very well, though you are a good-for-nothing creature.[11]

From the MARQUIS DE SAINT-SIMON,[1] Saturday 19 July 1755

Printed for the first time from the MS now WSL. Damer-Waller; the MS was sold Sotheby's 5 Dec. 1921 (first Waller Sale), lot 180, to Wells; given by him to Thomas Conolly, of Chicago, from whom WSL acquired it in 1937.

À Londres le 19 juillet 1755.

JE NE vous envoie mon ouvrage,[2] Monsieur, qu'avec une capitulation dont les articles doivent être fort étendus: premièrement que vous me prometterez de bonne foi de m'en dire votre avis, et que

7. Elizabeth Rich (ca 1716–95), m. (1749) Sir George Lyttelton, 5th Bt, 1751; cr. (1756) Bn Lyttelton.

8. Berkeley Square.

9. The grotto, 'decorated with large glassy cinders,' is described in [Joseph Heely,] *A Description of Hagley, Envil and the Leasowes*, Birmingham, n.d., pp. 88–90.

10. Charles Lyttelton (1714–68), dean of Exeter Cathedral, 1748; Bp of Carlisle, 1762; Lord Lyttelton's brother and HW's friend and correspondent (*ante* 28 Aug. 1734 OS, n. 1).

11. The postscript is by Elizabeth Rich, Lady Lyttelton.

1. Maximilien-Henri de Saint-Simon (1720–99), Marquis de Sandricourt, also called Marquis de Saint-Simon; soldier and man of letters.

2. A French translation of Swift's *Tale*

contre l'usage ordinaire vous ne me payerez pas par un compliment; 2e que pour me prouver l'attention que vous avez apporté à la lecture, vous voudrez bien mettre en marge ou en bas des pages qui sont disposés à ces effets les notes que vous croirez nécessaires et les corrections que vous trouverez à faire.*

*Nota. Si la traduction était si mauvaise qu'elle ne valût rien, vous vous engagez à le dire librement; je ne vous en demanderai pas la démonstration; il suffira de votre jugement.[3]

Si je n'avais pas déjà rempli une page des articles de ma capitulation,[4] je continuerais encore à vous fatiguer de mes inquiétudes, mais j'en reste là, et, persuadé que je suis en bonne main, je n'arrêterai plus mon imagination sur le sort de mon ouvrage, et je la laisserai se promener avec liberté dans le beau champ que votre amitié lui a ouvert. Ces premières démonstrations d'estime et d'amitié se reçoivent toujours avec vivacité mais il faut de la solidité dans le caractère pour la fixer. N'allez pas, je vous prie, faire tort à votre nation, et que la franchise et la droiture que je reconnais être ses vertus principales ne me laissent rien à désirer de ce côté de votre part, vous m'avez témoigné librement et sans affectation des sentiments d'amitié qui m'ont infiniment flatté. Je me suis mis en frais pour y répondre et j'ai payé de bonne foi ces sentiments par un retour très sincère, ainsi je vous prie de ne point vous en dédire et de me permettre de vous continuer l'expression d'un véritable attachement avec lequel je veux toujours être, Monsieur,

Votre très humble et très obéissant serviteur,

LE MARQUIS DE ST-SIMON

of a Tub. HW wrote Richard Bentley 4 Aug. 1755: 'The Marquis de St-Simon, whom I mentioned to you, at a very first visit proposed to me to look over a translation he had made of *The Tale of a Tub*—the proposal was soon followed by a folio, and a letter of three sides to press me seriously to revise it' (CHUTE 241).

3. 'You shall judge of my scholar's competence. He translates *L'Estrange, Dryden*, and others, *l'étrange, Dryden*, etc. Then in the description of the tailor as an idol [in the second section of the *Tale*], and his goose as the symbol; he says in a note, that the *goose* means the dove, and is a concealed satire on the Holy Ghost' (ibid.). No written reply from HW to St-Simon survives. The translation was never published.

4. This paragraph begins on the second MS page of St-Simon's letter.

To Grosvenor Bedford, Thursday 21 August 1755

Printed from Toynbee iii. 332 (no source given). The history of the MS and its present whereabouts are not known.

Mistley,[1] August 21, 1755.

Dear Sir,

I HEAR by an express that Mr Swinburn[2] died last night. I can't defer a minute to give myself the pleasure of offering you to succeed him, not only according to my promise, but according to my inclination. You know, I believe, that I had some strong suspicions that the poor man who is gone, did not do me all the justice he might have done.[3] In putting my affairs into the hands of a friend,[4] those suspicions will be entirely removed; and I think it almost unnecessary to tell you, that within this month I was offered[5] first five hundred pounds, and then whatever I would ask, for the reversion of Mr Swinburn's place. No offer certainly would have made me break my promise to you; but without pretending to that merit, I must own that I am persuaded my interest will be much more promoted in your hands than it could be by anyone I might have accepted for the place. I shall be in town on Tuesday night, and hope to see you in Arlington Street on Wednesday morning, till when I beg nobody but Mrs Bedford,[6] to whom I desire my compliments, may know a word of this business.[7]

I am, dear Sir,
Ever yours,

Horace Walpole

1. Mistley Hall, Essex, the seat of Richard Rigby. HW arrived there 19 Aug. for a visit (Mann iv. 490 n. 1).

2. William Swinburn (d. 20 Aug. 1755), counsellor at law; HW's deputy usher of the Exchequer (GM 1755, xxv. 381; *Court and City Register*, 1755, p. 109).

3. Little is known about Swinburn. The Rev. Ferdinando Warner (1703–68) asked George Selwyn 20 Aug. 1747 to frank a letter to 'young Mr Hor. Walpole, to recommend me to Mr Swinbourn, his first clerk, who is a very active man in the vestry of St George's, Queens Square' (copy, now wsl, made in 1901 for Mrs Toynbee by George Pritchard, of Poole, then the owner of the original letter).

4. HW was devoted to Grosvenor Bedford's aunt, Anne Grosvenor (1679–1750), who was a friend of HW's mother. She and her sister Elizabeth Grosvenor, mother of Grosvenor Bedford, had been companions or governesses in the Walpole household (*ante* 29 Aug. 1743 OS, nn. 1 and 8; Paget Toynbee, 'Horace Walpole and "Mrs G.",' *TLS* 16 Dec. 1920, p. 858).

5. It is not known who made this offer.

TO LADY ESSEX,[1] Tuesday 2 September 1755

Printed for the first time from the MS bound in a collection of letters to Sir Charles Hanbury Williams, now WSL (vol. 64, f. 112). These letters were originally at Coldbrook Park, Monmouth, Williams's seat; they were sold to Sir Thomas Phillipps in 1841; later acquired by William H. Robinson Ltd, who sold them to WSL in 1949.

Strawberry Hill, Sept. 2d 1755.

Madam,

NOTHING can please me more than an opportunity of obeying your Ladyship's or Sir Charles Williams's[2] commands;[3] but you will give me leave to tell you that it is impossible at present, as it is just the wrong season of the year. The goldfish are full of spawn, and it would not only hurt a vast many to disturb the pond[4] now, but your Ladyship would be disappointed in those you attempted to send, as it would certainly kill them, when they are breeding. The beginning of winter or early in the spring is the best time. I have already given some for Russia to the late Ambassador,[5] and shall be very glad to oblige Sir Charles,[6] but I fear they will find it impossible to preserve them in so rigorous a climate. Mine are kept in a common natural gravel pit, where there is a spring; nor is there any trouble with them; I sometimes give them a little bread; but they require very little feeding.

I am Madam
Your Ladyship's most obedient humble servant

HOR. WALPOLE

6. Possibly 'Mrs Bedford, of Chippenham' (ca 1702–90) (GM 1790, lx pt i. 373).

7. Bedford accepted appointment as HW's deputy. HW's deed of appointment for Bedford as his deputy, dated 21 Aug. 1755, is now WSL.

---

1. Frances Hanbury Williams (1735–59); dau. of Sir Charles Hanbury Williams, m. (1754) William Anne Holles Capel, 4th E. of Essex (MONTAGU i. 207 n. 9).

2. Sir Charles Hanbury Williams (1708–59), K.B., 1744; diplomatist, wit, poet; M.P.; HW's correspondent.

3. They apparently wanted HW to send goldfish to Russia. Sir Charles had been named ambassador to St Petersburg in April 1755 (SELWYN 322). See n. 5 below.

4. Po-Yang, HW's Chinese name for the goldfish pond at SH (MONTAGU i. 134 n. 11).

5. Count Petr Grigor'evich Chernyshev, Russian ambassador to England 1746–55 (CHUTE 199 n. 14). HW wrote Richard Bentley 6 May of this year: 'Po-yang has great custom: I have lately given Count Perron [the Sardinian envoy to England] some goldfish, which he has carried in his post-chaise to Turin: he has already carried some before. The Russian minister

To Grosvenor Bedford, Thursday 16 October 1755

Printed for the first time from the MS now WSL. The MS descended in the Bedford family to Grosvenor Bedford's great-niece, Mrs Erskine, of Milton Lodge, Gillingham, Dorset; sold Sotheby's 15 Dec. 1932 (property of Mrs Erskine), lot 490 (with HW to the Printer of the *Gazetteer* Sept. 1762), to Maggs for WSL.

The date of the letter is established by the postmark and the year of Bedford's appointment as HW's deputy in the Exchequer.

Address: To Grosvenor Bedford Esq. at the Excise Office, London. *Postmark:* 17 OC. *Frank:* Free Hor. Walpole.

Strawberry Hill, Thursday.

Dear Sir,

I SHALL like exceedingly to have you live in my house at the Exchequer;[1] and if you will call on me on Saturday morning next in Arlington Street, we will settle it; I don't think you will dislike the terms.

Yours ever

H. W.

To Grosvenor Bedford, Thursday 24 June 1756

Printed from the MS now WSL. First printed, Toynbee *Supp.* i. 71–2. The MS was sold Sotheby's 30 April [1 May] 1914 (Admiral Baker Sale), lot 349, to W. V. Daniell; resold Sotheby's 8 [11] April 1918 (Wheatley Sale), lot 1186 (with other Walpole family papers), to Edwards; offered by Maggs, Cat. Nos 370 (autumn 1918), lot 2098; 399 (Christmas 1920), lot 3447; 441 (1923), lot 2136; and 488 (spring 1927), lot 634; sold by Samuel Loveman, of Brooklyn, to WSL, 1935.

Endorsed in an unidentified hand, in ink: To Grosvenor Bedford Esq.

Address (in an unidentified hand, in pencil): To Grosvenor Bedford, Esq. in

has asked me for some too, but I doubt their succeeding there' (ibid. 225–6).

6. Sir Charles wrote Lady Essex 2 Oct. 1755 that 'Though you sent me no gold-fish, Lord Chesterfield has' (Williams MSS, vol. 76, f. 116, now WSL).

1. In New Palace Yard, Westminster. The house was one of the emoluments of the office of the usher of the Exchequer, to which HW had been appointed 31 Jan. 1738 (*Calendar of Treasury Books and Papers, 1735–1738,* comp. W. A. Shaw, 1900, p. 624).

Palace Yard Gate near Westminster Hall Gate, London. *Frank:* Free H. Walpole.
Memoranda (in an unidentified hand): £25
18.10
10.
53.10

Strawberry Hill, June 24, 1756.

Dear Sir,

As I CANNOT be in town for some days I should be obliged to you if you would call at Mr Le Gros's and Le Cras's[1] bankers in Bishopsgate Street, and with some of my money in your hands pay them three notes drawn on me in the names of Mr and Mrs Bernard,[2] amounting in all to £53. 10*s*. I hope Mrs Bedford and all your family are well. I will thank you too for what news you pick up relating to Byng[3] and Minorca.

Yours ever
H. Walpole

To Henry Fox, ? late October 1756

Printed for the first time from a photostat of the MS among the Holland House papers in the British Museum (Add. MS 51,404, f.182). For the history of the MS see *ante* 20 Aug. 1753.

This account of political events in the form of village gossip was presumably addressed to Fox but is unsigned. It must have been written between 13 Oct. 1756, when Fox announced his intention of resigning as secretary of state, and

1. Le Gros and Le Cras, of Bishopsgate Street, near Cornhill, are listed among the merchants in *A Complete Guide to all Persons who have any Trade or Concern with the City of London*, 1763, p. 150.

2. Possibly members of Richard Bentley's mother's family, who may have acted with the assistance of HW to pay Bentley's debts (Montagu i. 308 n. 2). Bentley had fled to Jersey, where he was a fugitive for debt. HW wrote George Montagu 26 July 1755 that Bentley was 'still a banished man. I have a scheme for bringing him back, but can get Mrs Tisiphone [Bentley's wife] into no kind of terms; and without tying her up from running him into new debts, it is in vain to recover him' (ibid. i. 172). Bentley was back in England within a year's time (ibid. i. 193).

3. Hon. John Byng (1704–57), Adm., 1756; M.P. His dispatch to the Admiralty on 25 May, giving his version of the encounter with the French fleet at Minorca, appears to have arrived in England on 16 June, but was not published in the *London Gazette* until 26 June. Rumours of his situation had reached England through dispatches of the French officers to their own government, arousing great indignation in London. For details of this long and unhappy episode see Conway i. 468–9 nn. 10–12 and Mann iv. *passim*.

13 Nov., when Fox formally resigned and William Pitt replaced him in office. In an interview with George II on 27 Oct., Fox was asked to see Pitt in an attempt to form a new ministry; but on 30 Oct. Fox acknowledged Pitt's firm unwillingness to join him. HW's fable was probably written soon after 27 Oct., the date of his letter to Fox encouraging him to 'take the Treasury' (SELWYN 128).

—you will the more easily believe this account, when I tell you, that on the last revolution in the family, there were living in the parish no less than six helpers,[1] whom old Tom[2] had persuaded his master[3] to discard; I send you their names, that you may inform yourself from any of the neighbours; they were, John Carter,[4] Will Standup,[5] Phil. Standup,[6] Jack Russel,[7] Tom Robins,[8] and Harry Fowkes:[9] the latter, who had been brought into the family by the old coachman Robin,[10] and who always retained great affection for his memory, and who so far from aspiring to be coachman himself, had often refused it,[11] was a fellow of great spirit and honesty: he had been courted into the best families in the village, but would never quit his master, till he found his Honour had rather have his neck broken by Thomas[12] and the bailiff,[13] than be driven by anybody else in a quiet manner. The case was much the same with the postilions;[14] for though Tom was reduced by his jealousy to associate the stable boys[15] with him, yet even they grew uneasy to him. He first introduced the little fellow[16] you mentioned, hoping, as he was a dwarf by nature, that he could never be preferred to the box. But even this supple pigmy grew offensive and was removed; and then old Tom persuaded his Honour to take for postilion the Worcestershire Giant,[17] as if whatever disqualified a man for any service, was a recommendation to his master's[18]—and indeed nothing was ever less fit to be employed than this long creature, who understood so little of the commonest business, that he thought hay was bought by the bushel, and beans by the load—.[19]

1. That is, those who since the fall of Sir Robert Walpole (1742) had held the office of secretary of state with or under the Duke of Newcastle. Lord Holdernesse (secretary of state for the south 1751–4, for the north 1754–61) is not included among the six 'helpers' because he had been retained in office.

2. Thomas Pelham Holles, 1st D. of Newcastle-upon-Tyne; secretary of state for the south 1724–48, for the north 1748–54; first lord of the Treasury 1754–11 Nov. 1756.

3. George II.

4. John Carteret (1690–1763), 2d Bn Carteret, 1695; 2d E. Granville, 1744; secretary of state for the south 1721–4, for the north 1742–4; lord president of the Council 1751–63.

5. William Stanhope (ca 1683–1756), cr. (1730) Bn and (1742) E. of Harrington; secretary of state for the north 1730–42, 1744–6; lord president of the Council 1742–5.

6. Philip Dormer Stanhope (1694–1773), 4th E. of Chesterfield, 1726; secretary of state for the north 1746–8.

7. John Russell (1710–71), 4th D. of

From LADY BROWN,[1] Sunday 28 November 1756

Printed from the MS now WSL. First printed, Toynbee *Supp.* iii. 141–2. Damer-Waller; the MS was sold Sotheby's 5 Dec. 1921 (first Waller Sale), lot 98 (with Sir John Fielding to HW March 1758), to Dobell; acquired from Maggs by WSL, ca 1932.

Bath, 28th November 1756.

THE Duchess of Norfolk[2] who left Bath this morning, has been so obliging as to desire me to charge her with the care of a pane of glass[3] I met with at an auction; the virtuosi tell me it has some merit, and if Mr Walpole should like it well enough to think it worthy of a place in a window at Strawberry Hill, his acceptance of it will give me great pleasure, and flatter my taste very much. I imagine you pass a good deal of your time there to absent yourself from the melancholy

Bedford, 1732; secretary of state for the south 1748–51; lord president of the Council 1763–5.

8. Sir Thomas Robinson (1695–1770), K.B., 1742; cr (1761) Bn Grantham; secretary of state for the south 1754–5.

9. Henry Fox. See headnote.

10. Sir Robert Walpole, who first gave Fox office (surveyor-general of Works, 1737–43) and persuaded Henry Pelham to make Fox a lord of the Treasury in 1743. See the ballad in MANN ii. 22 where Orford is called the 'Old Coachman.'

11. Fox was never invited by the King to form a ministry before Oct. 1756. Perhaps HW's statement is not meant to be taken literally; he may simply be saying in effect, 'he could have been first minister had he wanted to.'

12. Newcastle.

13. Philip Yorke (1690–1764), cr. (1733) Bn and (1754) E. of Hardwicke; lord chancellor 1737–56.

14. That is, those who had served Newcastle as chancellor of the Exchequer.

15. The junior lords of the Treasury.

16. Hon. Henry Bilson Legge (1708–64); lord of the Treasury 1746–9; chancellor of the Exchequer April 1754 – Nov. 1755, Nov. 1756 – April 1757, July 1757 – March 1761.

17. Sir George Lyttelton (1709–73), of Hagley Hall, Worcs; 5th Bt, 1751; cr. (1756) Bn Lyttelton; lord of the Treasury 1744–54; chancellor of the Exchequer Nov. 1755–Nov. 1756. In appearance he was extremely tall and thin.

18. Legge was dismissed from office in Nov. 1755 and replaced by Lyttelton. 'Not able to resist his devotion to the Duke of Newcastle, or the impulse of his own ambition, he [Lyttelton] accepted the office of chancellor of the Exchequer—had they dragged Dr Halley from his observatory, to make him vice-chamberlain . . . the choice would have been as judicious: they turned an absent poet to the management of the revenue, and employed a man as visionary as Don Quixote to combat Demosthenes!' (*Mem. Geo. II* ii. 63).

19. 'Poor Sir George never knew prices from duties, nor drawbacks from premiums' (HW to Conway 4 March, 1756, CONWAY i. 445).

1. Margaret Cecil (ca 1696–1782), m. Sir Robert Brown, cr. (1732) Bt.

2. Mary Blount (ca 1702–73), m. (1727) Edward Howard, 9th D. of Norfolk, 1732.

3. Not identified. Other presents from Lady Brown were a head of Sir Robert Walpole on white cornelian, by Natter, and a 'silver Turkish ornament, taken by a Russian officer in the last war; brought over by Charles Lord Cathcart, and given by him to Margaret Lady Brown, and by her to Mr Walpole' ('Des. of SH,' *Works* ii. 480, 484).

confusion at London. The House of Lords seems to be a House of Invalids, for the reception of all disabled ministers; such a load of them in so short a time, was never created,[4] I believe, till now. As I am very desirous to advance as much as I can, the fortune as well as the reputation of my painter Worlidge,[5] I can't help regretting my want of interest with their new Lordships to prevail with them to come to Bath to set to Worlidge, as I believe they will have no other employment this winter, than to be drawn in their robes; but if I had any interest with any of them, my application now might be too late, as they certainly would not neglect an affair of so much importance to the world. But luckily for you, have now reflected that I have taken up too much of your time with my nonsense, so will end, and with a sincere truth that I am with the highest esteem, dear Sir,

Your obedient and much obliged humble servant,

M. BROWN

To the DUKE of BEDFORD, Saturday 1 January 1757

Printed for the first time from a photostat of the MS in the possession of the Duke of Bedford, Woburn Abbey.

Strawberry Hill, Jan. 1, 1757.

My Lord,

I FLATTER myself that your Grace will forgive this trouble, at the same time that I trust you will be so good as to grant my request.[1] My friend Mr Montagu's[2] parson[3] at Greatworth[4] is chaplain to his brother's[5] regiment in Ireland, and it will make Mr

4. Lord Hillsborough was created 17 Nov. Bn of Harwich; Sir George Lyttelton was created 18 Nov. Bn Lyttelton; Percy Wyndham-O'Brien was created 11 Dec. E. of Thomond (Irish peerage); William Blakeney was made K.B. 27 Nov. and created 18 Dec. Bn Blakeney (Irish peerage). See HW to Sir Horace Mann 29 Nov. 1756 (MANN v. 23–4).

5. Thomas Worlidge (1700–66), portrait painter and etcher (GRAY ii. 190 n. 14). Worlidge did not realize Lady Brown's ambition for him as a portrait painter; he became better known as an etcher 'in the manner of Rembrandt' (*Anecdotes of Painting, Works* iii. 451).

1. As Lord Lieutenant of Ireland.

2. George Montagu (ca 1713–80), HW's friend and correspondent.

3. Rev. James Miller (ca 1720–80), chaplain 59th Foot, 1756 (MONTAGU i. 383 n. 1; *Army Lists,* 1757, p. 141; GM 1780, l. 445).

4. 'A house hired by Mr George Montagu,' about four miles from Brackley, Northants (MONTAGU i. 146 n. 1).

5. Charles Montagu (d. 1777), Col. 59th Foot, 1755 (ibid. i. 31 n. 14; *Army Lists,* loc. cit.).

Montagu, and consequently me, very happy, if your Grace will give Mr James Miller (the clergyman's name) leave to be absent from the regiment now at Cork.[6] Were I writing to the Archbishop of Canterbury, I could plead with great truth that while they have their present colonel, even the souls of the regiment will not suffer by the absence of their chaplain.

I am, my Lord,
Your Grace's most obedient humble servant

Hor. Walpole

From the Duke of Bedford, Monday 3 January 1757

Printed for the first time from a photostat of the MS copy in the possession of the Duke of Bedford, Woburn Abbey. The original letter is missing.

Woburn Abbey, Jan. 3d 1757.

Dear Sir,

I am truly very sorry, that it will be impossible for me to comply with your request of giving Mr James Miller leave to be absent from the regiment he belongs to at Cork. I have laid it down as an unvariable rule, that every chaplain in Ireland, shall constantly attend his duty either by himself, or a proper deputy, to be approved of by me, and recommended to me by the officer commanding the regiment, through whom every request of this nature, must come to me.

Honourable Mr Walpole.

6. HW's request was denied (see following letter).

From WILLIAM PITT,[1] Sunday 27 February 1757

Printed from the MS now WSL. First printed, Toynbee *Supp.* ii. 99. Damer-Waller; the MS was sold Sotheby's 5 Dec. 1921 (first Waller Sale), lot 102, bought in; resold Christie's 15 Dec. 1947 (second Waller Sale), lot 4 (with three other letters from Pitt to HW), to Maggs for WSL.

The date was added by HW.

Sunday night, Feb. 27, 1757,
past nine at night.

MR Pitt presents a thousand respectful thanks to Mr Walpole for the honour of his obliging letter.[2] He is, at present so engaged in business, as not to allow him a moment to add more than repeated thanks and acknowledgments.

To LORD HOLDERNESSE,[1] Monday 18 April 1757

Printed for the first time from a photostat of the MS among the Leeds papers in the BM (Egerton MS 3438, f. 67), through the kind offices of Mr Patrick Doran.

Arlington Street, April 18, 1757.

My Lord,

YOUR Lordship, I hope, will forgive the trouble of this request, and will confer a particular obligation on me, if you will be so good as to be favourable to it. The Sieur Theobald Müntz,[2] ministre du regiment suisse de Boccard[3] in the French service in Corsica, is leaving that service and retiring to his own country. His brother,[4] a

1. (1708–78), cr. (1766) E. of Chatham; M.P.; at this time, secretary of state, southern department.

2. Missing. HW wrote John Chute late at night 27 Feb.: 'I have done nothing but traverse the town tonight from Sir R[ichard] Lyttelton's to the Speaker's, to Mr Pitt's' (CHUTE 97). HW was trying to stay the sentence in the court martial of Admiral Byng by the passage of a bill to absolve the members of the court martial from their oath of secrecy (*Mem. Geo. II* ii. 327–50).

---

1. Robert Darcy (1718–78), 4th E. of Holdernesse, 1722; secretary of state for the north 1754–61.

2. Not further identified.

3. François-Jean-Philippe de Boccard (1696–1782), Swiss officer in the French service; maréchal de camp 1748; 'colonel d'un régiment suisse à son nom' 1752; Lt-Gen. 1759 (*Dict. de biographie française* vi. 741–2).

4. Johann Heinrich Müntz (1727–98). HW wrote of him to Sir Horace Mann 9 Sept. 1758: 'I have a painter in the house, who is an engraver too, a mechanic, an everything. He was a Swiss engineer in the French service, but his regiment being broken at the peace, Mr [Richard] Bentley found him in the Isle of Jersey and fixed him with me' (MANN v. 239). See also M. H. Grant, *A Chronological History*

Protestant too, and a painter whom I employ, has solicited me to try to obtain a passport for him and his effects, to secure him and them in case he should be taken by any English ship or privateer, as he leaves Corsica on his return home. I must again entreat your Lordship to excuse the liberty I take in making this solicitation, and I am,

My Lord,

Your Lordship's most obedient humble servant

Hor. Walpole

To the Hon. George Grenville,[1] Friday 13 May 1757

Printed from a photostat of the MS in the William L. Clements Library, University of Michigan. First printed in *The Grenville Papers,* ed. W. J. Smith, 1852–3, i. 195. Reprinted, Cunningham iii. 75–6; Toynbee iv. 53–4. The MS was among the Grenville papers deposited by his descendants at Stowe; sold in a collection of papers from Stowe by the 2d Duke of Buckingham and Chandos to his attorney, Edwin James, who in turn sold this collection to John Murray in 1851; resold Sotheby's 14 Dec. 1926 ('other properties'), lot 394, to Pearson; acquired from them by the Clements Library, 1927.

Endorsed by Grenville: Mr H. Walpole May the 13th 1757. Answered d[itt]o.

Arlington Street, May 13th.

Dear Sir,

I FLATTER myself that you have goodness enough for me to excuse the liberty I am now taking. The ridiculous situation of this country for some months drew from me yesterday the enclosed thoughts,[2] which I beg you will be so good as to run over and return.

As it certainly was my intention, so it has been my endeavour to offend no man or set of men: it most assuredly was my desire to give no umbrage to you or your friends, and therefore I will beg you

of the Old English Landscape Painters, 1926–47, i. 62–3; Arts Council of Great Britain, *The Age of Neo-classicism,* 1972, pp. 866–7.

1. (1712–70), M.P.; first lord of the Treasury 1763–5. He resigned the treasurership of the Navy on 9 April 1757 when his brother-in-law, Pitt, and his brother, Lord Temple, were dismissed from the government.

2. *A Letter from Xo Ho, a Chinese Philosopher at London, to his Friend Lien Chi at Peking.* Written on 12 May, 'it was published on the 17th and immediately passed through five editions' (HW's 'Short Notes,' Gray i. 27; Montagu i. 207; *Works* i. 205–9; Hazen, *Bibl. of HW* 39–41; idem, *Cat. of HW's Lib.,* No. 2489).

freely to tell me if there is the least expression which can be disagreeable to you or them. The paper is a summary of melancholy truths,[3] but which, as my nature is rather inclined to smile, I have placed in a ridiculous light. If it should not displease your good heart, or should divert Mrs Grenville[4] for a moment, I should be happy; but I must beg the return of the enclosed copy, as I go out of town early tomorrow.[5]

I am Sir

Your most obedient servant

Hor. Walpole

From Lord Sandwich,[1] Friday 22 July 1757

Printed from a copy collated with the MS then (1939) in the possession of the 9th Earl of Sandwich, Hinchingbrooke, Huntingdon. First printed, Toynbee *Supp.* iii. 390.

Hinchingbrook, July 22, 1757.

Sir,

I RECEIVED the favour of yours,[2] and have wrote to Mr Waters[3] the executor of my grandmother's[4] will to inquire for the picture[5] you mention and not suffer it to be disposed of, and you will I hope excuse the liberty I take in begging you to accept of the original.[6]

3. As an example, the King, 'who dismissed a whole ministry because one of them did not humble himself enough before the throne, is gone into the country, without knowing who are to be his ministers' (*Works* i. 208).

4. Elizabeth Wyndham (d. 1769), m. (1749) Hon. George Grenville; sister of Lord Egremont.

5. Grenville's reply, dated 13 May, is missing; it was offered by Thomas Thorpe, Cat. of Autograph Letters, 1844, lot 896; sold Anderson Galleries 20 April 1904 (John H. V. Arnold Sale), lot 529; not further traced. The Anderson Galleries catalogue quotes the following extract: 'I perfectly agree with you in thinking the present state of this country a most melancholy one.'

1. John Montagu (1718–92), 4th E. of Sandwich, 1729; politician.

2. Missing.

3. Not further identified.

4. Elizabeth Wilmot (1674–1757), dau. of John Wilmot, 2d E. of Rochester; m. (1689) Edward Montagu, 3d E. of Sandwich, 1688. She died 1 July at Paris, where she had lived since the death of her husband.

5. Of Ninon Lenclos (HW). Ninon de Lenclos (1620–1705), French courtesan. The portrait, probably by Louis Elle, called Ferdinand *le vieux,* was given by Ninon to Lady Sandwich (More 6 and n. 2).

6. HW wrote John Chute 26 July 1757: 'Old Lady Sandwich is dead at Paris, and my Lord has given me her picture of Ninon L'Enclos; given it me in the prettiest manner in the world' (Chute 99–100). HW received the portrait, after some difficulties, ca 4 June 1758 (Conway i. 531 and illustration). It hung in the Great North Bedchamber at SH and was sold SH xx. 98 to Fuller for 125 guineas (not further traced). See *post* 9 Jan. 1773.

I can very sincerely assure you I make no sort of sacrifice in giving up a dead mistress, had it been a living one, you would not perhaps have found me so tractable; though the civilities I have received from you, would have laid me under great difficulty to refuse you that, or anything else in my possession. I am with the utmost truth and regard,

Your most obedient and most faithful servant

SANDWICH

From DAVID GARRICK,[1] Wednesday 3 August 1757

Printed from the MS now WSL, pasted in an extra-illustrated copy of the *Description of Strawberry Hill,* 1784, given by Mrs Damer to Sir Wathen Waller. First printed, Toynbee *Supp.* iii. 143. Reprinted in *The Letters of David Garrick,* ed. D. M. Little and G. M. Kahrl, Cambridge, Mass., 1963, i. 264–5. For the history of the extra-illustrated copy see Hazen, *SH Bibl.,* 1973 edn, p. xxvii, copy 33.

Dated by the reference to the 'express from London'; see n. 5 below.

Hampton,[2] Wednesday evening.

MR Garrick presents his respects to Mr Walpole, and begs to know if he has rec[eive]d any advice of the Duke's[3] beating the French,[4] for there is such a report here and confidently affirmed that Mr Walpole has had an express from London[5]—Mr Garrick could not have taken the liberty, had not the news been of so much consequence.

1. (1717–79), actor, playwright, and theatrical impresario.

2. In 1754 Garrick purchased a house at Hampton, not far from SH, where he subsequently spent his summers after the end of the London theatrical season (*Letters of David Garrick* i. 205 n. 4).

3. William Augustus (1721–65), D. of Cumberland; son of George II.

4. The Duke was in command of the army defending Hanover against the French under Marshal d'Estrées. The Battle of Hastenbeck, 24–6 July, was a reverse for the British (CONWAY i. 493; MANN v. 119 and nn.).

5. HW received an express from Henry Seymour Conway dated 'L[ittle] War[wick] Street, Thursday morning,' 4 Aug., mentioning details of the battle, which he relayed to Sir Horace Mann in his letter of the same date (CONWAY loc. cit.; see MANN loc. cit. n. 1 for earlier reports from the Continent).

TO CHARLES LYTTELTON, Thursday 4 August 1757

Printed from a photostat of the MS in the possession of Viscount Cobham, Hagley Hall, Stourbridge, Worcs. First printed in N&Q 1869, 4th ser., iii. 3. Reprinted, Toynbee iv. 81. The MS descended in the Lyttelton family to the present owner.

Strawberry Hill, Aug. 4, 1757.

Good Dean,[1]

I CANNOT send you *our Odes*[2] by the post, they are too large: I shall leave two copies in Hill Street[3] to be sent to Hagley;[4] I must beg you to desire my Lord[5] to accept one; and if he likes the type and paper,[6] I should hope that the next life he writes of Henry II (the present being I know engaged) he would let me print it.[7] I am much obliged to Cambridge for the kind reflections it made you make on my subject; as I have had the pleasure of being with you at Hagley, I had rather owe them to that place, which I am sure must raise more agreeable accompaniments than any other. Excuse my haste, I write in all the hurry of a *gros marchand.*

Yours ever

HOR. WALPOLE

1. Lyttelton was dean of Exeter Cathedral 1748–62.

2. *Odes by Mr Gray,* SH, 1757. HW states in his 'Journal of the Printing Office' that 1000 copies were printed by 3 Aug. (*Journal of the Printing-Office,* p. 3; Hazen, *SH Bibl.,* 1973, pp. ix, 27).

3. That is, at the house of his brother, Lord Lyttelton, in London.

4. Lord Lyttelton's seat near Stourbridge, Worcs.

5. Sir George Lyttelton had been created Bn Lyttelton in 1756.

6. The type is Caslon; the paper is a good 'trade paper' (Hazen, *SH Bibl.* 11, 26; *Journal of the Printing-Office,* pp. 95–6).

7. For HW's opinion of this life when it finally appeared in four volumes, 1767–71, see *ante* 30 Sept. 1754, n. 5. The printer was William Bowyer the younger (*post* 31 Aug. 1757).

From DAVID GARRICK, Friday 5 August 1757

Printed from a photostat of the MS in the Folger Shakespeare Library. First printed by Paget Toynbee in the *Times Literary Supplement,* Dec. 18, 1919, p. 767. Reprinted, *Journal of the Printing-Office,* p. 29; Toynbee *Supp.* iii. 144; *The Letters of David Garrick,* ed. D. M. Little and G. M. Kahrl, Cambridge, Mass., 1963, i. 265. Damer-Waller; the MS was sold Sotheby's 5 Dec. 1921 (first Waller Sale), lot 130, to Quaritch; subsequently acquired by Folger.

Dated by the publication of Gray's *Odes* at the SH Press. HW sent presentation copies to his friends on Thursday, 4 Aug.

Address: To the Honourable Mr Walpole at Twickenham.

Hampton, Friday.

MR Garrick presents his best respects to Mr Walpole and returns him ten thousand thanks for his most agreeable present[1]—He is greatly flattered by the small alteration[2] at the end of the second Ode.[3] Should Mr Gray be at Stoke Mr Garrick hopes to have the pleasure of seeing him there this week.[4]

1. A copy of *Odes by Mr Gray.*

2. *Plung'd* for *sunk* (HW); see following note.

3. The last line of *The Bard* reads 'Deep in the roaring tide he plung'd to endless night.' In one of his copies of the *Odes,* now in the Rothschild Collection, HW noted on 'plung'd': 'It was originally *sunk;* Mr Garrick advised *plung'd* as a more emphatic word on such an occasion' (*The Rothschild Library,* Cambridge, 1954, i. 268).

4. Gray left Cambridge 17 June and, after a visit to SH, spent almost six months at Stoke with his aunt Mrs Rogers. The Garricks stayed with Lady Cobham at Stoke manor house for three days in mid-August, 'much to my entertainment' (Gray to HW 10 Aug. 1757, GRAY ii. 99 and n. 10; *Correspondence of Thomas Gray,* ed. Paget Toynbee and Leonard Whibley, Oxford, 1935, ii. xxviii, 516; R. W. Ketton-Cremer, *Thomas Gray,* Cambridge, 1955, p. 156).

From ARTHUR ONSLOW,[1] Friday 5 August 1757

Printed from the MS now WSL. First printed, Toynbee *Supp.* iii. 144. Damer-Waller; the MS was sold Sotheby's 5 Dec. 1921 (first Waller Sale), lot 167 (with two other letters to HW), to Wells; given by him to Thomas Conolly, of Chicago, from whom WSL acquired it in 1937.

Ember Court,[2] 5 August 1757.

I AM particularly obliged to Mr Walpole by the present[3] he has made me today. I shall soon be at Strawberry Hill to thank him. When and from whence shall we have the comfort of good news?[4]

His faithful servant,

AR. ONSLOW

To LORD GEORGE SACKVILLE,[1] Saturday 6 August 1757

Printed from a photostat of the MS in the possession (1960) of Col. N. V. Stopford Sackville, Kettering, Northants. First printed in Hist. MSS Comm., 9th Report, App. iii (*Stopford Sackville MSS*), 1884, p. 9. Reprinted in Hist. MSS Comm., *Stopford Sackville MSS,* 1904–10, i. 43–4; Toynbee iv. 82–3 (salutation, closing, and signature omitted in all three printings).

Arlington Street, Aug. 6, 1757.

My Lord,

I AM PERHAPS doing a very impertinent thing and very malapropos giving myself an air of consequence; but it is of consequence to me not to forfeit your good opinion very innocently. I came to town last night, where I have not been two days together these three weeks or more. The bookseller,[2] who printed my simple

1. (1691–1768), M.P.; Speaker of the House of Commons 1728–61.

2. The manor of Imber or Ember Court, near Thames Ditton, Surrey, was settled on Anne Bridges by her uncle Henry Bridges when she married Onslow in 1720 (Owen Manning, *History and Antiquities of . . . Surrey,* 1804–14, i. 459; *Vict. Co. Hist. Surrey,* 1902–16, iii. 464–5).

3. A copy of *Odes by Mr Gray*. This gift is noteworthy because HW had quarrelled with Onslow in the House of Commons nine years earlier ('Short Notes,' GRAY i. 20).

4. See *ante* 3 Aug. 1757.

1. (after 1770, Germain) (1716–85), cr. (1782) Vct Sackville; M.P.

2. See following note.

Chinese letter,[3] told me with a very significant look that he heard I had writ something else since, with which it seems I had not trusted him. This was a letter from the Elysian fields.[4] It struck me that the Speaker[5] had a few days ago with more earnestness than I then minded, pressed me to tell him who did write it. I told him very honestly that I neither knew nor had ever inquired. I read it when it came out, and did not admire it enough ever to inquire. Since I came home I have sent for it and read it—and that makes me now trouble your Lordship. I would flatter myself even as an author that it is not like me—In the impertinences to some for whom I have the greatest regard[6] I am most sure it is most unlike me. I can guess no reason for its being imputed to me but its being a letter like the Chinese one.

My dear Lord (I hope I may say so) I am not apt to be serious; I am on this head and very much hurt. I never thought any kind of my writing worth preserving; I should beg this letter may be, that if the most distant day could bring out the least trace of that Elysian letter being mine, my honour which I most seriously give you that I know not the least tittle relating to it, and my own hand and name may rise in judgment against me. When I have said this, I hope you will not tell how much I am punished for my writing follies, and that I, who care not a great deal for what is said of me that is true, am so liable to be wounded by lies.

I am my Lord
Your Lordship's most obedient humble servant

HOR. WALPOLE

3. *A Letter from Xo Ho* (*ante* 13 May 1757, n. 2). The first edition was printed 'for N. Middleton, in the Strand,' and four subsequent editions by Josiah Graham (fl. 1737–57) (GRAY ii. 51 n. 4). HW's regular bookseller was William Bathoe (d. 1768), who may have supervised the printing (Hazen, *Bibl. of HW* 41).

4. *Letter from the late Earl of H[arringto]n, in the Elysian Shades, to His Grace the Duke of D[orse]t*, announced in the *London Magazine*, 1757, xxvi. 368. HW's copy is Hazen, *Cat of HW's Lib.*, No. 2146:3:12.

5. Arthur Onslow.

6. The Duke of Dorset was Sackville's father.

From CHARLES STANHOPE,[1] Monday 22 August 1757

Printed from the MS now WSL. First printed, Toynbee *Supp.* iii. 145. Damer-Waller; the MS was sold Sotheby's 5 Dec. 1921 (first Waller Sale), lot 183, to Wells; given by him to Thomas Conolly, of Chicago, from whom WSL acquired it in 1937.

The year of the letter is established by the date of Lady Townshend's visit to SH (see n. 3 below).

Monday, Aug. 22d.

Sir,

LADY TOWNSHEND[2] is so well pleased with the amusements she lately found in your learned retreat at Strawberry Hill,[3] that she is desirous of renewing the pleasure she met with there, and has promised me at her return to her seat at Richmond, to give me notice of the day she will choose for that purpose, that I may have the pleasure at the same time of attending upon you both, and that in the elegant phrase of that reverend divine Beza,[4] addressed to his friends Candida and Auderbert[5] I may there, *integrisq[ue] frui integer duobus,*[6] who am,

Dear Sir,

Your most humble and obedient servant,

C. STANHOPE

1. (1673–1760), M.P.; under-secretary of state 1714–17.

2. *Ante* 25 Aug. 1744 OS, n. 1.

3. Lady Townshend dined at SH 19 Aug. 1757 in a company of friends and was shown the newly established printing-office, where a few lines were printed in her honour to show the manner of composing for the press (*Journal of the Printing-Office,* p. 4; Hazen, *SH Bibl.* 152).

4. Théodore de Bèze (1519–1605), French reformer.

5. In *De sua in Candidem et Audebertum benevolentia,* in his *Poemata,* Leyden, 1757, pp. 114–15.

6. 'Take undiminished delight in the company of two virtuous people.'

TO LORD LYTTELTON, Thursday 25 August 1757

Printed from a photostat of the MS in the possession of Viscount Cobham, Hagley Hall, Stourbridge, Worcs. First printed in *Memoirs and Correspondence of George, Lord Lyttelton,* ed. Robert Phillimore, 1845, ii. 563–7. Reprinted, Cunningham iii. 96–9 (signature omitted); Toynbee iv. 84–8; extracts printed in A. C. C. Gaussen, *A Later Pepys,* 1904, i. 194. The MS descended in the Lyttelton family to the present owner.

Strawberry Hill, Aug. 25, 1757.

My Lord,

IT IS A SATISFACTION one can't often receive, to show a thing of great merit[1] to a man of great taste. Your Lordship's approbation is conclusive, and it stamps a disgrace on the age, who have not given themselves the trouble to see any beauties in these odes of Mr Gray—they have cast their eyes over them, found them obscure,[2] and looked no farther. Yet perhaps no composition ever had more sublime beauties than are in each. I agree with your Lordship in preferring the last[3] upon the whole; the three first stanzas and half, down to *agonizing King,* are in my opinion equal to anything in any language I understand. Yet the three last of the first ode[4] please me very near as much. The description of Shakespear is worthy [of] Shakespear: the account of Milton's blindness, though perhaps not strictly defensible, is very majestic, the character of Dryden's poetry is as animated as what it paints. I can even like the epithet *Orient;* as the East is the empire of fancy and poesy, I would allow its livery to be erected into a colour. I think *blue-eyed Pleasures* as allowable. When Homer gave eyes of what hue he pleased to his Queen-Goddesses, sure Mr Gray may tinge those of their handmaids. In answer to your Lordship's objection to *many-twinkling* in that beautiful epode, I will quote authority to which you will yield. As Greek as the expression is, it struck Mrs Garrick;[5] and she says on that whole picture, that Mr Gray is the only poet who ever understood dancing.

1. *Odes by Mr Gray,* SH, 1757.
2. HW remarked to Sir Horace Mann 4 Aug. 1757: 'They are Greek, they are Pindaric, they are sublime—consequently I fear a little obscure' (MANN v. 120).
3. *The Bard.*
4. *The Progress of Poesy.*
5. Eva Maria Veigel (1724–1822), called 'Violette,' m. (1749) David Garrick; dancer. For her date of birth see Carola Oman, *David Garrick,* 1958, pp. 118–19, 123.

These faults I think I can defend, and can excuse others, even the general obscurity of the latter, for I do not see it in the first; the subject of it has been taken for music; it is the power and progress of harmonious poetry.[6] I think his objection to prefixing a title to it was wrong—that Mr Cooke[7] published an ode with such a title: If the *Louis the Great,*[8] whom Voltaire has discovered in Hungary, had not disappeared from history of himself, would not Louis Quatorze have annihilated him?[9] I was aware that the second would at first have darknesses, and prevailed for the insertion of what notes there are, and would have had more; Mr Gray said, whatever wanted explanation, did not deserve it; but that sentence was never so far from being an axiom as in the present case. Not to mention how he had shackled himself with strophe, antistrophe, and epode, (yet acquitting himself nobly) the nature of prophecy forbade his naming his kings. To me they are apparent enough—yet I am far from thinking either piece perfect, though with what faults they have, I hold them in the first rank of genius and poetry. The second strophe of the first ode is inexcusable, nor do I wonder your Lordship blames it; even when one does understand it, perhaps the last line[10] is too turgid. I am not fond of the antistrophe that follows. In the second ode he made some corrections for the worse: *brave* Urien was originally *stern; brave* is insipid and commonplace. In the third antistrophe, *leave me unbless'd, unpitied,* stood at first, *leave your despairing Caradoc.* But the capital faults in my opinion are these. What punishment was it to Edward the First to hear that his grandson would conquer France? or is so common an event as Edward the Third being deserted on his death-bed[11] worthy being made part of a curse that was to avenge a nation—I can't cast my eye here, without crying out on those beautiful lines that follow, *Fair smiles the morn!* Though the images are extremely complicated, what painting in the whirlwind

6. The titles by which the *Odes* are now known first appeared in *Poems by Mr Gray,* 1768.

7. Thomas Cooke (1703–56), author of *An Ode on the Powers of Poetry,* 1751.

8. Louis I (1326–82), called 'Le Grand,' K. of Hungary 1342–82.

9. Voltaire noted in his *Essai sur les mœurs et l'esprit des nations* that Louis *le Grand* 'est presque ignoré en Europe: il n'avait pas régné sur des hommes qui sussent transmettre sa gloire aux nations' (*Œuvres complètes,* ed. L.-E.-D. Moland, 1877–85, xii. 233). Voltaire's *Le Siècle de Louis XIV,* Berlin, 1751, was published by Dodsley in 1752.

10. 'Th' unconquerable mind, and freedom's holy flame.'

11. Edward III, grandson of Edward I, was deserted by his courtiers; his mistress took the rings from his fingers and left him dying (*Chronicon Angliæ,* ed. E. M. Thompson, 1874, pp. 142–4).

likened to a lion lying in ambush for his evening prey, *in grim repose!* Thirst and hunger mocking Richard II, appear to me too ludicrously like the devils in *The Tempest*[12] that whisk away the banquet from the shipwrecked Dukes. From thence to the conclusion of Queen Elizabeth's portrait, which he has faithfully copied from Speed[13] in the passage where she mumbled [*sic*] the Polish ambassador,[14] I admire: I can even allow that image of Rapture hovering like an ancient grotesque, though it strictly has little meaning—but there I take my leave; the last stanza has no beauties for me—I even think its obscurity fortunate, for the allusions to Spenser, Shakespear, Milton are not only weak, but the two last returning again, after appearing so gloriously in the first ode, and with so much fainter colours, enervate the whole conclusion.

Your Lordship sees that I am no enthusiast to Mr Gray; his great lustre has not dazzled me, as his obscurity seems to have blinded his cotemporaries. Indeed, I do not think that they ever admired him except in his *Churchyard*,[15] though the Eton Ode[16] was far its superior, and is certainly not obscure. The Eton Ode is perfect: these, of more masterly execution, have defects. Yet not to admire them is total want of taste. I have an aversion to tame poetry. At best perhaps the art is the sublimest of the *difficiles nugæ*:[17] to measure or rhyme prose, is trifling without being difficult.

I am sensible, that encouraged by your Lordship's criticism, I have indulged myself in it too much, and I would as willingly keep silence on the melancholy situation of our country,[18] sunk—whither! but there is to me a private part of it, now become a public one, and one that should, and I will trust in God, may yet be reserved for the

12. Act III, scene iii.

13. John Speed (ca 1552–1629), historian; author of *The History of Great Britaine*, 1611.

14. Pawel Dzialyński, Polish ambassador to England 1597 (*Polski Słownik Biograficzny*, Krakow, 1935– , vi. 95; Jozef Jasnowski, *England and Poland in the XVIth and XVIIth Centuries*, 1948, pp. 23–5). Thomas Gray's note, in his *Poems*, 1768, p. 68, reads: 'Speed relating an audience given by Queen Elizabeth to Paul Dzialinski, ambassador of Poland, says: "And thus she, lion-like rising, daunted the malapert orator no less with her stately port and majestical deporture, than with the tartness of her princely checks." ' The passage continues: 'and turning to the train of her attendants, thus said, God's death, my Lords, (for that was her oath ever in anger) I have been enforced this day to scour up my old Latin, that hath lain long in rusting' (Speed, op. cit. IX. xxiv. 871).

15. *An Elegy Wrote in a Country Church Yard*, published anonymously in 1751.

16. *Ode on a Distant Prospect of Eton College*, 1747, also appeared anonymously.

17. 'Difficult trifling verse.'

18. See *ante* 3 Aug. 1757.

public in a happier light, on whom I cannot keep silence, dear Mr Conway![19] Your Lordship asks my opinion—alas! my Lord, you have spoken my opinion—is France so vulnerable? Can we afford to risk our best officers, our best ships, our best soldiers? What, if they perish? Is our danger so remote, that we must send for it, mark its route with our own best blood?—I tremble as an Englishman and more as a friend. What must poor Lady Ailesbury[20] do, who sees the most reasonable system of happiness and the most perfect in every shape that ever existed, exposed to such imminent peril! my heart bleeds for her. Adieu! my Lord, this is a theme that cuts short all other reflections! My best compliments to my Lady and the Dean;[21] I grieve for the ill-health of the former. There is a question I must still ask; how does King Henry?[22] I ask this as a reader, not as a printer; not as Elzevir[23] Horace, as Mr Conway calls me, but as

Your Lordship's admirer
and obedient humble servant

Horace Walpole

From Lord Lyttelton, Wednesday 31 August 1757

Printed from the MS now wsl. First printed, Toynbee *Supp.* ii. 100–2. Damer-Waller; the MS was sold Sotheby's 5 Dec. 1921 (first Waller Sale), lot 155, to Maggs; offered by them, Cat. Nos 471 (1925), lot 2927; 501 (spring 1928), lot 426; resold Sotheby's 18 Dec. 1929 (various properties), lot 631; offered by Tregaskis, Cat. Nos 980 (1930), lot 211; 1013 (1935), lot 132; resold by Maggs to wsl, 1936.

Hagley, August 31, 1757.

Dear Sir,

I AM PROUD that the obscurity thrown over some parts of it has not hindered me from seeing and admiring the bright and glorious flame of poetical fire in Mr Gray's Odes, when you tell me

19. General Conway, HW's cousin, had been sent with Sir John Mordaunt to attack Rochefort; see Conway i. 495–520, *passim*.

20. Caroline Campbell (1721–1803), m. 1 (1739) Charles Bruce, 3d E. of Ailesbury; m. 2 (1747) Hon. Henry Seymour Conway.

21. Charles Lyttelton, dean of Exeter Cathedral.

22. Lyttelton was writing a life of Henry II (*ante* 30 Sept. 1754).

23. Louis Elzevir (1540–1617), Dutch printer.

it has escaped the eye of the public. But why should any spots remain in this sun? The second strophe of the first Ode may be easily altered and made very clear. I have no objection to the antistrophe but that I fear *to repeat their Chiefs* is not English. All the rest is very fine, especially the four first and three last verses. Q. Are the people of Chili *dusky?* Nothing ever exceeded the three last stanzas in greatness of imagination or nobleness of expression; but I cannot allow *Orient* to be made a colour. I think too that Dryden's horses had spirit enough and were very well managed, but I don't think their necks were *cloath'd in thunder.* However I would not desire to alter that expression, because by the loss of it the picture would suffer, and a poet is not obliged to draw his characters with the exactness of a critic or an historian. I agree with Mrs Garrick that the idea conveyed by *many-twinkling* feet is proper and just; but the composition of the word is against all rules of language. We may say *ever-twinkling* but not *many-twinkling. Many-coloured* is right, because that is only a poetical manner of expressing a thing which is *of many colours* and the compound is clear at first sight to the reader; whereas to understand *many-twinkling* we must give *many* the idea of *often* or *swiftly,* which it does not naturally contain. And with regard to *blue-eyed pleasures* I must observe to you, with the profound erudition of a great critic, that it was not arbitrarily, or from mere caprice, that Homer gave grey eyes to Minerva, and black ones to Juno. In the first there is usually more sharpness and sagacity, and more majesty in the last. Jupiter for the same reason had also black eyes. But I appeal to you whether the pleasures are not blue, black, and hazel-eyed.

The faults you find with the second Ode[1] are indeed great, but yet the disgraces that attended on the last years of Edward the Third, to which I suppose the author alludes in the second antistrophe, are a vengeance which the Welsh bard might triumph in foreseeing; but they ought to be expressed with more clearness and distinction from the common fate of Kings *to be forsaken on their death-beds. Stay oh! stay,* in the third antistrophe apparently refers to Edward the First who is named just before, and not to the bards, which obscurity would not be removed by restoring the line you mention *Leave your despairing Caradoc,* but may be cleared by some alteration expressing that he now addresses the bards. All the last stanza from *Fond impious Man*

1. *The Bard.*

in my opinion is very sublime and the poem cannot end better or in a manner more striking to the imagination of the reader than with the two last lines. The first part of the stanza I confess is obscure, but yet I understood it at the first reading, and perhaps the revival of poetry in this nation under kings of Welsh blood was a necessary consolation to make the bard die triumphant, for which reason those lines should not be left out, though they may be strengthened a little and made less obscure.

I am full of anxiety for Mr Conway, and feel for Lady Ailesbury with the sensibility of a friend who knows her happiness is at stake and how uncommonly great that happiness is. I also fear for the public if this expedition should prove as unfortunate as others have done, but if there be a reasonable hope of success there may be less danger in attacking than only defending. He who always parries and never thrusts, as my fencing master told me, will be certainly killed at last. But whether instead of wounding our enemy we are not going to run upon his sword I don't know. *That* depends upon intelligence which can only be known to the Cabinet Council. My greatest apprehension is that however practicable at first the design may have been, delay has made it impracticable now.

Adieu, dear Sir: Lady Lyttleton I think is now pretty well. She and the Dean desire their compliments. I am scribbling a little at my History,[2] but the printing goes on very slowly. Mr Bowyer[3] is not so good a printer as you. I am afraid besides the faults of the author the work will suffer a little by those of the press.

Believe me ever,
Dear Sir,
Your most affectionate and most obedient humble servant,

LYTTELTON

2. Of King Henry II. The printing was apparently going on while the work was being written, but the first volumes were not published until 1767.

3. William Bowyer (1699–1777), the younger, printer (John Nichols, *Anecdotes of William Bowyer*, 1782, pp. 384, 425–7).

TO CHARLES O'HARA,[1] Saturday 17 September 1757

Printed from HW's *Fugitive Pieces in Verse and Prose,* SH, 1758, pp. 206–16. Reprinted in GM 1781, li. 257–9; *European Magazine* 1785, viii. 253–6; *Works* i. 212–17; Toynbee *Supp.* i. 79–86. The history of the MS and its present whereabouts are not known.

Strawberry Hill, Sept. 17, 1757.

Sir,

I SHOULD have thanked you the instant I received the honour of your obliging letter,[2] if you had not told me you was setting out for Ireland: I am now in pain lest this should not come to your hands, as you gave me no direction, and I should be extremely sorry that you should think me capable, Sir, of neglecting to show my gratitude for the trouble you have given yourself. I cannot think of taking the liberty to give you any more, though I own the inscriptions you have sent me have not cleared away the difficulties relating to the Countess of Desmond.[3]—On the contrary, they make me doubt

1. (ca 1705–76), of Nymphsfield Manor, Annaghmore, Co. Sligo, Ireland; high sheriff of Co. Sligo 1740 and 1756; M.P. (Ireland) Ballinakill 1761–8, Armagh 1769–76; friend of Edmund Burke and Henry Seymour Conway (Foster, *Alumni Oxon.;* [Great Britain, Parliament, House of Commons], *Members of Parliament,* 1878, Pt II, pp. 667–8; W. G. Wood-Martin, *History of Sligo,* Dublin, 1882–92, iii. 498; R. J. S. Hoffman, *Edmund Burke . . . Correspondence with Charles O'Hara, 1761–1776,* Philadelphia, 1956, pp. 5–8; Burke, *Landed Gentry,* 4th edn, 1868, p. 1111).

2. Missing; enclosed with it was a letter dated 23 Aug. 1757 from an unknown correspondent to O'Hara, written from O'Hara's seat at Nymphsfield. O'Hara, who was in England at this time, had evidently asked this correspondent to transcribe for him the inscriptions on the O'Connor monument at Sligo. The enclosure, along with HW's reply to O'Hara's (missing) letter, was printed in *Fugitive Pieces* and *Works* under the heading: 'An Inquiry into the Person and Age of the long-lived Countess of Desmond.' HW prefaced this 'Inquiry' as follows: 'Having a few years ago had a curiosity to inform myself of the particulars of the life of the very aged Countess of Desmond, I was much surprised to find no certain account of so extraordinary a person; neither exactly how long she lived, nor even who she was; the few circumstances related of her depending on mere tradition. At last I was informed that she was buried at Sligo in Ireland, and a gentleman of that place was so kind as to procure for me the following inscriptions on the monument there; which however soon convinced me of that supposition being a mistake, as will appear by the observations in my letter, in consequence of this which contained the epitaph.'

3. Catherine Fitzgerald (d. 1604), dau. of John Fitzgerald of Dromana, Lord of the Decies, and Ellen, dau. of John Fitzgibbon, the White Knight; m. (ca 1505–34), as his second wife, Thomas Fitzthomas Fitzgerald (1454–1534), 11th E. of Desmond (OSSORY i. 317 n. 8; GEC iv. 249–50; Charles Smith, *Ancient and Present State of the County and City of Cork,* Dublin, 1750, ii. 36; Richard Sainthill, *The Old Countess of Desmond,* Dublin, 1861–3, *passim; Dublin Review* Feb. 1862, li. 51–91).

whether the lady interred at Sligo was the person reported to have lived to such an immense age. If you will excuse me, I will state my objections.

I have often heard that the aged Lady Desmond lived to one hundred and sixty-two or sixty-three years. In the account of her picture at Windsor,[4] they give her but one hundred and fifty years. Sir William Temple,[5] from the relation of Lord Leicester, reduces it to one hundred and forty; adding, 'That she had been married out of England in the reign of Edward the Fourth, and, being reduced to great poverty by the ruin of the Irish family into which she married, came from Bristol to London towards the end of the reign of James the First to beg relief from Court.'

This account by no means corresponds either with the monument at Sligo, or the new Irish peerage by Lodge.[6] The great particular (besides that of her wonderful age) which interested me in this inquiry, was the tradition which says that the long-lived Lady Desmond had danced with Richard the Third, and always affirmed that he was a very well-made man. It is supposed that this was the same lady with whom the old Lady Dacre[7] had conversed, and from whose testimony she gave the same account.

In the catalogue of the ancient Earls of Desmond,[8] inserted in the

4. See Pote's account of Windsor Castle, p. 418 (HW). 'In this room [the Queen's dressing room] is a closet in which are several small paintings, particularly a painting of the countess of Desmond, who lived as is said, to the age of one hundred and fifty within a few days' (Joseph Pote, *History and Antiquities of Windsor Castle,* Eton, 1749, p. 418). HW noted in his copy, now WSL, of Pote (Hazen, *Cat. of HW's Lib.*, No. 637): 'This is not the Countess of Desmond, but an old woman by Rembrandt, given to King Charles I by Sir Rob. Kerr, Earl of Ancram.' This information, in expanded form, appears in a printed 'Note' inserted in some copies of *Fugitive Pieces* (following p. 216) and in *Works* i. 217. A 'drawing of Rembrandt's mother from the picture at Windsor, called the Countess of Desmond; by Müntz' hung in HW's bedroom at SH ('Des. of SH,' *Works* ii. 453). Rembrandt's 'Portrait of his Mother' was painted at Leyden ca 1629–30 on an oaken panel; it was given to Charles I by Robert Ker, 1st E. of Ancram, one of the personal attendants of the King who was made a gentleman of the Bedchamber in 1625, when Charles became King (Lionel Cust, *The Royal Collection of Paintings,* vol. II, *Windsor Castle,* 1906; Abraham Van der Doort, *Catalogue . . . of King Charles the First's Capital Collection of Pictures,* 1757, p. 150, No. 101).

5. See his essay on health and long life (HW). Sir William Temple (1628–99), cr. (1666) Bt; statesman and author. In his essay 'Of Health and Long Life,' *Miscellanea,* 1701, pp. 124–5, he quotes the 'late Robert [Sidney (1595–1677), 16th] Earl of Leicester.'

6. John Lodge (d. 1774), archivist; deputy keeper of the records in Birmingham Tower, Dublin, 1751. His *Peerage of Ireland,* 4 vols, was published in 1754. HW's copy is Hazen, op. cit., No. 660.

7. Anne Sackville (d. 1595), m. (ca 1558) Gregory Fiennes (1539–94), 10th Lord Dacre of the South.

8. See Lodge, *Peerage,* 1789 edn (enlarged by Mervyn Archdall), i. 63–77.

pedigree of Kildare, I can find no one who married an Englishwoman near the period in question: but that we will waive; it might have been a mistake of Sir William, or his authority, the Earl of Leicester. Her poverty might be as erroneous, if Lodge's account be true,[9] that she left three hundred pounds to the chapel at Sligo, the tomb in which, as the inscription says, she erected in 1624. But here is the greatest difficulty: if she was one hundred and forty in 1636, according to Lodge,[10] the era of her death, (which by the way was in King Charles's and not in King James's reign) she was born in 1496. Gerald Earl of Desmond, her first husband, died according to the *Peerage* in 1583.[11] She was therefore eighty-seven when she married O'Connor of Sligo.[12]—that is possible.—if she lived to one hundred and forty, she might be in the vigour of her age (at least not dislike the vigour of his) at eighty-seven. The Earl of Desmond's first wife, says Lodge, (for our Lady Eleanor was his second) died in 1564:[13] if he remarried the next day, his bride must have been sixty-eight, and yet she had a son and five daughters by him.[14] I fear with all her juvenile powers, she must have been past breeding at sixty-eight.

These accounts tally as little with her dancing with Richard the Third; he died in 1485, and by my computation she was not born till 1496. If we suppose that she died twelve years sooner, *viz.* in 1624, at which time the tomb was erected, and which would coincide with Sir William Temple's date of her death in the reign of James; and if we give her one hundred and fifty years, according to the Windsor account, she would then have been born in 1474, and consequently was eleven years old at the death of King Richard: but this supposition labours with as many difficulties. She could not have been married in the reign of Edward the Fourth, scarcely have danced with his brother; and it is as little probable that she had much remembrance of his person, the point, I own, in which I am most inter-

9. Vol. 1. page 19 (HW). Ibid. i. 75.

10. Ibid. i. 75n.

11. Ibid. i. 74n. Eleanor Butler (ca 1546–1636), m. 1 (ca 1568), as his second wife, Gerald Fitzjames Fitzgerald (ca 1533–83), 14th E. of Desmond, 1558 (attainted 1582); m. 2 (ca 1597) Sir Donogh O'Connor Sligo. This is not the 'long-lived' Countess of Desmond who is the subject of HW's inquiry.

12. Sir Donogh (or Donnogh) O'Connor Sligo (or Sligah) (d. 1609), Kt, 1604 (GEC iv. 253–4; W. A. Shaw, *The Knights of England,* 1906, ii. 131).

13. 'His first wife Joan, only daughter of James, the eleventh Earl of Desmond, and widow of James, Earl of Ormond . . . died in 1564' (*Peerage,* 1789, i. 75). Joan Fitzgerald (d. 2 Jan. 1564/5), dau. of James, 10th E. of Desmond; m. 1 James Butler (d. 1546), 9th E. of Ossory and Ormond; m. 2 Sir Francis Bryan (d. 1550); m. 3 (1550 or 1551) Gerald, 14th E. of Desmond.

14. They are listed in Lodge's *Peerage,* 1789, i. 75.

ested,[15] not at all crediting the accounts of his deformity, from which Buck[16] has so well defended him, both by the silence of Comines,[17] who mentions the beauty of King Edward,[18] and was too sincere to have passed over such remarkable ugliness in a foreigner, and from Dr Shaw's[19] appeal to the people before the Protector's face, whether his Highness was not a comely prince and the exact image of his father. The power that could enslave them, could not have kept them from laughing at such an apostrophe, had the Protector been as ill-shapen as the Lancastrian historians[20] represent him. Lady Desmond's testimony adds great weight to this defence.

But the more we accommodate her age to that of Richard the Third, the less it will suit with that of her first husband. If she was born in 1474, her having children by him (Gerald Earl of Desmond) becomes vastly more improbable.

It is very remarkable, Sir, that neither her tomb, nor Lodge, should take notice of this extraordinary person's age; and I own if I knew how to consult him without trespassing on your good-nature and civility, I should be very glad to state the foregoing difficulties to him. But I fear I have already taken too great freedom with your indulgence, and am, etc.,

H. W.

PS. Since I finished my letter, a new idea has started, for discovering who this very old Lady Desmond was, at least whose wife she was, supposing the person buried at Sligo not to be her. Thomas the sixth Earl of Desmond[21] was forced to give up the Earldom: but it

15. This is one of the earliest references to the interest that led HW to publish *Historic Doubts . . . of King Richard the Third* in 1768.

16. Sir George Buck (d. 1623), in his *History of the Life and Reigne of Richard the Third,* 1646, pp. 79–80. HW's copy of the 1647 edition, now in the BM, is Hazen, op. cit., No. 475.

17. Philippe de Comines (1447–1511), sieur d'Argenton.

18. 'King Edward was not a man of any great management or foresight, but of an invincible courage, and the most beautiful prince my eyes ever beheld' (Comines, *Memoirs,* trans. Thomas Uvedale, 1712, i. 250). HW's copy, now WSL, is Hazen, op. cit., No. 1639.

19. Ralph Shaw (or Shaa) (d. 1484), S.T.B.; prebendary of London, 1477. He preached a sermon at St Paul's Cross 22 June 1483, saying 'this is the father's own figure' (John Le Neve, *Fasti Ecclesiæ Anglicanæ,* Oxford, 1854, ii. 372; Sir Thomas More, *Works,* 1557, pp. 60–1; Sir George Buck, op. cit. 80).

20. Sir Thomas More in his *History of King Richard III* and John Rous (ca 1411–91) in his *Historia Regum Angliæ* (first published in 1716).

21. Thomas Fitz John (ca 1386–1420), 5th E. of Desmond, 1400. Because of an imprudent marriage he was forced to give up the earldom in 1418.

is not improbable that his descendants might use the title, as he certainly left issue. His son died, says Lodge[22] in 1452, leaving two sons John and Maurice. John being born at least in 1451, would be above thirty at the end of Edward the Fourth. If his wife was seventeen in the last year of that King, she would have been born in 1466. If therefore she died about 1625, she would be one hundred and fifty-nine. This approaches to the common notion of her age, as the ruin of the branch of the family into which she married, does to Sir William Temple's. A few years more or less in certain parts of this hypothesis, would but adjust it still better to the accounts of her. Her husband being only a titular Earl solves the difficulty of the silence of genealogists on so extraordinary a person.

Still we should be to learn[23] of what family she herself was: and I find a new evidence, which agreeing with Sir William Temple's account, seems to clash a little with my last supposition. This authority is no less than Sir Walter Raleigh's, who in the fifth chapter of the first book of his *History of the World,* says expressly, that he himself 'knew the old Countess of Desmond of Inchiquin, who lived in the year 1589, and many years since, who was married in Edward the Fourth's time, *and held her jointure from all the Earls of Desmond since then;* and that this is true, all the noblemen and gentlemen of Munster can witness.'[24] Her holding a jointure from all the Earls of Desmond would imply that her husband was not of the titular line, but of that in possession: yet that difficulty is not so great, as no such lady being mentioned in the pedigree. By Sir Walter's words it is probable that she was dead when he wrote that account of her. His *History* was first printed in 1614; this makes the era of her death much earlier than I had supposed; but having allowed her near one hundred and sixty years, taking away ten or twelve will make my hypothesis agree better with Sir William Temple's account, and does not at all destroy the assumption of her being the wife of only a titular Earl. However, all these are conjectures, which I should be glad to have ascertained or confuted by any curious person, who could produce authentic testimonies of the

22. Vol. i. page 14 (HW). *Peerage,* 1789, i. 67.

23. *Sic;* presumably HW intended something like 'we should be glad to learn.'

24. Raleigh, *The History of the World,* 1614, Book I, chap. 5, p. 78. HW's copy is Hazen, op. cit. No. 2063. This reference and that in Fynes Moryson's *Itinerary,* 1617, Part III, Book I, chap. iii, p. 41, are the earliest printed references to the alleged great age of Lady Desmond.

birth, death, and family, of this very remarkable lady; and to excite or assist which was the only purpose of this disquisition.

Having communicated these observations to the Rev. Dr Charles Lyttelton Dean of Exeter, he soon afterwards found and gave me the following extract from page 36 of Smith's natural and civil history of the County of Cork, printed at Dublin, 1750. 8vo.[25]

'Thomas the thirteenth Earl of Desmond,[26] brother to Maurice, the eleventh Earl,[27] died this year (1534) at Rathkeile, being of a very great age, and was buried at Youghall. He married, first, Ellen[28] daughter of McCarty of Muskerry, by whom he had a son, Maurice, who died *vitâ patris.*—The Earl's second wife was Catherine Fitzgerald, daughter of the Fitzgeralds of the house of Drumana in the county of Waterford. This Catherine was the Countess that lived so long, of whom Sir Walter Raleigh makes mention in his *History of the World,* and was reputed to live to one hundred and forty years of age.'

This is the most positive evidence we have; the author quotes Russel's MS.[29] If she was of the Fitzgeralds of Waterford, it will not in strictness agree with Sir William Temple's relation of her being married out of England; by which we should naturally suppose that she was born of English blood—Yet his account is so vague, that it ought not to be set against absolute assertion, supposing the Russel MS to be of good authority enough to support what it is quoted to support in 1750.

Upon the whole, and to reduce this lady's age as low as possible, making it at the same time coincide with the most probable accounts, we will suppose that she was married at fifteen in 1483, the last year of Edward the Fourth, and that she died in 1612, two years before the publication of Sir Walter Raleigh's *History,* she will then have been no less than[30] one hundred and forty-five years of age, a particularity singular enough to excite, and, I hope, to excuse this inquiry.[31]

25. Charles Smith, *Ancient and Present State of the County and City of Cork,* Dublin, 1750, ii. 36.

26. His name was James, and he was the twelfth Earl (HW). Actually the 11th Earl; see n. 3 above.

27. Maurice Fitzthomas Fitzgerald (d. 1520), 9th E. of Desmond, 1487.

28. See Lodge's *Peerage;* vol. 1. p. 16 (HW). Actually Shela (Gille), dau. of Cormac *Laidir* McTeige MacCarthy, Lord of Muskerry.

29. Smith, op. cit. ii. 36n.

30. Lord Bacon, says Fuller, computed her age to be one hundred and forty at least; and added, that she three times had a new set of teeth; for so I understand *ter vices dentisse,* not that she recovered them three times after casting them, as Fuller translates it, which is giving her four sets of teeth. *Worthies in Northumb.* p. 310 (HW).

31. I cannot omit an anecdote, though too extraordinary to be given as authen-

TO GEORGE SELWYN,[1] Sunday 2 October 1757

Printed for the first time from the MS now WSL. The MS was sold Sotheby's 29 April 1969 (property of a Lady), lot 384, to Seven Gables for WSL; a note pasted underneath the MS suggests that the letter was once owned by 'Lady Vincent.'

Dated by the note HW wrote later in the day (SELWYN 138–9).

Strawberry Hill, Sunday.

Dear Sir,

WHETHER Matson[2] is in the way to Bath or not, I am very willing to believe it is, and as ready to make it so. I cannot set out from hence before tomorrow sennight the 10th but will be with you the day after,[3] with this proviso, that if my Lord Orford[4] sends for me to Lynn before that, I must go; but I trust he will not. I will not trouble you now with a word more, as I shall be in town on Tuesday morning, and hope to find you still there.[5] Adieu! Dear Sir

Yours ever

H. W.

tic, relating to this lady. In an original MS written by Robert the second Earl of Leicester, (from whom Sir W. Temple says he received the account of Lady Desmond) and containing memorandums of remarkable facts, it is said that that old Countess [actually Eleanor, widow of the 11th Earl] came to England to solicit a pension at the end of Queen Elizabeth's reign, and was so poor that she walked from Bristol to London; her daughter being too decrepit to go on foot, was carried in a cart. 'The Countess, adds Lord Leicester, might have lived much longer had she not met with a kind of violent death; for she would needs climb a nut-tree to gather nuts; so falling down, she hurt her thigh, which brought a fever, and that fever brought death.' Lord Leicester fixes her death to the end of that reign (HW's note, first printed in *Works*).

1. George Augustus Selwyn (1719–91), wit and politician; HW's friend and correspondent.

2. Selwyn's seat on Robins Wood Hill, two miles SE of Gloucester (SELWYN 120 n. 3).

3. HW gave up his visit to Bath (ibid. 143).

4. George, 3d E. of Orford, HW's nephew.

5. HW wrote Selwyn 6 Oct. that 'It was impossible for me to get to town on Monday night; and I was as sorry to find you gone on Tuesday' (ibid. 139).

From DAVID GARRICK, Thursday 6 October 1757

Printed from a photostat of the MS in the Folger Shakespeare Library. First printed, *Journal of the Printing-Office,* p. 29. Reprinted, Toynbee *Supp.* iii. 146; *The Letters of David Garrick,* ed. D. M. Little and G. M. Kahrl, Cambridge, Mass., 1963, i. 268–9. Damer-Waller; the MS was sold Sotheby's 5 Dec. 1921 (first Waller Sale), lot 129, to Quaritch; subsequently acquired by Folger.

Address: To the Honourable Mr Walpole at Twickenham, Middlesex. *Postmark:* 10 OC. SAFFRON WALDEN.

Newmarket, October the 6th 1757.

Dear Sir,

I AM AT this place, seeing a new species of men, whose acquaintance may hereafter be of some use to me. I am most prodigiously flattered by your opinion of the verses to Mr Gray[1]—they were printed in the *Chronicle* of last Saturday, but very inaccurately and they were thrust into the most obscure corner of the paper—As I am at such a distance from Mr Gray,[2] I cannot know his sentiments upon the occasion, but you have my free leave to dispose of 'em, as you shall please, for they and their author are always at your service.[3] As my name will be of little consequence to Mr Gray on the sonnet, I would not choose to have it printed with it.[4]

I am
Ever, Sir,
Your most obedient and much obliged humble servant,

D. GARRICK

1. Garrick's complimentary verses *To Mr Gray, on His Odes* were 'occasioned by his odes being but moderately well received by the public' and were first printed anonymously in the *London Chronicle* 29 Sept.–1 Oct. 1757 (*Journal of the Printing -Office,* pp. 5–6, 29–30).

2. Gray was visiting his aunt at Stoke Poges (*ante* 5 Aug. 1757, n. 4).

3. Sixty copies of the verses were printed at the SH Press 17–26 Oct., on both sides of a quarto leaf (Hazen, *SH Bibl.* 164–7; Mary E. Knapp, *A Checklist of Verse by David Garrick,* Charlottesville, 1955, No. 179).

4. Garrick's name does not appear on the verses.

From the REV. JOSEPH SPENCE, Thursday 27 October 1757

Printed from the MS now WSL. First printed, Toynbee *Supp.* ii. 103–5. Damer-Waller; the MS was sold Sotheby's 5 Dec. 1921 (first Waller Sale), lot 182, to Maggs; offered by them, Cat. Nos 421 (spring 1922), lot 719; 459 (1925), lot 639; 492 (summer 1927), lot 1158; 522 (summer 1929), lot 1203; sold by them to WSL, 1933.

Bifleet,[1] Oct. 27, [17]57.

Dear Sir,

I HAVE old Notredame[2] ready packed up, against he is called for: what I mentioned in the larger work of Crescembeni[3] is only the same thing repeated word for word. I find in the former that Richard I[4] lived for some time in the Court of Raimond Berengarius,[5] the last Count of Provence of that name: where he fell in love with his daughter Eleonara,[6] and the Provençal poetry (then about its height); so far, as to marry the former,[7] and practise the latter. That in his return from the Holy War, he was made prisoner by the Duke of Austria;[8] and during his confinement there, wrote *several* sonnets complaining of his barons for not redeeming him: some of which are preserved among the MSS collections from the Provençal poets, both in the Lorenzo Library at Florence, and in the Vatican at Rome.[9] After his return home, Anselm Faidit,[10] one of the most eminent among the Provençal poets, lived in his court, was much

1. Byfleet, Surrey, where Spence lived for twenty years.

2. Jean de Notredame (d. 1590), author of *Les vies des plus célèbres . . . poètes provençaux qui ont floury du temps des comtes de Provence,* Lyon, 1575.

3. Giovanni Mario Crescimbeni (1663–1728), author of *Dell'Istoria della volgar poesia,* 6 vols, Venice, 1730–1. HW did not own this or Notredame's work.

4. (1157–1199), 'the Lion-Heart,' K. of England 1189–99.

5. Raymond Bérenger V (1205–45), Count of Provence (Fernand Benoît, *Recueil des actes des comtes de Provence,* 1925, i. xxix–xxxv).

6. Eleanor of Provence (ca 1223–91), dau. of Raymond Bérenger V.

7. She was the queen of Henry III, not Richard I, who married Berengaria, dau. of Sancho VI of Navarre, in 1191. See *post* 6 Feb. 1764.

8. Leopold V (1157–94). Richard was made a prisoner 20 Dec. 1192 and confined at Durenstein, about 45 miles from Vienna (Lionel Landon, *Itinerary of King Richard I,* 1935, p. 71 [Pipe Roll Society, *Publications,* vol. LI]).

9. HW asked Sir Horace Mann in Florence to have copies made of Richard's poems in both libraries for use in his *Catalogue of the Royal and Noble Authors in England,* SH, 1758 (HW to Mann 20 Nov. 1757, MANN v. 156–7).

10. Gaucelm Faidit (d. ca 1220), troubadour.

favoured by him, and wrote a fine poem on his death.[11] Crescembeni's translation of Notredame, Art. 41 and 14,[12] who gives you the second stanza of one of Richard I's *serventesis,*[13] as follows

Or sachan ben mos homs e mos Barons,
Anglez, Normans, Peytavins, e Gascons;
Qu' yeu non ay ia si pavre compagnon
Que per aver lou laussess' en preson.[14]

Or as he translates it:

Or saccian ben miei uomini, miei Baroni
Normanni, Inglesi, del Poetu, e Guasconi,
Ch'io già non hò si povero compagno,
Che per aver, lo lassassi in prigione.

He says, there are some of his *serventesi* in both the above-mentioned libraries; and mentions in particular, Cod. 3204, in the Vatican:[15] but I suppose the taste of it above will be as much as you may possibly desire, of this lion-hearted poet's works. I long to see your ten royal, and other noble writers;[16] and may the press at Strawberry Hill ever flourish and abound, is the prayer of,

Sir,

Your most obedient humble servant,

JO. SPENCE

Tassoni[17] in his *Consid.* p. 489, and Redi[18] in his *Annotaz.* p. 98, mention this King as a poet; and quote from him: and will you

11. 'Fortz chausa es que tot lo major dan.' The text of this, the most famous of Gaucelm's poems, is given in Jean Mouzat, *Les poèmes de Gaucelm Faidit,* 1965, pp. 415–18.

12. Crescimbeni, op. cit. ii. 95–6, 43–5.

13. *Serventese,* 'a form of poem or lay, usually satirical, employed by the troubadours of the Middle Ages' (OED *sub* 'sirvente').

14. 'Now well know, my men and my barons,
English, Normans, Poiterins, and Gascons,
That I have not indeed a companion so poor
That to have [gold] I would leave him in prison.'

15. There is no poem by Richard I in this manuscript, but two poems by Rigaut de Barbezieux (or Richart de Berbezil or Berbesin) and Richard de Tarascon (MANN v. 169 and nn. 4–6).

16. HW does not acknowledge the help he received from Spence in his article on Richard I in his *Royal and Noble Authors (Works* i. 251–5).

17. Alessandro Tassoni (1565–1635), author of *Considerazioni sopra le rime del Petrarca,* Modena, 1609.

18. Francesco Redi (1626–98), author of *Bacco in Toscana,* Florence, 1685, which includes *Annotazioni di Francesco Redi Aretino accademico della crusca al ditirambo.*

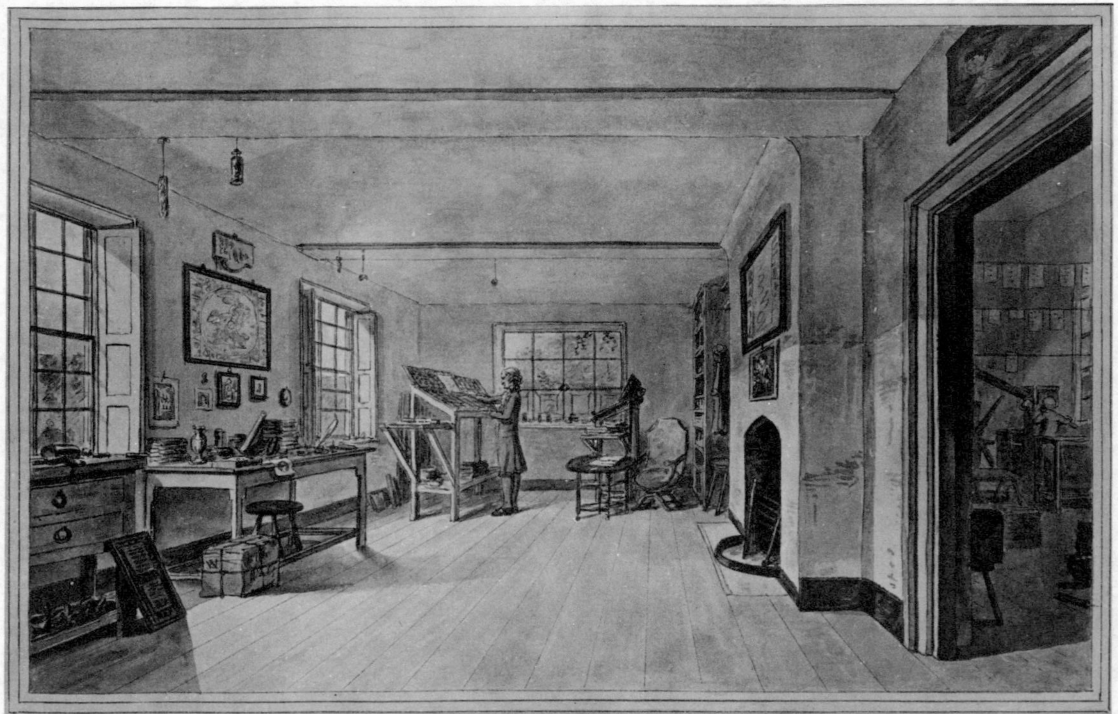

Inside of the PRINTING-HOUSE at Strawberry-hill.

THE PRINTING HOUSE AT STRAWBERRY HILL

believe one pitiful monk (if Hoveden[19] was a monk, for I vow I don't know), before all these great names and authorities?

To GROSVENOR BEDFORD, Wednesday 9 November 1757

Printed from Cunningham iii. 223 (misdated), where the letter was first printed. Reprinted, Toynbee iv. 261–2. The history of the MS and its present whereabouts are not known.

Cunningham placed the letter among those of May 1759, and by an oversight Mrs Toynbee allowed it to remain there in her edition. Her correction (Toynbee xvi. xxvi, n. 1) points out that the true date is established by the references to the setting-up of the SH Press in June 1757 and to McArdell's engraving of HW's portrait by Reynolds, also 1757. During the second half of 1757, the '9th' of the month occurs on a Wednesday only in November.

Strawberry Hill, Wednesday, 9th.

Dear Sir,

I MUST desire you will speak to Mr Tonson[1] to send me another parcel of paper for my printing, but I wish he would order it to be carefully examined, because in the last parcel there were several thin sheets interspersed. As I shall be in town the end of this week, I shall be glad if he would have the bills made up of the expenses of the press, etc. that I may pay them.[2]

I shall be much obliged too if you will call as soon as you can at M'Ardell's[3] in Henrietta Street, and take my picture from him.[4] I am extremely angry, for I heard he has told people of the print. If the plate is finished, be so good as to take it away, and all the impressions he has taken off, for I will not let him keep one. If it is not finished, I shall be most unwilling to leave the print with him. If he pretends he stays for the inscription, I will have nothing but these words, *Horace Walpole, youngest son of Sir Robert Walpole, Earl*

19. Roger of Hoveden (fl. 1174–1201), chronicler. Spence presumably refers to Hoveden's account of Richard I in *Rogeri Hovedeni Annalium pars prior, et posterior,* edited by Sir Henry Savile in his *Rerum anglicarum scriptores post Bedam praecipui,* 1596.

---

1. Jacob Tonson (d. 1767), bookseller. He, along with Dodsley, was HW's chief adviser in setting up the SH Press (CHUTE 98).

2. Although many of the bills connected with the Press are still with HW's *Journal of the Printing-Office,* now WSL, this bill is not among them.

3. James McArdell (ca 1729–65), engraver in mezzotint.

4. McArdell's engraving, dated 1757, was made from either the second (at Ragley) or third (at Bowood) version of the portrait by Reynolds (C. K. Adams and W. S. Lewis, 'The Portraits of Horace Walpole,' *Walpole Society* 1970, xlii. 15).

of Orford.[5] I must beg you will not leave it with him an hour, unless he locks it up, and denies to everybody there is any such thing. I am extremely provoked at him, and very sorry to give you so much trouble.

TO GROSVENOR BEDFORD, Saturday 26 November 1757

Printed from Cunningham iii. 118–19, where the letter was first printed. Reprinted, Toynbee iv. 114.

Dated by the reference to 'Monday next' (28 Nov.), when the verses enclosed in this letter appeared in the *Public Advertiser.*

Saturday.

Dear Sir,

I BEG you will get the enclosed stanzas inserted in the *Public Advertiser* on Monday next,[1] just as I have written them. If not in the *Public,* then in the *Daily Advertiser.* My name must not be mentioned, nor anything but the initial letters H. C.[2]

I am just going out of town, and shall not return till late on Wednesday. If you should have anything particular to say, write me a line to Strawberry.

Yours ever,

H. W.

5. The mezzotint, bearing the inscription as ordered by HW, is reproduced in COLE i. 64.

1. They were printed in the *Public Advertiser* of Monday, 28 Nov.

2. For Henry Conway, HW's cousin. The verses were prompted by criticisms of Conway for the failure of the expedition against Rochefort, which had been led by Sir John Mordaunt and himself. They vary slightly from those enclosed in HW to Conway ca 25 Nov. 1757 (CONWAY i. 522–3), where HW called the verses 'a most hasty performance, literally conceived and executed between Hammersmith and Hyde Park Corner.'

To Andrew Coltee Ducarel,[1] Sunday 25 December 1757

Printed from Nichols, *Lit. Anec.* iv. 700, where the letter was first printed. Reprinted, Cunningham iii. 120–1 (signature and part of closing omitted); Toynbee iv. 115–16. The history of the MS and its present whereabouts are not known.

Endorsed by Ducarel: Mr Horace Walpole, concerning the MS at Lambeth, which contains the only known illumination of King Edward V, etc., since engraved, by Mr Walpole in his *Royal and Noble Authors.*

Arlington Street, Dec. 25, 1757.

Sir,

THE Dean of Exeter[2] having showed me a letter in which you desire the name of the MS which contains the illumination I wished to see, I take the liberty of troubling you with this. The book is called, '*The Dictes and Sayings of the Philosophers; translated out of Latyn into Frenshe, by Messire Jehan de Teonville; and from thence rendered into English, by Earl Rivers.*'[3]—I am perfectly ashamed, Sir, of giving you so much trouble; but your extreme civility and good-nature, and your great disposition to assist anything that relates to literature, encouraged me to make my application to you; and the politeness with which you received it I shall always acknowledge with the greatest gratitude.—The Dean desired me to make his excuses to you for not writing himself; and my Lord Lyttelton returns you a thousand thanks for your kind offers of communication,[4] and proposes to wait on you himself, and talk those matters over with you. I shall not fail of paying my respects to you on Friday next, at one o'clock; and am, Sir,

Your most obliged and most obedient humble servant,

Hor. Walpole

1. (1713–85), D.C.L. (Oxon), 1742; antiquary; appointed Keeper of the Archiepiscopal Library at Lambeth Palace 3 May 1757.

2. Charles Lyttelton.

3. Mubashshir ibn Fātik, *The Dictes and Sayings of the Philosophers,* tr. Anthony Wydevill (ca 1440–83), 2d E. Rivers, from the French version of Guillaume de Tignonville (d. 1414), 1477; the first book published in England by William Caxton. HW used as the frontispiece to his *Royal and Noble Authors* the illumination of Rivers presenting the book to Edward IV; the plate was engraved by Grignion. The MS, a verbatim

To Andrew Coltee Ducarel, Thursday 12 January 1758

Printed from the MS now WSL. First printed in Nichols, *Lit. Anec.* iv. 700. Reprinted, Cunningham iii. 123–4 (closing and signature omitted); Toynbee iv. 120. The MS was sold Sotheby's 6 [9] Feb. 1865 (John Saintsbury Sale), lot 947, to John Dillon; resold Sotheby's 7 June 1869 (Dillon Sale), lot 638 (in an extra-illustrated set of Park's edition of HW's *Royal and Noble Authors,* 1806), to Ellis; resold Anderson Galleries Nov. 1912 (Hoe Sale, Pt VI), lot 3236, to George D. Smith; offered in his cat. [1914], lot 991; resold by E. Weyhe to WSL, 1937.

Endorsed by Ducarel: 12 Jan. 1758—Mr Hor. ‹Walpole› about the drawing represe‹nting Edward› IV & V etc. in the MS Li‹brary at› Lambeth—since engrav‹ed.› Frontispiece to his *Noble ‹Authors.›*

Address: To Dr Ducarel at Doctors Commons.

Arlington Street, Jan. 12th 1758.

Sir,

I HAVE the pleasure to let you know that his Grace the Archbishop[1] has with the greatest politeness and goodness sent me word by the Dean of Exeter[2] that he gives me leave to have the illumination[3] copied either at your chambers, or at my own house, giving you a receipt for it. As the former would be so inconvenient to me as to render this favour useless, I have accepted the latter with great joy, and will send a gentleman of the Exchequer, my own deputy,[4] to you, Sir, on Monday next with my receipt, and shall beg the favour of you to deliver the MS to him, Mr Bedford.

I would wait on you myself, but have caught cold at the visit I made you yesterday, and am besides going to Strawberry Hill, from whence I propose to bring for you a little print which was never sold,

copy of Caxton's printed edition of the *Dictes* published in Nov. 1477 and dated about six weeks later, belonged to Edward IV (M. R. James and Claude Jenkins, *Descriptive Catalogue of the Manuscripts in the Library of Lambeth Palace,* Cambridge, 1930, p. 412).

4. Presumably relating to Lyttleton's work on a life of Henry II (*ante* 30 Sept. 1754).

5. HW mentioned to George Montagu 20 April 1756 'the fruits of my last party to Strawberry; Dick Edgcumbe, George Selwyn and Williams were with me; we composed a coat of arms for the two clubs at White's' (MONTAGU i. 186). The design described by HW was engraved by Charles Grignion; it is reproduced in [W. B. Boulton,] *The History of White's,* 1892, i. 78.

---

1. Matthew Hutton (1693–1758), Abp of Canterbury, 13 April 1757

2. Charles Lyttelton. The letter is missing.

3. See previous letter.

4. Grosvenor Bedford.

and not to be had from anybody else, which is, the arms of the two clubs at Arthur's;[5] a print exceedingly in request last year. When I have more leisure, for at this time of the year I am much hurried, I shall be able, I believe, to pick you out some other curiosities, and am,

Sir

Your obedient servant

Hor. Walpole

From David Garrick, Monday 23 January 1758

Printed from a photostat of the MS in the Folger Shakespeare Library. First printed, Toynbee *Supp.* i. 87–8n. Reprinted, *The Letters of David Garrick,* ed. D. M. Little and G. M. Kahrl, Cambridge, Mass., 1963, i. 277–8. Damer-Waller; the MS was sold Sotheby's 5 Dec. 1921 (first Waller Sale), lot 128, to Quaritch; subsequently acquired by Folger.

The letter was dated 1757 by Garrick, but the reference to Hentzner's 'Itinerary' and HW's reply (*post* ca 24 Jan. 1758) establish the correct year as 1758. HW's MS draft of his reply is written on the verso of this letter.

Drury Lane Theatre, January 23, 175[8].

Dear Sir,

I HAVE taken the liberty to trouble you in behalf of Dryden Leach[1] the printer, a man to whom I have done some service, and who has ever behaved himself with the greatest integrity. I have been very uneasy at the offence which, he tells me, you think him guilty of, and therefore I have taken some pains to get at the bottom of it. I have now accomplished it, and when I have the pleasure of seeing you, I will tell you the particulars. The copy of the Itinerary,[2] that was made use of for the extracts in the Magazine,[3] was that you gave to *Lord Bath.*[4] I could wish that you would take no notice of

1. Master printer in London 1759–63; son and successor to Francis Leach, of Eliot's Court (H. R. Plomer, G. H. Bushnell, and E. R. McC. Dix, *A Dictionary of the Printers and Booksellers Who Were at Work in England . . . from 1726 to 1775,* Oxford, 1932, p. 151). He had large interests in several newspapers. For his arrest in 1763 on the false charge of publishing the *North Briton,* No. 45, see Mann vi. 188 n. 20.

2. *A Journey into England, by Paul Hentzner, in the Year 1598* had been printed at the SH Press in Oct. 1757 (Hazen, *SH Bibl.* 31).

3. *London Magazine* Dec. 1757, xxvi. 595–6, 631–2. All but one extract had appeared, also without HW's permission, in the *Monthly Review* Nov. 1757, xvii. 453–8.

4. William Pulteney (1684–1764), cr. (1742) E. of Bath. His copy of Hentzner's

this information till I have seen you, as there is something of consequence to a very ingenious young man[5] may depend upon it. Leach is very unhappy at his suffering so much in your opinion, and I assure you, that I would not have undertaken his justification had not I undeniable proofs of his innocence.

I am,

Dear Sir,

Your most obliged and most obedient humble servant,

D. GARRICK

PS. Our theatrical pens and paper are execrable: and I am now writing with the whole *dramatis personæ* about me.

TO DAVID GARRICK, ca Tuesday 24 January 1758

Printed from a photostat of the MS draft, written on the verso of the previous letter from Garrick to HW, now in the Folger Shakespeare Library. First printed, Toynbee *Supp.* i. 87–8. The whereabouts of the letter that went through the post is not known.

I COULD almost wish that Leach were in fault, that I might show you my readiness to comply with any request of yours, but I have no right to call it forgiving him when he is innocent.[1] He must forgive me. I had already heard that Mr Murphy was the person who hurried Hentznerus to the printer. Another time I should hope he would not be so eager to inflict upon me the honours of the Magazine. Your time is precious, even mine is much occupied, and therefore I will now only bid you good night.

Yours, etc.

Journey has not been located. Garrick had written John Hawkesworth ca Dec. 1757: 'I must desire you not to let Mr Walpole's book go out of your hands, for some friend has lent one of 'em to a printer, who has published several extracts from it, and given offence, to the honourable editor—therefore pray keep it to yourself' (*Letters of Garrick*, ed. Little and Kahrl, i. 271).

5. Arthur Murphy (1727–1805), author and actor (identified by HW's reply *post* ca 24 Jan. 1758).

1. HW's reasons for thinking that Leach had been involved in printing the unauthorized extracts from Hentzner's *Journey* are not known.

From SIR JOHN FIELDING,[1] March 1758

Printed from Toynbee *Supp.* iii. 147–8, where the letter was first printed. Damer-Waller; the MS was sold Sotheby's 5 Dec. 1921 (first Waller Sale), lot 98 (with Lady Brown to HW 28 Nov. 1756), to Dobell; *penes* A. R. Leslie-Melville in 1935; not further traced.

Endorsed by HW: From blind Justice Fielding, March 1758.

Address: To H. Warpool Esquire at his house in Arlinton Street.

Sir,

I WAS favoured with your obliging letter,[2] and as it is on the most interesting subject in the world, I sincerely wish the plan[3] could reap any advantage from my warmest endeavours, for it is an evil that reproaches our humanity, and its continuance reflects much on the good sense of this nation. I am pleased to think you have taken it in hand, and should be very glad to have the honour of a conference with you on the occasion, but shall leave this for your appointing. That the distresses of persecuted debtors[4] have not before now been relieved, is certainly not owing to want of humanity in general, but to the few to whom their distresses are known, for did not the reflections of the benevolent sometimes lead them into prisons, the cases of debtors would remain a secret to all, but their merciless prosecutors; that you may succeed in this work is the most ardent wish of, Sir,

Your most obedient and the public's faithful servant,

J. FIELDING

1. (1721–80), Kt, 1761; blind magistrate; half-brother of Henry Fielding.
2. Missing.
3. Presumably a scheme for the relief of debtors, but not further identified.
4. HW had been made aware of the distress of debtors by the cases of King Theodore of Corsica, imprisoned for debt in 1749, and of Richard Bentley, who was a fugitive for debt in 1753–6 (*ante* 23 Feb. 1753, nn. 2–3, and 24 June 1756, n. 2; MANN iv. 164 n. 10, 373–4).

TO CHARLES LYTTELTON, Thursday 23 March 1758

Printed from a photostat of the MS in the possession of Viscount Cobham, Hagley Hall, Stourbridge, Worcs. First printed in N&Q 1869, 4th ser., iii. 3. Reprinted, Toynbee iv. 129–30. The MS descended in the Lyttelton family to the present owner.

Strawberry Hill, March 23d 1758.

Dear Sir,

YOUR letter[1] found Mr Ward[2] here, and though a word from you would be strongest recommendation, his own quickness and knowledge had already made such way with me, that I cannot assume the merit of having liked him on any account but his own. I wish I had had more materials worth his notice; what he thought so, I have lent him.

Mr Whitworth[3] promised[4] to furnish me with the accounts I asked after Easter;[5] my haste is not immediate; if he is very dilatory, as I expect, I shall trouble you to quicken him again.[6] My own book is still likely to drag on for three weeks:[7] you may believe I shall transmit one of the first to you, less indeed from thinking it has any merit, than in hopes that you will send me your corrections, in case I should be obliged to make another edition from the faults of the first sketch.

Well! there is another Archbishop dead![8] will none of their deaths operate to your deanery?[9] Are you always to serve everybody, and are you never to be served? Must some future Mr Ward tell how much you promoted every work of learning, and yet how much

1. Missing.

2. Cæsar Ward (ca 1711–59), printer and bookseller (Robert Davies, *A Memoir of the York Press,* 1868, pp. 247–60; CHATTERTON 26 n. 10; MASON ii. 294 n. 17).

3. Probably Charles Whitworth (ca 1721–78), of Leybourne, Kent, and Blackford, Somerset; Kt, 1768; M.P. He was a nephew of Charles, 1st Bn Whitworth (1675–1725), and doubtless helped HW with the biographical account of his uncle in HW's advertisement to *An Account of Russia as it was in the Year 1710. By Charles Lord Whitworth,* SH, Sept. 1758 (Hazen, *SH Bibl.* 42).

4. Not in any recorded letter.

5. 26 March in 1758.

6. When Lyttelton 'quickened' him earlier is not known, nor why he was in a position to do so.

7. *A Catalogue of the Royal and Noble Authors of England* was finished by 15 April (Hazen, op. cit. 35).

8. Matthew Hutton, Abp of Canterbury, died 19 March 1758 (GM 1758, xxviii. 146).

9. Lyttelton had been Dean of Exeter since 1748. The 'yearly value' of the deanery in 1762 was £500 (*The Correspondence of King George the Third,* ed. Sir John Fortescue, 1927–8, i. 36).

the learned world lost by your not having greater power of being a patron? It is believed that *St Durham*[10] goes to Canterbury,[11] and St Asaph[12] follows him; I don't fancy St Asaph for you, but considering the ages of London[13] and Winchester,[14] can no regulation be made for you when those vacancies shall happen—why not get a promise? Cure your cough, be promised and be a Bishop[15]—so prays

Your affectionate Beadsman,

The Abbot of Strawberry

From Lord Royston,[1] ? late April 1758

Printed for the first time from the MS now wsl, acquired from Gabriel Wells in 1932; its earlier history is not known.

Dated conjecturally by the reference to HW's 'present' (see n. 2 below).

LORD Royston presents his compliments to Mr Walpole, and returns him many thanks for his most agreeable present,[2] and for the honour he has done him.

10. Richard Trevor (1707–71), Bp of Durham 1752–71. The value of the see was £6,000 a year (ibid.).

11. Thomas Secker (*post* 21 May 1758, n. 3), Bp of Oxford, became Abp of Canterbury 21 April 1758.

12. Robert Hay Drummond (1711–76), Bp of St Asaph, 1748; of Salisbury, June 1761; Abp of York, Oct. 1761. The value of the see of St Asaph was £1,400 a year (Fortescue, op. cit. i. 42).

13. Thomas Sherlock (1678–1761), Bp of London 1748–61. The value of the see was £4,000 a year (ibid. i.38).

14. Benjamin Hoadley (1676–1761), Bp of Winchester 1734–61. The value of the see was £5,000 a year (ibid. i. 41).

15. Lyttelton became Bp of Carlisle in 1762, at £1,300 a year (ibid. i. 35), but never advanced to a more lucrative see.

1. Philip Yorke (1720–90), styled Vct Royston 1754–64; 2d E. of Hardwicke, 1764; M.P.

2. Possibly a presentation copy of HW's *Catalogue of the Royal and Noble Authors of England,* which he finished printing at the SH Press on 15 April 1758 (Hazen, *SH Bibl.* 35).

To the DUKE of DEVONSHIRE,[1] Monday 24 April 1758

Printed for the first time from a photostat of the MS at Chatsworth House, Derbyshire, kindly furnished by the Duke of Devonshire.

Dated by the King's move to Kensington on 26 April.

Endorsed in an unidentified hand: April 24, 1758.

Arlington Street, Monday night.

My Lord,

I AM ashamed to trouble your Grace with a trifling request, but which will oblige me much if you will be so good as to grant it. It is to give me an order to the Housekeeper[2] of Kensington Palace to let me see the Queen's closet and stay as long as I please. As the King is to go to Kensington on Wednesday,[3] I should be glad to have this permission tomorrow morning; it is particularly to see a picture by Holbein of Lord Vaux,[4] one of the noble authors with whom I troubled you, and on whose account I am sorry your Grace thought it necessary to call here today; they did not deserve so much honour.

I am my Lord

Your Grace's most obedient humble servant

HOR. WALPOLE

1. William Cavendish (1720–64), 4th D. of Devonshire, 1755; lord chamberlain of the Household 1757–62.

2. Mrs Jane Keene (d. 1762) (*Court and City Register,* 1758, p. 77; GM 1762, xxxii. 46).

3. 'Yesterday, at one o'clock, his Majesty and the Royal family removed from St James's to Kensington for the summer' (*Daily Adv.,* Thursday, 27 April 1758).

4. Nicholas Vaux (ca 1460–1523), cr. (1523) Bn Vaux; see HW's *Catalogue of the Royal and Noble Authors,* SH, 1758, i. 66–8. The picture of him is No. 17 in 'A Catalogue of the Pictures, Drawings, Limnings, Enamels, Models in Wax, and the Ivory Carvings, etc. at Kensington, in Queen Caroline's Closet, next the State Bedchamber' (George Bickham, *Deliciæ Britannicæ,* 2d edn, [?1755], p. 33; see also *A Catalogue of the Pictures and Drawings in the Closet of the late Queen Caroline,* 1758, p. 2).

To the Rev. Thomas Birch,[1] Thursday 4 May 1758

Printed from a photostat of the MS in the BM (Add. MS 4320, f. 99). First printed, Wright iii. 351. Reprinted, Cunningham iii. 133; Toynbee iv. 133 (closing and signature omitted in Wright, Cunningham, and Toynbee). The MS was among the Birch papers bequeathed to the BM on his death in 1766.

Address: To the Reverend Dr Birch in Norfolk Street. *Postmark:* PENNY POST PAID. The name 'Hinton' on the back is possibly that of a postal carrier.

Arlington Street, May 4th 1758.

Sir,

I THOUGHT myself very unlucky in being abroad, when you was so good as to call here t'other day. I not only lost the pleasure of your company, but the opportunity of obtaining from you (what however I will not despair of) any remarks you may have made on the many errors which I fear you found in my book.[2] The hurry in which it was written, my natural carelessness and insufficience must have produced many faults and mistakes. As the curiosity of the world, raised I believe only by the smallness of the number printed, makes it necessary for me to provide another edition,[3] I should be much obliged to whoever would be enough my friend to point out my wrong judgments and inaccuracies—I know nobody, Sir, more capable of both offices than yourself, and yet I have no pretensions to ask so great a favour,[4] unless your own zeal for the cause of literature should prompt you to undertake a little of this task. I shall be always ready to correct my faults, never to defend them. I am Sir

Your most obedient servant

Hor. Walpole

1. (1705–66), antiquary and divine; secretary of the Royal Society 1752–65.

2. *A Catalogue of the Royal and Noble Authors of England,* which HW had written in less than five months in 1757 (HW's 'Short Notes,' Gray i. 29).

3. 300 copies were completed at the SH Press by 15 April 1758; an edition of 2,000 copies was published by Dodsley, dated 1759 (Hazen, *SH Bibl.* 35–6).

4. HW wrote Birch *post* 8 July 1758: 'As you have been so good as to favour me with your assistance, I flatter myself you will excuse my begging it once more.'

To Andrew Coltee Ducarel, Sunday 21 May 1758

Printed from the MS now wsl. First printed, Nichols, *Lit. Anec.* iv. 700–1 (misdated 'June, 1758'). Reprinted, Wright iii. 358; Cunningham iii. 139 (signature omitted in Wright and Cunningham); Toynbee iv. 142 (likewise misdated); Toynbee *Supp.* iii. 1. The MS was owned by Mrs Drage, of Rodd Court, Presteigne, in 1925; *penes* Mrs Radford, of Hampstead, 1936; sold Sotheby's 16 Nov. 1943 (property of Mrs Radford), lot 181, to Maggs for wsl.

The date-line in the MS is now partially torn away, but is supplied from Dr Toynbee's text.

Endorsed by Ducarel: Mr Horace Walpole. Thanks for my MS observations on his *Anecdotes of Paintings.*[1]

〈Strawberry Hill, May 21,〉 1758.

Sir,

I AM very much obliged to you for the remarks and hints you have sent me on my *Catalogue;*[2] they will be of use to me; and any observations of my friends I shall be very thankful for and disposed to employ, to make my book, what it is extremely far from being, more perfect.

I was very glad to hear, Sir, that the present Lord Archbishop of Canterbury[3] has continued you in an employment,[4] for which nobody is so fit, and in which nobody would be so useful. I wish all manner of success to, as well as continuance of, your labours and am Sir

Your obedient humble servant

Hor. Walpole

1. An error for *Catalogue of the Royal and Noble Authors* (see following note). Since *Anecdotes of Painting* was not published until 15 Feb. 1762, the endorsement must have been made after that date.

2. *Of the Royal and Noble Authors.* Ducarel's letter is missing.

3. Thomas Secker (1693–1768), confirmed as Abp of Canterbury 21 April 1758.

4. On 3 May 1757 Abp Hutton had appointed Ducarel keeper of the archiepiscopal library at Lambeth Palace, a post he held until his death in 1785.

TO DAVID MALLET,[1] Sunday 21 May 1758

Printed for the first time from the MS now WSL. The MS was presumably acquired by John Murray, the publisher of HW's *Memoires . . . of George II,* 1822; owned in 1936 by his descendant, Sir John Murray, of 50 Albemarle Street, London; sold Sotheby's 11 May 1970 (property of Sir John Murray), lot 226, to Seven Gables for WSL.

Strawberry Hill, May 21st 1758.

Dear Sir,

I AM extremely obliged to you for the trouble you have given yourself on my account, and thank you for the papers[2] you sent to my house. I don't know whether it would not be proper for me to acknowledge the civility I have received from the Governors of the Museum:[3] if it is customary, you will be so good as to tell me, for I would not be wanting in any respect to them, nor yet trouble them unnecessarily. I shall be in town on Thursday, and if you would have me write a few lines to Dr Maty,[4] be so good as to let me have a note from you, if it is not too much to ask you to call in Arlington Street on so idle an affair, but I hope you see that I am glad to catch at any opportunity of assuring you how much I am

Sir

Your obliged and obedient humble servant

HOR. WALPOLE

1. (ca 1705–65), Scottish poet, playwright, and miscellaneous writer.

2. Possibly materials for the second edition of HW's *Catalogue of the Royal and Noble Authors.* HW wrote Henry Zouch 12 Jan. 1759 that Mallet had contributed a story about Lord Suffolk (CHATTERTON 25).

3. The British Museum, established in 1753.

4. Matthew Maty (1718–76), at this time under-librarian and keeper of the printed books in the BM; principal librarian, 1772. No letters from HW to him have been found; one from him to HW was sold SH vi. 128 to Sir William Heygate (not further traced).

From CÆSAR WARD,[1] Wednesday 7 June 1758

Printed from the MS now WSL. First printed, Toynbee *Supp.* iii. 148–50. Damer-Waller; the MS was sold Sotheby's 5 Dec. 1921 (first Waller Sale), lot 193, to Wells; given by him to Thomas Conolly, of Chicago, from whom WSL acquired it in 1937.

York, 7 June [17]58.

Sir,

IN ORDER to clear up the point in question, I beg leave to begin with your postscript.[2] That Lord Herbert of Chepstow[3] had a seat in the H[ouse] of Lords, the 20th of May 1642, is matter of conjecture: that he had not, I think, is matter of evidence: because

1. At the beginning of the 9th volume of *Parliamentary History,* is a very accurate account of the state of the peerage,[4] but no mention made therein of L[ord] Herbert of Chepstow (for so he was styled by the Parliament who allowed the validity of no honours granted by the King after the Lord Keeper Littleton[5] had carried off the Great Seal, in May 1642), nor is it at all likely that, at such a time of jealousy, the King would have summoned him to Parliament, both his father[6] and himself being notoriously avowed Papists.

2. In Dugdale's *Summons*[7] a catalogue is given of all the peers summoned to the Long Parliament, and though there were 14 Earls' eldest sons called up by their fathers' baronies, yet Lord Herbert of Chepstow's name is not to be found there.

1. (ca 1711–59), printer and bookseller (*ante* 23 March 1758, n. 2).

2. HW's (missing) letter to Ward evidently concerned the forthcoming second edition of his *Catalogue of the Royal and Noble Authors.*

3. Edward Somerset (ca 1603–67), styled Lord Herbert 1628–45 and E. of Glamorgan 1645–6; 2d M. of Worcester, 1646. He is included in *Royal and Noble Authors,* SH, 1758, i. 207–15.

4. 'A State of the Peerage at this Time [1640,]' in *The Parliamentary or Constitutional History of England . . . from the earliest Times to the Restoration of King Charles II,* 1751–61, ix. 1–11. HW's copy is Hazen, *Cat. of HW's Lib.,* No. 1596. He used it extensively in his 'Book of Materials,' 1759.

5. Edward Littleton (1589–1645), cr. (1641) Bn Lyttelton of Mounslow; lord keeper, 1641.

6. Henry Somerset (ca 1576–1646), styled Lord Herbert 1598–1604; summoned to Parliament as Lord Herbert 1604; 5th E. of Worcester, 1628; cr. (1642) M. of Worcester. He is mentioned in *Parl. Hist.* ix. 2, 'Henry Somerset, Earl of Worcester, Lord Herbert of Chepstow,' as taking part with the King against the Parliament; see also ibid. ix. 9.

7. Sir William Dugdale, *A Perfect Copy of all Summons of the Nobility to the Great Councils and Parliaments of this Realm,* 1685, pp. 561–2.

3. In Dugdale's *Baronage*,[8] vol. 2, Lord Herbert of Cherbury[9] is spoke of as a person zealously attached to the King[10]—but neither in his nor Collins's *Baronage*,[11] is any mention of Lord Glamorgan's being called up *vitâ patris*.

Thus much may, perhaps, be sufficient to evince that there were not two Lord Herberts in the House, when this offensive speech was made there;[12] and consequently etc.

The ascribing this speech to Lord H[erbert] of C[hirbury] in the *Parliamentary History* and censure thereupon, is founded upon the Lords Journals; and the reason why no authority is cited for it, is because the work itself is an abstract of the Journals, unless where other vouchers are cited. Add to this, that in the 13th volume of *Parliamentary History*, p. 49, is a letter from the Lords who joined the King at Oxford, and formed the convention there, to the Scots Privy Council,[13] wherein it is affirmed that *not one recusant had signed that letter*,[14] and yet there is a *Lord Herbert's name among the subscribers* to it, which could be no other than Cherbury for the reasons before given.[15]

In opposition to this Whitlocke,[16] Ant[hony] Wood,[17] and *General Dictionary*[18] are produced. And upon comparing the assertion of the first of them (for the other two are copiers only, and therefore

8. *The Baronage of England*, 3 vols in 2, 1675–6.

9. Edward Herbert (1583–1648), cr. (1629) Bn Herbert of Chirbury, co. Salop. He is included in *Royal and Noble Authors* i. 188–92.

10. Dugdale writes that he was 'no less ready to serve his sovereign, than his noble father and grandfather ever really did.' He manifested 'his true loyalty unto his now Majesty King Charles the Second' by his efforts to have the King restored to the throne (*Baronage of England*, iii. 262).

11. Arthur Collins, *The English Baronage*, 1727.

12. HW's note on this speech in the 2d edn of *Royal and Noble Authors* is quoted in n. 21 below; see also HW to Henry Zouch 3 Aug. 1758 (CHATTERTON 5).

13. 'A Letter from the Lords at Oxford to the Scots Privy Council, touching their Expedition into England, and showing how few Peers were left at Westminster,' *Parl. Hist.* xiii. 49–52.

14. 'Whereas the House of Peers consists of above an hundred, besides minors and recusant lords, neither of which keep us company in this address to your Lordships' (ibid. xiii. 50).

15. This 'Herbert' was doubtless Edward Somerset, Lord Herbert of Chepstow, and not Lord Herbert of Chirbury who remained neutral during the civil wars.

16. Sir Bulstrode Whitelocke (1605–75), in *Memorials of the English Affairs*, 1682. HW did not have a copy of this work.

17. Anthony à Wood (1632–95), in *Athenæ Oxonienses*, 2 vols, 1691–2. HW's copy, now WSL, is Hazen, op. cit., No. 584.

18. Pierre Bayle's *General Dictionary*, tr. J. P. Bernard, Thomas Birch *et al.*, 10 vols, 1734–41. HW's copy is ibid., No. 2039. HW's Commonplace Book, 1750 (now WSL), contains many extracts from Bayle.

all three make but one evidence) with the Commons Journals, of 25 Feb. 1644/5, p. 62, col. 1, I find that Lord Herbert of Cherbury had a weekly allowance voted him of £20 for *his present subsistence,*[19] but without any mention of *his having been spoiled by the King's forces,* which is Whitlocke's own addition.[20] There is no doubt, however, of his *then* having left the royal party.

Thus, Sir, it appears to me, that the evidence of Lord Herbert's being a Royalist and being a Parliamentarian, stands upon an equal footing. Now, as the letter, to the Scots Privy Council above cited, bears date in February 1643/4, which is a whole year prior to the vote of the Parliament in his favour, the obvious conclusion seems to me [to] be this, that his Lordship, like many other well-intentioned peers and commoners, finding the King's designs, upon a nearer examination, to be subversive of the liberties of their country, determined to leave him, and join the Parliament, and that in consequence thereof he might suffer so much from the Cavaliers, as to induce the Commons to take him into their protection.[21]

I fear this long epistle will make you repent your having raised so troublesome a correspondent; and, in hopes of your pardon, I beg leave to subscribe myself,

Sir,

Your most obliged humble servant,

CÆSAR WARD

19. 'Resolved, etc. That twenty pounds per week shall be allowed unto the Lord Cherbury for his present subsistence' (*Journals of the House of Commons* iv. 62).

20. 'An Allowance was given to the Lord Herbert of Cherbury, for his livelihood, having been spoiled by the King's forces' (Whitelocke, op. cit. 129).

21. 'In the *Parliamentary History* it is said that Lord Herbert offended the House of Lords by a speech in behalf of the King, and that he attended his Majesty at York. Yet the very next year, on a closer insight into the spirit of that party, he quitted them, and was a great sufferer in his fortune from their vengeance' (HW's note in the 2d edn of *Royal and Noble Authors* i. 214).

TO LORD LYTTELTON, Sunday 25 June 1758

Printed from *Memoirs and Correspondence of George, Lord Lyttelton,* ed. Robert Phillimore, 1845, ii. 576–7, where the letter (misdated 'June 20th 1758') was first printed. Reprinted, Cunningham iii. 145 (closing and signature omitted); Toynbee iv. 150 (likewise misdated in both). The MS was sold Sotheby's 27 Feb. 1882 (Valuable Collection of Autograph Letters Sale), lot 170, to Doeg; not further traced.

Dated by the description of the MS in the Sotheby's auction catalogue cited above, which is corroborated by HW to H. S. Conway 16 June 1758 (see n. 2 below).

Strawberry Hill, June 2[5]th 1758.

My Lord,

I WAS unluckily at Park Place[1] when your Lordship sent to my house in town; and I more unluckily still left Park Place the very day your Lordship was expected there.[2] I twice waited on you in Hill Street,[3] to thank you for the great favour of lending me your history,[4] which I am sorry I kept longer than you intended; but you must not wonder. I read it with as great attention as pleasure: it is not a book to skim, but to learn by heart, if one means to learn anything of England—you call it the history of Henry II. It is literally the history of our constitution, and will last much longer than I fear the latter will; for alas! my Lord, your style, which will fix and preserve our language, cannot do what language cannot do, reform the nature of man. I beg to know whither I shall send this book, too valuable to be left in a careless manner with a servant. I repeat my warmest thanks, and am, my Lord,

Your Lordship's much obliged,

and most obedient humble servant,

HOR. WALPOLE

1. The seat of HW's cousin Henry Seymour Conway, near Henley.

2. HW wrote Conway 16 June 1758: 'The Churchills will be with you next Wednesday [21 June], and I believe I too; . . . I must be back at Strawberry on Friday night' (CONWAY i. 537).

3. Lyttelton's house in Berkeley Square.

4. The printing of Lyttelton's *History of the Life of King Henry the Second* was apparently proceeding while the work was being written, since the four volumes were not published until 1767–71 (*ante* 30 Sept. 1754, n. 5, and 31 Aug. 1757).

To the Rev. Thomas Birch, Saturday 8 July 1758

Printed from a photostat of the MS in the British Museum (Add. MS 4320, f. 101). First printed, Wright iii. 368. Reprinted, Cunningham iii. 147; Toynbee iv. 153–4 (closing and signature omitted in all three editions). The MS was among the Birch papers bequeathed to the BM on his death in 1766.

Address: To the Reverend Dr Birch in Norfolk Street.

Arlington Street, July 8th 1758.

Sir,

As you have been so good as to favour me with your assistance,[1] I flatter myself you will excuse my begging it once more. I am told that you mentioned to Dr Jortin,[2] a Lord Mountjoy[3] who lived in the reign of Henry VIII, as an author. Will you be so good as to tell me anything you know of him and what he wrote. I shall entreat the favour of this notice as soon as possibly you can, because my book[4] is printing off and I am afraid of being past the place where he must come in. I am just going out of town, but a line put into the post any night before nine o'clock, will find me next morning at Strawberry Hill.

I am Sir

Your obliged humble servant

Hor. Walpole

1. See *ante* 4 May 1758.

2. John Jortin (1698–1770), critic and historian; author of *The Life of Erasmus,* 2 vols. 1758–60.

3. William Blount (ca 1478–1534), 4th Bn Mountjoy, 1485. Erasmus dedicated his *Adages* to him and he addressed three Latin letters to Erasmus. Two of Mountjoy's letters to Henry VIII are printed in Samuel Bentley's *Excerpta historica,* 1831, pp. 286–9.

4. The 2d edn of *Royal and Noble Authors.* HW did not include Mountjoy in it.

TO DAVID HUME,[1] Saturday 15 July 1758

Printed from a photostat of the MS in the possession of the Royal Society of Edinburgh, furnished through the good offices of Mr W. H. Rutherford. First printed in *Letters of Eminent Persons addressed to David Hume,* ed. J.H. Burton, 1849, pp. 1–6. Reprinted, Cunningham iii. 150–3; Toynbee iv. 158–62. The MS was among Hume's papers which passed to his nephew, David Hume, the younger, who bequeathed them to the Royal Society of Edinburgh on his death in 1839.

Strawberry Hill, July 15th 1758.

Sir,

IT IS impossible to trouble my Lady Hervey[2] with transcribing what I wish to say[3] in answer to your kind objections to a very few passages in my *Catalogue:*[4] yet as I cannot deny myself the pleasure and indeed the duty of making some reply to such undeserved civilities from a gentleman of your abilities, you must excuse me, Sir, if I take the liberty of addressing my letter directly to you. It is, I assure you neither with vanity nor presumption: even your flattery, Sir, cannot make me forget the distance between the author of the best history of England[5] and a compiler of English writers. Were it known what countenance I have received from men of such talents as Mr Hume and Sir David Dalrymple,[6] I should with reason be suspected of partiality to Scotland—What I did say of your country,[7] Sir, was dictated by conviction, before the least selfishness or gratitude could have biased me.

I must premise, Sir, that what I am going to say is not directly to defend what you criticize; it is rather an explanation which I owe to such criticisms, and to apologize for not correcting my work in consequence of your remarks; but unhappily for me, the greater part

1. (1711–76), philosopher and historian.

2. Mary Lepell (1700–68), m. (1720) John, Lord Hervey of Ickworth; HW's correspondent.

3. That is, she would have kept HW's letter and sent Hume a copy of it.

4. *Of the Royal and Noble Authors,* SH, 1758. Hume's letter to Lady Hervey with his 'objections' is missing.

5. *The History of England,* 6 vols, 1754–62. The first two volumes were published in 1754–7. HW's copy is Hazen, *Cat. of HW's Lib.,* No. 3328. For his candid opinion of Hume as a historian ('that superficial mountebank') see *post* 27 Oct. 1783.

6. (1726–92), 3d Bt, 1751; lord of session as Lord Hailes, 1776; jurist and antiquary; HW's correspondent.

7. In the introduction to the Scottish section of *Royal and Noble Authors* ii. 182.

of your notes regard passages in pages already printed off for the future edition. I will touch them in order.

I perceive by what you and others have said to me, Sir, that the freedom I have taken with Sir Philip Sidney,[8] is what gives most offence: yet I think if my words are duly weighed, it will be found that my words are too strong, rather than my argument weak. I say, *when we at this distance of time inquire what prodigious merits excited such admiration.* What admiration? why, that all the learned of Europe praised him, all the poets of England lamented his death, the republic of Poland thought of him for their king.[9] I allow Sir Philip great valour, and, from some of his performances good sense; but, dear Sir, compare his talents with the admiration they occasioned, and that in no unlettered, no unpolished age, and can we at this distance help wondering at the vastness of his character? Allowing as much sense to Sir Philip as his warmest admirers can demand for him, surely this country has produced many men of far greater abilities who have by no means met with a proportionate share of applause. It were a vain parade to name them—take Lord Bacon[10] alone, who I believe of all our writers except Newton[11] is most known to foreigners, and to whom Sir Philip was a puny child in genius, how far was he from attaining an equal degree of fame and honour? To say the truth, I attribute the great admiration of Sir Philip Sidney to his having so much merit and learning for a man of his rank;[12]

> *Rarus enim fermè sensus communis in illâ*
> *Fortunâ*—[13]

Indeed, Sir, if your good sense and philosophy did not raise you above being blinded, I should suspect that you had conceived still

8. In his article on Sir Fulke Greville, Lord Brooke, the biographer of Sir Philip Sidney (1554–86), in *Royal and Noble Authors* i. 163–6.

9. 'So that whereas (through the fame of his high deserts) he was then [1586], or rather before, in election for the crown of Poland, the Queen of England refused to further his advancement, not out of emulation, but out of fear to lose the jewel of her times' (Anthony à Wood, *Athenæ Oxonienses,* 2d edn, 1721, i. 227).

10. Francis Bacon (1561–1626).

11. Isaac Newton (1642–1727).

12. He was the eldest son of Sir Henry Sidney (1529–86), K.G., 1564, by Mary, dau. of John Dudley, D. of Northumberland; his uncle was Robert Dudley, cr. (1564) E. of Leicester. He was knighted in Jan. 1583 to represent John Casimir, Count Palatine of the Rhine, at his installation by proxy as Knight of the Garter, no one of lower rank than a knight-bachelor being allowed this honour (Elias Ashmole, *The Institution . . . of the most noble Order of the Garter,* 1672, pp. 436, 438; J. M. Osborn, *Young Philip Sidney 1572–1577,* New Haven, 1972, p. 509).

13. 'For in that station of life concern for others is usually rare indeed' (Juvenal, *Satires* viii. 73).

more undeserved esteem, from the same surprise, for another author, who is the only one, that by being compared with Sir Philip Sidney, could make me think the latter a very great man. I have already thrown in a note[14] to illustrate my argument, and to excuse myself to some gentlemen who thought that I had not paid attention enough to Sir Philip's *Defence of Poesy*—but whether one or two particular tracts are a little better or not than I have represented his general writings, it does not affect the scope of my reasoning, the whole result of which is, as I said, that he was not a great man in proportion to his fame.

I will not be equally diffuse in my defence of the character of Lord Falkland;[15] the same kind of answer must serve for that too. The greatest part of page 194,[16] was intended as an answer to your objection, Sir, as I apprehended it would be made. When the King originally and the patriots subsequently had drawn upon their country all the violences of a civil war, it might be just abstractedly, but I think was not right for the consequences it might have, to consider that the King was become the party aggrieved. I cannot but be of opinion that assisting an oppressed king is in reality helping him to tyranny. It is the nature of man and power not to be content with being restored to their due and former rights. And however illegal and tyrannous the conduct of a victorious Parliament may be, I should think it more likely to come to its rational senses, than a victorious king—perhaps mine are principles rather than arguments—On the coolest examination of myself and of the history of these times, I think I should have been one of the last to have had recourse to arms, because an encroaching prince can never take such strides as a triumphant one, but I should have been one of the last too to lay them down for the reasons I have given you. As to the trifling affair of the clean shirt,[17] it was Whitlocke,[18] as I have quoted

14. *Royal and Noble Authors*, 2d edn, i. 183n (*Works* i. 342).

15. Lucius Cary (1610–43), 2d Vct Falkland, 1633.

16. Of the second volume. HW's argument begins on p. 193 (*Works* i. 501–2): 'It is certain that the ingenious Mr Hume has shown that both King James and King Charles acted upon precedents of prerogative which they found established —yet will this neither justify them nor Lord Falkland.'

17. 'His putting on a clean shirt to be killed in, is no proof of sense either in his Lordship, or in the historian, who thought it worth relating' (*Royal and Noble Authors* ii. 195).

18. Bulstrode Whitelocke, in *Memorials of the English Affairs*, new edn, 1732, p. 73: 'the Lord Falkland, secretary of state, in the morning of the fight, called for a clean shirt, and being asked the reason of it, answered, *that if he were slain in the battle, they should not find his body in foul linen*.'

him, page 195, and not Lord Clarendon[19] that mentioned it; and I was glad it was Whitlocke, to show that I equally blamed the republican and royalist writers for thinking Lord Falkland of consequence enough to have every little circumstance relating to him recorded.

For the transaction of the King and Glamorgan,[20] I must own Sir you have helped me to a strong argument against the King which I had overlooked, as I had another, which I have mentioned in my new edition,[21] though a fault not equally culpable, in my opinion,—the indulgences granted to the Catholics. If the argument I have proposed in the note, page 213[22] does not seem a strong one to you for the reality of Glamorgan's commission, I might use more words but I fear without conveying more conviction.

The reference to the *General Dictionary*[23] was certainly wrong, though too late for me now to correct. Instead of vol. 3, page 359, I ought to have referred to vol. 10, page 76,[23a] where, if not a new or satisfactory account, is at least so long a discussion, that I should have thought myself unpardonable to repeat it, as I had nothing new to offer on either side of the question. But, Sir, this is only a single and a slight mistake in comparison of the many which I fear still remain. As my work has been so fortunate to find some favour, it would look like a boast to mention how rapidly it was compiled and composed,[24] and I must waive my truest apology rather than plead it with an air of arrogance.

But now, Sir, though I can a little defend myself against myself, what sort of apology shall I use for the liberty I have taken with you?

19. Edward Hyde (1609–74), cr. (1660) Bn Hyde and (1661) E. of Clarendon; in his *History of the Rebellion and Civil Wars in England,* Oxford, 1702–7, ii. 270–7, he eulogizes Lord Falkland.

20. By which the Earl of Glamorgan was empowered to raise an army of Irish rebels and foreign Catholics for the assistance of Charles I ([Thomas Birch], *An Inquiry into the Share, which King Charles I had in the Transactions of the Earl of Glamorgan,* 2d edn, 1756, pp. 14–26; Irish Manuscripts Commission, *Commentarius Rinuccinianus . . . 1645–1649,* Dublin, 1932–49, i. 545–8).

21. *Royal and Noble Authors,* 2d edn, i. 236n.

22. 'If the Earl had abused the King's powers before, how came his Majesty to trust him again? To trust him with blank powers? And of a nature so unknown? The House of Lords did not question the reality of the second commission, which yet was more incredible than the former; especially if the former had been forged' (*Royal and Noble Authors* i. 213n).

23. Compiled by Pierre Bayle (*ante* 7 June 1758, n. 18). HW's copy is Hazen, *Cat. of HW's Lib.,* No. 2039. The references to pages in vols 3 and 10 are to a discussion of Charles I's authorship of *Icon Basilike.*

23a. HW included this reference in *Royal and Noble Authors,* 2d edn, i. 47n.

24. 'In less than five months' (HW's 'Short Notes,' Gray i. 29).

a liberty which you have reprimanded in the genteelest though severest manner, by your gentle observations on a work so faulty as mine. When you allow that I am at all justifiable in mistaking your sense, I must not retract, and therefore I will only say that the words *conduct much more natural could not however, procure Lord Halifax*[25] *the character of integrity,*[26] did seem to me to say that though his trimming more probably flowed from integrity than policy, *yet* it could not attain the reputation of the former. In general too I must own that you seemed to make him figure as a more considerable minister than I had thought him—for thus, Sir, one compares one's own scanty and superficial reading with the study of an historian who has long and diligently weighed every circumstance. All men are not fortunate like me to write from slight knowledge and then to be examined with the mildest good nature by men far more able and better informed!

I am sensible, Sir, that I have transgressed all bounds—I meant to thank you, and to explain myself; instead of that, I have wearied you, while I was amusing myself with the pleasure of talking to a man whose works I have so long admired.

I am Sir

Your much obliged and most obedient humble servant

HOR. WALPOLE

25. George Savile (1633–95), cr. (1682) M. of Halifax.

26. HW began his account of Halifax: 'A man more remarkable for his wit than his steadiness, and whom an ingenious modern historian has erected into a principal character in the reign of Charles the Second.' On 'modern' HW added this note: 'Mr Hume; who observes that the Marquis's variations might be the effects of his integrity, rather than of his ambition. They might; but it is doubtful' (*Royal and Noble Authors* ii. 86). HW did not alter the text or note in later editions (*Works* i. 420).

From DAVID HUME, Wednesday 2 August 1758

Printed from the MS now WSL. First printed, Toynbee *Supp.* iii. 151–3. Reprinted in *The Letters of David Hume,* ed. J. Y. T. Greig, Oxford, 1932, i. 284–5. Damer-Waller; the MS was sold Sotheby's 5 Dec. 1921 (first Waller Sale), lot 149, bought in; resold Christie's 15 Dec. 1947 (second Waller Sale), lot 18, to Maggs for WSL.

Edinburgh, 2d August 1758.

Sir,

I WAS very agreeably surprised, in returning from a jaunt in the country, to find the letter,[1] with which you had honoured me. I did not indeed entertain any doubt of your patience of criticism.[2] Those who are to reach great beauties, are seldom reluctant to hear of small faults. But a man must be endowed with some qualities, even above those of a good writer, and have these too fortified by education in the best company, to regard a criticism as an obligation, and to take thence an opportunity of commencing a friendly correspondence with the person, who had presumed to censure his writings.

I should be ashamed, after you had set me so good an example, not to make you acknowledgments for the remark, which you have made[3] on my negligence in not quoting my authorities. I own that I was so much the less excusable for not taking this precaution, that such an exactness would have cost no trouble; and it would have been easy for me, after I had noted and marked all the passages, on which I founded my narration, to write the references on the margin. But I was seduced by the example of all the best historians even among the moderns, such as Matchiavel,[4] Fra Paolo,[5] Davila,[6]

1. *Ante* 15 July 1758.

2. Of HW's *Catalogue of the Royal and Noble Authors,* SH, 1758.

3. In *Royal and Noble Authors* ii. 87, which continues HW's 'character' of Halifax: 'But when old histories are re-written, it is necessary to set persons and facts in new lights from what they were seen by cotemporaries. Voltaire, speaking of Dupleix, says, that he was the first who introduced the custom of quoting his authorities in the margin, "précaution absolument necessaire, quand on n'écrit pas l'histoire de son temps." However, the dictator of this sentence, and author of that beautiful essay on universal history, has totally forgot his own rule, and has indeed left that work a most charming bird's-eye landscape, where one views the whole in picturesque confusion, and imagines the objects more delightful than they are in reality, and when examined separately.'

4. Niccolò Machiavelli (1469–1527), author of *Istorie fiorentine,* Florence, 1532.

Bentivoglio;[7] without considering that that practice was more modern than their time, and having been once introduced, ought to be followed by every writer. And though it be easy for the falsest and most partial historian to load his margin with quotations, nor is there any other certain method of assuring one's self of the fidelity of an author than to read most of the original writers of any period; yet the reader has reason to expect that the most material facts, at least all such as are any way new, should be supported by the proper authorities. I am preparing for the press a new volume of history, from the commencement of Henry VII to the union of the two Crowns;[8] and have there been very careful to obviate this objection.

At the same time, that I submit to this censure, I hope, Sir, you will permit me to reclaim[9] against another sentiment, which you have rather insinuated than advanced; as if it were superfluous to re-write the English history, or publish on that subject anything which has ever before in any shape appeared in print. If no man is to know the English story but by perusing all those monuments, which remain of it, few will be able to attain that useful and agreeable erudition. The original books, which instruct us in the reign of Queen Elizabeth alone, would require six months reading at the rate of ten hours a day; and most people, even after taking all this pains, would attain but a very confused idea of the transactions of that period. But what must foreigners do to get some notion of our history? What must posterity, after these monuments have farther multiplied upon us? What must the far greatest part of ourselves, who have neither leisure nor inclination for such a laborious and disagreeable study? To allege therefore the number of historical monuments against composing a history seems not much better founded, than if one should give it as a reason for not building a house, that he lay near a quarry. Though my writings should fail of convincing the world of the propriety of this attempt, I am persuaded, Sir, that if your leisure permitted you to undertake such a

5. Paolo Sarpi (1552–1623), author of *Historia del Concilio Tridentino,* London, 1619.

6. Enrico (or Arrigo) Caterino Davila (1576–1631), author of *Historia delle guerre civili di Francia,* Venice, 1630.

7. Guido Bentivoglio (1579–1644), author of *Della guerra di Fiandra,* Cologne, 1632–9.

8. *The History of England, under the House of Tudor,* 2 vols, 1759. He did add references to his authorities.

9. 'Protest' (OED *sub* 'reclaim' ii. 7b).

work, your own country, as well as the learned throughout all Europe, would acknowledge the obligation. I have the honour to be,

Sir,

Your most obedient and most humble servant,

DAVID HUME

TO GROSVENOR BEDFORD, Tuesday 29 August 1758

Printed from the MS now WSL. First printed, Cunningham iii. 166. Reprinted, Toynbee iv. 180. The MS descended in the Bedford family to Grosvenor Bedford's great-niece, Mrs Erskine, of Milton Lodge, Gillingham, Dorset; sold Sotheby's 15 Nov. 1932 (property of Mrs Erskine), lot 493, to Maggs for WSL.

Strawberry Hill, Aug. 29, 1758.

Dear Sir,

AS YOU know a good deal more of Somerset House than I do,[1] I will beg you some day as you go by, to call there, and inquire carefully of the keeper of the King's pictures,[2] or of the housekeeper,[3] if there is any such thing as a picture of Lord Wimbledon[4] there. In an old MS of Vertue,[5] I find this memorandum;

Among the King's pictures at Somerset House, a picture of Colonel Cecil Viscount Wimbledon ætat. 37. anno 1610. Corn. Johnson[6] pinx.

You may imagine why I am solicitous to see this portrait.

Adieu! Dear Sir
Yours ever

H. WALPOLE

1. Bedford's aunt, Anne Grosvenor (1679–1750), had been housekeeper of Somerset House 1739–50 (*ante* 29 Aug. 1743, n. 8).

2. Stephen Slaughter (d. 1765), keeper and surveyor of the King's pictures (*Court and City Register,* 1758, p. 80; DALRYMPLE 95 n. 10).

3. Mrs Catherine Brietzcke, wardrobe-keeper and keeper of the royal apartments at Somerset House (*Court and City Register,* 1758, pp. 77, 79).

4. Edward Cecil (1572–1638), cr. (1625) Vct Wimbledon.

5. George Vertue (1684–1756), engraver and antiquary. On 22 Aug. 1758 HW bought from Vertue's widow some forty volumes of his MSS, which were the basis of his *Anecdotes of Painting* ('Short Notes,' GRAY i. 33).

6. Cornelius Johnson (or Jonson) (1593–ca 1664), portrait painter. HW omitted the '(qu)' that Vertue added after 'pinx.' (*Walpole Society* 1930, xviii. 54). It is un-

TO DAVID MALLET, Friday 8 September 1758

Printed from a photostat of the MS kindly furnished by the late Sir John Murray. First printed, Cunningham iii. 167–8. Reprinted, Toynbee iv. 183. The MS was presumably acquired by John Murray, the publisher of HW's *Memoires . . . of George II,* 1822; owned in 1936 by his descendant, Sir John Murray, of 50 Albemarle Street, London; sold Sotheby's 11 May 1970 (property of Sir John Murray), lot 227, to John Wilson; offered by Paul Richards, Cat. Nos 54 (1970), lot 13; 63 (1971), lot 49; not further traced.

Strawberry Hill, Sept. 8, 1758.

Dear Sir,

THE pamphlet I mentioned to you t'other day, of which I could not remember the title, is called, *Reflections concerning Innate Moral Principles, written in French by the late Lord Bolinbroke,*[1] *and translated into English.* Printed in both languages. 1752.

May I mention this as Lord Bolinbroke's?

Be so good as to tell Mrs Mallet[2] how extremely obliged I am for her note,[3] and I hope she knows that I have scarce been in town two days this whole summer. When she returns, she shall have no reason to think me insensible to her goodness. I am, Sir, hers

And your most obedient humble servant

HOR. WALPOLE

likely that Johnson at the age of 17 painted a portrait of Wimbledon (A. J. Finberg, 'A Chronological List of Portraits by Cornelius Johnson, or Jonson,' *Walpole Society* 1922, x. 3–7). HW does not mention any portrait of Wimbledon in his *Anecdotes* nor in his later editions of *Royal and Noble Authors.*

1. Henry St John (1678–1751), cr. (1712) Vct Bolingbroke. Mallet did not include this work in his edition of Bolingbroke's *Works,* 5 vols, 1754, but HW mentioned it in the 2d edn of his *Royal and Noble Authors,* 1759, ii. 143 (*Works* i. 450), with the statement that it had 'been published in his Lordship's name, but I do not know on what authority.' HW's copy of the *Reflections* is Hazen, *Cat. of HW's Lib.,* No. 1608:13:11.

2. Lucy Elstob (ca 1716–95), m. as his 2d wife (1742) David Mallet (GM 1742, xii. 546).

3. Missing.

From LADY TOWNSHEND, Saturday 21 October 1758

Printed from the MS now WSL. First printed, Toynbee *Supp.* ii. 109. Reprinted, Toynbee *Supp.* iii. 154-5. For the history of the MS see *ante* 30 Sept. 1743 OS.

The day of the month is established by HW's letter of Tuesday, 24 Oct. 1758, to Sir Horace Mann (MANN v. 251).

Endorsed by HW: Oct. 1758.

Whitehall,[1] Saturday evening.

LADY Townshend's compliments to Mr Walpole, and as she is very sensible that he is always master of the greatest fortitude, she ventures to inform him that this day an express arrived at Whitehall with an account[2] of the defeat of the Hanoverians[3] under Counts Issenbourg[4] and Oberg[5] near Cassel, by the Prince of Sobiize.[6] The Duke of Marborough,[7] Marq[uess] of Blandford,[8] Colo[nel] Wade[9] and Capt. Tuffnel[10] are all down with the camp fever and bloody flux.

If[11] Lady T[ownshen]d hears how the King supports it she will be sure to let Mr Walpole know, as she is apprehensive he will be under the utmost uneasiness.

1. Lady Townshend had taken a house in Whitehall in 1744 (*ante* ca March 1745, n. 3).

2. A 'Copy of the letter written from the camp of the Prince de Soubise, at Lutterberg, October 10' was printed in the *Daily Adv.* 23 Oct.

3. The Hanoverians and the Hessians were defeated at Lutterberg 10 Oct. 1758 (MANN v. 251, 254).

4. Johann Casimir (1715–59), Prinz von Isenburg, Hessian Lt-Gen., 1758 (ibid. v. 251 n. 9).

5. Christian Ludwig von Oberg (1689–1778), Hanoverian Maj.-Gen., 1754 (ibid. n. 10).

6. Charles de Rohan (1715–87), Prince de Soubise; Maréchal de France, 19 Oct. 1758.

7. Charles Spencer (1706–58), 5th E. of Sunderland, 1729; 2d D. of Marlborough, 1733; Lt-Gen., 1758. He died of a fever at Münster 20 Oct.

8. George Spencer (1739–1817), styled M. of Blandford until 1758; 3d D. of Marlborough, 1758; Capt. 20th Foot, 1756.

9. George Wade, Lt-Col. 3d Dragoon Guards, 1751 (*Army Lists,* 1758, p. 24).

10. Charles Tuffnall, Lt, 1755; Captain Royal Horse Guards, 1759 (ibid., 1759, p. 17; 1760, p. 17).

11. In the MS this paragraph, apparently added as an afterthought, is separated from the text above by the date-line.

To the Duke of Newcastle,[1] Sunday 12 November 1758

Printed from a photostat of the MS among the Newcastle papers in the British Museum (Add. MS 32,885, ff. 308–9). First printed (inaccurately and with omissions), *Works* ii. 371–3. Reprinted, Toynbee iv. 214–16. The Newcastle papers descended in the Pelham family to the 4th Earl of Chichester, who presented them to the British Museum in 1886.

Endorsed by Hugh Valence Jones: November 12th 1758. Mr H. Walpole.

Nov. 12, 1758.

My Lord,

SOME time ago Mr West[2] by your Grace's order treated with me for the sale of my place in the Custom House,[3] which bringing in to me at the very lowest thirteen hundred per ann. with the contingence of 100 per ann. more on the death of Mrs Leneve,[4] besides other advantages which I shall mention presently, was thought worth by those who understand, and whom I consulted on, these kinds of things, from fourteen to fifteen thousand pounds. The affair, as I understood, went off on my brother,[5] who has the reversion after me, expecting much more for his small share and great reversion, than was thought reasonable.

This being a brief state of the case, I have now thought of a plan, by which I believe I could accommodate your Grace in a much easier manner; and which I shall here propose to be accepted or rejected as your Grace shall think proper.

1. Thomas Pelham Holles (1693–1768), 2d Bn Pelham; cr. (1715) D. of Newcastle-upon-Tyne; prime minister 1754–6, 1757–62.

2. James West (ca 1703–72), politician and antiquary; joint secretary to the Treasury 1746–62; M.P.

3. Shortly before 5 April 1755, West, acting for Newcastle, met with HW and told him he was prepared to make him a considerable offer for his place in the Customs. The offer to be made was, unknown to HW, on behalf of the Earl of Ashburnham. At another meeting before 9 April, HW told West he would accept an offer of no less than £20,000 for the place, provided his brother Sir Edward, with whom he shared the collectorship, could be made agreeable. Ashburnham apparently accepted HW's terms and asked that approaches be made to Sir Edward, but the transaction did not occur for the reason HW states below (G. L. Lam, 'Walpole and the Duke of Newcastle,' in *Horace Walpole: Writer, Politician, and Connoisseur,* ed. W. H. Smith, New Haven, 1967, pp. 75–8 and documents cited there).

4. Isabella Le Neve (ca 1686–1759), governess-companion in the Walpole family (Montagu i. 62 n. 27).

5. Sir Edward Walpole.

The post of Master of the Mint, held at present by Mr Chetwynd,[6] is, I think reckoned at £1200 per ann.[7] If it is less, even £1000 I will exchange mine for it on the following terms. If your Grace will give me the reversion of the Master of the Mint, after Mr Chetwynd, for my life, I will immediately on his death resign my share and profits of the place in the Custom House to whomever your Grace pleases. That is, I will give up fourteen hundred a year precarious for 1200, or 1000, certain: on which your Grace will please to make these observations. If my brother will not part with his contingency, whoever shall have my share, will still be a great gainer. For instance; the Master of the Mint must be given to somebody: if to me, I give in lieu, to your Grace or your nominee, my profits (I believe, greater than those) besides what I hinted at above, viz: In our place there are seven or 8 places[8] alternately in mine and my brother's gift, of which two at least are *very good:* I shall give up my nominations with my place—if my brother can be satisfied, all the nominations would come to your Grace. If Mr Chetwynd outlives me, as my profits would go to another if not exchanged by me, not a farthing of money would be thrown away; and when Mr Chetwynd shall drop, his place will be in your Grace's disposal as it is at present. If my brother dies before me and Mr Chetwynd, the whole profit of the Custom House place will be in your Grace's disposal, and I shall be to wait for Mr Chetwynd's reversion, or to die myself; neither of which will be of any consequence but to myself. In short, my Lord, instead of paying me a large sum of money as was before proposed, your Grace will only have the trouble of asking the King to consent to my exchange of my place, that your Grace may have the very fair pretence of asking at the same time for two or three lives in the Custom House place, which on this agreement with me your Grace would ensure to your family and would be a handsome provision for a younger son of my Lord Lincoln.[9] And as I should

6. William Richard Chetwynd (? 1683–1770), 3d Vct Chetwynd, 1767; Master of the Mint 1744–69; M.P.

7. Chetwynd officially received £650 a year 'for himself and 3 clerks,' but the total income of the post was doubtless much greater (*Court and City Register*, 1758, p. 219).

8. A chief deputy, three clerks, and three receivers by deputation.

9. Henry Fiennes Clinton (after 1768, Pelham Clinton) (1720–94), 9th E. of Lincoln; 2d D. of Newcastle-under-Lyne, 1768; HW's correspondent. He had four sons: George, Lord Clinton (1745–52), Henry Fiennes Pelham Clinton (1750–78), Thomas Pelham Clinton (1752–95), who succeeded his father as 3d D. of Newcastle-under-Lyne, and John Pelham Clinton (1755–81), M.P. (Collins, *Peerage*, 1812, ii. 215).

be ready to resign mine (by far the largest and only considerable share) I should suppose his Majesty would not refuse your Grace a suit so advantageous to you, and which then you would have so reasonable a foundation for asking.

There is one thing more I ought to mention. I don't know the exact value of Mr Chetwynd's place: it may be more than I have stated it; and I have no thoughts of making any clandestine advantage. If it should exceed 13 or £1400 per ann. I by no means desire to be a gainer in income, and shall readily agree to pay to whomever your Grace pleases as much as it shall exceed my present place: as on the other hand, if it falls short, I am content to be the sufferer.

I have treated this exchange, my Lord, as very advantageous to your Grace; and it certainly would be exceedingly so: yet I do not mean either to be artful for my own profit; or to pretend to make any court by it. It would be below me not to deal frankly with your Grace: I have neither ambition nor avarice to satisfy: I have as much from the government as I desire or have any pretensions to; I want no more: but I do wish to be secure for my life and to keep nearly what I have. If I can keep it honourably, as I should by this exchange, I should be glad—If I cannot, I shall be content with much less, for I would do nothing unworthy of me, to obtain any advantage. Your Grace sent to me in a very handsome manner before; I hope my compliance then, and the much better proposal for your Grace that I make now,[10] mark my attention and desire of obliging your Grace, in which without any disguise, I mean, my Lord, at once to pay a civility to you, and to secure myself in a way which leaves me nothing to be ashamed of, and gives your Grace some reason to be satisfied with my plain dealing, and which in a word would be as creditable to you as it will be little expensive.

I am my Lord
Your Grace's most obedient humble servant

HOR. WALPOLE

PS. If your Grace wants any farther explanation, I will do myself the honour to wait on you when ever you please to order me.

10. Nothing came of HW's proposal; no reply from Newcastle has been found.

TO ROBERT DODSLEY, Monday 20 November 1758

Printed for the first time from the MS now WSL. HW wrote this note on Richard Bentley's letter to Dodsley 20 Nov. 1758, which follows below. Bentley's letter was printed in part in Hazen, *SH Bibl.* 48. The MS is laid in a copy of Lucan's *Pharsalia,* SH, 1760, purchased from Sir Robert Abdy, Bt, by Maggs for WSL, 1938.

Address (by Bentley): To Mr Dodsley, Bookseller in Pall Mall, London. *Postmark:* 21 NO. *Frank:* Free Hor. Walpole.

Mr Dodsley,

I SHALL be in town on Wednesday, and if you will call on me Thursday or Friday with your opinion, we will settle this affair.[1]

Yours etc.

HOR. WALPOLE

[Bentley's letter]

Strawberry Hill, November 20, 1758.

Mr Dodsley,

IF WE print the Lucan in quarto, it is to be considered that the notes[2] are not complete, and it will be called an imperfect edition, to remedy which I think it will be advisable to revert to my father's[3] design of printing Grotius's[4] notes along with his own, by which means a number of notes I had discarded as being only relative to Grotius will find their place again. But to prepare this for the press, I must be at the trouble of transcribing pretty near the whole work, a toil I would willingly contrive should pay me a little better.

No doubt you are the best judge of how many we are likely to dispose at home, but when I talked to Mr Franklyn[5] upon our first

1. The printing of Lucan's *Pharsalia* (Hazen, *SH Bibl.* 46–9).

2. The title-page of the SH Lucan reads, 'Cum notis Hugonis Grotii, et Richardi Bentleii.'

3. Richard Bentley (1662–1742), D.D.; classical scholar and controversialist; Master of Trinity College, Cambridge; father of Richard Bentley (1708–82), HW's correspondent and writer of the present letter.

4. Huig de Groot (1583–1645), called Hugo Grotius; writer and statesman.

5. Probably Richard Francklin (d. 1765), formerly printer of *The Craftsman,* who was HW's tenant at SH, or possibly Thomas Francklin (1721–84), D.D., Regius Professor of Greek at Cambridge 1750–9.

scheme of printing it in 8vo,[6] he said he had no doubt but half the edition might be disposed of in Holland. I should be glad to know your opinion.

Suppose therefore we were to print 500 at 12*s*. each, the trade to sell again at 16. I imagine the account would stand thus:

Paper	84-0-0
Advertisements[7]	10-0-0
500 books[8] at 12*s*. each	300-0-0
Profit to the bookseller[9]	

If you agree to this proposal, we can begin upon it immediately. I am,

Sir,

Your humble servant,

R. BENTLEY[10]

6. 'At first it was intended to print only the notes in octavo without the text' (HW's entry, 11 Dec. 1758, in *Journal of the Printing-Office*, p. 7).

7. Advertisements for the SH Lucan appeared in the *Daily Adv*. 9, 10, and 12 Jan. 1761 and in the *London Chronicle* 6–8, 8–10, 13–15, and 20–22 Jan. 1761.

8. Five hundred copies, in royal quarto, were printed at the SH Press 11 Dec. 1758 – 4 Oct. 1760 and published 8 Jan. 1761. Dodsley, who seems to have acted simply as HW's agent in selling the book, received 350 copies, of which 51 were for presentation by HW. Of the 150 copies not sent to Dodsley, at least 91 were imperfect and had to be completed later by HW's printer William Pratt (*post* ca June 1762; Hazen, op. cit. 46–8).

9. By the end of 1764 Dodsley had sold only 118 copies (ibid. 48). It would appear that his profit was about the same as Bentley's (see next note).

10. 'Mr Bentley printed his Lucan at Mr W's press at Strawberry Hill, by which Mr B. told me he got about £40' (William Cole's *Athenæ Cantabrigienses* MS in the BM, quoted in Nichols, *Lit. Illus*. viii. 573).

From ALLAN RAMSAY,[1] Thursday 1759

Printed from the MS now WSL. First printed, Toynbee *Supp.* iii. 163–4. Damer-Waller; the MS was sold Sotheby's 5 Dec. 1921 (first Waller Sale), lot 174, bought in; resold Christie's 15 Dec. 1947 (second Waller Sale), lot 21, to Maggs for WSL.

Dated by HW's endorsement.

Endorsed by HW: From Mr Ramsay, the Painter, 1759, about Mr Charles Townshend's picture.

Address: To the Honourable Horatio Walpole, Esq.

Memoranda (by HW, in pencil, concerning SH):

coal hole
lock to pink room[2]
floors
lanthorn[3]
The Screen drawn[4]

Soho Square, Thursday forenoon.

Dear Sir,

THE etiquette of painting prohibits us to go abroad to any but the Royal Family[5] except *in cases of necessity.* I am sorry to find that I have at this time so true an excuse for following my own inclination of obeying your commands and waiting on Mr Townshend,[6] and will be with him on Monday at 10 if I hear nothing to the contrary. I am with great respect,

Dear Sir,

Your most obliged and most humble servant,

ALLAN RAMSAY

1. (1713–84), painter. In 1758 he painted a portrait of HW, now WSL (C. K. Adams and W. S. Lewis, 'The Portraits of Horace Walpole,' *Walpole Society* 1968–70, xlii. 17–18; reproduced in MORE 9).

2. A watercolour drawing by Richard Bentley, now WSL, shows that the Star Chamber was papered with pink paper at this time. Paget Toynbee, in *SH Accounts,* p. 68, confuses the Pink Room with the Red Bedchamber.

3. The Gothic lantern, now WSL, which hung in the well of the staircase at SH. Bentley's design for it, also WSL, is re-

TO GEORGE SELWYN, ca 1759

Printed for the first time from the MS now WSL, acquired from Goodspeed's in 1968. The earlier history of the MS is not known.

Dated conjecturally by HW's letter of 23 Aug. 1759 to Selwyn (SELWYN 155).

Address: To Mr Selwyn.

I AM this minute come to town, and have neither fire nor dinner; if you and Mr Williams[1] dine anywhere together, not at Arthur's,[2] may I dine with you?

FROM DAVID MALLET, ca 1759

Printed from Toynbee *Supp.* iii. 164–5, where the letter was first printed. Damer-Waller; the MS was sold Sotheby's 5 Dec. 1921 (first Waller Sale), lot 156 (with Mallet to HW ca 1759 *bis* and 15 July 1761), to Maggs; offered by them, Cat. Nos 433 (Christmas 1922) and 471 (1925); not further traced.

Dated conjecturally by the reference to Mallet's *Edwin and Emma,* published ca 21 March 1760 (see n. 1 below).

Address: For the Honourable Horace Walpole.

MR Mallet presents his compliments to Mr Walpole, and begs that he would send him an—epithet.

The word sheltering[1] is not very liquid; but it has some meaning; and he cannot find another that has any. Was there ever such a distress? or such a request? He had altered two stanzas[2]—which he

produced in W. S. Lewis, *Collector's Progress,* New York, 1951, opp. p. 159. HW wrote George Montagu 11 June 1753: 'I have filled Mr Bentley's Gothic lanthorn with painted glass, which casts the most venerable gloom on the stairs that was ever seen since the days of Abelard' (MONTAGU i. 150–1).

4. Possibly a preliminary sketch for the screen in the Holbein Chamber that is also WSL and is, like the drawing of the lantern, in the portfolio of Bentley's designs for SH now at Farmington.

5. Upon his return from Italy in 1757 Ramsay was employed by the Prince of Wales as his portrait painter.

6. Hon. Charles Townshend (1725–67). Ramsay and Townshend were both members of the 'Select Society' of Edinburgh, founded by Ramsay and a few friends in 1754. The 'necessity' mentioned above was probably jocose: Ramsay wanted to paint Townshend. No portrait of him, however, is listed in Alastair Smart, *The Life and Art of Allan Ramsay,* 1952.

1. George James ('Gilly') Williams (ca 1719–1805), a member with Selwyn and Lord Edgcumbe of HW's 'out of town party' at SH.

2. That is, Robert Arthur's or White's club in St James's. Why HW did not want to dine at Arthur's is unexplained.

1. In the second line of Mallet's ballad *Edwin and Emma,* printed anonymously in March 1760 by Baskerville:

agrees wanted alteration. As an *author,* he thinks the other things may stand as they are: and at this, Mr W, as an author too, will not be much surprised.

From DAVID MALLET, ca 1759 *bis*

Printed from Toynbee *Supp.* iii. 165, where the letter was first printed. For the history of the MS and the date argument see the previous letter.

Tuesday.

Dear Sir,

MY BEING troublesome to you, on this occasion, is certainly a mark of my esteem. However, I will not say with the constable, in Shakespear, 'that were I ten times more troublesome, I should most willingly bestow it all on your worship.'[1]

The word, sheltering,[2] must stand, I fear; because I cannot find another appropriated epithet: at which I own I am surprised.

Who love nor pity knew[3]—is an improvement: and I gladly adopt it.

How I have altered the two stanzas, to which your objections were most reasonable, you will find in the enclosed paper.[4] Be so good as to say, whether I have succeeded.

A great cold forces me to trouble you with all this, in writing. I am,

Dear Sir,

Your obliged and most humble servant

D. MALLET

Far in the windings of a vale,
Fast by a sheltering wood,
The safe retreat of health and peace,
An humble cottage stood.

See Philip Gaskell, *John Baskerville, A Bibliography,* Cambridge, 1959, p. 29. HW quoted twice from *Edwin and Emma* (MONTAGU ii. 307; OSSORY ii. 540).

2. Not identified.

---

1. Dogberry in *Much Ado About Nothing* III. v. 23–5: 'If I were as tedious as a king, I could find in my heart to bestow it all of your worship.'

2. See previous letter, n. 1.

3. In the tenth stanza of *Edwin and Emma:*

The father, too, a sordid man,
Who love nor pity knew,
Was all-unfeeling as the clod,
From whence his riches grew.

4. Missing.

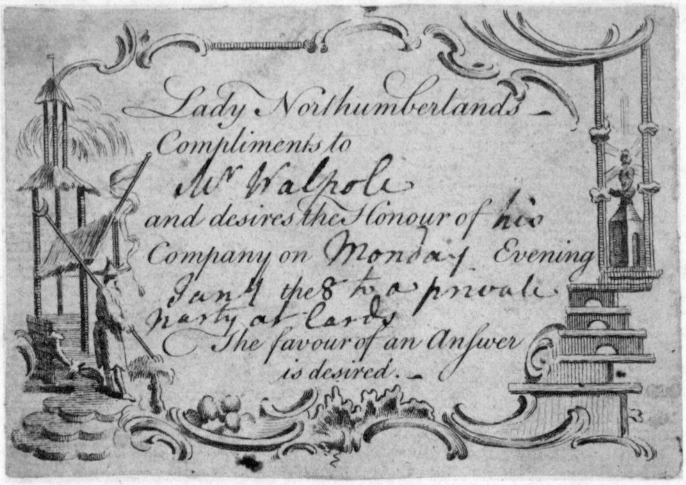

LADY NORTHUMBERLAND'S INVITATION CARD

From LADY NORTHUMBERLAND,[1] ?January 1759

Printed for the first time from the MS (an invitation card) pasted in an extra-illustrated copy, now WSL, of *A Description of the Villa of Mr Horace Walpole*, SH, 1784 (see illustration). For the history of this copy see Hazen, *SH Bibl.* 127, copy 10.

The year of the invitation is conjectural. 'Monday evening January the 8' occurred in 1753 and 1759, the only two years possible for this invitation to have been issued by Lady Northumberland. 1759 seems the more likely year, since Richard Bentley, who designed the card, was then at the height of his activity. HW had established a social life with his Twickenham neighbours by that time.

LADY Northumberland's compliments to Mr Walpole and desires the honour of his company on Monday evening January the 8 to a private party at cards. The favour of an answer[2] is desired.

To the HON. HENRY BILSON LEGGE,[1] Saturday 3 February 1759

Printed from *Works* ii. 373–4, where the letter was first printed. Reprinted, Toynbee iv. 237–8. The history of the MS and its present whereabouts are not known.

Arlington Street, Feb. 3, 1759.

Sir,

UPON hearing a motion yesterday in the House of Commons for an account of the produce of the tax on places,[2] I sent for my deputy[3] and asked what I had paid. He told me that nothing had been demanded; that he had been ready to pay whatever should be

1. Lady Elizabeth Seymour (1716–76), m. (1740) Hugh Smithson, 4th Bt, 2d E. of Northumberland, 1750; cr. (1766) D. of Northumberland. Their Middlesex seat, Syon House, near Isleworth, was only a short distance from SH.

2. Missing.

---

1. (1708–64), chancellor of the Exchequer 1754–55, 1756–61; M.P.

2. It was ordered 'that the proper officer do lay before this House, the Book of Register, in which all the money paid into the Exchequer, for the duties on offices and pensions, are entered and registered' (*Journals of the House of Commons* xxviii. 397). The tax imposed in 1757 by the act of 31 Geo. II, c. 22, amounted to one shilling per pound of all salaries, fees, and perquisites of offices exceeding £100 (*Statutes at Large*, ed. Owen Ruffhead, 1763–1800, viii. 212; MANN v. 199).

3. Grosvenor Bedford, HW's deputy usher of the Exchequer.

required, as I had given him positive orders, and to answer to the extent of the value of my place whenever it should be inquired into. You will excuse my troubling you with this now, since on one hand I don't know on what method the Treasury have fixed for taxing the places in the Exchequer; and on the other, if I did, I would not send my assessment[4] *just now,* lest it should look as if I had had any design of evading the tax, and only paid for fear of the inquiry. I must appeal to you, Sir, how very groundless such a suspicion would be. I can scarce expect that anything I say should make an impression on anybody, and yet I believe you may recollect, that when such a tax was first talked of, I told you how far I was from wishing it should not be imposed; that I thought persons who had a good deal from the government ought to pay towards carrying it on, and that we in employments could afford it better than many on whom the weight of taxes fell very heavily. I must bear my brother[5] witness that he entirely agreed with me in these sentiments.

When this tax was to be voted, I again spoke to you upon it, Sir, and said, though I was very ready to pay myself, I hoped it would not be extended to little offices, where salaries were small, and the business great: and I mentioned to you a difficulty that might, by inadvertence, be laid upon me, if I was rated according to my bills, which, including all that I pay to the King's workmen and tradesmen, would, if valued in that manner, impose a greater duty upon me than my whole income would amount to. This you told me could never be the case; and I only mention it now, to show that I no more conceal what I said *for* myself, than I sought to avoid any encumbrance to which I ought to be subject. You concluded the conversation with saying, that no method of taxing places was yet settled, and that it would be a very difficult matter to adjust.

Do excuse my repeating all this detail, and be so good as to keep this letter, if it should be necessary for my justification. There is but one thing in the world that I have any pretense to be proud of, and that is, my disinterestedness. It would hurt me beyond measure to have it for one moment called in question. My carelessness about money had made me quite forget the tax since last year, or I should

4. On 14 April 1759 Bedford listed in his account book under cash disbursed the sum of £13.2.0 'by the tax upon places.' In 1760 the entry was made on 20 Dec., 'By the place tax paid to the 5th April 1760 £85.' The same sum was entered for 1761 and 1762 (Grosvenor Bedford's MS 'Account Books,' 1758–62, now WSL).

5. Sir Edward Walpole.

have again applied to you for directions—but I do protest I had rather give up the place than have one man in England think that I meant to avoid paying my share.

I am, Sir,
Your most obedient humble servant,
HOR. WALPOLE

TO GROSVENOR BEDFORD, Saturday 3 February 1759

Printed from Cunningham iii. 206–7, where the letter was first printed. Reprinted, Toynbee iv. 238–9. The history of the MS and its present whereabouts are not known.

Arlington Street, Feb. 3, 1759.

Dear Sir,

I AM glad the time is not lapsed when I should have paid the tax.[1] I have writ to Mr Legge[2] for directions, and in the meantime can give you no other than to pay whatever shall be demanded, and to answer *any* questions that are asked, as I at first desired you to do. I am very indifferent about the money, exceedingly delicate not to take any advantage of exemption. It may be in the power of many persons to hurt my fortune, but it shall never be in their power to touch my character for disinterestedness. You can be my witness ever since you came into the office,[3] how scrupulous I have been not to take any improper advantage, and how constantly I have enjoined you not to think of my interest, but where I had the most exact right. Adieu!

Yours ever,
H. WALPOLE

1. The 'place tax' was to be levied twice a year, the first payment being due on or before 10 Oct. and the second on or before 5 April (*Statutes at Large*, ed. Owen Ruffhead, 1763–1800, viii. 214).

2. See previous letter.

3. Bedford became HW's deputy in the Exchequer in Aug. 1755 (*ante* 21 Aug. 1755).

From the REV. WILLIAM HARRIS,[1] Wednesday 7 February 1759

Printed from the MS now WSL. First printed, Toynbee *Supp.* iii. 155–7. Damer-Waller; the MS was sold Sotheby's 5 Dec. 1921 (first Waller Sale), lot 140 (with Harris to HW 25 Oct. 1760), to Wells; given by him to Thomas Conolly, of Chicago, from whom WSL acquired it in 1937.

Address: To the Hon. Horace Walpole, Esq., in London. *Postmark:* 9 FE. HONITON.

Honiton,[2] Feb. 7, 1759.

Sir,

THE pleasure you have given and the honour you have done me in your *Catalogue of Royal and Noble Authors,*[3] induce me to offer you the enclosed. If it meets with your approbation, I may, perhaps add, or remark some other things in your volumes, which I shall again read with fresh pleasure and delight.

I am, Sir,
With great esteem,
Your faithful humble servant,
WILL. HARRIS

[Enclosure]

Omission in the English *Catalogue of Royal and Noble Authors.*

Ford Lord Grey, afterwards Earl of Tankerville,[4] a vile man, wrote *The Secret History of the Rye-House Plot.* This work was printed in 1754, in a thin octavo.[5]

In the Irish *Catalogue.*

John Shute Barrington, Viscount Barrington,[6] wrote *The Rights*

1. (1720–70), D.D., 1765; biographer of James I, Charles I, Cromwell, and Charles II.

2. Harris was minister to the nonconformist congregation at Luppitt, near Honiton, Devon.

3. In his *Catalogue of the Royal and Noble Authors,* 2d edn, 1759, i. 42–7, HW included references to Harris's *An Historical and Critical Account of . . . James I,* 1753, and *An Historical and Critical Account of . . . Charles I,* 1758. HW's copies of these works are Hazen, *Cat. of HW's Lib.,* Nos 1643 and 1644.

4. Ford Grey (1655–1701), 3d Bn Grey of Warke, 1675; cr. (1695) E. of Tankerville.

5. HW's copy is Hazen, op. cit., No. 1608:71:2. HW included an article on Grey in subsequent editions of *Royal and Noble Authors* (*Works* i. 472).

6. John Shute Barrington (1678–1734), cr. (1720) Vct Barrington; M.P.

of the Protestant Dissenters, in answer to Sir Humphry Mackworth, two parts, quarto, 1704, 1705.[7] *Miscellanea sacra,* 2 vol., 8vo, 1725.[8] *Essay on the Several Dispensations of God to Mankind,* 8vo, 2d edition, 1732,[9] with several others, whose titles I cannot recollect.

It is objected, by some ingenious gentlemen, that Lord Clarendon by no means deserved the eulogiums bestowed on him by the author of the *Catalogue*.

Can the adviser of the sale of Dunkirk, and the promoter of persecution against great multitudes of his fellow subjects, say they, in any sense be deemed the chancellor of human nature?[10] Can a man whose every page demonstrates the party man and bigot deserve so illustrious a character?

In a blank page of his answer to Cressy, styled *Animadversions upon a Book styled Fanaticism* etc.,[11] in my possession, I read what follows: 'It appears from this piece, as well as the survey of Hobbs's *Leviathan,*[12] that Lord Clarendon's talents were good for controversy. Had he been an ecclesiastic, 'tis not to be doubted but he would have made a much better figure in polemical divinity, than he did in politics, in which his skill was but small.' If this is true, he ranks with his friend Lord Falkland.[13]

In vol. 2d, p. 56, for Peck's *Desiderata curiosa,*[14] read Peck's *Memoirs of Cromwell;*[15] I'm sure it is not in my edition of the former, and that it is in the latter, as well as in Howard's *Papers.*[16]

7. *The Rights of Protestant Dissenters. . . . The Case of the Dissenters Reviewed,* 1704; . . . *A Vindication of their Right to an Absolute Toleration, from the Objections of Sir H. Mackworth, in his Treatise, entitled, Peace at Home,* 1705.

8. HW's copy is Hazen, op. cit., No. 107.

9. HW's copy is ibid., No. 106; his copies of the 1st edn, 1728, are ibid., Nos 1608:19:2 and 1608:22:2. HW included a brief article on Barrington in subsequent editions of *Royal and Noble Authors* (*Works* i. 523).

10. In the article on 'Edward Hyde, Earl of Clarendon' HW wrote that 'For his comprehensive knowledge of mankind [Clarendon was] styled *The chancellor of human nature*' (*Royal and Noble Authors,* 1759, ii. 17).

11. *Animadversions upon a Book, intituled, Fanaticism fanatically Imputed to the Catholick Church, by Dr Stillingfleet, and the Imputation Refuted and Retorted by S[erenus] C[ressy]. By a Person of Honour,* 1673.

12. *A Brief View and Survey of the Dangerous and Pernicious Errors to Church and State, in Mr Hobbes's Book, entitled Leviathan,* Oxford, 1676.

13. See *ante* 15 July 1758 and n. 15.

14. Francis Peck, *Desiderata curiosa,* 2 vols, 1732–5. HW's copy, now WSL, is Hazen, op. cit., No. 578.

15. *Memoirs of the Life and Actions of Oliver Cromwell,* 1740. HW's copy, now WSL, is Hazen, op. cit., No. 467. In his article on the 1st Earl of Shaftesbury, HW wrote that Shaftesbury's 'character' of the Hon. Henry Hastings, second son of the 4th Earl of Huntingdon, was 'printed originally in Peck's *Desiderata curiosa,* and lately in the *Connoisseur,* vol. 3.' As Harris correctly points out, it first appeared in Peck's *Memoirs of . . . Cromwell,* 'to all which is added, a collection of divers curious historical pieces relating to

From John Sharp,[1] Friday 9 February 1759

Printed from the MS now wsl. First printed in *The Correspondence of Gray, Walpole, West, and Ashton*, ed. Paget Toynbee, Oxford, 1915, ii. 179–81. Reprinted, Toynbee *Supp.* iii. 157–8. Damer-Waller; the MS was sold Sotheby's 5 Dec. 1921 (first Waller Sale), lot 181 (with another letter), to Maggs; offered by them, Cat. No. 471 (1925), lot 3090; sold by E. G. Friehold to A. H. Reed, of Dunedin, New Zealand, from whom wsl acquired it in 1938.

C[orpus] C[hristi] C[ollege,] C[ambridge], Feb. 9, 1759.

Sir,

THE enclosed is a copy of an original letter, written by King Edward the Sixth and preserved in the manuscript library of this College.[2] I take the liberty of a fellow citizen in the republic of letters (to use your own elegant allusion[3]), in communicating to you this trifle, in return for that present of great curiosity as well as real value, with which you have lately favoured us,[4] and which you must allow *us* to call so, your *Catalogue of Royal and Noble Authors. Neque enim soli judicant, qui maligne legunt,*[5] says Pliny in your own manner. The citizens of no mean city in the commonwealth of learning read and judge otherwise. The great pleasure I received in the perusal of your work, excited me to examine those original papers belonging to us which you refer to;[6] I found letters of King

Cromwell and a great number of other remarkable persons (after the manner of *Desiderata curiosa* vol. I and II),' pp. 89–91; it was also printed in *The Connoisseur,* No. 81, of 14 Aug. 1755. HW did not make this correction in subsequent editions of *Royal and Noble Authors.*

16. See Leonard Howard, *A Collection of Letters and State Papers from the Original Manuscripts of Many Princes, Great Personages, and Statesmen,* 1753–6, pt i. 152–5. HW's copy is Hazen, op. cit., No. 86.

---

1. (ca 1729–72), D.D. (Cantab.), 1766; Fellow of Corpus Christi College 1753–72 (Venn, *Alumni Cantab.*). HW wrote Thomas Gray 15 Feb. 1759: 'Who and what sort of man is a Mr Sharp of Bennet? I have received a most obliging and genteel letter from him. . . . I have answered his, but should like to know a little more about him' (Gray ii. 104).

2. Edward VI's letter of 30 May 1547 to Catherine Parr is Parker MS 119, No. 8, in the library of Corpus Christi College (ibid. n. 4).

3. In the advertisement to *Royal and Noble Authors* HW wrote that 'no man ever wished to see the government of letters under any form but that of a republic. As a citizen of that commonwealth, I propose my sentiments for the revision of any decree, of any honorary sentence, as I think fit: my fellow citizens, equally free, will vote according to their opinions' (*Works* i. 249).

4. Sharp's copy of *Royal and Noble Authors* is no longer at Corpus Christi College (information kindly communicated by the late A. N. L. Munby, Librarian of King's College).

5. 'To be sure, those who read to find fault are not the only judges' (Pliny the younger, *Letters,* IX. xxxviii).

6. In *Royal and Noble Authors* i. 13n, 21n, and 37, citing manuscripts of Henry VIII, Catherine Parr, and Elizabeth I.

Henry the Fourth, Queen Elizabeth, and the Duke of Somerset,[7] but they are rather mandates and warrants and have only the sign manual. The enclosed is of a different kind; 'tis titled in the hand of Archbishop Parker[8] who was chaplain to Ann Boleyn,[9] *'Epistola scripta manu propria serenissimi regis Edwardi VI^{ti} ad dominam Catherinam reginam relictam regis Henrici octavi.'* The Archbishop seems to have been his preceptor on this occasion, and the manner of the whole confirms the justness of your remarks on this King's education.[10] I will not detain you longer, Sir, on this trifle, which you will scarce think worth inserting in the next edition of your work.[11] But if you are desirous of my making farther researches, and consulting any other repositories at this place, I shall be very willing to impart what I may find to your purpose. We hope to see another volume of your work, and that many of the present nobility will make a conspicuous figure in it, such as the Earl of Chesterfield,[12] Earl of Hardwicke,[13] Lord Lyttleton,[14] Lord Royston,[15] with some farther additions to the account of the late Lord Hervey.[16]

I am, Sir,
With great respect,
Yours,

J. SHARP

[Enclosure]

Epistola scripta manu propria serenissimi Regis Edwardi sexti ad Dominam Katherinam Reginā Relictā Regis Henrici octavi:

Cū non procul abs te abessē et quotidie me te visurum sperarē mihi optimū videbatur non omnino ad te literas dare. Literæ enim

7. Edward Seymour (ca 1500–52), cr. (1547) D. of Somerset; Protector.

8. Matthew Parker (1504–75), Master of Corpus Christi College, Cambridge, 1544; Abp of Canterbury, 1559. He gave his great library to the College; see James Nasmith, *Catalogus Librorum Manuscriptorum . . . legavit . . . Matthæus Parker,* Cambridge, 1777, p. 176.

9. Anne Boleyn (1507–36), m. (1533) Henry VIII of England.

10. 'Historians tell us, that Henry, during the life of Prince Arthur, was designed by his father for Archbishop of Canterbury. How far his education was carried with that view, I know not' (*Royal and Noble Authors, Works* i. 259).

11. HW did not insert it.

12. Philip Dormer Stanhope (1694–1773), 4th E. of Chesterfield, 1726. HW included an article on him in later editions (*Works* i. 535–8).

13. Philip Yorke (1690–1764), cr. (1754) E. of Hardwicke. HW, who disliked him, did not include him in later editions.

14. George Lyttelton (1709–73), cr. (1756) Bn Lyttelton. HW included an article on him in later editions (*Works* i. 539–40).

sunt cujusdam et memoriæ et benevolentiæ longe absentiū signa. Sed ego petitione tua tandem accensus non potui non ad te literas mittere. Primū ut tibi gratū faciam, deinde vero ut tuis literis respondeā benevolentia plenis quas e sancto Jacobo ad me misisti. In quibus primū ponis ante oculos tuū amorē erga patrē meū nobilissimæ memoriæ regē, deinde benevolentiā erga me, ac postremo pietatem scientiam atque doctrinam in sacris literis. Perge igitur in tuo bono incepto et prosequere patrem amore diuturno, ac exhibe mihi tanta signa benevolentiæ quæ semper hactenus in te sensi, et ne desinas amare et legere sacras literas et semper in eis legendis persevera. In primo enim indicas officium bonæ conjugis et subjecta in secundo ostendis laudem amicitiæ tuæ et in tertio tuā pietatē erga Deū. Quare cū ames patrem non possū non te vehementer laudare, cū me ames non te iterū diligere et cum verbum Dei ames te colā et mirabor ex animo. Quare si quod sit quo possū tibi gratum facto vel verbo facere libenter prestabo. Vale. Tricessimo Maii.[17]

A copy, taken off from the original in the library of C[orpus] C[hristi] C[ollege,] C[ambridge] by John Sharp, M.A., Fellow of C.C.C.C., January 15, 1759.[18]

15. Philip Yorke (1720–90), 2d E. of Hardwicke, 1764. Sharp apparently failed to realize that HW did not include holders of courtesy titles.

16. John Hervey (1696–1743), Bn Hervey of Ickworth, 1733. HW added the titles of eight works by Hervey.

17. 'Letter written with his own hand by the most serene King Edward VI to Lady Catherine, Queen, relict of King Henry VIII:

'Not being far from you and flattering myself daily that I might see you, it seemed to me the best course not to send you any letters at all. Letters indeed are marks of remembrance and good will which someone sends to persons long absent. But touched at last by your petition, I am no longer able to refrain from writing you, in the first place simply to oblige you, and in the second that I might truly respond to your letter so full of good will which you sent me from St James's, in which first you show your love for my father the King of most noble memory, then your kind feelings towards me, and lastly your piety, knowledge, and learning in the holy scriptures. Persist therefore in your good undertaking; continue to adorn the memory of my father with your lasting love, continue to show me such marks of benevolence as I have ever sensed in you, and do not cease to cherish and read the sacred scriptures; ever persist in reading them. In the first instance indeed you show the dutifulness of a good spouse and subject, in the second the worth of your friendship, and in the third your piety toward God. Whereas you love my father, I cannot refrain from praising you vehemently; whereas you love me, again I must esteem you; and whereas you love the word of God, I must revere and admire you. If it be at all in my power, I shall henceforth be prepared to oblige you in any way, whether by word or deed.
Farewell. 30 May.'

18. This endorsement in Sharp's hand appears on the 'copy' (an exact tracing of the original MS) enclosed with his letter to HW. Our text of Edward VI's letter is printed from a transcript (in a different hand) that Sharp also enclosed. This transcript is endorsed on the verso: 'An original letter in French of Anne de Boullan to her father (in Benet Library).'

From LORD CORKE,[1] Wednesday 14 February 1759

Printed from the MS now WSL. First printed, Toynbee *Supp.* iii. 159. Damer-Waller; the MS was sold Sotheby's 5 Dec. 1921 (first Waller Sale), lot 111A (with the Hon. Charles Hamilton to HW 31 Jan. 1784), to Wells; given by him to Thomas Conolly, of Chicago, from whom WSL acquired it in 1937.

Marlbro' Street, Feb. 14, 1759.

Sir,

I MOST humbly thank you for your very obliging and polite letter.[2] Your name must stamp honour wherever it is impressed. The liberty I have taken with it, is the result of my own opinion, which however erroneous in other cases, will be allowed to be right in all attempts of doing justice to your distinguished character. I live in the ambitious hope of being more known to you, for none of your friends can be more sincere admirers of you than is, Sir,

Your very obedient and obliged humble servant,

CORKE & ORRERY

1. John Boyle (1707–62), 5th E. of Orrery, 1731; 5th E. of Corke, 1753; author. HW's opinion of him appears in his letter of 1 Dec. 1754 to Sir Horace Mann (MANN iv. 454), and he is favourably noticed in *Royal and Noble Authors* (*Works* i. 459–60). His copy of *Royal and Noble Authors,* 2d edn, 1759, was offered by Quaritch, Cat. No. 371 (1922), lot 696; it contained a note by Corke on the fly-leaf of vol. I: 'In this edition there are some lives (they are marked in each volume with a star *) which are not in the first edition. There are also some additions in several lives, and alterations. I keep both editions. The first as the gift of the author, the second as a more perfect work. C and O' (information kindly furnished by the late A. N. L. Munby). See *ante* 4 Nov. 1753, n. 4.

2. Missing. Corke's public mention of HW that inspired HW's letter has not been traced.

From LADY NORTHUMBERLAND, MONDAY ?19 March 1759

Printed from the MS now WSL. First printed, Toynbee *Supp.* iii. 160. Damer-Waller; the MS was sold Sotheby's 5 Dec. 1921 (first Waller Sale), lot 166 (with Ds of Norfolk to HW 20 Nov. 1768), to Wells; given by him to Thomas Conolly, of Chicago, from whom WSL acquired it in 1937.

Dated conjecturally by the reference to 'the book,' presumably HW's *Fugitive Pieces,* which he began distributing 17 March 1759 (see n. 2 below).

Syon,[1] Monday morning.

Sir,

IT IS impossible for me to express how infinitely I think myself obliged to you for the book[2] and *Catalogue*[3] you have been so good as to send me and equally so to say how much pleasure I promise myself from the perusal of the first, a pleasure which I am sure to receive from any work of an author whose genius is equal to the perfect esteem I feel for him and this I assure you, Sir, is saying a great deal. The *Catalogue* too I have the utmost satisfaction in receiving and am truly grateful for your gratifying my impertinent curiosity upon that subject. I am with the utmost truth, Sir,

Your most obliged and obedient humble servant,

ELIZABETH NORTHUMBERLAND

1. Syon House, near Isleworth, the seat of the Earl of Northumberland.

2. Presumably HW's *Fugitive Pieces in Verse and Prose,* printed at SH 24 April–13 July 1758, but not distributed until 17 March 1759 (Hazen, *SH Bibl.* 39; 'Short Notes,' GRAY i. 31).

3. *A Catalogue of the Royal and Noble Authors.* Lady Northumberland's copy, signed 'E. Northumberland' in the first volume, is now WSL (Hazen, op. cit. 36, copy 2).

TO GEORGE SELWYN, ca Saturday 9 June 1759

Printed for the first time from the MS now WSL, acquired from Goodspeed's in 1968. The earlier history of the MS is not known.

Dated approximately by HW's letter of 5 June 1759 to Selwyn (SELWYN 154; see n. 1 below).

Address: To Mr Selwyn.

I AM extremely obliged to you as I did not doubt I should be, and if you will give me leave to say so, approve entirely your determination.[1] As there is no hurry, I shall have an opportunity of talking to you more: in the meantime I must anticipate Mr Bentley's thanks by making them for him.

From LORD HUNTINGDON,[1] Wednesday 13 June 1759

Printed from the MS now WSL. First printed, Toynbee *Supp.* iii. 160–1. Damer-Waller; the MS was sold Sotheby's 5 Dec. 1921 (first Waller Sale), lot 151 (with Huntingdon to HW n.d.), to Wells; given by him to Thomas Conolly, of Chicago, from whom WSL acquired it in 1937.

June 13th 1759.

LORD Huntingdon called yesterday upon Mr Walpole to thank him for his literary present.[2] He acknowledges himself doubly obliged to Mr Walpole for it: very much for the entertainment it afforded him as a reader; but much more for the satisfaction he feels, at being authorized by his declaration to esteem it a mark of his confidence and friendship.

1. HW wrote Selwyn 5 June 1759 to propose his friend Richard Bentley as successor to Selwyn's present deputy. Selwyn evidently approved this plan, although there is no positive evidence that Bentley later assumed the post (SELWYN 154 and n. 2).

---

1. Francis Hastings (1729–89), 10th E. of Huntingdon, 1746.

2. Possibly *Royal and Noble Authors,* in which there is a complimentary notice of Francis Hastings (ca 1514–60), 2d E. of Huntingdon; more probably *Fugitive Pieces,* since HW's friendship with (and high opinion of) Huntingdon would have prompted the gift of *Royal and Noble Authors* when it was printed the previous year.

From THOMAS FARMER,[1] Monday 27 August 1759

Printed from the MS now WSL, preserved with the Journal of the SH Press. First printed, *Journal of the Printing-Office,* pp. 79–80. Damer-Waller; the Journal was sold Sotheby's 5 Dec. 1921 (first Waller Sale), lot 52, to Sir Robert Abdy, Bt; resold by Maggs to WSL, 1933.

August 27, 1759, Strawberry Hill.

Honoured Sir,

HAVING now managed your Press for six weeks, and thereby become acquainted with your business of this sort, I hereby offer to engage myself faithfully and diligently to work your Press for two years more certain from the date hereof, upon your agreeing to pay me one guinea per week, as my wages for such service.

And for your satisfaction that I am fully resolved to be steady in your service, and not to be corrupted, or tempted from it in that time, I do agree, that you shall retain my first three months wages in your own hands 'til the end of the said two years; and that such retained wages shall be forfeited to you, in case before the end of the said two years I desert your service.

I do further agree to instruct in the art of printing, during the said two years, any young man you shall appoint to attend upon me,[2] upon your agreeing to pay me, as a gratuity for the same, two guineas at the end of the first year, and three guineas more at the end of the second year.

And I do agree to sign and execute with you the following[3] articles, whenever you shall please to require, in such legal form as a counsellor at law shall advise. I am, with dutiful respect, honoured Sir,

Your most obliged and obedient servant,

(signed) THOMAS FARMER

1. HW's fourth printer at SH (16 July 1759 – 2 Dec. 1761). He finished Lucan's *Pharsalia,* printed the catalogues of the pictures in the Holbein Chamber at SH and of the pictures in the collections of the Duke of Devonshire, Gen. Guise, and Sir Paul Methuen, and vol. I and two-thirds of vol. II of the *Anecdotes of Painting,* when he ran away for getting 'into debt and two girls with child' (MONTAGU i. 411). For HW's relations with Farmer see *Journal of the Printing-Office,* pp. 79–82.

2. Joseph Forrester, son of John Forrester, a gardener at Twickenham, was taken as an apprentice on 18 July 1759, two days after Farmer came to the Press (ibid. 9, 83–4).

3. *Sic,* for 'foregoing.'

To the Hon. Horatio Walpole, Esq.

August 27, 1759.

I do agree to perform my part of the foregoing articles.

(signed) HOR. WALPOLE

Witnesses[4]
R. Bentley[5]
J.H. Müntz[6]

TO LADY TOWNSHEND, Wednesday 12 September 1759

Printed for the first time from the MS now WSL. For the history of the MS see *ante* 25 Aug. 1744 OS.

Dated by the references to Roger Townshend's death and HW's return from the Vyne, which are mentioned in his letter of 13 Sept. 1759 to H. S. Conway (CONWAY ii. 27).

Endorsed in an unidentified hand: Sept. 1759 Horace Walpole to Visc[ounte]ss Townshend.

Arlington Street, Wednesday night.

MY LADY Townshend must undoubtedly think it extraordinary that one who has always professed so much regard for her and her family, should be the last to condole with her on the melancholy occasion of her present misfortune.[1] I would hope, if she has done me the honour to think of me, that she must be sure, as was the case, that I was not in a place or situation to hear of it sooner,[2] or that I should have been one of the first to express, what I am one of the warmest to feel, my concern for whatever afflicts her. The truth is, Madam, I have been rambling about, have been at the Vine,[3] at Salisbury, at Wilton[4] and two or three other places, and not knowing how to have them directed to me, I had ordered the newspapers and my letters to be kept till my return. It was but last night I did return,[5] and heard the truth of what I most sincerely lament. I

4. This word is in HW's hand.

5. Richard Bentley (1708–82), HW's correspondent.

6. Johann Heinrich Müntz (*ante* 18 April 1757, n. 4).

1. Her youngest son, Lt-Col. the Hon. Roger Townshend (ca 1731–59), had been killed at Ticonderoga 25 July 1759.

2. The news of Townshend's death reached England ca 8 Sept. (*Daily Adv.* 10 Sept.).

3. The Vyne, Hants, the seat of HW's friend and correspondent John Chute.

4. Lord Pembroke's seat, near Salisbury.

5. To SH.

came to town too late this evening to take the liberty of calling at her Ladyship's door to inquire after her; and indeed was desirous of explaining an appearance of neglect of which I flatter myself I am totally incapable. It would be too much trouble to her Ladyship to write a word herself in answer to this, but I flatter myself she will be so good as to let Mrs Runnington[6] send me a particular account how she does; nobody can be more interested in her Ladyship's welfare, and whenever he knows that it will not be improper, Mr Walpole will have the honour of calling,[7] though he owns he is afraid to see how much a nature so tender and affectionate is struck with the loss of so very amiable and deserving a young man.[8]

To Lady Townshend, Friday 21 September 1759

Printed for the first time from the MS now wsl. For the history of the MS see *ante* 25 Aug. 1744 OS.

Endorsed in an unidentified hand: September 21, 1759 Hor. Walpole to Visc[ounte]ss Townshend.

Strawberry Hill, Sept. 21, 1759.

Madam,

It is a melancholy offering I here make to your Ladyship, yet, I flatter myself, an acceptable one to your sensibility. You asked me t'other day[1] who could draw a design best for a monument to your brave son. I told your Ladyship then and think so, that the common designs of tombs are poor, improper and without invention. With your taste I am sure you would like something new; yet without letting that novelty run into tawdry or caprice. The more simplicity

6. Probably 'Dorcas,' Lady Townshend's 'woman' until sometime before 1766 (Selwyn 70 n. 16).

7. HW called on Lady Townshend the next day: 'I passed this whole morning most deliciously at my Lady T[ownshend]'s' (HW to Conway 13 Sept. 1759, Conway ii. 27).

8. 'Poor Roger, for whom she is not concerned, has given her a hint that her hero George may be mortal too' (ibid.). General George Townshend, who was at this time with Wolfe at Quebec, wrote to his wife 6 Sept. 1759 of 'the melancholy news I received the day before yesterday . . . of my poor brother's death. . . . I have wrote a line to poor Lady Townshend to comfort her by convincing her of my own health and safety' (Hist. MSS Comm., 11th Report, App. iv [*Townshend MSS*], 1887, pp. 308–9).

1. Doubtless when HW called on Lady Townshend 13 Sept. (see previous letter, n. 7). HW wrote Lord Strafford the same day: 'she affects grief—but not so much for the son she has lost, as for t'other that she may lose' (Chute 295).

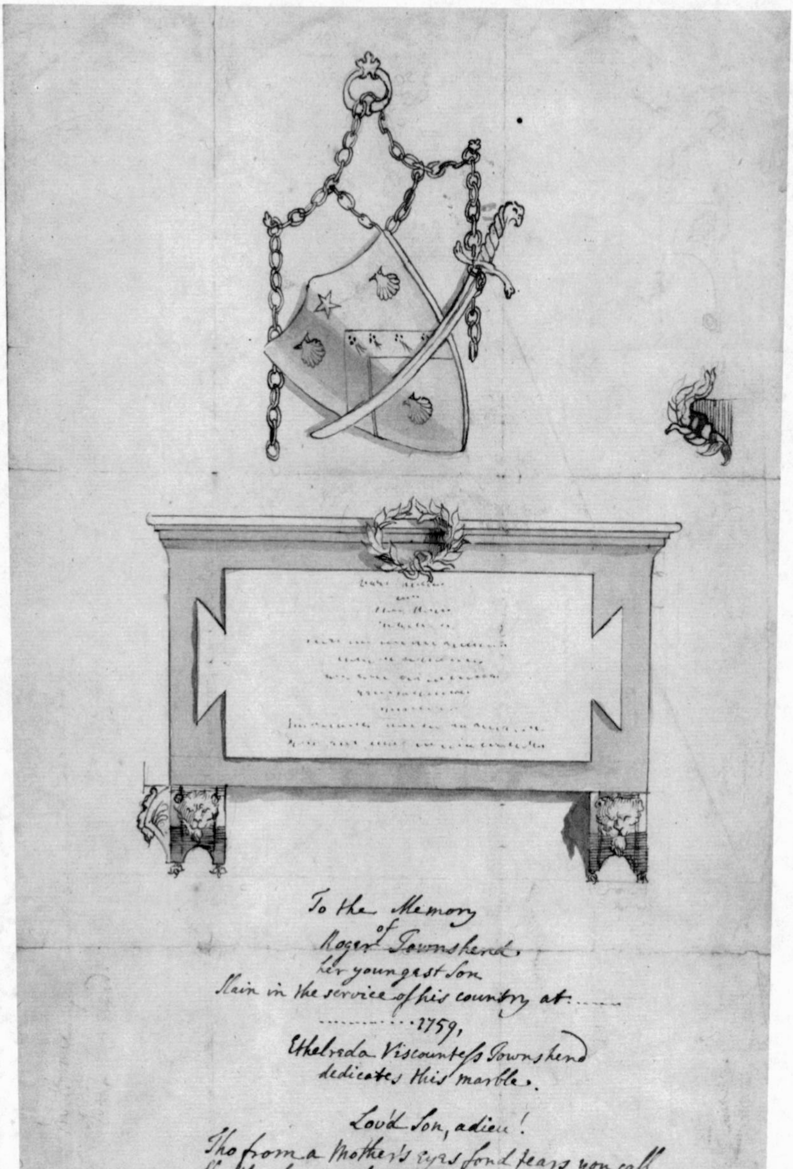
To the Memory
of
Roger Townshend
her youngest Son
Slain in the service of his country at......
..........1759,
Ethelreda Viscountess Townshend
dedicates this marble.
Lov'd Son, adieu!
Tho from a Mother's eyes fond tears you call,
She thanks you, that without a blush they fall.

BENTLEY'S DESIGN FOR
ROGER TOWNSHEND'S MONUMENT

and modesty there is in this sort of things, the more they are touching. I am not vain enough to think that there is any taste in what I have scratched out, but at least it is decent.

I have taken the liberty to sketch out an epitaph too, in which, wishing to give at once a picture of your Ladyship's amiable grief and fortitude, I have tried to blend the heroism of a Spartan mother[2] with the tenderness of an English one.

I am Madam
Your Ladyship's most faithful humble servant

HOR. WALPOLE

PS. My own draught was so rude, that I begged Mr Bentley[3] to draw the enclosed.

[Enclosure][4]

To the Memory
of
Roger Townshend
her youngest Son
Slain in the service of his country at . . . .
. 1759,
Ethelreda Viscountess Townshend
dedicates this marble.

Lov'd Son, adieu!
Tho' from a Mother's eyes fond tears you call,
She thanks you, that without a blush they fall.

2. 'My Lady T[ownshend] who has not learning enough to copy a Spartan mother, has lost her youngest son' (ibid. 294).

3. Richard Bentley, HW's correspondent.

4. See illustration. 'I gave my Lady Townshend an epitaph and design for a tomb for her youngest son killed at Ticonderoga; neither were used' (HW's 'Short Notes,' GRAY i. 34). The monument erected in 1762 by Lady Townshend in the south aisle of Westminster Abbey was designed by Robert Adam and executed by Thomas Carter and Johannes Eckstein. It consists of a pyramid of red and white marble against which stand, like caryatids, two Indians, one holding a gun, the other a tomahawk. They bear a sarcophagus on which is a bas-relief representing Townshend, and the British soldiers surrounding him, in Roman costume, with a view of Fort Ticonderoga in the distance. The inscription reads: 'This monument was erected by a disconsolate parent, the Lady Viscountess Townshend, to the memory of her fifth son, the Honourable Lieutenant-

From Lady Townshend, Wednesday 17 October 1759

Printed from the MS now wsl. First printed, Toynbee *Supp.* ii. 115. For the history of the MS see *ante* 30 Sept. 1743 OS.

The year is established by 'the taking of Quebeck' in Sept. 1759.

Address (in an unidentified hand): To the Honourable Horatio Walpole at Strawberry Hill near Twickenham. *Postmark:* 17 OC. PS.

White Hall, October the 17th.

Lady Townshend's compliments to Mr Walpole and begs he will believe that it is from the knowledge she has of his goodness to her and of his humanity in general that she is very sure he will now share in her joy when she acquaints him that Mr Townshend[1] is safe and well and has most miraculously been preserved in the midst of the most desperate enterprise in the taking of Quebeck in which he has made a glorious figure.[2]

Colonel Roger Townshend, who was killed by a cannon-ball on the 25th of July 1759, in the 28th year of his age, as he was reconnoitring the French lines at Ticonderoga, in North America. From the parent, the brother, and the friend, his sociable and amiable manners, his enterprising bravery, and the integrity of his heart, may claim the tribute of affliction. Yet, stranger, weep not; for, though premature his death, his life was glorious, enrolling him with the names of those immortal statesmen and commanders whose wisdom and intrepidity, in the course of this comprehensive and successful war, have extended the commerce, enlarged the dominions, and upheld the majesty of these Kingdoms, beyond the idea of any former age' ([William Combe or Rudolph Ackermann], *The History of the Abbey Church of St Peter's, Westminster,* 1812, ii. 42–3 and illustration, ii. 40; E. W. Brayley, *The History and Antiquities of the Abbey Church of St Peter, Westminster,* 1818–23, ii. 240; A. P. Stanley, *Historical Memorials of Westminster Abbey,* 5th edn, 1882, p. 236, n. 4; *London Chronicle* 2–4 Nov. 1762, xii. 438).

1. Hon. George Townshend (1724–1807), 4th Vct Townshend, 1764; cr. (1787) M. Townshend; Col. 64th Foot 9 June–Dec. 1759; Lady Townshend's eldest son.

2. Townshend was appointed Jan. 1759 to command a brigade under Gen. Wolfe in the expedition to Quebec and assumed command of the army on Wolfe's death. He took part in the successful assault on the Plains of Abraham 13 Sept. and received the surrender of Quebec 18 Sept. News of the victory reached London 16 Oct. (Mann v. 337–8; C. V. F. Townshend, *The Military Life of Field-Marshal George First Marquess Townshend,* 1901, pp. 232–41). Townshend himself wrote modestly to his wife, Lady Ferrers, from Quebec 20 Sept.: 'We have gained a great day, the particulars you will read in the public gazette. Though I was not in the warmest part of the action; yet I had more shots near me than in any other action I've seen' (Hist. MSS Comm., 11th Report, App. iv [*Townshend MSS,*] 1887, p. 313).

From JOHANN HEINRICH MÜNTZ,[1] Monday 12 November 1759

Printed from the MS now WSL, with the original spelling and punctuation preserved. First printed, Toynbee *Supp.* ii. 115–16. Damer-Waller; the MS was sold Sotheby's 5 Dec. 1921 (first Waller Sale), lot 163, to Wells; given by him to Thomas Conolly, of Chicago, from whom WSL acquired it in 1937.

This monday Nov^{er}. 12 in the afternoon 1759.

Sir,

IF I HAVE forgot myself, that I must know; If I have behaved improperly,[2] the world must judge of: any body that is bold enough, without reason to compare me to a Lyer and with acrimony, shall never see me behave otherways. for the grace you seem to accord me, to stay in your house till i am settled, I must mark you my aknoledgment, I shall get away all my things by to morow morning. I really believe not to Deserve all the monney y have remitted me Sir, viz. two notes making fifty guineas, and ten guineas more in gold. I am very glad you dit beforehand what I wanted to propose to you, for I Repeat it once more that I think myself injured, far more than ever befell me. I am fully determined to obey your commands, except chance and fate should so ordre, as to see you in the streets. for the Lottery ticket, you may be sure S^{r}. I shall never put in any claim. I was prepared for all this, this good while ago, if you thought me so little acquainted with mankind and their different passions it is not mi fault. you might better have judged of my way of thinking, if you took me for a fool or a knave you must answer for it to your self; Protection i never wanted, to purchase it at the rate I did for these last fiffteen month past. Protection of the house of co͞mons I never stood in need of. I Dare to go *tete Levee* every wheres. You

1. (1727–98), Swiss painter employed by HW 1755–9 (*ante* 18 April 1757, n. 4).

2. The details of Müntz's misconduct which caused HW to dismiss him are not known. He seems to have become involved with a female servant of HW's whom he is said to have later married. HW wrote George Montagu 17 Nov. 1759 that the reason for his dismissal was 'nothing but a tolerable quantity of ingratitude on his side, both to me and Mr Bentley. The story is rather too long for a letter; the substance was, most extreme impertinence to me, concluded by an abusive letter against Mr Bentley. . . . In short, I turned his head, and was forced to turn him out of doors. You shall see the *documents,* as it is the fashion to call proof-papers' (MONTAGU i. 259; see also 'Short Notes,' GRAY i. 34 and n. 233). No other 'documents' related to this affair have been found.

would oblige me to appoint, some body to visit all my thing, There might be some thing that might belong to you (though i know of nothing positively yet it is better that every one have what belongs to him in time.) if you will mark or name any thing you want you shall have it.

as your hand writing is very well known to me, it was not necessary to saign your name. as mine is not allways so uniform, i think fit to subscrib

J. H. MÜNTZ[3]

From WILLIAM PITT (later LORD CHATHAM), Saturday 17 November 1759

Printed from *Works* ii. 374–5, where the letter was first printed. The history of the MS and its present whereabouts are not known.

St James's Square, Nov. 17, 1759.

MR PITT presents his compliments to Mr Walpole, and is extremely sorry to have been abroad when Mr Walpole has twice done him the honour to call. He is going out of town this morning, and will be very glad to receive any commands[1] of Mr Walpole next week, at the time he shall please to name.

3. A note in Müntz's MS 'Vasen en Urnen,' 1772 (in the Victoria and Albert Museum), suggests that Müntz nevertheless retained a good opinion of HW: 'This gentleman was the youngest son of the famous knight Robert Walpole, Lord of Oxford [*sic*], prime minister of England. All the vases owned by the son were gifts to the minister. They represent the good taste of the knight. The son is not less an art-lover, scholar, man of taste and knowledgeable, and he knows how to treasure the objects' (translation from the Dutch kindly furnished by Dr Michael McCarthy).

1. See following letter.

To William Pitt (later Lord Chatham), Monday 19 November 1759

Printed from *Works* ii. 375–6, where the letter was first printed. Reprinted, *Monthly Review*, 1798, n.s., xxvii. 61–2; Cunningham iii. 267–8 (signature omitted); Toynbee iv. 324–5; extract printed in Paget Toynbee, 'Horace Walpole and Pitt,' *Times Literary Supplement* 15 March 1923, p. 179. The history of the MS and its present whereabouts are not known.

Nov. 19, 1759.

Sir,

On my coming to town,[1] I did myself the honour of waiting on you and Lady Hesther Pitt,[2] and though I think myself extremely distinguished by your obliging note,[3] I should be sorry for having given you the trouble of writing it, if it did not *lend* me a very pardonable opportunity of saying what I much wished to express, but thought myself too private a person, and of too little consequence to take the liberty to say. In short, Sir, I was eager to congratulate you on the lustre you have thrown on this country; I wished to thank you for the security you have fixed to me of enjoying the happiness I do enjoy. You have placed England in a situation in which it never saw itself—a task the more difficult, as you had not to improve, but recover. In a trifling book written two or three years ago, I said (speaking of the name in the world the most venerable to me), 'Sixteen unfortunate and inglorious years since his removal have already written his eulogium.'[4] It is but justice to you, Sir, to add, that that period ended when your administration began. Sir, don't take this for flattery; there is nothing in your power to give that I would accept—nay, there is nothing I could envy, but what I believe you would scarce offer me, your glory. This may sound very vain and insolent, but consider, Sir, what a monarch is a man who wants nothing; consider how he looks down on one who is only the most illustrious man in Britain.—But, Sir, freedoms apart, insignificant as I am, probably it must be some satisfaction to a great mind like yours, to receive incense when you are sure there is no

1. 7 Nov. (Montagu i. 253).

2. Lady Hester Grenville (1720–1803), m. (1754) William Pitt; cr. (1761) Bns Chatham s.j.

3. See previous letter.

4. *Royal and Noble Authors*, account of Sir Robert Walpole (HW). See *Works* i. 447.

flattery blended with it: and what must any Englishman be that could give you a minute's satisfaction, and would hesitate!

Adieu, Sir—I am unambitious, I am disinterested—but I am vain. You have by your notice,[5] uncanvassed, unexpected, and at the period when you certainly could have the least temptation to stoop down to me, flattered me in the most agreeable manner. If there could arrive the moment, when you could be nobody and I anybody, you cannot imagine how grateful I would be. In the meantime permit me to be, as I have been ever since I had the honour of knowing you,

Sir,

Your most obedient humble servant,

HOR. WALPOLE

From WILLIAM PITT (later LORD CHATHAM), Tuesday 20 November 1759

Printed from the MS now WSL. First printed in Paget Toynbee, 'Horace Walpole and Pitt,' *Times Literary Supplement* 15 March 1923, p. 179. Reprinted, Toynbee *Supp.* iii. 162–3. For the history of the MS see *ante* 27 Feb. 1757.

November the 20th 1759.

Dear Sir,

THE impressions I am under from the honour of your letter[1] are too sensible not to call for expression. As often as I have read it, (for tis best to confess) I do indulge myself in the frequent repetition, I am at some loss to decide which sort of pleasure such a letter is made to excite the most; that delight which springs from wit, *agrément* and beauty of style, or the serious and deep-felt satisfaction which the possession of so kind and honourable a testimony must convey.[2] I can however assure you that intoxicating as the charm is, I am, as yet, truly sensible and well acquainted with my own undeservings, but if my head holds out, after farther perusing the dangerous contents of a piece full of so much friendship and

5. His note of 17 Nov. 1759 to HW.

---

1. *Ante* 19 Nov. 1759.
2. HW still spoke of Pitt many years later as the 'great minister who carried our glory to its highest pitch' (HW's draft of a letter to William Mason ca 1 Feb. 1784, MASON ii. 351).

beauty, I shall begin to think a little more advantageously. In the meantime, the letter itself shall take its place in my library, between Pliny[3] and Voiture,[4] to the no small jealousy of both; while the writer will, I hope, give me leave to place him in the grateful and lasting remembrance of one who is with perfect esteem and respectful consideration,

Dear Sir,

Your most obedient and affectionate humble servant,

W. Pitt

To Lord Cardigan,[1] ?Tuesday 20 November ?1759

Printed from Toynbee iii. 131–2, where the letter was first printed from a copy of the MS then (1903) in the possession of the Earl of Home; not further traced. The MS may have passed to the Home family when the second daughter of Elizabeth, Duchess of Buccleuch (only surviving daughter and heiress of Lord Cardigan), married the 10th Earl of Home in 1798.

The letter was placed by Mrs Toynbee in 1752, the year Lord Cardigan was appointed governor and constable of Windsor Castle. However, a similar mention of 'Mr Bevan' in Lord Hertford to HW 1 Sept. 1759 (see n. 4 below) indicates that 1759 is probably the correct year.

Arlington Street, Nov. 20.

My Lord,

IS NOT it very ungrateful to take advantage from your goodness to give you new trouble? or may I plead that I could receive no advantage from that kindness *but* by giving you new trouble? I will tell your Lordship the case and then you shall try whether you think I am pardonable or not.

Mr Boyce, who kept Colonel Brown's[2] courts,[3] died last Thurs-

3. Pliny the younger (ca 62–ca 113).

4. Vincent Voiture (1598–1648), courtier and letter-writer.

1. George Montagu (before 1749, Brudenell) (1712–90), 4th E. of Cardigan, 1732; cr. (1766) D. of Montagu; governor and constable of Windsor Castle 1752–90.

2. Both men are unidentified.

3. As constable of Windsor Castle, Lord Cardigan was responsible for the administration of the forest laws in the Great Park and Forest of Windsor. A number of officials held employment under him to preserve not only the King's peace but also his 'vert and venison.' Courts dealing with minor offences were held in the Castle at suitable intervals, more serious cases were heard less frequently, and the Supreme Court met once a year (T. E. Harwood, *Windsor Old and New,* printed privately, 1929, pp. 30, 140; information kindly furnished by Sir Owen Morshead).

day. Your Lordship flattered me, that if Colonel Brown, upon inquiry, found himself disengaged, he would employ Mr Bevan.[4] I dare say no more, nor shall I venture to wait upon you again, till you have forgot how impertinent I am, and shall only remember that

I am

Your Lordship's most obedient humble servant,

HOR. WALPOLE

TO ?HENRY READE,[1] ca 1760

Printed for the first time from the MS now WSL. For the history of the MS see *ante* 29 Aug. 1743 OS. The text of the letter appears to be incomplete: it is written on the recto of a sheet from which the conjugate leaf has been torn off. The letter seems to be addressed to Henry Reade, although the provenance of the MS suggests that it may actually have been sent to HW's deputy, Grosvenor Bedford, who also held a post in the Exchequer.

Dated conjecturally; HW was at this time gathering information for *Anecdotes of Painting* (see n. 4 below). In 1758 Reade sent HW a copy, now WSL, of Duwes's *An Introductorie for to lerne to Rede, to Pronounce, and to Speake Frenche trewly, compyled for . . . The Lady Mary of England,* [?1539] (Hazen, *Cat. of HW's Lib.,* No. 118). The only other letter in their correspondence that has been found is *post* 1 May 1761.

To ask Mr Reade, if Lord Lincoln[2] has any picture of Elizabeth Countess of Lincoln,[3] daughter of the Earl of Kildare in the time of Queen Elizabeth. When Mr Walpole has the pleasure of seeing Mr Reade, he will tell him why he asked.[4]

4. Possibly the son of Arthur Bevan (ca 1688–1743), of Laugharne, co. Carmarthen; M.P. Carmarthen 1727–41. HW had apparently written to his cousin, Lord Hertford, in August to ask him 'to employ Mr Bevan in keeping [his] courts in Suffolk' on Hertford's estates (CONWAY ii. 25 and nn. 5–6).

1. (d. 1762), comptroller of duties on houses in the Tax Office of the Exchequer (*Court and City Register,* 1758, p. 111; GM 1762, xxxii. 600).

2. 2d D. of Newcastle-under-Lyne, 1768; HW's correspondent. He was auditor of the Exchequer 1751–94.

3. Lady Elizabeth Fitzgerald (ca 1528–90), youngest dau. of Gerald (1487–1534), 9th E. of Kildare, 1513; m. 1 (1543) Sir Anthony Browne; m. 2 (1552), as his third wife, Edward Clinton, otherwise Fiennes, cr. (1572) E. of Lincoln. The only portrait of her mentioned in *Anecdotes of Painting,* 1762–71, i. 135n, was at Woburn Abbey. It was attributed to Cornelius Ketel, but has since been attributed to Hans Eworth (Lionel Cust, 'The Painter HE (Hans Eworth),' *Walpole Society* 1913, ii. 16, 31).

4. HW was engaged in collecting material for his *Anecdotes of Painting.* He recorded in his 'Short Notes': 'Jan. 1 [1760]. I began the lives of English artists from Vertue's MSS' (GRAY i. 34).

To the REV. MICHAEL LORT,[1] Thursday 24 January 1760

Printed for the first time from a photostat of the MS bound into Lort's copy of HW's *Catalogue of the Royal and Noble Authors,* 2d edn, 1759, now in the Bodleian Library (Vet. A.S.e. 947). Its earlier history is not known. The letter antedates the rest of HW's correspondence with Lort which is printed in CHATTERTON; it was answered by Lort in a letter of 7 Feb. 1760 (ibid. 137–9).

Arlington Street, Jan. 24, 1760.

Sir,

AFTER giving yourself the trouble of making remarks on my *Catalogue,*[2] with a sight of which Mr Cumberland[3] has favoured me, you must not be surprised at receiving the additional trouble of my thanks. The information I get lays me under great obligation to you, as I shall certainly profit of it, if ever I find it necessary to reprint my book:[4] this is a real obligation; yet perhaps as an author it is natural for me to be full as well pleased with some marks of your approbation. However, Sir, as I wish it was still more deserving of your applause, I should have been glad if you had been more severe to it, for I correct it readily, as often as I am told of its faults, except such faults as I don't desire to have it exempt from. Some notices even of the curious ones I have received from you, Sir, I had picked up since the work was last printed; I have got Puttenham,[5] and Warburton's book;[6] and I knew of Lord Barrington's works,[7] but was desired by his son[8] not to mention him. The pamphlet said to be my father's,[9] if his, at least he did not remember. Lady

1. (1725–90), antiquary and divine; Fellow of Trinity College, Cambridge, 1750–81 and Regius professor of Greek 1759–71; F.S.A., 1755.

2. *Of the Royal and Noble Authors;* see headnote.

3. Richard Cumberland (1732–1811), dramatist. Lort's letter of 22 Dec. 1759 to Cumberland with his comments on *Royal and Noble Authors* is printed in CHATTERTON 364–71.

4. HW's use of Lort's information is indicated in the footnotes ibid.

5. *The Arte of English Poesie,* 1589, by George Puttenham (d. 1590) (see ibid. 365 and n. 6). HW's copy, now WSL, is Hazen, *Cat. of HW's Lib.,* No. 2456:1.

6. *A Critical and Philosophical Enquiry into the Causes of Prodigies and Miracles,* 1727, by William Warburton (1698–1779), Bp of Gloucester, 1760 (see CHATTERTON 368 and n. 39). HW's copy, now WSL, is Hazen, op. cit., No. 211.

7. See *ante* 7 Feb. 1759, nn. 6–9.

8. William Wildman Barrington Shute (1717–93), 2d Vct Barrington, 1734.

9. *A Letter to the Examiner, Suggesting Proper Heads for the Vindicating His Masters,* 1714; the author has not been identified, but it was apparently not Sir Robert Walpole (CHATTERTON 370 and n. 54).

Masham[10] was no peeress: she was an authoress, and has had a claim put in for her to the *Whole Duty of Man.*[11] Lord Coleraine[12] is quite new to me as an author; considering how diligent he or his son[13] were to print and have engraved every thing relating to them, I wonder they did not make those writings more public. The story of the Duchess of Newcastle[14] and her man John[15] is very entertaining; I never heard it before—but I will not tire you, Sir, in particularizing my obligations, but it will add to those I have to Mr Cumberland if he procures me, Sir, a nearer acquaintance with you.

I am Sir

Your most obliged humble servant

Hor. Walpole

To the 4th Duke of Devonshire, Monday 18 February 1760

Printed for the first time from a photostat of the MS at Chatsworth House, Derbyshire, kindly furnished by the Duke of Devonshire.

Arlington Street, Feb. 18, 1760.

My Lord,

Your Grace knows enough of me, I believe, to know that I am not apt to ask favours, even where I might have pretensions. I certainly have no right to ask any of your Grace, nor am I going to take any such liberty. I would only, and even that is presumption, put your Grace in mind of something which I think so well of you, as to trust you will not be angry with me for reminding you of, and which I am sure it is only your ignorance of the case that has pre-

10. Damaris Cudworth (1659–1708), m. (1685) Sir Francis Masham, 3d Bt (see ibid. 370 and n. 57).

11. Published in 1658, attributed to Richard Allestree (1619–81). HW's copies are Hazen, op. cit., Nos 867 and 1389.

12. Hugh Hare (ca 1606–67), 1st Bn Coleraine; translator of G. F. Loredano's *The Ascents of the Soul,* 1681 (see Chatterton 371 and nn. 58, 60).

13. Henry Hare (1636–1708), 2d Bn Coleraine, 1667; antiquary.

14. Margaret Lucas (1617–73), m. (1645), as his second wife, William Cavendish, M. of Newcastle; cr. (1665) D. of Newcastle.

15. John Rolleston, Newcastle's secretary (Chatterton 368 n. 37). According to the story, he slept in the Duchess's bedchamber closet, ready to record any of her literary inspirations (see ibid. 367–8 and n. 38). HW added this anecdote to *Royal and Noble Authors* (*Works* i. 383).

vented you from thinking of already. In short, my Lord, I have some suspicions, and they are mere suspicions, for I never heard one word of it from themselves, that Mr Churchill[1] and Lady Mary[2] are far from easy in their affairs. He has been so unlucky in marrying a favourite daughter of Sir Robert Walpole, as to be involved in a lawsuit for her fortune,[3] and to be likely to lose part, if not the whole of it. He has had other losses; and the Duke of Newcastle[4] was so unkind as to give away even the reversion of a place which she holds only for the life of another person. Your Grace knows the steadiness of his behaviour to the Government, as a member of Parliament,[5] and opportunity of serving the King which he has always bought very dearly, without the least recompense, and even without asking the least.

As Mr Churchill has the honour of your Grace's friendship, if he has never mentioned these circumstances to you, it is, my Lord, at least an amiable modesty; and I should wrong that virtue, if I did not give you my honour in the most solemn manner, that the step I now take is absolutely without his knowledge, or suggestion or connivance, even in the most indirect manner. My concern for a sister and her children[6] whom I love, and my own incapacity of serving them, alone dictated this application, which, if unsuccessful, will at least, I flatter myself, carry its excuse along with it.

If your Grace should be so good as to go one step beyond pardoning me, and should ask, what you could do for them, it would be decent in me, to leave that wholly to your Grace: though if I might even suggest anything to you, it would be a simple hint, that as Colonel Pelham[7] is very old, you might not perhaps, my Lord, if

1. Charles Churchill (ca 1720–1812), HW's brother-in-law.

2. Lady Maria Walpole (ca 1725–1801), m. (1746) Charles Churchill; HW's half-sister, being the illegitimate daughter of Sir Robert Walpole by Maria Skerrett, whom he married in 1738.

3. Sir Robert's will (1741) provided that £12,000 invested in 3½ percent annuities by Maria Skerrett before their marriage (to which he was entitled) be held for their daughter until her own marriage, as likewise lands in the counties of Somerset and Shropshire, and all of his jewels except those otherwise disposed of (P.C.C. – 91 Seymour).

4. First lord of the Treasury 1754–56, 1757–62.

5. Churchill was M.P. for Stockbridge 1741–47, Milborne Port 1747–54, and Great Marlow 1754–61.

6. The Churchills had five sons and two daughters.

7. James Pelham (ca 1683–1761), of Crowhurst, Sussex; Lt-Col. 1st Foot Guards, 1716; M.P.; secretary (ca 1720–61) to the lord chamberlain of the Household, a post held by the Duke of Devonshire since 1757.

you have nobody else in your view, think Mr Churchill is proper to succeed him.[8]

I must retract what I said in the beginning of my letter, that I had no favour to ask. I must entreat your Grace, not to mention this to Mr Churchill. I don't know how he would take my troubling you in his behalf. Besides, if this hint should have any good fortune, I should wish Mr Churchill to have the pride of thinking that he was solely indebted to your Grace's favour.

I am my Lord

Your Grace's most obedient humble servant

Hor. Walpole

To Lady Northumberland, Wednesday 2 April 1760

Printed from a photostat of the MS in the possession of the Duke of Northumberland, Alnwick Castle, Northumberland, kindly furnished by Mr D. P. Graham. First printed in Helen Sard Hughes, 'Another Letter by Horace Walpole,' *Modern Language Notes*, 1928, xliii. 320. The MS is preserved among the Percy family papers (vol. 32, p. 170) at Alnwick Castle.

Strawberry Hill, April 2d 1760.

Madam,

The account of *Percy-Heralds* which I had the honour to mention to your Ladyship yesterday, is in a book called *A Collection of Curious Discourses Written by Eminent Antiquarians upon Several Heads in our English Antiquities.*[1] These pieces were published by T. Hearne in 1720. In one of the tracts called *The Duty and Office of an Herald of Armes*[2] it is said p. 263. that in the time of King Henry IV among a few others was *Percy-Herald:* and in the reign of Edward IV p. 265. that the Earl of Northumberland had *Northumberland-Herald:* as he had given under Henry VII when it is particularly recorded that none even of the great peers had her-

8. He was succeeded by his deputy, the Duke's friend Sir Robert Wilmot (d. 1772) (*Court and City Register*, 1760, p. 75; 1763, p. 79).

1. *A Collection of Curious Discourses, Written by Eminent Antiquaries*, Oxford, 1720, by Thomas Hearne (1678–1735). HW's copy is Hazen, *Cat. of HW's Lib.*, No. 657.

2. *A Discourse of the Dutye and Office of an Heraulde of Armes, Written by Frauncis Thynne Lancaster Heraulde*, 1605.

alds but the Earl of Northumberland; even the Lord Marquis (of Worcester) having but a pursevant.[3] I flatter myself that these additional proofs of the greatness of your Ladyship's house will not be unacceptable, as the discovery is a satisfaction to and an evidence of the attachment of

Madam

Your Ladyship's most obliged and
obedient humble servant and tenant

Hor. Walpole

To ? the Rev. Christopher Wilson,[1] Tuesday 29 April 1760

Printed from the MS now wsl. First printed (inaccurately) in Sotheby's Cat. of 5 May 1900. Reprinted, Toynbee iv. 375–6 (closing and signature omitted). The MS was sold Sotheby's 5 May 1900, lot 236, to Denholm; resold Sotheby's 30 Jan. [1 Feb.] 1918 (Denholm Sale), lot 380, to Maggs; offered by them, Cat. Nos 370 (autumn 1918), lot 2097; 399 (Christmas 1920), lot 3446; 441 (1923), lot 2135; 488 (spring 1927), lot 633; 516 (spring 1929), lot 593; resold by Walter T. Spencer to wsl, 1932.

Ascribed conjecturally to Christopher Wilson from the endorsement.

Endorsed in an unidentified hand: Chr. (Bp) Wilson—marr[ie]d Bp Gibsons dau[ghte]r.[2]

Arlington Street, April 29, 1760.

Sir,

I AM much obliged to you for the favour of your letter[3] communicated to me by our friend Dr Ducarel.[4] It is particularly pleasing to me to receive information from a gentleman, *Sir, of your knowledge and character;* and if ever my *Catalogue*[5] should want another edition, I shall undoubtedly be proud of correcting it

3. 'A junior heraldic officer attendant on the heralds; also one attached to a particular nobleman' (oed *sub* 'pursuivant' 1).

1. (ca 1714–92), D.D., 1753; canon residentiary of St Paul's, 1758; Bp of Bristol 1783–92 (Venn, *Alumni Cantab.;* Nichols, *Lit. Anec.* ix. 519–20; John LeNeve, *Fasti Ecclesiæ Anglicanæ,* Oxford, 1854, i. 220).

2. Anne Gibson (d. 1789), youngest dau. of Edmund Gibson (1669–1748), Bp of London 1723–48; m. Christopher Wilson (gm 1789, lix pt i. 471; Norman Sykes, *Edmund Gibson,* 1926, p. 378).

3. Missing.

4. HW's correspondent (*ante* 29 April 1760).

5. *Of the Royal and Noble Authors.*

by the lights you have bestowed on me. One article I cannot help repeating out of your letter, because I do not quite understand the drift of it—It is the *quære* on Lord Hervey's *Epistle*[6] for Miss Howe[7] to Mr Lowther.[8] If you doubt the designation of it, I can assure you, Sir, it was so intended. I was well acquainted with my Lord Hervey, and am very intimate with several of his family,[9] who know the fact as I have reported it.[10]

I am Sir

Your obliged and obedient humble servant

Hor. Walpole

From Lord Holdernesse, Thursday 3 July 1760

Printed from the MS now wsl. First printed, Toynbee *Supp.* ii. 117. Damer-Waller; the MS was sold Sotheby's 5 Dec. 1921 (first Waller Sale), lot 147, to Wells; given by him to Thomas Conolly, of Chicago, from whom wsl acquired it in 1937.

Sion Hill,[1] July 3d 1760.

Dear Sir,

I am infinitely obliged to you for the trouble you have given yourself about the plan,[2] and am so much pleased with the ornaments you propose that I shall send orders tonight for the immediate execution of them. I hope I shall soon have an opportunity of thanking you in person. I go to London tonight where I shall wait with some

6. 'Monimia to Philocles,' one of Hervey's four *Epistles in the Manner of Ovid* (*Royal and Noble Authors,* 2d edn, 1759, ii. 148; Dodsley's *Collection of Poems,* 1755, iv. 82–9; Ossory iii. 256).

7. Sophia Howe (d. 1726), maid of honour to the Ps of Wales, afterwards Q. Caroline (*Historical Register . . . Chronological Diary,* 1726, p. 15).

8. Hon. Anthony Lowther (d. 1741), son of 1st Vct Lonsdale; M.P.

9. Particularly his widow, Lady Hervey.

10. Miss Howe had 'conceived a violent attachment to . . . Mr Lowther,' thinking her love returned; but on finding him at length indifferent, she 'laid herself at the door of Mr Lowther's house' in despair and died soon after 'raving mad' (*The Autobiography and Correspondence of Mary Granville, Mrs Delany,* ed. Lady Llanover, 1861–2, vi. 163).

1. Syon Hill, Lord Holdernesse's seat at Isleworth, Middlesex.

2. The sketch for a Gothic room, probably at Aston, Lord Holdernesse's seat in Yorkshire. HW wrote George Montagu 4 July 1760: 'Mr Bentley has sketched a very pretty Gothic room for Lord Holderness, and orders are gone to execute it directly in Yorkshire. The first draught was Mason's, but as he does not pretend to much skill, we were desired to correct—I say *we,* for I chose the ornaments' (Montagu i. 285).

anxiety for the next letters, as it is very probable there has been a general action in Hesse[3] by this time.

I ever am with the truest regard,

Dear Sir,

Your most obedient humble servant,

HOLDERNESSE

Honourable Hor. Walpole.

TO UNKNOWN, ca Friday 15 August 1760

Printed for the first time from a photostat of the MS (a fragment of a draft in pencil, apparently for an otherwise missing letter) on the back page of Lord Hertford's letter of 10 Aug. 1760 to HW (BM Add. MS 23,218, f. 31 verso; see CONWAY ii. 67). The letter was probably written just after HW's recovery from an attack of gout which he suffered ca 4–14 Aug. 1760; see MONTAGU i. 291 and MANN v. 432.

As I now conclude I am to live an hundred years longer, I am making intimate friendships with all the children I ⟨ ⟩ my co-temporaries, whom ⟨ ⟩ with whom I intended to say ⟨ ⟩ the friends who are going out of the world.

To the 4th DUKE OF DEVONSHIRE, Tuesday 2 September 1760

Printed for the first time from a photostat of the MS at Chatsworth House, Derbyshire, kindly furnished by the Duke of Devonshire.

Arlington Street Sept. 2d 1760.

My Lord,

I SHOULD be very ungrateful, if I was not sensible to all your Grace's goodness to me at Chatsworth,[1] and I hope you will not think me officious in returning you my thanks. But your Grace will

3. On the Schwalm, where Prince Ferdinand and Broglie were opposed from 27 June to 7 July (*London Chronicle* 5–8 July, viii. 30, *sub* 'Hague, July 3'; *Daily Adv.* 11 July). Prince Ferdinand wrote Holdernesse 29 June, describing his situation: 'Les deux armées se trouvent vis à vis l'une de l'autre, à la distance de deux heures de chemin' (MANN v. 419 n. 4).

1. Where HW arrived 25 Aug. and stayed four days (MONTAGU i. 295). For his long account of Chatsworth see *Country Seats* 28–9.

be convinced of my feeling it, when you find I trust enough to it to be more troublesome to you. If you have no objection, I should be glad when your pictures come to town to Collevaux's,[2] if you would give me leave to have a copy in little of James V and his Queen;[3] as there are no other pictures of them, they are a great curiosity. I was extremely obliged to your Grace and Lord John[4] for the trouble he gave himself in showing me Hardwicke.[5] I cannot say it effaces Chatsworth; I think the mere situation of the latter much the finer—you will forgive this preference when both are your own. I was however pleased with the magnificence of your great grandmother[6] enough to think of her in the chaise afterwards, and I offer your Grace the fruits of my meditation:

Epitaph[7]
for Elizabeth of Hardwicke
Countess of Shrewsbury;

Four times the nuptial bed she warm'd,
And ev'ry time so well perform'd,
That when Death spoil'd each husband's billing,
He left the widow ev'ry shilling.
Sad was the dame, but not dejected;
Five stately mansions she erected
With more than royal pomp, to vary
The prison of her captive, Mary.
When Hardwicke's tow'rs shall bow their head,
Nor mass be more in Worksop said,
When Bolsover's fair frame shall tend,
Like Old-Coates, to its mould'ring end,

2. Collevause, 'picture cleaner in Maiden Lane' (HW's 'Book of Materials,' 1759, pp. 90, 124).

3. James V of Scotland (1512–42), m. Mary of Guise (1515–60). According to HW's note in his priced copy of the 'Des. of SH,' 1774, he paid Wale 5 guineas for making the drawing. It was sold SH xx. 59 to Forster for £3.

4. Lord John Cavendish (1732–96), the Duke's younger brother; statesman.

5. Hardwick Hall, near Chesterfield, Derbyshire, another of the Duke's seats. HW describes it at length in *Country Seats* 29–30.

6. Elizabeth Hardwick (ca 1520–1608), m. 1 (1532) Robert Barlow (or Barley) (d. 1533); m. 2 (1547) Sir William Cavendish (d. 1557); m. 3 (ca 1559) Sir William St Loe (d. 1564 or 1565); m. 4 (1568) George Talbot, 6th E. of Shrewsbury (ca 1522–90) (E. C. Williams, *Bess of Hardwick,* 1959, pp. 1, 5–8, 14, 36, 39–40, 57, 62, 194; GEC). 'Bess of Hardwick' built Hardwick Hall 1591–7.

7. HW sent this epitaph, with minor variations, to George Montagu 1 Sept. 1760 (MONTAGU i. 298, where it is annotated).

When Chatsworth knows no Candish bounties,
Let Fame forget this costly Countess.

I am my Lord

Your Grace's most obedient and most obliged humble servant

HOR. WALPOLE

PS. I a little repent not accepting the offer your Grace was so good as to make me of letting Mr Payne[8] draw a bit of Haddon[9] for me: the house is so great a curiosity to an antiquarian that I own I should be glad of one or two little views of it—but as it is too ugly and bad to employ Mr Payne upon, if he has any clerk who could make a sketch of the inner court, particularly of the right-hand corner within where are those strange disjointed pieces of arches;[10] and a slight view of the whole building of the garden side from the water below,[11] I should be very glad to pay him for them; but I know not how to give your Grace the trouble of this commission—you must take care how you let antiquaries into your house; they always fall in love with the ugliest thing they see.

8. James Paine (ca 1716–89), architect employed by the 4th Duke to carry out his great scheme of reconstructing Chatsworth. His treatise *Plans, Elevations and Sections, of Noblemen and Gentlemen's Houses*, 1767, included his plans executed for Chatsworth (Francis Thompson, *A History of Chatsworth*, 1949, p. 89; H. M. Colvin, *A Biographical Dictionary of English Architects, 1660–1840*, 1954, pp. 429–34).

9. Haddon Hall, Derbyshire, described by HW as 'an ancient seat belonging to the Duke of Rutland. . . . It is very low and can never have been a tolerable house' (*Country Seats* 29).

10. 'Within the court in a corner is a strange confusion of half arches and beams, that imply the greatest ignorance in the art' (ibid.). These architectural features are fully described and illustrated in Christopher Hussey, 'Haddon Hall, Derbyshire—II,' *Country Life*, 1949, cvi. 1746 and fig. 14. A drawing of the inner court was apparently made for HW; see *post* 27 Aug. 1782.

11. Illustrated *Country Life*, cvi. 1884, fig. 1.

To Lord Bute,[1] Monday 20 October 1760

Printed from Toynbee *Supp.* i. 94–5, where the letter was first printed. The MS was sold Sotheby's 10 April 1895 (Frampton Sale), lot 243, to Thomson; re-sold Sotheby's 3 Dec. 1913 (Eliot Reed Sale), lot 373, to Maggs; offered by them, Cat. No. 320 (Jan.–Feb. 1914), lot 769; not further traced.

The letter is recorded in Bute's letterbook in the BM (Add. MS 36,796, p. 54) as follows: 'Desires to be presented to the Prince of Wales. Received a visit from the Duke of York' (information kindly communicated by Prof. John B. Shipley).

Strawberry Hill, Oct. 20, 1760.

My Lord,

WHEN one has been very negligent of one's duty, there is nothing so awkward as to know how to set about correcting one's self. Your Lordship's goodness, I must trust, will supply what I really cannot frame a set of words to excuse. The privacy of my situation, the little consequence I am of, a total want of ambition, content and indolence, have all concurred to make me so faulty as never to have had the honour of kissing his Royal Highness the Prince of Wales's[2] hand; and having omitted it on the first opportunity, I was ashamed to ask permission without any pretence to do it afterwards. I must beg your Lordship's favour to obtain that leave for me now; and you will forgive my troubling your Lordship with explaining the reason of my present request.[3]

His Royal Highness the Duke of York[4] did me the unexpected honour of coming the week before last to see my small house here.[5] It was certainly my duty to wait on his Royal Highness immediately and offer him my most humble thanks. But not having had the honour of being presented to his Royal Highness the Prince of Wales, I was afraid that an abrupt intrusion of myself without asking leave, would be thought an impertinent and officious forwardness. As no want of duty or affection for the Royal Family has prevented my showing myself among the number of their servants, and

1. John Stuart (1713–92), 3d E. of Bute, 1723; tutor to George, P. of Wales, 1755; first lord of the Treasury 1762–3.

2. George, Prince of Wales, later George III.

3. Bute was Groom of the Stole to the Prince of Wales 1756–60. HW was advised by a 'jury of court matrons, that is, courtiers,' to write him to explain his reason for wanting to kiss hands at this time (MONTAGU i. 306).

4. Edward Augustus (1739–67), cr. (1760) D. of York; younger brother of George III.

5. The Duke of York went to SH 10 Oct.; for a full account see MONTAGU i. 304.

as I am most glad of embracing any opportunity of expressing my zeal and gratitude, I flatter myself that his Royal Highness the Prince will admit me to the honour of kissing his hand next Sunday;[6] and that gracious leave will be heightened to me, if I have the satisfaction of owing it to your Lordship's kindness.

As my behaviour is dictated by the most respectful and disinterested duty to his Royal Highness the Prince, her Royal Highness the Princess,[7] and their family, and this application suggested by personal regard for your Lordship, I presume to hope that both will be graciously and favourably interpreted.

I am, my Lord,

Your Lordship's most obedient humble servant,

Hor. Walpole

From Lord Bute, Wednesday 22 October 1760

Printed from a photostat of the MS in the Cardiff Public Library, Cardiff, Wales, kindly furnished by Mr G. A. Dart through the good offices of Prof. John B. Shipley. First printed, Toynbee *Supp.* i. 94, n. 1. Damer-Waller; the MS was sold Sotheby's 5 Dec. 1921 (first Waller Sale), lot 101, to Mild; later acquired by the Cardiff Public Library.

Lond[on], Oct. 22, 1760.

Sir,

I CAN with truth assure you that the perusal of your letter[1] gave me great pleasure; gentlemen of your birth and character ought not to be unknown to the Prince of Wales. I rejoice therefore at the accidental visit[2] that draws you out of your retirement. Though you may entirely depend on any good office of mine, yet I must not lay claim to merit I have no pretensions to. Such is the Prince's disposition that you could not have failed of meeting with a gracious reception, though you had not previously intimated your intentions

6. 26 Oct. The King died suddenly the day before, but HW kissed hands on the 28th 'with all England,' which he found more 'comfortable . . . than to have all England ask why one kisses hands' (ibid. i. 310–11, 313).

7. Augusta (1719–72) of Saxe-Gotha, m. (1736) Frederick Louis (1707–51), P. of Wales.

1. *Ante* 20 Oct. 1760.

2. By the Duke of York.

to me; not but I feel most sensibly the polite and flattering attention you show me. I have the honour to be, Sir, with great regard,

Your most obedient humble servant,

BUTE

TO THOMAS BRAND,[1] Saturday 25 October 1760

Printed from HW's transcript in his 'Book of Materials,' 1786, p. 11, now WSL. First printed, Toynbee *Supp.* i. 96. Reprinted in *Horace Walpole's Miscellany 1786–1795*, ed. L. E. Troide, New Haven, 1978, p. 22. Damer-Waller; the 'Book of Materials' was sold Sotheby's 5 Dec. 1921 (first Waller Sale), lot 57, to Maggs for Henry C. Folger; acquired by WSL in exchange with the Folger Shakespeare Library, 1950.

Dated on the assumption that the letter was written the day George II died. HW's transcript, made at least 26 years after he sent the original, is prefaced by his note: 'When George II died, Mr H. W. wrote this note to Mr Brand, who was a remarkable laugher.'

Dear Brand,

YOU love laughing; there is a King dead; can you help coming to town?

From the REV. WILLIAM HARRIS, Saturday 25 October 1760

Printed from the MS now WSL. First printed, Toynbee *Supp.* iii. 166. For the history of the MS see *ante* 7 Feb. 1759.

Address: To the Honourable Horace Walpole, Esq., in London. *Postmark:* 27 OC. HONITON.

Honiton, Oct. 25, 1760.

Sir,

LOOKING into the *State Trials*,[1] I found the proceedings against Sir John Hollis,[2] and others, in reading of which and comparing it with your account of Lord Clare,[3] I find you have been led

1. (1718–70), of The Hoo, Kimpton, Herts; M.P. HW referred to him in a letter to William Cole 15 Nov. 1770 as 'my particular acquaintance, and our old schoolfellow' at Eton (COLE i. 198 and n. 2).

1. See n. 5 below.

2. John Holles (1564–1637), cr. (1616) Bn Houghton and (1624) E. of Clare.

3. In *Royal and Noble Authors*, 2d edn, 1759, ii. 157, where HW refers the reader to the *Biographia Britannica*, 7

into a very great mistake by trusting to the *Biographia* and others.[4] You'll pardon this freedom, and believe me to be,

Sir,

Your very humble servant,

WILL. HARRIS

State Trials, Vol. I. p. 327. 2d edit.[5]

There is great ground to complain of the carelessness and inaccuracy of the *Biographia,* as I have found on examination.

Cromwell[6] is in the press.

TO LORD BUTE, Monday 15 December 1760

Printed from a photostat of the MS in the possession of Lord Bute, Mount Stuart, near Rothesay, Isle of Bute, kindly furnished through the good offices of Miss C. M. Armet. First printed, *Works* ii. 376–7. Reprinted, *Monthly Review,* 1798, 2d ser., xxvii. 62; Toynbee v. 11–12; *Horace Walpole's Fugitive Verses,* ed. W. S. Lewis, 1931, p. 136.

Endorsed in an unidentified hand: Mr H. Walpole Dec. 15, 1760.

Arlington Street, Dec. 15th 1760.

My Lord,

HAVING heard that his Majesty was curious about his pictures, I recollected some catalogues of the royal collections, which I had a little share in publishing a few years ago.[1] I dare not presume

vols, 1747–66, and to Arthur Collins, *Historical Collections of the Noble Families of Cavendishe, Holles, Vere, Harley, and Ogle . . . ,* 1752. HW's copies of these works are Hazen, *Cat. of HW's Lib.,* Nos 2041 and 56R.

4. HW, following the account in *Biographia Britannica* iv. 2639–40, states that 'Holles was disgraced and imprisoned . . . for having a private conference with Garnet and another Jesuit at their execution' (*Royal and Noble Authors* ii. 159).

5. *A Complete Collection of State-Trials, and Proceedings for High-Treason, and other Crimes and Misdemeanours,* 2d edn, 1730, first published in 4 vols, folio, 1719. HW's copy, now WSL, is an abridgment (6 vols, 1720) of the 1719 edition and does not include Holles's trial (Hazen, op. cit., No. 1724).

6. *An Historical and Critical Account of the Life of Oliver Cromwell,* 1762. HW's presentation copy from Harris is Hazen, op. cit. No. 1645.

1. *The Catalogue and Description of King Charles the First's Capital Collection of Pictures,* 1757, compiled by Abraham Van der Doort, and *A Catalogue of the Collection of Pictures etc. belonging to King James the Second; to which is added a Catalogue of the Pictures . . . in the Closet of the late Queen Caroline, with their exact Measures; and also of the Principal Pictures in the Palace at Ken-*

to offer them to his Majesty myself; but I take the liberty of sending them to your Lordship, that if you should think they may contribute to his Majesty's information or amusement, they may come to his hand more properly from your Lordship than they could do from me. I have added some notes that illustrate a few particulars.

Having dabbled a good deal in this kind of things, if there is any point in which I could be of use to your Lordship for his Majesty's satisfaction, I should be very ready and happy to employ my little knowledge or pains. And permit me to say, my Lord, your Lordship cannot command anybody who will execute your orders more cheerfully or more disinterestedly; or that will trouble you less with any solicitation—an explanation that even esteem and sincerity are forced to make to one in your Lordship's situation. The mere love of the arts and the joy of seeing on the throne a prince of taste are my only inducements for offering my slender services.[2] I know myself too well to think I can ever be of any use but as a virtuoso and antiquarian; a character I should formerly have called very insignificant, though now my pride, since his Majesty vouchsafes to patronize the arts, and your Lordship has the honour of countenancing genius—a rank, of which, at most, I can be but an admirer.

I have the honour of being

My Lord

Your Lordship's most obedient humble servant,

Hor. Walpole

sington, 1758, compiled by W. Chiffinch. Both works were prepared for the press by George Vertue and published by William Bathoe. HW wrote the introductions to them (Hazen, *Bibl. of HW* 120–2). See following letter, n. 1.

2. How earnestly HW wished to forward some great work on English art and antiquities under royal patronage is shown by his verses addressed to the King, 'The Garland,' which he sent anonymously to Lady Bute ('Short Notes,' 16 July 1761, Gray i. 36). His preface (1762) to *Anecdotes of Painting* contains the following compliment to the King: 'the Throne itself is now the altar of the graces; and whoever sacrifices to them becomingly, is sure that his offerings will be smiled upon by a prince, who is at once the example and patron of accomplishments' (*Works* iii. 8).

From LORD BUTE, Wednesday 17 December 1760

Printed from *Works* ii. 377, where the letter was first printed. Reprinted, *Monthly Review,* 1798, 2d ser., xxvii. 62–3. The history of the MS and its present whereabouts are not known.

Dec. 17, 1760.

Sir,

I HAVE presented the book[1] sent me to his Majesty, and mentioned the very polite and respectful manner you expressed yourself in with regard to him. The catalogue came very opportunely, for the King had just given orders to the Duke of Devonshire[2] to make out exact lists of all the pictures in the royal palaces. His Majesty's great fondness for the arts will, I hope, soon have a striking effect in this country. I with gratitude acknowledge the assistance they have been of to me during many years of absolute solitude: other matters much less agreeable now demand my whole attention; depend upon it, therefore, I shall presume on your generosity, and use the freedom you give me, without remorse or hesitation; fully satisfied, that whatever you shall please to undertake, will be executed in a much superior manner to any attempts of mine, even in the days of liberty and quiet. I am sorry before I finish this scrawl to be forced to enter my protest against an expression in yours.[3] Men of your character and ability are by no means confined to any one study: quick parts and superior talents become useful in every occupation they are applied to; with these, according to Marshal Saxe,[4] little things amaze, and great ones do not surprise.

I am, Sir,

Your obedient humble servant,

BUTE

1. HW's present of the catalogues mentioned in the previous letter; bound with them was *A Catalogue of the Curious Collection of Pictures of George Villiers, Duke of Buckingham,* 1758, containing an introduction by HW. The set, 'bound in one volume in old calf, with the royal monogram on sides, rebacked, with the bookplate of George III,' is now in the BM (Hazen, *Cat. of HW's Lib.*, No. 2479).

2. Lord chamberlain of the Household 1757–62.

3. 'I know myself too well to think I can ever be of any use but as a virtuoso and antiquarian' (*ante* 15 Dec. 1760).

4. Hermann-Maurice (1696–1750), Comte de Saxe; Maréchal de France.

From WILLIAM PITT (later LORD CHATHAM), Wednesday 7 January 1761

Printed from the MS now WSL. First printed, Toynbee *Supp.* ii. 118. Damer-Waller; the MS was sold Sotheby's 5 Dec. 1921 (first Waller Sale), lot 102, bought in; resold Christie's 15 Dec. 1947 (second Waller Sale), lot 4, to Maggs for WSL.

Endorsed by HW: From W. Pitt, Lord Chatham.

Memoranda (by HW, in pencil):

However,[1] I advise the Reader, not only on this picture of mine, but on most other minor pieces, whether portraits or histories, not to give too much credit to the possessors of them—I have found few of them that could stand the test, either in their character or pretensions.

Well, Lady < soon glad 'tis> over
< > sighing for a scornfull Lover
< > sword
Sure, you may be < >d had Hastings heart
Been touch'd by Cupid's most invenom'd dart.

Is. Oliver by himself[2]
Chanc. Wriothesley[3] Holbein[4]
Sir Benj. Rudyard[5] Hoskins[6]
K. of Denmark[7] P. Oliver[8]
Q[ueen] Is. Oliver[9]
D. of Richmond
Family of More[10]

1. Apparently notes for HW's *Anecdotes of Painting.* The first two passages are very faint, and the readings are conjectural.

2. A miniature self-portrait by Isaac Oliver (ca 1556–1617) in HW's collection was sold SH xiv. 85 to the 13th Earl of Derby for £21. It is owned by the present Lord Derby (Graham Reynolds, *Nicholas Hilliard and Isaac Oliver,* 1971, No. 135).

3. Thomas Wriothesley (1505–50), K.G., 1545; lord chancellor 1544–7; cr. (1547) E. of Southampton.

4. A portrait of Wriothesley 'after H. Holbein,' supposed to be a copy of the picture destroyed by fire at Cowdray Park in 1793, is now in the Fitzwilliam Museum, Cambridge (GEC *sub* Southampton, xii pt i. 122). A miniature of Wriothesley by Samuel Cooper was sold SH xiv. 99 to Samuel Rogers for £10.10.0.

5. Benjamin Rudyerd (1572–1658), Kt, 1618; politician and poet.

6. John Hoskins (d. 1664), miniature painter. 'Colonel Sothby has a head of Sir Benjamin Rudyard by him' (*Anecdotes of Painting, Works* iii. 255).

7. Presumably Christian IV (1577–1648), K. of Denmark 1588–1648.

8. Peter Oliver (1594–1648), eldest son of Isaac Oliver; painter. No portrait of Christian IV by him is known.

9. A miniature of Anne (1574–1619) of Denmark, m. (1589) James I of England, by Isaac Oliver was sold SH xiv. 93 to the Duke of Buckingham for £11.0.6.

10. '[Andrew] De Loo had also the family-picture of Sir Thomas More, which was bought by his grandson Mr Roper' (*Anecdotes of Painting, Works* iii. 69n). This was probably a copy of the original family portrait, now lost (Paul Ganz, *The Paintings of Hans Holbein,* 1956, pp. 276–80).

St James's Square, Jan. 7th 1761.

MR PITT cannot defer expressing how sensible he is to the honour of Mr Walpole's remembrance, and desires he will accept his best thanks for the favour of his obliging present.[11] The edition is very beautiful.

From HENRY READE, Friday 1 May 1761

Printed from the MS now WSL. First printed, Toynbee *Supp.* ii. 97–8. Damer-Waller; the MS was sold Sotheby's 5 Dec. 1921 (first Waller Sale), lot 185, bought in; resold Christie's 15 Dec. 1947 (second Waller Sale), lot 27, to Maggs for WSL.

Exchequer, May 1st 1761.

Sir,

AGREEABLE to my promise I have sent you the instrument[1] that cleared the King of Corsica[2] from the King's Bench. Though the docket on the back, calls the schedule a copy, yet the handwriting at the bottom is original, as the Marshal[3] of the King's Bench informs me, who saw him sign it,[4] and who brought it to me yesterday.

I am, with the greatest respect,

Sir,

Your most obedient and obliged humble servant,

H. READE

Honourable Mr Walpole.

[Enclosure]

Surry, to wit, A schedule or inventory containing a full and true account of all the debts, effects, and estate, both real and personal (of what kind or nature soever), of Theodore

11. A copy of the SH edition of Lucan's *Pharsalia;* 500 copies were published 8 Jan. 1761 (Hazen, *SH Bibl.* 46).

1. A 'Copy of the Schedule of Baron de Newhoff,' dated 24 June 1755 (MS now WSL), printed below.

2. Theodore (1694–1756), Baron de Neuhoff; self-styled 'King of Corsica.' He was imprisoned in the King's Bench prison for debt in 1749. For HW's attempts to help him see *ante* 23 Feb. 1753.

3. John Ashton (d. 1768), marshal of the Court of King's Bench 1749–67 (*Court and City Register,* 1749–67, *passim*).

4. The signature is not that of King Theodore, but in the same hand as the rest of the document.

Stephen de Newhoff, a German from Westphalia and late of Mount Street, Grosvenor Square, now a prisoner in the King's Bench Prison, and a list of the names of all and every person and persons that are any wise (and how much) indebted unto him, the said Theodore Stephen Baron de Newhoff, and the witnesses that can prove the same, pursuant to an Act of Parliament made in the twenty eighth year of his present Majesty King George the Second, entitled an Act for Relief of Insolvent Debtors.

Debtors' Names and Places of Abode	Sums due.	How due and for what.	Witnesses and Vouchers thereof.
That he is entitled to the Kingdom of Corsica and hath no other estate or effects but in right of that Kingdom.			

The above written is a full and true schedule of all my estate and effects whatsoever except wearing apparel, bedding for myself and family, working tools, and necessary implements for my occupation and calling, and those in the whole not exceeding the value of ten pounds. Witness my hand this 24 day of June 1755

Th. Bn de Newhoff[5]

5. After Boswell visited HW 21 Jan. 1766, he noted in his journal: 'He [HW] had seen Theodore, but whether from pride or stupidity, he hardly spoke any. Horace has the original writing for getting him out of prison'; see *post* 20 Jan. 1766.

From LORD GRIMSTON,[1] Friday 8 May 1761

Printed from the MS now WSL. First printed, Toynbee *Supp.* iii. 167–8. Damer-Waller; the MS was sold Sotheby's 5 Dec. 1921 (first Waller Sale), lot 135, bought in; resold Christie's 15 Dec. 1947 (second Waller Sale), lot 53 (with Grimston to HW 7 June 1761), to Maggs for WSL.

Gorhambury,[2] 8th May 1761.

Sir,

I WAS favoured with yours[3] on Wednesday last, but was prevented answering it, the first post, and am glad you have put it in my power, to return you my thanks, for having justified my father's[4] young performance, in your late work;[5] and an opportunity of obliging you in anything, on that account. You are therefore extremely welcome to copy any of my pictures[6] here, but beg to be excused having the painter in my family, from the disagreeable circumstances on the like occasion, in my father's life time, and think he may easily be accommodated at St Albans. But imagine you under some mistake with regard to the picture, not knowing of any here of Sir *Nicholas*[7] (not Nathaniel)[8] Bacon, except a coloured bust, in the little cloister, and a portrait in the hall of Lord Bacon's[9] elder brother,[10] over the

1. Hon. James Grimston (1711–73), 2d Vct Grimston, 1756; M.P. St Albans 1754–61.

2. 'The seat of Lord Grimston, two miles from St Albans . . . is a most respectable and agreeable retirement, with an air of sober simplicity, yet calculated for great enjoyment' (HW's comment in *Country Seats* 21).

3. Missing.

4. William Grimston (ca 1683–1756), cr. (1719) Vct Grimston.

5. In the *Catalogue of the Royal and Noble Authors,* SH, 1758, ii. 214–15, HW mentions Grimston's 'young performance,' a play, written when a boy, called 'Love in a Hollow-Tree.' It was published in 1705 as *The Lawyer's Fortune: or, Love in a Hollow Tree;* 2d edn, 1736. HW apparently had two copies of the play (Hazen, *Cat. of HW's Lib.,* Nos 1896, 2861).

6. HW wanted to have Sir Nathaniel Bacon's self-portrait at Gorhambury engraved for *Anecdotes of Painting;* the engraving by Thomas Chambars appears in vol. I, 1762, opp. p. 163.

7. Nicholas Bacon (1509–79), of Redgrave and Gorhambury; Kt, 1558; lord keeper of the Great Seal, 1558–79.

8. Nathaniel Bacon (1585–1627), 7th son of Sir Nicholas Bacon, 1st Bt; K.B., 1626; painter. In *Anecdotes* i. 163–4, HW mistakenly says that he was 'a younger son of the [Lord] Keeper, and half-brother of the great Sir Francis,' confusing him with his uncle, Nathaniel Bacon (1547–1622), Kt, 1604, who was the second son of the Lord Keeper by his first wife (Bernard Denvir, 'Sir Nathaniel Bacon,' *Connoisseur,* 1956, cxxxvii. 116–19; *The Official Papers of Sir Nathaniel Bacon,* ed. H. W. Saunders, Camden Soc., 1915, 3d ser., xxvi. pp. xvii–xvix).

9. Francis Bacon (1561–1626), 5th and youngest son of the Lord Keeper; cr. (1618) Bn Verulam and (1621) Vct St Alban.

10. Sir Nicholas Bacon (ca 1540–1624), eldest son of the Lord Keeper; cr. (1611) Bt (the first person ever to hold that rank); Sir Francis Bacon's half-brother.

marble table, who perhaps may be the person you mean, by his succeeding to the baronetage, besides which, there are only two original pictures of Lord Bacon. Be assured you have given me no trouble, but great pleasure, being,

Sir,

Your most obliged humble servant,

GRIMSTON

TO LORD BUTE, Sunday 10 May 1761

Printed for the first time from a photostat of the MS in the possession of Lord Bute, Mount Stuart, near Rothesay, Isle of Bute, kindly furnished through the good offices of Miss C.M. Armet.

Arlington Street, May 10th 1761.

My Lord,

THE enclosed petition[1] from a young man[2] under sentence of death I must beg your Lordship to present to his Majesty. The case is truly a melancholy one. His father Dr Brett[3] is an aged clergyman in Ireland, of a very fair and respectable character, with a large family of daughters, who, besides the scandal brought on the profession of a divine of the Church of England, are likely to suffer extremely by the disgrace inflicted on them by their brother; the eldest particularly, who is sought in marriage, which she may lose though an advantageous one, if her brother suffers. Dr Brett would be happy if his Majesty would be so graciously good as to change the bitterness of death into banishment to the East Indies in either capacity of soldier or sailor.[4]

1. Missing.

2. John Brett. He was capitally convicted at the Old Bailey 7 May 1761 for forging and publishing a bill of exchange drawn upon Frazier and Co., merchants, with intent to defraud (*Daily Adv.* 8 May 1761; GM 1761, xxxi. 234).

3. Possibly the 'John Brett . . . doctor in divinity' who died in 1772 (Sir Arthur Vicars, *Index to the Prerogative Wills of Ireland, 1536–1810,* Dublin, 1897, p. 53).

4. Brett had been adjutant in the 49th Foot in 1755–7 (*Army Lists,* 1755, p. 68; 1757, p. 85). 'Sir William Moreton, Knight, recorder, made report to his Majesty of the prisoners under sentence of death in Newgate,' when John Brett was ordered for execution on 27 May (GM 1761, xxxi. 236; *Daily Adv.* 22 May 1761). See following letter.

Your Lordship, I hope, will forgive my taking this liberty, but an aged father at a distance recommending to me the life of his child was a commission my pity could not refuse,[5] and your Lordship's benevolent temper will I flatter myself excuse in

My Lord

Your Lordship's most obedient humble servant

Hor. Walpole

To Lord Bute, Wednesday 27 May 1761

Printed for the first time from a photostat of the MS in the possession of Lord Bute, Mount Stuart, near Rothesay, Isle of Bute, kindly furnished through the good offices of Miss C.M. Armet.

Endorsed in an unidentified hand: Mr H. Walpole. May 27, 1761.

Arlington Street, May 27th 1761.

My Lord,

While the fate of that unhappy young man, Brett, in whose favour I troubled your Lordship,[1] was yet in suspense, I declined even returning you my thanks for the honour of your obliging answer.[2] I could plead nothing for him but what I had pleaded, the commiseration to be felt for his family. It was too hard a task to acknowledge the justice of his sentence,[3] while there was a possibility of its being mitigated; I could not almost with the same breath say, 'My Lord, he has merited his fate—but save him!' Yet, my Lord, when my pity has had its full scope, and when I have done all that could be expected from me by his miserable father, it is a justice due to your Lordship to own that there has been nothing hard on your part, and that your not granting the request I asked, was, solely because it could not in the present case be granted. They who demand

5. Brett's letter to HW is missing; it is not known how he came to apply to HW.

1. See previous letter.

2. Missing.

3. 'Yesterday morning [27 May] about half an hour after 9 o'clock' John Brett was carried in a cart from Newgate to Tyburn. He 'was genteelly dressed in mourning, with a cockade in his hat, having formerly been an officer. At the place of execution he made a short speech to the populace, wherein he owned he was guilty of the crime for which he suffered, and hoped that others would take warning by him' (*Daily Adv.* 28 May 1761).

more than they ought to demand, are bound in honour to lay the ill success where it is due, on the cause in which they apply. I cannot say so much, my Lord, without going farther; if I have asked more than was reasonable, as the event has shown, I ought to ask your Lordship's pardon for putting the least difficulty upon your humanity, and I have no excuse but in my judging of your Lordship by my own heart; and you will allow me to say that when one asks a favour which one has no right to ask, it is at least a proof of the high idea one has of the person's good nature to whom one applies. That good nature, if it could have been exerted, I am persuaded, would. A most humane King, and a tender-hearted minister invite solicitations for the wretched, and when they cannot yield, will pity the object, and forgive the solicitor; this reign, I have full persuasion, will not be a season of discouraging that truly British principle, good nature. Your Lordship may see how much I trust to this opinion, by deferring so long to subscribe myself

My Lord

Your Lordship's most obedient humble servant

Hor. Walpole

From Lord Grimston, Sunday 7 June 1761

Printed from the MS now WSL. First printed, Toynbee *Supp.* iii. 168–9. For the history of the MS see *ante* 8 May 1761.

Gorhambury, 7 June.

Sir,

As you are so generous to look upon the small assistance that lay in my power to give Mr Chambers[1] towards completing your work, as an obligation to yourself, I assure you I shall esteem myself abundantly rewarded, by being honoured with a copy of it, and a print of the picture,[2] both which I shall endeavour to place to the best advantage. No one could be either easier accommodated, or

1. Thomas Chambars (ca 1724–89), engraver of Irish extraction, who engraved several heads for *Anecdotes of Painting* (Dalrymple 96 n. 12).

2. Of Sir Nathaniel Bacon (1585–1627), the painter (*ante* 8 May 1761, nn. 6 and 8).

better behaved, than Mr Chambers, for the short time of his continuance here, and I was particularly pleased nothing was wanting to make his drawing complete. If I should ever be able to serve you on the like or any other occasion, it will give great satisfaction to,

Sir,

Your most obedient humble servant,

GRIMSTON

TO LORD DACRE,[1] Tuesday 9 June 1761

Printed from Toynbee *Supp.* iii. 2–5, where the letter was first printed from a copy of the MS then (1925) in the possession of Field Marshal Sir Evelyn Wood; not further traced.

Arlington Street, June 9th 1761.

My dear Lord,

AFTER giving you and Lady Dacre[2] a thousand thanks for all your goodness and civilities to us,[3] I obey your commands in telling you the success of our expedition. It proved seventy-six measured miles, and yet we arrived here by half an hour after eight, just twelve hours and twenty minutes.

If Mr Shafto[4] had been to get a thousand pounds by us, we could not have been more fortunate, considering that excepting the auction at Pangbourne we accomplished all our objects, though we were forced to return from Hendon to Ware, where we left our servants to rest. Turning out of the great road to Puckeridge we found in a

1. Thomas Barrett Lennard (1717–86), 17th Bn Dacre, 1755.

2. Anna Maria Pratt (d. 1806), m. (1739) Thomas Barrett Lennard, 17th Bn Dacre; sister of Charles Pratt, later 1st E. Camden.

3. HW had just returned from a visit to Belhus, Lord Dacre's seat near Aveley, Essex; for his description of it see *Country Seats* 34. The Tudor mansion had been remodelled by Lord Dacre with the advice of HW and Sanderson Miller, in the Gothic style similar to that of SH. For an account of a previous visit to Belhus see HW to Richard Bentley 3 Nov. 1754 (CHUTE 183–4). Belhus was pulled down in 1954 (OSSORY i. 239 n. 5).

4. Jenison Shafto (ca 1728–71), 'gentleman jockey'; member of the Jockey Club; M.P. He had just won 1000 guineas from Hugo Meynell for wagering that he would find someone to ride 100 miles a day for 29 days successively. The bet was won 1 June, only fourteen horses having been used (Robert Black, *The Jockey Club*, 1891, i. 133–4; James Rice, *History of the British Turf*, 1879, i. 153–4; J. C. Whyte, *History of the British Turf*, 1840, i. 513; T. A. Cook, *A History of the English Turf*, [1901–4], ii. 246).

perpendicular hole the tops of the towers of Standon.[5] It appeared a ruinous old house with not the least trace of garden, pleasure grounds, or inhabitants, excepting farmers. We gave all over, having forgotten to inquire if any family resided there. We came to the great gate flanked with towers; two women came out of the side buildings and told us they belonged to the farmer. We asked if any of the Astons[6] lived there—'Oh! no! they have been all gone these five years.'—'What! and taken the furniture!'—'Yes, all.' This was fine hearing at the end of forty miles out of the way! 'Well! but can we see the chambers?'—'Yes! I believe you may; I will go and ask the gentleman within.'—'Who is the gentleman within?'—'Mr Kendal,[7] who teaches the school.' We crossed ourselves at finding a school instead of a piece of wedding tapestry—and yet this crossing brought us good luck. Another maid came—'Pray, child, is Mr Kendal a clergyman?'—'Humph! yes, Sir, he is coming.'—An elderly man in a grey frock came—we broke our minds to him. He was wondrously courteous, carried us into a great hall, where there was nothing at all, up a ruinous staircase where were no very execrable pictures of Henry VIII, Edward VI, Queen Elizabeth,[8] and Richard Weston,[9] Earl of Portland; thence into a vast dining-room whose walls could scarce support the remains of three Sybils whole lengths and a rag of tapestry with the story of Tobit, which we concluded passed in the neighbourhood for the marriage of Prince Arthur and Queen Catherine. However, inquiring further, he unlocked an ancient door, which to our great surprise proved the Popish chapel with vast numbers of trinkets and benches. We now saw we were in a seminary, which the good man did not at all disguise, but here was the tapestry covering one entire side of this chamber, which had been the great drawing-room. The arras is not very good, nor are the

5. 'Standon, within a mile of Puckeridge, an old seat of Lord Aston's, but now abandoned by the family and converted into a farmhouse and Popish seminary' (*Country Seats* 34).

6. Descendants of Sir Walter Aston (1584–1639), cr. (1627) Bn Aston of Forfar.

7. Richard Kendal (ca 1709–80), educated at Douai ca 1728; first president (ca 1752) of the school at Standon, established for the sons of the Catholic nobility and gentry. The Aston estates in this district were sold ca 1767 and the school transferred to Hare Street and later to Old Hall Green, near Ware (Joseph Gillow, *A Literary and Biographical History, or Bibliographical Dictionary of the English Catholics*, [1885–1902], i. 81–2, iv. 10–11).

8. 'A young lady richly dressed, which seems to be Queen Elizabeth' (*Country Seats* 34).

9. (1577–1635), cr. (1633) E. of Portland; his second dau. Mary m. (1629) Sir Walter Aston, 2d Bn Aston, 1639. In 1660 he inherited Standon.

figures portraits, but they are in the dresses of the time, and there is a deal of good history besides up and down the piece, as how the Princess arrived, and how those wise monarchs, King Henry VII and King Ferdinand, sat upon a joint throne and talked over the position. In[10] . . . -able relic if it was worth sixpence . . . with the rest of the Sybils, . . . and a small King James's Gothic . . .[11] with two orders of pillars . . . just fit my Lady Dacre's dressing-room to a hair, or by the addition of another order would be the very thing for your library—I dare say they would give it to you for half a dozen of your farmer's sons. There are some indifferent family pictures besides, and a curious whole length of my Lady Hatton[12] weeping over my Lord Chief Justice's coffin in a church.[13] The good old priest made us drink a glass of sherry with him, and we came away contented to Hatfield, where the Earl[14] was not, but we saw the mansion[15] and the curious picture of which Mr Coniers[16] told your Lordship. It is Henry VIII—if it is he—and one of his Queens in masquerade walking in a village near the Tower to see a country wedding. The figures are prettily done, with variety of habits and a yeoman of the guard in red laced with black.[17] I forgot to tell you that the whole road cross the country is the prettiest in the world, and sowed with at least one dozen substantial seats. I fear I have tired you, but so you ordered it.

Belleisle[18] is not taken nor the French come, at least my porter knows nothing of the first, nor Friar Kendal of the latter. Your pretty Hollars[19] arrived very safe—accept my thanks and my shame

10. At this point a piece of the MS has been cut out (Toynbee).

11. 'In the gallery is a pretty chimney piece of two orders, of King James's Gothic' (*Country Seats*, loc. cit.).

12. Lady Elizabeth Cecil (1578–1646), m. 1 Sir William Hatton; m. 2 (1598), as his second wife, Sir Edward Coke (1552–1634), lord chief justice.

13. Their thirty-six years of married life was notoriously unhappy. Lady Hatton is reported to have said at Coke's death, 'We shall never see his like again, praises be to God' (BM Harl. MS 7193, f. 16, quoted by S. E. Thorne, *Sir Edward Coke*, 1957, p. 4).

14. James Cecil (1713–80), 6th E. of Salisbury, 1728.

15. HW described Hatfield House as 'a noble pile of building, never modernized, but the inside now extremely out of repair' (*Country Seats* 35).

16. John Conyers (1717–75), M.P. (MONTAGU i. 92 n. 14).

17. 'In a closet a very curious picture, representing a wedding in a village by the Thames, with a view of the Tower of London. . . . On the foreground is a strutting figure said to be Henry VIII' (*Country Seats* 35).

18. The citadel of Belle-Île, off the French coast, surrendered 7 June 1761 to the attacking English forces (MANN v. 505 n. 7).

19. Three folio volumes containing 934 engravings by Wenceslaus Hollar (Hazen, *Cat. of HW's Lib.*, No. 3622).

for them again, and make my compliments to my Lady and Mrs Taylor,[20]

and I remain

Your Lordship's very affectionate humble servant

HOR. WALPOLE

PS. I hope Sir John Tirell[21] was well when you heard from him, and caught no cold at the fish pond.

From BISHOP PEARCE,[1] Friday 10 July 1761

Printed from the MS now WSL. First printed, Toynbee *Supp.* ii. 120–2. Damer-Waller; the MS was sold Sotheby's 5 Dec. 1921 (first Waller Sale), lot 171, to Quaritch; resold Sotheby's 22 Feb. 1949 (Harmsworth Sale), lot 5882, to Maggs for WSL.

Bromley, Kent, July 10, 1761.

Sir,

I RECEIVED the favour of your letter,[2] in which the offer which you make is very generous, and shows your proper regard to antiquity.

I am always very unwilling, that any monuments in the Abbey should be removed, to make room for those of the present age. Particularly with regard to that which is designed for Gen. Wolfe,[3] the whole Abbey was several times examined in company with Mr

20. Not identified.

21. Sir John Tyrrell (ca 1728–66), 5th Bt, 1735. HW's visit to his seat, Heron (or Herne), in East Horndon, Essex, is described in *Country Seats* 34.

1. Zachary Pearce (1690–1774), Bp of Bangor, 1748; Bp of Rochester, 1756; dean of Westminster, 1756.

2. Missing. HW wrote H. S. Conway 5 Aug. 1761: 'I heard lately, that Dr Pearce, a very learned personage, had consented to let the tomb of Aylmer de Valence, Earl of Pembroke, a very great personage, be removed for Wolfe's monument. . . . [I] wrote to his Lordship, expressing my concern that one of the finest and most ancient monuments in the Abbey should be removed, and begging, if it was removed, that he would bestow it on me, who would erect and preserve it here. After a fortnight's deliberation, the Bishop sent me an answer, civil indeed, and commending my zeal for antiquity!' (CONWAY ii. 110–11).

3. Parliament had voted 21 Nov. 1759 to erect a monument to Wolfe in the Abbey (*Journals of the House of Commons* xxviii. 643).

Wilton,[4] the architect of Gen. Wolfe's monument: and, as it is to be 28 feet in heighth and 15 in breadth, it was extremely difficult to find a place for it. But at last the architect expressed a great desire of having leave to remove an old monument, which appears ruinous, and had no inscription by which it might be known,[5] for whom it was designed, though it had the appearance of being designed for a Knight Templar.

With this desire of Mr Wilton we complied, though much unwillingly, but insisting, that the old monument, when removed, should be set up again over against the place, where it now stands; and that it should be done at Mr Wilton's expense, as the Church of Westminster takes no money in this (as in other cases), for leave to erect the new monument.

Within these three months it has been found out, that the old monument was erected to the memory of Aylmer de Valence Earl of Pembroke;[6] and it has given me some concern to find, that what we thought the monument of some unknown person, is now known to be that of one distinguished for his honours, and mentioned in English history. I heartily wish, that another place could be found, and shall still endeavour to persuade the architect to be content with another.

But, whatever success I may have in this endeavour, I hope, that the monument of Aylmer de Valence will be decently placed,[7] and put into a more durable condition, very near to its present place, not above (as I think) ten feet from it.

I have given you, Sir, this account, that you may judge, how unwilling we are to do anything in the Abbey, which may be a preju-

4. Joseph Wilton (1722–1803), sculptor. His first public monument was Wolfe's, which he was commissioned to do in 1760, but did not finish until 1772. Wilton was one of the forty original members of the Royal Academy of Arts appointed by George III in 1768.

5. 'Observe, that not only the man who shows the tombs names it everyday, but that there is a draught of it at large in Dart's *Westminster*' (CONWAY ii. 111).

6. Aymer de Valence (ca 1270–1324), regarded as E. Pembroke, 1307. He was an important figure of the reign of Edward II.

7. The monument remained in its original position on the north side of the choir of the Abbey, but the tomb of the Abbot Esteney was dislodged in order to make room for General Wolfe's monument. J. P. Neale, in his drawing of Aymer de Valence's monument, shows through its arch a group of figures of the Wolfe monument (E. W. Brayley, *The History and Antiquities of the Abbey Church of St Peter, Westminster*, 1818–23, ii. 202, 274–5 and pl. XLIII; A. P. Stanley, *Historical Memorials of Westminster Abbey*, 4th edn, 1876, pp. 254–5; Jocelyn Perkins, *Westminster Abbey the Empire's Crown*, 1937, pp. 85, 152, 282–3).

dice to antiquity; and may see, that we are disposed to pay all due regard to the relics of the great, who are deposited with us in that royal church.

I cannot conclude this letter, without taking an opportunity of making my acknowledgments to you for the[8] generous and disinterested share, which you take at Strawberry Hill in promoting learning, and giving to the world good editions of learned works.[9]

I am, Sir,

Your very respectful and humble servant,

Zʏ ROCHESTER

From DAVID MALLET, Wednesday 15 July 1761

Printed from Toynbee *Supp.* iii. 169, where the letter was first printed from the MS in the Waller Collection. For the history of the MS see Mallet to HW ca 1759.

The year is determined on the assumption that the 'Westminster Hall ticket' desired by Mallet was for the Coronation of George III (see n. 3 below).

July 15th, 9 at night.

A thousand thanks, dear Sir, for your very obliging answer to my note.[1] Instead of asking the Duke of Ancaster[2] whom you do not know; which would be the most disagreeable thing in the world for either a great favour or a small: please only to ask any of the peers who are your acquaintance for a Westminster Hall ticket.[3] Every Lord will have a certain number allowed him. Methinks I ask like a sturdy beggar: but it is only to save you the trouble of reading a long insipidly civil letter; which in the end could only tell you with more circumstance, not with more truth, that I am

Most faithfully,

Your humble servant,

D. MALLET

8. 'Your' crossed out in the MS.

9. HW did not overlook Pearce's condescending first and last paragraphs in the summary of the letter he sent to Conway (CONWAY, loc. cit.).

---

1. Both missing.

2. Peregrine Bertie (1714–78), 3d D. of Ancaster, 1742; lord great chamberlain at the Coronation, 22 Sept. 1761.

3. Doubtless for the Coronation of George III and Queen Charlotte, the date of which had just been announced (CONWAY ii. 96 and n. 14).

TO GROSVENOR BEDFORD, ca Saturday 18 July 1761

Printed for the first time from the MS now WSL. The MS descended in the Bedford family to Grosvenor Bedford's great-niece, Mrs Erskine, of Milton Lodge, Gillingham, Dorset; sold Sotheby's 15 Nov. 1932 (property of Mrs Erskine), lot 488, to Maggs for WSL.

Dated conjecturally; see n. 1 below.

Dear Sir,

DON'T give yourself the trouble of coming to town; I sent this morning to tell Mrs Bedford that I shall be in town again next week, and then or afterwards, what I wanted,[1] will do just as well. I am going out of town now, therefore pray don't put yourself to any inconvenience, for I assure you, there is no matter of hurry.

Yours etc.

H. W.

TO GROSVENOR BEDFORD, Sunday 19 July 1761

Printed from a photostat of Bedford's copy of HW's letter and verses, kindly supplied by the late Sir John Murray, 50 Albemarle Street, London. First printed, *Quarterly Review,* 1852, xc. 312. Reprinted, Cunningham iii. 415–16; Toynbee v. 79–80; Hazen, *Bibl. of HW* 165 (the letter only). The verses were reprinted in *Horace Walpole's Fugitive Verses,* ed. W. S. Lewis, 1931, pp. 134–5. The original letter in HW's hand is missing; in 1852 it was apparently among Bedford's papers in the possession of Mrs Bedford, of Upper Seymour Street, the widow of Grosvenor Bedford's grandson.

Dated by HW's reference to 'The Garland' in his 'Short Notes,' 16 July 1761 (see n. 1 below).

Strawb[erry Hill], Sunday.

Dear Sir,

I WILL beg you to copy the following lines[1] for me, and bring or send them, whichever is most convenient to you, to my house

1. Perhaps HW wanted to arrange for the use of Bedford's house in Palace Yard during the Coronation; several friends were invited there to see the procession (*post* 23 Sept. 1761). Possibly he wanted only to deliver 'The Garland' to Bedford (see following letter).

1. 'July 16 [1761], wrote "The Garland," a poem on the King, and sent it to Lady Bute, but not in my own hand, nor with my name, nor did I ever own it' ('Short Notes,' GRAY i. 36). The verses were an attempt to further HW's hopes of being useful to the King 'as a virtuoso and antiquarian' (*ante* 15 Dec. 1760).

in Arlington Street on Tuesday morning—Pray don't mention them to anybody.

Yours etc.

H. W.

I hope you did not suffer by all the trouble I gave you yesterday.[2]

[Enclosure]

The Garland.

In private life, where virtues safely bloom,
What flow'rs diffuse their favourite perfume?
  Devotion first the garland's front commands,
Like some fair lily borne by angel hands.
Next, Filial Love submissive warmth displays,
Like heliotropes, that court their parent rays.
Friendship, that yields its fragrance but to those
That near approach it, like the tender rose.
As royal amaranths, unchanging Truth;
And violet-like, the bashful blush of youth.
Chaste Purity, by no loose heat misled,
Like virgin snowdrops in a winter bed.
Prudence, the sensitive, whose leaves remove
When hands too curious would their texture prove.
Bounty full-flush'd at once with fruit and flow'r,
As citrons give and promise ev'ry hour.
Soft Pity last, whose dews promiscuous fall,
Like lavish eglantines, refreshing all.
  How blest a cottage where such virtues dwell!
To heav'n ascends the salutary smell:
But should such virtues round imperial state
Their cordial gales in balmy clouds dilate;
Nations a long-lost paradise would own,
And happiness reclaim her proper throne.
Hate, discord, war, and each foul ill would cease,
And laurel'd conquest only lead to peace.
  'Ah! vain idea!' cries the servile bard,

2. Bedford may have come to town on 18 July as a result of the previous letter.

Who lies for hire, and flatters for reward:
'Such I have sung of—such have never seen—
My Kings were visions—and a dream my Queen.
Point out the charming phantom.'—One there is;
Unnam'd, the world will own the garland His:
Truth so exactly wove the wreath for one,
It must become his honest brow—or none.

TO HENRY FOX, Saturday ?19 September 1761

Printed from a photostat of the MS in the Bodleian Library (MS Toynbee c. 1, f. 4). First printed, Toynbee xv. 443. The MS was *penes* Mrs Alfred Morrison in 1905; offered by Maggs, Cat. Nos 368 (summer 1918), lot 1436; 396 (autumn 1920), lot 2671; 439 (1923), lot 1169; subsequently acquired by Paget Toynbee, who gave it to the Bodleian.

Dated conjecturally. The letter must have been written before 3 May 1762 when Fox's wife, Lady Caroline, was created Baroness Holland. The event for which HW was trying to obtain another 'ticket' was probably the coronation of George III and Queen Charlotte, which took place on Tuesday, 22 Sept. 1761 (*ante* 15 July 1761, n. 3).

Saturday night late.

Dear Sir,

I SEND you an expeditious answer that you may lose no time in other applications.[1] It is out of my power to serve you and Lady Caroline,[2] zealously as I wish for both. I am earnestly suing myself for another person,[3] at present with very small hopes, and with not much better hereafter. It will perhaps surprise you but I literally have not yet obtained a single ticket for any person. I was too modest at first with my own particular friends, knowing how they would be tormented, and the consequence has been literally as I tell you.

I write in so uneasy a posture that you will excuse my saying more than that I wish you better interest than that of

Yours ever

H. W.

1. For tickets to attend the Coronation (see heading).

2. Lady Georgiana Caroline Lennox (1723–74), m. (1744) Henry Fox, 1st Bn Holland; cr. (1762) Bns Holland, s.j.

3. David Mallet had solicited HW for a 'Westminster Hall ticket,' but it is not certain that he is the 'person' HW had in mind (*ante* 15 July 1761).

To Grosvenor Bedford, Wednesday 23 September 1761

Printed from the MS now WSL. First printed, Cunningham iii. 436. Reprinted, Toynbee v. 109–10. The MS descended in the Bedford family to Grosvenor Bedford's great-niece, Mrs Erskine, of Milton Lodge, Gillingham, Dorset; sold Sotheby's 15 Nov. 1932 (property of Mrs Erskine), lot 487, to Maggs for WSL.

The MS is dated (in pencil, probably by Bedford) September 23, 1761. According to Cunningham, Bedford noted: 'Mr Walpole's friends invited by Mr Grosv[eno]r Bedford to his house in Palace Yard to see the coronation in 1761: Lady Hervey, Lady Hertford, Lady Anne Conway, Mr Chute, Mrs Clive, Mr Raftor, Lady Townshend and Master, Miss Hotham and her maid.' Bedford's note is no longer preserved with the MS.

My dear Sir,

TEN thousand thanks to you for all your goodness and all your trouble; I can never say enough to you for the obliging kindness you have shown me.[1] I fear you will suffer by it; tell me how you do today, and if you have got a good night's rest. Compose yourself till you are perfectly recovered. Pray make my thanks too to Miss Bedford and your sons,[2] who have had nothing but plague with me. Adieu!

Your much obliged and sincere friend

HOR. WALPOLE

Don't wonder I was so impatient to get away; I was fatigued to death;[3] but got home perfectly well and am quite so.

1. HW had spent the night of 21 Sept. at Bedford's house 'at the gate of Westminster Hall' (HW to H. S. Conway 25 Sept. 1761, CONWAY ii. 123). For his description of the Coronation see MONTAGU i. 386–9 and MANN v. 534–6.

2. One of the sons, Charles Bedford (ca 1742–1814), became a clerk to his father in 1763 and succeeded Joseph Tullie (d. 1774), who had succeeded Grosvenor Bedford, as deputy usher of the Exchequer (GRAY ii. 256; GM 1814, lxxxiv pt i. 701).

3. 'Indeed, one had need be a handsome young peeress, not to be fatigued to death with it' (HW to Sir Horace Mann 28 Sept. 1761, MANN v. 534).

From UNKNOWN, ?1762

Printed for the first time from a photostat of the MS at Nostell Priory, Wakefield, Yorks, kindly furnished by the late Hon. Charles Winn. The MS (possibly an enclosure, for which no covering letter has been found) was preserved by HW in two folio volumes 'containing a mass of letters . . . and various memorials concerning painters and engravers that have exercised their practice in England,' sold in the London sale of 1842, lot 1121; later in the possession of the Hon. Charles Winn at Nostell Priory, now property of the National Trust.

Dated conjecturally on the assumption that the MS was sent to HW for possible use in the second edition of *Anecdotes of Painting* (Hazen, *SH Bibl.* 62). The information was not included.

Address: For the Honourable Horatio Walpole Esq., Arlington Street.

Proceedings in Parliament against Inigo Jones,[1] not strictly an *impeachment*, but *charge:*[2]

Journal of H[ouse of] C[ommons] 25 November 1640
19 May 1641
19 July——
20 July——
10 May 1642
11 May——
28 May 1646[3]
1 June——[4]

As to the books and medals etc. at St James's: Journal of H. C. 30 July 1649,[5] and, especially, see Whitelock's *Memorials,* pages 415–416.[6]

1. (1573–1652), architect; surveyor of the works and commissioner for buildings.

2. In December 1641 Jones appeared before the House of Lords to answer a charge brought against him by the parishioners of St Gregory's, a church whose structure adjoined one corner of St Paul's Cathedral. The charge alleged that he had demolished part of their church and should be forced to rebuild it. Jones's defence was vague and procrastinating, but he was not impeached. The parishioners were eventually placated and permitted to rebuild St Gregory's (J. A. Gotch, *Inigo Jones,* 1928, pp. 154–60; John Summerson, *Inigo Jones,* Harmondsworth, 1966, p. 136; DNB).

3. 'An ordinance for granting a pardon unto Inigo Jones, of London, Esquire, for his delinquency, and for discharge of the sequestration of his estate, was this day read' (*Journals of the House of Commons* iv. 557).

4. 'An ordinance for discharge of the delinquency of Mr Inigo Jones' was carried to the Lords (ibid. iv. 560).

5. 'Resolved, etc. that the medals and models at St James's be not sold, till the House take further order. Ordered, that it be referred to the Council of State, to take care that the books, and the medals, at St James's, be not sold or embezzled' (ibid. vi. 272).

6. On 30 July 1649 Bulstrode Whitelocke was prevailed upon to become the

TO UNKNOWN, ca 1762

Printed from the MS now WSL, removed from an extra-illustrated copy of Thomas Moore's *Memoirs of the Life of . . . Sheridan,* 1825. First printed in *Seven Letters Written by Sterne and his Friends,* ed. W. D. Cooper, 1844, p. 14. Reprinted, Toynbee xv. 451–2. The MS in 1844 was in the possession of John Hall Stevenson's great-grandson, John Thomas Wharton, of Skelton Castle, near Guisborough, Yorks; sold Sotheby's 12 June 1899 (William Wright Sale), lot 1442, to Maggs; resold Sotheby's 25 May 1954 (Lady Wavertree Sale), lot 266, to Maggs for WSL.

Address: To [name crossed out].

Dear Sir,

I RETURN you Mr Hall's[1] verses,[2] which I was forced to take into the country with me, as I had not time to read them over carefully in town. They entertained me extremely, as Mr Hall's works always do. He has a vast deal of original humour and wit, and nobody admires him more than I do. I should wish he would change the words *Strawberry Hill*[3] for the title of any convent or abbey, because it would send a great many impertinent people to inquire after the supposed MS, and I am so tired with curious fools, that I should be seriously sorry to be troubled with more. They would really believe I had some old MSS and would want to see them—and I should be forced to deny it, which would look as if I disavowed a knowledge of the poems, and that would have an air of disliking the works of an author for whom I have so much regard and esteem. I beg you will assure Mr Hall how much I think myself honoured by his notice and communication. If all authors had as much parts and good sense as he has, I should not be so sick of them as I am. My own follies have drawn them upon me, or what is worse, to me; and as I wish to be quiet, and no more in question, it will be a real obligation, if he

keeper of the books and precious medals at St James's, in order to preserve them from embezzlement. 'I did accept of the trouble . . . and therein was encouraged and much persuaded to it by Mr Selden, who swore that if I did not undertake the charge of them, all those rare monuments of antiquity, . . . would be lost' (Whitelocke, *Memorials of the English Affairs,* new edn, 1732, pp. 415–16).

1. John Hall (later Hall Stevenson) (1718–85), of Skelton Castle, Yorks; author of *Crazy Tales* and other satirical poems.

2. Evidently the MS volume of verses, now WSL, that included 'A Collection of Monkish Epitaphs from an Ancient Manuscript at Strawberry Hill.' Nearly all of the 'Collection' was first published in *The Works of John Hall-Stevenson,* 1795, ii. 171–215.

3. The reference to SH is omitted in the printed text.

will be so good as to omit Strawberry Hill, where his works will always be most welcome,[4] and whither I am sure he would be sorry to send me fools he justly despises.

I am dear Sir

Yours most sincerely

H. Walpole

PS. I hope your leg is better, and that you take more care of it.

From Lord Bute, Saturday 13 February 1762

Printed from *Works* ii. 378, where the letter was first printed. Reprinted, *Monthly Review,* 1798, xxvii. 63; Cunningham iii. 484, n. 1; Toynbee v. 174, n. 1; *The Correspondence of Gray, Walpole, West and Ashton,* ed. Paget Toynbee, Oxford, 1915, ii. 210, n. 4. The history of the MS and its present whereabouts are not known.

Dated by HW's letter to Bute *post* 15 Feb. 1762.

Saturday.

Lord Bute presents his compliments to Mr Walpole, and returns him a thousand thanks for the very agreeable present[1] he has made him. In looking over it, Lord Bute observes Mr Walpole has mixed several curious remarks on the customs, etc. of the times he treats of;[2] a thing much wanted, and that has never yet been executed,

4. HW's library included eight titles identified by him as being written by Hall, including the *Works,* 3 vols, published posthumously (Hazen, *Cat. of HW's Lib.,* Nos 2959, 3222:2, 4, 6, 9, 10).

---

1. Doubtless an advance copy of the first two volumes of *Anecdotes of Painting,* which was not published until 15 Feb. 1762 (Hazen, *SH Bibl.* 55).

2. Such as HW's remarks on the 'proud, warlike, and ignorant nobility' in the reigns of the first two Edwards: 'Rich plate, even to the enamelling on gold, rich stuffs, and curious armour were carried to excess, while their chairs were mere pedestals, their clothes were encumbrances, and they knew no use of steel but as it served for safety or destruction. Their houses, for there was no medium between castles and hovels, implied the dangers of society, not the sweets of it; and whenever peace left them leisure to think of modes, they seemed to imagine that fashion consisted in transfiguring the human body, instead of adding grace to it. While the men wore shoes so long and picked, that they were forced to support the points by chains from their middle; the ladies erected such pyramids on their heads, that the face became the centre of the body; and they were hardened to these preposterous inconveniences by their priests, who, instead of leaving them to be cured by the fickleness of fashions, or by the trouble of them, denounced God's judgments on follies against which a little

except in parts by Peck,[3] etc. Such a general work would be not only very agreeable, but instructive:—the French have attempted it;[4] the Russians are about it;[5] and Lord Bute has been informed, Mr Walpole is well furnished with materials for such a noble work.[6]

TO LORD BUTE, Monday 15 February 1762

Printed from a photostat of the MS in the Simon Gratz Collection, Historical Society of Pennsylvania. First printed, *Works* ii. 378–9. Reprinted, *Monthly Review,* 1798, xxvii. 63–4; Cunningham iii. 484–5 (closing and signature omitted); Toynbee v. 174–6. The MS was given by Simon Gratz to the Historical Society of Pennsylvania ca 1920; its previous history is not known.

The MS is endorsed, erroneously, in pencil: 'to Lord Egremont.'

Arlington Street, Feb. 15, 1762.

My Lord,

I AM sensible how little time your Lordship can have to throw away on reading idle letters, or letters of compliment: yet as it would be too great want of respect to your Lordship not to make some sort of reply to the note[1] you have done me the honour to send me, I thought I could couch what I have to say in fewer words by writing, than in troubling you with a visit, which might come unseasonably, and a letter you may read at any moment when you are most idle. I had already, my Lord, detained you too long, by sending you a book, which I could not flatter myself you would turn over in

laughter and a little common sense had been more effectual sermons. It was not far distant, I think, from the period of which I am speaking, that the ladies wore looking-glasses about the same height of their bodies, with that, on which the men displayed such indecent symbols' (*Anecdotes, Works* iii. 28–9).

3. Francis Peck (1692–1743), antiquary; author of *Desiderata curiosa,* 1732–5, *Academia tertia Anglicana,* 1727, and other antiquarian works.

4. Montfaucon's *Monuments de la monarchie française* is mentioned in HW's reply to Bute (see following letter), and was suggested by Dr Ducarel as a model for a similar work on the antiquities of England (*post* 23 Feb. 1762). Thomas Gray advised HW how to proceed with such a work (Gray to HW 28 Feb. 1762, GRAY ii. 122–3).

5. Not explained.

6. According to Mary Berry, HW began to draw up a plan, 21 Feb. 1762, for 'Collections for a History of the Manners, Customs, Habits, Fashions, Ceremonies, etc., of England' in a large memorandum book extant ca 1798 (*Works* v. 400). The memorandum book has since disappeared. HW's notes were arranged alphabetically by subjects: 'Coats of Arms, Arms and Armour, Armies,' etc.; 'Anecdotes relating to Hours' appear in HW's 'Book of Materials,' 1759, p. 9.

1. *Ante* 13 Feb. 1762.

such a season of business: by the manner in which you have considered it, you have shown me, that your very minutes of amusement you try to turn to the advantage of your country. It was this pleasing prospect of patronage to the arts, that tempted me to offer you my pebble towards the new structure. I am flattered that you have taken notice of the only ambition I have; I should be more flattered if I could contribute to the least of your Lordship's designs for illustrating Britain.

The hint that your Lordship is so good as to give me for a work like Montfaucon's *Monuments de la monarchie françoise,*[2] has long been a subject that I have wished to see executed; nor in point of materials do I think it would be a very difficult one. The chief impediment was the expense, too great for a private fortune. The extravagant prices extorted by English artists is a discouragement to all public undertakings. Drawings from paintings, tombs etc. would be very dear. To have them engraved as they ought to be, would exceed the compass of a much ampler income than mine, which, though equal to my largest wish, cannot measure itself with the rapacity of our performers.

But, my Lord, if his Majesty was pleased to command such a work, on so laudable an idea as your Lordship's, nobody would be more ready than myself to give his assistance. I own, I think I could be of use in it, in collecting or pointing out materials; and I would take any trouble in aiding, supervising, or directing such a plan. Pardon me, my Lord, if I offer no more; I mean, that I do not undertake the part of composition. I have already trespassed too much upon the indulgence of the public; I wish not to disgust them with hearing of me and reading me. It is time for me to have done; and when I shall have completed, as I almost have, the history of the arts, on which I am now engaged,[3] I did not purpose to tempt again the patience of mankind. But the case is very different with regard to my trouble. My whole fortune is from the bounty of the Crown and from the public:[4] it would ill become me to spare any pains for

2. 5 vols, 1729–33, by Bernard de Montfaucon (1655–1741). An abridged version translated into English was published in London in 1750; HW's copy is Hazen, *Cat. of HW's Lib.*, No. 3683.

3. That is, *Anecdotes of Painting*. HW finished the *Catalogue of Engravers*, published together with the third volume of the *Anecdotes*, 10 Oct. 1762 ('Short Notes,' GRAY i. 38).

4. For a summary of HW's finances see his 'Account of my Conduct relative to the Places I Hold under Government, and towards Ministers' (*Works* ii. 364–70).

the King's glory, or for the honour and satisfaction of my country;[5] and give me leave to add, my Lord, it would be an ungrateful return for the distinction with which your Lordship has condescended to honour me, if I withheld such trifling aid as mine, when it might in the least tend to adorn your Lordship's administration. From me, my Lord, permit me to say, these are not words of course or of compliment; this is not the language of flattery; your Lordship knows I have no views, perhaps knows, that, insignificant as it is, my praise is never detached from my esteem; and when you have raised, as I trust you will, real monuments of glory, the most contemptible characters in the inscription dedicated by your country, may not be the testimony of

My Lord,

Your Lordship's most obedient humble servant

Horace Walpole

From Andrew Coltee Ducarel, Tuesday 23 February 1762

Printed from a photostat of the MS at Nostell Priory, Wakefield, Yorks, kindly furnished by the late Hon. Charles Winn. First printed, Nichols, *Lit. Anec.* iv. 701–3 (closing omitted). For the history of the MS see *ante* ?1762. Ducarel's MS draft of this letter, including his notes for the 'two enclosed papers,' was sold Sotheby's 29 Oct. 1962 (property of a gentleman), lot 231 (with the MS drafts of Ducarel to HW 27 Feb. 1762, 20 May 1762, and 6 Feb. 1768), to Quaritch; acquired from them by WSL, 1963.

Address: To the Hon. Horace Walpole Esq.

Doctors Commons, Feb. 23, 1762.

Sir,

I BEG leave to return you my most sincere thanks for your very kind present of your *Anecdotes of Painting in England;*[1] a work full of learning which has given me an infinite satisfaction.

5. HW's unfulfilled hopes to be the English Montfaucon are summarized in W. S. Lewis, *Horace Walpole,* 1961, p. 154.

1. Ducarel's set of the *Anecdotes,* 5 vols in 3, was sold Sotheby's 7 April 1786 (Ducarel Sale), lot 987, to Egerton; not further traced.

I herewith, Sir, beg leave to trouble you with the two enclosed papers A. and B.[2]—A. contains some remarks on Vol. I which I hope will not be unacceptable.

As your observations are entirely new, it has occurred to me that it would not be altogether impossible including what you mention in the *Anecdotes* to draw up a list of pictures etc. relating to the hist[ory] and antiquities of England (in the manner of Montfaucon's *Monumens de la monarchie françoise*)[3] *from the Conquest to the present time*—and this occasions my troubling you with the paper marked B. To begin at the Conquest—the tapestries at Bayeux and Montfaucon's representations of Will[iam the] Conqueror, his wife, and two sons (French Edit. plate 55–56 to 64), would bring it down to Will[iam] Rufus.[4] Of Henry I and his queen[5] are two fine figures in stone at the west end of Rochester Cathedral, hitherto unnoticed, first discovered by the late Dr Thorpe[6] M.D. when he was writing the hist[ory] of that town and diocese—all whose MSS, finished for the press, are now (1762) in the hands of his son John Thorpe[7] of Bexley in Kent Esq., my particular friend, who intends shortly to publish them.

The Reverend Dr Free[8] informed me some time since, that there is now some tapestry, in a room near the House of Commons,[9] which, he says, represents the Crusades of King Richard the First. These I have never seen but only mention to you the notice I have received from that gentleman.

Perhaps, Sir, upon a strict search of the Harleian and other MSS, public and private, farther discoveries might be made towards such a work, and I know nothing so likely to bring it about, as the *Anecdotes* on painting with which you have been so kind as to oblige the world—a book which will set the learned upon a close examina-

2. Printed below.

3. See previous letter, n. 2.

4. William II (?1056–1100), 3d son of the Conqueror, called 'Rufus.'

5. Henry I (1068–1135), 4th son of the Conqueror, m. Matilda (1080–1118) of Scotland, who was crowned 11 Nov. 1100.

6. John Thorpe (1682–1750), M.D., F.R.S.

7. (1715–92), F.S.A. He edited his father's MSS, one volume of which he published in 1769 as *Registrum Roffense;* a supplement, *Custumale Roffense,* appeared in 1788. Plate XXXVI of this volume shows the figures of Henry I and Matilda carved on either side of the west door of Rochester Cathedral.

8. John Free (1711–91), D.D., 1744 (Nichols, *Lit. Anec.* v. 687–95; GM 1791, lxi. pt ii. 876, 966–8, 1048).

9. No such room has been identified.

tion of their ancient paintings and drawings and do eternal honour to its author. I beg leave to subscribe myself with great truth,

Sir,

Your most obedient and most obliged humble servant,

AND. COLTEE DUCAREL

Hon. Horace Walpole Esq.

PS. I have this moment seen a copy of a letter from Mr Berch,[10] a counsellor, keeper of the Queen of Sweden's[11] cabinet of medals and an eminent antiquary, to a gentleman[12] in London, dated Stockholm, Jan. 15, 1762—from whence I copied the following passage, viz.

'Mr Beylon[13] (a Swiss gentleman who I find is Reader to the Queen) est depuis quelques semaines avec la cour à Uhbricks Dahl. Autant que je puis prévoir, il ne vous fournira pas d'autre moyen de servir la Reine que par les monnaies courantes du Roi George III, dont assurément elle n'a pas une seule pièce dans son cabinet. La médaille du couronnement de L.L.M.M. ne serait pas moins agréable; et celle du Roi de Prusse,[14] son cher frère. Ajoutez-y, s'il vous plaît, pour moi, le Prince Ferdinand,[15] ce brave capitaine, et Mr Horace Walpole.'[16]

[Enclosures]

A. Observations on Mr Walpole's *Anecdotes of Painting in England* by Dr Ducarel Feb. 23, 1762

Vol. 1. preface pag. xi. note. A clergyman has suggested to me that he thinks it would have been better to have left out *the nature of* in that note and to have let it run *whether the second person was* etc.

10. Carl Reinhold Berch (1706–77), Swedish antiquary, numismatist, and historian (*Svenskt Biografiskt Lexikon*, Stockholm, 1918– , iii. 309–18).

11. Luise Ulrike (1720–82), m. (1744) Adolf Frederik, K. of Sweden, 1751 (MANN ii. 62 n. 12).

12. Not identified.

13. Jean François Beylon (1717–79), Reader to Queen Luise Ulrike, 1760, and to King Gustav III, 1772 (*Svenskt Biografiskt Lexikon*, iv. 127–32).

14. Frederick II (1712–86) the Great, K. of Prussia 1740–86.

15. Prince Ferdinand (1721–92) of Brunswick.

16. No medal of HW is known to have been struck; possibly Sir Robert Walpole was meant.

Vol. 1. p. 13 note. There seems to be an inaccuracy of expression in saying *The lions were originally leopards.*[17]

Vol. 1. p. 24 l. 14—It is a mistake that oil colours grow black when on proper ground and rightly prepared though not guarded by glass or any other way—nor does it follow that being covered with glass it must be miniature; for oil colours will, if properly prepared, endure as well with as without a glass.[18]

Vol. 1st. p. 25 l. 18 *When they painted*—to—*gum only*. By this must be meant the white of the egg, which with the juice of the tender twigs of a young fig-tree was long before in use in illuminating manuscripts, and mixed with whiting finely washed and ground, the white of egg being first prepared.

Vol. 1 p. 26 l. 7 Cimabue[19] must have used the white and not the yolk, if he expected it should bind the colours; for the yolk contains an oil not inclined to dry—and besides, the yolk would vitiate the white, the blue, the purple and the violet.

temp. Hen. V
In the long gallery at Lambeth are the two following original pictures in oil
viz. Q. Katherine wife of Henry V
Abp Chicheley[20]

Marriage of Henry VII

Vol. 1 p. 51 Anecdote concerning that picture communicated to Dr Ducarel by Mr Geo. Vertue Jan. 28, 1754.

viz. 'That Lord Pomfret bought this picture of one Old Sykes[21] above 30 years ago, which Sykes dealt in pictures and was a noted tricker—that he (Sykes) gave it that name, well knowing how to give names to pictures

17. See following letter.

18. Ibid.

19. Giovanni Cimabue (?1240–?1302), Florentine painter.

20. Henry Chichele or Chicheley (?1362–1443), Abp of Canterbury, 1414. In the 2d edn of the *Anecdotes*, 1765, i. 35, HW mentioned these pictures: 'In the long gallery at Lambeth is an ancient portrait of Queen Catherine of Valois, and another of Archbishop Chicheley.'

21. William Sykes (ca 1659–1724), painter and picture dealer (Vertue Note Books, *Walpole Society* 1929–30, xviii. 142, 146; *Historical Register . . . Chronological Diary*, 1725, p. 4).

to make them sell—that Geo. Vertue had carefully examined that picture, Lord Pomfret having once a design that he should engrave it, which was not done because Vertue could not spare time to go to Easton for that purpose—that Lord Pomfret had often promised him to send it to London to be engraven which he never did—that upon the strictest examination Vertue could never be convinced that the man was Hen. VII, the face not appearing to him like any of the pictures he had seen of that king—that as to the woman, she had pomegranates upon her clothes, which certainly did not belong to her—that the church in which they are married, as represented in the picture, did not appear to be any English church, and that, upon the whole, it was suspected, at the time that Lord Pomfret bought it, that Old Sykes, who was a rogue, had caused the figures and representation of the marriage, to be added to the representation of the inside of a church, Old Sykes having before been guilty of many pranks of that sort.'[22]

Vol. 1st p. 21 l. 6 Concerning painting in the time of the two first Edwards.

In Dart's *Hist. of Canterbury Cathedral*[23]—appendix, p. 3, No. 5. Bibliotheca Cotton Galba E. IV., fol. 103: nova opera in Ecclesia et in Curia temp. Henrici Prioris ab A.D. 1285 usque ad annum 1290. I find this hint concerning painting temp. Edw. I. viz. 'Camera magni Prioris, cum pictura.'

Hon. Horace Walpole Esq.

B. Memorand. of some ancient drawings relating to the hist. of England in the Harleian MSS—

Harleian MSS.

No. 1498-2- picture of Hen. VII (giving a book to John Islipp,[24] Abbot of Westminster) who is called Moost Cristen

No. 1499-3- drawings of ancient kings

No. 1766-3- picture of Lydgate[25]

No. 1892-26- ancient British saints

22. HW did not change his account of this picture, which he had bought at Lord Pomfret's sale for 84 guineas (Gray ii. 68 n. 12; Mann iv. 390 n. 10). See following letter.

23. John Dart, *The History and Antiquities of the Cathedral Church of Canterbury*, 1726. HW's copy is Hazen, *Cat. of HW's Lib.*, No. 428.

24. John Islip (d. 1532), Abbot of Westminster, 1500.

25. John Lydgate (ca 1370–ca 1451), poet.

No. 2278-3- picture of Hen. VI as a child
ibid.-4-5-6 Hen. VI and pictures of ancient architecture, habits, weapons, etc.
No. 2358-14-15- old English dresses
No. 4826-1- picture of Lydgate
No. 1319 ancient drawings relating to the hist. of England
No. 1349-3- drawings of Edward III with all his children

temp. Hen. VI
Besides this Pyne[26] has engraven (from the Charter of Eaton College) a representation of Hen. VI and the Houses of Lords and Commons sitting together.

temp. Edw. IV
Mr Walpole has likewise engraven (from a MS in the Lambeth Library) a representation of Edward IV and V, Richard Duke of Gloucester, etc.

For some other English antiquities engraven by Montfaucon I beg leave to refer you to the Postscript of my *Tour through Normandy*.[27]

Hon. Horace Walpole Esq.

26. John Pine (1690–1756), engraver (*Bryan's Dict. of Painters and Engravers*, 1903–5, iv. 121).

27. London, 1754. HW's copy is Hazen, *Cat. of HW's Lib.*, No. 668:6.

TO ANDREW COLTEE DUCAREL, Wednesday 24 February 1762

Printed from the MS now WSL. First printed, Nichols, *Lit. Anec.* iv. 703–4 (closing omitted). Reprinted, Cunningham iii. 487–8; Toynbee v. 178–9 (closing and signature omitted in Cunningham and Toynbee). The MS apparently passed from Ducarel to John Nichols; sold Sotheby's 18 Nov. 1929 (J. G. Nichols Sale), lot 241, to Francis Edwards; resold by them to WSL, 1932.

Address: To Dr Ducarel at Doctors Commons. *Postmark:* PENNY POST PAID.

Feb. 24, 1762.

Sir,

I AM glad my books have at all amused you, and am much obliged to you for your notes and communications. Your thought of an English Montfaucon accords perfectly with a design I have long had of attempting something of that kind,[1] in which too I have been lately encouraged,[2] and therefore I will beg you at your leisure, as they shall occur, to make little notes of customs, fashions, and portraits, relating to our history and manners.

Your work on vicarages,[3] I am persuaded, will be very useful, as everything you undertake is, and curious.

After the medals I lent Mr Perry,[4] I have a little reason to take it ill, that he has entirely neglected me; he has published a number, and sent it to several persons, and never to me.[5] I wanted to see him too, because I know of two very curious medals, which I could borrow for him. He does not deserve it at my hands, but I will not defraud the public of anything valuable, and therefore if he will call on me any morning, but a Sunday or Monday, between eleven and twelve, I will speak to him of them.

With regard to one or two of your remarks.

1. George Vertue also had a similar idea in 1748: 'As Monfaucon has published monuments of France, etc. so I have long thought such a book would be acceptable to the public' (Vertue Note Books, *Walpole Society* 1951–2, xxx. 144).

2. By Lord Bute and Thomas Gray (*ante* 13 Feb. 1762 and n. 4).

3. *A Repertory of the Endowments of Vicarages in the Diocese of Canterbury* was published in 1763 as a specimen of the proposed general repertory of the endowments of all vicarages. The diocese of Rochester was later included and published as *A Repertory of the Endowments of Vicarages in the Dioceses of Canterbury and Rochester,* 1782.

4. Francis Perry (d. 1765), engraver (*Bryan's Dict. of Painters and Engravers,* 1903–5, iv. 98).

5. Perry had not yet completed the 'number' in his *Series of English Medals* that mentioned HW's medals (see following letter, n. 15).

I have not said that *real* lions were originally leopards—I have said that lions in arms, that is, *painted* lions, were leopards, and it is fact, and no inaccuracy. Paint a leopard yellow, and it becomes a lion.

You say, colours *rightly* prepared do not grow black—the art would be much obliged for such a preparation. I have not said that oil colours would not endure with a glass—on the contrary, I believe they would last the longer.

I am much amazed at Vertue's blunders about my marriage of Henry VII. His account is a heap of ridiculous contradictions. He said, *Sykes knowing how to give names to pictures to make them sell,* called this the marriage of Henry VII and afterwards, he said, Sykes had the figures inserted in an old picture of a church. He must have known little indeed, Sir, if he had not known how to name a picture that he had painted on purpose that he might call it so! That Vertue on the strictest examination could not be convinced that the man was Henry VII not being like any of his pictures. Unluckily he is extremely like the shilling,[5a] which is much more authentic than any picture of Henry VII—but here Sykes seems to have been extremely deficient in his tricks: did he order the figure to be painted like Henry VII and yet could not get it painted like him, which was the easiest part of the task? Yet how came he to get the Queen painted like, whose representations are much scarcer than those of her husband?[6] And how came Sykes to have pomegranates painted on her robe, only to puzzle the cause?[7] It is not worth adding, that I should much sooner believe the church was painted to the figures than the figures to the church. They are hard and antique; the church in a better style, and at least more fresh. If Vertue had made no better criticisms than these, I would never have taken so much trouble with his MSS. Adieu! Sir

I am

Your obliged humble servant

Hor. Walpole

5a. The coinage of 1504–9 introduced one new coin, the shilling, described by C.W.C. Oman, *Coinage of England,* Oxford, 1931, p. 242, and illustrated pl. XXV (7).

6. Torregiano's effigy on her tomb in Westminster Abbey and a half-length painting by an unknown artist are noted in the National Portrait Gallery's *Catalogue,* 1932, *sub* Elizabeth of York. She is shown in the painting holding the White Rose of York.

7. Thomas Gray called pomegranates 'a fashionable pattern for embroidery and

From ANDREW COLTEE DUCAREL, Saturday 27 February 1762

Printed from a photostat of the MS at Nostell Priory, Wakefield, Yorks, kindly furnished by the late Hon. Charles Winn. First printed, Nichols, *Lit. Anec.* iv. 704–5 (closing omitted). Reprinted, Toynbee *Supp.* iii. 171–2 (signature omitted). For the history of the MS see *ante* ?1762. Ducarel's MS draft of this letter is now WSL; for its history see *ante* 23 Feb. 1762.

Doctors Commons, Feb. 27, 1762.

Sir,

IN ANSWER to your obliging letter of the 24th, I am very glad to find that my thoughts of an English Montfaucon accords with your design of attempting something of that kind; and I will, with great pleasure, send you, from time to time, such notes as I may have made of customs, fashions, portraits etc. relating to our history and manners—and I dare say your *Anecdotes on Painting* will occasion the learned to look into those matters, and daily furnish you with new discoveries.

At present, Sir, I can only add a hint (to vol. 1 p. 14) which confirms Windsor's being a place of note long before the time of Edward III, taken from a memorandum I have of a record in the Tower, viz. Rotulus Franciæ de anno 16 Hen. III memb. 3. *De Capella de Windlesor paveanda et depingenda Teste Rege apud Burdegalam 20 Septembris.*[1] I will moreover carefully examine the Lambeth MSS in my custody and send you every notice I can to forward that great work.

There is in that valuable library a curious MS (No. 279)[2] representing Death's Dance, finely illuminated on vellum, with verses in French seemingly as old as the time of Edward III.[3] It is not a procession—each division contains only two figures, as Death and the Pope, Death and an emperor, Death and a king etc.—and the verses

brocades about that time' (Gray to HW 3 March 1754, GRAY ii. 78). It is probable that Vertue thought the White Rose should have been the symbol depicted.

1. 'French scroll of the year 16 Henry III [1232], parchment 3. Of paving and painting the Chapel at Windsor, attested by the King at Bordeaux 20 September.'

2. 'This is a book printed at Paris in Gothic types, and contains 35 most curious and highly finished illuminations, descriptive of each dialogue between Death and the character whom he addresses.' The publisher was A. Verard (Lambeth Palace, *Catalogue of the Archiepiscopal Manuscripts in the Library*, 1812, p. 38).

3. K. of England 1327–77.

of Lydgate (printed in Dugdale's *St Paul,* p. 289, edit. 1658)[4] may, for ought I know, have been translated from that very manuscript; but I do not assert it, as I have not compared the MS with Dugdale.

To the hints in my last give me leave, Sir, to add the following ones—as to[5]

William the Conqueror

The MS account of the tapestries at Bayeux, drawn up by the late Mr Smart Lethieullier[6] (which is pretty long, and different from Montfaucon's) is now in the hands of my friend Mr Tyndall[7] of Doctors Commons, who purchased it at the auction[8] of Mr Lethieullier's books.

Henry I

In my last[9] I mentioned 2 figures of Hen. I and his Queen at the west end of Rochester Cathedral; instead of *figures* read *heads.*

Henry III

Mr Hodsall[10] has had the good fortune to meet with *a gold coin* of Henry III.[11] It is said to be undoubtedly of him—I have not seen it—Perry the engraver who has seen it gave me this information.

Edward III

I have been lately assured that Sir Charles Frederick[12] has in his collection a brass medal of Edward III.[13]

4. See CHATTERTON 143–4.

5. This paragraph is omitted in Toynbee.

6. (1701–60), antiquary and art collector (C. H. I. Chown, 'Smart Lethieullier,' *Essex Review,* 1927, xxxvi. 1–20).

7. Thomas Tyndall (d. ca 1766), F. R. S., F. S. A. (A. C. Ducarel, *Anglo-Norman Antiquities,* 1767, p. vii).

8. 23–29 Feb. 1761 (British Museum, *List of Catalogues of English Book Sales, 1676–1900,* 1915, p. 68; Chown, op. cit. 16).

9. *Ante* 23 Feb. 1762.

10. Edward Hodsoll (d. 1794), a 'banker in the Strand, and possessed of a most curious collection of coins and medals' (Nichols, *Lit. Anec.* iv. 704n; F. G. H. Price, *Handbook of London Bankers,* 1890–1, *sub* Stirling, p. 158; GM 1794, lxiv pt ii. 966).

11. A coinage, called gold pennies, current in all transactions at the rate of 20 pennies of sterlings, according to a writ dated at Chester 16 Aug. 1257. These coins were unpopular and, being of pure gold, were readily melted down and became extremely rare (R. L. Kenyon, *The Gold Coins of England,* 1884, pp. 14–15).

12. (1709–85), K. B., 1761; surveyor-general of the Ordnance 1750–82; M. P. (see Chown, op. cit. 15).

13. Perhaps a reference to John Dassier's medal in copper 'published' in 1731; there were no contemporary medals of Edward III (*Anecdotes, Works* iii. 481–2; [John Pinkerton,] *The Medallic History of England,* 1790, pp. 1–6; pls I, II).

As to the remarks contained in my last, if any of them have given you the least uneasiness, I am very sorry for it—Vertue's note about your picture of Hen. VII I sent you just as Vertue gave it me—for I was so far from laying any stress upon it, and from believing it not to be Hen. VII's marriage that I went twice to Easton[14] on purpose to see that picture, and was long since convinced that it is not only what you say, but likewise one of the finest English historical picture[s] I ever yet beheld.

This letter, Sir, will be delivered to you by Perry (who also brought my last to your house)—you will find that he is so far from having finished one number (which is to contain 3 plates) as you was informed, that he has only finished one plate and begun another, both which he will show you.[15] He is an honest, ingenious and modest man, and I hope you will not withdraw your favour from him. I have the honour to remain,

Sir,

Your most obedient humble servant,

AND. COLTEE DUCAREL

Hon. Horace Walpole Esq.

From the REV. CHARLES PARKIN,[1] ca March 1762

Printed for the first time from a photostat of the MS at Nostell Priory, Wakefield, Yorks, kindly furnished by the late Hon. Charles Winn. For the history of the MS see *ante* ?1762.

Dated approximately by the publication of the first two volumes of *Anecdotes of Painting* 15 Feb. 1762 (Hazen, *SH Bibl.* 55).

Endorsed by HW: Not inserted yet [in pencil, crossed out]. Inserted [in ink].

Address: To the Honourable Horatio Walpole Esq.

Oxburgh, 1762.

Sir,

I HAVE read with great pleasure and satisfaction your *Anecdotes,* lent me by my good friend the Recorder of Lynn,[2] and as I have

14. Easton Neston, Northants (MONTAGU i. 5 n. 13).

15. He had engraved the plates for Ducarel's *A Series of above Two Hundred Anglo-Gallic . . . Coins,* 1757, and was in the process of publishing *A Series of English Medals* (CHATTERTON 157 and n. 18).

1. (1689–1765), rector of Oxburgh, Norfolk, 1717; antiquary.

2. Henry Partridge (1711–93), Recorder of Lynn, 1745 (Hamon Le Strange, *Norfolk Official Lists,* Norwich, 1890, p. 200; Sir Bernard Burke, *Landed Gentry,* 4th

met with some things on the same subject, take this liberty of communicating them, relying on pardon, as a brother antiquary.

Anecd[otes], vol. 1, p. 6–12.[3] I find a charter or grant in the 28 of Hen. III—Js. Edw°. filio Odonis, de quâdam pipâ Subterranea aque, ex Aquaductu Regis apud Westmonaster̃.[4]—A°. 32 a patent—Rex cepit in manum suam Tot. libertat. Civitatis Londoñ. et eam commisit Will°. de Haverhull,[5] et Edwardo de Westmoñ.[6] custod̃. dat. ap[d]. Oxoñ. 25 Aug[i].[7]—Haverhull was the King's Treasurer A°. 29, and probably also at this time.

Anecd[otes], v. 1, p. 12.[8] In the 36 of Hen. III—John de Somercote had a patent for the Custody of the Mint—Custos Cambij p. tot. regnum.[9]

Anecd[otes], p. 14, v. 1, and p. 17.[10] King Edward the Confessor granted Windsor (being Royal Demeans) to the Abbey of Westminster on the 5th of the Calends of January in his 25 year just before his death. King William I, on his accession prevailed on the Abbot and Convent to exchange it for other lands,[11] being delighted with the site of it, 'Maxime utilis et commodus est visus propter contiguam aquam, et situam venationibus aptams'[12] (as he expresses it in his charter to the said monastery) and after naming the Lordships etc. that he gave them; he mentions the gift of £100 of silver to complete and finish the building of the Abbey, and then adds—'Ob reverentiam nimis amoris quem Ego in ipsum Inclitum Regem Edwardum habueram, Tumbum ejus et Regine juxta eum posite,

edn, 1868, p. 1157; GM 1793, lxiii pt ii. 1057).

3. This citation appears in the MS as a footnote marked (a).

4. 'To James Edward Fitz-Odo, of a certain subterranean water-pipe, out of the King's aqueduct at Westminster.'

5. William de Haverhull or Haverhill, treasurer 1240–52 under Henry III.

6. Edward Fitz-Odo, master of the King's works at Westminster (*Anecdotes* i. 9n).

7. 'The King took in his hand all of the liberties of the city of London and committed it to William de Haverhull and Edward of Westminster, custodians, given at Oxford 25 Aug.'

8. This citation appears in the MS as a footnote marked (b).

9. HW added this information about Somercote in a footnote to the 2d edn, i. 13.

10. This citation appears in the MS as a footnote marked (c).

11. The manor of Old Windsor, which was part of 'the ancient demesne of the Crown,' and long the property of the Saxon kings, was bequeathed to Westminster Abbey by Edward the Confessor about a week before his death, but recovered by William the Conqueror in an exchange. Although alienated several times, it always reverted to the Crown (T. E. Harwood, *Windsor Old and New*, privately printed, 1929, p. 289).

12. 'It is seen to be of the greatest usefulness and convenience because of the adjacent water and a location suitable for hunting.'

ex auro et argento fabrili opere, artificiosi Decoris mirifice operiri feci.'[13]

Amongst the lands etc. granted to this Abbey and confirmed by him, is that of land and houses by Godwin[14] called Greatsyd, and his son Ealfwin (in London) with the consent of the late King Edward. This Godwin was Master Mason to King Edward and—præ erat Cæmentarijs illius Eubesie,[15] as the aforesaid grant testifies—and in the 56 of Hen. III—Rob^s. de Beverlaco Carpentar̃. Rx principale et visor operatioñ. Regis.[16]

As you have taken notice of painted glass, I shall observe some things that I thought curious of that kind, some few years past in the church of Walpole St Peter in Norf[olk]. In the east window of the south aisle is the figure of a knight on his knees, with a great broad belt over his shoulder, and a large broadsword hanging from it, and this label—'Tu Sis memor mei, Jacobe in presentia Dej.'[17] This is the figure of Sir Tho. Daniel,[18] a person of great eminency in the reigns of Hen. VI, and Edward IV, who married Margaret a sister of John Howard, the first Duke of Norfolk of that family, in the 27 of Hen. VI. He had a patent to be Constable of the Castle of Rising in Norf[olk], Keeper of the Forest, and Chase and Warren, then held by Ralph Lord Cromwell[19] (Lord Treasurer) on his death, or vacancy etc. In the 16 of Edward IV [he] had licence to found the chantry of St James in this church.[20]

Here in this south aisle in a window, is a representation of the Supreme Being, in a long purple gown, resting his right hand on a wand of gold, pointing out the first finger of his left hand (as dictating) to the Virgin Mary, who is on a seat with a pen in her hand, and paper before her; the Deity stands at the entrance of a castle with a wall about it embattled, and many angels are looking down

13. 'Because of the reverence—the exceeding love—which I had had for the illustrious King Edward, I caused his tomb and that of his Queen beside it to be covered over with skillful workmanship in gold and silver, wonderfully and artistically ornamented.'

14. Not further identified.

15. 'Before that was mason to the famous Eubesius.'

16. 'Robert de Beverley, King's principal carpenter and overseer of the King's works.'

17. 'May you be mindful of me, James, in the presence of God.'

18. Constable of Castle Rising, 1448 (Le Strange, op. cit. 250; Francis Blomefield and Charles Parkin, *An Essay towards a Topographical History of . . . Norfolk*, 1805–10, ix. 112–13).

19. Ralph de Cromwell (ca 1403–55), 3d Lord Cromwell; constable of Castle Rising, 1431; lord high treasurer 1433–43.

20. See Blomefield and Parkin, op. cit. ix. 113–14.

from the turrets; there is a great degree of majesty in this figure of the Deity, and the painter seems to have been animated with the same spirit as Phidias, in his figure of Jupiter Olympius, from the verses of Homer—Ἦ καὶ κυανέῃσιν ἐπ' etc. Homer, *Iliad,* Lib. 1.[21]

In the east window of the north aisle (where the dormitory of the ancient family of De Rochford[22] was) is the effigies of Ralph Lord Cromwell of Tateshale on his knees in armour, on his surtout—argent a bend ingrailed azure, and a chief gules (his own arms), also that of his lady, who by the arms on her vest—quarterly or and gules, a bordure sable bezanty—appears to have been a Rochford. Here also are 2 of the Rochfords in armour, and their ladies, one a Cromwell, the other a Goddard, all well executed.

At the east end of the north aisle of the church of Outwell[23] in Norf[olk] are well preserved and curiously painted in the windows, several saints etc. in full length—St Ethelbert the King and Martyr, St Edward the Confessor, St Edmund the King and Martyr, St Etheldreda, St Michael, St George, the 3 Wise Men with their offerings, the Virgin Mary teaching the Child Jesus to read, and our Saviour etc. This chapel was built,[24] and thus beautified (as I take it) by John Fincham Esq.[25] of this town, who married Elizab[eth] daughter and sole heir of Tho. Derham Esq.[26] by Alice his wife, daughter and coheir of Gilbert Haultoff a baron of the Exchequer in the reign of Hen. VI, and built in that of Edward IV.

As I have some curious pictures of my own, I will take the liberty to name some of them to you—St Jerome on board, a very antique piece, near 4 feet long, and a yard broad, his upper part naked, holding between his hands a skull, his Book of Meditations by him with a crucifix; in a grotto, his cardinal's hat, and lion by him. The nerves, sinews, beard, and his emaciated face etc. is admirable, the hand or performer, I know not.—King Hen. VIII, an half length, a yard in height and 2 feet 4 inches broad, with a black bonnet ornamented with jewels in a gown with open sleeves, at the opening, and at his neck, there is some fur, adorned with many jewels etc. with a noble collar of the same, agreeable to what you

21. 'Then truly the son of Chronos spake and bowed his dark brow in assent; the ambrosial locks flowed down from the king's immortal head, and he made great Olympus tremble' (*Iliad* i. 528–30). See Blomefield and Parkin, op. cit. ix. 114.

22. See ibid. ix. 108, 115.

23. St Clement's Church (ibid. vii. 470–3).

24. The Fincham Chapel was added between 1461 and 1483.

25. See 'Fincham's pedigree, of Outwell,' ibid. vii. 462, 473.

26. M. P. Lynn, 1406.

mention of ballast rubies in your 2d vol. p. 65.[27] This is allowed to be by Holben,[28] and on it are these following profane verses as a compliment:

Si talis pictâ prodit sub Imagine princeps,
Quale putas verum Corpus habere decus.
Mens divina latet, tenti sub Corpore Regis,
Numinis hæc forma est, Effigiesq Dej.[29]

One of Corñ. Janson,[30] 2 feet 7 inches high, and 2 broad, being the great Duke of Bucks[31] in King Charles I reign, in armour, and the Garter over it.

One on board in chiaroscuro, about 20 inches broad, and 2 feet, 2 inches long; in the centre on a pedestal or altar, stands a winged angel with a sack of money, and on the altar is wrote, *Albe Mens Gading;* not far from the altar stand 2 principal figures, on their heads large white hats and feathers, just before them is a lady or gentlewoman on her knees as a supplicant, and supported by a man in a broad brim hat; to him the Queen seems to point; probably the painter, Rubens; with a great group of persons above 20 in miniature, in high and low life; their dress, ardour, and humour is admirable and not to be described.

Also a picture on canvas, somewhat less than the last, being a Biggen[32] of Flanders in her proper habit, and in a closet. The shade of her face under her veil etc. is highly beautiful, and is looked upon as a capital piece; I have not judgment sufficient to know the painter. Some years past, I bought these 2 last pictures, and after I had, Dr Hebburn[33] came to do the same, and said he should have procured them for your great and worthy father.

27. The 'inestimable collar of rubies' or 'great collar of ballast rubies' that 'had belonged to Henry VIII' (*Anecdotes* ii. 65–6).

28. Possibly a copy of the Holbein portrait of Henry VIII at Castle Howard painted in 1542 (Paul Ganz, *The Paintings of Hans Holbein,* 1956, p. 254, No. 119).

29. 'If such a prince appears in the painted image, you may judge what splendour the true body has. The godlike mind lies hidden, held within the body of the King; this is the figure of divine majesty and the likeness of God.'

30. Cornelius Johnson (or Jonson van Ceulen) (1593 – ca 1662) (CHUTE 73 n. 33).

31. George Villiers (1592–1628), cr. (1623) D. of Buckingham. See C. R. Cammell, 'George Villiers First Duke of Buckingham,' *Connoisseur,* 1936, xcviii. 127.

32. Beguine, the name for the members of a lay sisterhood which began in the Low Countries in the 13th century; they wore a sombre habit and headdress (E. W. McDonnell, *Beguines and Beghards in Medieval Culture,* New Brunswick, N.J., 1954, pp. 3–7, 205; OED).

33. George Hepburn (or Hepborne) (ca 1670–1760), of King's Lynn; M.D.; Sir Robert Walpole's physician (William Richards, *The History of Lynn,* Lynn, 1812, ii. 1028–32; GM 1760, xxx. 46; Nichols, *Lit. Anec.* iii. 650; R. W. Ketton-Cremer, *Country Neighbourhood,* 1951, pp. 49, 203).

I have 2 or 3 more agreeable pieces, but as I know not the painter, I shall only observe that Tho. Lant[34] mentioned by you, p. 165, vol. 1, was Portcullis Pursuivant at Arms. I have a MS entitled—The Armoury of Nobility etc. first gathered etc. by R^t^. Cooke[35] Clarencieux King of Armes, and corrected etc. by R^t^. Glover,[36] Somerset Herauld, and lastly augmented with the Knights of the Garter, by Tho. Lant Portcullis etc. A^o^. Dom^i^. 1589, but I query if it was ever printed.

If you'll excuse the freedom I have here taken, it will be a favour conferred on,

Sir,

Your obedient humble servant,

CHA. PARKIN

From JOHN HAWKINS,[1] Monday 1 March 1762

Printed from the MS now WSL. First printed, Toynbee *Supp.* iii. 173–4. Damer-Waller; the MS was sold Sotheby's 5 Dec. 1921 (first Waller Sale), lot 141, to Maggs; offered by them, Cat. 473 (1926), lot 262; acquired by Henry C. Folger; Folger Shakespeare Library to WSL, by exchange, 1950.

Memoranda (by HW, in pencil, possibly a list of letters to be written):

Mr Hawkins
Lord Kaymes
Mr Gray

Twickenham, 1st March 1762.

Dear Sir,

I HAD made my acknowledgments for the curious and most acceptable present the *Anecdotes* before now, but that I have been in the daily hope of being able to do it in person, for which purpose I have sent to Strawberry Hill, but though I hear you sometimes come thither on Sunday, I have been so unfortunate as to miss you.[2] I am as much edified as delighted with the book and have more to

34. (ca 1556–1600), Portcullis pursuivant, 1588. His 'Armoury of Nobility' is BM Add. MS 4959.

35. (d. ca 1593), Clarencieux King of Arms, 1567.

36. (1544–88), Somerset herald, 1571.

1. (1719–89), Kt, 1772; historian of music and biographer of Dr Samuel Johnson; HW's neighbour at Twickenham.

2. HW wrote to George Montagu, 'Arlington Street, March 9th,' that he had not been at SH for 'above a month, nor ever was so long absent' (MONTAGU ii. 20–1).

say about it than a letter would contain. Something however I must not conceal from you and that is that the Bishop of Gloucester[3] has taken fire at a passage in it which to several of his friends he has declared he looks on as a *malignant unprovoked attack on him,* and with a spirit as resolute as that which animated *Becket* he has vowed revenge. I am further told that a new edition of Pope[4] now in Baskervile's press[5] is the intended vehicle for his abuse, for abuse I pronounce it; all controversy must be that comes from that quarter.

The passage I own I cannot find unless it is that pertinent reflection on the folly of hypothesis-making in the 27th page of Vol. I,[6] a reflection which I never could forbear to make on looking into either the *Alliance between Church and State* or the *Divine Legation,*[6a] though my author tells me it is something more direct in a passage where *Brown Willis* and *Hearne* and the *Phœnicians* are mentioned together; you have my information just as I received it and I give it you thus only to enable you to recur to the passage.[7]

As much as I admire the Bishop's learning and parts I never had the least opinion of his judgment and to sum up his character I think that with all the haughtiness of a *Scaliger*[8] or a *Bentley*[9] towards his adversaries, he has shown himself capable of such meanness and servility in his Dedication of his and *Pope's* Shakespeare[10] to Mrs *Allen,*[11] a plain well meaning woman and nothing more, as no honest man could practise, by honesty I mean sincerity and integrity, the want of which, in most of the concerns of life no degree of parts or knowledge will atone for.

I have forborne to mention this matter to anyone for as the Bishop

3. William Warburton (1698–1779), Bp of Gloucester, 1760.

4. Pope's *Works,* edited by Warburton, had been published in 9 vols, 1751.

5. The Baskerville edition was never published (GRAY i. 38 n. 260).

6. 'Curious facts are all I aim at relating, never attempting to establish an hypothesis, which of all kind of visions can nourish itself the most easily without any. The passion for systems did not introduce more errors into the old philosophy, than hypothesis has crowded into history and antiquities' (*Anecdotes* i. 27).

6a. HW's copies of *The Alliance between Church and State,* 1736, and *The Divine Legation of Moses Demonstrated,* vol. I, 1738 (vol. II, 1741), are Hazen, *Cat. of HW's Lib.,* Nos 1608: 34: 1 and 1425.

7. HW discusses Warburton in the most spirited passage in 'Short Notes' (GRAY i. 38–9).

8. Giulio Cesare Scaligero (1484–1558), scholar and controversialist.

9. Dr Richard Bentley (1662–1742), classical scholar.

10. First published in 1747.

11. Elizabeth Holder (ca 1698–1766), m. (1737), as his second wife, Ralph Allen (1694–1764), whose niece, Gertrude Tucker, had married Warburton in 1746 (Benjamin Boyce, *The Benevolent Man: A Life of Ralph Allen of Bath,* Cambridge, Mass., 1967, pp. 71, 165, 295).

has communicated his design but to a single person,[12] to talk of it would discover my author.

Mr Garrick called on me this morning to borrow your book, which he is impatient to read and I have promised to lend him next Saturday.[13]

Be pleased to let me know when I may wait on you at Strawberry Hill who am

Your most obliged humble servant,

JOHN HAWKINS

TO LORD KAMES,[1] Tuesday 2 March 1762

Printed from a photostat of the MS in the Scottish Record Office, Edinburgh, kindly furnished by Mr C. T. McInnes (Abercairny Collection 564). First printed in I. S. Ross, *Lord Kames and the Scotland of his Day,* Oxford, 1972, p. 284. The MS descended in the Home of Kames family to Major J. S. Home Drummond Moray of Abercairny, who deposited the collection of family papers in the Scottish Record Office.

Arlington Street, March 2d 1762.

My Lord,

UNKNOWN as I am to your Lordship, and as I fear I have no title but to be, it cannot but appear a very singular honour, that I have received from Mr Kincaid, by your Lordship's order, the agreeable and flattering present, which your Lordship I perceive by the Introduction too modestly calls only, *Elements of Criticism.*[2]

I have been formerly honoured, I believe, by presents from the same respectable hand,[3] but as they were sent to me without your Lordship's name, I thought it would be taking too great a liberty

12. Warburton wrote his complaints to David Garrick 17 Feb. 1762, and they were conveyed to HW (GRAY i. 39 n. 265). He also wrote in similar terms to Mason (BM Add. MS 32,563 ff. 12–14).

13. Garrick later acquired a copy of the *Anecdotes,* the first two volumes of which were sold with his library at Sotheby's 16 Dec. 1908 (Hazen, *SH Bibl.* 67, copy 8).

1. Henry Home (1696–1782), lord of session as Lord Kames, 1752; jurist and miscellaneous writer.

2. Edinburgh, 3 vols, 1762. HW's copy is Hazen, *Cat. of HW's Lib.,* No. 2895. Late in 1760 Kames had tried to get the diplomatist Hans Stanley, a mutual friend, to pass on part of a draft of the *Elements* for HW's comments, but Stanley apparently demurred (Ross, op. cit. 284).

3. No other works by Kames appear in the SH records.

to offer your Lordship my thanks—but this permission I trust is now granted to me, and I embrace it with zeal and with satisfaction. It was but yesterday I received the last welcome gift, and consequently cannot have had time to read so much as would justify my entering into a particular detail of the pleasure a work from so able, learned and masterly a hand must give me; but I could not delay a moment to assure your Lordship how highly I think myself distinguished by such notice; and which I must beg leave to say, deprives me of one satisfaction, that of concurring *disinterestedly* in the general applause bestowed on your Lordship's writings. If there were faults in them, my Lord, could I see them? You have made me too vain, to leave me impartial. You must be content, my Lord, to receive admiration from the world; you have imprinted a stronger sensation on me, gratitude; and it is with that feeling in the most pleasing degree that I profess myself

My Lord

Your Lordship's most obliged humble servant

Hor. Walpole

From Sir Thomas Reeve,[1] Thursday 4 March 1762

Printed for the first time from a photostat of the MS at Nostell Priory, Wakefield, Yorks, kindly furnished by the late Hon. Charles Winn. For the history of the MS see *ante* ?1762.

March the 4th 1762.

Sir,

Doubtless you will be surprised on finding yourself addressed by one who has not the honour of being known to you, but the occasion of it will I hope excuse my giving you this trouble, to which I am encouraged by having formerly when I lived at Windsor been acquainted with Sir Edward Walpole.[2]

I have with great pleasure read the *Anecdotes of Painting* with which you have lately favoured the world. And supposing that you intend to go on with it and bring it down to the present time thought

1. (d. 1777), Kt, 1756; Sheriff of Berks (Montagu ii. 105 n. 9).

2. Reeve's name is mentioned in Sir Edward Walpole's family letters (now wsl) of 1753. Sir Edward was then living near him at Frogmore, Windsor.

it might not be improper to acquaint you that I for some time have been making a collection of painters' heads and lives of which I have got upwards of three hundred English and others, most of them of my own drawing, some of which by your books I take to be scarce; some I took out of Dr Mead's[3] collection with whom I was very intimate; among them are a mezzotinto print of Hen. Giles,[4] a head of Artimesia Gentileschi;[5] now, Sir, if you like to see them and find any that will be of service to you, you will be very welcome to make use of them.[6]

I am, Sir,

Your most obedient servant,

THOS REEVE

PS. I am curious to know what piece it is that Sandart[7] wants to complete his set of Holbein's drawings of our Saviour's sufferings, for I have in my possession one by the same hand, a folio leaf on which are two representations of Christ, which I had with some others from Basil.

If you favour me with a line please to direct for Sir Thomas Reeve at Holliport near Maidenhead, Berks.

3. Richard Mead (1673–1754), M.D., whose collection of books, drawings, and sculpture was one of the largest of his time. The prints and drawings were sold 13 Jan. 1755 (COLE i. 172 n. 53). Reeve's uncle, Sir Thomas Reeve (d. 1737), Chief Justice of Common Pleas, had married a relative of Mead, Arabella Foote, who left a legacy to Mead. The elder Sir Thomas Reeve left part of his estate to the younger Reeve who later lived at Maidenhead (T. E. Harwood, *Windsor Old and New*, 1929, pp. 153–4).

4. Henry Giles (or Gyles) (ca 1640–1709), glass painter; HW refers to him in *Anecdotes, Works* iii. 158.

5. Artemisia Gentileschi (1597– ca 1651), Italian painter (ibid. iii. 242; Thieme and Becker xiii. 408–9).

6. HW wrote George Montagu 3 Oct. 1763 of his 'ridiculous' and disappointing call on Reeve, whom he had found 'a man about thirty in age and twelve in understanding' (MONTAGU ii. 105–6).

7. Joachim von Sandrart (1606–88), author of *Academia nobilissimae artis pictoriae,* Nuremberg, 1683. HW wrote in *Anecdotes,* SH, 1762, i. 75: 'Sandrart had drawings by Holbein of Christ's passion, in folio; two of them were wanting; in his book he offers 200 florins to whoever will produce and sell them to him. p. 241.' HW's copy of Sandrart is Hazen, *Cat. of HW's Lib.*, No. 3630.

From LORD KAMES, ca Saturday 6 March 1762

Printed from Toynbee *Supp.* iii. 312–13, where the letter was first printed from the MS in the Waller Collection. Damer-Waller; the MS was sold Sotheby's 5 Dec. 1921 (first Waller Sale) lot 153, to Oppenheim; not further traced.

Dated approximately by HW's letter to Kames *ante* 2 March 1762.

Sir,

THE present you received of my book[1] was a tribute paid to distinguished merit, so natural and withal so small, that I little thought of being even thanked for it.[2] And yet you testify to so much gratitude in the finest expressions, that I could not help blushing at every line. And I found myself so much inferior in this cordial intercourse, that I thought of withdrawing myself from it altogether by silence. But this resolution did not sit easy upon me; and I must acknowledge your goodness, however short I may fall in expressing my sense of it. Imagine only my heart to be like your own, and then you'll easily conceive my gratitude to be of the purest kind.

At the same time, to you, Sir, I will not be guilty of any disguise. And though the trifling present was the only opportunity I could have of testifying my sense of your merit in the literary way, yet I dare not say my motive was altogether disinterested. An author generally flatters himself with more than one edition; and as your humanity is well known to the world, I fairly laid the plot to have your corrections and improvements in a future edition,[3] if ever the book should be entitled to that honour. It will probably be my last work,[4] for I am growing old; and as I wish to have some reputation by it, nothing will give me greater satisfaction than the hopes of being assisted by men of distinguished taste and knowledge.

I am with the utmost sincerity and gratitude,

My dear Sir,

Your obliged humble servant,

HENRY HOME

1. *Elements of Criticism,* 3 vols, Edinburgh, 1762.

2. *Ante* 2 March 1762.

3. Seven editions of *Elements of Criticism* were published at Edinburgh between 1762 and 1788 (BM Cat.). HW did not offer any 'corrections and improvements.'

4. Kames published several other works after 1762, including *Sketches of the History of Man,* 1774.

From BISHOP LYTTELTON, ca Friday 12 March 1762

Printed for the first time from a photostat of the MS at Nostell Priory, Wakefield, Yorks, kindly furnished by the late Hon. Charles Winn. For the history of the MS see *ante* ?1762.

Dated approximately by the enclosed letter of 11 March 1762 from William Richardson to Lyttelton.

Address: Honourable Mr Walpole, Arlington Street.

THE Bishop of Carlisle[1] received this packet[2] yesterday. If Mr Walpole would have any farther inquiries made at Lincoln, he will write again to Dr Richardson.[3]

[Enclosures]

E[mmanuel] C[ollege], March 11, 1762.

My Lord,

ON MY return to Cambridge I sent your papers down to Lincoln, that there might be no mistake: the answer I here enclose.[4] The person[5] employed I presume you saw, when you was at Lincoln. His father[6] (whose corrections he has made use of) was a very diligent and curious antiquary; of whose writing the son has now a valuable collection, in a large folio, of what is most worth preserving of the Roman and Saxon antiquities of that church and city. He was Master of the Fabric, or (if you choose it rather) Clerk of the Works. I should have deferred the inquiry till I went down myself, but that I thought the answer might be wanted sooner.

If your Lordship has any further commands, either in this or any other way, they will be with pleasure executed by

Your Lordship's most obedient servant,

W. RICHARDSON

1. Lyttelton was elected Bp of Carlisle 1 March and consecrated 21 March 1762.

2. Letters from William Richardson to Lyttelton and from Thomas Sympson to Richardson are with the present letter. They concern the inscription on a gravestone at Lincoln.

3. William Richardson (1698–1775), D.D., 1735; Master of Emmanuel College, Cambridge, 1736–75; precentor of Lincoln Cathedral, 1760; antiquary.

4. See below.

5. Thomas Sympson (ca 1726–86), prebendary of Lincoln 1759–86 (Venn, *Alumni Cantab.;* John Le Neve, *Fasti Ecclesiæ Anglicanæ,* Oxford, 1854, ii. 110).

6. Thomas Sympson (fl. 1740–50), Master of the Works at Lincoln Cathedral (COLE i. 10 n. 68).

My compliments to Mr Pitt.[7]

Address: To the Reverend Dr Richardson, Master of Emanuel College, Cambridge.
Endorsed in a different hand: Torn at Caxton.

Lincoln, March 6, [17]62.

Honoured Sir,

I HAVE examined the gravestone very carefully this mom. but the letters are so filled up with mortar that I am in doubt about some letters, though I employed a couple of men an hour in cleaning it; however the inscription is nearly perfect except the date. I have sent my reading corrected by my father's which was taken upwards of 20 years ago when perhaps it was more intelligible.

It is in Sax[on] characters engraven on the stone and circumscribes a beautiful portraiture lying under a canopy of tabernacle work; in the area there are compasses, a square and other instruments belonging to his profession all engraven in the free stone.

Hic jacet Ricardus de Gaynsbourgh olym Cementarius hujus Ecclesiæ qui obiit . . . u . Kalendarum Junii An . . . ini . . . . .[8]

My father's copy reads 12 after *obiit,* also *annodomini* 13 . . . The date according to his copy is you perceive imperfect but I cannot trace any remains of the date upon the stone.

The Chancellor[9] was so kind as to send me Mr Essex's[10] survey as soon as he received it from you.

The court martial[11] is fixed on Friday the 19th inst[ant] and is said to be occasioned by a very silly affair and will in all probability end in nothing. I suppose you have seen the letters which passed

7. Probably William Pitt, E. of Chatham, but possibly Lyttelton's nephew, Thomas Pitt (1737–93), cr. (1784) Bn Camelford.

8. The inscription is given in full in COLE i. 10; see also ibid. i. 12 n. 6.

9. John Taylor (1704–66), classical scholar; chancellor of the diocese of Lincoln 1744–66.

10. Probably James Essex (1722–84), builder and architect. His survey was possibly for the extensive repairs at Lincoln Cathedral for which he had accepted a commission in 1761 (DNB).

11. A general court martial of Phillips Glover, Lt-Col. of the south battalion of the Lincolnshire militia, 'for behaving in a manner unbecoming an officer, and a gentleman, to Captain Richard Gardiner,' was held at Lincoln 19–24 March. Glover was found not guilty, but was reprimanded for 'having used some expressions . . . not strictly becoming an officer, which appear to have proceeded from warmth, occasioned in part by some provocation on the part of Captain Gardiner' (GM 1762, xxxii. 154).

upon the affair which sufficiently explain it. The Captain[12] printed them.

I hope, Sir, you have had good health this winter and I wish you a continuance of it.

I beg my respects to Mr Richardson[13] and I am,

Honoured Sir,

Your faithful and most obedient servant,

T. SYMPSON

I should be glad to know what use Mr Walpole has for this inscrip[tion].

TO JOHN RATCLIFFE,[1] ? mid-March 1762

Printed from the MS now WSL. First printed (without the list of prints), Toynbee *Supp.* ii. 248–9. The MS was at one time in the possession of the print-seller and engraver John Thane (1748–1818); not further traced until offered by Tregaskis, Cat. 934 (Feb. 1927), lot 528; sold by them to WSL, 1931.

Dated conjecturally 'May 1762' by Toynbee, who notes that the letter was written from SH, but publication of the first two volumes of *Anecdotes* took place 15 Feb., and HW was at SH a month later (HW to Lady Ailesbury 15 March 1762, CONWAY ii. 155). By this date the bound copy of *Anecdotes* for Ratcliffe could have been ready as HW 'hope[d] to find.'

Address: To Mr John Ratcliffe in East Lane, Rotherhithe. *Postmark:* ‹ISLEWORTH›.

Sir,

THE above is the list[2] of the prints you was so obliging as to give me. You received I hope a parcel of about 150 that I sent to you on Thursday, but as I was come out of town before the messenger returned, I have heard nothing of them.

12. Richard Gardiner (1723–81), Capt. 115th Marines, 1757, who thought himself to be a natural son of HW's eldest brother, Robert (MANN ii. 507 n. 6; *Army Lists*, 1758, p. 139; R. W. Ketton-Cremer, *Norfolk Portraits*, 1944, pp. 110–39).

13. Presumably Robert Richardson (1732–81), only son of William Richardson; prebendary of Lincoln (DNB *sub* William Richardson).

1. (d. 1776), book collector, who kept a chandler's shop in Southwark. His collection of Caxtons and black-letter books was sold at Christie's 27 March–6 April 1776 (T. F. Dibdin, *Bibliomania*, 1809, pp. 54–7; GM 1812, lxxxii pt i. 114).

2. Printed below.

I have found two or three books here which I hope will please you, and will bring them the first time I go to London, which cannot be this week; but by that time I hope to find my *Anecdotes of Painting* bound for you.[3] I wish I knew how late in date you go in collecting the works of old printers; or if any other kind of books would be acceptable to you,[4] as I wish for nothing more than an opportunity of returning your great civilities. If you favour me with a line, direct to me at Strawberry Hill Twickenham.

I am Sir

Your most obliged humble servant

Horace Walpole

List of prints I received from Mr Ratcliffe.

John Quarles
Gondomar
Jeremy Rich
Lord Orrery
Richard III
Duchess of Richmond
Dr Young
W. Ramesey
W. Lilly
Maj. Erskine
Lady Elinor Temple
Darcy Wentworth
Lancelot Cœlson
Rob. Turner
M. Gen. Harison
Another, Jer. Rich, different
Hen. Oxenden
Countess of Kent
John Heydon
John Archer
Samson Lennard
Dr Cameron
Moses Brown
Fr. Bugg
Edw. Hatton
J. Playford
W. Walker
F. K. Cibizen
Gilb. Primrose
W. Addy
Th. Brodrick
Chr. Terne
W. Bluck
James Drake
W. Cockburn
Sam. Bolton
J. Hopkins
Jane Q of Scotl[and]
J. Earl of Somerset
Marg. of Richmond
J. Duke of Somerset
J. Bulwar
G. Parker
J. Warburton
Sir John Houblon
Duchess of Somerset
Ernest D. of York
Countess of Seafort
Earl of Macclesfield
Count Bothmar
Charles I
Dervorguilla
John Baliol
Brian Boiroimbe
George Taylor
Edward Bright
W. Walker
Lord Osborne and 2 sisters
W. Parsons
Ch. Ratcliffe
Portraits of Ch. I's progeny
Christ and Angels by Faithorne

3. A mark of special favour. HW's binder is not known.

4. Copies of Hentzner's *Journey*, *Fugitive Pieces*, and *Anecdotes* are listed in Christie's sale catalogue, *Bibliotheca Ratcliffiana. A Catalogue of the Elegant and Truly Valuable Library of John Ratcliffe, Esq. late of Bermondsey, deceased,* 1776.

Capt. Saltonstall
Lord Wharton
Tobias Venner
Rob. Morison
Cutbert Mayn
Rob. Turner, different
G. Withers
T. Stapleton
Abdiah Cole
Francis Moore
——— Cockain
Mr Perkins
W. Atkins
Mrs Burnet
T. Dilworth
J. Dunton
K. Robert II
Th. Nigel
Nath. Bailey
Dr Poole
J. Clark
D. Taintarier
Henry Evans
Sir Barth. Shower
John Seddon
James Robinson
John Fryer
Q. Eliz. Burleigh
and Walsingham
Batty Langly
James Graham
Ambr. Godfrey
Mrs Marg. Nichol
Sir W. Reade
Lords Justices
Fred. K. of Prussia
Prince Eugene
Princess Sophia
James D. of York
Charles II
John Kenrick
Sir Rob. Raymond
St Dunstan
Lord Rochester
Princess Dow. of Orange
5 anonymous portraits
III.

From LADY NORTHUMBERLAND, mid-March 1762

Printed for the first time from the MS (an invitation card) pasted in an extra-illustrated copy, now WSL, of HW's *Fugitive Pieces*, SH, 1758. For the history of this copy see Hazen, *SH Bibl.* 41, copy 9.

Between 1756 and 1766, when Lady Northumberland became a duchess, 1 April occurred on Thursday only in 1762.

LADY Northumberland's compliments to Mr Walpole and desires the honour of his company to play at cards Thursday, April the 1st.

From UNKNOWN, Monday 19 April 1762

Printed for the first time from a photostat of the MS at Nostell Priory, Wakefield, Yorks, kindly furnished by the late Hon. Charles Winn. For the history of the MS see *ante* ?1762.

London, April 19th 1762.

A person totally unknown to the Honourable Mr Walpole begs leave to return him thanks, for the pleasure his late *Anecdotes of Painting* have given him, and hopes he will excuse this trouble.

You have called Petitot[1] a Frenchman and have no particulars of his painting here in Charles I time of any consequence.[2] I presume you had when you wrote this life, forgot that in *The Lives of the Painters who have lived since, or were omitted by De Piles* by J. B., Printed for T. Payne, Mews Gate, 1755, is a particular account of Petitot.[3] If you please to refer to the above book, which is chiefly taken from a French author, you will find that Petitot was born at Geneva, that he was indebted to Sir Theodore Mayern[4] for his principal colours and the means of vitrifying them, was introduced by him to Charles I who gave him a lodging at Whitehall, that he stayed here till the King's death, and many other particulars. I beg leave likewise to remark that though you have judged proper to omit the lives of the Simons,[5] yet perhaps you will in the succeeding volumes, find some opportunity of mentioning that they were Englishmen.[6] This is necessary as your books will fall into many hands who have never seen Virtue's account of them,[7] and will therefore believe the positive assertion of the Abbé Du Bos,[8] who in the chapter in which he treats of climates unfavourable to the arts, has a passage to this effect:

1. Jean Petitot (1607–91), painter in enamel.

2. In *Anecdotes,* SH, 1762, ii. 132. In the 2d edn, 1765, ii. 150–5, HW corrected and expanded the account of Petitot, using the information his correspondent gives here.

3. The account of Petitot occurs on pp. 56–61 of *The Lives of the Most Eminent Modern Painters who have Lived since, or were Omitted by Mons. de Piles,* 1754, by J[ames] B[urgess], which is bound with Roger de Piles, *The Art of Painting . . . To Which is Added, an Essay towards an English School,* 3d edn, Printed for T. Payne [?1750] in the Yale Library copy. See Hazen, *Cat. of HW's Lib.*, Nos 308 and 1608: 78.

4. Sir Theodore Turquet de Mayerne (1573–1655), Swiss physician. He was called to London in 1611 to be first physician to James I, occupying his leisure with chemical experiments concerning pigments and enamels (J. A. van de Graaf, *Het de Mayerne manuscript als bron voor de schildertechniek van de barok,* Mijdrecht, 1958, p. 3 and *passim*).

5. Thomas Simon (1618–65) and his elder brother Abraham (1617–92), medallists. Thomas became engraver to the London mint in 1645, engraving medals for Charles I and for Cromwell, who appointed him chief engraver. Abraham, who modelled portraits in wax, was his collaborator (Helen Farquhar, 'Thomas Simon,' *Numismatic Chronicle,* 1932, 5th ser., xii. 274–310; idem, 'New Light on Thomas Simon,' ibid., 1936, 5th ser., xvi. 210–34; Thieme and Becker xxxi. 52; DNB).

6. HW had mentioned Thomas Simon in his article on Briot in *Anecdotes* ii. 42, noting that 'Briot returned to France about 1642, having formed that excellent scholar Thomas Simon'; he is mentioned again, ii. 140, in the article on Rogiers.

7. George Vertue, *Medals, Coins, Great Seals, and Other Works of Thomas Simon,* 1753; 2d edn, 1780.

8. Jean-Baptiste Du Bos (1670–1742), called Abbé; diplomatist and historian (*Dict. de biographie française* xi. 1006–7).

'The medals struck under Cromwell and Charles II were good work, but were done by Roiters of Antwerp, Gibbons's countryman who was for some time the principal sculptor in London.'[9]

The passage is in the 2d vol. of *Critical Reflections, on Poetry Painting and Music.* I quote it by memory, not having the book by me. Indeed Vertue's account of the Simonses, fully proves your account of his manner of writing to be just; it is so confused that, I remember, after having read it, I could scarce find out what country they were born in. If you should think proper to take any notice of the reflections Abbé Le Blanc[10] has thrown on Hogarth and other English artists in one of his letters; you may remember that Monsieur Rouquet's[11] *L'État des arts en Angleterre,* 1755, contains passages which may be urged against him.[12] The author of the supplement to De Piles says David Teniers[13], Junior, was in England.[14] Excuse extreme haste.

TO LORD BUTE, Tuesday 20 April 1762

Printed from the MS now WSL. First printed, Toynbee v. 197–8. The MS was sold in 1929 by Sabin to Gabriel Wells, who sold it to WSL, 1932; its earlier history is not known. The letter was printed by Mrs Toynbee as 'To the Earl of Egremont (?),' but it is now believed that the recipient was Bute.

Endorsed, in ink, in an unidentified hand: Mr H. Walpole April 1762.

Endorsed, in pencil, in an unidentified hand: To Lord Egremont.

Arlington Street, April 20th 1762.

My Lord,

I MUST entreat your Lordship to be assured that in what I am going to say I have neither positive nor negative view; and only

9. 'The medals struck in England in Cromwell's time, and those made there under Charles II and James II were very good work, but done by a stranger: this was Roëttiers of Antwerp, Guibbons's countryman, who was for a considerable time the principal sculptor in London' (Du Bos, *Critical Reflections on Poetry, Painting and Music,* tr. Thomas Nugent, 1748, ii. 114).

10. Jean-Bernard Le Blanc (1707–81). The 'reflections' occur in a letter written from London to the Abbé Du Bos in Le Blanc's *Lettres,* nouv. edn, Amsterdam, 1751, i. 211–22.

11. Jean-André Rouquet (1701–58), Swiss miniaturist and enameller; friend of Hogarth.

12. Rouquet tried to explain the humours of the English artists to his own countrymen; see particularly pp. 42–52 for his remarks on Hogarth. His work was translated into English in 1755, shortly after the Paris edition appeared.

13. David Teniers the younger (1610–90), Flemish painter.

14. See Burgess, op. cit. 63–4.

lay the following information before you, as I think it mine and every man's duty to contribute their mite to the service of his Majesty and his country.

I happened lately to have in my hands the journal of the Admiral Earl of Sandwich,[1] when he was Ambassador at Madrid, negotiating a truce between Spain and Portugal.[2] He sets down a very exact relation of the then force of each country, as he received it from Don Gulielmo Cascar, a Scotch Sergeant-Major of Battalia, in the Spanish army in Badajoz; and adds this particular passage from the same intelligence;

'The climate (he is speaking of the war on the frontiers of Portugal) too is very unfit for war, there being only *two months,* viz. April and May, fit for a campania, and then begins drowth and heat, that it is impossible for an army to be kept together in; and at the latter end of the year the season is temperate enough again, but then the rains are so uncertain, sometimes coming earlier (in September) sometimes later, and when they come, they make the country so soft, that the artillery cannot stir, but must stay where the rain finds them, what design soever they are upon.'

'He says (adds Lord Sandwich) the armies usually retire to the quarters from the hot season about July 15th.'

I will beg your Lordship not to mention this intelligence as coming from me. If it is of any use[3] to your Lordship, or of any service in general, I am satisfied, and am

My Lord

Your Lordship's most obedient humble servant

Hor. Walpole

1. Edward Montagu (1625–72), cr. (1660) E. of Sandwich; ambassador to Spain 1666–8.

2. He arrived at Lisbon 12 Jan. 1668 to negotiate the truce between Spain and Portugal; a treaty was signed 1 Feb. 1668 (F. R. Harris, *The Life of Edward Mountagu, K. G. First Earl of Sandwich,* 1912, ii. 126–32). HW made 'Extracts' (now WSL) from this MS journal, described in Dalrymple 132 n. 6; see also *post* Sept. 1762, n. 4.

3. On 8 April 1762 the Portuguese ambassador in London requested English support against the recent Spanish invasion of Portugal. HW wrote to Sir Horace Mann 13 April: 'Portugal cries out for help, and our troops are going thither; but I don't think that every Spanish soldier in the world will march to Lisbon' (Mann vi. 23–4 and n. 4).

TO LADY HENRIETTA CECILIA WEST,[1] before Tuesday 4 May 1762

Printed for the first time from a photostat of the MS in the Halsey Collection, Hertfordshire County Record Office, Hertford, through the kind offices of Col. W. Le Hardy. The MS descended in the Johnston family to Frederica Johnston (b. 1818), who married Thomas Plumer Halsey in 1839; it descended in the Halsey family to Sir Walter Halsey, 2d Bt, who deposited it in the Herts County Record Office.

Dated by the marriage of Lady Henrietta Cecilia West to Col. James Johnston 4 May 1762.

Endorsed in an unidentified hand: Horace Walpole.

Memorandum (in another hand): General and Lady Cecilia Johnston are the characters drawn in this sketch by Hor. Walpole.

Dear Madam,

I AM going to make you an extraordinary request—don't be frightened; it cannot be a gallant one; a vestal could not think *that* extraordinary; those young ladies were only bound to refuse; no mortal ever took an oath not to ask them the question. In short, Madam, I am going to write a romance but want the principal ingredients, a hero and a heroine. In the early ages of romance, nobody pretended to draw natural characters, but were at liberty to make their chief personages as perfect as they pleased. At this time of day the world demands a little more probability, and yet in their hearts they don't give up the requisition of something wonderfully near perfection. This puzzles me terribly: I have examined all my acquaintance, and yet I am not above half way. Ladies I find without number possessed of every virtue and beauty that I could desire; but the men are far from being so complete. Though one meets with a hero at every corner, yet they have all some fault or other that clashes with my scheme. General Clive[2] is as brave as Orondates,[3] but he is not quite so tall, or so handsome as I could wish. My Lord Granby,[4] with a soul as great as Alexander's, and as noble a countenance, thinks too much like that monarch that

1. (1727–1817), dau. of John West, 1st E. de la Warr; m. (1762) Col. (afterwards Gen.) James Johnston (ca 1721 *or* 1724–97) (CHUTE 305 nn. 11, 12).

2. Robert Clive (1725–74), cr. (15 March 1762) Bn Clive; Maj.-Gen. in the East India Company's service.

3. Prince Oroondates, the lover of Statira, widow of Alexander the Great, in La Calprenède's romance *Cassandre*.

4. John Manners (1721–70), styled M. of Granby; army officer; M. P.

Bacchus' blessings are a treasure,
Drinking is the soldier's pleasure;[5]

a system incompatible with a true lover's ritual; and though champagne does but expand his heart to his friends, I never read that a hero had anything to do with friends, but to talk to them of his mistress. I have heard of another warrior, whose valour is equal to that of Amadis,[6] and who is of the just height of a hero, that is very tall, who is admirably well-made, and as constant, as if there was but one woman in the world.—You will wonder that I am not contented—should not you think this was the very hero I sought? I own I am difficult: I will tell you my objections: the warrior in question I am told has light hair—in all my practice I never read of the first person in a romance that had not black or at least very dark locks. Melancholy don't sit at its ease upon a fair eyebrow; and at least till the last leaf, you know, Madam, a lover is not to presume to be in good spirits. But I have a stronger prejudice; I call it by its true name: the charming champion I have described *is not an Englishman:*[7] my scene is to lie in Britain; it would be preposterous to fetch my hero from t'other side of the water, though the sea he should cross were no wider than the Irish channel. Besides, I am so scrupulously attached to my own country, that meaning to describe a faultless knight, I cannot let it be supposed that such a character could exist out of Albion. To tell you the truth, I have formed ideas in my own brain both of the hero and the heroine that I should like to employ; and if I cannot match them with two living objects, adieu my romance! I will not abate a single feature, no, nor the air of a feature; and therefore if you are impatient for my work, as to be sure you are already, you must find out a gentleman and a lady who tally exactly to the measures I am going to give you. Don't tell me it is impossible, and that there neither is, nor ever was such a pair, and that it is not your business to realize my visions. Consider how you will be rewarded for your pains; you will read the best novel that

5. Dryden's *Alexander's Feast; or the Power of Musique. An Ode, in Honour of St Cecilia's Day,* 1697, iii. 56–7; set to music by Handel and first performed at Covent Garden 19 Feb. 1736 (P. H. Lang, *George Frideric Handel,* New York, 1966, p. 291).

6. Amadis de Gaule, the hero of a 15th-century prose romance in which Amadis, the flower of chivalry, rescues Oriana, daughter of Lisuarte, King of Great Britain, from the Emperor of Rome who seeks her hand in marriage.

7. Col. Johnston, born in Dublin, was known as 'Irish' Johnston to distinguish him from his kinsman of the same name. His father, Capt. George Johnston, was a Scottish army agent stationed in Ireland.

ever was written; you will become an intimate friend of the heroine; and as you cannot expect with all your merit to shake the fidelity of the most constant lover that ever existed, you will despise all the rest of mankind, and so be secure from the torments of a passion that some time or other would certainly engage your heart. I come to the description.

The fair one must be of a proper height; it is usual to make her tall, but, *except yourself,* I never knew a woman that united majesty and softness. She shall not be tall. I should be inclined to have her complection of the lily hue with a small quantity of roses, but as there is likely to be more sympathy if there is some resemblance in their skins, and as it is written that the hero must be dark, the lady if you please shall be of that proportionate brown that suits the softer sex. Her hair, not black as his, but dark enough to make her skin seem fairer than it is. For the roses, leave them as above, with a reserve for blushes, that every now and then may make her appear still more beautiful. Her eyes are to be sweetly grave, and must not pretend to interfere too much with the graces, that I determine shall inhabit her smiles chiefly. Her nose is to be slender, and a little elevated—a straight one is more perfect, but does not bestow so sensible an air. Her teeth small, white and even; the shape of her face towards an oval—not too exact, because I will not have her undistinguishable from every Statira upon record. Her behaviour in general must be reserved, cheerful with her particular friends; happy, only when her lover is present. She must have a sweet voice, but know it so little, as even to be awkward when forced to sing. She must play on the lute, to divert solitude, as a great queen[8] said; and lest she should be too modern with all these excellencies, she must work admirably. She must have more learning than is necessary for a woman; and this for a whim of my own; I intend she shall read the histories of all countries to be convinced that nothing was ever so perfect as her lover—but she must keep her knowledge a secret from everybody but him. She must be gentle and compassionate; and if I write a second volume, she must be a fond mother. One thing more I require, which indeed I believe was never demanded for a romance before—she must be extremely sensible—I hurry over this, lest you should not believe that I really in-

8. Presumably Elizabeth I, who played the lute.

tend such a work as I promise you. Oh! I had forgot; when her lover is summoned to battle, she must bear it with uncommon fortitude, that is, she must prefer his honour to her own peace; she must seem to think of nothing but his glory while he lives, reserving all grief, till, which I don't design shall ever happen, she may be so miserable as to lose him. Her temper, and I will add no more, must be of the smoothest evenness, and never, unless you insist upon it, must be ruffled with a thought of asperity, except against the enemies of her lover; for I intend he shall have some (though he will never deserve them) just to give him an opportunity of exerting the greatness of his mind in bearing injuries. Now for him.

He may be as tall as you please—no, I will not give you an unlimited commission in that respect, I have a reason; but he may be taller than me, sure that is tall enough! His complexion, I have told you, Madam, must be brown, but warm: his forehead, manly and exactly shaped: his nose and mouth as you would wish them; his teeth fine, his eyes serious, black, and with as much languor as becomes a lover: his hair, jet; and the contour of his face as uncommonly pleasing as you can draw it—You see, having humoured my own taste in the lady, I know how to be indulgent to yours. He must be strong without an air of robustness; I will not have him the least fat, though I am not so partial to leanness, as not to be satisfied if he is just what everybody would think the right medium. I anticipate you in prescribing that his legs and feet must be very handsome. He must have a courage which nothing can daunt; in short, I will let him fear nothing but reproach, as I will have him, contrary perhaps to the rules of heroic love, be jealous only of his honour: yet with all his intrepidity, let him be as cool as if he had patience to write a romance, instead of being the object of it. He must have a tone of voice so sweet that it would persuade without argument; and as much eloquence as would convince without any embellishment. He must seem without passions for everything but his mistress; for whatever else he does, is to appear the result of reason and reflection; yet to prevent his good sense from giving him too wise an air for a romantic being, I will allow you to let him seem very absent—his humanity if you will, shall never be known but by the effects. You are a woman, Madam, and I beg your pardon, will I fear insist upon some trifling qualities—why, let him trifle; he shall play upon the German flute, if you please, I don't much care; he shall be as idle in the country with women, as if he was not formed for the greatest actions; he shall plant bowers; he shall make songs on you and your admirers—nay, I will let him descend to draw patterns for his mistress's work;—but when I or his country call, he shall—why, he shall behave with more propriety and dignity that all your Rinaldos[9] put together;—and I will tell you what you will like still less, he shall be insensible to all the arts and enchanting allurements of Armidas and Calypsos, and their maids of honour, though the former were as beautiful as my Lady Coventry,[10] and the latter more charming than the virgins attending her Royal Highness. In short, Madam, he shall be a pearl—and if you cannot find me such a couple as I wot of, I wish—and I cannot wish you a more tedious punishment, instead of my romance, may you be obliged to take up with Sir Charles Grandison![11]

I am, Madam,
notwithstanding my menaces,
Your devoted humble servant

HOR. WALPOLE

From LADY HENRIETTA CECILIA WEST, before Tuesday 4 May 1762

Printed from the MS now WSL. First printed, Toynbee *Supp.* iii. 317–18. Damer-Waller; the MS was sold Sotheby's 5 Dec. 1921 (first Waller Sale), lot 152, to Wells; given by him to Thomas Conolly, of Chicago, from whom WSL acquired it in 1937.

For the dating of the letter, see the previous letter.

Dear Sir,

IN THE first hurry of reading your delightful letter I felt I should be much less frightened had you made me a gallant request than that you seemed about to propose. The first, vestal-like, to be sure

9. Rinaldo, Prince of Este and lover of Armida, in Tasso's *Jerusalem Delivered,* whose valour decides the final battle for Jerusalem. Armida, the beautiful enchantress, was sent to allure the Christian knights, among whom was Rinaldo. Handel's *Rinaldo,* with libretto by Giacomo Rossi, was first performed at the Haymarket Theatre 24 Feb. 1711 (Lang, op. cit. 118–19).

10. Maria Gunning (1732–60), m. (1752) George William Coventry, 6th E. of Coventry, 1751.

11. The hero of Richardson's novel, 1753–4.

I should have refused, and there wants no great parts to say no, though infinite virtue, when the requester is so charmingly agreeable. But the more danger the more honour. Therefore you may believe I am sadly disappointed not to have it in my power to give the world so convincing a proof of my chastity. You cannot guess my concern when I found I was to give you a pattern hero for your romance, because I was certain I have not an idea worthy your pen nor know a man perfect enough to be the hero of your history. The latter I own a mistake occasioned by suffering my first thoughts to wander far from my own country, and fixing on a hero who I conceive has every requisite for a modern attachment, but who I doubt would fail in romantic constancy, as I have heard Orondates and those gentlemen were all male Lucretias, and I am terribly afraid my hero, if occasion offered, would not follow the example of Joseph.[1] The heroes of our days preach us a doctrine they do not practise and presume we are to be contented with the constancy of their hearts. Indeed in all my search after perfection I find none but the charming description you have drawn of the adorable pearl worthy of a place in your romance. As I should be flattered to live forever do me the honour to introduce me in your history, an humble attendant on the beautiful heroine, adoring the virtues of the faultless hero, and, dear Sir, at least extol my judgment by owning I am one of your greatest admirers and devoted humble servants.

H. C. WEST

From LADY NORTHUMBERLAND, ? mid-May 1762

Printed for the first time from the MS (an invitation card) pasted in an extra-illustrated copy, now WSL, of HW's *Fugitive Pieces,* SH, 1758. For the history of this copy see Hazen, *SH Bibl.* 41, copy 9.

Between 1756 and 1766, when Lady Northumberland became a duchess, 5 June occurred on Saturday only in 1762.

LADY Northumberland's compliments to Mr Walpole and desires the honour of his company to play at cards on Saturday, June the 5. The favour of an answer[1] is desired.

1. In Genesis 39, where he resists the advances of Potiphar's wife.

1. Missing.

From ANDREW COLTEE DUCAREL, Thursday 20 May 1762

Printed from Ducarel's MS draft, now WSL. First printed, Nichols, *Lit. Anec.* iv. 705. For the history of the MS draft see *ante* 23 Feb. 1762. The original letter sent to HW is missing; it doubtless included a salutation and some introductory remarks about the text that is printed here.

Doctors Commons, May 20, 1762.

Ancient King of England

About a month ago, I saw a beautiful ancient psalter, full of illuminations (formerly presented to the Grey Friars of Norwich[1] by Lady Clifton)[2] belonging to Matt[hew] Duane, Esq.;[3] containing *inter alia* a fine drawing of an ancient king of England sitting on his throne, designed perhaps for Henry III.

Gloucester, old picture at

When I was at Gloucester, in 1732, I there saw a large piece of painting, on board, representing the Day of Judgment,[4] newly found hid behind a wall and about 8 feet square, in which our Saviour's wounds in particular seemed to be extremely well represented. But when done or by whom, ⟨I⟩ know not and whether in oil colours I do not at present recollect.

Earl of Egmont's[5] Collection

Extract of a letter to Dr Ducarel from the Reverend Mr Morant[6] of Colchester, dat[ed] March 1, 1762.

1. The convent at Norwich was founded in 1226 and suppressed in 1538 when it was claimed by the Duke of Norfolk (Bartholomæi de Cotton, *Historia Anglicana,* ed. H. R. Luard, 1859, p. 113; Edward Hutton, *The Franciscans in England,* 1926, pp. 72, 288–9).

2. Lady Margaret Howard (d. 1433), m. 1 (after 1390) Constantine de Clifton, Lord Clifton; m. 2 Sir Gilbert Talbot (GEC iii. 308).

3. (1707–85), lawyer, coin collector, and antiquary (OSSORY ii. 200 n. 18).

4. The picture in Gloucester is described as 'painted on plank oak, on a white plaster ground. There are no signs of linen upon the joints. The colours appear to have been tempera or distemper; certainly not oil. The back-ground is in some parts flat gold, and in others blue sky.' 'The entire height of the whole work is 7 feet 6½ inches' (George Scharf, Jr, 'Observations on a Picture in Gloucester Cathedral,' *Archæologia,* 1855, xxxvi. 372 and illustration).

5. John Perceval (1683–1748), cr. (1733) E. of Egmont.

6. Philip Morant (1700–70), historian and antiquary.

'Mr Walpole is a promoter of everything that is curious. There are undoubtedly many valuable paintings in many parts of England. Col. Coniers[7] was lately telling me of a curious one at Hatfeild House,[8] which is in danger of perishing; and there may be others in the same house, and others [elsewhere]. Illuminations in MSS come within Mr Walpole's plan. The late Earl of Egmont, in his travels through England, took notes, upon loose papers, of all the curious pictures and paintings he observed anywhere. In 1734 I transcribed for Mr Knapton[9] in a folio white paper book, most of the Earl of Egmont's notes, I think in an alphabetical order: but what is become of it I cannot tell.'

Saxon drawings

In a MS belonging to the Lambeth Library (No. 200) there is *inter al.* a Latin treatise, *De virginitate* (by Aldhelmus),[10] written in Saxon characters; at the beginning of it is a very neat and elegant Saxon drawing of a priest presenting several virgins to some archbishop or bishop. N. B. The only Saxon drawings (engraven) that I can now call to mind are those of a Saxon book in the Bodleian Library, entitled *Cædmon's Paraphrase of the Book of Genesis*.[11]

AND. COLTEE DUCAREL

7. John Conyers (1717–75), M.P.

8. See *ante* 9 June 1761 and n. 17.

9. George Knapton (1698–1778), portrait painter; surveyor and keeper of the King's pictures, 1765.

10. Aldhelm (ca 639–709), Bp of Sherborne. His treatise *De laudibus virginitatis* was addressed to the Abbess of Barking and her nuns.

11. Presumably Franciscus Junius's *Cædmonis monachi paraphrasis poetica Genesios ac præcipuarum sacræ paginæ historiarum*, Amsterdam, 1655. A copy of this book, as well as the Cædmon MS itself (MS Junius XI), was in the Bodleian. It included a series of engraved plates which were also published in *Figuræ quædam antiquæ ex Cædmonis monachi paraphraseos in Genesin*, Oxford, 1754; Ducarel may have had in mind the latter work.

From WILLIAM PRATT,[1] ca June 1762

Printed from the MS now WSL, preserved with the Journal of the SH Press. First printed, *Journal of the Printing-Office,* p. 86. For the history of the Journal see *ante* 27 Aug. 1759.

Pratt came to live at SH on 29 May 1762 and immediately began 'completing imperfect copies of former [SH] editions' (*Journal of the Printing-Office,* p. 10). This note evidently refers to his work completing the second state of the SH edition of Lucan's *Pharsalia* (Hazen, *SH Bibl.* 49).

MAY it please your Honour,
There are ninety-one books, excepting titles and dedications, of Lucani.[2]

To LORD ILCHESTER,[1] Thursday 10 June 1762

Printed for the first time from a photostat of the MS among the Holland House papers in the British Museum (Add. MS 51,349, f. 142). For the history of the MS see *ante* 20 Aug. 1753.

Arlington Street, June 10th 1762.

My Lord,

YOU are very good to put me in mind of what I had not forgot, and certainly shall not forget,[2] but shall hold myself in readiness to obey Mr Bateman's first summons.[3] I hope for your Lordship's sake and ours that we shall have some rain before we set out,[4] but if I am blown to Redlynch in a whirlwind of dust, I will not fail.

I am my Lord
Your Lordship's most obedient humble servant

HOR. WALPOLE

1. HW's fifth printer at SH, 1761–4.
2. See *ante* 20 Nov. 1758, n. 8.

---

1. Stephen Fox (1704–76), cr. (1741) Bn Ilchester and (1756) E. of Ilchester; M.P.
2. Ilchester had invited HW to visit him at Redlynch House, Ilchester's seat near Bruton, Somerset. HW had expected to go there 'the very beginning of July,' but the visit, which lasted about a fortnight, did not take place until mid-July (MONTAGU ii. 34; *post* 29 July 1762). See *Country Seats* 41–8.
3. As HW makes no other reference to visiting Redlynch with his friend Richard ('Dicky') Bateman, the collector and antiquary, he may have gone alone. HW wrote letters to Bateman on 19 and 26 August 1762, but they have not been found (CONWAY ii. 167 and n. 13).
4. William Cole wrote HW from Bletchley, Bucks, 31 July 1762: 'I am sorry to

From JOHN DAVIDSON,[1] Friday 23 July 1762

Printed for the first time from a photostat of the MS at Nostell Priory, Wakefield, Yorks, kindly furnished by the late Hon. Charles Winn. For the history of the MS see *ante* ?1762.

Memorandum (by HW, in pencil): Not inserted yet.[2]

Edinburgh, 23d July 1762.

Sir,

IN THE short time I had to glance over your curious and elegant book on painting I do not remember to have met with any notice of the artist mentioned by Blaise Vigenère[3] on ciphers whom I read of in Paul Colomiez's[4] Κειμηλια *Literaria* p. 73 ed. 1669.[5] 'Telle était aussi l'écriture et les traits d'un peintre anglais nommé *Oeillarde*,[6] d'autant plus à émerveiller, que cela se faisait avec un pinceau fait des poils de la queue d'un écureuil, qui ne resiste ni ne soutient pas comme ferait une plume de corbeau qui est très ferme.'[7] The author is mentioning very minute pieces of art when he takes notice of this painter. I cannot get either Vigenère or your performance at present, so I presume to give you this note and am with very great regard,

Sir,

Your most obedient humble servant,

JOHN DAVIDSON

hear Strawberry Hill is in the same state with us in this part of the country, where there is not a blade of grass to be seen, and hardly any water for the cattle. We have been daily tantalized with rain, but not a drop has fallen here to any purpose these three months: though, by accounts, other places have had very plentiful showers' (COLE i. 14–15).

1. (d. 1797), of Haltree; Writer to the Signet in Edinburgh; antiquary.

2. See n. 6 below.

3. Blaise de Vigenère (1523–96), author of *Traicté des chiffres, ou secrètes manières d'escrire*, 1586.

4. Paul Colomiès (or Colomesius) (1638–92), librarian of Lambeth Palace; vicar of Eynsford, Kent, 1687–91 (A. C. Ducarel, *The History and Antiquities of the Archiepiscopal Palace of Lambeth*, 1785, pp. 67–8, in *Bibliotheca Topographica Britannica*, ed. John Nichols, 1780-1800, vol. ii; Edward Hasted, *The History . . . of Kent*, 2d edn, Canterbury, 1797–1801, ii. 539).

5. In his *Opuscula*, Utrecht, 1669.

6. Nicholas Hilliard (ca 1547–1619), miniature painter. Davidson had apparently overlooked the article on Hilliard which appeared in the 1st edn of *Anecdotes* i. 148–52, which did not, however, include the remarks of Vigenère. HW inserted these notes in the 2d edn, i. 161–2. See also John Pope-Hennessy, *A Lecture on Nicholas Hilliard*, 1949, p. 14; Graham Reynolds, *Nicholas Hilliard and Isaac Oliver*, 1971, pp. 11–14.

7. Colomiès, *Keimēlia literaria* ('Literary Treasures'), in his *Opuscula*, chap. xxxiii.

8. George Jamesone (ca 1588–1644), of

The Honourable Horace Walpole Esq.

PS. A relation of George Jameson,[8] a Scots painter in Ch[arles] I time, is picking up anecdotes of his life and works which he proposes to send you if you reckon him worthy of a place in your 3d volume.

TO LORD ILCHESTER, Thursday 29 July 1762

Printed from a photostat of the MS among the Holland House papers in the British Museum (Add. MS 51,349, f. 146). First printed in *Letters to Henry Fox, Lord Holland,* ed. Lord Ilchester, Roxburghe Club, 1915, pp. 153–4. Reprinted, Toynbee *Supp.* i. 100–2. For the history of the MS see *ante* 20 Aug. 1753.

Strawberry Hill, July 29th 1762.

My Lord,

WHEN people disoblige one, they hate one; when they oblige one, they are full of thanks. The latter is some amends for the former, and therefore I take it as of course. Otherwise I must be miserably ashamed, when I find your Lordship thanking me for passing the most agreeable fortnight imaginable.[1] Why, if you was the crossest of beings, and Lady Ilchester[2] the worst bred, and Lady Susan[3] the most disagreeable, do you think that showing me Redlinch,[4] Melbury,[5] Sherburn[6] and Mr Hoare's,[7] would not have con-

Aberdeen; portrait painter; see *post* 11 Sept. 1762.

1. See *ante* 10 June 1762.

2. Elizabeth Strangways Horner (1723–92), m. (1736) Lord Ilchester.

3. Lady Susan Fox Strangways (1743–1827), eldest dau. of Lord Ilchester, m. (1764) William O'Brien, an actor.

4. Redlynch House, Somerset, Ilchester's seat, 'a comely dwelling, a new stone house with good rooms and convenient. . . . The park is filled with a particular breed of cows, which have a pretty effect. Their whole fore and hinder parts are black or brown, and the bodies milk white, divided in such straight lines, that they look as if they had a sheet flung over them, whence they are called, sheet-cows' (HW's description in *Country Seats* 44).

5. Another seat of Ilchester's, in Dorset; 'a sumptuous old seat in a fine situation, the house ancient, but modernized. . . . A lake is near the house, and a noble grove of large old trees, as there are in the park; and without it, a charming wood of 200 acres, cut into wild walks, with a natural water, and two beautiful cascades. . . . The kitchen and servants' hall are very spacious . . . in one of the orange trees in the court, I saw a goldfinch sitting on its nest, close to the house' (ibid. 47–8).

6. Sherborne, Lord Digby's seat in Dorset, 'an indifferent house, but pretty' (ibid. 46).

7. Stourhead in Wilts, seat of Henry Hoare (1705–85). 'The whole composes one of the most picturesque scenes in the world' (ibid. 43–4).

tented me? Come again? yes, I will, and shall like it so much, that I expect you will be all gratitude—But you are not quite so well with Strawberry as with me; I have done nothing but abuse it since I came home; I[8] have called it hovel, and cottage, and told it that it was not worthy of standing in the housekeeper's room at Melbury; I have mortified the Thames, that used to fancy itself the only water in the world, with asking for its cascades, and telling it how paltry it looked without the ruins of a castle on Richmond Hill—I have broken all my orange-trees with hunting for goldfinches' nests, and tore my sheets with hanging them cross my cows—in short, I am so out of humour since I came home, and so envious, that I believe I shall murder a couple of my neighbours and cram them into a pit with a grate over them,[9] that I may have something at least like what I have been seeing. If you have a mind, my Lord, to make me any reparation for the damage you have done me, you must at least send me Lady Fanny.[10] My compliments to her and all Paradise, my love to Miss Cheek,[11] and my hate to Mr Berkeley.[12]

I am my Lord

Your Lordship's most obliged,
though angry, humble servant

HOR. WALPOLE

8. 'And' in Toynbee.

9. 'On the edge of the lawn before the house [at Stourhead] is a grate over a cave into which Charles Lord Stourton thrust the bodies of the two Hargills, whom he had murdered, and for which he was executed in the reign of Queen Mary' (ibid. 41).

10. Lady Frances Muriel Fox Strangways (1755–1814), youngest dau. of Lord Ilchester, m. (1777) Richard Quin, cr. (1822) E. of Dunraven.

11. Joanna Cheeke (1721–1819), m. (1763), as his second wife, William Melliar (ca 1720–72), of Castle Cary, Somerset; friend and companion to Lady Ilchester and Lady Holland (OSSORY i. 198 n. 4).

12. Probably the Hon. Charles Berkeley (d. 1765), brother of John, 5th Bn Berkeley. He owned property at Bruton, near Redlynch, and sold it to Ilchester ca 1749 (W. Phelps, *The History and Antiquities of Somersetshire*, 1839, i. 230–1).

From JOHN SHARP, Friday 13 August 1762

Printed for the first time from a photostat of the MS at Nostell Priory, Wakefield, Yorks, kindly furnished by the late Hon. Charles Winn. For the history of the MS see *ante* ?1762.

Address: To the Hon. Hor. Walpole Esq. at Strawberry Hill near Twickenham Middlesex. *Postmark:* 14 AV. CAMBRIDGE.

Memorandum (by HW): Not inserted yet.[1]

Benet College,[2] Cambridge, August 13, 1762.

Sir,

THE enclosed remarks[3] were made by a gentleman of my acquaintance[4] on reading your *Anecdotes of Painting* and at my request were put into writing by him, in order that I might forward 'em to you, who have a claim from every man of letters, and will not I hope be displeased with this little tribute from,

Sir,

Your obliged humble servant,

J. SHARP

To THOMAS WARTON,[1] Saturday 21 August 1762

Printed from John Wooll, *Biographical Memoirs of the late Reverend Joseph Warton, D.D.,* 1806, pp. 281–3, where the letter was first printed. Reprinted, Cunningham iv. 15–16; Toynbee v. 236–8. The history of the MS and its present whereabouts are not known. Among HW's memoranda on the MS of Lady Hertford to HW 14 Aug. 1762 is a list of letters written about that time; it includes 'Mr Warton [August] 21.'

Strawberry Hill, Aug. 21st 1762.

Sir,

I WAS last week surprised with a very unexpected present in your name;[2] and still more, when, upon examining it, I found myself so much and so undeservedly distinguished by your approbation.[3] I

1. That is, to be included in the 2d edn of *Anecdotes of Painting.*

2. Corpus Christi College, referred to in the eighteenth century as Benet because of its proximity to St Benedict's Church (*ante* 9 Feb. 1759, n. 1).

3. Missing.

4. Not identified.

1. (1728–90), historian of English poetry; professor of poetry at Oxford 1756–66.

certainly ought to have thanked you immediately, but I chose to defer my acknowledgments till I had read your volumes very attentively. The praise you have bestowed on me, debars me, Sir, from doing all the justice I ought to your work: the pleasure I received from it would seem to have grown out of the satisfaction I felt in what, if it would not be ungrateful, I should be humble enough to call flattery; for how can you, Sir, approve such hasty, superficial writings as mine, you, who in the same pursuits are so much more correct, and have gone so much deeper? for instance, compare your account of Gothic architecture with mine; I have scarce skimmed the subject; you have ascertained all its periods.[4] If my *Anecdotes* should ever want another edition, I shall take the liberty of referring the readers to your chronicle of our buildings.[5]

With regard to the Dance of Death,[6] I must confess you have not convinced me. Vertue (for it was he not I that first doubted of that painting at Basil) persuaded me by the arguments I found in his MSS, and which I have given,[7] that Holbein was not the author. The latter's prints, as executed by Hollar,[8] confirmed me in that opinion: and you must forgive me if I still think the taste of them superior to Albert Durer. This is mere matter of opinion, and of no consequence, and the only point in your book, Sir, in which I do not submit to you and agree with you.

You will not be sorry to be informed, Sir, that in the library of the Antiquarian Society there is a large and very good print of Nonsuch,[9] giving a tolerable idea of that pile, which was not the case of Speed's[10] confused scrap. I have myself drawings of the two old

2. Warton's *Observations on the Fairy Queen of Spenser,* 2d edn, 2 vols, 1762. HW's copy, now WSL, with his corrections and marginalia, is Hazen, *Cat. of HW's Lib.,* No. 1840.

3. Warton refers to HW's *Catalogue of the Royal and Noble Authors* and to 'Mr Walpole's valuable and entertaining anecdotes of ancient painting' (*Observations* ii. 233; see also ibid. ii. 50, 109, 117–18).

4. Warton describes 'the Saxon style,' 'the Gothic Saxon,' 'Absolute Gothic,' 'Ornamental Gothic,' and 'Florid Gothic,' ibid. ii. 186–94, giving some examples.

5. HW did not add such a reference in the 2d edn of *Anecdotes.*

6. In the churchyard of the Dominican convent at Basle (*Observations* ii. 117–20). In a footnote Warton respectfully questions HW's dismissal of Holbein as the artist.

7. In *Anecdotes of Painting* i. 74–5.

8. See CHATTERTON 146 nn. 26–7; 156–7.

9. In Surrey, built by Henry VIII; pulled down about 1670 (Society of Antiquaries, *Vetusta monumenta,* vol. ii, 1789, pl. XXIV; Georg Braun and Franz Hogenberg, *Civitates orbis terrarum,* Cologne, [1572]–1618, vol. v, pl. I; CHATTERTON 75 n. 15).

10. John Speed (ca 1552–1629), historian and cartographer. In *The Theatre of the Empire of Great Britaine,* new edn, 1676, p. 11, he wrote that 'albeit the County [Surrey] is barren of cities or

palaces of Richmond[11] and Greenwich;[12] and should be glad to show them[13] to you, if at any time of leisure you would favour me with a visit here. You would see some attempts at Gothic, some miniatures of scenes which I am pleased to find you love—cloisters, screens, round towers, and a printing house, all indeed of baby dimensions, would put you a little in mind of the age of Caxton[14] and Wynken. You might play at fancying yourself in a castle described by Spenser. You see, Sir, by the persuasions I employ, how much I wish to tempt you hither! I am, Sir,

Your most obliged and obedient servant,

HOR. WALPOLE

PS. You know to be sure that in Ames's *Typogr. Antiquities*[15] are specified all the works of Stephen Hawes.[16]

towns of great estate, yet is she stored with many princely houses . . . of some she may well say, no shire hath none such, as is None-such indeed.' Speed's view of Nonsuch is a border illustration on the accompanying map of Surrey.

11. Built by Henry VII (CHATTERTON 73, 75; *Vetusta monumenta,* vol. ii, pl. XXIII).

12. Built in 1433 by Humphrey, Duke of Gloucester, at whose death it reverted to the Crown (CHATTERTON 71–2; *Vetusta monumenta,* vol. ii, pl. XXV).

13. The two drawings were in a portfolio of drawings by Vertue and others, sold London 1268 to Smith for £31.10.0; they were resold Sotheby's 5 March 1862, lots 57 and 96.

14. Who learned the new art of printing at Cologne in order to print his English translation of Le Fèvre's *Le Recueil des histoires de Troyes,* Bruges, 1475. Wynkyn de Worde probably accompanied Caxton to England in 1476, when he became his apprentice. HW compared himself to Caxton on other occasions; see HW to Mason 21 July 1772 and 8 July 1782 (MASON i. 40, ii. 263).

15. Joseph Ames, *Typographical Antiquities: Being an Historical Account of Printing in England,* 1749. HW's annotated copy, now WSL, is Hazen, op. cit., No. 261.

16. (ca 1475–1530), poet. In his 'Book of Materials,' 1759, p. 178, HW listed the works of Hawes and noted that *The Temple of Glass* was referred to 'in Warton's notes on Spenser v. 1.'

To the PRINTER OF THE *Gazetteer*,[1] September 1762

Printed from the MS now WSL. First printed in the *Gazetteer and London Daily Advertiser* 21 Sept. 1762 (signature and postscript omitted). HW doubtless sent the MS to his deputy Grosvenor Bedford to copy and forward; for its subsequent history see *ante* 16 Oct. 1755.

Sir,

I HAVE lately been informed by a Spanish merchant of the following circumstance relating to the management of bees in Spain, which I am glad to communicate to my countrymen.[2]

It is well known that bees are a most profitable commodity in Spain, and might be so to a much greater degree than they are in England. There is little, indeed scarce any, expense attending them, and if it was not for the absurd and ungrateful custom of destroying such swarms yearly, they might be propagated to a vast extent.[3] The poorest people might make fortunes by them; women and girls might easily manage them.

The material difference between the Spanish practice and ours, is this.[4] They never kill their bees, but drive them down to the bottom of the hive with smoke of rosemary, and then with a knife cut the combs, and take them out afterwards with a ladle, and shut the top

1. HW originally wrote 'London Chronicle.' The printer of the *Gazetteer* was Charles Greene Say (ca 1721–75), and the publisher was William Owen (d. 1793) (Nichols, *Lit. Anec.* iii. 654–5; H. R. Plomer *et al.*, *A Dictionary of the Printers and Booksellers . . . 1726 to 1775*, Oxford, 1930, p. 222; R. L. Haig, *The Gazetteer 1735–1797*, Carbondale, Ill., 1960, pp. 30, 36).

2. HW knew no Spanish merchant and is merely following the then current practice of inventing a merchant or other authority to gain credence and give freshness to the writer's views. HW's knowledge of bees in Spain was acquired from Lord Sandwich's diary quoted below (third paragraph). HW's MSS also contain many references to Samuel Hartlib, author of *The Reformed Common-Wealth of Bees*, 1655, in which Hartlib quotes Varro (*De Re Rustica* III, xvi) on the great revenue raised by apiculture in Spain; HW's two copies of Hartlib's work are Hazen, *Cat. of HW's Lib.*, Nos 125:4 and 1071.

3. The common method of taking the honey and wax was by smothering the bees with brimstone-matches, in a hole in the ground under the hive, or by drowning (Royal Dublin Society, *Instructions for Managing Bees*, Dublin, 1733, pp. 33–4; see also Robert Maxwell, *The Practical Bee-Master . . . the Management of Bees . . . without Killing Them for their Honey*, Edinburgh, 1750, pp. 106–7; John Gedde, *The English Apiary*, 1721, p. 104; Stephen White, *Collateral Bee-Boxes*, 1756, pp. 34–5).

4. The remainder of this paragraph is copied almost verbatim from the MS diary of Admiral Edward Montagu, 1st Earl of Sandwich, lent to HW 'by his descendant, John [4th] Earl of Sandwich. 1762' (HW's 'Extracts . . . from . . . Manuscripts . . . of Admiral Edward, Earl of Sandwich,' Vol. 8, now WSL; *ante* 20 April 1762, n. 2).

of the hive again; but they never take above half the honey, that the bees may have some foundation to go to work upon again.

This practice has something so good-natured in it, that I cannot doubt but it will gain ground in an age, whose best improvements have been made in common sense and humanity to brutes. The Turks, barbarians to us in every other respect, have long been more polished by this ruling tenderness: but to our honour, cruelty is everyday more and more exploded; and it has proved by fact, contrary to the ridiculous opinion of our progenitors, that the greatest bravery is consistent with the greatest good-nature. Few[5] animals are more serviceable to men than bees. We repay their services with destruction. I hope to see an end to this practice, especially as the experience of Spain evinces that sparing them is more profitable. I cannot flatter myself with equal[6] hopes of knowing that no more lobsters are roasted or boiled alive.[7] Avarice is capable of being corrected, if it finds its account—but gluttony is totally deaf. I am Sir

Your humble servant

APICIUS

PS. As the world seems desirous of being reformed, and as notices are every day conveyed to the public by the newspapers, I hope it will be sufficient to put a stop to the practice, that an eminent physician observing the great increase of consumptions of late among the common people, found upon inquiry that the porter and beer sold in alehouses is fined with verdigrease, which must produce gradual destruction of the species.[8]

5. 'No' crossed out in the MS.

6. 'The' crossed out in the MS.

7. HW's concern for animals and insects extended to moths and flies; see DALRYMPLE 70.

8. Dr Robert James, in his *Medicinal Dictionary*, 1743–5, vol. I, *sub* 'Ærugo' and 'Es', defined 'verdigrease' as 'rust of any metal, particularly of copper,' and warned of the danger of using copper as a utensil for domestic purposes: 'this metal, and especially its rust, are reckoned poisons;' the symptoms include 'difficulty of breathing.'

To Grosvenor Bedford, Thursday 9 September 1762

Printed from Cunningham iv. 21–2, where the letter was first printed. Reprinted, Toynbee v. 245–6. The history of the MS and its present whereabouts are not known.

Strawberry Hill, Sept. 9, 1762.

Dear Sir,

I MUST trouble you in an affair in which it is not easy, I fear, to assist me. My servant, Henry Jones,[1] is grown old and wants to retire. If you could find a very good servant for me, it would be of great use. I will tell you exactly what sort of man I want. He is to be steward and butler, not my gentleman, nor have anything to do with dressing me, or with my clothes, but is to wait at table and at tea. His chief-business will be to look after my family, in which he must be strict; and he must understand buying and selling, for what I shall chiefly expect, will be, that he shall bring me every Saturday night the house-bills for the week, and every month those of the other tradesmen and servants. For these reasons which I cannot dispense with, I choose to have a grave servant of forty, or near it, with a very good character, and I should wish, not married. When you inquire, be so good as not to let it be known that it is for me; as I do not like to have servants present themselves, whom I should probably not care to take. The wages I shall make little difficulty about, if it is one that I can depend upon for being careful in my family, and letting there be no waste. I shall be in town on Monday night, and if you will call on me on Tuesday or Wednesday mornings, I will talk to you farther, for though I should be glad to have this servant soon,[2] I am in no particular haste. Adieu, dear Sir!

Yours ever,

H. W.

1. 'Harry,' HW's servant 1752–62. His retirement was doubtless hastened by the fact that he was held responsible for the fire that occurred the night before in the servant's hall at SH. HW wrote Conway 9 Sept.: 'The chimney of the new Gallery . . . was on fire at eight o'clock. Harry had quarrelled with the other servants, and would not sit in the kitchen; and to keep up his anger had lighted a vast fire in the servants' hall, which is under the gallery. The chimney took fire; and if Margaret had not smelt it with the first nose that ever a servant had, a quarter of an hour had set us in a blaze' (Conway ii. 175).

2. Favre, a Swiss, became the servant who performed most of the duties speci-

PS. One material condition will be, that he is not to have friends coming to my house after him.

From Andrew Coltee Ducarel, Thursday 9 September 1762

Printed from Nichols, *Lit. Anec.* viii. 509, where the letter was first printed. The history of the MS and its present whereabouts are not known.

Doctors Commons, Sept. 9, 1762.

Sir,

SINCE I had the honour of waiting upon you, Mr Blennerhasset[1] has acquainted me that you had some thoughts of being in town for a few days next week. As the weather is still pretty warm, if it is agreeable to you to see the Lambeth Library[2] this year, I will, with great pleasure, wait upon you there any morning next week which you shall appoint, between 12 and 3 o'clock.[3]—Though it seems almost impossible to make any additions to your immense treasure of antiquities, yet I cannot help acquainting you that the two following curiosities are to be disposed of—1. an ancient beautiful candlestick (from some church in Kent), inlaid with gold and silver, with several inscriptions in characters of the XIIth century; 2. an ancient pyx box,[4] with Jesus on the cross and the twelve Apostles finely enamelled, and quite perfect. They belong to Mr Carmey[5] (who lives near Ranelagh House[6] at Chelsea), who will wait upon you with them whenever you please.[7] I have not seen these curiosities, and therefore can only send you the account he gave me of them this morning. I have the honour to remain, etc.

A. C. Ducarel

fied by HW. He is first mentioned in a letter from HW to Lord Hertford 3 Aug. 1764 (Conway ii. 418), and at intervals thereafter until 1771, when he disappears from the correspondence. He was the head servant at the Arlington Street house and was left in full charge during HW's absences (Montagu ii. 172; Du Deffand v. 376–81; More 82, 104).

1. Perhaps William Blennerhassett, author of *A New History of England . . . to the End of the Reign of King George I,* 6 vols, Newcastle-upon-Tyne, privately printed, 1751. A William Blennerhasset 'of Cumberland' died 19 Feb. 1765 (GM 1765, xxxv. 98).

2. Ducarel was Keeper of the Archiepiscopal Library at Lambeth Palace 1757–85.

3. HW probably did not see the library at this time. He returned from a visit with the Conways at Park Place ca 22 September (Montagu ii. 44).

4. 'The vessel in which the host or consecrated bread of the sacrament is reserved' (OED *sub* 'pyx' 2).

From JOHN JAMISONE,[1] Saturday 11 September 1762

Printed for the first time from a photostat of the MS at Nostell Priory, Wakefield, Yorks, kindly furnished by the late Hon. Charles Winn. For the history of the MS see *ante* ?1762.

Address: To the Honourable Horatio Walpole Esq. London.

Leith, 11 September 1762.

Sir,

MR DAVIDSON of Edinburgh did me the favour sometime ago to mention to you[2] my purpose of attempting to tell in a true light the merits of George Jamesone,[3] painter, my kinsman. This accompanies an essay[4] to that effect to which I hope your known candour and humanity will give favourable acceptance. However partial I may be to the man I can assure you I have asserted nothing but what is either sufficiently authenticated by vouchers in my possession or concerts with my own knowledge. Mr Davidson told me you was so good to propose inserting Jamesone's life in the second edition of your second volume. But would it not further diffuse his fame if it was inserted in your third volume which no doubt will also admit of a second edition. But this I submit to your better judgment.[5] If anything I have sent you needs explanation, I will readily undertake it. If your next publication is to be any time deferred in this interval I may be able to learn something further. I am sorry that I could not send you a drawing from my picture of my friend, in his features there are expressions of his mind. If I can search out anything here

5. Angel Carmey, 'a foreigner long resident here, and a great dealer in coins, medals, antiquities, etc.' (Nichols, *Lit. Illus.* iii. 544n).

6. Near Chelsea College, erected ca 1691 by Richard, 1st Earl of Ranelagh, and taken down in 1805 (H. B. Wheatley, *London Past and Present,* 1891, iii. 149).

7. HW does not appear to have purchased these articles; they are not mentioned in the *Description of SH,* 1784.

1. (d. 1807), of Leith; wine merchant (*Scots Magazine,* 1807, lxix. 158; *Williamson's Directory for . . . Edinburgh, Canongate, Leith, and Suburbs,* Edinburgh, 1774, 'Leith Directory,' p. 113).

2. John Davidson to HW *ante* 23 July 1762.

3. (ca 1589–1644), of Aberdeen; portrait painter. HW had made inquiries of Sir David Dalrymple the previous year for information about this artist; see DALRYMPLE 75.

4. See following letter.

5. HW included an article on George Jamesone in the *Additional Lives* for Vol. II, pp. 2–6, and in *Anecdotes,* 2d edn, ii. 116–20, with the note: 'The materials of this article were communicated by Mr John Jamisone, wine-merchant in Leith.' The account of Jamesone was favourably noticed in the *Critical Review,* 1768, xxv. 57–8.

for your amusement I will on every occasion receive your commands with respect and execute them with pleasure. This accompanies the etching[6] and elegy[7] mentioned in the essay which goes under another cover. I am, Sir,

Your most obedient and most humble servant,

JNO. JAMISONE

Direct for John Jamisone in Quality Street, Leith.

[Enclosure]

Sub Obitum Viri Spectatissimi,
GEORGII JAMESONI,
ABREDONENSIS,
Pictoris Eminentissimi,

Lachrymæ.

Gentis Apollo suæ fuit ut Buchananus, Apelles
  Solus eras Patriæ sic, JAMESONE, tuæ.
Rara avis in nostris oris: Tibi mille colores,
  Ora tibi soli pingere viva datum.
At Te nulla manus poterit sat pingere; nempe
  Lampada cui tradas nulla reperta manus.
Quin si forte tuas vatum quis carmine laudes
  Tentet, id ingenii vim superabit opus.
Quicquid erit, salve pictorum gloria, salve:
  Æternumque vale Phosphore Scotigenum:
Phosphore, namque tua ars tenebris prius obsita cæcis,
  Fors nitidum cernet Te Præeunte diem.

Tumulus Ejusdem.

Conditur hic tumulo JAMESONUS Pictor, & una
  Cum Domino jacet hic Ars quoque tecta suo.

6. Of Jamesone, his wife Isobel Tosche, and their young child, by John Alexander, 1728, after George Jamesone's painting of ?1635 (not 1623). The etching is no longer preserved with this letter. The painting is now at Fyvie Castle, Aberdeenshire (Duncan Thomson, *The Life and Art of George Jamesone,* Oxford, 1974, pp. 117–18, No. 114).

7. Printed below; one of three elegies on the death of Jamesone written by David Wedderburn (Peter Murray, 'On the Tercentenary of George Jamesone,' *Aberdeen Univ. Review,* 1944–6, xxxi. 80). The sheet on which the elegy is printed is preserved with this letter.

Hujus ni renovent cineres Phœnicis Apellem;
Inque urna hac coeant Ortus & Interitus.

Ejusdem Encomium meritissimum.

Si pietas prudens, pia si prudentia, vitæ
Si probitas, omni si sine labe fides;
Partaque si graphio Magnatum gratia, dotes
Nobilis ingenii siquid honoris habent;
Si nitor in pretio est morum cultusque decori,
Et tenuem prompta sæpe levasse manu;
Æmula si Belgis Italisve peritia dextræ
Artifici laudem conciliare queat:
Omne tulit punctum JAMESONUS, Zeuxe vel ipso
Teste; vel hoc majus Græcia si quid habet.

Amoris indissolubilis ergo

DAVID WEDDERBURNUS.[8]

****

Ad Exemplar ABREDONIÆ Impressum per *Edwardum Rabanum,* 1644.

8. David Wedderburn (1580–1646), poet laureate of Aberdeen, 1620.

From JOHN JAMISONE, Saturday 11 September 1762 *bis*

Printed for the first time from a photostat of the MS at Nostell Priory, Wakefield, Yorks, kindly furnished by the late Hon. Charles Winn. For the history of the MS see *ante* ?1762.

This note appears at the end of the seven-page 'Essay' on George Jamesone, printed below.

Leith, 11 September 1762.

Sir,

I HAVE wrote you by this post[1] and sent a printed copy of the above elegy,[2] and the etching of the forementioned picture,[3] and always respectfully am,

Sir,

Your most obedient and most humble servant

JNO. JAMISONE

To the Honourable Horatio Walpole Esq.

Essay[4] towards a Character of the late George Jamesone, Painter, and his works

He was son of Andrew Jamesone, an ingenious architect, and was born at Aberdeen in Scotland in the year 1586[5] and justly deserves to be ranked in the first class of painters of British parents[6] and of British birth. His talents early discovered themselves. He studied under Sir Peter Paul Ruben[s] at Antwerp,[6a] was condisciple with Van Dyck, between whose works and Jamesone's there is such re-

1. See previous letter.

2. 'Sub Obitum Viri Spectatissimi, Georgii Jamesoni, Abredonensis, Pictoris Eminentissimi, Lachrymæ,' mentioned at the end of the 'Essay' on Jamesone printed below.

3. See previous letter, n. 6. HW had the etching copied by Alexander Bannerman for the plate which illustrates the article on Jamesone in *Anecdotes of Painting,* 2d edn, facing ii. 116.

4. Written by Jamisone, but the MS (doubtless a transcription) is in a different hand.

5. He was probably born in late 1589 or early 1590 (Duncan Thomson, *The Life and Art of George Jamesone,* Oxford, 1974, p. 14.

6. His father, Andrew Jamesone, was a mason in Aberdeen who married Marjory Anderson in 1585 (ibid. 13).

6a. No evidence has been found to support this claim.

semblance that they have often been mistaken for Van Dyck's.

His particular characteristic is delicacy and softness. He had a clear and beautiful colouring, with a fine harmony in his shades which he made with little colour by the help of a varnish, so that the pencil seldom appears; his clothes were of even-wove linen smoothly primed with a proper tone to forward the harmony of his shades.

His portraits which for the most part are somewhat less than life bear to be looked at very near and have likeways a fine effect at a distance.

When King Charles the First made a visit to Scotland in 1633, the magistrates of Edinburgh knowing his Majesty's taste and love of painting got Jamesone to make drawings of a series of the Scots Kings for his Majesty's entertainment, which so forcibly struck him, that inquiring after the author, his Majesty employed him to draw his picture,[6b] with which he was so pleased that he bestowed upon him a diamond ring from his own finger with other honorary marks of his royal approbation.

It is remarkable that he always painted himself with his hat on, partly in imitation of his master Ruben[s], or rather occasioned by the King's permitting him to sit covered when he drew his picture, being told that our painter was in use to wear his hat, when at work for the benefits of his eyesight.

Sir Colin Campbell[7] of Glenorchy, ancestor to the present Earl of Breadalbin,[8] was his chief and early patron, who he accompanied in his travails, at whose seat of Taymouth[9] is a large collection of his heads a catalogue whereof is contained in the following authentic extract copied verbatim:

Excerpt from a manuscript vellum book[10] in the
possession of the Earl of Breadalbane, of the
genealogy of the house of Glenorchy, first
collected, and thereafter begun to be written in
the month of June 1598.

Page 52 / Anno 1635 } 'Item the said Sir Coline Campbell (8th Laird of Glenorchy) gave unto George Jamesone painter in Edinburgh, for King Robert and King David Bruysses, Kings of Scotland, and

6b. Charles I was in Edinburgh in June 1633 for his Scottish coronation, but this portrait is unsubstantiated (ibid. 6).

7. (ca 1577–1640), 2d Bt, 1631.

8. John Campbell (1696–1782), 3d E. of Breadalbane and Holland, 1752.

9. Taymouth Castle, in Perthshire.

10. The so-called 'Black Book of Taymouth' (William Bowie, *The Black Book of Taymouth*, ed. C. N. Innes, Edinburgh, 1855, p. 77). See also Thomson, op. cit. 103–7, Nos 71–92.

Charles the first King of Great Brittane France and Ireland, and his Ma^{teis} Quein; and for nine more of the Queins of Scotland, their portraits, quhilks are sett up in the Hall of Balloch (now Taymouth) the sum of tua hundreth thrie Scor punds.

Mair the said Sir Coline gave to the said George Jamesone for the Knight of Lochow's Lady, and the first Countess of Argylle and Six of the Ladys of Glenurquhay their portraits, and the said Sir Coline his own portrait, quhilks are sett up in the Chalmer of Deass of Balloch, Ane hundreth four Scoire punds.'

Mem^{d}.

In the same year 1635 the said George Jamesone painted a large genealogical tree of the family of Glenorchy—8 feet long, and 5 five [*sic*] broad, containing in miniature, the portraits of Sir Duncan Campbell[11] of Lochow, of Archibald Campbell,[12] his eldest son, first Earl of Argylle;[13] and of Sir Coline Campbell,[14] his second son, first Laird of Glenorchy, together with the portraits of eight successive Knights Lairds of Glenorchy, with the branches of their inter-marriages and of these of their sons and daughters, beautifully illuminated.[15]

At the bottom of which tree the following words are painted on a label or scroll, viz.

'The Genealogie of the hous of Glenurquhie whereof is descendit sundrie Nobill and worthie houses. 1635'

GJ amesone faciebat

11. (d. 1453), of Lochow; 1st Lord Campbell, 1445; Kt, 1448 (*Scots Peerage* i. 331).

12. (d. before 1440), eldest son of Sir Duncan Campbell (ibid. i. 331–2).

13. Colin Campbell (d. 1493), 2d Lord Campbell, cr. (1457) E. of Argyll. He was the only son of Archibald Campbell and grandson of Sir Duncan Campbell of Lochow (GEC).

14. (d. ca 1475), second son of Sir Duncan Campbell; half-brother of Archibald Campbell and uncle of the 1st E. of Argyll; 1st Laird of Glenurchy, 1432 (*Scots Peerage* i. 331, ii. 174–5).

15. 'Fanciful and often grotesque portraits of Sir Colin, first of Glenurchy, his father Duncan, Lord Campbell of Lochaw, his nephew [Colin], first Earl of Argyll, and of the second, third, fourth, fifth, sixth, seventh, and eighth Lairds of Glenurchy are given in the *Black Book of Taymouth,* and portraits of them also appear in the Genealogical Tree at Taymouth Castle painted in 1635 by George Jamesone' (*Scots Peerage* ii. 175). The painting is now in the Scottish National Portrait Gallery; see Thomson, op. cit. 107–9, No. 93.

Besides the foregoing there are eleven portraits of lords and ladies of the first families in Scotland, painted in the years 1636 and 1637 in the possession of the Earl of Breadalbane at Taymouth.[15a]

From the above extract we are ascertained that Jamesone received no more for each of these heads than twenty pound Scots or one pound thirteen shillings and four pence English and yet it can be proved from our public records that he died possessed of an easy fortune which he left to his three daughters two of whom were honourably married, one of them named Mary[16] was as dexterous at the needle as her father at the pencil, the fine sewings yet extant which used to be hung out on festivals in St Nicholas' Church Aberdeen being her hand of work. Mr Thomson[17] of Portlethen descended of this Mary has a fine original picture of her father by himself.[18]

As he was indefatigable in his business his works are everywhere, several full and a great many half lengths and heads without number, so that the houses of the families in Scotland of any note are adorned with his pictures.

Mr John Alexander,[19] limner in Edinburgh, his great grandson, is in possession of several of his family pictures drawn by himself. In one of these on the same board (for he painted as well on board, especially in his first performances, as on cloth) with himself and young son is Isabella Tosh,[20] his wife, a beautiful woman who survived him, an etching whereof is herewith transmitted.[21] Another of him from life in his school with sketches both of history and landscape with a portrait of King Charles the First, his Queen, his own wife, and four others of his works from life.[21a] All done in miniature,

15a. See ibid. 109–13, Nos 94–104.

16. Mary Jamesone (d. 1684), fourth dau. of George Jamesone, m. 1 (1664) John Burnet; m. 2 (1669) James Gregory; m. 3 (1677) Baillie George Eddie (or Ædie) (ibid. 23, 41–3; M. W. Brockwell, *George Jamesone and Some Primitive Scottish Painters,* privately printed, 1939, pp. 28–9; DNB *sub* James Gregory). Only three of Jamesone's four daughters were named as heirs to his estate, and only two (Marjory, the eldest, who married John Alexander, an advocate; and Mary) lived to adulthood.

17. James Thomson (d. 1767), of Portlethen, Kincardine (*Scots Magazine,* 1767, xxix. 109).

18. Apparently not an original, but a copy; see following letter.

19. (fl. 1715–52), sometimes called Alexander Jamesone; Scottish painter and engraver. He is said to have been the great-grandson of George Jamesone (*Bryan's Dict. of Painters and Engravers,* 1903–5, i. 18, iii. 105; Thieme and Becker i. 265–6).

20. Isobel Tosche (d. 1680), m. 1 (ca 1625) George Jamesone; m. 2 (1649) Robert Cruikshank, merchant and bailie of Aberdeen (Thomson, op. cit. 22, 42).

21. See n. 3 above.

21a. See Thomson, op. cit. 116–17, No. 112.

for he also excelled in that way as is evident from the genealogical tree of the Glenorchy family, with many others extant, particularly three small ones for the Haddington family in the possession of Thomas Hamilton[22] of Fala Esq. and a fine one for and by himself, 12 by 10 inches, in the possession of John Jamesone,[22a] wine merchant in Leith, collector of these anecdotes.

There are many of his pictures in both Colleges of Aberdeen. The Sibyls there[23] which it is said he drew from living beauties of that city are pregnant instances of his capability. In the collection of Mr Baird[24] of Auchmedden in Aberdeenshire is a full length of three young ladies, cousins of the families of Argyle, Erroll, and Kinnoul, their ages are marked on the margin of the picture to be six, seven, and eight. This gentleman has a whole length in little of William Earl of Pembroke,[25] highly finished by our painter, though some ascribe it to Van Dyck. At Mr Lindsay's[26] of Wormeston in Fife is a double half length of two boys of that family from the life of five and three years old, playing with a dog painted in 1636.

He also did some landscapes and a perspective view of the city of Edinburgh with a Neptune in the foreground.

He finished an exquisite full length for King Charles the First which he expected the magistrates of Aberdeen would purchase for their hall, but for which they offered him so vilifying a price that in a pet he carried it to Edinburgh and sold it to a gentleman of the north of England in whose family it remained not many years ago. But the gentleman's name is at present unknown.

He had several scholars. The best was Michael Wright[27], a Scotsman who drew the judges at full length at Guild Hall and who is recorded among the painters of the English school, though no mention is made there of Jamestone his master, which is the more to be wondered at since his picture in the Gallery at Florence[28] amongst the illustrious painters has been long held in great estimation.

22. Possibly Thomas Hamilton (d. 1774), who died at Wellwood, Fife (GM 1774, xliv. 46); doubtless a member of the Hamilton family, Earls of Haddington.

22a. Now in the Scottish National Portrait Gallery; see Thomson, op. cit. 117, No. 113.

23. That is, King's College, Aberdeen.

24. William Baird (d. 1775), of Auchmedden, Aberdeen (*Scots Magazine,* 1775, xxxvii. 110).

25. William Herbert (1580–1630), 3d E. of Pembroke, 1601.

26. George Lindsay (ca 1690–1764), of Wormistone, Fife (ibid., 1764, xxvi. 56).

27. Joseph Michael Wright (ca 1623–1700), Scottish portrait painter (Thieme and Becker xxxvi. 281; Thomson, op. cit. 32, 72–4).

28. The Uffizi.

Had the Abbé du Bos[29] been acquainted with his works he had not so freely charged the Britons with want of genius, or had at least ranked our North Britons with his British contemporaries.

The sweetness of his disposition and many other good qualities procured him universal esteem. Nor has the sister art of poetry in that age been wanting to celebrate his fame, as will appear by the following epigram addressed to him and Latin elegy composed on his death, first printed at Aberdeen in 1644[29a] which year he changed this life for a better, having died of the stone at Edinburgh aged 58, and was honourably interred in the Gray Friers churchyard there, but still without any monument.

Arcturi Johnstoni[30] Regii Medici Epigramma
Ad Georgium Jamisonum Pictorem eminentissimum
de Anna Cambella[31] Heroina Marchionissa Huntlæa

Illustres, ars quotquot habet tua, prome colores,
Pingere Cambellam Si, Jamisone! paras.
Frons Ebori pectusque nivi, sint colla ligustris
Æmula, Pæstanis tinge labella rosis.
Ille genis color eniteat, quo mixta corallis
Marmora, vel quali candida poma rubent.
Cæsaries auro rutilet: debetur ocellis,
Qualis inest gemmis sideribusque, nitor.
Forma Supercilii sit, qualem Cypridis arcus,
Vel Triviæ, leviter cum sinuatur, habet.
Sed, Pictor! Suspende manum; Subtilius omni
Stamine, quod tentas hic simulare, vides.
Cedit Appolineo Vulsus de vertice crinis,
Cedit Apellea linea ducta manu.
Pinge Supercilium sine fastu, pinge pudicos
Huic oculos, totam da sine labe Deam:
Ut careat nævo, formæ nil deme vel adde,
Fac similem tantum, qua potes arte, sui.

29. Jean-Baptiste Du Bos (1670–1742), author of *Critical Reflections on Poetry, Painting and Music*, tr. Thomas Nugent, 1748 (*ante* 19 April 1762, nn. 8, 9).

29a. It was first printed in *Epigrammata Arturi Ionstoni Scoti, Medici Regii*, Aberdeen, 1632, pp. 20–1.

30. Arthur Johnston (1587–1641), M.D., 1610; rector of King's College, Aberdeen, 1637; writer of Latin verse.

31. Anne Campbell (1594–1638), dau. of Archibald Campbell, 7th E. of Argyll; m. (1607) George Gordon, 2d M. of Huntly, 1636.

Extracted from the edition of Johnston's works[32] printed at Middleburgh in 1642.

The picture of the above lady is extant in the collection of the Duke of Gordon[33] and there is a fine three-quarter picture for Doctor Johnston himself in the Newton College of Aberdeen,[34] both by our painter.

Sub obitum Viri Spectatissimi,
Georgii Jamesoni
Abredonensis
Pictoris Eminentissimi
Lachrymæ etc. etc.

From JOHN JAMISONE, Thursday 23 September 1762

Printed for the first time from a photostat of the MS at Nostell Priory, Wakefield, Yorks, kindly furnished by the late Hon. Charles Winn. For the history of the MS see *ante* ?1762.

Leith, 23 September 1762.

Sir,

BY LAST post I had the honour to receive your obliging favour;[1] accept of my sincere thanks for the place you are to allow in your works for Jameson's life.

My candour will not permit me to conceal a discovery I made within these few days that the picture I mentioned of him in the possession of Mr Thomson of Portlethen (whatever that gentleman may think) is not an original[2] but a copy and that not a good one.

In tracing the works of Jamesone I fell in with the year 1612. That which I sent you the print of is dated 1623,[3] and I had the pleasure to perceive a remarkable improvement in those done from 1630 to

32. *Arturi Ionstoni Scoti Medici Regii Poemata Omnia,* Middelburg, 1642.

33. Alexander Gordon (1743–1827), 4th D. of Gordon, 1752. The portrait is possibly that now at Goodwood House; see Thomson, op. cit. 86–7, No. 16.

34. Now in the collection of Marischal College, University of Aberdeen; see ibid. 90–1, No. 27.

1. Missing.

2. See previous letter, nn. 17, 18.

3. See *ante* 11 Sept. 1762, n. 6.

the time of his death, and that the greatest number which I have seen or got accounts of are done in that period. I very respectfully am,

Sir,

Your most obedient and most humble servant,

Jno. Jamisone

To the Honourable Horatio Walpole.

To Grosvenor Bedford, Friday 24 September 1762

Printed from Cunningham iv. 22, where the letter was first printed. Reprinted, Toynbee v. 246. The history of the MS and its present whereabouts are not known.

Strawberry Hill, Sept. 24, 1762.

Dear Sir,

I WOULD not trouble you with the enclosed commissions, but as I think you pass by both doors almost every day. Be so good as to inquire if the persons mentioned in these advertisements[1] are really objects of charity, and if they are, I will beg you to leave a guinea for each, and put it to my account. Yours ever,

H. W.

1. One of them may have appeared in the *Daily Adv.* 21 Sept., dated 'St Paul's Coffee-House Sept. 20 1762': 'A charitable contribution is humbly requested for a poor creature now lying in St George's hospital, having lost all she was possessed of in the world by the late fire in Pulteney Street; and who to avoid perishing in the flames, threw herself together with a little boy out of a two pair of stairs window. . . . She has not a rag of clothes to put on, nor either money or relations to assist her, but is a woman of an unexceptionable character, as the people of this house can testify.'

Reverendus Admodum CAROLUS LYTTELTON
Nuper Episcopus Carlioleusis et Societatis Antiquariorum Præses
Honoris & Gratitudinis Ergo
Voluit Soc. Ant. Lond. 1770.

CHARLES LYTTELTON, BISHOP OF CARLISLE,
AFTER FRANCIS COTES

TO BISHOP LYTTELTON, Saturday 25 September 1762

Printed for the first time from a photostat of the MS in the Worcestershire Record Office, Shirehall, Worcester, kindly furnished by the 4th Baron Hampton. The MS may have been given by Lyttelton or his descendants to the Pakington family because of the letter's reference to the 'portrait of Sir John Perrot at Sir Herbert Pakington's' (see n. 3 below); it descended in the Pakington family to the 5th Baron Hampton, who deposited the collection of Pakington family papers in the Worcestershire Record Office before his death in 1974.

Strawberry Hill, Sept. 25th 1762.

My good Lord,

BY THIS time I think you are settled at Hagley,[1] that is, in due course have left your diocese for Paradise, whither I must address a petition to you, as if you had been a popish prelate, and were already canonized. I once mentioned to you that Vertue says[2] there is a portrait of Sir John Perrot[3] at Sir Herbert Packington's.[4] You would oblige me much if you could ascertain it. The folk of the house may not know it; the marks and tokens are that he was very like his supposed father Harry VIII.

As I have not heard a word of your nephew[5] this twelvemonth, that is, a fortnight ago, when Mrs Anne[6] his aunt told me he was to set out next day, I conclude he is with you. My compliments to him, and my respects to your Lord-Brother.[7] Pitt[8] told me you was not en-

1. The seat of the Lyttelton family, near Stourbridge, Worcs.

2. In Vertue Note Books, *Walpole Society* 1937–8, xxvi. 62, with HW's marginal note 'a Drawing from it in Mr Walpole's collection by Chamber [Thomas Chambars].'

3. (ca 1527–92), lord deputy of Ireland, reputed to be the son of Henry VIII, whom he resembled in appearance. The portrait is presumably that engraved by Valentine Green, after the drawing by George Powle, which appeared in T. R. Nash, *Collections for the History of Worcestershire,* 1781–2, i. 350; it was in the possession of Herbert Stuart Pakington, 4th Baron Hampton, and the Hon. Dorothy Pakington in 1948.

4. Sir Herbert Perrot Pakington (ca 1701–48), 5th Bt, 1727, of Westwood Park, Worcs; M.P. He was succeeded by his son Sir John Pakington (ca 1722 – 30 Nov. 1762). HW did not know who occupied Westwood Park at this time, as he admitted to Lyttelton *post* 16 Oct. 1762.

5. Thomas Pitt (1737–93), cr. (1784) Bn Camelford. He had settled at Twickenham in April 1762. HW wrote Mann 29 Aug. 1762: 'I will make your compliments to Palazzo Pitti, when I see it; but he has scarce been here; he is not well, and drinking waters at Sunning Hill' (MANN vi. 73.)

6. Anne Pitt (1712–81), sister of William Pitt, cr. (1766) E. of Chatham; HW's correspondent (MORE 1 n. 1).

7. George, 1st Bn Lyttelton.

8. Probably William Pitt, 1st E. of Chatham, who was Bishop Lyttelton's brother-in-law and Thomas Pitt's uncle.

chanted with Rose Castle[9]—I am glad of it; sue for translation: if a bishop is to be the husband of one wife, at least he ought to wed from inclination. Pray choose a spouse, my Lord, nearer town. Your old landlady Exeter[10] is to be disposed of, but I think you had enough of her in her husband's time. Adieu! my Lord,

Your obedient humble servant

HOR. WALPOLE

TO BISHOP LYTTELTON, Saturday 16 October 1762

Printed for the first time from a photostat of the MS in the Worcestershire Record Office, Shirehall, Worcester, kindly furnished by the 4th Baron Hampton. For the history of the MS see *ante* 25 Sept. 1762.

Strawberry Hill, Oct. 16, 1762.

My very good and obliging Lord,

I THANK you heartily for your kind letter[1] and information, and for recovering my ancestor,[2] though I find he is no more like Harry VIII than I his spare descendant.

I know nothing of whom the seat belongs to[3]—consequently if I am absurd you will excuse me. I cannot help asking if there is any possibility of purchasing that picture; if not, whether one could have it to town to be copied?[4] Don't trouble yourself to write an answer to these questions, but bring the response yourself.

Next I must make due acknowledgments to Mr Sandys[5] for the

9. The official residence of the Bishops of Carlisle (Samuel Jefferson, *The History and Antiquities of Carlisle*, 1838, pp. 371–83).

10. 'Of which he was Dean' (MS note in an unidentified hand). Lyttelton had been dean of Exeter 1748–62 while George Lavington was Bishop. Lavington died 13 Sept. 1762 and was succeeded by Frederick Keppel, nominated 14 Oct. and consecrated 7 Nov. 1762 (John Le Neve, *Fasti Ecclesiæ Anglicanæ*, Oxford, 1854, i. 382, 388; MANN vi. 94 n. 14).

1. Missing.

2. Sir John Perrot. HW's maternal grandmother, Elizabeth Philipps Shorter, was descended from John Philipps, cr. (1621) Bt, of Pickton, who married as his first wife Anne, dau. of Sir John Perrot (GEC *sub* John Philipps).

3. See previous letter, n. 4.

4. HW had to be satisfied with a copy 'in black and white chalk, by Chambars'; it hung in the Great North Bedchamber at SH (*Des. of SH, Works* ii. 497). The copy was sold SH xx. 112 to Horace Rodd for £5.15.6 and is now WSL. HW wrote on the back, 'Sir John Perrot Lord Deputy of Ireland,' and his secretary Kirgate added below, 'From the original at Sir Herbert Perrot Packington's at Westwood Worcestershire.'

trouble he has been so good as to take. When he comes to town, I will wait on him and thank him in person. His discovery is not one to me; I have given a short article of Butler[6] as a painter in my second volume;[7] it is certain he did paint. I am sorry all his genius flowed through his pen and that none passed into his pencil[8]—however, I am such a bigot, that I should be strangely happy with a scrap of his performance, which Mr Sandys flatters me is attainable; I should not scruple giving more than it is worth.[9] In short, I have opened so many veins of virtu, that it is amazing what trumpery is necessary to my felicity! One grows attached to men of abilities because they have executed fine works, and then grows fond of bad things because they were performed by men of abilities, though it ought to be a reason for disliking them—and yet men are not happy, though they have so many ways of reconciling themselves to what should disgust them!

Your nephew[10] will be most welcome; in the first place for his own sake, in the second for mine, which whether you will believe it or not, weighs most with me. I want him exceedingly, and till I do not, I shall not wish for him disinterestedly. The board of works stands still, from the absence of the surveyor.[11]

My Lord Lyttelton, I hope, comes back quite established in his health. Does he bring King Henry complete?[12] or are we to have nothing this winter but *Britons* and *North Britons*?[13] Adieu, my dear Lord, I am truly obliged to you, and

Your Lordship's most faithful humble servant

HOR. WALPOLE

5. Possibly the Hon. Edwin Sandys (1726–97), 2d Bn Sandys, 1770; M.P.

6. Samuel Butler (1612–80), poet.

7. *Anecdotes of Painting,* 1st edn, ii. 126–7.

8. Butler spent some of his early years as clerk to Thomas Jeffries, a justice of the peace in Earls Croome, Worcs, when he showed an inclination to painting. 'I have seen formerly in the mansion-house here [Earls Croome] some portraits of the family, said to have been painted by Butler; but going not many years since to inquire for them, I found them made use of to stop up windows. They had no other merit than that of being painted by the author of *Hudibras*' (T. R. Nash, *Collections for the History of Worcestershire,* 1781–2, i. 267).

9. No evidence has been found that HW ever possessed any of Butler's paintings.

10. Presumably Thomas Lyttelton.

11. Thomas Pitt, whom HW referred to as 'my present architect' (CONWAY ii. 198). He had informed Mann 13 April that Pitt 'draws Gothic with taste, and is already engaged on the ornaments of my Cabinet and Gallery' (MANN vi. 25). Pitt had been away 'drinking waters at Sunning Hill' for his health (ibid. vi. 73).

12. The first two volumes of Lord Lyttelton's *History of the Life of King Henry the Second* did not appear until 1767.

13. *The Briton,* edited by Tobias Smollett, was published from 29 May 1762 to 12 Feb. 1763; *The North Briton,* edited

From JOHN BASKERVILLE,[1] Tuesday 2 November 1762

Printed from a photostat of the MS in the Timmins Collection, Birmingham Reference Library. First printed in Nichols, *Lit. Anec.* iii. 452–4. Reprinted, GM 1810, lxxx pt ii. 521–2; William Hutton, *The History of Birmingham,* 1819, pp. 126–9; T. B. Reed, *A History of the Old English Letter Foundries, etc.,* 1887, pp. 278–9; Ralph Straus and R. K. Dent, *John Baskerville,* 1907, pp. 99–100; Toynbee *Supp.* iii. 174–7; Walpole Printing Office, *Specimens of Work Recently Issued from the Press,* New Rochelle, N.Y., 1931, pp. [3–4]; Leonard Jay, *Letters of the Famous 18th Century Printer John Baskerville of Birmingham,* Birmingham, 1932, pp. 19–21; William Bennett, *John Baskerville, The Birmingham Printer: His Press, Relations, and Friends,* Birmingham, 1937–9, i. 126–7 (passages omitted); J. H. Benton, *John Baskerville, Type-Founder and Printer 1706–1775,* New York, 1944, pp. 67–70; *Minor Lives,* ed. E. L. Hart, Cambridge, Mass., 1971, p. 297. The MS is untraced until sold Sotheby's 10 June 1869 (John Dillon Sale), lot 73, to John Waller; subsequently acquired by Samuel Timmins, whose Baskerville collection was bequeathed to Robert Dent in 1903 and later presented to the Birmingham Reference Library. A facsimile of the MS was printed for the Baskerville Club at Cambridge ca 1907.

Address: To the Honourable Horace Walpole Esq. Member of Parliament; in Arlington Street London. *Postmark:* 4 NO. BIRMINGHAM.

Easy Hill,[2] Birmingham, 2d November 1762.

Sir,

AS THE patron and encourager of arts, and particularly that of printing, I have taken the liberty of sending you a specimen[3] of mine, begun ten years ago at the age of forty-seven; and prosecuted ever since with the utmost care and attention; on the strongest presumption that if I could fairly excel in this divine art; it would make my affairs easy, or at least give me bread. But alas! in both I was mistaken. The booksellers do not choose to encourage me, though I have offered them as low terms as I could possibly live by; nor dare I attempt an old copy, till a lawsuit relating to that affair is determined.[4]

by John Wilkes and others, first appeared 5 June 1762 and continued irregularly until 11 May 1771.

---

1. (1706–75), type-founder and printer.

2. Baskerville's small estate NE of Birmingham, where he built a house for himself in 1745 and spent the rest of his life. There he set up his press and typefoundry, which was several times enlarged until at his death it included twenty-three complete founts (Ralph Straus and R. K. Dent, *John Baskerville,* 1907, pp. 9, 14–18).

3. The specimen of the *Bible,* with proposals, 1759; reissued 1760 (Philip Gaskell, *John Baskerville, a Bibliography,* Cambridge, Eng., 1959, pp. 8–9, No. viii). A copy of the 1760 reissue is in the Birmingham Reference Library.

4. Baskerville wrote to an unknown correspondent 4 Jan. 1757 that the booksellers claimed 'an absolute right in copies

The University of Cambridge have given me a grant to print there 8vo and 12mo Common Prayer Books;[5] but under such shackles as greatly hurt me: I pay them for the former twenty, and for the latter twelve pound ten shillings the thousand, and to the Stationer's Company thirty-two pound for their permission to print one edition of the Psalms in metre to the small Prayer Book:[6] add to this the great expense of double and treble carriage; and the inconvenience of a printing house an hundred miles off. All this summer I have had nothing to print at home. My folio Bible[7] is pretty far advanced at Cambridge, which will cost me near £2,000, all hired at 5 p. cent. If this does not sell, I shall be obliged to sacrifice a small patrimony[8] which brings me in ⟨£ 74⟩[9] a year to this business of printing; which I am heartily tired of, and repent I ev⟨er⟩ attempted. It is surely a particular hardship that I should not get bread in my own country (and it is too late to go abroad) after having acquired the reputation of excelling in the most useful art known to mankind; while every one who excels as a player, fiddler, dancer etc. not only lives in affluence but has it [in] their power to save a fortune.

I have sent a few specimens (same as the enclosed) to the courts of Russia and Denmark, and shall endeavour to do the same to most of the courts in Europe;[10] in hopes of finding in some one of them a purchaser of the whole scheme, on the condition of my never attempting another type. I was saying this to a particular friend,[11] who reproached me with not giving my own country the preference, as it would (he was pleased to say) be a national reproach to lose it: I told him, nothing but the greatest necessity would put me upon it; and even then, I should resign it with the utmost reluctance. He observed, the Parliament had given a handsome premium for a quack

of books, as old as even Milton and Shakespeare; the former of which I did design to have printed, but am deterred by Mr Tonson and Co. threatening me with a bill in Chancery if I attempt it' (quoted in Straus and Dent, op. cit. 98). No further information about the lawsuit has been found.

5. In Jan. 1758 Baskerville publicly announced that he had 'obtained from the University of Cambridge, full powers to print . . . octavo Common-prayer-books on a large fine Royal paper . . . and one edition of a folio Bible' (*Birmingham Gazette*, extracts quoted in ibid. 47).

6. *The Whole Book of Psalms, Collected into English Metre . . . (By Permission of the Stationer's Company)*, Birmingham, 1762 (Gaskell, op. cit. 39–40, No. 21).

7. *The Holy Bible*, Cambridge, 1763 (ibid. 44–5, No. 26).

8. Baskerville was 'heir to a paternal estate of £60 *per annum*, which fifty years after [1756], while in his own possession, had increased to £90' (Nichols, *Lit. Anec.* iii. 450).

9. The MS is torn at this point; the amount is supplied from Nichols's text of the letter.

10. A copy of the specimen of the *Bible*, 1760, is in the Royal Library at Stockholm (Gaskell, op. cit. 9).

11. Not identified.

medicine;[12] and he doubted not, if my affair was properly brought before the House of Commons, but some regard would be paid to it; I replied, I durst not presume to petition the House, unless encouraged by some of the members, who might do me the honour to promote it, of which I saw not the least hopes or probability.

Thus, Sir, I have taken the liberty of laying before you my affairs, without the least aggravation; and humbly hope [for] your patronage:[13] To whom can I apply for protection but the great, who alone have it in their power to serve me?

I rely on your candour as a lover of the arts to excuse this presumption in

Your most obedient and most humble servant,

JOHN BASKERVILLE

PS. The folding of the specimens will be taken out by laying them a short time between damped papers. N.B. the ink, presses, chases, moulds for casting and all the apparatus for printing were made in my own shops.

12. Doubtless a reference to Joanna Stephens (d. 1774), who, by an Act of Parliament in 1739 (12 Geo. II, c. 23), received payment of £5,000 for her secret remedy 'for the cure of the stone' (Stephen Hales, *An Account of Some Experiments and Observations on Mrs Stephens's Medicines for Dissolving the Stone,* [1740], pp. 38–42, 48). Sir Robert Walpole and his brother Horatio, Lord Walpole, both of whom suffered from the stone, are known to have taken Mrs Stephens's medicines (MANN ii. 566; David d'Escherny, *A Treatise of the Causes and Symptoms of the Stone,* 1755, pp. 53–4).

13. Nothing came of this letter, although HW's name appears in the list of subscribers to *Paradise Lost,* 1758, printed by Baskerville. HW's library included copies of eight or nine works from Baskerville's press (Hazen, *Cat. of HW's Lib.,* Nos 300, 1927, 2187, 2196, 2197, 2206, 2208, 2482, and 3889).

To Lord Bute, Monday 14 March 1763

Printed from *Works* ii. 380, where the letter was first printed. Reprinted, Toynbee v. 292. The history of the MS and its present whereabouts are not known.

Arlington Street, March 14, 1763.

My Lord,

As it is now near five months since your Lordship signed my orders, I should be glad if your Lordship would please to direct the payment of the money.[1]

I am, my Lord,
Your Lordship's obedient humble servant,

Hor. Walpole

From Samuel Martin,[1] Tuesday 15 March 1763

Printed for the first time from the MS now WSL. The MS was sold by the Waldegrave family to Richard Bentley, the publisher, ca 1843; resold from the estate of his grandson, Richard Bentley the younger, to WSL, 1937.

Treasury Chambers, 15 March 1763.

Mr Martin's compliments to Mr Horace Walpole; and acquaints him that it is the fault of the Treasury people that Mr Martin did not sign the letter, he having been ordered by Lord Bute to do it a considerable time ago and having given directions at the Treasury accordingly that the proper letter should be prepared

1. Money due to HW as usher of the Exchequer. He believed that the payments had been withheld because of his refusal to vote in favour of the peace preliminaries in 1762 and because of the letter he sent to Henry Fox 21 Nov. 1762, concerning political matters affecting HW's family (Selwyn 168–70 and n. 8). 'There were truths enough to displease, and they did not escape Fox. The consequence to me was, that by his influence with [Samuel] Martin, Secretary of the Treasury, my payments were stopped for some months, nor made but on my writing to Lord Bute himself' (*Mem. Geo. III* i. 171). See following letter.

1. (1714–88), secretary to the Treasury 1756–7, 1758–63; M.P. In 1763 he obtained through Lord Bute the reversion of HW's ushership of the Exchequer, and HW later referred to him as 'my reversionary heir' (Mason i. 71 and n. 19).

for his signing; indeed he thought he had actually signed it. But on finding the contrary this day, he has just now set his hand to the issuing letter.

TO LORD BUTE, Wednesday 16 March 1763

Printed from a copy by the late Sir Shane Leslie, Bt, in 1941 of the MS then in the possession of the Hon. Mrs Clive Pearson, Parham Park, Pulborough, Sussex. First printed, *Works* ii. 380. Reprinted, Toynbee v. 292. The MS was *penes* Maggs in 1904; later acquired by Sir Herbert H. Raphael, Bt, who inserted it in an extra-illustrated copy of Cunningham's edition of HW's *Letters*, 18 vols, folio; this copy was sold Sotheby's 4 Feb. 1919 (Raphael Sale), lot 311, to Bumpus for Lord Cowdray, the father of the Hon. Clive Pearson; bequeathed by his widow, the Hon. Mrs Pearson, to her daughter, Mrs P. A. Tritton, of Parham Park, in 1974.

Arlington Street, March 16, 1763.

My Lord,

I AM very sensible of your Lordship's obliging civility in immediately ordering my money on my application. It was by no means from want of respect to your Lordship, that that application was not made sooner; but for above twenty years that I have held the office, it has been the constant practice to write to the first secretary[1] to desire his letter, when the Lords have signed the orders, and the payment has seldom been delayed above a fortnight after.

If your Lordship should approve of it, I had much rather, as my bills become due, apply to your Lordship than to anybody else, unless your Lordship please to give any other directions.

I am my Lord
Your Lordship's most obedient humble servant
HOR. WALPOLE

1. Of the Treasury, at this time Samuel Martin.

TO UNKNOWN, ca Friday 8 April 1763

Printed from a photostat of the MS in the Pierpont Morgan Library. First printed, Toynbee v. 299. The MS was sold Sotheby's 28 Nov. 1890 (Manners Sale), lot 447, to Barker; *penes* J. Pearson and Co., London, 1904; subsequently acquired by J. P. Morgan.

Dated approximately by Lord Waldegrave's death on 8 April 1763 (see n. 1 below).

Dear Sir,

THE medical people certainly give us little hopes of poor Lord Waldegrave,[1] though they owned last night that all the symptoms were less unfavourable than in the morning.[2] If I was not thoroughly persuaded of their ignorance, it would be very impertinent in me to form any opinion, not founded on theirs; yet till their arguments are clearer and more satisfactory, I shall not despair. His head is so perfectly unaffected by his disorder, that I cannot conceive how his danger should be so imminent; as they affirm that the bodily symptoms are not of half the consequence in this disorder as those are of the head. His tranquillity they own is his best chance. It is unalterable; his temper, goodness, reason, and patience double what one feels on the prospect of losing him. I am just going thither, and if I should find any material alteration, will let you know.

Yours ever

H. W.

1. James Waldegrave (1715–63), styled Vct Chewton 1729–41; 2d E. Waldegrave, 1741; K.G. In 1759 he had married HW's niece, Maria Walpole. He died of smallpox on the afternoon of 8 April 1763, having been ill for about two weeks. Sir Edward Wilmot and Dr Cæsar Hawkins attended him (MONTAGU ii. 58–9; MANN vi. 126–8).

2. 'Last night we had some glimmerings of hope. The most desponding of the faculty flattered us a little' (HW to Montagu 'Friday night late,' 8 April 1763, MONTAGU ii. 58).

To the Contessa Rena,[1] ca Saturday 9 April 1763

Printed from the MS now WSL. First printed, Toynbee v. 309–10. The MS was *penes* W. V. Daniell in 1904; later acquired by C. Francis Gaskill, who sold it in a collection to WSL, 1939.

Dated approximately by the death of Lord Waldegrave on 8 April 1763.

MONSIEUR Walpole est très sensible aux bontés de Madame la Comtesse Rena,[2] et la remercie infiniment de la peine qu'elle s'est bien voulu donner pour savoir de ses nouvelles et de celles de Madame sa nièce.[3] La pauvre Milady Waldegrave est aussi touchée qu'elle doit l'être d'une perte si grande: elle pleure le meilleur mari, l'amant le plus tendre, et l'homme le plus respectable de son siècle. Monsieur Walpole qui ne quitte pas une nièce si véritablement affligée, aura l'honneur de remercier en personne Madame Rena quand il retournera à la ville.[4] En attendant, il l'assure de sa vive reconnaissance et de son respect.

To Lord Egremont,[1] Wednesday 20 April 1763

Printed for the first time from a photostat of the MS at Petworth House, Petworth, Sussex, kindly furnished by the late 1st Bn Egremont (d. 1972). The MS descended in the Wyndham family, the former owners of Petworth House, now property of the National Trust.

Arlington Street, April 20th 1763.

My Lord,

LADY Waldegrave has desired me to tell your Lordship how sensible she is of the very kind and obliging offer that your Lordship has been so good as to make her of the house at Petersham,[2] but she will

1. 'A Florentine, who had been long in England; had originally been mistress (at Florence where she was wife of a wine-merchant) of Lord Pembroke, and afterwards here of the Earl of March and Ruglen, and occasionally of others' (HW's note on his letter to Mann 14 April 1769, MANN vii. 106 n. 7).

2. The Rena's letter is missing.

3. Maria Walpole (1736–1807), second dau. of Sir Edward Walpole; m. 1 (1759) James Waldegrave, 2d E. Waldegrave; m. 2 (1766) William Henry, D. of Gloucester. See previous letter.

4. HW took Lady Waldegrave to SH 9 April and returned to Arlington Street 18 April. The Rena's letter was one of a 'thousand letters of condolence' that HW told Montagu he must answer (MONTAGU ii. 59, 63, 67).

---

1. Sir Charles Wyndham (1710 – 21 Aug. 1763), 4th Bt, 1740; 2d E. of Egremont, 1750; M.P.

2. Across the Thames from SH. Lady Waldegrave's elder sister, Laura Keppel, wrote to her aunt, Jane Clement, ?18 Sept. 1775: 'At Petersham there is nothing

not by any means think of depriving your Lordship of a place which she is sure must be so convenient and agreeable to you. The civility was so great (and uncommon, except by its coming from your Lordship) that she hopes you will not think her thanks mere expressions of form, but a real gratitude, with which she is the more touched, as she flatters herself that your Lordship's esteem for Lord Waldegrave had some share in this goodness, as well as your natural politeness.

It would not be proper for me, my Lord, to take the liberty of adding my own thanks on this occasion, though nobody is more bound by any goodness shown to my niece, than, my Lord,

Your Lordship's most obedient humble servant

HOR. WALPOLE

From LORD EGREMONT, Thursday 21 April 1763

Printed from the MS now WSL. First printed, Toynbee *Supp.* iii. 177. Damer-Waller; the MS was sold Sotheby's 5 Dec. 1921 (first Waller Sale), lot 120 (with lot 121), to Wells; given by him to Thomas Conolly, of Chicago, from whom WSL acquired it in 1937.

Piccadilly,[1] April 21, 1763.

Sir,

I RETURN you all the thanks I owe for the obliging letter you honoured me with yesterday, and I feel as I ought Lady Waldegrave's goodness in doing justice to the esteem, friendship, and respect which I have ever felt for a friend[2] whom I shall ever regret. As to the house at Petersham from the moment I knew her Ladyship had thoughts of it I thought of it no more, and still beg that she will accept of an offer which I assure you did not proceed from compliment but from very sincere regard, unless some other motive besides civility to me should make her Ladyship choose not to inhabit the house: I should not inhabit it with any satisfaction if I knew

but people of quality, and therefore 'tis the fittest place for them [the Waldegrave sisters] to live' (MS now WSL; see also Daniel Lysons, *The Environs of London,* 1792–6, i. 399–403).

1. Egremont House, Picadilly.
2. Lord Waldegrave.

that her Ladyship was thereby deprived of a place she liked. I have the honour to be,

Sir,

Your most obedient and most humble servant,

EGREMONT

TO LORD EGREMONT, Thursday 21 April 1763

Printed for the first time from a photostat of the MS at Petworth House, Petworth, Sussex, kindly furnished by the late 1st Bn Egremont (d. 1972). For the history of the MS see *ante* 20 April 1763.

Arlington Street, April 21st 1763.

My Lord,

AS SOON as I had seen Lady Waldegrave, I did myself the honour of waiting on your Lordship, that you might not have the trouble of writing any more, which I beg your Lordship would not think it necessary to do.

Lady Waldegrave renews her most grateful thanks for your Lordship's goodness, but is very happy that without putting you to any inconvenience, she can accommodate herself, as she finds that Mrs Pritchard's[1] house,[2] with the opportunity of being near mine, will suit her. In her unhappy situation nothing could give her so much satisfaction as such testimonial as your Lordship's to the character of Lord Waldegrave.

I have the honour to be, My Lord

Your Lordship's most obedient humble servant

HOR. WALPOLE

1. Hannah Vaughan (1711–68), m. (*ante* 1733) William Pritchard; actress.

2. Ragman's Castle, a small house at Twickenham that Mrs Pritchard bought ca 1755 and remodelled (R. S. Cobbett, *Memorials of Twickenham*, 1872, pp. 246–7; Edward Ironside, *The History and Antiquities of Twickenham*, 1797, p. 86, in *Bibliotheca Topographica Britannica*, vol. X). HW wrote George Montagu 22 April 1763: 'I have taken Mrs Pritchard's house for Lady Waldegrave; I offered her to live with me at Strawberry, but with her usual good sense she declined it, as she thought the children would be troublesome' (MONTAGU ii. 69).

From JOHN JAMISONE, Saturday 14 May 1763

Printed for the first time from a photostat of the MS at Nostell Priory, Wakefield, Yorks, kindly furnished by the late Hon. Charles Winn. For the history of the MS see *ante* ?1762.

Memoranda (by HW, in pencil):[1]

2 [family portraits of] Savages
Qu[een] Eliz[abeth] arms and devices
pious mottoes [on the wall]
[offices were part of a] nunnery
wall [next] to road
Concert [of birds by] Mario di Fiori
handsome balustrade [to the stairs] E[arl] of Sand[wich] arms
good head round [of a young man] like Holbein
odd [picture like] Ch[arles] I in red v[ery] fine
Copy of Misers [by Quentin Matsys] at Houghton
5 [small Egyptian] idols
Cromwell's arms
old view of Mount Edgc[umbe]
Ralph D[uke] of Montagu
his wife Lady Northumb[erland]
[4th] Lord Sandw[ich by] Liotard
a French lady, prob[ably] Lady Sandw[ich]
Adm[iral's] red velvet bed
Ch[arles] II of Spain ridic. boy
his mother as nun writing
Ebony Cabinet and brass
Noble old drawing room, ceiling like college halls, tapestry after cartoons
Mrs Ruperta Howe [in] riding clothes
Cath[erine] of Portug[al] handsome, being a Vandyck imitation
2 ‹long . . . copy of Olivers›
Lord Rochester [Head of the] Admiral
Death of E[arl] of Sandw[ich by] Peckitt, and
[head of a] Dey of Algiers
fine Vandeveld black and white
Scot[t] paintings [in the] great room
view of Alexandria
Vandevelde other sea pieces
[Scott's 'Engagement of the] Lion and Eliz[abeth'] fine
Lady Rochester

1. These almost illegible notes were made during a visit to Hinchingbrooke, Lord Sandwich's seat, 31 May 1763 (MONTAGU ii. 79). HW used them to write his account of Hinchingbrooke in *Country Seats* 49–50.

Admiral when young
Lady Sandwich [by] Mr Dahl
Duchess of Bourbon
Lady Hinchinbrook
Mon[c]k[e] oval [and] Cromwell [heads]
Sea drawings best drawing room
Ch[arles] II
2d Earl [by] Lely and good
Duchess of Cleveland
George II [by] Shackleton
large Scot[t of engagement between Admiral] Anson
and Jonquière
D[uke] of Cumb[erland by] Reynolds
Admiral, head bad, rest good
Arms [in glass by] Peckitt
⟨ ⟩

Memoranda (by HW, in ink):[2]

H. T.
Lady Blandf[or]d
Lady Egremont
Tailor
Domino
Lord Exeter
6-6-0
1-1-0
3-6
Ticket
qualification

Leith, 14 May 1763.

Sir,

I HAD the pleasure of writing to you in September last,[3] in answer to your favour 18th of that month.[4] I have been sometime in possession of Mr Jamesone the painter's last will[4a] written with his own hand, in July 1641, and which breathes that spirit of piety which

2. These notes relate to HW's preparations for the masquerade and fireworks at Richmond House 6 June 1763. He wrote Conway 28 May: 'Write, the moment you receive this, to your tailor to get you a sober purple domino as I have done, and it will make you a couple of summer waistcoats' (CONWAY ii. 206). The day after the masquerade he described to Mann the 'magnificent entertainment . . . with suppers spread, the houses covered and filled with people, the bridge, the garden full of masks . . . about six hundred' (MANN vi. 148–9).

3. *Ante* 23 Sept. 1762.

4. Missing.

4a. Not known to have survived; see Duncan Thomson, *The Life and Art of George Jamesone*, Oxford, 1974, p. 7.

was the characteristic of the times and that benevolence which was so natural to himself. He provides kindly for his wife and children, leaves many legacies to his friends and relations (particularly to Lord Rothes[5] the King's picture from head to foot[6] and Mary with Martha in one piece; to William Murray[7] the medals in his coffer), makes a handsome provision for his natural daughter[8] and bestows liberally to the poor. That he should have been in condition to do all this is wonderful since in the bosom of his will enumerating the debts due to him he charges Lady Haddington[9] for her husband's picture, a full length, and Lady Seton's[10] of the same, frames and all, three hundred marks, and Lord Maxwell[11] for his own picture and his Lady's to their knees, one hundred marks, both Scots money.[12]

I have likewise a memorandum written and signed by him mentioning a manuscript in his possession containing two hundred leaves of parchment of excellent write adorned with diverse histories of our Saviour curiously limned, which he values at one hundred pounds sterling, an enormous sum in these days. What sort [of] a book this has been we are at a loss to find out, as there is nothing analogous to it extant in any of our repositories, which makes us regret the loss of so curious and valuable a piece of antiquity. I would be glad to have your opinion about it. And I beg you will do me the favour as to let me know when the second edition of your *Anecdotes*

5. John Leslie (ca 1600–41), 6th E. of Rothes, 1611.

6. See *ante* 11 Sept. 1762 *bis,* n. 6b. In Alexander Carnegie's 'Catalogue of some of the Works of George Jamieson, Painter' (transcribed in 1797) a portrait of Charles I is listed as being in the possession of 'Mr Jamieson, wine merchant in Leith,' HW's correspondent (M. W. Brockwell, *George Jamesone and Some Primitive Scottish Painters,* privately printed, 1939, p. 33).

7. (ca 1600 – ca 1653), cr. (1643) E. of Dysart, but styled William Murray, Esq. as late as 1651; tutor and secretary to Charles, P. of Wales, afterwards Charles I; gentleman of the Bedchamber, 1626.

8. Jamesone's daughter Elizabeth is said to have been illegitimate, but she was baptized 6 Feb. 1630 as a legitimate child (Thomson, op. cit. 7).

9. Lady Jean Gordon (d. 1655), m. (14 Jan. 1640) Thomas Hamilton (1600 – 30 Aug. 1640), 2d E. of Haddington, 1637.

10. Lady Henrietta Gordon (d. 1651), m. 1 (1639) George Seton, styled Lord Seton; m. 2 (1649), as his first wife, John Stewart (?1624–66), 2d E. of Traquair, 1659; Lady Haddington's sister.

11. Robert Maxwell (1586–1646), 9th Bn Maxwell, 1613; cr. (1620) E. of Nithsdale; m. (1619) Elizabeth Beaumont (d. 1671).

12. 'For full-length portraits of Lord Haddington and Lady Seton he appears to have charged 300 marks (£17 12*s.* 6*d.*); and for Lord and Lady Maxwell "to the knees" 100 marks (£5 17*s.* 6*d.*)' (*Scottish Notes and Queries* 1927, 3d ser., v. 58).

13. The second edition of *Anecdotes of Painting* was published in June 1767, the first edition of vol. III and the *Catalogue of Engravers* on 6 Feb. 1764 (Hazen, *SH Bibl.* 55, 62).

will be published and when the third and fourth tomes[13] on that subject, which are much longed for. I have the honour of being,

Sir,

Your most obedient and most humble servant,

JNO. JAMISONE

To the HON. ROBERT HAMPDEN,[1] ca June 1763

Printed for the first time from a photostat of a copy of the letter made by Louis de Joncourt, bound in the copy of HW's *Fugitive Pieces* presented to the Prince of Orange in June 1763 and now in the Koninklijke Bibliotheek, The Hague (press-mark 192. C. 9).

Joncourt, librarian to the Prince of Orange, included the following explanation with the text of the letter: 'Ce volume a été donné de la part de l'auteur à la bibliothèque de S.A.S. Monseigneur le Prince d'Orange[2] etc. par Monsieur Wolters,[3] agent de sa Majesté Britannique à Rotterdam. Mr Walpole, auteur de cet ouvrage, l'ayant fait imprimer dans son imprimerie de Strawberry Hill, et ne le donnant qu'à ses amis, sans permettre qu'il entrat dans le commerce de la librairie; Mr Wolters engagea Monsieur Hampden[4] né Trevor à en demander un exemplaire à l'auteur. Mr Walpole le lui envoya avec le billet suivant . . . .

'Cet exemplaire que Mr Hampden avait demandé comme pour lui m'a été remis, avec le billet que j'ai copié, en juin 1763.

Louis de Joncourt
Bibliothécaire de S.A.S.'

MR Walpole sends Mr Hampden the book,[5] as he was ordered, though much ashamed of transmitting such a trifle to so great a person, and only preferring obedience to delicacy. If Mr Hampden

1. Hon. Robert Trevor (after 1754, Hampden) (1706–83), 4th Bn Trevor, 1764; cr. (1776) Vct Hampden; secretary of embassy at The Hague 1736–9, under HW's uncle Horatio Walpole; envoy extraordinary to Holland 1739–41; envoy extraordinary and plenipotentiary 1741–7 (D. B. Horn, *British Diplomatic Representatives 1689–1789,* pp. 163–4; MANN i. 281 n. 12). He owned a fine collection of drawings and prints; HW's 'Drawings and Designs by Richard Bentley,' now WSL, contains a drawing of 'a frame for butterflies for Mr Trevor Hampden' (Hazen, *Cat. of HW's Lib.,* No. 3585).

2. William V (1748–1806), Prince of Orange 1751–95.

3. Richard Wolters (1713–71), British agent at Rotterdam (D. B. Horn, *The British Diplomatic Service 1689–1789,* Oxford, 1961, pp. 274–5; *The Fourth Earl of Sandwich, Diplomatic Correspondence 1763–1765,* ed. Frank Spencer, Manchester, 1961, pp. 105–6).

4. 'Depuis il a herité du titre de Lord Trevor' (MS note added by Joncourt).

5. *Fugitive Pieces in Verse and Prose,* SH, 1758.

approves it, and will return it, Mr Walpole will have it richly bound,[6] as a mark of more respect.

TO BISHOP LYTTELTON, Sunday 10 July 1763

Printed from a photostat of the MS in the possession of Viscount Cobham, Hagley Hall, Stourbridge, Worcs. First printed in N&Q 1869, 4th ser., iii. 3–4. Reprinted, Toynbee v. 348–50. The MS descended in the Lyttelton family to the present owner.

Strawberry Hill, July 10th 1763.

My good Lord,

YOU are ever kind and obliging to me, and indulge my virtuoso humour with as much charity, as if a passion for collecting were a Christian want. I thank you much for the letter[1] on King James's death: it shall certainly make its appearance with the rest of your bounties. At present that volume is postponed; I have got a most delectable work to print, which I had great difficulty to obtain, and which I must use while I can have it. It is the life of the famous Lord Herbert of Cherbury, written by himself[2]—one of the most curious pieces my eyes ever beheld—but I will not forestall the amusement it will give you.

Do I confound it, or is the print of Master Prideaux, the same with that of Master Basset?[3] I have some such notion: if it is, I have it.[4] If not, I will inquire of Ramsay. As to your nephew,[5] he is a lost

6. HW's offer was apparently not taken; the binding of the volume is mottled calf, not 'richly bound.'

---

1. Missing.

2. *The Life of Edward Lord Herbert of Cherbury, Written by Himself*. HW wrote Montagu 16 July 1764: 'I found it a year ago at Lady Hertford's, to whom Lady Powis had lent it. . . . I begged to have it to print—Lord Powis, sensible of the extravagance, refused. I insisted, he persisted. . . . I sat down and wrote a flattering dedication to Lord Powis, which I knew he would swallow. He did, and gave up his ancestor' (MONTAGU ii. 129–30). The printing of *Life* was completed 27 Jan. 1764, but HW did not begin distributing copies until July (Hazen, *SH Bibl.* 70).

3. Doubtless John Prideaux Basset (1744–56). Allan Ramsay's portrait of him in Van Dyck dress, hat in hand, with his hound beside him, was engraved by John Faber, junior (*BM Cat. of Engraved British Portraits* i. 133; *The Autobiography and Correspondence of Mary Granville, Mrs Delany*, ed. Lady Llanover, 1861–2, iii. 431–2; *The Connoisseur*, 1953, cxxxi. 113 and frontispiece facing p. 73).

4. It does not appear in the SH records.

5. Thomas Pitt, afterwards Bn Camelford, who lived near SH at his villa facetiously called the Palazzo Pitti.

thing; I have not set eyes on him this fortnight; he has deserted Palazzo Pitti; at least has abandoned me. Nay, I do not guess when we shall meet, for this day sennight I begin a ramble[6] to George Montagu's, Drayton, Burleigh, Ely, Peterborough, and I don't know where. This is to occupy the time, while they finish what remains to paint and gild of the gallery. This is very necessary, for with impatience I have spoiled half the frames that are new gilt, and do ten times more harm than I mean to do good. However, I see shore; three weeks will terminate all the workmen have to do—I shall long to have your Lordship see it, though I shall blush, for it is much more splendid than I intended, and too magnificent for me.

Mr Borlase,[7] I believe, knows your Lordship has some partiality for me. He honours me far beyond my deserts; forgets how little share I can claim in the *Anecdotes,* as greatly the largest part was owing to Vertue.

If I have any time towards the end of the summer, I will certainly visit the Museum;[8] I have much business there; but you will allow, my good Lord, that it is not from idleness that I have neglected going thither. I am not apt to be idle; few people have done so much of nothing, or have been so constantly employed, though indeed about trifles. I have almost tired myself, it is true, and yet I do not hitherto find my activity much relaxed.

You do not mention Rose Castle:[9] is it in disgrace? —well, be it so. Change it for Hartlebury or Farnham Castles[10]—to these Pitt and I can come with our Gothic trowels.

News I can send you none, for none I know. I seldom in summer do know an event that has happened since 1600. It is one of those ancient truths that

I am your Lordship's
Most bounden servant and poor beadsman
Hor. Walpole

6. For accounts of this tour, which took place 17–26 July, see Montagu ii. 84–92, 332–47, and *Country Seats* 51–60.

7. Rev. William Borlase (1695–1772), rector of Ludgvan, Cornwall, 1722–72; F.R.S., 1750; antiquary.

8. The British Museum. HW makes no mention of visiting it in the late summer.

9. The official residence of the Bishop of Carlisle.

10. The residences of the more richly endowed Bishops of Worcester and Winchester.

From WILLIAM PRATT, Thursday 14 July 1763

Printed from the MS now WSL, preserved with the Journal of the SH Press. First printed, *Journal of the Printing-Office,* p. 85. For the history of the Journal see *ante* 27 Aug. 1759.

July 14th 1763.

May it please your Honour,

HAVING an immediate occasion for three guineas[1] should esteem it as a great favour if you would be so good as to let me have it tonight[2] which will be of great service to

Your Honour's most obedient humble servant,

WM. PRATT

To ANDREW COLTEE DUCAREL, Monday 8 August 1763

Printed from a photostat of the MS in the Hornby Library, Liverpool City Libraries. First printed in Nichols, *Lit. Anec.* iv. 706. Reprinted, Wright iv. 293; Cunningham iv. 102; Toynbee v. 356 (closing and signature omitted in Wright, Cunningham, and Toynbee). The previous history of the MS is not known.

Endorsed by Ducarel: Aug. 8, 1763. Mr Walpole—Thanks for some hints I had given him about his *Anecdotes* on painters.

Postmark: 10 AV. ISLEWORTH.

Strawberry Hill, Aug. 8, 1763.

Sir,

I HAVE been rambling about the country,[1] or should not have so long deferred to answer the favour of your letter.[2] I thank you for the notices in it and have profited of them. I am much obliged to

1. His wages for six weeks as HW's printer.
2. This was doubtless only one of many favours asked by Pratt. He appears to have been in debt for lodging as well, according to the papers and accounts relating to him that are preserved with the Journal of the SH Press.

1. The 'ramble' mentioned to Charles Lyttelton *ante* 10 July 1763.
2. Missing.

you too for the drawings you intended me,[3] but I have since had a letter from Mr Churchill,[4] and he does not mention them.

I am Sir
Your obliged humble servant
HOR. WALPOLE

From WILLIAM BATHOE,[1] Saturday 27 August 1763

Printed from the MS now WSL, preserved with the Journal of the SH Press. First printed, *Journal of the Printing Office,* p. 85. Reprinted Toynbee *Supp.* iii. 178.

London, August 27, 1763.

Sir,

ENCLOSED is the account[2] of the whole money paid to Mr Pratt[3] and his wife. I believe I have not omitted anything. Mr Hillier[4] tells me today that he has some names of engravers which he intends sending to you very soon.[5] He likewise has prints of them if you should want any of them. I am,

Sir,
Your most obedient humble servant,
W. BATHOE

The prints and *Catalogue*[6] I sent by the waterman.

3. Not explained.

4. Charles Churchill (?1720–1812), HW's brother-in-law. His letter is missing.

1. (d. 1768), bookseller in the Strand, near Exeter Exchange. He was connected with several of HW's publications and at this time acted as his adviser in the management of the SH Press (CHATTERTON 123 n. 16).

2. No longer preserved with the letter.

3. William Pratt, HW's printer at SH 1761–4 (*ante* ca June 1762). HW wrote Selwyn 28 Sept. 1763: 'I must have my bookseller come from London and examine my printing-house. . . . I don't know whether I am robbed, nor how I may have suffered by this fellow and a drunken wife' (SELWYN 172). Pratt worked at the Press into Oct. 1764, perhaps settling his past debts, as the records show that he received payment 'in full of all demands' on 19 Sept. 1764 and was paid again on 17 Oct. 1764 for four weeks' printing (*Journal of the Printing-Office,* pp. 84–6).

4. Nathaniel Hillier (ca 1707–83), merchant, of Pancras Lane; collector of prints and drawings; HW's correspondent.

5. Hillier wrote HW 29 Aug. 1763, sending him a list of engravers and their works for possible use in preparing his *Catalogue of Engravers* (CHATTERTON 63–8). But the printing of the *Catalogue* had already been finished 9 May, and therefore the list was 'not inserted' (ibid. 63; Hazen *SH Bibl.* 55).

6. Presumably the *Catalogue of Engravers,* dated 1763 but not published

To the Hon. George Grenville, Wednesday 7 September 1763

Printed from the MS now wsl. First printed in *The Grenville Papers,* ed. W. J. Smith, 1852–3, ii. 113. Reprinted, Cunningham iv. 113; Toynbee v. 371 (closing omitted in all editions). The MS was among the Grenville papers desposited at Stowe by his descendants; sold in a collection of papers from Stowe by the 2d Duke of Buckingham and Chandos to his attorney, Edwin James, who in turn sold this collection to John Murray in 1851; resold Sotheby's 11 May 1970 (property of Sir John Murray), lot 228, to Seven Gables for wsl.

Strawberry Hill, Sept. 7th 1763.

Dear Sir,

THOUGH I am sensible I have no pretensions for asking you a favour, and indeed should be very unwilling to trespass on your good nature, yet I flatter myself I shall not be thought quite impertinent in interceding for a person, who I can answer has neither been to blame nor any way deserved punishment; and therefore I think you, Sir, will be ready to save him from great prejudice. The person is my deputy Mr Grosvenor Bedford,[1] who above five and twenty years ago was appointed collector of the Customs in Philadelphia by my father.[2] I hear he is threatened to be turned out.[3] If the least fault can be laid to his charge, I do not desire to have him protected. If there cannot, I am too well persuaded, Sir, of your justice, not to be sure you will be pleased to protect him. When I have appealed to your good nature and justice, it would be impertinent to say more than that I am

Dear Sir

Your most obedient humble servant

Hor. Walpole

until 6 Feb. 1764. Bathoe, who sold the *Catalogue,* had perhaps been given printed sheets to look over in advance of publication. HW wrote William Cole 8 Oct. 1763 that 'the volume of *Engravers* is printed off and has been some time; I only wait for some of the plates' (Cole i. 47).

1. For Grosvenor Bedford's appointment as HW's deputy usher of the Exchequer see *ante* 21 Aug. 1755.

2. Bedford's name appears in the Customs Book (vol. XIII, p. 310) under the date 29 June 1732 as follows: 'Treasury order for royal letters patent. Grosvenor Bedford, collector of customs, Philadelphia, America.' Under the date 22 Feb. 1732/3 (vol. XIII, p. 362), he is listed as receiving £160 per annum for the post ([Great Britain, Public Record Office,] *Calendar of Treasury Books and Papers 1731–1734,* 1898, pp. 357, 474; W. T. Root, *Relations of Pennsylvania with the Brit-*

From the HON. GEORGE GRENVILLE, Thursday 8 September 1763

Printed from a photostat of the MS copy, in Grenville's Letter Book 1763–70, among the Stowe MSS in the Henry E. Huntington Library. First printed in *The Grenville Papers,* ed. W. J. Smith, 1852–3, ii. 113–15. Grenville's Letter Book was among the Grenville papers deposited at Stowe by his descendants; it remained in the family's possession until 1921; sold in a collection of Stowe MSS by the Museum Bookstore, London, to Henry E. Huntington, 1925. The original letter is missing.

Downing Street, 8th September 1763.

Dear Sir,

YOU certainly have the two best claims that can be made to every mark of regard and attention which is in my power to grant; I mean your own merit, and the friendship you have shown to me, joined to my warm sense of them, and my earnest desire to comply with any wish of yours.

I have never heard of any complaint against Mr Grosvenor Bedford, or of any desire to turn him out; but by the office which you tell me he holds in North America, I believe I know the state of the case, which I will inform you of, that you may be enabled to judge of it yourself.[1] Heavy complaints were last year made in Parliament, of the state of our revenues in North America, which amount to between £1000 and £2000 a year, the collecting of which cost upon the establishment of the Customs in Great Britain between £7000 and £8000 a year. This, it was urged, arose from the making all these officers sinecures in England. When I came to the Treasury[2] I directed

ish Government 1696–1765, New York, 1912, pp. 72–3). Bedford was the only collector of customs in North America officially authorized (by his special warrant) to act entirely by deputy, and therefore not required to be present in person at the port (T. C. Barrow, *Trade and Empire: The British Customs Service in Colonial America 1660–1775,* Cambridge, Mass., 1967, pp. 76, 131, 297 n. 44).

3. See following letter.

1. In his *Memoirs* HW wrote of this episode: 'I had heard that American [customs] officers were to repair thither, or forfeit their places. My deputy, who enjoyed a sinecure in Philadelphia (I think it was), came to me in a fright, and begged I would intercede for his being excused. . . . I would not ask his being excused, but wrote to Mr Grenville to beg that if no fault was alleged against my deputy, and the order was not general, he might not be laid under the cruel necessity of throwing up his employment. Mr Grenville civilly answered that he knew of no such order or intention; that he would inquire into it, and no particular hardship should be laid on the person I interceded for' (*Mem. Geo. III* ii. 4–5).

2. Grenville, who had been first lord of the Admiralty since Oct. 1762, became first lord of the Treasury 13 April 1763.

the Commissioners of the Customs to be written to, that they might inform us how that revenue might be improved, and to what causes they attributed the present diminished state of it.[3] In their report, the principal cause which they assigned was the absence of the officers, who lived in England by leave from the Treasury, which they proposed should be recalled.[4] This we complied with, and ordered them all to their duty,[5] and the Commissioners of the Customs to present others in the room of such as should not obey. I take it for granted that this is Mr Bedford's case.[6] If it is, it will be attended with difficulty to make an exception, as they are every one of them applying to be excepted out of the order.[7] You will see the nature of that difficulty by what I have stated. If it is not so, or if Mr Bedford can suggest to me any proper means of obviating it without overturning the whole regulation,[8] he will do me a sensible pleasure, as it will put it in my power to do an act of kindness to one you recommend, and to express in this instance, as I wish to do in every other, the sentiments of sincere regard and attachment, with which I am ever,

My dear Sir, etc.

G[EORGE] G[RENVILLE]

3. On 21 May 1763 the Treasury asked the commissioners of customs to consider the revenue in America, and on 14 July it requested a list of customs officers serving in the colonies (T. C. Barrow, *Trade and Empire: The British Customs Service in Colonial America 1660–1775,* Cambridge, Mass., 1967, p. 177).

4. The commissioners' report, presented to the Treasury 22 July, stated that the efficiency of the customs service was impaired by many officers being absent on leave for one reason or another. The report recommended that the absentees be ordered back to duty (ibid. 177–8).

5. Grenville's order that all customs officers proceed to their posts in America is BM Add. MS 38,335, f. 155.

6. The general policy was that customs officers were not permitted the regular use of deputies to act in their place, but Grosvenor Bedford's special warrant specifically allowed him to operate by deputy (ibid. 314–15 n. 73; *ante* 7 Sept. 1763, n. 2).

7. John Bindley, one of the commissioners of excise, wrote to Charles Jenkinson, joint secretary to the Treasury, 9 Sept. 1763: 'One Grosvenor Bedford a very honest fellow is under an apprehension that his place in Philadelphia which he had held 30 years may be taken away in case of any new arrangement there. He therefore entreated me to mention him as my friend to you and as a man I believe deserving of protection' (*The Jenkinson Papers 1760–1766,* ed. N. S. Jucker, 1949, p. 188).

8. An exception was made for Bedford, presumably because of the special warrant he held, and he managed to keep the post until his death in 1771.

To Lady Temple,[1] ca Friday 20 January 1764

Printed from a photostat of the MS in the possession of Mr Robert H. Taylor, Princeton, New Jersey, kindly furnished by the late Sir John Murray. First printed in *The Grenville Papers,* ed. W. J. Smith, 1852–3, ii. 252–3. Reprinted, Cunningham iv. 175; Toynbee v. 446. The MS was among the Temple papers preserved at Stowe; sold in a collection of papers from Stowe by the 2d Duke of Buckingham and Chandos to his attorney, Edwin James, who in turn sold this collection to John Murray in 1851; resold Sotheby's 11 May 1970 (property of Sir John Murray), lot 229 (with HW to Lady Temple 28 Jan. 1764), to Hofmann and Freeman; acquired from them by Mr Taylor, Sept. 1970.

Dated approximately by the following letter.

Endorsed in an unidentified hand: Horace Walpole to Countess Temple on receiving from her her poems to be printed under his care at Strawberry Hill.

MR Walpole cannot express how much he is obliged and honoured by the trust Lady Temple is so good as to put in him, nor will her Ladyship's modesty let her be a proper judge how great that is. He will say no more now, but that, more than slight corrections in measure would destroy the chief merit of the poems,[2] which consists in the beautiful ease and negligence of the composition: a merit which correction may take away, but can never bestow. To do real justice to these poems, they should be compared with the first thoughts and sketches of other great poets. Mr Addison with infinite labour accomplished a few fine poems[3]—but what does your Ladyship think were his rough draughts?

1. Anne Chambers (ca 1709–77), m. (1737) Richard Grenville (after 1752, Grenville Temple) (1711–79), styled Vct Cobham 1749–52; 1st E. Temple, 1752.

2. 'Anna Chamber, Countess Temple, was forty years old before she discovered in herself a turn for genteel versification, which she executed with facility, and decked with the amiable graces of her own benevolent mind. A few copies of her select "Poems" were printed at Strawberry Hill, in 1764' (HW's *Catalogue of the Royal and Noble Authors of England, Works* i. 541). The original MS of one of Lady Temple's poems is bound in HW's copy of the *Poems,* now WSL (Hazen, *SH Bibl.* 76, copy 1).

3. HW owned a copy of Addison's *Miscellaneous Works in Verse and Prose,* 1726 (Hazen, *Cat. of HW's Lib.,* No. 1844).

TO LADY TEMPLE, Saturday 28 January 1764

Printed from a photostat of the MS in the possession of Mr Robert H. Taylor, Princeton, New Jersey, kindly furnished by the late Sir John Murray. First printed in *The Grenville Papers,* ed. W. J. Smith, 1852–3, ii. 256–7. Reprinted, Cunningham iv. 175; Toynbee v. 447. For the history of the MS see *ante* ca 20 Jan. 1764.

Jan. 28, 1764.

I HAVE now, Madam, very carefully studied your Ladyship's poems, in which, as I told you,[1] I can find no faults, but in the longer metre. This I have tried to supply here and there by a syllable, or by little inversions, which mend the cadence; and these I submit to your Ladyship's judgment,[2] as mere mechanic corrections, and not at all as improving the ease and natural grace of the original, much less the poetry, which perhaps suffers by my dull criticisms. Your Ladyship will probably improve on my hints, for your own genteel pen is much more likely to strike out proper alterations, than I who work by dull rules can do. One thing I am sure of, that larger changes than I have ventured to make, would entirely prejudice the agreeable air of your verses, which is so much and so peculiarly your own. When I have the honour of seeing you, I will hope for farther orders as to the impression,[3] which I trust will not be so rigidly confined as you first proposed.

I am Madam
Your most obedient and most
sensibly obliged humble servant

HOR. WALPOLE

1. See previous letter.

2. In returning the MS of the *Poems* to Lady Temple with his corrections, HW presumably included a copy of his prefatory verses addressed to her beginning 'Long had been lost enchanting Sappho's lyre.' The MS in HW's hand, signed 'Horace Walpole' and dated 'January 26th 1764,' was preserved with the present letter and is now in the possession of Mr Robert H. Taylor, Princeton, New Jersey.

3. HW finished printing 100 copies of *Poems by Anna Chamber Countess Temple* at the SH Press 23 April 1764 (Hazen, *SH Bibl.* 74).

From JOHN BOWLE,[1] Monday 6 February 1764

Printed for the first time from the MS now WSL. The MS was presumably sold SH vi. 141 to Thorpe; offered by him, Cat. of Autograph Letters, 1843, lot 3925; sold Puttick and Simpson 12 March 1862 (Extraordinary Collection of Autograph Letters Sale), lot 713 (with HW to John Hutchins 26 Feb. 1771), to Boone; not further traced until resold Christie's 29 July 1971 (property of the Trustees of the 7th Duke of Newcastle), lot 525, to Seven Gables for WSL. Bowle's MS draft of this letter, bound in his 'Travelling Book' (letter copybook), is in the Bowle-Evans Collection, University of Cape Town Library; for the history of this collection see R. F. M. Immelman, *The Bowle-Evans Collection in the University of Cape Town Library,* Rondebosch, South Africa, privately printed, 1958, pp. [iv], 4.

Address (from Bowle's draft): To Horace Walpole Esq. to the care of Messrs Dodsley in Pall Mall, London.

February 6, 1764.

Sir,

I CANNOT resist a violent impulse urging me on to write to you. I beg pardon for the intrusion of a stranger, who will offer nothing but with the greatest deference to your better judgment. Know then, Sir, that I have with singular pleasure but a few days past perused your *Catalogue of Royal and Noble Authors,* and from what I read at the end of your Advertisement[2] am induced to this. In your said work I have noted these omissions, and without a miracle the former could not have found a place in your book. This is a curious autograph on vellum of the Princess Elizabeth entitled *Quid Christus sit et Quam ob rem in mundum venerit. Sermo Bernardini Ochini ex Italico in Latinum Conversus.* 'Tis dedicated to her brother Edward the Sixth in an elegant epistle, is wrote in a good hand,[3] which has been compared with her other performance at the British Museum,[4] and 'tis plain from hence that she was greatly im-

1. (1725–88), F.S.A., 1776; vicar of Idmiston, Wilts; editor of *Don Quixote*.

2. 'I never mean to offer my opinion but with submission to better judgments. . . . I propose my sentiments for the revision of any decree, of any honorary sentence, as I think fit: my fellow-citizens [in the republic of letters], equally free, will vote according to their opinions' (*Royal and Noble Authors,* 2d edn, 1759, i. vi–vii).

3. 'Elizabeth translated an Italian sermon of Occhines, which she transcribed in a hand of great beauty, and sent to her royal brother, as a new year's gift. The dedication is dated Enfield, December 30, but the year is not specified; the MS is now in the Bodleian Library' (Agnes Strickland, *Lives of the Queens of England,* 1842–8, vi. 53).

4. HW made many additions to the list of Elizabeth's works in the 1787 edition of *Royal and Noble Authors,* including three letters to her brother Edward in the BM (Harleian MS 6986, Nos 11–13); the Bodleian MS is not mentioned.

proved in her writing. This has been for somewhat more than two years added to the treasures of the Bodlejan. There are two of her orations to the Oxonians preserved in Wood's *Historia et Antiq.* in the years 65 and 92,[5] the former of which is extant in *Humphredi Vita Juelli,* p. 244.[6]

Perhaps it would be no loss to letters were all the writings of James the First buried in everlasting oblivion: but certainly you did not designedly omit his first sally of authorship—*The Essayes of a Prentise in the Divine Art of Poesie, Edinburgh,* 1585, 4to.[7] 'Tis a work worthy of him and no one else; for who can with any patience read his 'Reulis and Cautelis to be eschewit in Scottis Poesie'?

You will probably be surprised to be told of another of our English kings being an author, and what is more a poet. Such was Richard the Third, if any credit is to be given to a poem called 'The Rising to the Crowne of Richard the Third: Written by Himself,' so it is asserted in the separate title. This at the end of *Licia, or Poems of Love, in Honour of the Admirable and Singular Virtues of his Lady to the Imitation of the best Latin Poets and Others. Whereunto is added The Rising* etc. This is the whole of the title (the motto excepted). There is no mention of author, printer, place, or year.[8] The dedication to Lady Mollineux[9] is dated September 4, 1593. This precarious authority is of much the same nature with yours for placing Edward II among the Royal Authors.[10]— Is not Charles Howard[11] Earl of Carlisle to be added to your list of learned noblemen? Did he not write, as well as publish his three *Embassies*[12] to Muscovy, Sweden,

5. That is, 1565 and 1592; see Anthony à Wood (1632–95), *Historia et antiquitates Universitatis Oxoniensis,* Oxford, 1674, i. 289, 306. The first oration is recorded under the year 1566.

6. 'Illustrissimæ Reginæ Elizabethæ ad Oxonienses oratio,' in Laurence Humphrey (?1527–90), *Ioannis Ivelli Angli, Episcopi Sarisburiensis vita & mors, eiusq.,* 1573 pp. 244–5.

7. An earlier issue of the *Essayes* published at Edinburgh is dated 1584 (BM Cat.).

8. Both *Licia* and 'The Rising to the Crowne of Richard the Third' were written by Giles Fletcher, the elder (1546–1611). The book was printed by John Legate at Cambridge, probably in 1593. It is a very rare work, only three copies being known (G. R. Barnes, *A List of Books Printed in Cambridge at the University Press 1521–1800,* Cambridge, 1935, p. 8; *The English Works of Giles Fletcher, the Elder,* ed. L. E. Berry, Madison, Wisconsin, 1964, pp. 69–72).

9. 'To the worthy, kind, wise, and virtuous Lady, the Lady Mollineux; wife to the Right Worshipful Sir Richard Mollineux Knight' (Fletcher's *Works,* op. cit. 74). Frances Gerard (d. 1620), m. (ca 1590) Sir Richard Molyneux (ca 1560–1622), cr. (1611) Bt.

10. See *Royal and Noble Authors* i. 8–9.

11. (ca 1629–85), cr. (1661) E. of Carlisle.

12. *A Relation of Three Embassies from his sacred Majestie Charles II to the great Duke of Muscovie, the King of Sweden, and the King of Denmark. Performed by the Right Hon[oura]ble the Earle of Carlisle in the Years 1663 & 1664.*

and Denmark? I have not the book to refer to, but some account of it may be seen in Hartley's *Catalogue* G. 68 (which by the way seems to be wrong dated)[13] and in Clavel's ditto, fol[io], 1695, p. 47.[14]

Though Ant. à Wood says nothing of Tiptoft[15] Earl of Worcester, for the reason you mention, in his *Athenæ*,[16] yet he has a pretty copious account of him in his *Hist. et Antiq. Oxon.*, pages 50, 75, v. 2.[17]

Excuse me, Sir, for saying you have much mistaken *Crescimbeni*.[18] Surely he deserves not the appellation of a miserable historian. You have not sufficiently distinguished betwixt the original writer and the translator[19] here. Indeed one shall hardly anywhere meet with such horrid blunders, such foul anachronisms as present themselves in the two articles mentioned by you. But even the historian (if Crescimbeni be true to his original) is free from some mistakes you have imputed to him. I do not find in the page you refer to—Eleanor wife of Edward the Third.[20] *Crescimbeni's* words are—la seconda genita Eliona, overo Lionora [fu maritata] ad Errico terzo [o come altri scrivono, Odoardo Re d'Inghilterra. *Nostre-dame* was misled to this possibly by Londino].[21] Here is no mention of Edward the Third's name, nor in the account of Richard. Turn once more to your authority—la terza Sancia a Riccardo parimente d'Inghilterra.[22] Observe, Sir, he does not say RE d'Inghilterra, and as he explains

Written by an Attendant on the Embassies, and Published with his L[ordshi]ps Approbation, 1669. Carlisle's 'attendant' was Guy Miège (see following letter, n. 6).

13. John Hartley, *Catalogus universalis librorum*, 1699, p. G 68. Carlisle's *Embassies* is misdated 1661.

14. Robert Clavell (d. 1711), *A Catalogue of Books Printed in England since the Dreadful Fire of London in 1666. To the End of Michaelmas Term, 1695*, 4th edn, 1696, p. 47.

15. John Tiptoft (1427–70), 2d Lord Tiptoft; cr. (1449) E. of Worcester. See *Royal and Noble Authors* i. 59–66.

16. *Athenæ Oxonienses*, 2 vols, 1691–2.

17. *Historia et antiquitates Universitatis Oxoniensis* ii. 50, 75–6.

18. Giovanni Mario Crescimbeni (1663–1728) (*ante* 27 Oct. 1757, n. 3). HW refers to him as a 'miserable historian' in his article on Richard I in *Royal and Noble Authors* i. 5.

19. The second volume of Crescimbeni's *Dell' Istoria della volgar poesia*, Venice, 1730–1, contains his Italian translation of Jean de Notredame's *Les vies des plus célèbres et anciens poètes provençaux*, Lyon, 1575.

20. In his article on Richard I HW wrote: 'Crescimbeni's account is a heap of blunders. Richard married Berengaria daughter of Sancho King of Navarre; and no Princess of Provence. In the life of the very Raimond here mentioned, p. 76, Crescimbeni makes the same Eleanor wife of Edward III and Sanchia, the third daughter, wife of Richard I' (*Royal and Noble Authors* i. 4).

21. In the article on 'Ramondo Berlinghieri,' *Dell' Istoria* ii. 72 (HW's 'p. 76' is an error). Eleanor (ca 1223–91), daughter of Raymond Bérenger IV, Count of Provence, married Henry III of England in 1236; Raymond's daughter Sancha (d. 1261) married Richard (1209–72), Earl of Cornwall, in 1243.

22. *Dell' Istoria* ii. 72.

himself 'tis clear he did not mean him. His first annotazione, also p. 96,[23] is a farther collateral proof of this.

And now, Sir, I have only to add that I shall be very sorry to have advanced anything that you may think impertinent, or justly reprehensible. And as I have just pointed out a slight error of yours, I should be glad to be set right in any mistake of my own. If there be anything in this worthy of your notice, and you will please to make use of the underwritten direction, it will come safe to the hands of one who is an admirer of your writings, and as such takes the liberty of subscribing himself

Your most humble servant,

IGNOTUS

PS. If you think proper to answer this, please to direct to Andrew Smith Esq. at Mr Easton's in the Market Place, Sarum. If you do not the writer will think himself justly liable to the censure of the Italian adage—Chi scrive a chi non risponde, od e matto, o ha bisogna.[24] Whatever be the event as he has no thoughts of offending, and as this is known only to himself, he shall make himself easy.

To Horace Walpole Esq.

23. The article on 'Riccardo Re d'Inghilterra' is in *Dell' Istoria* ii. 95–6 (the annotations in this edition, published after Crescimbeni's death, were written by A. F. Seghezzi and Pietro Caterino Zeno). The first annotation on p. 96 points out that Raymond Bérenger's daughter Eleanor was married to Henry III or to Edward King of England, and that Sanchia was married to 'Riccardo Suddetto' who was afterwards King of the Romans.

24. 'He who writes to one who does not reply, either is mad, or has need of something.'

To John Bowle, Saturday 11 February 1764

Printed for the first time from a photostat of the MS pasted in the 'Epistolarium Bowleanum' (a volume of original letters addressed to Bowle), in the Bowle-Evans Collection, University of Cape Town Library. For the history of this collection see the previous letter.

Endorsed by Bowle: See the letter that gave rise to this correspondence in the Travelling Book,[1] J. B. Jan. 20, [17]82.

Address: To Andrew Smith Esq. at Mr Easton's in the Market Place Salisbury. *Frank:* Free Hor. Walpole. *Postmark:* 11 FE.

Arlington Street, Feb. 11th 1764.

Sir,

If you knew me better, you would not suspect me of so much ill breeding or ingratitude as to be capable of not thanking you for the favour of your letter. I am certainly much obliged to you for your informations and corrections, and should my *Catalogue* ever be reprinted,[2] it shall profit by both. I am far from being able to make any work of mine so perfect as I wish it; but in the kind of works in which I have dealt, it is next to impossible for any man to make them near perfection at first. I have wished for and solicited new lights and assistance, and have ever been thankful for receiving them. It has happened to me several times to be furnished with additional materials by gentlemen, like yourself, Sir, unknown to me:[3] but I never was guilty of not owning the obligation by immediate answers. It is only when I have been abused, that I have been silent—those debts indeed I do not intend to repay. In truth, less of this has fallen to my share than I had reason to expect. The trifles I have offered to the public have been in general much more favourably received than they deserved.

The autograph of Queen Elizabeth is new to me. The title of King James's first work I have noted down in my own copy, having only seen the collection since my last edition.[4]

You have raised my curiosity, Sir, extremely about Richard III. I

1. See heading to the previous letter.

2. In 1787 HW printed a quarto edition of *Royal and Noble Authors* which included 'Pieces omitted in the foregoing *Catalogue* . . . and discovered since the volume was printed' and other additions (*Works* i. 526–67). See HW to John Pinkerton 29 June 1787 (Chatterton 292–4).

3. See *ante* ca March 1762, 4 March 1762, and 19 April 1762.

4. HW did not include these items among the 'Pieces omitted' (see n. 2 above).

never heard the least intimation of the piece you mention, and am sorry it rests solely on its own authority. Yet I cannot but suppose there must be some *intrinsic* marks of originality in it, if genuine. Such a man could not easily have written a very common poem. Such a soul must have stamped some marks of itself on its composition, though perhaps no marks of poetry—for Richard, I imagine, did not, like the King of Prussia,[5] write verses only to prove he was an universal genius, which unluckily the latter is not; I am sure not a poet. May I ask where the volume called *Licia* is to be found? is it in the Bodleian Library, or in your possession, Sir? if in the latter, I would fain flatter myself from the goodness you have had for me already that some time or other, when most convenient to you, I might be favoured with a sight of it. I will take the greatest care of it, and return it as quickly as you shall prescribe.

Charles Earl of Carlisle was not an author: the relation of his travels was set forth by one of his attendants.[6]

I will not now pretend to say that I may not have mistaken, and consequently spoken too slightly of Crescimbeni, because I have not the book itself. It was lent to me,[7] and gave me the idea I have expressed. His inaccuracy in the persons he mentions I thought very gross, which you will allow, Sir, is a pretty considerable fault in an historian. However, before I think of another edition, I will certainly reexamine the passage, and as certainly correct myself if I have been mistaken.[8]

It would be very unreasonable, Sir, and yet perhaps not extraordinary, if the encouragement you have given me should make me draw again upon your knowledge and good nature. There is another work of my press, for I cannot call it my own work, which I doubt is subject to still more mistakes and faults than my *Catalogue of Royal and Noble Authors,* the materials of the former being newer and much less discussed. I mean the *Anecdotes of Painting.* If these volumes, Sir, should ever fall in your way, you would add to the

5. Frederick II, K. of Prussia 1740–86. An unauthorized edition of his *Œuvres du philosophe de Sans-Souci* appeared in 1760 (DALRYMPLE 68; MANN v. 403–4, 413).

6. Guy Miège (1644 – ca 1718), author of Carlisle's *Embassies,* 1669 (see previous letter, n. 12). A native of Lausanne, he was undersecretary to Carlisle on his missions.

7. By Joseph Spence (*ante* 27 Oct. 1757). HW may have been misled partly by the errors in Spence's letter to him.

8. Although he was 'mistaken' about the facts Bowle pointed out, HW did not alter the passage in the 1787 edition of *Royal and Noble Authors.*

obligation you have already conferred on me, by either pointing out any errors, or contributing to the collection. You seem, Sir, to have truly a public spirit, and therefore I trust will not think my request very unreasonable.

I am Sir
Your much obliged humble servant
Hor. Walpole

From John Drumgold,[1] Wednesday 15 February 1764

Printed from the MS now wsl. First printed, Toynbee *Supp.* iii. 179–82. Damer-Waller; the MS was sold Sotheby's 5 Dec. 1921 (first Waller Sale), lot 116 (with lot 115), to Wells; given by him to Thomas Conolly, of Chicago, from whom wsl acquired it in 1937.

Address: To the Honourable Horace Walpole at his house, Arlington Street, London.

À Paris le 15 février 1764.

Je profite, Monsieur, avec grand plaisir de l'occasion du Sieur Prault[2] qui va à Londres, pour me rappeler dans votre souvenir. Je ne puis pas m'empêcher de rire quand je pense que c'est à vous que j'écris, et que c'est par un imprimeur que j'écris. Je vous prie donc de vouloir bien marquer quelques bontés à votre confrère. Il va à Londres pour les affaires de son commerce et si vous avez besoin à Paris d'un correspondant pour les nouveautés, ou pour tout autre chose de son district, je puis vous répondre de son intelligence et de sa probité.

Autre chose qui vous regarde encore, M. de la Curne de Sainte-Palaye,[3] mon ami particulier, et l'un de nos académiciens des plus

1. (or Dromgold) (1718–81), born in Paris of Irish parents; educated at the Collège de Navarre and professor of rhetoric there, 1740; aide-de-camp to the Comte de Clermont, 1758, and Col. of cavalry; secretary to the Duc de Nivernais on the peace mission in London, 1762; commandant of the École Militaire, 1763; poet and literary critic (*Dict. de biographie française* xi. 795; Richard Hayes, *Biographical Dictionary of Irishmen in France,* Dublin, 1949, pp. 73–4). HW met Drumgold during his visits to Paris and owned several of his literary works (Hazen, *Cat. of HW's Lib.*, No. 3920).

2. Laurent-François Prault (d. 1780), Paris bookseller, or Marcel Prault, well-known Paris publisher in 1768.

3. Jean-Baptiste de la Curne de Sainte-Palaye (1697–1781), linguist, literary historian, and antiquary.

distingués,[4] me charge de m'adresser à vous pour avoir réponse à la question suivante. Vous avez imprimé dans votre ouvrage *Of the Royal Authors,* un poème provençal de Richard *Cœur-de-Lion.*[5] M. de Sainte-Palaye, qui vous devez connaître par ses mémoires dans l'Académie des Inscriptions,[6] et par le jour qu'il a répandu sur notre ancienne chevalerie,[7] et nos vieux romanciers,[8] travaille actuellement à un glossaire de l'ancienne langue française.[9] Il a vu paraître il y a quelques années dans un ouvrage périodique à Londres[10] le poème provençal de Richard. On le disait tiré d'un recueil d'anciennes poésies françaises qui se trouvait en Angleterre, qui contenait d'autres pièces inconnues et curieuses, et l'on demandait l'explication du poème du Roi Richard. M. de Sainte-Palaye offrit de donner cette explication et demanda qu'on lui envoya le premier vers seulement des pièces anciennes que l'on disait renfermées dans le recueil. Il n'a jamais pu avoir de réponse. Vous êtes plus à portée qu'un autre de lui rendre ce service. M. de Sainte-Palaye a le sonnet de Richard que vous avez rapporté. En lui citant le premier vers des autres poésies manuscrites annoncées dans l'ouvrage périodique, dont je viens de parler, M. de Sainte-Palaye verrait s'il les connaît ou non. Il travaille depuis longtemps à un glossaire complet de l'ancien français, comme je vous ai dit, et la connaissance de ces anciennes pièces lui est nécessaire.

Vous m'avez voulu faire l'honneur, lorsque j'étais à Londres, l'hiver dernier,[11] de faire imprimer chez vous, quelques-unes de mes

4. Sainte-Palaye was admitted to the Académie des Inscriptions in 1724 and to the Académie Française in 1758 (NBG).

5. The poem, said to have been written by Richard I, had been brought to HW's attention by Joseph Spence (*ante* 27 Oct. 1757). Copies of the MS in the Laurentian Library at Florence were sent to HW by Sir Horace Mann (MANN v. 157, 169, 186) and it was printed in *Royal and Noble Authors,* 2d edn, 1759, i. 6–8. Mann wrote HW 25 March 1758 that 'St Palais, who has taken the most pains to interpret the old Provençal language, is uncertain in many cases' about the meaning of the poem (ibid. v. 186).

6. The Académie des Inscriptions et Belles-Lettres, founded in 1663.

7. *Mémoires sur l'ancienne chevalerie, considérée comme un établissement politique et militaire,* 2 vols, 1759. HW's copy is Hazen, op. cit., No. 809. A third volume was published in 1781.

8. *Histoire littéraire des troubadours,* 3 vols, 1774. HW's copy, now in the BM, is Hazen, op. cit., No. 3113. He wrote Lady Ossory 23 Nov. 1774: 'It is very curious, I have longed for it several years, and yet am cruelly disappointed' (OSSORY i. 218).

9. *Glossaire de l'ancienne langue française,* announced in a prospectus, 1756, but never completed by Sainte-Palaye. The *Dictionnaire historique de l'ancien langage français* based on his work was published in 10 vols, 1875–82.

10. Not identified.

11. HW wrote Montagu 17 May 1763 about a breakfast party at SH for Madame de Boufflers which Drumgold could not attend due to illness (MONTAGU ii, 71–2). He was in London 1762–3 as secretary to the Duc de Nivernais.

faibles productions,[12] mais, vous désiriez réellement faire paraître quelque chose de M. de Nivernois.[13] À l'egard du dernier vous pourrez avoir contentement. Voici comment. Il y a du temps que je m'occupe à mettre ensemble quelques réflexions sur l'origine, la nature et la composition des langues françaises et anglaises comparativement entr'elles.[14] Pour servir de preuve à cet objet, j'ai traduit différents morceaux des poètes anglais de tous les âges, et des vieux français ⟨ de fai⟩re[15] paraître cet ouvrage d'abord en Angleterre, parce que ⟨c'est⟩ un droit naturel. Ce sera pour ainsi dire, l'histoire de la langue, les originaux étant cités. M. de Nivernois m'a donné un morceau qu'il a composé sur les poètes provençaux, les troubadours. Il a traduit en vers des morceaux charmants de leur poésie, et vous sentez qu'ils n'ont pas perdu entre ces mains. Le tout pourra faire deux petits in-12°, et j'avoue que je serais flatté qu'ils portassent le nom de *Strawberry Hill*. J'ai de plus une raison particulière. Vous savez que je me suis établi *votre traducteur*. Comme je prends depuis *Gower*[16] jusqu'à nos jours, je m'arrêterai à vous, et je serais bien aise de savoir si mon idée vous plaît, parce que j'aurais dessein d'y joindre une petite reconnaissance poétique *à mon imprimeur*. Mes amis ici sont on ne peut pas plus contents de ce qu'ils ont vu de Gower, de Chaucer et de quelques autres. Mais, si vous acceptez la proposition, je vous prierai de vouloir bien être non seulement *le correcteur de l'impression,* mais, bien plus encore des choses.[17] Marquez-moi, je vous prie, ce que vous en pensez, parce que si cela ne vous duisait[17a] pas, je prendrais d'autres mesures.

Adieu, Monsieur, et recevez, je vous prie, les assurances bien sincères de l'hommage de votre plus fidèle serviteur,

Dromgold

12. HW never printed any work by Drumgold at SH, but the 'Portrait de Jean Comte de Granville. Traduit de l'Anglois de Monsieur Walpole par Monsieur le Colonel Drumgold' was included in *Works* i. 32.

13. Louis-Jules-Barbon Mancini-Mazarini (1716–98), Duc de Nivernais; French ambassador to England 1762–3; HW's friend and correspondent. Nivernais' French translation of HW's *Essay on Modern Gardening* was printed at SH in 1785 (*post* 6 Jan., 1 Feb., 30 April 1785).

14. This comparative study was apparently never published.

15. There is a tear in the MS at this point.

16. John Gower (ca 1325–1408), English poet.

17. The words 'et je l'abandonnerai entièrement' have been written over.

17a. Apparently so spelled in the MS, but the sense seems to be 'convenait.'

PS. M. Prault vous remettra de ma part trois petites gravures[18] qui sont des chefs-d'œuvres en ce gen⟨re.⟩ Cela ne vaut pas cependant ce que vous m'avez donné de vos impressions.

From JOHN BOWLE, Thursday 16 February 1764

Printed for the first time from a photostat of Bowle's MS draft, bound in his 'Travelling Book' in the Bowles-Evans Collection, University of Cape Town Library. For the history of this collection see *ante* 6 Feb. 1764. The original letter actually sent to HW is missing; it was offered by Thorpe, Cat. of Autograph Letters, 1843, lot 405; 1844, lot 187; not further traced.

Idmerston near Sarum, February 16, 1764.

Sir,

As I have the satisfaction to find my first letter not unacceptable, I shall without reserve open myself to you. I am, Sir, a clergyman, and have for several years past, without any emolument to myself been a humble retainer in the service of letters. Dr Douglas[1] in his book against Lauder[2] has mentioned my assistance to him.[3] Thus much for the trifling article of self. As to that of Elizabeth I have only to add that I had the luck to meet with this some years back at Ayliffe's[4] sale at Blandford, and at the librarian Mr Owen's[5] earnest request I gave it to the Bodlejan. The transcript of the dedication I have by me, and is at your service if you desire it. I have reason to think it was some time or other stole out of the Cotton Library,[6] for in the inside of the cover occurs the word Tiberius, and the books

18. Not identified.

1. John Douglas (1721–1807), D.D.; Bp of Carlisle 1787–91, of Salisbury 1791–1807.

2. William Lauder (d. 1771), whose *Essay on Milton's Use and Imitation of the Moderns in his Paradise Lost,* 1750, charged Milton with plagiarism, on the basis of documents which Lauder had forged.

3. Douglas's *Milton Vindicated from the Charge of Plagiarism,* 1751, exposed Lauder's forgeries. On pp. 52–3 Douglas acknowledges Bowle's assistance and pays tribute to his learning. Douglas's letters to Bowle in 1749–50 concerning the forgeries are in the Bowle-Evans Collection, University of Cape Town Library.

4. John Ayliffe (ca 1723–59), of Blandford Forum, Dorset, whose estate was sold to meet his debts when he was convicted of forgery (GM 1759, xxix. 548–9, 578–80).

5. Humphrey Owen (1702–68), librarian of the Bodleian 1747–68; principal of Jesus College, Oxford, 1763–8 (Foster, *Alumni Oxon.*).

6. The collection of MSS formed by Sir Robert Bruce Cotton (1571–1631). It was purchased from the Cotton family by the government in 1707 and in 1753 was removed to the British Museum.

there were ranged, if I have been rightly informed, by the names of the twelve Cæsars.[7] To no purpose I presume would it be for you to seek for *Licia,* but, Sir, as I have raised your curiosity I shall with much pleasure contrive to convey the book to you some time this spring as possibly, I may visit London. And here, Sir, I cannot avoid mentioning to you the utility of some scheme, if such could be struck out by the booksellers, and they would certainly find their account in it, of furnishing their labourers of the quill with such rare books, as they must frequently stand in need of in the prosecution of their studies. Their undertakings must unavoidably be often retarded or imperfectly executed on account of the want of that assistance, which from such and such books might most certainly be furnished to them.

I have only cursorily looked over the 2 volumes of your *Anecdotes.*[8] The serious perusal of them is a pleasure I hope to have hereafter. I have this past winter knowing nothing of your last publication made a list of English sculptors or such as have resided in England from 1591 to the end of the last century: but this consisting of but 25 I should hardly think worthy of your notice. However I have marked as far as my few books would give me any accounts their first and last performances. I presume, Sir, you specify the time when chalcography first made its appearance among us.[9] I do not love to affect singularity, but I cannot help informing you that I have a book printed Lond. 1545 in which there are cuts that have greatly the appearance of copper.[10] I have carefully compared it with two foreign printed books of the years 1555 and 1563 abounding with several beautiful wooden cuts and the workmanship appears in the lines and execution very different from these. This is carrying the account itself to a more distant period of time than I have read of and indeed to several years before the discovery of the rolling press: how they worked of[f] their plates before the invention of this useful engine I have never learnt. I should think myself happy if in anything I could

7. In the original library the volumes were kept in fourteen presses above which were busts of the twelve Cæsars and of Cleopatra and Faustina.

8. The first two volumes of *Anecdotes of Painting,* SH, 1762.

9. 'The first [English] book that appeared with cuts from copperplates, at least the first, that so industrious an inquirer as Mr Ames had observed, was "The Birth of Mankind, otherwyse called, The Woman's Book," dedicated to Queen Catherine and published by Thomas Raynalde in 1540, with many small copper cuts, but to these no name was affixed' (HW's *Catalogue of Engravers,* 2d edn, SH, 1765, p. 5).

10. HW's first article on individual engravers mentions '*Thomæ Gemini Lysiensis compendiosa totius Anatomes delineatio, ære exarata,* folio 1545' (ibid. 6).

be of service to you in your literary pursuits, and have the honour though unknown to you of subscribing myself

Your most obedient humble servant,

J. BOWLE

TO JOHN BOWLE, Saturday 25 February 1764

Printed for the first time from a photostat of the MS pasted in the 'Epistolarium Bowleanum,' in the Bowle-Evans Collection, University of Cape Town Library. For the history of this collection see *ante* 6 Feb. 1764.

Address: To the Reverend Mr Bowle at Idmerston near Salisbury. *Frank:* Free Hor. Walpole. *Postmark:* 25 FE.

Arlington Street, Feb. 25, 1764.

Sir,

IT WILL not be a small addition to the obligations you have laid on me already,[1] if you let me have the satisfaction of being acquainted with you when you come to London. Your profession is a recommendation of itself, and the dignity of it must be increased in my eyes in finding you amused with pursuits like my own.

The booksellers of London, I fear, will not be induced to come into your plan of keeping curious books by them. Any man who lives on the spot as I do, and sees that nothing but new trash of the most despicable kinds has, I had almost said, any vent, knows how little encouragement there is for whatever has been out of fashion for a month; and I assure you, Sir, most of our booksellers have no views but of profit.

Give me leave to repeat to you that I am much obliged to your kind informations, and that I am, Sir,

Your most obedient humble servant

HOR. WALPOLE

1. See *ante* 6 Feb. and 16 Feb. 1764.

TO GROSVENOR BEDFORD, Wednesday 29 February 1764

Printed from Cunningham iv. 200, where the letter was first printed. Reprinted, Toynbee vi. 23. The history of the MS and its present whereabouts are not known.

Feb. 29, 1764.

Dear Sir,

I WILL get you to send one of the porters of the Exchequer, in whom you have most confidence, with the enclosed three guineas. Two are for the prisoners that are sick in the new jail, Southwark;[1] the other for those in the common side of the Marshalsea prison.[2] He must not say from whom he comes, but in the name of A.B., and don't let him go into the prison, for the jail distemper[3] is there.

I want some gilt paper and a penknife. Yours ever,

H.W.

From COUNT VORONTSOV,[1] Wednesday 28 March 1764

Printed from Toynbee *Supp.* iii. 182, where the letter was first printed. The history of the MS and its present whereabouts are not known.

À Londres ce 28 mars 1764.

Monsieur,

ON NE saurait être plus sensible que je le suis de la bonté que vous avez eu de satisfaire mon désir en m'envoyant les ouvrages[2] qui m'étaient connus de reputation et qui me causeront une vraie sat-

1. The County Gaol, Southwark, known as the New Gaol, 'situated in a populous neighborhood, I did not wonder to see in March 1776 several felons sick on the floors. No bedding nor straw; no infirmary' (John Howard, *The State of the Prisons in England and Wales,* 1777, p. 233).

2. In High Street, Southwark, adjoining the King's Bench prison where debtors were brought who had been arrested for the lowest sums. 'There are, in the whole, near sixty rooms; and yet only six of them now left for common-side debtors' (ibid. 205–6).

3. Jail fever, a virulent type of typhus fever, endemic in crowded jails (John Pringle, 'An Account of Several Persons Seized with the Gaol-fever,' in the Royal Society's *Philosophical Transactions,* 1753, xlviii. 42–55).

---

1. Alexander Romanovich Vorontsov (1741–1805), Russian ambassador to the Empire 1761–2, to England 1762–4 (MANN vi. 55 n. 27).

2. Apparently presentation copies of works by HW; these copies have not been located.

isfaction à lire, lorsque je serai un peu plus versé dans la langue que vous avez si enrichi, Monsieur, par vos productions que je ne l'ai été jusqu'à présent. Je ne suis pas moins flatté du billet[3] obligéant dont vous m'avez honoré; permettez que vous en marquant ma reconnaissance, j'aie la satisfaction de vous renouveler les assurances de la parfaite considération avec laquelle j'ai l'honneur d'être,

Monsieur,

Votre très humble et très obéissant serviteur,

COMTE ALEXANDRE DE W<ORONZOW>

TO ARTHUR ONSLOW, Saturday 31 March 1764

Printed from a photostat of the MS, kindly furnished by the late 6th Earl of Onslow, bound in a volume of 'Private Papers O[nslow] 1630–1863' deposited in the Guildford Muniment Room, Castle Arch, Guildford, Surrey. First printed in C. E. Vulliamy, *The Onslow Family*, 1953, pp. 151–2 (one passage omitted). The MS descended in the Onslow family to the late Lord Onslow; deposited in the Guildford Muniment Room, with a collection of Onslow family papers, by the Dowager Countess of Onslow in 1972.

Strawberry Hill, March 31, 1764.

Sir,

I CANNOT express how much I am obliged to you for the great trouble you have been so good as to give yourself. I have so slender a title to it, that I cannot help attributing a little of it to your love of and zeal for the arts. This sounds ungrateful: but I do not know how to assume to myself alone the pains you have taken. All I can do, both to pay the debt of the arts and my own, is, to improve my next edition[1] by your communications[2]—at the same time that I must do justice to Vertue,[3] by taking from him to myself many of the faults, at least, omissions that you blame. My fear of making so trifling and uninteresting a work too prolix, prevailed on me to omit many stories that he had collected, especially on the less shining artists, for I think, Sir, you and I differ in nothing but when you ascribe more merit to our English performers than I do. Some of

3. Missing.

1. Of *Anecdotes of Painting.*
2. Onslow's letter to HW is missing.
3. George Vertue, whose MSS, acquired by HW in 1758, were the basis of *Anecdotes of Painting* (*ante* 29 Aug. 1758, n. 5).

their paintings and some of their drawings, have and may have, a degree of merit, but when compared with the works of really great masters, I fear we ought not to say much for our friends.

Richardson,[4] Thornhill,[5] and other painters, whom, as you observe, Sir, I have omitted, are reserved for the last volume.[6] The etchings of the first, some of which I have, intended to mention in his life there, he being so much more known as a painter than engraver; and though I have now and then mentioned a person in both capacities, it is but seldom, nor, as I said before, did I care to swell my volumes too much. I have been reproached already for saying so much on the artists of this country, for it is not everybody, Sir, that has your candour and indulgence.

Among the many curious notices, Sir, which you have sent me, I must particularly thank you for the anecdotes relating to T. Britton.[7] I have a print of him,[8] and have long wished to know more of him; for I cannot, like my censors, think it an offence to tell anybody what they did not know before.[9] Ferg's[10] works I am well acquainted with and have always admired as inferior to few masters who have come into this country. Of Van Straaten[11] and Wollaston[12] I knew nothing. They shall not be forgotten, nor your relation Mr Hillier,[13] for an account of whom I am extremely obliged to you.

I do not grudge the pains this work has cost me, while you, Sir, and a few other curious and good-natured persons are pleased with it. Had I not undertaken it, Vertue's manuscripts might have perished, and the work have remained impracticable. Such as it is, there will always be men glad of even such a history of the arts in their own country. They have flourished so little here, that I question

4. Jonathan Richardson, the elder (1665–1745).

5. Sir James Thornhill (1675–1734).

6. The fourth volume of *Anecdotes* was printed in 1771 but not published until 1780 (Hazen, *SH Bibl.* 63). In the article on Richardson, pp. 15–19, HW mentions 'a few etchings by his hand, particularly two or three of Milton, and his own head.' The account of Thornhill is on pp. 20–3.

7. Thomas Britton (ca 1654–1714), the celebrated 'musical small-coal man.' His portrait was painted twice by J[?ohn] Wollaston. HW added an account of him in *Anecdotes,* 2d edn, iii. 145–6.

8. Engraved by Grignion after Woolaston; it is bound in HW's copy, now WSL, of *Anecdotes,* 2d edn, iii. 145, with a long note in HW's hand.

9. The rest of this paragraph is omitted by Vulliamy.

10. Franz de Paula Ferg (1689–1740), Viennese marine and landscape painter, who lived in England ca 1720–40. See *Anecdotes* iv. 25–6.

11. Hendrik van der Straaten (ca 1665–1722), landscape painter, included in *Anecdotes,* 2d edn, iii. 144.

12. J[?ohn] Wollaston or Woolaston (b. ca 1672), portrait painter (*Anecdotes,* 2d edn, iii. 145–6; J. Kerslake, *Early Georgian Portraits,* 1977, i. 305).

13. Not identified; HW did not include him in the 2d edn of *Anecdotes.*

whether any man who could perform the task better, would have condescended to it. The assistance of gentlemen, curious, communicative and able, like you, Sir, may enable me to make the next edition more worthy of appearing in public. It is for that public, Sir, that I beg you to continue your cooperation, and, if you do not think it too much trouble, pray do not apprehend that you can tire me, who reap such benefit from your correspondence and who am Sir

Your bounden and much obliged humble servant

Hor. Walpole

From James West,[1] Saturday 31 March 1764

Printed from the MS now WSL. First printed, Toynbee *Supp.* iii. 183–4. Damer-Waller; the MS was sold Sotheby's 5 Dec. 1921 (first Waller Sale), lot 195, to Wells; given by him to Thomas Conolly, of Chicago, from whom WSL acquired it in 1937.

March 31, 1764, Covent Garden.

Dear Sir,

I AM just returned from a most delightful morning at Strawberry Hill, and owe you infinite thanks for the entertainment, instruction and erudition received there. You have truly made amends for your villainous *Augustan* reflections on Gothic taste, in your books,[2] where by the by, is more wit, than ought to assemble with true antiquity; however I forgive you, whether the manes of Leland,[3] Camden[4] and Hearne[5] will or no, the young antiquary Bishop[6] with you, can best tell: though I have still my fears that Tully, Horace or Pliny will still lay some claim to Strawberry. Your library instructs, your gallery delights, and your cabinet makes one wonder, how all the fine things

1. (1703–72), F.S.A.; P.R.S. 1768–72; M.P.; politician and antiquary. 'He had a very curious collection of old pictures, English coins, English prints, and MSS' (HW to Cole 7 July 1772, Cole i. 265). For HW's purchases at the sale of his collection in 1773 see ibid. i. 300, 305.

2. West presumably has in mind the recently published volumes of *Anecdotes of Painting*.

3. John Leland (ca 1506–52), antiquary.

4. William Camden (1551–1623), historian and antiquary; author of *Britannia,* 1586.

5. Thomas Hearne (1678–1735), antiquary; editor of Leland and Camden.

6. Charles Lyttelton, Bp of Carlisle, who was a fellow of the Society of Antiquaries. HW informed Lord Hertford 5 April 1764: 'The Bishop of Carlisle has been with me two days at Strawberry' (Conway ii. 362).

of this country should come there. But let me ask you who did the ceiling of the gallery, and the wainscotting, gilding and glass work of it.[7]

The world owe you much for the accounts of English painters and engravers, give me leave to ask if you have any register of the works of Raphael, Corregio, Titian, Rubens, Vandyke etc. *in England,* and where *deposited.*[8] It would help us idle travellers much in our studio, and begin to grow fond of the mother, when we grow too old for the daughters. We are now in the pleasing recollection of what satisfaction we received at Strawber[r]y, which is not more the object of delight, than its master is, of the true respect of,

Dear Sir,

Your much obliged and most obedient faithful servant,

J. WEST

From SIR WILLIAM MUSGRAVE,[1] Tuesday 3 April 1764

Printed from the MS now WSL. First printed, Toynbee *Supp.* iii. 184. Damer-Waller; the MS was sold Sotheby's 5 Dec. 1921 (first Waller Sale), lot 164, to Wells; given by him to Thomas Conolly, of Chicago, from whom WSL acquired it in 1937.

Cleveland Row, Tuesday, 3 April 1764.

SIR Wm. Musgrave presents his compliments to Mr Walpole and has taken the liberty to send him a short specimen of the intended catalogue of English heads.[2] Sir Wm. relies upon Mr Walpole's usual

7. For 'the ceiling of the Gallery' HW paid Thomas Bromwich (d. 1787), the fashionable decorator, £115.0.0 on 2 April 1763; for 'the five painted tops of the Gallery windows and the yellow star in the ceiling of the Cabinet' he paid William Peckitt (1731–95), glass painter, originally a carver and gilder of York, £34.14.0 on 15 May 1762 (*Strawberry Hill Accounts . . . kept by Mr Horace Walpole,* ed. Paget Toynbee, Oxford, 1927, p. 9). Among the West MSS at Alscott Park, near Stratford-upon-Avon, is a sheet containing sketches of Gothic 'patterns of Strawberry Hill' (information from the late Sir Lewis Namier).

8. HW recorded many works by these painters in his 'Visits to Country Seats,' but had no 'register' of them.

1. (1735–1800), 6th Bt, 1755; barrister and antiquary.

2. Published in 1769, 2 vols in 4, as *A Biographical History of England, from Egbert the Great to the Revolution,* by the Rev. James Granger (1723–76), vicar of Shiplake, Oxon. It was dedicated to HW, who assisted Granger in the work (COLE i. 151–2, 156–7, 164; MANN vii. 211 and n. 17). HW's copies, now WSL and in the Princeton Univ. Library, are Hazen, *Cat. of HW's Lib.,* Nos 541 and 3813.

goodness to excuse his giving him so much trouble—but Mr Granger (who is engaged in this undertaking) is now in town and would think himself very unhappy if he should be obliged to return without putting himself and his work under Mr Walpole's protection and receiving from him that assistance and advice which he could not hope for in a like degree from any other quarter.

As soon as Mr Granger has finished transcribing Mr West's collection[3] he will do himself the honour to wait upon Mr Walpole for his commands.[4]

From JOHN BROMFIELD,[1] Sunday 8 April 1764

Printed for the first time from a photostat of Bromfield's MS copy, kindly furnished by Mr Francis Russell. The copy, bound with Bromfield's copies of his letters to HW 14 April and 16 May 1764 and of his 'Notes, Strictures, and Corrections etc.' on *Anecdotes of Painting,* is in the possession of a lady in England who wishes to remain anonymous; see Hazen, *Cat. of HW's Lib.,* No. 2534. The history and present whereabouts of the letter actually sent to HW are not known.

The year of the letter is determined by Bromfield's letter to HW *post* 16 May 1764.

Petworth, April 8.

MR BROMFIELD presents his compliments to Mr Walpole; has sent enclosed as many sheets,[2] as could be contained conveniently under one cover; and will by the next post, send the re-

3. See previous letter, n. 1. HW wrote in his 'Book of Materials,' 1771 (now WSL), pp. 1–2: 'I had been thirty years collecting English heads, and ranged mine according to the several reigns. Mr Granger of Shiplake, who had begun a collection, took the hint, and after ranging Sir W[illiam] Musgrave's collection in that method, and making a catalogue from thence and from mine and Mr West's collections, published a biographic list down to the Revolution.'

4. See *post* 24 April 1764.

1. (ca 1726–92), only son of John Bromfield of Lewes, Sussex; educ. Trinity College, Oxford; antiquary (*Sussex Archæological Collections,* 1862, xiv. 244; Foster, *Alumni Oxon.*).

2. 'In my packet of April 8th I enclosed ten quarto sheets which . . . relate to about 40 pages only of the first vol. [of *Anecdotes of Painting*]' (Bromfield to HW *post* 14 April 1764). This was doubtless part of the 'manuscript in sheets, written by Mr Bloomfield [*sic*], from Lord Egremont's, at Petworth, to Horace Walpole, relative to a new edition of the *Anecdotes of Painting in England,* very interesting and curious,' sold SH vi. 124 to Thorpe; offered by Thorpe, Cat. of MSS, 1844, lot 397 (with 'two letters to Horace Walpole, relating to the valuable collection of pictures of Lord Egremont at Petworth'); not traced since 1855. See Hazen, *Cat. of HW's Lib.,* No. 2534. The copy of the 'Notes, Strictures, and Corrections etc.' in Bromfield's hand (see

mainder, with a letter[3] to apologize for so long, and unlucky a delay; which, as it was not only involuntary, but unavoidable, he flatters himself, will meet with the readier pardon.

From JOHN BROMFIELD, Saturday 14 April 1764

Printed for the first time from a photostat of Bromfield's MS copy, kindly furnished by Mr Francis Russell. For the history of the MS and its present whereabouts see *ante* 8 April 1764. For the letter actually sent to HW see ibid. n. 2.

The year of the letter is determined by Bromfield's letter to HW *post* 16 May 1764.

Petworth, April 14th.

THE obliging manner, in which you express your acceptance of my proposed assistance, might justly have demanded a more ready, and more early acknowledgment of your favour of February 23.[1] It is with pain that I reflect on the suspense, that, so long, and unexpected a silence must necessarily have occasioned; but, having been attacked immediately after the receipt of your letter, by an epidemic disorder which has been almost general in these parts, and which, though of no long continuance, having left an uncommon giddiness in my head, I have till these few days past, found myself quite incapable of drawing into order, and transcribing, my notes, that were before scattered in loose detached pieces; the moment, however, that I found myself in any degree equal to the task, I resumed the work; and although I am sensible that you will think the inequality of the writing relishes not a little of the before-mentioned giddiness, like the Archbishop of Granada's homily in *Gil Blas*,[2] yet, I flatter myself, that your good nature will overlook the inaccuracy of the writing, in consideration of the above accident.

The first four sheets, and half the fifth were written above six

heading) consists of forty-eight quarto sheets closely written on both sides, containing many elaborate and detailed comments on the first two volumes of *Anecdotes*.

3. *Post* 14 April 1764.

1. Missing.

2. After suffering a stroke of apoplexy, the Archbishop wrote a homily which Gil Blas judged to be below standard; his criticism resulted in his dismissal from the Archbishop's service (Le Sage, *Histoire de Gil Blas de Santillane*, Book VII, Chap. iv).

months since, and should have been written over again; but apprehending that a longer delay might be more disagreeable, than any inaccuracy of hand, or composition, I have adventured to trespass on your good nature, by sending those few sheets in their original rough form, rather than make you ⟨ ⟩ a longer space.

In my packet of April 8th I enclosed ten quarto sheets which, as they relate to about 40 pages only of the first vol.[3] might justly give the most terrible apprehensions of what is to follow; and perhaps, may appear too formidable, to be adventured on as a reader. I must observe, therefore, th⟨at⟩ as the first vol. has engrossed seven-eighths of my observations, so the first 40 o⟨dd⟩ pages of that volume take up three-fourths of that quantity.

My motives, in undertaking this work, I have already mentioned; it may not, therefore, be improper, in this place, to observe, that having no view nor pride to appear as a coadjutor, in a work, the whole merit of which is justly due, and ought to be attributed to the generous editor alone, I with great pleasure, submit the whole of those notes, etc., to your sole use. I am perfectly sensible, that most of them are too prolix for the public view; and therefore beg that you would make use of such only, as you may yourself approve;[4] and that you would abbreviate, new-model, or abridge even those, in such manner as may best suit your conveniency or taste.

I have been tediously minute in my criticism, but, be pleased to remember, that they are intended, in great part, for your private use alone, and not for the public, or I should not have been so free; besides, as they are submitted to your own censure and correction, you are quite at liberty to dash out the unnecessary, trifling, or faulty passages.

I have sometimes brought tedious quotations from history to prove to you particular facts; such, for instance, as that Windsor was a favourite royal residence long before Henry III's days;[5] but it is by no means necessary to insert such articles in your work. They are inserted merely to convince and satisfy yourself and therefore a single line, by way of note, may suffice, just to observe, that Windsor was evidently a royal seat before the Conquest, and a stronghold presently after; perhaps with a view to render the royal residence more secure.

3. Of *Anecdotes of Painting*.

4. HW appears to have made little or no use of Bromfield's lengthy criticisms.

5. Henry I established Windsor Castle as a royal residence ca 1107–10 (T. E. Harwood, *Windsor Old and New*, privately printed, 1929, pp. 78–9).

In some places I have not set down my authority; that is, where I have only found the note in my memoranda, and the author's name has been omitted, or when I well knew the truth of the position, though I could not recollect the authority for it.

In some passages, I may seem to have idly trifled with your time and patience, by making long digressions from the point; but this I presume, that I have never done but with a view of hinting to you reasons, and authorities, for supporting my own opinion, when I have adventured to dissent from yours, or the author's, and although they may appear, of themselves, not to merit much notice, yet, whatever may tend to correct, or improve, such a work as the *Anecdotes,* etc., is certainly worth a single reading, at least.

After all, I fear, that I must necessarily plead guilty to the charges of prolixity and digression, as I have sometimes taken up a page, nay two or three pages, merely with a view of convincing you of the necessity or propriety of altering or omitting in your next edition a single passage, or perhaps a word.

The hints, with respect to the words *fast, gestes, vestiges,* and *ostensible,* or *ostensibly,* and such like, are in a more particular manner submitted to your own private judgment; for, they ought, by no means, to have any place in public, either by way of note, supplement, or appendix. On this subject, it may not be improper, once for all to observe, that foreign words, terms, and modes of expression, are frequently admitted in the epistolary style, and in works of humour, etc., as well as in pieces destined for the stage, with advantage; but, in a serious historical deduction of facts, in a narrative of the progress of the arts, in Britain only, I presume, that exotic expressions can hardly be allowed admissible.

With regard to my own observations, etc., I have so little time to revise my own sheets, that, I fear, you will frequently find me tripping; my eagerness to come to a conclusion has probably rendered some of the articles a little confused. Two, I have already observed; the first of which is that I have, on the picture of the marriage of Henry VI,[6] said that the Princess of Castile,[7] wife of Edmond Langley, Duke of York, left no issue; though I have in the proper place marked it as faulty; and the other is, in the composition of the article relative to

6. See *Anecdotes* i. 33–5 and GRAY ii. 68 n. 12.

7. Isabel (ca 1355–92) of Castile, m. (1372) Edmund (Plantagenet), cr. (1385) D. of York. Their marriage produced two sons: Edward, 2d D. of York, and Richard, cr. (1414) E. of Cambridge.

the picture of Margaret, Arthur, and Henry Tudor, by Mabuse;[8] where I have omitted my third reason for dissenting from the author of the *Anecdotes*.

It may also appear odd, that I have sometimes addressed myself, or my observations to Mr Walpole, sometimes to the author, and sometimes perhaps to the reader. But, having written most of those articles above six months since, and many of them being composed by pieces at several times, it will not appear surprising if the connection between the several passages should not always be preserved perfect or entire.

Several particulars I have taken the liberty to refer to your own determination, assisted by some of our more rare historians, from your own library; for being only a temporary resident here, having retired to my relations[9] for the recovery of my health, which had suffered greatly by a long and painful illness in London, I have no conveniency of forming a study, or of keeping any great number of books with me, and this place is so ill furnished, as to be incapable of supplying the deficiency ⟨of⟩ any private gentleman's library. So that I am generally compelled to trespass ⟨on⟩ the good nature of Lord Winterton,[10] for whatever books his library affords, which indeed are not many, and those few, except the classics, are mostly modern, as his house at Shillingley was built only for a month's residence in the summer, and his Lordship is not yet come to a resolution where to build a larger.

You may probably ask me, what is become of the noble library of the ancient Percies at Petworth once open to every man of learning and merit; to which, I am compelled to answer, with a heavy heart, that from the inauspicious hour when it fell into the hands ⟨of⟩ the Wyndhams,[11] it became totally useless to the world. The door of the library is kept as closed as that of the late owner's kitchen and cellar.

On the subject of this family, give me leave to observe, that although it may appear odd ⟨to⟩ you, that some of the capital, and a great number of the other, paintings in the Earl of Egremont's house

8. See *Anecdotes* i. 49–50.

9. A Mrs Bromfield, who was living at Petworth in 1762 and paid the window tax on eleven windows, may have been the relative Bromfield was visiting (*Sussex Archæological Collections*, 1961, xcix. 111).

10. Edward Turnour Garth (after 1744, Garth Turnour) (1734–88), of Shillinglee Park, Sussex; cr. (1761) Bn and (1766) E. Winterton (Ireland); M.P.; F.R.S., 1767.

11. In 1750 Petworth passed into the possession of Sir Charles Wyndham, 2d E. of Egremont. At his death 21 Aug. 1763 it became the property of his son, George O'Brien Wyndham (1751–1837), 3d E. of Egremont.

at Petworth are unknown; yet it will not appear so extraordinary when you recollect that Josceline Percy, the last Earl of Northumberland,[12] left an heiress[13] in her childhood; that Charles Duke of Somerset[14] who married that lady, was quite < > though a man of excellent understanding; and that having survived the heiress of Percy and renounced his only son[15] by her, he married again in his old age; and having survived all the servants that were possessed of accurate lists of the paintings, he refused to grant new lists, or copies, to the new servants, so that when he died half the portraits were quite unknown by the family; and the servants and agents of Duke Algernoon, having on his accession to the title, etc., carried off all the papers that could be found, for purposes relative to their master's claim to the whole Percy estate; when they were reclaimed, on the Duke's death, no perfect list could be found among them by the next heir, the late Earl of Egremont[16]—and though it's probable there were several in the house at Duke Charles' death, and that they were carried off by Duke Algernoon's agents, yet nothing of the kind could be procured from the present Countess of Northumberland.[17] One old list was found of some particular pieces, a copy of which was delivered by the Earl of Egremont to his groom of the chambers[18] on his first coming into possession of the house at Petworth, for the information of strangers. On hearing that a list was given out, and that it was a comprehensive one, I gave the person a handsome gratuity for the liberty of copying it; but, though I had been persuaded that it contained the details of the whole collection, I found that it fell short of two-thirds, when I came to make the transcript. However, as it points out the painters of several notable pieces, and as the noble owners have always made a difficulty of giving or permitting copies to be taken, I imagined that it might not be unacceptable to you,

12. Joceline Percy (1644–70), 5th E. of Northumberland, 1668.

13. Lady Elizabeth Percy (1667–1722), m. 1 (1679) Henry Cavendish (afterwards Percy) (1663–1680), styled E. of Ogle, 1676; m. 2 (secretly, 1681) Thomas Thynne (d. 1682); m. 3 (1682) Charles Seymour (1662–1748), 6th D. of Somerset, 1678.

14. Known as 'the proud Duke.' He m. (1726), as his second wife, Lady Charlotte Finch (1693–1773).

15. Algernon Seymour (1684–1750), 7th D. of Somerset, 1748; cr. (1749) E. of Egremont.

16. Who was Duke Algernon's nephew (the Duke had no surviving son). The Duke's sister, Lady Catherine Seymour (d. 1731), had married Sir William Wyndham, 3d Bt, in 1708; Sir Charles Wyndham, 2d E. of Egremont, was their son.

17. Lady Elizabeth Seymour (1716–76), only dau. of Algernon Seymour, 7th D. of Somerset; m. (1740) Sir Hugh Smithson (after 1750, Percy) (1715–86), 4th Bt, 1733, 2d E. of Northumberland, n.c., 1750, cr. (1766) D. of Northumberland. She inherited the northern estates of the Percy family, including Alnwick Castle, in 1750.

18. Not identified

and shall therefore enclose a copy[19] with the last packet of those papers. I have since my purchase of this copy had an opportunity of collating mine with the original and find only that Lord Egremont has added three or four pieces from his own collection, which additional pieces I shall mark. Since taking this copy, I purchased the liberty of going with an ingenious young fellow to take the dimensions of the most remarkable pieces and to view them at my own leisure—by whose assistance I took an exact catalogue of all the pieces then in the house, but unluckily, Lord Egremont had sent up a considerable number to be cleaned and new-framed, and her Ladyship's[20] fancy altered so often, that though I had specified in my catalogue where and on what side of each room the several pictures hung, yet in six month's time this punctuality became of no use, most of the pictures being removed and the pieces from the upper apartment exchanged places with those in the lower; however, if with this inconvenience and another of much worse consequence, *videlicet* that of being unable to discover the names, either of the painter, or the painted in a great number of portraits, you should think it important enough to be worth your reading, I'll do myself the honour to transcribe and send it you, by the first opportunity.

But, to return to the *Anecdotes,* I must observe, that on a hasty revisal, I find that I have omitted many little particulars that I am obliged to throw into the form of a supplement, and to place it at the conclusion of the notes on the first volume.

I have submitted to your decision whether there be any room or place for Catherine of Arragon, in the emblematical picture of the establishment of the House of Tudor, or not. You may, therefore, if you think with me, that she has no place there, suppress all that relates to that princess; which will be a great saving of time and paper; but if you think, that she is there represented, then you may insert what part you please, or the whole. The rest of that essay, except a few incidental conjectures, will hardly admit of a doubt.

The second picture, on the marriage of Henry VI, has given rise to many conjectures. You will be pleased to select what you approve, and suppress the rest, unless you should rather choose to lay the whole before the public for their determination.

As to the third, I have done little more than doubt; what author-

19. Apparently never sent; see *post* 16 May 1764.

20. Hon. Alicia Maria Carpenter (d. 1794), m. 1 (1751) Sir Charles Wyndham, 2d E. of Egremont; m. 2 (1767) Hans Moritz, Graf von Brühl.

ity those doubts may have with you, time only can determine. I am obliged to send this with only the remainder of the first vol. and two or three articles of the supplement, as I cannot transcribe more for a day or two, but I flatter myself that in two or three days more, I shall be able to send the remainder of the supplement, the whole notes on the second vol. and the catalogue of Lord Egremont's pictures.

I have the honour to be with great respect,

Sir,

Your most obedient humble servant,

JOHN BROMFIELD

From SIR DAVID DALRYMPLE,[1] Tuesday 17 April 1764

Printed from a photostat of the MS in the Historical Society of Pennsylvania. First printed in R. H. Carnie, 'A Missing Hailes-Walpole Letter,' N&Q 1957, ccii. 75–6. The MS was offered by Thorpe, Cat. of Autograph Letters, 1843, lot 1008; 1844, lot 539; subsequently acquired by the Historical Society of Pennsylvania. This is the reply to HW's letter of 9 April 1764 to Dalrymple (DALRYMPLE 100–1).

Edinburgh, 17th April 1764.

I AM much obliged to you, dear Sir, for the trouble you take about the prints of Nanteuil.[2] I wish heartily that I had any opportunity of being serviceable to you in the same way or in any other. If Mr Bathoe[3] will send the prints addressed to me, to the house of Mrs St Clair,[4] Greek Street, Soho, they will come safe to me. My only fear is lest they should be crumpled or folded, but as Mr Bathoe is a man of the trade he will I hope take care of this.

Dr Reid[5] is a professor at Aberdeen no less celebrated for his

1. (1726–92), 3d Bt, 1751; lord of session as Lord Hailes, 1766; Scottish jurist and antiquary. The rest of HW's correspondence with him is printed in DALRYMPLE.

2. Robert Nanteuil (ca 1623–78), painter and engraver. See DALRYMPLE 100 and nn. 5–11 concerning the seven prints by Nanteuil.

3. William Bathoe (d. 1768), bookseller, who had located impressions of the prints Dalrymple wanted.

4. Janet Dalrymple (1698–1766), m. 1 Sir John Baird (1685–1745), 2d Bt, 1737; m. 2 Gen. the Hon. James St Clair (1688–1762). She was Dalrymple's aunt.

5. Thomas Reid (1710–96), D.D., professor of philosophy at King's College, Aberdeen, 1751–64.

modest reserved character than for his learning. They talk of him as one of the persons who are put in the lists to supply the chair of Mr Smith[6] of Glasgow who travels with the Duke of Buccleugh.[7] I am afraid Mr Charles Townshend[8] will make a very indifferent *compagnon de voyage* out of a very able professor of ethics. Mr Smith has extensive knowledge and in particular has much of what may be termed constitutional knowledge, but he is awkward and has so bad an ear that he will never learn to express himself intelligibly in French.

I shall take care to let Dr Reid know that you have received his present.[9]

I am much obliged to you for your offer as to John Hales.[10] I am not sure whether you mean to say that a friend of yours has a picture or only a print of him:[11] if it is only a print, I am afraid it will be some poor thing, and if it be good, I should be afraid of its being hurt in the copying.

You have here enclosed some slight notices concerning your third volume of painters.[12] They will serve to show that I have had the pleasure of reading that work, and they will do no more. Adieu, dear Sir.

Believe me with great respect

Your most obedient and obliged servant,

DAV. DALRYMPLE

6. Adam Smith (1723–90), political economist, who escorted HW to the Scots College in Paris in 1766 ('Paris Journals,' DU DEFFAND v. 307). Reid succeeded him as professor of moral philosophy at Glasgow in May 1764.

7. Henry Scott (1746–1812), 3d D. of Buccleuch, 1751. Smith was tutor to Buccleuch during his travels in France Feb. 1764 – Oct. 1766 (John Rae, *Life of Adam Smith,* 1895, p. 174), and HW met them both in Paris (DU DEFFAND v. 'Paris Journals,' *passim*).

8. Hon. Charles Townshend (1725–67), Buccleuch's stepfather, who had married, as her second husband, Lady Dalkeith in 1755. Smith was Townshend's choice to be Buccleuch's tutor and he arranged the terms (Rae, op. cit. 164–5).

9. A copy of Reid's *An Inquiry into the Human Mind, on the Principles of Common Sense,* Edinburgh, 1764. HW's copy is Hazen, *Cat. of HW's Lib.*, No. 1602.

10. John Hales (1584–1656), fellow of Eton and man of letters.

11. HW's letter reads: 'I forgot to tell you, Sir, that I know no picture of Mr John Hales of Eton, nor have I a print of him; but I know a gentleman who has, and who I dare say would lend it me to be copied, if that will do' (DALRYMPLE 101 and nn. 14, 15).

12. The third volume of *Anecdotes of Painting* was published on 6 Feb. 1764 (Hazen, *SH Bibl.* 55).

From the REV. JAMES GRANGER,[1] Tuesday 24 April 1764

Printed from *Letters between the Rev. James Granger . . . and Many of the Most Eminent Literary Men of his Time,* ed. J. P. Malcolm, 1805, pp. 5–7, where the letter was first printed. The MS was in the possession of W. Richardson, printseller in the Strand, in 1805; sold Puttick and Simpson 4 June 1867 (Collection of . . . Autograph Letters Sale), lot 433 (with other Granger MSS), to Loddy; not further traced.

Shiplake, April 24, 1764.

Sir,

I WRITE this letter with great diffidence, lest what is meant as respect might be taken for impertinence. Yesterday Mr Simon Fanshawe[2] was so kind as to lend me your two last volumes of *Anecdotes of Painting,* etc. which I take the liberty to mention, that, if in turning over my alphabetical catalogue,[3] you should condescend to honour it with any addition or alteration that may readily occur to you, you might not give yourself the trouble of altering or inserting anything that I can do myself by the help of your books.

These two volumes I have eagerly devoured, and shall in reading them over a second time endeavour to digest them. I find upon this cursory view of them, that I have misplaced John Barefoot[4] and the landlady of Louse Hall[5] in the list which I sent, which I did almost against conviction, implicitly relying on the authority of a gentleman[6] in London, who I had reason to believe knew much better where to place them than myself.

As the heads I have do not deserve the name of a collection, permit me, Sir, to add my mite towards yours: the widow in the Gospel[7] did not cast hers into the treasury with more alacrity.

The pleasure I have received from your works has more than compensated any humble offering that is, or ever can be, in my power to

1. (1723–76), vicar of Shiplake, Oxon; author of *A Biographical History of England,* 1769; print collector and antiquary. His addiction to extra-illustrating books contributed the term 'Grangerizing' to the language.

2. (1716–77), M.P.

3. Granger was preparing the materials for his *Biographical History of England* (*ante* 3 April 1764, n. 2).

4. 'Letter-doctor to the University of Oxford' (Granger, *Biographical History,* 3d edn, 1779, iv. 200–1).

5. 'Mother Louse; an old woman . . . at Louse Hall, an alehouse near Oxford, which was kept by this matron' (ibid. iv. 217).

6. Presumably Sir William Musgrave.

7. Mark 12. 42–4, Luke 21. 2–4.

make you. I cannot help repeating, that I am ashamed of putting so rude a sketch as my catalogue into your hands, being extremely sensible of its incorrectness; but that sensibility would have quickened my diligence in correcting it, if I had carried it into the country with me. But here, Sir, I labour under many disadvantages, as the not having access to a large library, and as there is not one in the narrow circle of my acquaintance that can give me any assistance; but, on the contrary, they are rather inclined to laugh at me for undertaking a work, of the utility of which they have no conception.

I am, Sir, etc.

JAMES GRANGER

PS. I have generally taken the whole, or part, of the inscription of a print literally as it stands, which will account for the different spelling of names and other inaccuracies.

The head of A. Ross[8] is taken from the title of his continuation of Sir Walter Raleigh's *History*, fol., 1652.[9] The engraver's name did not stand originally where it now is, but at some distance from the head: I removed it with my own hand.

The head of Sir Toby Mathews[10] was prefixed to his *Letters*, printed with the *Character of Lucy, Countess of Carlisle*, 1660, small 8vo.[11]

8. Alexander Ross (1591–1654), chaplain to Charles I; miscellaneous writer.

9. *The History of the World: The Second Part, in Six Books: Being a Continuation of the . . . History of Sir Walter Raleigh*, 1652. The portrait of Ross is by J. Goddard.

10. Sir Tobie Matthew (1577–1655), Kt, 1623; diplomatist and author; M.P.

11. *A Collection of Letters, Made by Sr Tobie Mathews Kt. With a Character of the Most Excellent Lady, Lucy, Countesse of Carleile*, 1660. The engraved portrait of Matthew is by James Gammon.

From JOHN BROMFIELD, Wednesday 16 May 1764

Printed for the first time from a photostat of Bromfield's MS copy, kindly furnished by Mr Francis Russell. For the history of the MS and its present whereabouts see *ante* 8 April 1764. For the letter actually sent to HW see ibid. n. 2.

Petworth, Sussex, May the 16th 1764.

Sir,

YOUR favour of April 17th[1] gave me a most sincere pleasure; and while it inspired me with a desire of sending you a more perfect list of the pictures now at Lord Egremont's, than that which I took two or three years since, it has prevented my acknowledging its receipt in due time; a fault to which I acquiesced with less difficulty, as I found, that the impressions of the *Anecdotes* was too forward to receive any correction;[2] and likewise, that some of the errata were not general.

Lady Egremont[3] has, by her return into Sussex, put it out of my power, at present, to correct and enlarge my catalogue of 1761. So that, I must beg your candour to excuse what has been an involuntary omission. Such as it is, I shall send it by an early post, not having quite transcribed it; nor indeed have I room in this cover, in which I have included three sheets of supplement to the first vol. of the *Anecdotes,* and five sheets of notes etc. on the second volume.

The most obliging manner in which you are pleased to express your acceptance of my petty assistance is sufficient, were the subject much more valuable. You are generously pleased to declare, that you are sorry, that you could not avail yourself of a more early acquaintance with me, etc. I wish, Sir, that while you are doing honour to your own noble spirit, by expressing sentiments worthy of yourself, you do not rouse a latent spark of vanity in me, for who can resist a temptation so soothing to self-love as *laudari a laudato viro?*[4]

1. Missing.

2. The printing of the first volume of *Anecdotes of Painting,* 2d edn, was finished 22 Sept. 1763; the printing of the second volume was begun 30 Jan. 1764 and may have been completed by the date of this letter (Hazen, *SH Bibl.* 62).

3. See *ante* 14 April 1764, n. 20.

4. *Lætus sum laudari me abs te, pater, a laudato viro:* 'Praise from you, my father, a much lauded man, makes me glad indeed' (Nævius, *Hector proficiscens,* fragment 2).

I dare not presume to appear in public in any shape as a coadjutor to the noble editor of the *Anecdotes;* that you are pleased to accept the petty services in question must be the utmost of my ambition; nor do I think it a trifle, that I have presumed to attempt the part your polite namesake of the Augustan court once modestly bespoke,

Fungar vice cotis, acutum
Reddere quæ ferrum valet, exors ipsa secandi.[5]

With respect to the enclosed sheets, in my notes I have taken particular care to consult the Errata,[6] that I might insert none that stood corrected; but I am utterly incapable of discovering what could be the meaning of the variations in the copy before me from that of yours. That from whence I have made extracts hath all the appearance of being genuine.

It is not indeed my property, but ⟨it⟩ was sent me by Lord Winterton,[7] on its first coming out, for my perusal, and afterwards, when he had read it at his own leisure, I took it again with a view to what I have since executed. I expect to see his Lordship in the country in a short space, and will then learn where he bought it: and should there appear any farther reason to suspect a surreptitious edition, I have no doubt but that he will give me leave to send the books to Arlington Street, or wherever you shall please to order them. In the meantime, I must own that, this variation excepted, I see no reason at present to doubt the book's being genuine; however, to put them to the only test I could think of, I compared all the errata in the tables at the end of each volume with their respective places in the body of the work, and found that they tallied exactly except that in the table at the end of the first vol. we find this article: p. 101, line 4, for *Southwash* read *Southwark.* But in page 101, line 4, it is printed properly Southwark. Whether it may stand thus in your copy may soon be determined.[7a]

Perhaps, after all, the corrector of the press may have neglected to

5. 'I'll serve as a whetstone which, unable of itself to cut, makes iron sharp' (Horace, *Ars poetica* 304–5).

6. The *Anecdotes* contains pages of 'Errata' at the end of the first and second volumes.

7. See *ante* 14 April 1764, n. 10.

7a. No copy examined has the reading 'Southwash' and no copy with 'Southwash' has ever been reported. The erratum may have been added to correct the wrong reading in only a very few copies. Perhaps no copy finally distributed had the error; the printer, Thomas Farmer, may have corrected the error in his final proofing without informing HW, who made up the Errata from whatever errors he noticed during final review of the sheets.

correct the proof sheets so completely as he ought to have done at first; but, when part of the impression had been printed off, may have seen his error and corrected such faults as occurred at the top or bottom of each page, which might be done without great trouble or loss of time; or otherwise, the rascal employed in the printing office may (according to their laudable custom) have printed off a number of sheets as proofs only, which they may afterwards have made up into volumes and sold to the booksellers 'with all their imperfections on their heads,' as the ghost of Hamlet expresses it.[8]

Something of this kind I should suspect to be the case; for, I own, that on the most exact scrutiny I can see no reason to suppose the copy before me to be part of a spurious edition, at least in any other sense than the above.

With respect to the papers which I have here enclosed, I must own that I am really vexed with myself, on a cool revisal, for having filled up the three sheets of supplement with so much useless and unnecessary matter; but a little patience and much of the sponge will relieve you.

June 3d.

I have seen Lord Winterton, who informs me, that he bought his two volumes of the *Anecdotes* of Robson,[9] bookseller to the Princess of Wales.[10] Whenever his Lordship shall send me the two last volumes, I will endeavour to obey your commands as to them.

Your obliging invitation does me too much honour for me not to seize that permission of paying my respects to you when I shall be in London; but, as that time may be somewhat distant, I should be proud of executing any commands that you may be pleased to honour me with here. As to making any observations on your other works, I fear that I am very unequal to the task; but if you are pleased to think otherwise, I shall obey the first notice of your commands.

I must own, that I have never had the pleasure of seeing any but

8. *Hamlet* I. v. 78–9.

9. James Robson (1733–1806), bookseller in New Bond Street.

10. Augusta (1719–72) of Saxe-Gotha, m. (1736) Frederick Louis (1707–51), P. of Wales.

11. *A Catalogue of the Royal and Noble Authors of England,* 2 vols, SH, 1758. Bromfield's finely-bound copies of several SH Press books, including a presentation copy of *Anecdotes,* were among the books from his library sold by Egerton in 1798.

your *Royal and Noble Authors,*[11] which work, as it gave me several agreeable hours' amusement, as well as information, I could not resist the temptation of marking some particulars, and collecting the titles of several works and authors that I did not see in that *Catalogue;* I even adventured so far as to write to you on the occasion, but, on better consideration, suppressed the letter, as thinking it an impertinence.

April 14th 1765.

Sir,

I most sincerely beg pardon for my long but involuntary silence; the enclosed papers were written near a year ago, as well as the preceding part of this letter, with intent that they should be sent to you immediately; but, being flattered with new and vain hopes of executing the list of paintings at Petworth House, I unhappily postponed sending them till I had delayed so long, that I was really ashamed of doing it till it could be done complete, and which I have never been able to perform, the late great changes in the family, and alterations in the several apartments, having succeeded so rapidly that it was impossible to say where a picture that was here today should be next month.

To this state of uncertainty several particulars in my own private affairs, joined to an indisposition of my own having added their influence, I was obliged to renounce all thoughts of this work till a more happy season, which I flattered myself with finding this spring; but a letter which a gentleman,[12] a near relation of mine, received from the Duchess Dowager of Somerset[13] two or three days since, has given me so much uneasiness, that I could no longer defer writing to you upon it, as it turns chiefly on a former letter,[14] which I am said to have written to you, and which has given great offence to Mr and Mrs Grenville;[15] the particulars, if you will give me leave, I purpose to mention by the next post.[16]

12. Not identified.

13. See *ante* 14 April 1764, n. 14.

14. Presumably *ante* 14 April 1764, in which Bromfield declared that from the time Petworth 'fell into the hands of the Wyndhams' the 'noble library of the ancient Percies . . . became totally useless to the world.'

15. Elizabeth Wyndham (d. 1769), m. (1749) Hon. George Grenville; sister of the 2d E. of Egremont.

16. Missing; no later letters between HW and Bromfield have been found.

I once more beg pardon for my past long silence, and would have written to have asked it before, but could not presume to take that liberty.

I have the honour to be,
Sir,
Your most obliged and obedient humble servant,
JOHN BROMFIELD

From THOMAS PITT,[1] Friday 25 May 1764

Printed from a photostat of Pitt's MS copy (sent by him to George Grenville) among the Grenville papers in the British Museum (Add. MS 57,816, f. 104). First printed in *Additional Grenville Papers 1763–1765*, ed. J. R. G. Tomlinson, Manchester, 1962, p. 130. This copy in Pitt's hand was apparently among the papers deposited by Grenville's descendants at Stowe; sold, in a collection of papers from Stowe, by the 2d Duke of Buckingham and Chandos to his attorney, Edwin James, who in turn sold this collection to John Murray in 1851; acquired by the British Museum from John Murray, the publishers, in 1972. The original letter sent to HW is missing; Pitt's copy of the letter retained by himself is among the Dropmore papers in the British Museum (Add. MS 59,487, f. 9).

Endorsed: Copy of a letter to Mr H. Walpole May 25th 1764.

B[oconno]ck, May 25th 1764.

Dear Sir,

BY THE last post I received a very long letter from Mr Grenville[2] in which he expresses great uneasiness at a report which has been maliciously raised and industriously propagated by his enemies, charging him with having said in the conversation which passed at my house[3] 'that if Mr Conway voted in Parl[iamen]t according to his

1. (1737–93), of Boconnoc, Cornwall; cr. (1784) Bn Camelford; lord of the Admiralty 1763–5; M.P. He was the only surviving son of Thomas Pitt, the elder brother of William Pitt (later Earl of Chatham), and was the nephew of HW's friend and correspondent Charles Lyttelton, Bishop of Carlisle.

2. Hon. George Grenville, Thomas Pitt's first cousin once removed, at this time first lord of the Treasury. Grenville's letter to Pitt 15 May 1764 is printed in *The Grenville Papers*, ed. W. J. Smith, 1852–3, ii. 320–4.

3. On 3 Dec. 1763 Grenville met with HW at Pitt's house for the purpose of arranging an interview between himself and Henry Conway. The King had asked Grenville 'to speak to Mr Conway, and endeavour to make him explicit upon the occasion . . . whether he did actually mean to join the Opposition [in Parliament], or that the votes he had given upon the late questions [of general war-

conscience he was unfit to have any command in the King's army.' And what makes this report the more painful to him is that they have added to this falsehood one I am sure as great to acquire to themselves credit, namely that this report has not been discouraged by you.[4] I have taken the liberty to send you a copy[5] of my answer[6] to Mr Grenville's letter which will recall the transaction to your mind. I will not therefore trouble you with anything further upon the subject than to beg of you if you agree with me in the state I have given of the conversation, that you will use your endeavours to put a stop to a groundless report which seems to occasion uneasiness to a person I know you esteem. I hope you enjoy this fine weather in full perfection at Strawberry and that it has been a means of reestablishing your health.

I am, dear Sir,

Your very affectionate humble servant,

T[HOS.] P[ITT][7]

rants] were merely from opinion, and that in other measures he would fairly and roundly support the King's government. Mr Grenville approved of this expedient, and sent to desire a meeting with Mr Conway, through the means of Mr Thomas Pitt, who was to mention it to Mr Walpole' (ibid. ii. 231; see also *Mem. Geo. III* i. 272–3).

4. 'It has been reported industriously, that when I met Mr Horace Walpole at your house I told him that if General Conway voted in Parliament according to his conscience he was unfit to have any command in the King's army, and it has been said that this absurd and monstrous falsehood has not been discouraged by Mr Walpole himself' (Grenville to Pitt 15 May, *Grenville Papers* ii. 320).

5. Missing.

6. Dated 25 May; printed ibid. ii. 324–7. Pitt assured Grenville that 'the facts are, I believe, precisely as you represent them.'

7. HW enclosed this letter and apparently also a copy of his long reply to it (see following letter) when he wrote to Conway 5 June, referring to Pitt's letter as 'the enclosed *mandate*. You will see *my masters* order me, as a subaltern of the Exchequer, to drop you and defend them —but you will see too, that, instead of obeying, *I have given warning*' (CONWAY ii. 395–6 and n. 3; see also *Mem. Geo. III* ii. 8).

To Thomas Pitt, Tuesday 5 June 1764

Printed from a photostat of the MS kindly furnished by the late Sir John Murray. First printed in *The Grenville Papers*, ed. W. J. Smith, 1852–3, ii. 335–44. Reprinted, Cunningham iv. 238–45; Toynbee vi. 68–77. The MS was sent by Pitt to George Grenville and was among the Grenville papers deposited at Stowe by his descendants; sold in a collection of papers from Stowe by the 2d Duke of Buckingham and Chandos to his attorney, Edwin James, who in turn sold this collection to John Murray in 1851; resold Sotheby's 11 May 1970 (property of Sir John Murray), lot 231, to John Wilson; not further traced. Pitt's copy of the letter (in a different hand) is among the Dropmore papers in the British Museum (Add. MS 59,487, ff. 10–15).

Endorsed in an unidentified hand: Mr Walpole to Mr Thomas Pitt.

Strawberry Hill, June 5th 1764.

Dear Sir,

YOU tell me a report has been maliciously raised and propagated by Mr Grenville's enemies, that in the conversation which passed at your house, Mr Grenville said, that if Mr Conway voted in Parliament according to his conscience, he was unfit to have any command in the King's army. You add, that what makes this report more painful to Mr Grenville, is, that I am said not to have discouraged it: and you conclude with desiring, if I agree with your state of that conversation (which you send me, to refresh my memory) that I would use my endeavours to put a stop to a groundless report.

I will begin with telling you that I am far from having forgot the conversation you mention. At the very time it passed, I thought it so extraordinary, that the next day I wrote down an account of it; as I did also of what I heard passed at Mr Grenville's[1] on the same subject. I have it at this moment lying before me, and therefore can speak very accurately on that topic.

If therefore you ask me whether Mr Grenville said *totidem verbis* that if Mr Conway voted in Parliament according to his conscience, he was unfit to have any command in the army? I answer directly and truly, No: I never heard him say those words, nor have I certainly ever said he did. Yet I think the report may easily have arisen from

1. The interview between Grenville and Conway took place late in the evening of 4 Dec. 1763, the day after HW had talked with Grenville at Pitt's house. The Duke of Richmond accompanied Conway at this meeting (*Grenville Papers* ii. 233–4; *Mem. Geo. III* i. 273–4).

what he assuredly did say, and which I avow I have said, he said. Mr Grenville said twice, *the King cannot trust his army in the hands of those that are against his measures.* Now give me leave to put *you* a little in mind. The expression of *the King not trusting his army in such hands,* you first dropped yourself in my room.[2] You cannot forget the surprise it occasioned in me, or the answer I made you. Did I not, I ask you upon your honour, reply, 'Good God! Mr Pitt, what are you going to do with the army? or what do you think Mr Conway is going to do? Do you think he is going into rebellion? if the tenor of Mr Conway's services and character do not entitle him to be trusted with a regiment, I do not know what can entitle any man to one. Is he factious? What do you think he is going to do?'[3] Mr Grenville at night in your room *twice* used the same expression of *not trusting the army in such hands.* I did then and still think them the most extraordinary words ever used by [an] English minister. I repeated the same answer that I had made to you. I appeal to you yourself whether this is not most strictly true. When I saw Mr Conway, I told him of these words before Lady Ailesbury;[4] I mentioned them to the Duke of Devonshire;[5] I believe when it was agreed the Duke of Richmond[6] should be present at the conversation between Mr Grenville and Mr Conway,[7] I told them to his Grace, but of this I will not be positive. I do know that to prevent any mistakes thereafter, I set down the very words; and I am glad I did so. That paper has been seen by those who will bear me witness that it is no new account, nor do you or Mr Grenville I dare to say suspect me capable of having written it now and calling it an old account; nor could it be necessary: I desired to have you for witness to my conversation with Mr Grenville, being so much convinced of the rigid strictness of your honour, that, though much more Mr

2. This meeting at HW's house took place shortly before 3 Dec. 1763.

3. In *Mem. Geo. III* i. 271, HW wrote that Thomas Pitt had told him 'it could not be suffered to have men in the King's service acting against him,—and then [he] dropped this unguarded expression, *the King could not trust his army in such hands.* I started! "Good God!" said I, "Mr Pitt, what are they going to do with the army? to what use is it to be put, if a man of Mr Conway's virtue, and tried loyalty and bravery, cannot be trusted with a regiment! You alarm me!" He beat about backwards and forwards; sometimes it was offers and promises, sometimes threats; but I had taken my part, and had got hold of words I was determined not to part with or forget.'

4. Conway's wife.

5. William Cavendish, 4th D. of Devonshire; HW's occasional correspondent and Conway's intimate friend.

6. Charles Lennox (1735–1806), 3d D. of Richmond, 1750; HW's correspondent. He was married to Lady Ailesbury's daughter by her first marriage.

7. See n. 1 above.

Grenville's friend than mine, I was sure you would do me justice, if it should be necessary to appeal to you.[8] I do appeal to you in the most solemn manner, nay, I appeal to Mr Grenville himself, whether every syllable that I have here stated to you be not most scrupulously and conscientiously true, not only in syllables but in sense and purport, for I would scorn to report words however true, which yet, by adding to or taking from, I should set in a different light from that in which they were intended by the speaker.

I now come to the case as you state it, which in general agrees very much with my own paper: but we differ widely in the conclusions we draw from what passed. You allow I insisted principally upon the high point of honour and delicacy of sentiment in Mr Conway, and that I thought him incapable *in any situation* of doing anything but from mere motives of conscience and honour? Has he not acted invariably, as I foretold! has he not sacrificed his fortune to his conscience? and do you not *ipsissimis verbis* own, that it would have been an absurdity in Mr Grenville to say Mr Conway was unfit to have any command in the King's army, if he voted according to his conscience; unless indeed, *his conscience* leading him to a systematical opposition to the King's government, *in that case Mr Grenville may be construed to have said,* that *such* a *conscience* must render it very difficult and unlikely for him to continue long in his situation. Without dwelling on the words *such a conscience* (though a man acting uniformly in opposition against his interest may be supposed as conscientious as a man acting uniformly with his interest for government) it is evident from your words and opinion, that if Mr Conway's conscience led him to opposition, he probably would be removed. If therefore Mr Conway's conscience led him not to systematical opposition, but to opposition to one single measure, and yet he has been dismissed, will not the world say with reason, indeed can it say otherwise? than that Mr Grenville's declared opinion led him to remove officers for systematical opposition from conscience, and that the practice has been to remove them for one single conscientious vote? and unless Mr Grenville declares (which I, if authorized,

8. HW wrote in *Mem. Geo. III* i. 272 that he told Pitt: 'I will wait on him [Grenville], upon condition a third person is present. I do not desire it may be a friend of mine and not his; you are a friend of both; and though justly much more attached to him than to me, I am persuaded, if any difference should arise between us in the relation of the interview, you have too much honour not to do strict justice to either.'

will publish with pleasure) that he had no hand in the removal of Mr Conway, I do not see how anybody can help thinking that Mr Grenville's opinion and practice went together. You approve the wisdom of removing men in the former case—I wonder you did even in speculation—surely the execution has not convinced you of the wisdom of this measure, which has so much offended mankind, and has intimidated nobody. From all this you must see clearly, that if I contradicted the essence of the report, I must contradict you and the truth, who agree together.

You allow I was positive in opinion, that Mr Conway neither was nor intended to be in opposition: I was most assuredly of that opinion, am now convinced I was in the right, as in every question that did not relate to the warrants he voted with the administration. In the next point, which is matter of opinion, you think Mr Grenville showed every mark of kindness and friendly disposition to Mr Conway. Give me leave to say it did not strike me in that light. Mr Grenville, with greath warmth and eagerness persisted in thinking Mr Conway rooted in opposition, which occasioned, what you own, my repeated declarations of believing the contrary. This did not strike me as any great mark of kindness or confidence to either Mr Conway or me. Less did I think it kind to insist with the vehemence Mr Grenville used, on positive declarations from Mr Conway. Such demands appear to me highly unconstitutional, and therefore I do not see how they can be made with friendship to the party. Those demands of positive declaration were, I believe, made before the Duke of Richmond,[9] as well as to me.

You know I went so far as [to] tell you that Mr Conway was, I firmly believed, not only not in opposition, but should he be ever so ill-used, and the ministry should propose a question which he thought right for this country, he would vote for it. I remain exactly of the same opinion. He has been as ill, as hardly, and as unjustly used as every man was; and yet he will do what he thinks right, though his behaviour may serve his bitterest enemies; for he will never suffer his personal resentments to carry him to do a wrong thing, even to his foes; much less towards his country. When I say he has been ill-used, I repeat with great sincerity, and you who have known, and are so good as to allow my real regard to Mr Grenville, will believe me, that few things would give me more pleasure than to be assured

9. See postscript below.

that the dismission of Mr Conway was without Mr Grenville's consent or approbation.[10]

You say that below the bar of the House of Lords Mr Grenville told you and me that Mr Conway had declared that he was not then engaged nor did at that time intend to engage in any system of opposition; but at the same time desired not to be understood to intend to separate himself from the Dukes of Grafton and Devonshire, to whom he was obliged.[11] This agrees with the message I myself delivered to Mr Grenville from Mr Conway; that he was in no opposition, nor thought of being in any; but in answer to Mr Grenville's question, whether there was anything he would like, he declared he would accept nothing, while those Dukes were dissatisfied with the administration. Both your state of the case and mine, which agree together, do not at all coincide with Mr Grenville's letter to Lord Hertford, that he had found Mr Conway's connections with his friends *unbounded*.[12]

I have omitted, for the last, one passage, which I had forgotten in my own memorandums, which yet from your assertion, who I am sure will adhere in every point to the strict matter of fact, let it affect whom it will, I am not only persuaded passed, but I think I recollect it myself from the circumstance of the particular day on which it passed. You say Mr Grenville told me that a regular system of opposition to government would render any one unfit for a high rank in military command; and that in some instances, as in cases of tumult and insurrections such a man would be more dangerous to the King and Commonwealth. I am sure I do not remember the

10. 'After long search and much information, I cannot fix the deed on any single man. . . . The King often afterwards protested to Lord Hertford that his ministers forced him to it. Grenville declared that his Majesty was more eager for it than any of them' (ibid. i. 320). Grenville had succeeded in delaying the King's dismissal of Conway from the Bedchamber and from the command of his regiment, but Grenville eventually acquiesced in it. The dismissal took place 20 April.

11. On 5 Dec. 1763, following his interview with Grenville, Conway wrote his brother Lord Hertford that he had told Grenville he was 'determined to take the part I should choose hereafter without making myself responsible for it to any person whatever, and should only add that my obligations to some particular persons, and I named the Dukes of Devonshire and Grafton, who were understood to be in Opposition, were such that if hereafter I should happen in any degree to differ from them, I should steer my conduct so as not to be in any shape the better for it' (MS now WSL).

12. In his letter to Hertford 18 April 1764, Grenville referred to Conway's 'unbounded attachment to others' (*Grenville Papers* ii. 297). Hertford reported the contents of the letter to HW 30 April (CONWAY ii. 385).

word *Commonwealth* being used; though, if you assert it, I cannot take upon me to say it was not used, for I remember this salvo but imperfectly. I know the day of the conversation was after the tumult on the burning of the *North Briton:*[13] Mr Grenville was much flustered, and very likely applied the case of the day to the subject we were discussing; and if he did, it probably made the less impression on me, because my mind had been already struck with the same singular words from you *before* the tumult happened; and therefore when I heard them repeated by a minister, it was natural for me to conclude you had heard them from his mouth, as you came to me with a message from him: and I am bold to declare, such words in the mouth of a minister are to me exceedingly alarming. As such I have repeated them; and I leave you who know me, to judge, whether I will retract anything I have said, which I am particularly authorized, by having taken down the words, to affirm are true, and to the very substance of which you agree, as I am sure you will to the precise words, being thus put in mind of them; especially as you own you are not exact in the very words.

I love and honour Mr Conway above any man in the world: I would lay down my life for him: and shall I see him every day basely and falsely traduced in newspapers and libels, and not say what I know is true, when it sets his character in so fair and noble a light? I am asked to discourage reports. I am ready to discourage such as are *not* true and do *not* come from me. Mr Grenville is welcome to publish this letter; it will be the fullest answer to anything that is said against him, without foundation. Let Mr Grenville in his turn discourage and disavow the infamous calumnies published against Mr Conway, the authors of which I dare to say are unknown to Mr Grenville; but who not content with seeing Mr Conway's fortune ruined, would stab his reputation likewise—Thank God, they cannot fix a blemish upon it. I will certainly bear witness to it as much as lies in me. Fear or favour shall not intimidate or warp my friendship. Yet I wish Mr Grenville so well, that I will take the liberty of giving him through you this piece of advice. It is high time for the administration to discountenance and disclaim the language held by all

13. For an account of this episode 3 Dec. 1763 see MANN vi. 187–8 and nn. 10, 11.

the writers on their side, particularly by the author of the *Address to the Public,*[14] *that officers are to be dismissed for their behaviour in Parliament.* Such doctrines are new, and never were *avowed* before. They clash with all parliamentary freedom; they render the condition of officers in Parliament most abject, slavish and dishonourable; they alarm all thinking men—and I will do them the justice to say, do not seem universally the sentiments of ministers themselves, as so many generals and officers in Parliament, who are avowedly in opposition, retain their commissions;[15] a circumstance that makes the singling out of Mr Conway, who was not in opposition, look more like the effect of private pique and resentment somewhere or other, I don't know where, than a settled determination to make officers in general the absolute tools of the ministry.

I will now conclude this tedious letter, with adding by your leave a few words on myself. It has more than once been insinuated to me, that I might ruin myself, if I took Mr Conway's part. I do Mr Grenville the justice to declare that I believe him incapable of countenancing such insinuations. Come they from whom they will, I despise them. My place is a patent for life,[16] and as much my property by law, as your estate is yours—Oh! but I have been told, the payments may be delayed or stopped[17]—they may by violence or injustice; and that insinuation I despise likewise. Mr Grenville's civilities and regularity on those occasions I acknowledge with gratitude, though I disclaim all dependence, all paying of court—I would fling up my patent tomorrow, if it was capable of making me do one servile act, if it deterred me one moment from following the dictates of conscience and friendship. Both in Parliament and out of it I will say and do what I think right and honest. I was born free, and will live and die so, in spite of patents and places. I may be ruined as Mr Conway has been, but I will preserve my honour inviolate. If I did not, I might receive you here with more magnificence, but I had rather receive you, as I hope to do, without a blush. You know the passion I have

14. *An Address to the Public on the Late Dismission of a General Officer,* by William Guthrie (1708–70), a hack-writer for the government; it was published 24 May ('Short Notes,' GRAY i. 40 and n. 267).

15. For example, Lord Frederick Cavendish, Col. 34th Foot, and Lord Albemarle, Col. 3d Dragoons, who went into opposition in 1762. See *Grenville Papers* ii. 234.

16. The ushership of the Exchequer, given to him by his father in 1738 ('Short Notes,' GRAY i. 7 and n. 35).

17. See *ante* 14 March 1763 and n. 1.

for Strawberry Hill; but trust me, at this moment I know I could with pleasure see it sold, if reduced to it by suffering for my country and my principles. Remember this, my dear Sir, you, who are much younger[18] and have longer to live than me. It is this satisfaction of conscience which sweetens every evil, and makes Mr Conway at this instant the happiest man in England.

I am your sincere and affectionate humble servant,

HORACE WALPOLE

PS. I am so desirous of not saying a syllable that is not strictly true, that I choose to contradict in a postscript, rather than erase, one passage in which I had said what I *believed* had passed. On showing this letter to the Duke of Richmond, his Grace says, he cannot say that before him Mr Grenville made a demand of a positive declaration, though he expressed a strong desire that Mr Conway would declare what his general system was. If I have therefore stated the argument too strongly, I willingly retract so much, as is overcharged; though I must own I see little difference between a minister demanding a positive declaration of a member of Parliament, and expressing a strong desire of a declaration; because if a minister will take upon himself to catechize members of Parliament, he must know that either the gentler or rougher method will be effectual, or both will be resisted. The Duke says he remembers very well my telling him the words *cannot trust his army* etc., *before* his Grace saw Mr Grenville.[19]

18. HW was then forty-six, Pitt twenty-seven.

19. Pitt enclosed this letter when he wrote to Grenville 10 June (*Additional Grenville Papers 1763–1765*, ed. J. R. G. Tomlinson, Manchester, 1962, p. 134). For Grenville's comments on it, in his reply to Pitt 19 June, see *Grenville Papers* ii. 353–60.

From THOMAS PITT, Sunday 10 June 1764

Printed from a photostat of Pitt's MS copy (sent by him to George Grenville) among the Grenville papers in the British Museum (Add. MS 57,816, ff. 106–9). First printed in *The Grenville Papers,* ed. W. J. Smith, 1852–3, ii. 346–52. This copy in Pitt's hand was apparently among the papers deposited by Grenville's descendants at Stowe; sold, in a collection of papers from Stowe, by the 2d Duke of Buckingham and Chandos to his attorney, Edwin James, who in turn sold this collection to John Murray in 1851; acquired by the British Museum from John Murray, the publishers, in 1972. The original letter sent to HW is missing; Pitt's draught of the letter, which contains a long crossed-out passage, is among the Dropmore papers in the British Museum (Add. MS 59,487, ff. 16–20).

Endorsed by Pitt: Copy of a letter to Mr Horrace Walpole [in a different hand] from Mr Thomas Pitt.

Boconnock, June 10th 1764.

Dear Sir,

I HAVE just received your answer to my letter of the 25th which contains matter of various kinds. The matter of fact is what I am principally concerned in, and is therefore what I shall first begin with. I must still, as I did before, declare that I am totally unable to charge my memory with particular words in a long conversation, which I had not the precaution at the time to write down, but which is fresh enough in my mind not to suffer any material circumstance to escape me. And this I think it necessary to premise, I am sure you will do me the justice to believe, not with an intention to misrepresent, disguise, or conceal, but from that regard for truth which I ever have, and I hope ever shall esteem above all ties and obligations whatsoever, and which, as it should make me most scrupulously testify against myself, so it should against my father, my brother or my friend. Having said thus much, I proceed to the circumstance about which you appeal to me. I do perfectly well remember, in conversation with you, justifying the removal of Mr Conway, from the danger there appeared to me at this time, supposing him to be in a systematical opposition to Government, in trusting in his hands an important military command. I remember you took me up eagerly, and replied, I verily believe the words you mention. 'Good God! Mr Pitt, what do you intend to do with the army? or what do you think Mr Conway is going to do with the army?' etc. I do very well remember the same sort of expression falling from Mr Grenville, of apprehension from the army being in the hands of persons in systematical opposition to the King's measures, I dare say in the terms you make use of, as you remember them so distinctly,[1] 'that the King cannot trust his army in the hands of those that are against his measures,' and I very well remember he applied the instance of the tumult in the City, to show how dangerous it would be for the safety of the King (I will not swear he added the word *Commonwealth,* though I hope I know him well enough to be persuaded that he never disunited their interests in his thoughts), to trust the defence of the King against a tumult raised upon account of burning the *N[orth] Briton* to a person who was known publicly to have defended the cause of the author of that paper;[2] to which you replied to this effect, 'that you thought, from Mr Conway's character, that defence might nevertheless be trusted to him with safety.'

This was, Sir, indeed the whole scope of Mr Grenville's conversation, as it appeared to me, upon my honour, viz., that Mr Conway seemed to be in a systematical opposition; that he wished to be enabled to say it was otherwise; that if it was so, he could not see there was that difference between a military and civil employment that would render it possible for Mr Conway long to continue in his situation. He did frequently explain his sentiments with regard to the injustice of removing any man from his employment for a single vote, or conscientious opposition to a particular measure; and though I declare myself ignorant what part he may have taken in Mr Conway's affair,[3] yet I will take upon me to say, had he seen that gentleman's conduct in the light you represent it in, perhaps, with great truth and justice, he would not[3a] have been a party to what has happened.

The report which Mr Grenville resents, and for the falsehood of which he appeals to me, and for which I likewise appeal to you, is this, 'that if Mr Conway voted in Parliament according to his conscience he was unfit to have any command in the King's army.' This report is false. Mr Grenville did, on the contrary, repeatedly declare —what I have heard him say a hundred times upon other occasions—

1. Grenville wrote Pitt 19 June 1764: 'I am confident that I did not make use of those words to Mr Walpole, which, if I had done it twice I should not have totally forgotten' (*Grenville Papers* ii. 354).

2. The author of the *North Briton*, No. 45, was John Wilkes (1725–97), M.P.

3. See previous letter, n. 10.

3a. The MS reads 'would not only not.'

that from difference of opinions a man might give his vote against Government, in particular instances, without being in opposition to Government, and consequently would not render himself *unfit* for any trust from government, civil or military. If, on the other hand, the report had been that Mr Grenville had declared what you mention, 'that the King cannot trust his army in the hands of those that are against his measures,' I protest, though I do not recollect the particular words which I dare say you have set down with truth and exactness, I do remember the sense of them well enough to declare that I understood that to be his opinion then delivered at my house; but give me leave to say it widely differs, not only in *terms,* but in *essence,* from the other proposition. An opposition to the King's measures, his motives for which he is the only judge of, would, in the latter case, be the reason to render him unfit for a high rank in military command, and not his having voted according to his conscience.

Alarming would it be, indeed, to every friend to liberty if we could conceive an English Minister uniting the two propositions, 'that an officer voting in Parliament according to his conscience was *therefore* unfit to serve,' and 'that the King did not dare to trust his army in any hands but of such as were ready at any time to vote in Parliament against their consciences.' But, Sir, there are different opinions and different convictions. A minister who means honestly by his King and country, and is conscious of the integrity of his own intentions, will make use of every constitutional method to carry his purposes into effect. He will be apt to suspect those of sinister views who oppose his measures, which he knows are well intentioned; at least he will endeavour to prevent the means that are taken to oppose and render them abortive, even though he should not suspect the principles of those who oppose. On the other hand, those who from principle and conscience condemn the measures of the minister, will be apt to suspect the minister of bad intentions towards the public, and will, in consequence of that conviction, endeavour to discredit and diminish his influence, and to oppose his measures.

I do not find, my dear Sir, that we differ about matters of fact, though we, indeed, differ widely in our conclusions. Perhaps we may be both of us warped in our reasonings by our partialities; but as *matters of fact* are the immediate objects of our consideration, to the truth of which I am appealed to on both sides, and which are not the objects of partiality, I am glad to be able, with the strictest adherence to truth, to join issue with both parties.

The report raised against Mr Grenville is, by your own concession, not true, viz., 'that if Mr Conway voted in Parliament according to his conscience he was unfit to have any command in the King's army.'

What you assert I *believe* to be true, in the *very words* in which you repeat them; I am ready to *attest* the truth of the *sense* of them, as delivered in that conversation which passed at my house, viz., 'that the King cannot trust his army in the hands of those who are against his measures.'

The first of these propositions is, I hope, on both sides confuted. The second is a text which may bear a comment according to the different conceptions, prejudices, and passions of mankind, though, in the sense in which I understand it, it is neither new or unconstitutional. I, for one, do from my heart believe the contrary doctrine of the absolute immunity and independence of the army to be much more new and dangerous to the constitution. However, I avoid entering further than is necessary upon this subject, as I know I have not the happiness to agree with you in it, and as I am not called upon to give my sentiments and opinion concerning it.

With regard to your unshaken and disinterested friendship for Mr Conway, it is such as well becomes the generosity and disinterestedness of your character, and those persons, whoever they were, who have endeavoured to throw unworthy insinuations into your mind by menaces of oppression and injustice, must have known as little of Mr Grenville, if they thought he could countenance such an idea, as they did of you if they thought you could be affected by it. No, Sir, I have the honour to live in friendship with Mr Grenville; I love and esteem him much. I will freely own he is the only attachment I have to any public or political situation; but could I once suppose him capable of taking so base and unjust an advantage over a man to punish him for a conduct which does him honour, I should renounce all connection with him, from that hour, as the lowest and most unworthy of men.[4]

In the meantime you will do me the justice to believe that, whether he is minister or no minister, as long as I continue to think of him as you know I do at present, I shall never fail to give him every mark of comfort, support, and feeble assistance in my power, under the great load of calumny and misrepresentation which, from

4. Pitt enclosed a copy of this letter (BM Add. MS 57, 816, ff. 106–9) in his letter of 10 June to Grenville (ibid. f. 105). Grenville returned 'my sincerest thanks for the very kind expressions of your good opinion and friendship towards me, in your letter to Mr Walpole' (*Grenville Papers* ii. 359–60).

quarters you have no dealings with, are every day heaped upon him. In short, I shall endeavour to imitate your own virtues, which will, I doubt not, give me that cheerfulness and self-satisfaction which you promise as the reward of an unblemished conduct.

I am, dear Sir, etc. etc.

THOS. PITT[5]

TO LORD MARCH,[1] mid-June 1764

Printed for the first time from a photostat of the MS (a note written on the back of a 9-of-clubs playing-card) in the Cely-Trevilian Collection, Society of Antiquaries, London. The previous history of the MS is not known.

Dated approximately by March's attendance at the dinner at SH 18 June 1764 (see n. 2 below).

MR Walpole hopes Lord March is so good as not to forget that he promised Mr Walpole to do him the honour of dining at Strawberry Hill next Monday 18th.[2]

5. In his reply to Pitt 19 June, Grenville declared that 'after what I have met with . . . I will have no farther intercourse with Mr Walpole upon this subject, neither directly nor through the channel of anyone else' (ibid. ii. 359).

1. William Douglas (1725–1810), 3d E. of March, 1731; 4th D. of Queensberry, 1778; 'Old Q.'

2. HW described the occasion to George Montagu 18 June 1764: 'Strawberry . . . has been more sumptuous today than ordinary, and banqueted their representative majesties of France and Spain. I had Monsieur and Madame de Guerchy, Mademoiselle de Nangis their daughter, two other French gentlemen, the Prince of Masserano, his brother and secretary, Lord March, George Selwyn, Mrs Anne Pitt and my niece Waldegrave. . . . Indeed everything succeeded to a hair' (MONTAGU ii. 126–7).

To the DUKE OF NEWCASTLE, Saturday 28 July 1764

Printed from a photostat of the MS in the British Museum (Add. MS 32, 960, f. 429). First printed in *Horace Walpole: Writer, Politician, and Connoisseur*, ed. W. H. Smith, New Haven, 1967, p. 80.

Dated by the endorsement.

Endorsed by Thomas Hurdis:[1] R[eceived] July 28th 1764. Mr Hora[ce] Walpole.

MR Walpole thinks himself very unfortunate in not having been able to make use of the permission the Duke of Newcastle has given him of waiting on his Grace;[2] but Mr Walpole has been and is confined with a rash and fever, but flatters himself that by the end of next week he shall be able to pay his duty to his Grace at Claremont.[3]

From the DUKE OF NEWCASTLE, Saturday 28 July 1764

Printed for the first time from a photostat of the MS copy in Thomas Hurdis's hand in the British Museum (Add. MS 32,960, f. 419). An extract from the letter was printed in *Horace Walpole: Writer, Politician, and Connoisseur*, ed. W. H. Smith, New Haven, 1967. p. 80.

Endorsed by Hurdis: Copy to Honourable Horatio Walpole July 28th 1764.

Claremont, July 28th 1764.

Dear Sir,

I WAS, and am, extremely flattered with the hopes of the honour of seeing you here; I am much concerned for the cause of its being deferred. I hope, however, that the end of next week will be the latest,[1] and that your health will be perfectly reestablished by that time.

1. Rev. Thomas Hurdis (ca 1707–84), D.D., 1766; prebendary of Chichester 1755–84 and canon of Windsor 1766–84 (Foster, *Alumni Oxon.;* Venn, *Alumni Cantab.*). He was for '40 years private secretary and domestic chaplain to the . . . D. of Newcastle' (GM 1784, liv pt i. 316).

2. Newcastle's letter of 25 July inviting HW to visit him at Claremont was answered the next day; both letters are missing. Richard Turner, Newcastle's London steward, wrote Thomas Hurdis 26 July: 'Mr Walpole has sent his compliments to my Lord Duke and will endeavour to wait on his Grace' (BM Add. MS 32,960, f. 407).

3. Newcastle's seat in Surrey, 15 miles from London and 9 miles from SH *via* Kingston. See following letter.

1. Newcastle wrote the Duke of Devonshire 4 Aug. 1764: 'I expect the honour of a visit from Mr Horace Walpole, who was so good, as to desire to come here, I

As I am sometimes abroad, I must beg to have a note the night before,[2] and I will certainly be at home. The satisfaction, I propose to myself, will be incomplete, if I have not the honour of your company in the morning, and at dinner;[3] and if you will not allow me, to return you my thanks very soon at Marble Hall,[4] and to have the pleasure of seeing the beauties of that place.

I am with great truth and respect,

Dear Sir,

Your most obedient humble servant,

HOLLES NEWCASTLE

Honourable Horatio Walpole.

To GROSVENOR BEDFORD, Monday 30 July 1764

Printed from Cunningham iv. 256, where the letter was first printed. Reprinted, Toynbee vi. 94–5. The history of the MS and its present whereabouts are not known.

July 30, 1764.

Dear Sir,

I DID not know that the watch-coats[1] were bought of Mr Mann.[2] I should be very glad to oblige Mr Jackson,[3] and will in anything else; but I don't see how I can deal with anybody else, as Mr Edward

believe, to talk a little upon our present situation; and, as I understand, with some view, if possible, to bring about an union with the Duke of Bedford. . . . Mr Horace Walpole could never come here at a better time; for I received, yesterday, the prettiest pamphlet, wrote, I suppose, by him, upon the cruel treatment of General Conway, that I ever read' (BM Add. MS 32,961, ff. 42–3). HW's *A Counter-Address to the Public, on the late Dismission of a General Officer* was published 2 Aug. (Hazen, *Bibl. of HW* 50).

2. No such note from HW has been found.

3. HW wrote Lord Hertford 'August 4th': 'I have dined today at Claremont, where I little thought I should dine, but whither *our* affairs have pretty naturally conducted me. . . . Our first meeting to be sure was awkward, yet I never saw a man conduct anything with more sense than he did' (CONWAY ii. 418–20).

4. Presumably he meant Strawberry Hill, although HW was often at nearby Marble Hill, Lady Suffolk's seat. For Newcastle's visit to SH see *post* 2 Oct. 1764.

1. 'A thick heavy cloak or coat worn by seamen, soldiers, or watchmen when on duty in bad weather' (OED).

2. James Mann (d. 15 April 1764), army clothier; Sir Horace Mann's younger brother.

3. Perhaps Thomas Jackson, clothier in Chambers Street, Goodman's Fields (Sir Ambrose Heal's Collection of Tradesmen's Cards, British Museum).

Mann[4] and his family continue the business, and I have such connections with them. I could wish you had not thought of this, as I would fain oblige Mr Jackson, and yet I cannot do anything—the Manns would take it ill.

I enclose the warrant, and a ticket[5] for Strawberry; and three advertisements,[6] which, at your leisure as you go into the City, I will beg you to inquire after, and if their cases are really compassionate, to give half a guinea for me to each, and to send a guinea to the common side of the Fleet Prison,[7] where they advertise their sickness,—but don't mention me.

Yours ever,

H. WALPOLE

From CHRISTOPHER WREN,[1] Friday 3 August 1764

Printed for the first time from the MS now WSL. The MS was probably in the lot of fifteen letters to HW from 'C. Wren' and others, sold SH vi. 139 to Thorpe; not further traced until sold by Maggs to WSL, 1932.

Endorsed by HW: Used.[2]

August 3d 1764, Wroxhall,[3] (near Warwick) Warwickshire.

Sir,

NOT being used to introduce myself into company, I have waited long for some better method of applying to you; but seeing no more reason to expect an opportunity's offering in any time to come,

4. Edward Louisa Mann (1702–75), of Linton, Kent; army clothier; collector of customs inwards ca 1752–75; Sir Horace Mann's older brother and HW's occasional correspondent (MANN i. 321 n. 22).

5. Of admission for visitors.

6. Two such newspaper appeals, one from 'a poor distressed widow, with three small children . . . all perishing for want of necessaries' and another from 'a poor tradesman, eighty-seven years of age, that is . . . plunged into prison for a small debt, and in great distress,' appeared in the *Daily Adv.* 25 July 1764.

7. The debtors' prison in Farringdon Street, which consisted of a 'master side' with private rooms for those that could afford them and a 'common side' for others confined there.

1. (1711–71), of Wroxall Abbey, Warwick; grandson of Sir Christopher Wren, the architect (J. W. Ryland, *Records of Wroxall Abbey and Manor Warwickshire,* 1903, pedigree following p. xl; Foster, *Alumni Oxon.*).

2. That is, information in the letter used by HW for the second edition of *Anecdotes of Painting*.

3. The Wroxall estates were purchased in 1713, when Wren was eighty-one years old, and it is doubtful whether he visited

than in what went before, I venture to take the liberty I now do; and hope you will permit me, without further apology, to enter upon my business.

In the *Anecdotes of Painting* you obliged the public with, I find very honourable mention in general made of my grandfather Sir Christopher Wren;[4] but not without some intermixtures which rather tend to his discredit.

I am persuaded you would rectify these in a future edition, if they appeared to you proceeding (as I think them) from mistakes.

You will not blame me, considering who I am, should I happen to be wrong; you will thank me, where I am right.

'The length of Sir Christopher's life enriched (you kindly say) the reigns of several princes; and disgraced the last.'[5]

It is true. Neither will the disgrace of the action here alluded to, be alleviated by the largeness of the sum Benson[6] advanced to procure it; because no money will be thought sufficient for such a job, considering Sir Christopher's extreme old age, and the irreproachable removal, which must soon have followed from it.

But a more shameful thing than the turning him out, was the manner of its being done, and Benson's strange behaviour, which not being commonly spoken of, at least not of late years, perhaps, you may never have heard.

The new Surveyor-General was scarcely known to be in office, I don't know but it might be the next day after his appointment, when he came to command my grandfather to leave his house:[7] he wanted to occupy it himself, he said; and threatened everybody (looking with sternness even at me, a child of about seven years old) that, if we were not all of us packed up, bag and baggage, by a day he named, he would *then* come with authority, and throw the goods out into the street.

the seat more than a few times; his son Christopher (1675–1747) was the first of the Wrens to take up residence there (Ryland, op. cit. xli–xlii).

4. See *Anecdotes*, 1st edn, iii. 89–93.

5. Ibid. iii. 89. 'At the age of 86 he was removed from being surveyor general of the works by George I!' (HW's note, ibid.).

6. William Benson (1682–1754), surveyor-general of the Works 1718–19; M.P. 'Mr B[enson] was a favourite of the Germans . . . so great, that Sir Christopher Wren . . . was turned out of his employment of being Master of the King's Works . . . to make way for this favourite of foreigners' (*The Memoirs of John Ker, of Kersland . . . Relating to Politics, Trade, and History*, 3d edn, 1727, ii. 110).

7. Wren lived in a house in Scotland Yard appropriated to the office of surveyor-general (John Ward, *Lives of the Professors of Gresham College*, 1740, p. 105).

My grandfather, not in the least discomposed, answered his rude visitor, with a mildness, that like 'music, had charms to soothe a savage beast.'[8]

'Threats are quite needless (said he); we will remove out of your way as fast as possible. I have a house of my own at Hampton Court,[9] where I can lay my head. To the King's pleasure I submit, and cheerfully resign to him what is his—and for yourself, Mr Benson, I give you joy of your post; and wish you may live to be more deserving of it, than any of your predecessors.[10]'

'A variety of knowledge (you proceed) proclaims, the universality; a multiplicity of works, the abundance; St Paul's, the greatness of his genius.'

Nobly said. And more than forty *Parentalia*-writers[11] could have expressed in forty of *their* books.

How sorry am I to find after this just eulogy a false taste attributed so unjustly.

I won't cavil at what seems to me however a paradox; that of a confessedly great genius's wanting a true taste; or wanting it, at some times, and on some certain occasions: but allowing the proposition true, so long as a servant is not above his master, Sir Christopher's taste is not to be condemned for what he was under an absolute necessity of doing.

For instance, in the first, you mention Hampton Court.[12] Now, Sir, I do assure you, upon my word, that I have heard my grandfather very much admired for accomplishing this work, *so, as it is.* Not that those gentlemen wanted a good taste; for theirs, was pretty much like your own, I believe; but, because they took upon them to know so perfectly well, who *the person* was, that the Surveyor had to please, at that time.

I wish I could tell you where the original design of Hampton Court palace, in my grandfather's own drawing, was to be seen. *This*

8. 'Music has charms to soothe a savage breast' (Congreve, *The Mourning Bride* I. i. 1).

9. 'He had another house, that belonged to the surveyor-general to the Crown, at Hampton Court; the enjoyment of which had been granted him by Queen Anne, and was held by an Exchequer lease, which descended to his son and heir' (Ward, op. cit. 105).

10. Benson's joy was short-lived; he was dismissed for incompetency in 1719 (*Wren Society* 1930, vii. 204).

11. *Parentalia: or Memoirs of the Family of the Wrens,* compiled by Christopher Wren (1675–1747) and published by Stephen Wren, 'with the care of Joseph Ames,' 1750. HW's copy is Hazen, *Cat. of HW's Lib.*, No. 1137.

12. 'Hampton Court was sacrificed to the god of false taste' (*Anecdotes* iii. 90).

the Queen (Mary) good Lady! mightily approved of, but had not influence enough to get executed.[13]

I remember somewhat of a cupola, and that is *all* I remember, for it was many years ago, and only for about two minutes time, that my father favoured me with the sight.

This, no doubt, fell at last, with all the rest, into the hands of one Master Stephen;[14] who sold, he knew not what, to the first bidders; and lumped many of the drawings,[15] in conjunction (comically enough) with tables, chairs, pamphlets, old books, and saddle-cloths.

'The tower of St Dunstan's church; and the church of St Mary's, at Warwick; you also hold in high disdain; and the last to be much the worst of the two.'[16]

Your judgment, for aught I can say, may be very right, on this tower, and this church. But are you sure the tower of St Dunstan's is Sir Christopher's?

I do not ask the question, as questions are sometimes asked, by the way of insult, and because one knows the contrary to be true: I really ask from ignorance of the truth; and because I have some notion of having heard, that a tower, or a steeple, had been tacked to one of his churches, since his time. I am far from asserting such a thing for fact; I know nothing of the matter; am acquainted with nobody now that can resolve me; am moreover old, and may be forgetful.

But for the church at Warwick, I can speak knowingly. It is the *tower* only that was my grandfather's.

The *church pretty well* escaped the fire; the parts which did not, were rebuilt by the mason of the town at that time; afterwards known by the name, and title of, Honest Frank Smith.[17]

13. Wren's first designs (1689) for adapting the old Tudor palace at Hampton Court for royal lodgings are illustrated in *Wren Society,* 1927, iv. 9–12 and plates IV–VII, XI–XII. The drawings are now in Sir John Soane's Museum and All Souls Collections (ibid. 77–80). The rebuilding was interrupted by Queen Mary's death in 1694, and later resumed until William III's death in 1702 (ibid. 10, 19–20, 38, 55).

14. Possibly Stephen Wren (b. 1722), son of Christopher Wren and half-brother of HW's correspondent (Ryland, op. cit. pedigree following p. xl).

15. The collection of coins and medals of Christopher Wren, 'together with the collection of drawings of architecture of the late Sir Christopher Wren, his father,' was sold by Abraham Langford, auctioneer in the Great Piazza, Covent Garden, 4–6 April 1749. The architectural drawings were lots 30–45 in the sale; lot 35 is listed in the sale catalogue as 'sixty-six drawings of Hampton Court, all pasted into a book.'

16. 'The tower of St Dunstan's church, attempted in the Gothic style with very poor success. The church of St Mary at Warwick, in the same manner, but still worse' (*Anecdotes* iii. 91).

17. A contemporary guide-book mentions 'the rare abilities of Messrs Smith, the builders, who finished this edifice A.D. 1704' (*Wren Society* 1933, x. 128).

He it was also that worked the tower, from a plan which my grandfather gave to his old friend, the Lord Digby.[18]

But Smith being under nobody's inspection, blundered egregiously in his performance; I can't say, what his blunders in particular were, but I know the general truth, that *so it was.*

And now, Sir, I think I have done speaking of Sir Christopher Wren, as an architect; and am heartily glad of it. For it is not in *that* light I wish him to be considered by you; although by the world he is rarely seen, or understood in any other.

The abundance of his works, and the grandeur of some of them, is manifestly the reason. But this abundance was owing to an accident, the fire of London, which threw him directly into such a heap of rubbish, as during his whole life, he could never extricate himself from.

I used his own phrase, in those words, a heap of rubbish. And if we, at this day, rightly consider, what you was pleased to call the universality of his genius, we shall sincerely lament, the strict confinement of it to a single object, and that too, in some respects, *beneath* him.

Oh! that he had never built anything but summer-houses for his own diversion; or, now and then, a palace at Winchester for the pleasure of a 'merry king'[19] who loved his company; (and by the by gave him first an estate, and afterwards the place at Court, merely to have the more of it) what helps and improvements in all the arts and sciences might not have been expected from such a working brain as his, when left at leisure to its own operations? I say, Sir, left at full leisure; and not to be perplexed, and harassed, as Sir Christopher was, from morning to night with the cares and fatigues of as busy a life as perhaps ever fell to any man's lot.

Besides these, what useful secrets might he have discovered in his particular profession; I mean, physic; which he had bred himself to, and seemed by nature peculiarly adapted?—but I shall run into a schoolboy's declamation, if I don't take care. In a word, Sir, I only meant to observe, that had Sir Christopher not been by accident so *great* an architect, he might have proved a greater blessing to man-

18. William Digby (ca 1662–1752), 5th Bn Digby of Geashill, 1686; M.P.

19. 'This palace was begun by the commands of King Charles the Second, (March 23, 1683) and prosecuted with that expedition, that the greatest part was covered in, and finished, as to the shell, before the King's decease, February 1684–5' (Wren, *Parentalia,* p. 325). HW called the palace 'one of the ugliest piles of building in the island' (*Anecdotes* iii. 92). For an account of this building see *Wren Society,* 1930, vii. 11–21.

kind; and latest posterity have enjoyed the benefit of his researches, when houses, churches, and monuments will be no more than *heaps of rubbish indeed;* or at best, only what Vanbrugh prophesied of his Blenheim, make glorious ruins.

I am ashamed of the length of my letter, and being such a stranger too; but I knew not how to manage matters more concisely. I have not said half what I thought to do neither—but 'tis enough, I believe.

Yet one thing only I would add (late as it is) if you will give me leave.

The story[20] of my grandfather's being carried once every year to see St Paul's is credible; may be supposed, very natural; and I should have no objection to its being universally received, but that I am well satisfied it is not true. Vertue[21] must have dreamt it.

The last time that I ever heard of his visiting St Paul's, was when he had business there; and went to lay the *last* stone to it, *with his own hands,* as he had laid the *first.*[22]

A piece of ceremony, not necessary, one may say; nevertheless what, I reckon, no man in the same case would have willingly omitted.

The time when this was, and somewhat about the ceremonial part, is mentioned somewhere in the *Parentalia,*[23] as well as I remember. But I do not remember that odd history book makes any memorandum of what had like to have proved a very *singular* conclusion of that day's work.

As Sir Christopher was coming down again, the stick he leaned upon, slipped beside the scaffold, and he was following after it, 'so many fathom deep, the very thought is dizziness'[24] but Mr Strong,[25]

20. In *Anecdotes* iii. 91.

21. George Vertue, whose MSS provided the basic material for the *Anecdotes.*

22. Sir Christopher Wren apparently presided over the laying of the foundation stone of St Paul's 21 June 1675, assisted by his mason, Thomas Strong (d. 1681). Sir Christopher's son is credited with laying the last stone of the lantern on 26 Oct. 1708, with the assistance of Wren's master mason, Edward Strong senior (ca 1652–1723). See *Wren Society,* 1937, xiv. ix–x; Robert Clutterbuck, *The History and Antiquities of the County of Hertford,* 1815–27, i. 167–8; Jane Lang, *Rebuilding St Paul's after the Great Fire of London,* 1956, pp. 79, 241.

23. A short account of the ceremony is given in *Parentalia,* p. 293, where Sir Christopher's son Christopher is said to have placed the 'highest or last stone on the top of the lantern' in the presence of Edward Strong and other masons.

24. Not identified. The story may be true; according to tradition Sir Christopher was hoisted up in a basket to the dome of St Paul's several times a week to supervise the construction (W. R. Matthews and W. M. Atkins, *A History of St Paul's Cathedral,* 1957, p. 192).

25. See n. 22 above.

his master mason, caught him in the critical moment up in his arms; and so saved (as my grandfather with a *smile* told him) 'an old man's life, not worth the saving.'

I don't know whether you will think this anecdote worth your reading; but as I have made it short, and mean to conclude with it, hope you will the sooner excuse, and let me have the honour of subscribing myself,

Sir,

Your most obedient humble servant,

CHRIST[R] WREN

TO CHRISTOPHER WREN, Thursday 9 August 1764

Printed from a photostat of the MS in the Berg Collection, New York Public Library. First printed, Toynbee vi. 103–7. The MS was sold Puttick and Simpson 12 March 1862 (Extraordinary Collection of Autograph Letters Sale), lot 712, to Holloway; resold Sotheby's 2 April 1875 (Interesting and Valuable Autograph Letters Sale), lot 542, to Naylor; *penes* Mrs Alfred Morrison in 1905; sold Sotheby's 15 April 1918 (Morrison Sale, Part II), lot 894, to Edwards; offered by Maggs, Cat. Nos 373 (Christmas 1918), lot 2649; 405 (summer 1921), lot 1384; 445 (Christmas 1923), lot 2972; 474 (summer 1926), lot 1336; 510 (autumn 1928), lot 2181; later acquired for the Berg Collection.

Strawberry Hill, Aug. 9th 1764.

Sir,

YOU do me justice in believing that I should receive any information from you with pleasure, and should be ready to give you any proper satisfaction that depends on me with regard to that great man, your grandfather. If I had not supposed, Sir, that you had exhausted the subject in that agreeable and instructive work the *Parentalia,* I should have taken the liberty of consulting you on the life of Sir Christopher Wren. I have already apologized in my *Anecdotes* for attempting an account of him,[1] as I could add nothing to what has already been written on his article.

1. 'I do not mean to be very minute in the account of Wren even as an architect. Every circumstance of his story has been written and repeated. . . . above all a descendant of his own has given us a folio, called *Parentalia,* which leaves nothing to be desired on this subject. Yet in a work of such a nature as this, men

When I began your letter, Sir, I own I was alarmed. The caution I have used on modern artists, lest I should give a moment's pain to their families, is evident. It has occasioned the latter volumes of my work being more dry, and perhaps less amusing than the former. It has even made me stop before I had completed my plan,[2] because to say the truth, there are exceedingly few of the latter painters on whom it is possible to bestow just panegyric, and I cannot sacrifice my veracity in compliment to their descendants. But when I had finished your letter, my apprehension was in great measure removed, as the little I have said in dispraise of Sir Christopher, cannot I think, Sir, reasonably give you any uneasiness.

I have said in my book, where I certainly did not mean to flatter him or you, that he was a genius. I have not said, nor can say consistently with truth, that he was faultless. Methinks even the few objections I have made to him confirm the encomiums—a general panegyric always passes for such, and does no honour to the person extolled. Criticism mixed with approbation is apt to make both appear sincere, though the former may not be just. My criticisms on Sir Christopher are given, and could not be given otherwise, but as matters of opinion. I am no standard of judgment. The sole question on the article of taste will be whether Sir Christopher or I knew best what taste is—weigh so inconsiderable judgment as mine, Sir, against Sir Christopher's, and you will soon be easy on that head.

You say, Sir, that it appears a paradox to you that a great genius should want true taste—Give me leave to differ with you and to give you my reasons. So far from being a paradox, the one almost appears to me a consequence of the other. I will not defend myself on the distinction I might fairly make, that Sir Christopher Wren was a genius in some respects, and wanted taste in others, which yet I presume is all I have said in effect; but it seems to me as if there was a sobriety in taste which would be a shackle on a genius. That there has been now and then a genius (for a genius itself is a curiosity) without taste, and often taste without genius, is evident from example. One of the greatest geniuses that ever existed, Shakespeare, undoubtedly wanted taste. In the very class, which is the subject of

would be disappointed, should they turn to it, and receive no satisfaction. They must be gratified, though my province becomes little more than that of a mere transcriber' (*Anecdotes,* 1st edn, iii. 89–90).

2. The fourth volume of *Anecdotes,* dealing with painters in the reigns of George I and George II, is dated 1771, but was not published until 1780. See *post* 4 Oct. 1780.

this letter, I mean, architecture, Inigo Jones seems to me to have had more taste than genius. A genius is original, invents. Taste selects, perhaps copies with judgment. If I am right, have I wronged your ancestor?

You impute to King William, Sir, the want of taste in Hampton Court—you therefore allow there was want of taste. Was I to blame, when observing that want of taste, I imputed it to the architect? you will perhaps urge the same plea for the palace at Winchester—Forgive me if I say that to prove Sir Christopher had a taste for erecting palaces equal to what he had for churches, some building ought to be specified in which he has exerted it. A prince may name some general style of building to his architect, but does not draw the design—and even if his choice is vicious; if the architect has taste, he will exert it even in an injudicious style. The truth is, the fault was in the age, and to that I have really imputed it, not to your grandfather. I shall however, Sir, on your information do justice to Sir Christopher, as I should be glad to do it if I was authorized in what I have heard, that he gave two other designs for St Paul's, preferable even to what is executed, but which were rejected by the Duchess of Portsmouth's[3] influence for interested reasons—I say, I will mention the fact of a superior plan for Hampton Court.[4]

With regard to the tower of St Dunstan's, I cannot at this moment resolve you from what book I took my authority; whether from any of those I have quoted, or from the printed table of Sir Christopher's designs for churches. If I can find or you can give me, Sir, any authority for contradicting it, I shall be most ready to satisfy you[5]—as I certainly will in all facts you disprove, and in matters of opinion, if you convince me. You have too good sense, Sir, to expect or require that I should unsay what I have said, for no reason but to pay a compliment to Sir Christopher's memory, which would do him no honour, and would make me ridiculous.

The church at Warwick shall certainly no longer be imputed to him by me.[6]

3. Louise-Renée de Penancoet de Kéroualle (1649–1734), cr. (1673) Bns Petersfield, Cts of Fareham, and Ds of Portsmouth; Charles II's mistress from 1671 until his death.

4. HW added the following footnote in *Anecdotes,* 2d edn, iii. 96: 'I have been assured by a descendant of Sir Christopher, that he gave another design for Hampton Court in a better taste, which Queen Mary wished to have had executed, but was overruled.'

5. HW did not revise the passage concerning the tower of St Dunstan-in-the-East in the second edition of *Anecdotes.*

6. HW corrected this imputation in a

As I mean in my next edition to do justice to Sir Christopher where it is due, I must here Sir do justice to Vertue, whose merit in the *Anecdotes* is real, while mine is only trifling and ornamental. The story of your grandfather being carried every year to St Paul's came not from Vertue, but from my having heard it often. It appeared very natural, and certainly cannot convey an idea of the smallest imputation. Would any man living have wondered if Milton had had his *Paradise Lost* read over to him every year?

I flatter myself, Sir, I have restored myself to your favour. It would vex me to have disobliged you undesignedly—but consider, Sir, how hardly an author would be circumstanced, if he was prohibited from speaking his opinion on public works, lest it should offend the descendants of the poets, architects, painters, etc. in question. Every public character, and such is an architect, is liable to be criticized. Nobody has been more censured than my own father—with all the veneration I feel for his memory, I never thought him perfect. You Sir justly hold Sir Christopher's talent for architecture far inferior to his other qualifications—while his moral virtues remain unblemished, you will not, I am sure, think, Sir, that it is of any consequence whether Hampton Court and Winchester are executed in the best taste, or not.

I am Sir

Your obedient humble servant

HOR. WALPOLE

To Christ. Wren Esq.

footnote to the second edition (iii. 97): 'I have been informed . . . by Sir Christopher's descendant, that the tower only of this church as it is at present was designed by his grandfather.'

TO WILLIAM PITT (later Lord Chatham), Wednesday 29 August 1764

Printed from *Correspondence of William Pitt, Earl of Chatham,* ed. W. S. Taylor and J. H. Pringle, 1838–40, ii. 292–3, where the letter was first printed from the MS then in the possession of the executors of Pitt's son, John, 2d Earl of Chatham. Reprinted, Wright iv. 449–50; Cunningham iv. 272; Toynbee vi. 117–18 (full closing and signature omitted in Wright, Cunningham, and Toynbee). The history of the MS and its present whereabouts are not known.

Arlington Street, August 29, 1764.

Sir,

AS YOU have always permitted me to offer you the trifles printed at my press,[1] I am glad to have one to send you of a little more consequence, than some in which I have had myself too great a share. The singularity of the work[2] I now trouble you with is greater merit than its rarity; though there are but two hundred copies printed, of which only half are mine. If it amuses an hour or two of your idle time, I am overpaid. My greatest ambition is to pay that respect, which every Englishman owes to your character and services; and therefore you must not wonder if an inconsiderable man seizes every opportunity, however awkwardly, of assuring you, that he is,

Sir,

Your most devoted humble servant,

HORACE WALPOLE

1. See Pitt's letter *ante* 7 Jan. 1761, thanking HW for a copy of Lucan's *Pharsalia* printed at the SH Press.

2. *The Life of Edward Lord Herbert of Cherbury, Written by Himself.* The printing of it was completed 27 Jan. 1764, but HW did not begin distributing copies until July (Hazen, *SH Bibl.* 70). See *ante* 10 July 1763 and n. 2.

From WILLIAM PITT (later Lord Chatham), Thursday 30 August 1764

Printed from the MS now WSL. First printed, Toynbee *Supp.* ii. 127. For the history of the MS see *ante* 27 Feb. 1757.

Dated by the previous letter.

Endorsed in an unidentified hand: Pitt.

Thursday past 3 o'clock.

MR PITT is just come to town[1] and has the pleasure to find Mr Walpole's most obliging and valuable present. He cannot defer a moment begging Mr Walpole to accept a thousand sincere thanks for the great honour of this flattering mark of his remembrance.

From the REV. THOMAS BIRCH, Thursday 30 August 1764

Printed from the MS now WSL. First printed, Cunningham iv. 274–5 (closing partially omitted). The MS was sold Sotheby's 21 Dec. 1853 (J. H. S. Pigott Sale), lot 1004, to Cunningham; not further traced until resold Sotheby's 17 Dec. 1956 (property of Mrs Eileen M. Garnett), lot 81, to Maggs for WSL.

Norfolk Street in the Strand, Aug. 30, 1764.

Sir,

THE enclosed is a copy of the letter of Sir William Herbert,[1] mentioned to you by Dr Watson,[2] which I had thoughts of sending you some time ago upon an accidental sight of your elegant edition of Lord Herbert's *Life* of himself, and remarking in it the passage where his Lordship speaks of Sir William, his father-in-law, as *being noted to be of a very high mind;*[3] of which you will think this letter a

1. Pitt spent most of his time at Hayes, his seat in Kent, during 1764–5, in an attempt to strengthen his failing health (Basil Williams, *The Life of William Pitt,* 1913, ii. 129).

---

1. (ca 1554–93), of St Julians, Monmouth; Kt, 1576. He was one of the 'undertakers' for the plantation of Munster, which, along with his property elsewhere, he left to his only child Mary, on the condition that she marry a Herbert. She became the wife of Edward Herbert, afterwards Lord Herbert of Chirbury, 28 Feb. 1599, when he was sixteen and she twenty-three (GEC vi. 442).

2. Probably William Watson (1715–87), Kt, 1786; F.R.S., 1741; physician and naturalist.

3. *The Life of Edward Lord Herbert of Cherbury, Written by Himself,* SH, 1764, p. 26.

full proof. The copy, from which I took what I send you, was in an old hand, and given me several years ago by William Jones[4] Esq., F.R.S. and an eminent mathematician, deceased.

I observed in Lord Herbert's *Life,* in a page which I have forgot, but you will easily recollect, that he speaks of a Court wit, who in your edition, I think, bears the name of Tom Cogge.[5] I am persuaded, that the person meant was Tho[mas] Carew[6] Esq., sometimes spelt *Cary* and *Carye,* of whom we have a volume of *Poems, Songs, and Sonnets, with a Masque.*[7] He was one of the gentlemen of the Privy Chamber to King Charles I and Sewer in Ordinary to his Majesty. His character is given by Lord Clarendon in the history of his own life.[8]

Monsieur Balagny,[9] who is said by Lord Herbert to have killed eight or nine men in single fight,[10] died himself of the wounds which he received in an encounter with Monsieur Pinocin, whom he killed in the streets of Paris in March 1611/2, as appears from Sir Ralph Winwood's *Memorials,*[11] Vol. III, p. 350, 353.

I am,
Sir,
Your most obedient and most humble servant,

THO. BIRCH

4. (1675–1749), F.R.S., 1712; author of *Synopsis Palmariorum Matheseos,* 1706, and editor of Newton's *Analysis per quantitatum series, fluxiones ac differentias,* 1711.

5. The name on p. 135 of the *Life* is Thomas Caage.

6. (ca 1595–1640), courtier and poet, who accompanied his friend Lord Herbert to the French court in 1619. See *The Autobiography of Edward, Lord Herbert of Cherbury,* ed. Sidney Lee, 2d edn, [1906], pp. xx, 106; *The Poems of Thomas Carew,* ed. Rhodes Dunlap, Oxford, 1949, pp. xxxi, xlii-xliii, lxxvi.

7. *Poems, Songs and Sonnets, Together with a Masque,* 4th edn, 1670 (reissue, 1671). HW's copy is Hazen, *Cat. of HW's Lib.,* No. 1889.

8. 'He was very much esteemed by the most eminent persons in the Court, and well looked upon by the King himself. . . . a person of a pleasant and facetious wit, and made many poems' (*Life of Edward Earl of Clarendon . . . Written by Himself,* Oxford, 1759, i. 36). HW's copy of the 1759 folio edition is Hazen, op. cit., No. 2.

9. Damien de Monluc (ca 1587–1612), Seigneur de Balagny. He was the son of Jean de Monluc (1545–1603), Seigneur de Balagny, Maréchal de France, 1594, and Renée de Clermont d'Amboise (d. 1595) (Joseph Jean, Comte de Broqua, *Le Maréchal de Monluc sa famille et son temps,* 1924, p. 305; La Chenaye-Desbois and Badier, *Dictionnaire de la noblesse,* 3d edn, 1863–76, xiv. 236–7; NBG).

10. See Lord Herbert's *Life,* pp. 69–70.

11. *Memorials of Affairs of State in the Reigns of Q. Elizabeth and K. James I,* edited by Edmund Sawyer from the papers of Sir Ralph Winwood (?1563–1617) and others, 3 vols, 1725. HW's copy is Hazen, op. cit., No. 1100.

[Enclosure]

Copy of a letter[12] of Sir William Herbert[13] of St Julian's in Monmouthshire to a gentleman of the family of Morgan of Glantyrnam.

From St Julian.

Sir,

PERUSE this letter in God's name. Be not disquieted. I reverence your hoary hair. Although in your son I find too much folly and lewdness, yet in you I expect gravity and wisdom. It hath pleased your son late at Bristol to deliver a challenge to a man of mine on the behalf of a gentleman, as he said, as good as myself. Who he was he named not, neither do I know: but if he be as good as myself, it must either be for virtue, for birth, for ability, or for calling and dignity. For virtue I think he meant not; for it is a matter that exceeds his judgment. If for birth, he must be the heir male of an earl, the heir in blood of ten earls; for in testimony thereof I bear their several coats; besides, he must be of the blood royal; for by my grandmother Devereux I am lineally and legitimately descended out of the body of Edward the Fourth.[14] If for ability, he must have a thousand pounds a year in possession, a thousand pounds a year more in expectation, and must have some thousands in substance besides. If for calling and dignity, he must be a knight, a lord of several signories in several kingdoms, a lieutenant of his county, and a counsellor of a province.

Now to lay all circumstances aside, be it known to your son, or to any man else, that if there be anyone who beareth the name of a gentleman, and whose words are of reputation in his country, that doth say, or dare say that I have done unjustly, spoken an untruth, stained my credit, or reputation in this matter or in any matter else, wherein your son is exasperated, I say, he lieth in his throat; and my sword shall maintain my word upon him in any place or province, wheresoever he dare, where I stand not sworn to observe the peace. But if they be such, as are within my governance, and over whom I

12. Printed in GM 1785, lv pt i. 32.

13. 'This gentleman's daughter and coheir Mary was married Febr[uary] 28, 1598 to Edward Herbert, afterwards Lord Herbert of Cherbury' (Birch's MS note).

14. Apparently not so; Sir William's great-great-grandfather (ca 1423–69), cr. (1468) E. of Pembroke, had married ca 1455 Anne, daughter of Sir Walter Devereux and sister of Sir Walter Devereux (d. 1485), Lord Ferrers, 1461. A later Walter Devereux (ca 1491–1558), Lord Ferrers, 1501, cr. (1550) Vct Hereford, married the step-granddaughter of Edward IV, but Sir William Herbert was not descended from him (DNB *sub* Sir William Herbert; GEC *sub* Bourchier, Dorset, Ferrers, Hereford, and Pembroke).

have authority, I will for their reformation chastise them with justice; and for their malapert misdemeanour bind them to their good behaviour. Of this sort I account your son and his like, against whom I will shortly direct my warrant, if this my warning will not reform him. And so I thought good to advertise you hereof and leave you to God.

Your loving cousin,

WILLIAM HERBERT

TO WILLIAM PITT (later LORD CHATHAM), ca Friday 31 August 1764

Printed for the first time from a photostat of the MS kindly furnished by the late Sir Edward Hoare, 7th Bt, through the good offices of Lt-Col. R. P. F. White. The MS passed from Sir Edward Hoare (d. 1969) to his son, Sir Timothy Edward Charles Hoare, 8th Bt, who deposited it in the Public Record Office, London, in 1972; its earlier history is not known.

Dated approximately by Pitt's letter to HW *ante* 30 Aug. 1764 which HW probably received the same day as he 'was dressing in haste to go out to dinner.'

MR Walpole was dressing in haste to go out to dinner, or should undoubtedly have immediately expressed his gratitude to Mr Pitt, both for the honour of accepting the book,[1] and for the trouble he was so good to give himself by writing. Mr Walpole cannot presume to hope that such trifling sheets should amuse Mr Pitt, but as the latter has permitted him to offer the productions of the Strawberry press, he depended upon the same indulgence, and he owns more officiously now than ever, though he flatters himself that Mr Pitt knows that Mr Walpole's homage has long been paid to his superior genius, and not to his situation.

1. *The Life of Edward Lord Herbert of Cherbury,* SH, 1764. See *ante* 29 Aug. and 30 Aug. 1764.

To the REV. THOMAS BIRCH, Monday 3 September 1764

Printed from a photostat of the MS in the British Museum (Add. MS 4320, f. 103). First printed, Wright iv. 452. Reprinted, Cunningham iv. 274–5; N&Q 1862, 3d ser., ii. 352; Toynbee vi. 120–1. The MS was among the Birch papers bequeathed to the BM on his death in 1766.

Dated by Birch's endorsement.

Endorsed by Birch: Sept. 3, 1764.

Address: To the Reverend Dr Birch in Norfolk Street in the Strand. *Postmark:* PENNY POST PAID.

Sir,

I AM extremely obliged to you for the favour of your letter,[1] and the enclosed curious one of Sir William Herbert. It would have made a very valuable addition to Lord Herbert's *Life,* which is now too late, as I have no hope that Lord Powis[2] will permit any more to be printed. There were indeed so very few, and but half of those for my share,[3] that I have not it in my power to offer you a copy, having disposed of my part. It is really a pity that so singular a curiosity should not be public—but I must not complain, as Lord Powis has been so good as to indulge my request thus far.

I am Sir

Your much obliged humble servant

HOR. WALPOLE

1. *Ante* 30 Aug. 1764.

2. Henry Arthur Herbert (ca 1703–72), cr. (1743) Bn Herbert and (1748) E. of Powis; M.P. See *ante* 10 July 1763, n. 2.

3. 100 of the 200 copies printed (*ante* 29 Aug. 1764).

From the DUKE OF NEWCASTLE, Saturday 29 September 1764

Printed for the first time from a photostat of the MS copy in Thomas Hurdis's hand in the British Museum (Add. MS 32,962, f. 169). An extract from the letter was printed in *Horace Walpole: Writer, Politician, and Connoisseur,* ed. W. H. Smith, New Haven, 1967, p. 81. The whereabouts of the letter actually sent to HW is not known.

Endorsed by Thomas Hurdis: Copy to Honourable Hora[tio] Walpole Esq. September 29th 1764.

Claremont, September 29th 1764.

Dear Sir,

THE Duchess of Newcastle's[1] ill state of health[2] has prevented my having the honour and pleasure of waiting upon you at Strawberry Hill; she is now, I thank God, a great deal better;[3] and, if you will give me leave, I will drink tea with you, on Tuesday morning next,[4] if it be convenient to you; if not, any other morning that you shall choose. I shall bring my nephew Onslow[5] with me: but I shall tell him, that I have some private business with you; so his coming will be attended with no inconvenience.

I propose to go to Gunnersbury,[6] on Monday. I was on Thursday at the Duke's,[7] to receive his commands, before he went to Newmarket. I thank God, the last accounts of the Duke of Devonshire[8]

1. Lady Henrietta Godolphin (d. 1776), m. (1717) Thomas Pelham Holles, cr. (1715) D. of Newcastle-upon-Tyne.

2. A fit of the gout, followed by a 'violent giddiness in her head and hysteric disorder' (Newcastle to Dr Cæsar Hawkins 18 Sept. 1764, BM Add. MS 33,068, f. 99). Newcastle wrote Lady Gage 2 Oct.: 'The Duchess of Newcastle . . . has been very ill, and has suffered very much, from several severe illnesses, as well as from the loss of her sister [the Duchess of Leeds, who died 3 Aug.], whom she loved very tenderly' (ibid., f. 125).

3. Newcastle wrote Lord Rockingham 29 Sept.: 'Your Lordship will be glad to hear, that, (thank God) the Duchess of Newcastle is greatly mended . . . [and] to be soon perfectly restored to her health. She has suffered greatly for some days with a violent pain in her stomach, bowels and back' (BM Add. MS 32,962, f. 166).

4. 2 Oct. See *post* 2 Oct. 1764 and n. 4.

5. George Onslow (1731–1814), 4th Bn Onslow, 1776; cr. (1801) E. of Onslow. In 1753 he had married Henrietta Shelley, Newcastle's niece.

6. The Princess Amelia's summer residence at Ealing, Middlesex.

7. The Duke of Cumberland, at Windsor Great Lodge (Cumberland to Newcastle 25 Sept., Newcastle to Lord John Cavendish 28 Sept., BM Add. MS 32,962, ff. 150, 164). The Duke of Cumberland proposed 'to go to town . . . Saturday afternoon [29 Sept.]' and on 'Sunday to Newmarket' (ibid.) The races began on 1 Oct. (*Daily Adv.* 2 Oct.).

8. William Cavendish, 4th D. of Devonshire, HW's occasional correspondent.

were more favourable than the former:[9] but I am in the utmost pain for him.

I am, dear Sir, with great respect,
Your obliged humble servant,
Holles Newcastle

Honourable Horatio Walpole Esq. at Strawberry Hill.

To the Duke of Newcastle, Saturday 29 September 1764

Printed from a photostat of the MS in the British Museum (Add. MS 32,962, f. 171). First printed, Toynbee vi. 122. An extract from the letter was printed in *Horace Walpole: Writer, Politician, and Connoisseur,* ed. W. H. Smith, New Haven, 1967, p. 81. The letter was apparently carried by the servant who brought the previous letter and was received by Newcastle the same day.

Dated by the endorsement.

Endorsed by Thomas Hurdis: September 29th 1764. Mr Hora[tio] Walpole. R[eceived].

My Lord,

I am quite confounded that your Grace should think it necessary to make any excuses to me, or give yourself the trouble to call on me. I must not refuse the honour you design me, though if it is only from your Grace's great goodness to me, I would beg to receive your commands at Claremont, and hope if your Grace thinks a visit to me necessary, that you will look upon it as made. May I beg your Grace will really choose which is most convenient to you, and as you go to Gunnersbury on Monday, permit one of your servants to call at my house, and let me know where it will be most convenient for me to obey your commands.

I rejoice at any favourable accounts of the poor Duke of Devon-

9. Devonshire's brother, Lord John Cavendish, wrote Newcastle from Spa 17 Sept.: 'Last Saturday [15 Sept.] . . . he was taken with a violent headache, and the next day was rather feverish . . . this has prevented the drinking the waters for two days' (BM Add. MS 32,962, f. 127). But Lord Frederick Cavendish reported to Newcastle 24 Sept. that 'there is infinite amendment, they had bled him, and his blood was good, of a *proper texture,* and not sizey' (BM Add. MS 33,068, f. 111).

shire; but I will say no more, as I am at Lady Suffolk's,[1] and have only Miss Hotham's[2] pen and paper to write with.

I am my Lord

Your Grace's most obliged and most obedient humble servant

HOR. WALPOLE

To the Duke of Newcastle, Tuesday 2 October 1764

Printed from a photostat of the MS in the British Museum (Add. MS 32,962, f. 191). First printed, Toynbee vi. 123–4. An extract from the letter was printed in *Horace Walpole: Writer, Politician, and Connoisseur,* ed. W. H. Smith, New Haven, 1967, p. 81.

Dated by the endorsement.

Endorsed by Thomas Hurdis: October 2d 1764. Mr Horatio Walpole. R[eceived].

My Lord,

THE weather is so bad, that I own I should have been in pain at seeing your Grace here today,[1] for fear of your getting cold,[2] and I earnestly entreat your Grace not to think of it this year, unless the weather settles to be much finer than it has been lately. Whenever you have any commands for me, I am ready at a moment's warning if you please to send for me. On Thursday I should be proud of the honour of seeing your Grace, but I am to have company[3] at dinner, who will probably come early to see the house, and might be troublesome to your Grace. If Friday is fine, and your Grace chooses it, I shall be happy to receive the honour you

1. Henrietta Hobart (ca 1688–1767), m. 1 (1706) Charles Howard (1675–1733), 9th E. of Suffolk, 1731; m. 2 (1735) Hon. George Berkeley (d. 1746); HW's occasional correspondent. She lived at Marble Hill, Twickenham.

2. Henrietta Gertrude Hotham (1753–1816), Lady Suffolk's great-niece and companion at Marble Hill, for whom HW wrote *The Magpie and Her Brood.* See *post* mid-October 1764, n. 1.

1. Newcastle had expected to drink tea with HW at SH on Tuesday morning, 2 Oct. (Newcastle to HW *ante* 29 Sept. 1764). His letter, giving his excuses for postponing the visit and asking HW to write a letter of recommendation for Dr Blanshard to Lord Hertford (see below), is missing.

2. Newcastle's fear of catching cold was notorious; see MONTAGU i. 323.

3. Not identified.

design me;[4] but I will not expect it, lest it should put your Grace to the least inconvenience.

I was unlucky in not receiving your Grace's orders sooner about Dr Blanshard,[5] having written to Lord Hertford but yesterday.[6] I shall however go to London on Friday after dinner, and will find some way of sending a letter to Paris, for I scarce ever write by the post and will take care to recommend Dr Blanshard in so strong a manner that it shall be very agreeable to him, and show the great regard I have to your Grace's commands.[7]

I am equally impatient with your Grace for more accounts from the Spa; I tremble, and yet am not without hopes.[8] The return of the Duke's old disorder,[9] which in a like case saved Lord Chesterfield,[10] raises one's spirits, and yet it is too early to be confident. If I should not have the honour of seeing your Grace on Friday, will you be so good as to let me know if I may have the pleasure of waiting on you any day next week!

I am with the greatest respect
My Lord
Your Grace's most obedient humble servant

HOR. WALPOLE

4. HW wrote Conway Friday, 5 Oct.: 'The Duke of Newcastle was come to breakfast with me, and had pulled out a letter from Lord Frederick [Cavendish], with a hopeless account of the poor Duke of Devonshire. Ere I could read it, Colonel Schutz called at the door and told my servant this fatal news!' (CONWAY ii. 445). The news, which proved to be false, was that the Duke of Cumberland had died at Newmarket. Newcastle went immediately to the Princess Amelia's at Gunnersbury, but the next day, after learning that the report was 'without any foundation,' he offered her his apologies for the mistake (BM Add. MS 32,962, f. 212).

5. Wilkinson Blanshard (1734–70), M.D., 1761; F.R.C.P., 1762; physician to St George's Hospital, 1766, where he succeeded Dr Richard Warren, the Duchess of Newcastle's physician (CONWAY ii. 442 nn. 2, 3; BM Add. MS 32,974, f. 171). See n. 1 above.

6. HW's letter of 1 Oct. to Hertford is missing.

7. On Friday morning, 5 Oct., before leaving SH for London, HW wrote to Hertford recommending Blanshard (CONWAY ii. 442).

8. 'The letters yesterday, from Spa, give a melancholy account of the poor Duke of Devonshire . . . I look on his case as a lost one!' (ibid. ii. 444–5).

9. 'The Duke of Devonshire . . . has suffered another stroke of the palsy, by which he has entirely lost the use of one hand and one side' (Charles Townshend to Lord Temple 4 Oct. 1764, in *The Grenville Papers*, ed. W. J. Smith, 1852–3, ii. 441). His condition improved during the next few days, but he relapsed on 28 Sept. and died four days later (BM Add. MS 32,962, f. 236; *Daily Adv.* 11 Oct.; GM 1764, xxxiv. 498).

10. Chesterfield visited Spa for two months in 1754. In a letter to the Bishop of Waterford 15 June 1754 he wrote that he had drunk the waters 'to the greatest benefit of my general state of health' (Chesterfield's *Letters*, ed. Bonamy Dobrée, 1932, v. 2118).

To Thomas Warton, Tuesday 9 October 1764

Printed from John Wooll, *Biographical Memoirs of the late Reverend Joseph Warton, D.D.*, 1806, pp. 296–7, where the letter was first printed. Reprinted, Cunningham iv. 279; Toynbee vi. 128–9. The history of the MS and its present whereabouts are not known.

Strawberry Hill, Oct. 9th 1764.

I SHOULD be very ungrateful, Sir, if I did not execute with much pleasure any orders you give me. My knowledge is extremely confined and trifling; but such information as I can give you, will always be at your service.

The most authentic picture of Margaret[1] Queen of Scotland is a whole length at Hampton Court. I have a small copy of the head by Vertue.[2] She has a round face, blue eyes, and brown hair, not light.

The original of her sister Mary[3] (with her second husband, Charles Brandon), which Vertue engraved while Lord Granville's,[4] is now mine;[5] her face is leaner and longer than in the print; her eyes blue, like her sister's, and her hair rather more dark. Vertue believed that the small head by Holbein, which I have, and was Richardson's,[6] and which is engraved among the *Illustrious Heads*[7] for Catharine Howard,[8] is the portrait of this Queen Mary; but it has no resemblance

1. Margaret Tudor (1489–1541), m. 1 (1503) James IV of Scotland; m. 2 (1514) Archibald Douglas, 6th E. of Angus; m. 3 (1528) Henry Stewart, 1st Bn Methven.

2. The picture at Hampton Court was a copy by Daniel Mytens of the lost original painted in 1515 (Ernest Law, *The Royal Gallery of Hampton Court,* 1898, p. 199). Vertue's copy, which hung in the Holbein Chamber at SH, was sold SH xx. 46 (with a portrait of Lady Jane Grey) to Town and Emanuel for £7. 7. 0.

3. Mary Tudor (1495–1533), m. 1 (1514) Louis XII of France; m. 2 (1515), as his third wife, Charles Brandon (ca 1484–1545), cr. (1514) D. of Suffolk.

4. John Carteret (1690–1763), 2d Bn Carteret, 1695; E. Granville, 1744.

5. HW bought the picture, which was in a frame designed by William Kent, at Lord Granville's sale for 19 guineas (MONTAGU ii. 53). It hung in the Gallery and was sold SH xxi. 94 to the Duke of Bedford for £535. 10. 0; it is still at Woburn Abbey. Vertue's engraving is pasted into HW's extra-illustrated copy, now WSL, of the *Des. of SH,* 1784 (Hazen, *SH Bibl.* 128, copy 12).

6. Jonathan Richardson, the elder (1665–1745), portrait painter. The greater part of his collection was sold in 1747, the remainder after the death of his son Jonathan in 1771 (*Anecdotes, Works* iii. 415).

7. Thomas Birch, *The Heads of Illustrious Persons of Great Britain Engraven by Mr Houbraken, and Mr Vertue,* 2 vols in one, 1743–51. HW's copy, now WSL, is Hazen, *Cat. of HW's Lib.*, No. 3637. The engraved portrait said to represent Catherine Howard appears facing p. 25 of Vol. I.

8. Catherine (Howard) (d. 1542), m. (1540) Henry VIII. In *Anecdotes of Paint-*

to the large one, which is unquestionably of her. In the two first pictures I mentioned, Margaret is much superior to Mary in point of beauty, though I think neither of them handsome; nor is any sense in either face. The picture supposed of Catharine Howard has much expression, but little beauty; the print resembles it very imperfectly. I am,

Sir,

Your most obedient humble servant,

HOR. WALPOLE

From LORD and LADY TEMPLE, mid-October 1764

Printed from the MS copy among the Grenville papers in the British Museum (Add. MS 57,821, ff. 162–3). First printed in *The Grenville Papers,* ed. W. J. Smith, 1852–3, ii. 189–90 (misdated 'December —, 1763'). The MS copy was among the Temple papers preserved at Stowe; sold in a collection of papers from Stowe by the 2d Duke of Buckingham and Chandos to his attorney, Edwin James, who in turn sold this collection to John Murray in 1851; acquired from his descendant, John Murray, by the British Museum in Nov. 1972. The original letter is missing.

Dated approximately by the printing of HW's 'verses' at the SH Press and by the prorogation of Parliament (see nn. 1 and 5 below).

LADY Temple is extremely obliged to Mr Walpole for his verses,[1] though they have occasioned a strange confusion amongst the winged kind at Stowe,[2] who took their flight to Marble Hill[3] some years ago; they think it very hard a parcel of chattering magpies should be produced to sing so much better: the creatures can prate, say they, what business have they to sing; if Lady Suffolk listens to

ing, HW described his picture as 'Cath. Howard, a miniature, damaged. It was Richardson's, who bought it out of the Arundelian collection' (*Works* iii. 79). The miniature is now in the Royal Collection at Windsor (Paul Ganz, *The Paintings of Hans Holbein,* 1956, p. 259).

1. *The Magpie and Her Brood, A Fable.* HW printed 200 copies at the SH Press 17 Oct. 1764 (Hazen, *SH Bibl.* 191–4). In 'Short Notes' he recorded: 'Oct. 15, wrote the "Fable of the Magpie and her Brood" for Miss Hotham, then near eleven years old, great-niece of Henrietta Hobart Countess Dowager of Suffolk' (GRAY i. 41). The copy sent to Lord and Lady Temple is apparently that in the Grenville Collection in the BM.

2. Lord Temple's seat.

3. Lady Suffolk's seat in Twickenham (HW to Newcastle *ante* 29 Sept. 1764, n. 1). Lord and Lady Temple had been married there 9 May 1737; at this time Miss Hotham was living at Marble Hill with her great-aunt.

the inhabitants of Strawberry Hill, she will never be able to bear the music of anybody else.

Lord T.[4] desires to thank you for your kind remembrance, and to assure you of his most affectionate respects. Before the Parliament meets, thanks to the prorogation,[5] he will be quite recovered of his lameness.[6] He already rides and walks very well.

TO THOMAS WARTON, Tuesday 30 October 1764

Printed from John Wooll, *Biographical Memoirs of the late Reverend Joseph Warton, D.D.*, 1806, p. 325, where the letter (misdated 'Oct. 30th, 1767') was first printed. Reprinted, Cunningham v. 72; Toynbee vii. 144 (likewise misdated, closing and signature omitted).

Wooll apparently misread the date of '1767'; the correct year is established by the reference to Lord Herbert of Chirbury's *Life*, SH, 1764 (see n. 6 below).

Strawberry Hill, Oct. 30th 176[4].

Sir,

I SHALL be very thankful for a transcript of the most material passages in Mr Beale's[1] pocket-book,[2] and of Hollar's letters,[3] if you will be so good as to employ any person to transcribe them, and let me know the expense when they are done. It is unlucky, with regard to the former, that Mr[s] Beale's[4] article is printed off, and

4. The rest of the letter is in Lord Temple's hand.

5. Parliament had been 'further prorogued' from 23 Aug. to 30 Oct. 1764 (*Journals of the House of Commons* xxix. 1059).

6. For another reference to Temple's lameness see HW to Montagu 7 July 1770 (MONTAGU ii. 314–15).

1. Charles Beale (b. 1631), lord of the manor of Walton, Bucks (Bucks Parish Register Society, *The Register of Walton*, Olney [1902], p. 9; Elizabeth Walsh, 'The Flatman Letters' [to Charles Beale], *Life and Letters*, 1949, lxi. 218–21). He 'took great interest in chemistry, especially the manufacture of colours, in which he did business with Lely and other painters of the day' (R. E. Graves in DNB *sub* Mary Beale).

2. One of more than thirty small almanac notebooks in which Beale kept a record of his business affairs and of his wife's painting. Vertue made extracts from seven of them which HW quoted in *Anecdotes of Painting*, 1st edn, iii. 67–77. Warton had evidently told HW about the existence of another of Beale's notebooks (now in the Bodleian Library), but HW made no use of it. One other notebook, in the National Portrait Gallery, is known to have survived (Ida Proctor, 'A Woman Artist of the Restoration,' *Country Life*, 1960, cxxvii. 1242).

3. Two letters from Wenceslaus Hollar (1607–77), the engraver, to John Aubrey, 1 Aug. 1665 and n. d. (MS Aubrey 12, ff. 174–5, in the Bodleian; information kindly communicated by Dr David Fairer). HW made no use of the letters.

4. Mary Cradock (1633–99), dau. of the Rev. John Cradock, rector of Barrow; m. (1651) Charles Beale; portrait painter. She

several other subsequent sheets, for the second edition.[5] And I must not expect that so trifling a work should go any farther. The sight of the pocket-book will, however, gratify my own curiosity, though I am much ashamed to give you so much trouble, Sir. You will permit me, I hope, in return, though a small one for so many favours, to send you a most singular book, of which I have lately been permitted to print two hundred copies (half only indeed for myself). It is the *Life*[6] of the famous Lord Herbert of Cherbury,[7] written by himself. You will not find him unworthy of keeping company with those paladins, of whom you have made such charming use in your notes on Spenser.[8] Pray let me know how I shall convey it to you. I am, Sir,

Your most obliged and obedient humble servant,

Hor. Walpole

To the Rev. James Merrick,[1] Saturday 1 December 1764

Printed from a photostat of the MS in the possession of Mrs Sarah Markham, Wotton-under-Edge, Gloucestershire. First printed, Toynbee *Supp.* i. 104–5. The MS was among the books and papers bequeathed by Merrick to the antiquary John Loveday (1711–89); it descended to Loveday's great-great-grandson, Dr Thomas Loveday, on whose death in 1966 it passed to his daughter, Mrs Markham.

Arlington Street, Dec. 1st 1764.

Sir,

It was a very sensible affliction to me to hear of your brother's[2] death, for whom I had a real and very great value. His worth, hu-

is said to have painted or copied about 1500 portraits (Elizabeth Walsh, 'Mary Beale,' *Burlington Magazine*, 1948, xc. 209; Gery Milner-Gibson-Cullum, 'Mary Beale,' *Proceedings of the Suffolk Institute of Archæology*, 1916–18, xvi. 229–41).

5. HW wrote William Cole 8 Nov. 1764: 'It is printed to past the middle of the third volume' (Cole i. 83). The article on Mary Beale remained unchanged in the second edition of *Anecdotes*.

6. *The Life of Lord Herbert of Cherbury, Written by Himself*, printed at the SH Press by 27 Jan. 1764 but not distributed till July 1764. The copy presented to Warton was sold Sotheby's 20 July 1906, lot 366; not further traced (Hazen, *SH Bibl.* 70–2).

7. 'Shirbury' in Wooll's edition.

8. See *ante* 21 Aug. 1762, n. 2.

1. (1720–69), son of Dr John Merrick (d. 1757), physician and sometime mayor of Reading; fellow of Trinity College, Oxford, 1745; poet and scholar.

2. John Merrick (ca 1705–64), B. Med. (Oxon), 1731; physician (Foster, *Alumni Oxon.*). He died 11 Nov. 1764 at Reading.

manity and good sense were very uncommon, and are a peculiar loss to any man whom he honoured with his friendship, as I flatter myself he did me; and nobody would have done more, willingly than I would, to preserve so valuable a life. His consummate knowledge in his profession convinced him *that* was impossible; and his philosophic resignation and tranquillity made *that* conviction no pain to him. He was so kind as to insist on my taking the picture[3] before he left Isleworth, much against my inclination, and only upon condition that he would let me restore it if he lived to return; a condition I heartily wish could have been accomplished! I shall now preserve it in memory of him with the highest esteem; but should you ever, Sir, come to Twickenham or to London, I hope you will give me an opportunity of showing my regard to Dr Merrick's memory, by expressing my satisfaction in seeing anybody so nearly related to him.

I am Sir

Your most obedient humble servant

HOR. WALPOLE

Turn over.

I beg pardon, Sir, if this letter is not properly addressed: I have an imperfect idea, Sir, that you are a divine;[4] but my uncertainty and the fear of occasioning any miscarriage to my letter, which would mortify me extremely, is the cause of so simple and indefinite a superscription,[5] which I hope you will be so good as to excuse.

3. Described by HW as 'the inside of a church, a very good Flemish picture on board; a legacy to Mr Walpole from Dr Meyrick at Isleworth' and hung in the Round Bedchamber ('Des. of SH,' *Works* ii. 505). In the SH sale catalogue, 1842, xxi. 20, the artist is listed as Steinwick (doubtless Hendrik van Steenwyck, the younger [ca 1580–1649], architectural painter of the Court of Charles I). The clause in Merrick's will reads: 'Also I give to the Honourable Horatio Walpole my large picture of a church by Antoine de l'Orme' (presumably Anthonie de Lorme [d. 1673], a painter of architectural subjects).

4. Merrick was ordained and preached occasionally, but was prevented by illness from holding a living (DNB).

5. No address appears on the letter.

From Allan Ramsay, Saturday 1765

Printed from the MS now wsl. First printed, Toynbee *Supp.* iii. 316–17 (dated conjecturally '[1764]'). Reprinted in *Strawberry Hill Accounts . . . Kept by Mr Horace Walpole,* ed. Paget Toynbee, Oxford, 1927, pp. 124–5; Alastair Smart, *The Life and Art of Allan Ramsay,* 1952, p. 111. Damer-Waller; the MS was sold Sotheby's 5 Dec. 1921 (first Waller Sale), lot 175, bought in; resold Christie's 15 Dec. 1947 (second Waller Sale), lot 21 (with Ramsay to HW 1759), to Maggs for wsl.

Dated approximately by HW's entries in *Strawberry Hill Accounts,* pp. 10–11: 'March 20 [1765] . . . paid Ramsay for pictures of my 2 nieces 84-0-0. . . . Aug. 26. for frame for the picture of Mrs Keppel and Lady Huntingtower, and other frames 23-1-6.'

On the last page of the MS are two pencil sketches of arches, possibly by HW.

Soho Square, Saturday afternoon.

Mr Ramsay presents his compliments to Mr Walpole, and will not let him be displeased, if it is in his power to prevent it. He will finish his nieces' pictures[1] in preference to those which were begun long before them, and which Mr Walpole may easily believe would not have been at this time unfinished, but from the utter impossibility of his doing more with his own hands than what he has actually done.

Mr Ramsay therefore desires to be informed whether the size[2] of 4-6 by 4-2, first given, be still to his mind; or if he chooses any alteration in it; that he may immediately give orders for a stretching frame to be ready for lining the heads after Mrs Capel[3] has given hers the last sitting, which he hopes will be as soon as she comes to town. He begs that Mrs Capel may come dressed in the manner she proposes to be painted, as he wants to make a sketch of her attitude upon paper as he has already done to Lady Huntingtower.[4]

1. 'Laura and Charlotte Walpole, eldest and youngest daughters of Sir Edward Walpole, and wives of Frederic Keppel Bishop of Exeter, and of Lionel Talmach Earl of Dysart; Mrs Keppel in white, Lady Dysart in pink: by Ramsay' ('Des. of SH,' *Works* ii. 461). The picture, which hung at the east end of the Gallery at SH, was sold SH xxi. 51 and bought in by Lord Waldegrave for £52.10.0. See J. L. Caw, 'Allan Ramsay, Portrait Painter, 1713–1784,' *Walpole Society* 1936–37, xxv. 61, and illustration.

2. Its dimensions when it was resold at the American Art Association-Anderson Galleries 25 April 1935 (Nathaniel Thayer Sale), lot 65, were given as 'Height, 63 inches; width, 55 inches.'

3. Laura Walpole (ca 1734–1813), m. (1758) Hon. Frederick Keppel, Bp of Exeter, 1762.

4. Charlotte Walpole (1738–89), m. (1760) Hon. Lionel Tollemache, styled Lord Huntingtower, 5th E. of Dysart, 1770.

THE HON. MRS KEPPEL AND
LADY HUNTINGTOWER, BY ALLAN RAMSAY, 1765

From LADY TOWNSHEND, Friday ?February 1765

Printed from the MS now WSL. First printed, Toynbee *Supp.* iii. 187–8. For the history of the MS see *ante* 30 Sept. 1743 OS.

Dated conjecturally by HW's 'long confinement' due to illness in 1765, and by the reference to 'Thursday the 28th of February' (28 Feb. occurred on Thursday in 1765).

Friday, one o'clock.

THE numbers of the most amiable of the human race which I am informed you are constantly surrounded or, more properly speaking, infested with, has prevented me from indulging my inclination in inquiring so often after your health since your long confinement[1] as I wished to do, being sensible how worth[i]ly I am most unpopular to that honourable society; therefore [I] hope you will forgive me for troubling you with this letter to assure you that I have been extremely concerned for the anxiety of mind and affliction that you have so long suffered, and flatter myself you will do me the justice to believe that my heart is so much the reverse of the Townshends[2] that I am capable of esteeming and valuing the few that I am obliged to; as I hear you now go out, I hope I shall have the pleasure of seeing you here[3] Saturday evening and Thursday the 28th of February.[4] As this is the only opportunity I have had some time of conversing with you in any way, I must beg it may be the excuse for the length of this letter and that you will believe me very sincerely

Your obedient humble servant,

E. TOWNSHEND

1. HW wrote Cole from SH 28 Feb. 1765 that he had been 'much out of order above a month with a very bad cold and cough, for which I am come hither to try change of air' (COLE i. 85). He reported to Lord Hertford 26 March: 'I have passed many days at Strawberry, to cure my cold (which it has done)' (CONWAY ii. 522). See also HW to Montagu 19 Feb. 1765 (MONTAGU ii. 147).

2. 'Since she was parted from her husband, she has broke with all his family' (HW to Mann 22 Oct. 1741 OS, MANN i. 173).

3. Her house in Whitehall (*ante* ca March 1745, n. 3).

4. HW was apparently still too much 'out of order' to attend; see n. 1 above.

To the Rev. Thomas Percy,[1] Tuesday 5 February 1765

Printed from a photostat of the MS in the British Museum (Add. MS 32,329, ff. 24–6). First printed, Toynbee vi. 181–5. The MS passed to Percy's descendants until it was sold Sotheby's 29 April 1884 (Percy Sale), lot 214 (with other letters to Percy), to Quaritch for the BM.

Address: To the Reverend Mr Percy at Easton Mauduit Northamptonshire by Wellingborough bag. *Postmark:* 5 FE. FREE. *Frank:* Free Hor. Walpole.

Arlington Street, Feb. 5th 1765.

Sir,

I HAVE received from Mr Dodsley[2] the flattering and very agreeable present of the *Reliques of Ancient Poetry;*[3] and though I have not had time yet to read the whole carefully, yet the transient perusal has given me so much pleasure, that I am impatient to make you my most grateful acknowledgments for so particular a favour. As I am personally unknown to you, Sir, I must regard it as a great distinction; and though you are so kind as to mark the cause of that distinction,[4] I cannot help fearing that you are too partial to me even as an author, and that the honour you have in several places done to my *Catalogue of Royal and Noble Authors,* is much beyond what that compilation deserves. Since however that collection has merited your notice, may I not hope, Sir, that you will not confine it to my book, but that when you come to London, you will let me have the honour of your acquaintance?[5]

Before I have the pleasure, that I promise myself, of talking over

1. (1729–1811), vicar of Easton Maudit, Northants, 1753, and rector of Wilby, Northants, 1756; dean of Carlisle, 1778–82; Bp of Dromore 1782–1811.

2. James Dodsley (1724–97), bookseller, whose older brother Robert had died in 1764; HW's occasional correspondent.

3. The announcement of Percy's forthcoming work had appeared in the *London Chronicle* 29–31 Jan. 1765, xvii. 106: 'In a few days will be published . . . *Reliques of Ancient English Poetry.* Consisting of old heroic ballads, songs, and other pieces of our earlier poets (chiefly in the lyric kind) together with some few of later date.' Publication of the three volumes by Dodsley was announced in the *Chronicle* 9–12 Feb., xvii. 151 (Dalrymple 106 n. 5). HW's presentation copy of the first edition, perhaps given away when he acquired later editions, does not appear in the SH records. His copies, now wsl, of the second edition, 1767 (a present from Percy), and the fourth edition, 1794, are Hazen, *Cat. of HW's Lib.,* Nos 2919 and 3455.

4. Doubtless in Percy's presentation inscription. The inscription in HW's copy of the second edition reads: 'To the Honourable Horace Walpole, these volumes containing specimens of the composition of some of his royal and noble authors are presented with great respect by the Editor.' Percy acknowledges his debt to *Royal and Noble Authors,* SH, 1758, in several places.

5. Percy wrote his friend Richard Farmer, who had given him substantial

with you a thousand curious things in your new publication, permit me, Sir, to mention a few points that particularly struck me. The good sense and conciseness of your dissertations[6] persuade me that these are not your sole productions.[7] I would not take the liberty to ask any impertinent questions, but you must allow me to hope that with so much knowledge, so accurate and judicious a talent for criticism, and so just a style, you will not confine yourself to this single publication nor to the mere office of an editor. Your observation on Lord Vaux[8] appears to me strongly founded. His poetry, as you remark, is undoubtedly more polished than is consonant to the age of Henry VII.[9] You know my authorities, Sir, for ascribing those poems to Lord Nicholas:[10] yet I prefer truth to any trifles of my own writing, and am willing to sacrifice my own account to what is more probable. If it is not too much to ask, I could wish, as I have little leisure, Sir, that you could ascertain this point for me, and even demonstrate to which specific Lord Vaux the poems belong. There is another of my noble authors, about whom I interest myself strangely; Lord Rochford.[11] Have you, Sir, in your researches ever met with any lines that you believe to be his?

I was not more pleased with anything than with your proofs, for so they certainly are, that Shakespeare's plays ought to be distinguished into *histories,* tragedies and comedies, and with your very just reflections on that subject.[12] They are a full answer to all Voltaire's impertinent criticisms[13] on our matchless poet.

assistance with the *Reliques,* 10 Feb. 1765: 'I have received two very flattering letters from two great favourites with the public (I mean as writers) viz. Lord Lyttleton and Mr Hor. Walpole; to whom I sent copies of my book: having by poor Shenstone been introduced to some acquaintance with the former: and wanting to commence one with the latter, (who by the bye answers my intentions in the most agreeable manner)' (*The Correspondence of Thomas Percy and Richard Farmer,* ed. Cleanth Brooks, Baton Rouge, Louisiana, 1946, pp. 82–3).

6. The *Reliques* included four essays on the ancient English minstrels, the origin of the English stage, the metre of *Piers Plowman's Visions,* and the ancient metrical romances. 'The dissertations too I think are sensible, concise, and unaffected' (HW to Joseph Warton *post* 16 March 1765).

7. Percy had published several earlier works. HW later acquired one of these: *Miscellaneous Pieces Relating to the Chinese,* 1762 (Hazen, op. cit., No. 1578).

8. Thomas Vaux (1509–56), 2d Bn Vaux of Harrowden, 1523.

9. See 'Additions and Corrections,' *Reliques,* 1765, iii. 335–7.

10. On the authority of Anthony à Wood, HW had attributed the poems to Lord Vaux's father, Sir Nicholas Vaux (ca 1460–1523), cr. (1523) Bn Vaux. See CHATTERTON 366 n. 20.

11. George Boleyn (d. 1536), styled Vct Rochford; brother of Anne Boleyn. See COLE i. 357–8; MASON i. 191.

12. In the essay 'On the Origin of the English Stage, etc.,' *Reliques* i. 127.

13. Notably in Letter XVIII, 'Sur la tragédie,' of his *Lettres philosophiques,* 1734. See *post* 21 June 1768.

The beginning of the second part of *Sir Cauline,*[14] as no doubt, Sir, you have observed, resembles the story of Tancred and Sigismonda;[15] as the ditty of *Glasgerion*[16] seems evidently to have given birth to the tragedy of *The Orphan,*[17] in which Polidore profits of Monimia's intended favours to Castalio.[18]

I will not make this first letter too long. With it I enclose an old ballad, which I write down from memory, and perhaps very incorrectly, for it is above five and twenty years since I learned it. I do not send it to you, Sir, as worthy to be published,[19] but merely as an addition to your collection, if it is not there already. I remember to have heard another, which was the exact counterpart to it, called *Giles Colin,*[20] but I do not recollect a single stanza.

If it should ever lie within my slender power to assist your studies or inquiries, I hope, Sir, you will command me. I love the cause, I have a passion for antiquity and literary amusements, and though I much doubt whether I shall ever engage in them again, farther than for my own private entertainment, I shall always be glad to contribute my mite to any gentleman, whose abilities and taste demand, like yours, to be encouraged.

I am Sir

Your much obliged humble servant

HOR. WALPOLE

14. *Reliques* i. 44–53.

15. In Boccaccio's *Decameron;* also the subject of Dryden's *Sigismonda and Guiscardo.*

16. *Reliques* iii. 43–8.

17. By Thomas Otway, first produced at the Dorset Garden Theatre in Feb. 1680 (*London Stage* Pt I, i. 285).

18. In the second edition of the *Reliques* iii. 43, Percy added this note: 'An ingenious friend thinks that the following old ditty [*Glasgerion*] . . . may possibly have given birth to the tragedy of the *Orphan,* in which Polidore intercepts Monimia's intended favours to Castalio.'

19. Percy did not include it in his second edition.

20. This ballad, with the title *Lady Alice,* appears in several versions in *English and Scottish Popular Ballads,* ed. F. J. Child, Boston, 1882–98, ii. 279–80, iii. 514–15, v. 225–6. It has the title *Giles Collins and Proud Lady Anna* in *Gammer Gurton's Garland,* 1810, pp. 38–9.

[Enclosure]

THE BALLAD OF LADY HOUNSIBELLE AND LORD LOVEL[21]

I fare you well, Lady Hounsibelle,
  For I must needs be gone;
And this time two year I'll meet you again,
  To end the true love we begun.

That's a long time, Lord Lovel, she said,
  To dwell in fair Scotland:
And so it is, Lady Hounsibelle,
  And to leave a fair lady alone.

He called unto his stable-groom
  To saddle his milk-white steed;
Hey down, Hey down, Hey, hey derry down,
  I wish my Lord Lovel good speed.

He had not been in fair Scotland
  Above half a year,
But a longing mind came over his head,
  Lady Hounsibelle he would go see her.

He had not been in fair London
  Above half a day,
But he heard the bells of the high chapel ring;
  They rung with a sesora.

He asked of a gentleman,
  That stood there all alone,
What made the bells of the high chapel ring,
  And the ladies to make such a moan.

The King's fair daughter is dead, he said,
  Whose name's Lady Hounsibelle;

21. In the MS this title has been added by Percy.

She died for love of a courteous young knight,
Whose name it is Lord Lovel.

Lady Hounsibelle died on the Easterday,
Lord Lovel on the morrow;
Lady Hounsibelle died for pure true love,
Lord Lovel he died for sorrow.

Lady Hounsibelle's buried in the chancel,
Lord Lovel in the choir;
Lady Hounsibelle's breast sprung up a rose,
Lord Lovel's a branch of sweet briar.

They grew till they grew to the top of the church,
And when they could grow no higher,
They grew till they grew to a true lover's knot,
And they both were tied together.

There came an old woman by,
Their blessing she did crave;
She cut her a branch of this true lover's knot,
And buried 'em both in a grave.[22]

To the Rev. Joseph Warton,[1] Saturday 16 March 1765

Printed from John Wooll, *Biographical Memoirs of the late Reverend Joseph Warton, D.D.*, 1806, pp. 301–3, where the letter was first printed. Reprinted, Cunningham iv. 331–2; Toynbee vi. 198–200 (closing and signature omitted in both). The history of the MS and its present whereabouts are not known.

Arlington Street, March 16th 1765.

Sir,

YOU have shown so much of what I fear I must call partiality to me, that I could not in conscience send you the trifle[2] that accompanies this till the unbiased public, who knew not the author,

22. 'NB. Compare this song with Giles Collin, Fair Margaret and Sweet William, Lord Thomas and Fair Annet' (MS Note in Percy's hand). The ballad, with many variations from HW's text, is printed as *Lord Lovel* in Child's *Ballads* ii. 207.

1. (1722–1800), older brother of Thomas Warton; D.D. (Oxon.), 1768; headmaster of Winchester College, 1766; prebendary of London, 1782, and of Winchester, 1788; poet and critic. At this time he was usher, or second master, at Winchester.

2. A copy of *The Castle of Otranto*, published 24 Dec. 1764 (Hazen, *Bibl. of HW* 52).

told me that it was not quite unworthy of being offered to you. Still I am not quite sure whether its ambition of copying the manners of an age which you love may not make you too favourable to it, or whether its awkward imitation of them may not subject it to your censure. In fact, it is but partially an imitation of ancient romances; being rather intended for an attempt to blend the marvellous of old story with the natural of modern novels. This was in great measure the plan of a work, which, to say the truth, was begun without any plan at all. But I will not trouble you, Sir, at present with enlarging on my design, which I have fully explained in a preface prepared for a second edition,[3] which the sale of the former makes me in an hurry to send out. I do not doubt, Sir, but you have with pleasure looked over more genuine remains of ancient days, the three volumes of old poems and ballads:[4] most of them are curious, and some charming. The dissertations too I think are sensible, concise, and unaffected. Let me recommend to you also the perusal of the life of Petrarch, of which two large volumes in quarto are already published by the Abbé de Sade,[5] with the promise of a third. Three quartos on Petrarch will not terrify a man of your curiosity, though, without omitting the memoirs and anecdotes of Petrarch's age, the most valuable part of the work, they might have been comprised in much less compass: many of the sonnets might have been sunk, and almost all his translations of them. Though Petrarch appears to have been far from a genius, singly excepting the harmonious beauty of his words, yet one forgives the partiality of a biographer, though Monsieur de Sade seems as much enchanted with Petrarch as the age was in which he lived, whilst their ignorance of good authors excuses their bigotry to the restorer of taste. You will not, I believe, be so thoroughly convinced as the biographer seems to be, of the authentic discovery of Laura's body, and the sonnet placed on her bosom. When a lady dies of the plague in the height of its ravages, it is not very probable that her family thought of interring poetry with her, or indeed of anything but burying her body as quickly as they could; nor is it more likely that a pestilential vault was opened afterwards for that purpose. I have no doubt but that the sonnet was

3. In the preface to the second edition, published 11 April 1765, HW acknowledged his authorship of the book (ibid. 54–5). 'It has succeeded so well, that I do not any longer entirely keep the secret' (HW to Cole 28 Feb. 1765, COLE i. 85).

4. Percy's *Reliques;* see previous letter.

5. Jacques-François-Paul-Aldonçe de Sade (1705–78), author of *Mémoires pour la vie de François Pétrarque,* 3 vols, Amsterdam, 1764–7. HW's copy is Hazen, *Cat. of HW's Lib.*, No. 932.

prepared and slipped into the tomb when they were determined to find her corpse. When you read the notes to the second volume, you will grow very impatient for Mons. de St Palaye's promised history of the troubadours.[6] Have we any manuscript that could throw light on that subject?

I cannot conclude, Sir, without reminding you of a hope you once gave me of seeing you in town or at Strawberry Hill. I go to Paris the end of May or beginning of June, for a few months,[7] where I should be happy if I could execute any literary commission for you. I am,

Sir,

Your obedient and obliged humble servant,

Hor. Walpole

To Jean-Baptiste-Jacques Élie de Beaumont,[1] Monday 18 March 1765

Printed from HW's MS draft, now WSL. First printed, *Works* v. 642–3. Reprinted, Wright v. 8–9; Cunningham iv. 332–3; Toynbee vi. 200–2 (closing and signature omitted in Wright and Cunningham). Damer-Waller; the MS draft was sold Sotheby's 5 Dec. 1921 (first Waller Sale), lot 16, to Maggs; offered by them, Cat. Nos 421 (spring 1922), lot 835; 459 (spring 1925), lot 748; 492 (summer 1927), lot 1233; offered by G. Michelmore and Co., Cat. of Shakespeareana [Dec. 1927], lot 694; acquired by Henry C. Folger, Oct. 1928; Folger Shakespeare Library to WSL by exchange, 1950. The original letter sent to Élie de Beaumont is missing.

The MS was edited by Mary Berry for the text printed in *Works* and contains notes in her hand.

Endorsed by HW: To Monsieur Beaumont with the *Castle of Otranto.*

Strawberry Hill, March 18th 1765.

Sir,

When I had the honour of seeing you here;[2] I believe I told you that I had written a novel,[3] in which I was flattered to find that I had touched an effusion of the heart in a manner[4] similar to a

6. See *ante* 15 Feb. 1764, nn. 3, 8.

7. HW did not leave London for Paris until 9 Sept. (*post* 5 Sept. 1765 and n. 1).

1. (1732–86), m. (1750) Anne-Louise Morin-Dumesnil (1729–83); French jurist.

2. HW informed Lord Hertford 9 Nov. 1764 that Élie de Beaumont had 'breakfasted here [SH] t'other morning, and pleased me exceedingly: he has great spirit and good humour' (Conway ii. 461).

3. *The Castle of Otranto.*

4. 'In a manner' substituted for 'very' in the MS.

passage in the charming letters[5] of the Marquis de Roselle.[6] I have since that time published my little story, but was so diffident of its merit, that I gave it as a translation from the Italian.[7] Still I should not have ventured to offer it to so great a mistress of the passions as Madame de Beaumont, if the approbation of London, that is, of a country to which she and you, Sir, are so good as to be partial, had not encouraged me to send it to you. After I have talked of the passions, and the natural effusions of the heart, how will you be surprised to find a narrative of the most improbable and absurd adventures! how will you be amazed to hear that a country, of whose good sense you have an opinion, should have applauded so wild a tale! But you must remember, Sir, that whatever good sense we have, we are not *yet in any light* chained down to precepts and inviolable laws.[8] All that Aristotle or his superior commentators, your authors, have taught us, has[8a] not yet subdued us to regularity: we still prefer the extravagant beauties of Shakespeare and Milton to the cold and well-disciplined merit of Addison, and even to the sober and correct march of Pope. Nay, it was but t'other day that we were transported to hear Churchill[9] rave in numbers less chastised than Dryden's, but still in numbers like Dryden's. You will not I hope think I apply these mighty names to my own case with any vanity, when it is only their enormities that I quote, and that in defence, not of myself, but of my countrymen, who have had good humour enough to approve[10] the visionary scenes and actors in the *Castle of Otranto*.

To tell you the truth, it was not so much my intention to recall the exploded marvels of ancient romance, as to blend the wonderful of old stories with the natural of modern novels.[11] The world is apt to wear out any plan whatever, and if the *Marquis de Roselle* had not appeared, I should have been inclined to say, that that species *had* been exhausted. Madame de Beaumont must forgive me if I add that Richardson had, to me at least, made that kind of writing in-

5. Written by Madame de Beaumont wife of this Élie de Beaumont (HW's note, crossed out in the MS by Mary Berry; see headnote).

6. *Lettres du Marquis de Roselle,* 1764, Mme Élie de Beaumont's epistolary novel, much admired by HW; see n. 12 below and MASON i. 7. HW's copy, now in the Bodleian Library, is Hazen, *Cat. of HW's Lib.,* No. 938.

7. The full title is: *The Castle of Otranto, A Story. Translated by William Marshal, Gent. from the Original Italian of Onuphrio Muralto, Canon of the Church of St Nicholas at Otranto.*

8. 'Rules' crossed out in the MS.

8a. 'Have' crossed out in the MS.

9. Charles Churchill (1731–64), author of *The Rosciad* and other satirical poems.

10. 'Applaud' crossed out in the MS.

11. This explanation is given in HW's preface to the second edition, published 11 April 1765.

supportable;[12] I thought the *nodus* was become *dignus vindice,* and that a god, at least a ghost, was absolutely necessary to frighten us out of too much senses. When I had so wicked a design,[13] no wonder if the execution was answerable. If I make you laugh, for I cannot flatter myself that I shall make you cry, I shall be content; at least I shall be satisfied, till I have the pleasure of seeing you, with putting you in mind of[14]

Sir

Your most devoted humble servant

Horace Walpole

PS. The passage I alluded to in the beginning of my letter is where Matilda owns her passion to Hippolita[15]—I mention it, as I fear so unequal a similitude would not strike Madame de Beaumont.

To Grosvenor Bedford, Thursday 5 September 1765

Printed from the MS now wsl. First printed, Cunningham iv. 401. Reprinted, Toynbee vi. 290–1. The MS descended in the Bedford family to Grosvenor Bedford's great-niece, Mrs Erskine, of Milton Lodge, Gillingham, Dorset; sold Sotheby's 15 Nov. 1932 (property of Mrs Erskine), lot 488, to Maggs for wsl.

Strawberry Hill, Sept. 5, 1765.

Dear Sir,

I SHALL set out for Paris next Monday,[1] but I could not go without taking a kind leave of you. I would not tell you the day sooner, because I would not disturb you if you are in the country, or lame;[2] and because though I shall be in London for two days, I have so much to do, that you would hardly find me at home.

I have recovered very much in this last fortnight, and except when

12. 'Madame de Beaumont . . . has lately written a very pretty novel . . . imitated too from an English standard, and in my opinion a most woeful one; I mean the works of [Samuel] Richardson, who wrote those deplorably tedious lamentations, *Clarissa* and *Sir Charles Grandison* . . . but Madame de Beaumont has almost avoided sermons, and almost reconciled sentiments and common sense' (HW to Mann 20 Dec. 1764, Mann vi. 271).

13. 'A design' substituted for 'an intention' in the MS.

14. 'Making you remember' crossed out in the MS.

15. In chapter iv of *The Castle of Otranto, Works* ii. 72–3.

1. 'Sept. 9. Set out from Arlington Street at half an hour after eight' ('Paris Journals,' du Deffand v. 258).

2. HW to Bedford *post* 20 Nov. 1765 indicates that Bedford had been suffering for some time from the gout.

I get up, or attempt to take a walk, which very soon tires me, am now free from everything but weakness.[3] Change of air and easy motion will I don't doubt soon quite restore me.

If you have any business with me, send a letter at any time to Arlington Street, and Favre,[4] whom I leave behind, will convey it to me.

Adieu! dear Sir; I most heartily wish you health and happiness, and am

Ever yours
HOR. WALPOLE

To the REV. JOHN HUTCHINS,[1] Sunday 22 September 1765

Printed from the MS now WSL. First printed in John Hutchins, *The History and Antiquities of the County of Dorset,* 3d edn, ed. William Shipp and J. W. Hodson, 1861–73, ii. 461–2. The MS apparently passed from Hutchins to John Nichols and remained in the Nichols family; sold Sotheby's 18 Nov. 1929 (J. G. Nichols Sale), lot 230, to Francis Edwards; resold by them to WSL, 1932.

The letter is listed in 'Paris Journals' as sent to England 30 Sept. 'by Lord Beauchamp' (DU DEFFAND v. 376).

Paris, Sept. 22d 1765.

Sir,

WHEN you see whence my letter is dated, I trust I shall need no other apology for not answering yours[2] sooner. My being here occasions what I am still more sorry for, the impossibility of complying with your request. I have some materials for the life of Sir James Thornhill, which as you rightly guessed, Sir, is reserved for a future volume of my *Anecdotes of Painting,* and which I have not yet begun.[3] Were I in England, you should certainly have the use of those materials, but they are locked up at my house in the country with the rest of my papers, which cannot be got at in my absence.

3. HW had reported to Lord Holland 15 July 1765: 'For these sixteen last days I have been confined to my room, and almost the whole time to my bed, with the gout in my head, stomach, and both feet' (SELWYN 192).

4. HW's head servant.

1. (1698–1773), rector of Wareham, Dorset, 1744; topographer.

2. Missing.

3. See *ante* 31 March 1764, nn. 5, 6.

The length of that absence is very uncertain, and will depend upon my health, which I came abroad to reestablish. In all probability I shall return at latest in the spring,[4] when, if it is not too late for your work, Sir, I shall be very ready to communicate what you want;[5] but when I come to mention Sir James Thornhill, I doubt I shall not rate him so high as you do when you call him *the English Raphael*—He had some merit, and we have had but few good painters, but surely Sir James was not one of the first class!

As I flatter myself, Sir, that my present situation will excuse my not being so useful to you as I wish to be, so I will assure you that you had no occasion to make any excuse to me for writing. I have too much respect for your profession, and wish too well to literary pursuits, not to oblige you if it was in my power: and I shall be extremely glad if I return time enough to lend any assistance to your work,[6] which I shall have great pleasure in perusing.

I am Sir

Your obedient humble servant

Hor. Walpole

4. HW left Paris 17 April 1766, reaching London 22 April ('Paris Journals,' du Deffand v. 314).

5. See *post* 10 May 1766, 17 Feb. 1767, and 26 Feb. 1771.

6. *History and Antiquities of the County of Dorset*, 2 vols, folio, 1774. HW's copy is Hazen, *Cat. of HW's Lib.*, No. 4. 'In the decline of life, when he had a reasonable prospect of seeing his History through the press, he was seized with a paralytic stroke, which . . . greatly debilitated him' ([George Bingham,] 'Biographical Anecdotes of the Reverend John Hutchins, M. A.,' in *Bibliotheca Topographica Britannica*, vol. VI, 1790, p. 18).

From WILLIAM HAMILTON,[1] Tuesday 15 October 1765

Printed for the first time from the MS now WSL. The MS was possibly one of the five letters from Hamilton to HW sold Sotheby's 24 April 1879 (John B. C. Healt Sale), lot 150, to Waller; not further traced until sold Phillips 20 Jan. 1976 (Miscellaneous Sale), lot 117 (with other letters and documents), to Pickering and Chatto, who resold it to the Seven Gables Bookshop, Inc.; acquired from Seven Gables by WSL, Nov. 1976.

Naples, October 15th 1765.

Dear Sir,

IT gave me great concern to hear that you had been so far indisposed as to have occasion for a warmer climate than ours; Lady Aylesbury[2] writes Mrs Hamilton[3] word that you are in France and propose going to the southern parts of that kingdom.[4] Of all the climates that I have experienced, surely none can be compared to this in winter. Should you therefore be tempted thus far, Mrs Hamilton and I can offer you a quiet apartment in a glorious situation overlooking the Bay of Naples. You shall be as retired as you please. In short, all I can say is that should it suit your convenience or inclination, you will make me most happy in accepting of an offer that comes from the bottom of a heart of one that is sincerely attached to you, and wishes for an opportunity to show you how sensible he is to your goodness to him upon many occasions. Hercu-

1. (1730–1803), K.B., 1772; M.P.; envoy to Naples 1764–1800; diplomatist and archæologist. This is the earliest extant letter in HW's correspondence with Hamilton; the rest of their correspondence is printed in CHUTE 403–47.

2. The wife of HW's intimate friend and correspondent Henry Seymour Conway.

3. Catherine Barlow (d. 1782), m. (1758), as his first wife, Sir William Hamilton, K.B., 1772.

4. At the end of June 1765 HW suffered the sharpest attack of gout he had yet experienced, and spent the next two months recuperating. He wrote Montagu 23 Aug.: 'My two months are up, and yet I recover my feet very slowly. . . . This duration of weakness makes me very impatient, as I wish much to be at Paris before the fine season is quite gone' (MONTAGU ii. 167). During the period of his intense political activity in 1764–5, he had promised himself the diversion of a trip to Paris as soon as it was possible to get away. 'I have so long set my mind upon it, that I am now childishly eager for it' (HW to Lord Holland 19 July 1765, SELWYN 196). Also he was disappointed that Conway and other friends had neglected to offer him a place in the new administration (see Appendix 7, CONWAY iii. 529–32). HW left London 9 Sept., arriving at Paris on the 13th ('Paris Journals,' DU DEFFAND v. 258, 260). He only made short trips outside Paris during his visit to France, which lasted until mid-April 1766 (ibid. v. 314).

laneum will afford you, as it does me, an inexhaustible fund of amusement, and you cannot stir a step without being in classic ground.[5] It is impossible to describe the effect this air has had upon Mrs Hamilton, having entirely lost all her complaints, and that effect was almost immediate. I send this letter to Sir Horace Mann, who knows where you are to be found.[6] You may easily imagine what pleasure it gives me to write once a week to my good friend Mr Conway instead of Lord Halifax.[7] Adieu, dear Sir, I will hope to see you; if not, pray let me have the satisfaction of hearing that you are well again.

Your most obedient and much obliged humble servant,

WM. HAMILTON

TO THOMAS BRAND, Saturday 19 October 1765

Printed from *Works* v. 643–5, where the letter was first printed. Reprinted, Wright v. 90–2; Cunningham iv. 425–7; Toynbee vi. 332–4 (closing omitted in Wright and Cunningham). The history of the MS and its present whereabouts are not known.

The letter is listed in 'Paris Journals' as sent to England 21 Oct. 'by Mr Taylor's servant' (DU DEFFAND v. 377).

Paris, October 19, 1765.

DON'T think I have forgot your commissions:[1] I mentioned them to old Mariette[2] this evening, who says he has got one of them, but never could meet with the other, and that it will be impossible

5. Excavation of the classical ruins of Herculaneum had begun in 1738. See HW to West 14 June 1740 NS, GRAY i. 222 and n. 4.

6. 'I have taken the liberty of enclosing a letter for Mr Walpole, which I will beg the favour of you to forward to him. Lady Aylesbury tells Mrs Hamilton that he is in France, but does not say where. . . . I am quite grieved to hear that Mr Walpole has been so ill, I have told him the charming effect this climate has had upon Mrs Hamilton, and I wish I could tempt him here, as I verily believe it might do him great service, for the winter is delightful here' (Hamilton to Mann, Naples, 15 Oct. 1765, cited in MANN vi. 354 n. 5). In his reply to Hamilton ca 15 Nov. 1765 (missing), HW presumably declined the invitation (CHUTE 405).

7. George Montagu (after 1741, Montagu Dunk) (1716–71), 2d E. of Halifax, 1739; secretary of state for the southern department 1763–5. On 10 July Conway had succeeded Halifax as secretary of state for the south, in the new administration headed by Lord Rockingham (MANN vi. 310 nn. 5, 9). Hamilton's diplomatic dispatches were sent weekly to the secretary of state for the southern department, whose territorial responsibility included the Kingdom of Naples.

---

1. Probably engravings, but the subjects are not identified.

2. Pierre-Jean Mariette (1694–1774), collector. See *post* 21 Nov. 1765, n. 1.

for me to find either at Paris. You know, I suppose, that he would as soon part with an eye as with anything in his own collection.

You may, if you please, suppose me extremely diverted here. Oh! exceedingly. In the first place, I have seen nothing; in the second, I have been confined this fortnight with a return of the gout in both feet; and in the third, I have not laughed since my Lady Hertford[3] went away. I assure you, you may come hither very safely, and be in no danger from mirth.[4] Laughing is as much out of fashion as *pantins*[5] or *bilboquets*.[6] Good folks, they have not time to laugh. There is God and the King to be pulled down first; and men and women, one and all, are devoutly employed in the demolition. They think me quite profane, for having any belief left. But this is not my only crime: I have told them, and am undone by it, that they have taken from us to admire the two dullest things we had, whisk and Richardson[7]—It is very true, and they want nothing but George Grenville to make their conversations, or rather dissertations, the most tiresome upon earth.[8] For Lord L[yttelton],[9] if he would come hither, and turn free-thinker once more, he would be reckoned the most agreeable man in France—next to Mr Hume,[10] who is the only thing in the world that they believe implicitly; which they must do, for I defy them to understand any language that he speaks.

If I could divest myself of my wicked and *unphilosophic* bent to laughing, I should do very well. They are very civil and obliging to me, and several of the women are very agreeable, and some of the men. The Duc de Nivernois[11] has been beyond measure kind to me, and scarce missed a day without coming to see me during my con-

3. Lady Isabella Fitzroy (1726–82), m. (1741) Francis Seymour Conway, cr. (1750) E. and (1793) M. of Hertford. Lord Hertford had been recalled as ambassador to Paris in July 1765 and returned to England, but Lady Hertford remained until 22 Sept. ('Paris Journals,' DU DEFFAND v. 263; MORE 45).

4. Brand was celebrated for his laughter; see *ante* 25 Oct. 1760.

5. Dancing puppets.

6. Puppets weighted so as always to recover their upright position.

7. HW wrote Selwyn 2 Dec. 1765: 'I have not hurt myself a little by laughing at whisk and Richardson, though I have steered clear of the chapter of Mr Hume; the only Trinity now in fashion here' (SELWYN 208–9).

8. The tediousness of Grenville's speeches was noted by HW in his letters to Lord Holland 19 July 1765 and 14 Nov. 1766 (ibid. 197, 237).

9. George, 1st Bn Lyttelton. 'Lord Lyttleton, the statesman, was a very absent man, of formal manners, who never laughed' ('Farington's Anecdotes,' DALRYMPLE 330).

10. David Hume, who was considered 'the liveliest young fellow in the world' when he arrived with Lord Hertford at the Embassy in Paris in 1763 (HW to Selwyn 7 March 1766, SELWYN 218). Hume was appointed secretary of the Embassy in 1765.

11. *Ante* 15 Feb. 1764, n. 13.

finement.[12] The Guerchys[13] are, as usual, all friendship. I had given entirely into supping, as I do not love rising early, and still less meat breakfasts. The misfortune is, that in several houses they dine, and in others sup.[14]

You will think it odd that I should want to laugh, when Wilkes,[15] Sterne,[16] and Foote[17] are here; but the first does not make me laugh, the second never could, and for the third, I choose to pay five shillings when I have a mind he should divert me. Besides, I certainly did not come in search of English; and yet the man I have liked the best in Paris is an Englishman, Lord Ossory,[18] who is one of the most sensible amiable young men I ever saw, with a great deal of Lord Tavistock[19] in his manner.

The joys of Fontainebleau I miss by my illness—*Paziènza!* If the gout deprived me of nothing better than a court.

The papers say the Duke of Dorset[20] is dead: what has he done for Lord George?[21] You cannot be so unconscionable as not to answer me. I don't ask who is to have his ribband;[22] nor how many bushels of fruit the Duke of Newcastle's dessert for the Hereditary Prince[23] contained, nor how often he kissed him for the sake of the *dear house of Brunswic*—No, keep your politics to yourselves; I want to know none of them:—when I do, and authentically, I will write to my Lady —[24] or Charles Townshend.

12. A statement confirmed by HW's 'Paris Journals.'

13. Claude-Louis-François de Regnier (1715–67), Comte de Guerchy; French ambassador to England 1763–7; m. (1740) Gabrielle-Lydie d'Harcourt (b. 1722). HW had 'banqueted' them at SH in June 1764 (*ante* mid-June 1764, n. 2).

14. 'I find no inconvenience, but dine at half an hour after two and sup at ten as easily as I did in England at my usual hours' (HW to Lady Suffolk 20 Sept. 1765, More 48).

15. John Wilkes, the politician.

16. Laurence Sterne, the novelist.

17. Samuel Foote (1720–77), comic actor and playwright.

18. John Fitzpatrick (1745–1818), 2d E. of Upper Ossory, 1758; M.P. HW recommended him to 'Gilly' Williams as 'one of the properest and most amiable young men I ever knew' (Selwyn 207). In 1769 he married the divorced Duchess of Grafton, HW's close friend and correspondent.

19. Francis Russell (1739–67), styled M. of Tavistock; M.P. He was a cousin of Lord Ossory.

20. Lionel Cranfield Sackville (1688–1765), 7th E. of Dorset, 1706; cr. (1720) D. of Dorset. He died 10 Oct. 1765.

21. Lord George Sackville (after 1770, Germain) (1716–85), youngest son of the 1st D. of Dorset; cr. (1782) Vct Sackville. He succeeded to the estate of Stoneland Lodge, Sussex, on the death of his father.

22. Dorset, K.G. 1714, was succeeded in that order 26 Dec. 1765 by Karl Wilhelm Ferdinand (1735–1806), Hereditary P. and later D. of Brunswick-Wolfenbüttel (W. A. Shaw, *The Knights of England,* 1906, i. 46).

23. Who was then in England.

24. Perhaps Lady Dalkeith (later Lady Greenwich), whom HW later referred to as 'that shrill *Morning Post*' (HW to Conway 16 Oct. 1774, Conway iii. 197–8). She was married to Charles Townshend, of whom it had been recently rumoured

Mrs Pitt's friend, Madame de Rochefort,[25] is one of my principal attachments, and very agreeable indeed. Madame de Mirepoix[26] another. For my admiration, Madame de Monaco[27]—but I believe you don't doubt my Lord [Hertford]'s taste in sensualities. March's passion, the Maréchale d'Estrées,[28] is affected, cross, and not at all handsome. The Princes of the Blood are pretty much retired, do not go to Portsmouth and Salisbury once a week, nor furnish every other paragraph to the newspapers. Their campaigns are confined to killing boars and stags, two or three hundred in a year.

Adieu! Mr Foley[29] is my banker; or it is still more sure if you send your letter to Mr Conway's office.

Yours ever,
Hor. Walpole

To Grosvenor Bedford, Wednesday 20 November 1765

Printed from Cunningham iv. 437, where the letter was first printed. Reprinted, Toynbee vi. 354. The history of the MS and its present whereabouts are not known.

The letter is listed in 'Paris Journals' as sent to England 23 Nov. 'by Duke of Richmond's servant' (du Deffand v. 377).

Paris, Nov. 20, 1765.

Dear Sir,

I SHOULD hope you was convinced that you need not at any time wait for business, to write to me. I am always happy to hear of you, and glad to receive your letters.

(falsely) that he was about to form a new administration with Lord Bute and Lord Holland (*The Grenville Papers*, ed. W. J. Smith, 1852–3, iii. 101).

25. Marie-Thérèse de Brancas (1716–82), m. 1 (1736) Jean-Anne-Vincent de Larlan de Kercadio, Comte de Rochefort; m. 2 (1782) Louis-Jules-Barbon Mancini-Mazarini, Duc de Nivernais. See HW to Anne Pitt 8 Oct. 1765 (More 53–4).

26. Anne-Marguerite-Gabrielle de Beauvau (1707–91), m. 1 (1721) Jacques-Henri de Lorraine, Prince de Lixin; m. 2 (1739) Gaston-Charles-Pierre Lévis de Lomagne, Marquis (Duc, 1751) de Mirepoix, Maréchal de France, 1757. See HW to Lady Hervey 15 Sept. 1765 (ibid. 47).

27. Marie-Catherine de Brignole (1739–1813), m. 1 (1757) Honoré-Camille-Léonor Goyon-de-Matignon de Grimaldi, P. of Monaco; m. 2 (1808) Louis-Joseph de Bourbon, Prince de Condé. See ibid.

28. Adélaïde-Félicité Brulart de Puisieulx de Sillery (1725–86), m. (1744) Louis-Charles-César le Tellier de Louvois, Maréchal-Duc d'Estrées.

29. Sir Robert Ralph Foley (ca 1727–82), cr. (1767) Bt; Paris banker.

I caught cold after I had been here a fortnight, and the gout returned in both feet, and in one of my eyes, with what gave me still more uneasiness, constant sickness at my stomach, so that I almost loathed every kind of food, and could bear no sort above two days together. Thank God! after six weeks all is over, my sickness is gone and my appetite returned. My feet continued long swelled, and my legs swelled so much every night, that I feared that weakness would remain, but it is gone too, and I have nothing to complain of now, but weakness. I wish you got as easily quit of this horrid distemper. My gout leaves no traces at all, though so severe while it stays.

I will beg you to keep the money[1] till my return, which will be when the severity of the winter is over; but I am grown a great coward, and dare not venture travelling in bad weather, nor risk being laid up on the road. I am not less afraid of the House of Commons, when I am persuaded long attendance would bring back the gout, of which I own my dread is extreme. The same apprehension will prevent my going more southward. I shall be very glad to be in my own house again. Adieu, dear Sir, and believe me ever

Most cordially and affectionately yours,

HORACE WALPOLE

1. Presumably accrual from his Exchequer places.

From PIERRE-JEAN MARIETTE,[1] Thursday 21 November 1765

Printed from the MS now WSL. First printed, Toynbee *Supp.* iii. 191. Damer-Waller; the MS was sold Sotheby's 5 Dec. 1921 (first Waller Sale), lot 160, passed; resold Christie's 15 Dec. 1947 (second Waller Sale), lot 55 (with other letters to HW), to Maggs for WSL.

Dated by the reference to Fonçemagne's dining with HW at Président Hénault's 20 Nov. 1765 (see n. 6 below).

Ce jeudi matin.

VOICI, Monsieur, la lettre que vous m'avez fait l'honneur de me demander[2] pour Saint-Denys.[3] C'est Monsieur de Foncemagne[4] qui l'écrit[5] et vous pouvez compter que vous serez très bien servi. Il me dit hier au soir qu'il avait eu ce jour-là même le plaisir de dîner avec vous[6] et que s'il eût su que vous eussiez eu besoin de sa recommandation il m'aurait enlevé la satisfaction que j'éprouve en vous donnant des preuves de mon zèle et du respect avec lequel j'ai l'honneur d'être,

Monsieur,

Votre très humble et très obéissant serviteur,

MARIETTE

1. (1694–1774), collector of prints and drawings and translator of HW's *Anecdotes of Painting* (DU DEFFAND i. 252 n. 13; *post* ca 8 Oct. 1767). He called on HW 28 Oct. and 1 Nov. 1765, and HW visited him and saw his collection on 2 Nov., 19 Nov., and 2 Dec. ('Paris Journals,' ibid. v. 268 n. 83, 269, 273, 279). William Cole, who was then also in Paris, wrote in his journal *sub* 28 Oct.: 'After dinner, Mr Mariette, grandson of the famous engraver of that name, and who left his family a good estate, came to drink coffee with Mr Walpole: he is an old man of between 60 and 70 years of age, a great connoisseur in painting, has a large collection of them as well as prints; and seemed to be well acquainted with all our best books of antiquity; especially such as had any prints in them, as Dugdale, King, etc.' (*A Journal of my Journey to Paris in the Year 1765*, ed. F. G. Stokes, 1931, pp. 100–1; see also COLE ii. 9 n. 11). For HW's purchases at Mariette's sale in 1775 see OSSORY i. 281–2 and Hazen, *Cat. of HW's Lib.*, No. 3867.

2. Presumably on 19 Nov., when HW visited Mariette (see n. 1 above).

3. 'Mr Walpole called upon me about 11 o'clock to carry me with him to the Royal Abbey of St Denis, about 5 miles from Paris' (Cole's *Journal*, p. 305; see pp. 305–21 for his account of their visit).

4. Étienne Lauréault de Fonçemagne (1694–1779), sub-govenor to the Duc de Chartres ca 1752–8; member of the Académie des Inscriptions et Belles-Lettres, 1722, and of the Académie Française, 1737 (NBG).

5. 'To the Prior of the Abbey, Father Chretien' (Cole's *Journal*, p. 305). Dom Jacques-Nicolas Chrestien, grand prieur de l'Abbaye de Saint-Denis 1763–6 (Félicie d'Ayzac, *Histoire de l'Abbaye de Saint-Denis*, 1860, i. cxxxi).

6. At Président Hénault's on 20 Nov. ('Paris Journals,' DU DEFFAND v. 273).